Thérèse of Lisieux

Thérèse of Lisieux

God's Gentle Warrior

THOMAS R. NEVIN

OXFORD
UNIVERSITY PRESS
2006

OXFORD
UNIVERSITY PRESS

Oxford University Press, Inc., publishes works that further
Oxford University's objective of excellence
in research, scholarship, and education.

Oxford   New York
Auckland   Cape Town   Dar es Salaam   Hong Kong   Karachi
Kuala Lumpur   Madrid   Melbourne   Mexico City   Nairobi
New Delhi   Shanghai   Taipei   Toronto

With offices in
Argentina   Austria   Brazil   Chile   Czech Republic   France   Greece
Guatemala   Hungary   Italy   Japan   Poland   Portugal   Singapore
South Korea   Switzerland   Thailand   Turkey   Ukraine   Vietnam

Published by Oxford University Press, Inc.
198 Madison Avenue, New York, New York 10016

www.oup.com

Oxford is a registered trademark of Oxford University Press

Frontispiece: Thérèse in 1895, the year of "Vivre d'Amour,"
the *offrande*, and her first autobiographical manuscript.
Copyright Office Central de Lisieux.

Library of Congress Cataloging-in-Publication Data
Nevin, Thomas R., 1944–
Thérèse of Lisieux : God's gentle warrior / Thomas R. Nevin.
   p.   cm.
Includes bibliographical references and index.
ISBN 978-0-19-530721-4
ISBN 0-19-530721-6
1. Thérèse, de Lisieux, Saint, 1873–1897.   2. Christian saints—France—
Lisieux—Biography.   3. Lisieux (France)—Biography.   I. Title.
BX4700.T5N48   2006
282.092—dc22   2006004339

For Bonnie and Jim and Mike

*. . . que les enseignements de Jésus sont
contraires aux sentiments de la nature,
sans le secours de sa grâce il serait
impossible non seulement de les mettre en
pratique mais encore de les comprendre.*

Preface: Not Another Hagiography

She has had enough of those, this very young woman who came to prefer bitter things to sweet and who, when told toward her life's end that she was not a good nun, responded: "To hear on my death-bed that I'm not a good nun, what joy! Nothing could please me more." This book departs from conventional treatments of Thérèse of Lisieux while keeping in focus the Catholic spirituality from which she grew and which she transformed during her life of twenty-four years.

It is addressed to the widest possible audience: first, to those who love and revere Thérèse and are interested in knowing more about her informative backgrounds; also and especially, to those of Christian faith who have found themselves either in spiritual dark-ness or indifference and are seeking the inspiration and guidance which she provides; and, not least, to those who feel or even affirm themselves to be outsiders to Christianity, including people who, in the secular spirit of the age, are inclined to respond to the very notion of sanctity with skepticism or scoffing. It is with the bitter, the dismissive, and the contemptuous that Thérèse sat down toward the close of her life.

At the beginning of this book, I sketch a background which usually finds no place in theresian studies but which seems both obvious and essential for approaching her. I review French Catholi-cism as it was during her time, particularly in the three generations preceding it. In that way, we are reminded of how Catholicism in France, reeling from the seismic blows of the Revolution and the Napoleonic aftermath, struggled to adjust itself to a rapidly ascen-dant and vaunting secularism. Scholarly studies of the Church in nineteenth-century France abound, depicting so-called *déchristianisation* in regional statistics and sociological shelvings. While giving them due nods, I prefer to give more attention to particular voices. As Voltaire, Diderot, and Rousseau portended the French Revolution, Chateaubriand, Lamennais, and Renan—each of them devoutly errant Christians—carried on its message but in inadequate, not to say perverse, ways.

Heeding them is not arbitrary. Thérèse, although a seeming latecomer to this story, plays a vital role in its unfolding because, sublimely free of intent, she rescued Catholicism from the doldrums into which it had sunk under the vigorously anticlerical Third Republic by answering in her fashion the claims of the postrevolutionary writers I have just named.

Rather than iterate the story of her life in strict sequence, I have chosen to recount it in a chapter's summary. It is complemented by another chapter which tells her mother's story, known to us in fifteen years of correspondence (never translated into English) up to the time of her death in 1877. As a kind of diary of a provincial bourgeoise and an industrious businesswoman, this account has its own value for anyone interested in how women fared before the articulations of modern feminism, but its particular worth for the present study is that it affords a close view into the home life from which Thérèse emerged. She had much in common with her mother but surpassed her into a void. At the time of this writing, both parents await beatification.

I have given an entire chapter to the Carmelites themselves, as an order and as a conventual community at Lisieux. As she was a Carmelite of the Discalced, or sandal-wearing, Order, it is helpful for us to know how Thérèse's conventual life was shaped and how she created a new perspective within it. At the same time, it is only fair to note that she could not have gone so far as she did without the daily presence of her Carmelite sisters. In their various ways, they informed her spirituality and, even by occasional resistance, gave it impetus. I consider her famous "little way" as a personal discovery and a communal enterprise, however aware or otherwise Thérèse's natural and spiritual sisters were about their parts in it. Much that we find in her writings derives from the Spanish Carmelite tradition and from the prescriptive texts of the order: the Carmelite Rule and Constitutions, the *Papier d'Exaction* as the protocol of daily life, the *Direction spirituelle*, and Madre Teresa's letter from Avila to her world of sisters, the *Camino de Perfección*.

This chapter also draws heavily upon the inexplicably neglected obituary notices known as *circulaires*, written by prioresses in Carmels around France and in French-speaking Carmels abroad. I have read more than four hundred of these portraits composed between the spring of 1888 and the summer of 1897, the span of Thérèse's time at the Lisieux Carmel. As they were read at meal times in the Carmel and were available for reading in the Carmel library, we know that Thérèse learned from them. Many could be called sketches of her own spirituality. Many are about young women as zealous as she, who, like her, died young. Some clearly gave inspiration to her writing, including the title of her best-known poem. These sisters, too, took the little way.

It was she, nonetheless, who revitalized Christianity itself. It would not be amiss to claim that she is the most beloved woman in modern history, certainly among Catholics. But she is both too easily embraced and too easily dismissed: a saint of common people, presumably, accessible to everyone and without the challenging (medieval) baggage of mysticism. (Even in the Carmel of her time, there was a kind of prejudice against the mystical life, as it was presumed to be *illuminisme*, Swedenborgian, and suspect.) She is one of us and, being so, she says that sainthood is for anybody. So say her devotees. And, by the same turn, she is sometimes dismissed as a simpering, if not simple-minded, creature, a mediocrity in intellect. Vita Sackville-West, in her "study in contrasts," *The Eagle and the Dove*, judged Teresa of Avila "highbrow" to the "lowbrow" Thérèse. Snobbishness aside, I have found some Catholics, including religious, put off by Thérèse because of her imputed flawlessness. She is the paradox of an extraordinarily ordinary person, a nobody who attained an arcane perfection. The problem for snobs might be the ordinariness, for others, the perfection. In the end, she turns out not to be one of us. People, like democracies, might feel the allure of the exceptional, but they will also hate it and seek to pull it down.

In this book, Thérèse is neither ordinary nor perfect. She appears with the flaws of greatness, both less and more than she has been taken to be. I have drawn, however, upon the documentation provided by some who knew her, the *Procès Informatif Ordinaire* (1910–1911) and the *Procès Apostolique* (1915–1917). On this end of that story, she has become a doctor of the Church, a fact that merits any number of examinations, and indeed, intellectualizing studies of her as a theologian keep coming in daunting abundance, though mostly in French. Well meant, some have a grim earnestness or, as Thérèse would say, they tend to crack the head and dry the heart.

In four of the book's chapters, apart from the biographical sketch, she has four profiles: as a writer sketching herself; as a dramatist and poet writing for the community; as a tubercular patient; and as an improvisatory theologian who effected what I am bold to call a Copernican change in Christian spirituality. Treating her as a theologian has become respectable, but the angle from which she is viewed in these pages may seem to some readers something else. I hope, in any case, to have taken at least a little inspiration from my subject's own *audace*.

As in any study of a life, there is a point where an ineffable mystery blocks the way to any certainties and because this study is up against the far greater mystery of divinity, I have sufficient cause to be humble. Prompted by a priest, Thérèse claimed only one spiritual director, Jesus, and said of him that he did not need books. The implication is devastating: do we need to read her? Does anyone need yet another book about her? Has everything been said? Is the icon with the roses not enough? Do we need to be reminded that roses bear thorns?

This book, preponderantly, is about the thorns amid those roses. As the Jesuits are fond of saying, there are many avenues to God (though an eminent Jesuit found within these pages insists that there is only Thérèse's way), and I believe there are many avenues to Thérèse. As mine deals substantially with her tunnel vision, this might be called a subterranean essay. It is not a story of faith and hope triumphant but of a darkness that left faith and hope wholly obscured from affirmation. It is about a void in which many people, Christians and others, find themselves today. Because she occupied darkness and void to the end of her life, Thérèse, as the Quakers would put it, speaks to our condition. Even so, and amazingly, at no time did she become an atheist.

She once said that she sought only the truth. A comparable sobriety seems required of anyone who dares to write of her. That extends to the cold and clammy facts of her medical history. I was once told that death left Thérèse's body uncorrupted. In this book, however, tubercular toxins render her intestinal tract gangrenous: more than corrupted, she is decaying before she dies. That may be an unsavory fact, but it remains a fact. When she was disinterred from a public cemetery in September 1910, only a few bones were still intact; the rest was dust. And yet the casque holding this dust has drawn countless thousands every year as it travels to lands far distant from France. Thérèse has an enduring global status, especially in the Southern Hemisphere countries, where Catholicism seeks new life, even as it is losing its old one in the Northern.

Another fact is that she died without belief in heaven, the terminus of the Christian faith. She also died without hope of getting there. What she kept to the end was a resilient love for God, even in her knowing that God was the creator of the darkness in which she was situated to the end.

Pope Leo XIII, at whose feet Thérèse once knelt, said upon opening the Vatican archives to scholarship that the Church had nothing to fear from the truth. I believe that is still the case. I hope that this book, no matter its degrees of success or failure, has moved in that direction.

All citations from Thérèse come from the *Oeuvres complètes* published by Le Cerf in 1992, with occasional references to the multivolume centenary edition, known as the NEC, and its extensive, invaluable notes. I have given each quotation first in the French and then in my own bracketed English so that the reader of French or the reader of a preferred translation can take issue with me. Except for secondary literature, cited in footnotes, the source is given parenthetically after the English. Unavoidably, every translation amounts to an interpretation. All translations are mine with the exception of the New Testament, here in the Authorized, or King James, Version, preferred for its poetry over today's banal renditions. Citations from the *Imitatio Christi* come from the translation by the once-notorious Lamennais, the edition Thérèse herself used without worry.

Of Thérèse's writings, I have given primacy to her autobiographical manuscripts, known simply as A, B, and C. Familiarly titled *The Story of a Soul*, they are the texts with which to begin and end any study of her. My sometimes cursory treatment of her other writings should not be construed as a slighting of them. Thérèse remains her own best commentator, and the writings inform one another richly. The poems might even be called prayers and the letters not infrequently become poetry in their flights of inspired imagery. The autobiographical texts are themselves three letters to three women. All her writings share a certain exhilaration, a brio of adolescent fervor conditioned by the fact that Thérèse had within Carmel's and her cell's walls only one evening hour every day in which to write. Hence, the compaction, direct and ever lucid.

A few words are due about lexical and related texts. In establishing likely denotations of words as Thérèse would have known and used them, I have consulted two contemporaneous sources: the first, a dictionary published in 1897, the year of her death: Louis-Nicholas Bescherelle's *Nouveau dictionnaire classique de la langue française*. The reason is simple: in our preponderantly secular "post-Christian" age, some words have lost a resonance they had only a century ago. An example is *anéantissement*, a weighty word in this study, which means according to Larousse (1993 edition) and *Le Petit Robert* "destruction, extermination, or annihilation." Well and good, but Bescherelle includes this entry: "Dévot [Devotional] État d'abaissement volontaire devant Dieu," a voluntary humbling of oneself before God. No modern dictionary carries such a denotation. Akin to that word is *néant*, which *Robert* generously glosses with citations from Pascal, Racine, and Lamartine and which Larousse identifies in the Sartrean void as that which is opposed to metaphysical being. From Bescherelle, we cull the theresian sense: "vide de l'âme, absence d'amour de Dieu," a void of the soul, an absence of God's love. Armed with such semantics, we can approach the obscurities of Thérèse's last months. Bescherelle's dictionary straddles admirably some chasms in diction opened by the contest between republicans and Christians, oppositions which animated France late in the nineteenth century.

The other source is generally recognized as the greatest of all French dictionaries and a monument in itself to philological endeavor, Émile Littré's four-volume *Dictionnaire de la langue française*, in an edition of 1883–1884. (Bescherelle's first edition spanned 1843–1846 and Littré's, 1863–1872.) Littré's value lies in the vast archaeological strata he established in the literary developments of words, including etymological notes. Where Bescherelle, a popularizer, is wide, Littré is deep. He, for example, indicates that the junction of love and *abandon*, one of the most important words in theresian semantics, goes back to the virtual beginnings of French literature, to Marie de France. From Littré, someone could compose a veritable lexicon of Carmel as it evolved from "the Spanish mothers" who brought the Discalced Order into early seventeenth-century France.

For the discussion of Thérèse and tuberculosis, I have read (and I cite) extensively the medical literature of the generation of doctors who were treating her as well as recent texts on pathology. How was this disease diagnosed and treated in the 1890s? What was the quality of treatment given at Carmel? Is it even certain that Thérèse had it rather than another sort of pulmonary infection? Does it matter? Yes, because tuberculosis sustained, as we shall see, a macabre aura about it, an almost sanctifying glamour. It helps to establish as clearly as we can the nature and course of Thérèse's physical suffering, much of it iatrogenic, because her spiritual itinerary moved closely with it. In brief, how did she deal with acute affliction and impending death? In discussing her theological development, I draw on sources demonstrably vital to her, such as the mystical literature of Carmel (San Juan de la Cruz, primarily) but also on texts she never read, such as the Thomist *Summa* and the *Theologia Deutsch*. Protestants such as Luther and Bonhoeffer have also informed my perspective. I have attempted to "read" her within a broad Christian continuum. It is not difficult to establish that, like some other saints, she is almost too unruly to be safe. Even those churchmen who write to prove that she can be fitted onto the procrustean bed of dogma do not deny that one of her prime epithets is *audace*, or daring. This study indicates how far that word went with Thérèse from Lisieux.

The selective annotated bibliography identifies books I consider informative, reliable, helpful, or dispensable, and to which readers, taking issue with my perspectives, might wish to repair for support or reassurance. A caveat: almost all of Thérèse's writings are accessible in English translations but most of the secondary works cited are available only in French. Although the best of all commentators on Thérèse is Thérèse, that happy fact does not quite overcome the inherent problems in crossing from one language into another.

It is a pleasure to thank those who have helped me as I pursued the Carmelite way and Thérèse's particular and audacious movement along it: Frs. Steven Payne and John Sullivan of the Institute for Carmelite Studies in Washington, D.C., for help in securing texts and addresses; Fr. Conrad de Meester, elder statesman of Carmelite writers on Thérèse, for charitable criticisms and insights; the staffs of *travailleuses missionaires* at the Foyer Martin and the Ermitage de Sainte-Thérèse at Lisieux for their hospitality and singing; and the Religieuses Oblates de Sainte Thérèse of the Maison Natale, Alençon, and the Oblates at Les Buissonnets, Lisieux, for their guidance and information.

For information on Fr. Pichon, S.J., I wish to thank his biographer, Mary Frances Coady. For helpful discussions, I am indebted to Fr. Philip Endean of Campion Hall, Oxford, and to my colleagues Sister Mary Ann Flannery, Dr. Doris Donnelly, the Reverend Donald Cozzens, and especially Dr. Hélène Sanko, for her memories of growing up in Third Republican France, with many details pertinent to the educational and medical practices of Thérèse's own time.

Fr. Matthias, of the Discalced Carmelite Friars at Holy Hill, Wisconsin, kindly supplied me with copies of the Martin family correspondence published in the *Vie thérésienne*, the indispensable journal for Thérèse's many admirers.

I am indebted to John Carroll University for a research leave and to the Grauel Fellowship Fund for supporting it. I owe much as well to my assistant at the computer, Cheryl Kelley.

I wish especially to thank Caroline Zilboorg of Clare Hall, Cambridge University for facilitating my lectures there on Thérèse over the course of four years, 2000–2003; Françoise Lejeune of the Université de Nantes for inviting me to lecture on Thérèse at a conference there (June 2001) on women and war; and the organizers of the Hawaii International Conference on Arts and Humanities, Honolulu, where I spoke on the *circulaires* of Carmel (January 2005).

The prioresses at the Carmel at Montigné (Bretagne) and the Carmel at Nantes (Loire-Atlantique) generously provided the records and annals of their communities in the time of Thérèse. I wish to thank them for their time, assistance, and hospitality.

I have also been kindly welcomed to discuss Thérèse and this writing with sisters of the Carmel proximate to the Jesuit university where I teach and write. Their enthusiasm, their informed insights about Thérèse and Carmelite life, and especially their prayers have been deeply gratifying.

By far the greatest debt I owe is to the archival staff at Lisieux's Carmel, who with unstinting efficiency provided me with the extraordinary materials of the Archives du Carmel. The staff also shared many perceptions and insights about Thérèse and a great deal about Carmelite life and tradition during the many weeks of my research there. I appreciated instruction in the delivery of *recto tono* for the reading of *circulaires* and demonstrative application of the *ventouse* as a device for treating tuberculosis. Two members of the staff read the entire manuscript and provided an abundance of detailed corrections and candid criticisms. Their charitable and keen attention immeasurably improved the final drafts. As Carmelites, they prefer to remain hidden and forgotten.

Finally, I wish to thank Cynthia Read and the staff at Oxford University Press, Theo Calderara, Julia TerMaat, and Stacey Hamilton, for their enthusiasm, assiduity, and steady good cheer.

Let me impress upon the reader that wrongheadedness, mistaken judgment, or errant interpretations of facts are entirely my production and my responsibility. As this is, among much else, a book about self-humbling, it is almost a pleasure to say that every one of its errors, whether unintended or willful or wicked, comes only from me, its author.

Contents

Abbreviations

A	The first autobiographical manuscript, 1895
AC	Archives of Carmel, which include all the *circulaires* cited
B	The second autobiographical manuscript, 1896
C	The third autobiographical manuscript, 1897
CF	*Correspondance familiale, 1863–1877*, letters of Zélie Martin (Lisieux: Carmel de Lisieux, 1958)
CG	*Correspondance gènèrale* of Thérèse of Lisieux (Paris: Cerf, Desclée de Brouwer, 1974)
CS	*Conseils et souvenirs* of Thérèse of Lisieux (Paris: Cerf, Desclée de Brouwer, 1973)
DE	*Derniers entretiens* of Thérèse of Lisieux (Paris: Cerf, Desclée de Brouwer, 1971)
HA	*Histoire d'une âme* (Bar-le-Duc: St. Paul, 1911)
LC	Letters of Thérèse's correspondents, numbered and published in CG
LD	Letters of various correspondents or contemporaries of Thérèse among themselves, published in chronology but without number in CG
LT	Letters of Thérèse, numbered and published in CG
NEC	*Nouvelle édition du centenaire*, an 8-volume edition of Thérèse's complete works (Paris: Cerf, Desclée de Brouwer, 1992)
NPHF	Notes prepared by Céline for Stéphane-Joseph Piat's *Histoire d'une famille* (Paris: Pierre Téqui, 1945)
NPPA	Notes prepared by Carmelites for the *Procès apostolique*

OC   *Oeuvres complètes*, a 1-volume edition of Thérèse's complete
       works (Paris: Cerf, Desclée de Brouwer, 1992)
PA   *Procès de béatification et canonisation: Apostolique*, hearings held in 1915–
       1917 for Thérèse's beatification and canonization (Rome:
       Teresianum, 1976)
PN   *Poèsies*, Thérèse's 54 poems (Paris: Cerf, Desclée de Brouwer, 1992)
PO   *Procès de béatification et canonisation: Ordinaire*, hearings held in 1910–
       1911 for Thérèse's beatification and canonization
       (Rome: Teresianum, 1973)
Pri   *Prières*, Thérèse's 21 prayers (Paris: Cerf, Desclée de Brouwer, 1992)
RP   *Récréations pieuses*, Thérèse's 8 plays (Paris: Cerf, Desclée de Brouwer,
       1992)
VT   *Vie thérésienne*, trimestral review published since 1961

Thérèse of Lisieux

I

After the Revolution

Catholicism in France before Thérèse

Tout vrai philosophe doit opter entre deux hypothèses, ou qu'il va se former une religion nouvelle, ou que le christianisme sera rajeuni de quelque manière extraordinaire [Every genuine thinker must choose between two suppositions, either that he is going to create a new religion or that Christianity will be revitalized in some extraordinary way].

—Joseph de Maistre, *Considérations
sur la France*, 1796

Three men over as many generations pursued de Maistre's second option. Each of them failed brilliantly. Their failures prepared the way for someone who had never read nor perhaps even heard of de Maistre, and who was so obscure, a young, inadequately educated woman, that her finding what has been called the "Columbus egg" of Christianity would have seemed even to herself dauntingly improbable. If that succession seems to give this narrative a fairytale aspect, it becomes more so as Chateaubriand, Lamennais, and Renan figure centrally in any chronicle of nineteenth-century French Catholicism, while Thérèse Martin, the Little Flower, Saint Thérèse of Lisieux would be marginal to it, and yet these men, who lived long and wrote much, are for the greater part forgotten, and she, dead at twenty-four, has become the most beloved woman in modern times.

She was from Normandy; Chateaubriand, Lamennais, and Renan from neighboring Brittany, one of the most fervently Catholic regions of France. That these men, who enjoyed considerable social profiles and even notoriety in their times, failed and that an inconspicuous, indeed hidden away woman succeeded in this modern version of a Grail quest, affords one of the caprices in which the history of thought and feeling abounds. Their profiles, all of them, are postrevolutionary and of the nineteenth century, a time when many minds were coursing de Maistre's first and much broader avenue, the invention of a new religion. Not a new religion strictly, but ideology, the secular ersatz for spirituality, exerted its sway, spouted its dogmas, predicted the future, and promised the generation of a new humankind. Utopian visions, whether from Fourier or Saint-Simon, from Marx or Comte, took their historical impetus from the French Revolution's overthrow of autocracy and caste privilege. The promissory note in utopianism, however, had been written many centuries before, within the greatest of all myths, when the serpent in the garden told its only human inhabitants that they would be like gods.

The three failed men were variously propelled, if not swept away, by the tide of that message. As this is a Christian's story, I have chosen to see them under three sorts of temptation, none of which is strictly comparable to those Christ faced in the wilderness but each of which St. Augustine identifies: the rage for feeling, *libido sentiendi*; for commanding, *libido dominandi*; for knowing, *libido sciendi*. As these men did not think, work, write in a vacuum, it is necessary to provide with each account some brief remarks on the political and spiritual life of their age.

Chateaubriand and the *Libido Sentiendi*

At 11 a.m. on Wednesday, October 16, 1793, despoilers broke into the massive tomb of King Louis XV in Saint-Denis, north of Paris. He had been lying there for nearly twenty years. When his casket was opened and his corpse released from its linen shrouds, the smell of putrefaction was overwhelming. The intruders fired pistols over the regal, rotten body so the gunpowder would cleanse the air. Sometime during that hour, the once queen, Marie-Antoinette, was losing her head.

These lurid proceedings are recorded among the voluminous notes behind *Génie du christianisme*, a farrago of ecclesiastical history and ritual, literary criticism, landscapes, and piety, all presented with intermittent but lengthy rhetorical effusions by François-René de Chateaubriand. To this day, he is reckoned the father of romanticism in nineteenth-century France. He wrote *Génie* in England, whither he had fled at age twenty-five, during the Jacobin republic of terror, in the year that proved so unpleasant to Louis XV and his daughter-in-law. He had secretly returned to France in 1801 but was able to emerge from proscription only after publishing *Atala*, a melancholy little fiction of thwarted passions between two noble savages in the American wilderness. It starts in Florida, proceeds to the Mississippi River, and concludes at Niagara Falls. He had initially intended to include *Atala* within *Génie* as a demonstration of his claim that literature could and should take up Christianity, its morals and its history, as sources of inspiration, shedding in that way the well-worn classicism which had exclusively dominated literary taste before the Revolution.

Few read *Génie du christianisme* today. Its author's *Mémoires d'outre-tombe*, a massive autobiography with engagingly close optics on eight decades of French history, goes on maintaining its hoary profile. The morbidly charming *Atala* runs second, awaiting French majors between *Candide* and *Lorenzaccio* on the reading lists. *Génie*, however, remains a vital historical gauge of both taste and spirituality in the first years under Bonaparte. It was published on April 14, 1802, just eight days after his regime altered the terms of its *concordat* with Rome, ending state repression of clerical life and practices but subordinating ecclesiastical power, including the papal, to the will of the civil government.

Roman Catholicism had been crippled and nearly destroyed by two weighty assaults in the previous generation. Identified with the corrupt absolutism of monarchy and aristocratic privilege, it had become the target of populist fury and official maleficence. The cause lay chiefly in the egregious wealth the Church had long amassed. Bishops, themselves of high lineage, and monastics had profited conspicuously, while countless parish priests subsisted in poverty. Many in the church hierarchy were cynical unbelievers, including the cardinal of Toulouse, who had been the prime minister of France. Thus was the Church exposed to Voltaire's withering gibes, which it had neither the strength nor the will to combat.

By official dispensation within the first year of the Revolution, on November 2, 1789, ecclesiastical properties were sold off, and in the following February the monastic orders were dissolved. The motion for selling came from an unbelieving bishop, Talleyrand, who was not alone among expedient clerics in riding the revolutionary wave. Clergy were brought under a constitution which had them elected and salaried. Pope Pius VI objected helplessly to these extraordinary reforms but officially condemned the constitution only after about half of France's parish priests, with no cue from Rome, had accepted its provisions under oath. Thereafter, Catholicism staggered on with three kinds of priests: those who had resisted the oath from the first, those who had taken it but retracted, and those who formed in effect a new state-run clergy.

The Church had to sustain more than political and economic disasters. Far more subtle than the constitutional contempt for the Church in this bizarrely unhappy history was the other enmity, which came from the makers of intellectual fashion, *les philosophes*, as they were long known and as Chateaubriand consistently denominates them. We would call them atheists or "secular humanists." To such minds, Christianity amounted to little more than a congeries of barbarous superstitions to which no rational person could honestly subscribe. Even some devout Catholics were embarrassed and repelled by folk-rooted devotions. In these practices and in the corruption of church officers, the Church was ridiculed mercilessly according to the enlightenment, or what in a darker age would be called the correctness, of the time.

In his *Journal*, André Gide, a Protestant, once noted that the effect of reading witty barbs against Catholicism by writers such as Diderot was to make him more sympathetic to the Church. Something of the same sort of reaction might have set in after the persecutions, but nationalism had first come into play against the Church. Anticlericalism was identified with the national defense against Catholic Austria, which went to war with France in May 1792. Pius VI was ineluctably identified with the counterrevolution. In the tumult of war, even the civil clergy were at risk and were fatally discredited when in the autumn of that year the revolutionary assembly introduced clerical marriage and recognized civil divorce. The First Republic invented a cult of reason under which priests not killed in their parishes were forced abroad or into hiding. While we might see in the republic the birth of the modern state, it would be amiss to underestimate the failure of this regime to dislocate the cultism, the subterranean irrationality of folk Catholicism by which alone the Church was able to survive the Revolution. As in its first generations under persecution, the Body of Christ was not chiefly its officers but its people, unobstreperous, tested, devout.

The mockery of clever unbelievers proved finally too weak to thrive because it could not fill the spiritual void which it had willy-nilly prepared. And the torments to which the Church was subjected during the Revolution's reactionary phase paradoxically strengthened it: many priests, having refused or having recanted on the oath of allegiance, continued the sacramental life of parishes by a kind of underground, and some provinces, notably the Vendée and Chateaubriand's Brittany, remained staunch in their adherence to the Church throughout the Jacobin period, the Directory, and the Consulate.

Chateaubriand had not written for believers but for skeptics, aging sophisticates still open to argument, vagrant youths, and anyone else who realized that France had lost its spiritual anchorage and that Robespierre's farcical cult of the Supreme Being had offered no mooring. He shrewdly dodged metaphysical and theological arguments, thus leaving *les philosophes* isolated and ignored. His appeal was primarily aesthetic, to convince the reader that in Christianity one would find an imperishable source of uplifting beauty, especially in its rituals, its architecture, and its scriptural mysteries.

No matter his many claims to the *poésie* of the Christian religion, it does not take the reader long to notice that Chateaubriand ignores the Christian God. In two volumes, Christ is given 3 pages out of 670 (in the Flammarion edition). That is because this writer's intent rests not merely upon appeals to outward beauties in Christian history and practice. It lies more deeply couched in appeals to this religion's indispensable contribution to social order. The Roman, one might say Ciceronian, accent upon the need for religion as a stay against chaos implies that the sincerity of one's beliefs does not constitute an issue; religion will always be attended by hypocrisy. What matters is a kind of idea of God, a centripetal force of social stability. Chateaubriand posed an argument from utility, both collective and individual: atheism helps no one and threatens the state with havoc and blood. France by 1801 had had enough of both. Anticipating Dostoevsky by three generations, Chateaubriand urged that without the moral constraints of theism, men can and will hurl themselves into innumerable crimes.[1]

It would be difficult to determine how much Chateaubriand in *Génie du christianisme* was reflecting an age exhausted by revolution and war, and how much he was shaping its articulation of a profound spiritual crisis. What remains clearly his own, his sensibility, affords us another perspective on this book. With tireless and tiresome iterations, its advertisable sensitivity is registered in two words, sublimity and tears.

In Christianity's life and art, he argues, we find an inexhaustible source of the sublime, something of such loftiness and grandeur that it provokes awe and reverence. That it would be, then, a perpetual source of higher distraction provides another hint about Chateaubriand's cultured, leisurely audience. It would have time to read. In order to shake his readership free of its old allegiance to classical literature, Chateaubriand makes pointlessly pejorative arguments at the expense of Homer and on behalf of Tasso and Milton. For instance, admitting equity in the "amours pures et sévères" of Odysseus and Penelope, he claims that Milton's Adam and Eve (she, though, weak and loquacious) are a superior couple because in them "la vraie religion a pu seule donner le caractère d'une tendresse aussi sainte, aussi sublime" ["the true religion alone has been able to give the stamp of such saintly, such sublime tenderness"].[2] The Christian epic hero is far superior to the pagan because the latter could never be more than "l'homme naturel." Charity confounds vanity: the humility of Tasso's Godefroi marks the first of Christian virtues, as the pride of Achilles or Agamemnon marks the first of vices.

Chateaubriand does not skirt the old question of why evil's depiction in literature is so much more engaging than any profile in goodness (Satan, not Adam, exemplifies grandeur in *Paradise Lost*); he is simply unaware of it. He intuited that his readers wanted uplift. Whatever the many merits of polytheistic classicism—and among them he finds some of Simone Weil's "intuitions pre-chrétiennes"—only Christianity can put you into the fields of hope. Hope of what? For the author, release from the destructive sway of passions, especially the pathology of eros.

Chateaubriand makes a claim for Christianity much like the one Lucretius made for Epicureanism, that it alone could save you from yourself, from all the sways of emotions, their costly turmoil, and the disgust with life which they entail. This could be Pascal speaking.[3] Augustine, a veteran in the passion wars, might have concurred, but here is how Chateaubriand puts it: "Ah! le christianisme est surtout un baume pour nos blessures, quand les passions, d'abord soulevées dans notre sein, commencent à s'apaiser, ou par l'infortune, ou par la durée. Il endort la douleur, il fortifie la résolution chancelante, il prévient les rechutes, en combattant, dans une âme à peine guérie, le dangereux pouvoir des souvenirs: il nous environne de paix et de lumière; il rétablit pour nous cette harmonie des choses célestes, que Pythagore entendait dans le silence de ses passions" ["Oh, Christianity is an especial balm for our wounds, when passions, once aroused in our breast, begin to be calmed, whether by adversity or by time. It puts suffering to sleep, fortifies faltering resolve, prevents relapses, by fighting in the scarcely cured soul the dangerous power of memories; it surrounds us with peace and light and restores for us this harmony of heavenly things which Pythagoras heard in the silence of his passions"].[4]

An aestheticized Christianity, then, performs as a narcosis for the overwrought, or at least for the egotists of romanticism who need from time to time to be rescued from themselves: the heart has treasons of which reason knows nothing. Readers of *Génie*'s encyclopedic celebration of Christian tradition will find nothing about the bearing of a cross nor would they guess that the promised aura of peace and light cannot be derived from the Sermon on the Mount. Not incidentally, Chateaubriand, abundant in patristic references, cites not one passage from the New Testament, but then the Bible was not in his day a book which the devout themselves were allowed to know. He would likely fail to convince anyone that he not only understands Christianity from without but lives it from within, that a need to escape from the expensive ardors of eroticism or any other self-indulgence does not in itself constitute a conversion nor a genuine penance, let alone an attention to the neediness of other sinners. Exhaustion does not stand in the same ledger with renunciation.

The duchess de Broglie, one of Chateaubriand's many aristocratic critics, may have hit the mark when she said that *Génie*'s popularity was a proof of the unbelief (*incrédulité*) of the age, "le produit d'une société toute factice" ["the product of a completely fake society"].[5] There remains something unsettlingly bogus and stagy about this work, not least because the sublimity supposedly bearing us up provokes in its agent a lachrymose enthusiasm, fitful and self-induced. Chateaubriand knew his rhetorical gift and abused it with self-hypnotic abandon. That does not detract from the urgent melancholy of a slavishness to the emotions, a fetter which Chateaubriand is (only) apparently attempting to escape. Yet, in a sense, he needs "the dangerous power of memories" which Christianity was presumably fending off, so that he can feel the more drawn to this religion. Had he wholly embraced it, he would not have been Chateaubriand. Neither would he have written this book.

Although he shows himself no friend of Rousseau, dismissing the paranoid *promeneur solitaire* for his unwholesome self-absorbing solitude, he, like Rousseau, is not so much a religious man as someone intoxicated with religion. *Génie's* celebration of Gothic architecture is credited with a revival in France of interest in things medieval, but that does not alter the plain fact that Chateaubriand was presenting a spectator Christianity, one for on-looking as the occasion of appreciative, exclamatory reveries and noticeable tears. Everything which he commends in Christian life amounts to a kind of trussing up, and the costuming of church and folk tradition remains only adornment.

All of these objections stand for naught, however, if we concede that, whatever its value as a mechanism of social order and control, religion's predominant purpose is therapeutic, that it serves not so much to offer the rigors of a hortatory moral vision as to ensure comfort for the unhappy, the anxious, the weary. Forlorn France at that century's turn labored under far more than weariness: it had become spiritually dispossessed, in a kind of Babylonian captivity of its own devising. Under the sway of ruthlessly secular authorities, the Church had gradually recovered for itself the bracing countercultural vitality of early Christian history, and it was this hardiness, the unshakable appeal of an irrational power, which Napoleon shrewdly saw fit to coopt with the *concordat*. He was also depriving counterrevolutionary foes like Austria of a potent ally in the papacy.

It may seem that Chateaubriand had all too conveniently served the first consul's intent with *Génie*. The book appealed to the educated public because it came not from a religious but from a thoroughly lay writer, one not trained in theology yet able to make a passable case for the affective might of the emotions as a sufficient basis for religious affirmation. In a *Défense* composed after the book underwent its first criticisms, Chateaubriand made much of being a layman, boldly citing Pascal and La Bruyère as his lay predecessors in defense of the faith. It was bootless for a critic like the comte de Salaberry to accuse him of a "charlatanisme des mots," of sustaining "sous une fausse modestie une vanité effrénée" ["under a false modesty an unbridled vanity"].[6] That unflinching, Rousseauist exposure of self, of personality, of emotional susceptibility, far from weakening Chateaubriand's partisanship, likely strengthened it. Any reader would feel at home with such foibles. The not infrequent argument from tears, if wearisome to the judicious, was at least tolerable and far preferable to any dispassionate show of metaphysics from that overworked mare, reason.

Those foibles, however, indicated to anyone concerned about the gravity of the author's religious belief that Chateaubriand wrote mostly for show: exhibits from Christianity's stores of art and cult, yes, but primarily exhibitions of self. On not a page of *Génie* is its composer out of sight. Neither hypocrisy nor insincerity is at issue here: Chateaubriand is always himself but it is not an integral self, as the following passage from his autobiography suggests. He refers to a sunset along the Virginia coast which he had observed during his 1791 voyage to America. It was recalled as one of *Génie*'s many occasions for proving God's existence from nature's beauties: "Quand je peignis ce tableau dont vous pouvez revoir l'ensemble dans le *Génie du christianisme*, mes sentiments religieux s'harmonisaient avec la scène; mais hélas!...ce n'était pas Dieu seul que je contemplais sur les flots dans la magnificence de ses oeuvres. Je voyais une femme inconnue et les miracles de son sourire; les beautés du ciel me semblaient écloses de son souffle; j'aurais vendu l'éternité pour une de ses caresses" ["When I depicted this scene the whole of which you can read in *Génie du christianisme*, my religious feelings harmonized with the setting, but alas!...it wasn't God alone that I contemplated on the waves in the magnificence of his works. I saw an unknown woman and the miracles of her smile; the beauties of the sky seemed to me blossomings of her breath; I would have sold eternity for one of her caresses"].[7]

There is more. As the Virginian sun set, Chateaubriand might have been thinking of God and that absurd phantom, but he was not so distant from the *philosophes* he later scorned in *Génie*. From 1793 to 1797, while writing on ancient and modern revolutions, he anticipated de Maistre's first question: what religion will replace Christianity? He concluded that Christianity's decline was irreversible and hoped that future humanity might attain "un degré de lumières et de connaissances morales suffisant pour n'avoir pas besoin de culte" ["a degree of enlightenment and moral awareness sufficient to dispense with religious worship"]. What more would Voltaire himself have prescribed?

It seems unfair to fault so youthful a writer for changing his mind and heart, but what matters is that Chateaubriand could not realize that their very mutability made them unreliable foundations for the ataraxia he presumably sought. What he aptly styled his religious feelings (*mes sentiments religieux*) were themselves inherently unstable. It is almost comically self-defeating for someone wanting a refuge from his emotions to presume that that refuge lies in an emotional exaltation directed toward religion. The fleetingness of that sublimity which his rhetorical "highs" attest could never be identified even with conviction, let alone creed.

Chateaubriand's *Mémoires*—the passage on Virginia dates from 1822— prove commendably sober toward his much younger self on that American shore as it exposes the pitfalls of an exclusively affective response to religion. He spares us the clumsy piety of a convert—he did not become one—but that fact only underscores the more imposingly the sentimentality, not even vibrant nor fanatical enough to be called religiosity, which is the driving engine of *Génie*. At a safe distance and in a jaded time, we can only read the rhetoric in this book as though it were coming from another race. We know egotism but expect it not to be so unabashedly silly and can only wonder about the tearfulness, affected or simply pathetic, which the writer makes a warrant for the truthfulness of his record.

Here we reach central questions for any study of Thérèse. Is the affective response to religion all in all deficient? Is Chateaubriand's exhibitionistic emotionalism the form which that response will likely tend to assume or can affectivity attain a less labile, more ripened development? What if we call that affectivity by the name of love, to which St. Paul gave primacy among Christian virtues? Does the affective life of a Christian, the subjective act of giving, take its character according to its subject or its object? Chateaubriand, as though seeking asylum, concerned himself not at all with Christ but only with the institutional props, the smells and bells of Christendom. What if one's emotive self were turned almost wholly toward the person of Christ? No less a hair shirt than Pascal had insisted that only the heart feels God; reason, never. And is the act of writing the occasion which prompts emotional exuberance? Is writing not so much the record of a passion as itself the passion? Perhaps when Chateaubriand put down his pen, he became a reasonably mediocre person.

Lamennais and the *Libido Dominandi*

When Napoleon went into exile and the monarchy was restored in France, the Church did not sit down at the banquet of reaction. Pius VII, a Benedictine by training, had weathered the overbearing and devious emperor with a forbearance just short of martyrdom. He became the first beloved pope of modern times and one of its shrewdest. He acknowledged the libertarianism unleashed by the Revolution and secured a *concordat* with Protestant Prussia on behalf of Catholics' freedom of religion, but the papacy had to come to terms with the ascendance of the state from a position of weakness requiring exquisite diplomacy. How the Church would maintain its authority before secular powers, especially those with Catholic cultures—Austria, France, Spain, Italy—became the predominant issue for nineteenth-century pontiffs.

The abiding legacy of 1789 was not its vaunted liberties and egalitarianism but a renewed and strengthened statism, the secular power to which Catholicism, an established but enfeebled religion, became subordinate. The fervor of revolution and reform in the nineteenth century might well be read as energy spent upon a renewal of the impulsions of 1789 against authoritarian structures, but those structures were themselves sustained, if not strengthened, by wars and nationalism. Catholicism, in its papacy, had to contend with both these overweening states and the ideological forces which were pounding at their gates.

To a degree, those ideologies picked up the remnant spiritual power of religion itself, recasting Christendom's legacy into new communitarian forms, some of them ironically modeled on medieval monasticism. Saint-Simon's last book (1825) proclaimed *Le nouveau christianisme*. Chateaubriand's aestheticism had made its case for ad hoc sublimity but had been found wanting by its pharisaical complacency, its total ignorance of the claims of justice. It is instructive that in their *Manifesto*, Marx, a convinced atheist, and Engels urged that they were not opposed to religion, only to bourgeois religion. The redemptive appeal and promise of faith had been coopted, if not aborted, by secularism and the ascendant bourgeoisie which sustained it.

That the Church could no longer remain on the defensive but was imperatively called to renewal by an offensive, was the prophetic insight of its most unruly son since Luther, Hugues Félicité Robert de La Mennais. Born in 1782, he had come of age in the midst of the Revolution's convulsive lurches toward imperial power, but his native Brittany, with its druidic conservatism, had fiercely resisted the centripetal power of the Jacobin capital. (Two vivid fictions, Balzac's *Les Chouans* and Hugo's *Quatre-vingt-treize* attest to this fact.) Like Chateaubriand, he spent an exile in England and began to write. By the time he became a priest, in 1816, he had published two books on the ecclesiastical crisis, neither of which lit fires but which indicate that early on he was mulling over the question which was to occupy the rest of his life: how Christianity was to be reformed to meet the challenge of a materialist age.

His most lengthy work came as early as 1817. *Essai sur l'indifférence en matière de religion* identified the malaise of an age as La Mennais saw it: its satanic zeitgeist. The vigorous parataxes of his writing rival Chateaubriand's rhetoric in their headiness. Indifference was neither doctrine nor doubt nor even an honest atheism; rather "une ignorance systématique, un sommeil volontaire de l'âme, qui épuise sa vigueur à résister à ses propres pensées, un engourdissement universel des facultés morales, une privation absolue d'idées sur ce qu'il importe le plus à l'homme de connoître [sic]" ["a systematic ignorance, the soul's voluntary slumber, which exhausts its power to resist its own thoughts, a universal numbing of moral awareness, a total privation of ideas about what most matters for someone to know"].[8] The *Essai* argued against three assumptions implicit in so-called indifferentism: that religion sufficed merely as a political institution; that, with all religions subject to relativism, only natural religion or deism was valid; and that with a revealed religion, one could be free to pick and choose among its fundamental truths—the latter, an attack upon Luther and Protestantism.

The book won La Mennais instant praise and prompted him to write three supplementary volumes with the same title. It would be interesting to know, given the subsequent and extreme turn of his thinking, whether it was his sharp denunciation of democracy which won clerical approval. "La démocratie la plus effrénée n'est que l'absence de tout ordre et de toute loi" ["The most unbridled democracy is only the absence of all order and law"], a government of passions which honors with its hate all that is superior to it: wealth, talent, genius, glory, and virtue itself.[9] It is a timeless plaint, as old as Plato, and it was sounded through the nineteenth century by Tocqueville, Burckhardt, and Nietzsche. La Mennais stands unique in this succession of protesters because he soon altered his views diametrically.

In 1825, his *De la religion considérée dans ses rapports avec l'ordre politique et social [Religion in Relation to the Sociopolitical Order]* claimed that Christianity had to be extended beyond private life and individual needs so as to inform political and social institutions. By then, he had become completely disillusioned with the Bourbon Restoration and resentful that the state had continued the Napoleonic practice of controlling the Church and keeping its clerics salaried as virtual hirelings. Ever more disdainful of the temporizing and compromised clerical powers in France, La Mennais realized that the only countervailing power to be set against the modern state lay in the papacy. The examples of two popes, Pius VI, who had been humiliated and broken by Napoleon, and Pius VII, who endured and outlasted him, informed the impetus of his vision, but Pius VII's discreet accommodation of the modern age, principally in the *concordats*, dismayed this Breton to a fury. The *concordats* tacitly affirmed the state's predominance over the religious life of its communities; no matter that in signing them, the pontiff was attempting to protect the freedoms of Catholics. While it would be fatuous to suppose that La Mennais, who died in 1854, foresaw such advances as the republican takeover of papal territories in 1869 or Bismarck's *Kulturkampf* against Rome in the 1880s, it would be fair to assume that he never underestimated the threat to Christianity posed by any government which, in his reckoning, could be called spiritually dead. That came to include them all.

La Mennais brought to the fore the central issue of how much Christianity was to render unto Caesar. The Caesar he saw in Restoration France was not martial and triumphant but corrupt and corrupting, and the Church could sustain itself and fulfill its forgotten holy mission only by unqualified secession from its alliance with the state. Nothing could have been more horrific to the vested powers within both civil and ecclesiastical offices than this gospel, which sundered church and state. Instead of two props for authority and order, one would be tilted against the other.

In effect, La Mennais was expecting the Church to seize a kind of cultural initiative, not by appending itself to modern liberal ideas of democracy and equality but by claiming them for its own. Not first with the idea but its most articulate proponent, he became convinced that Christianity was itself true democracy; it alone recognized the equality of all souls. After the collapse of the 1830 revolt, when revolutionaries realized one king had been substituted for another, this celebration of the people was much to the fore. Jules Michelet, in his *Introduction à l'histoire universelle* (1831), proclaimed *le peuple* the anonymous victor of modern times, when revolutions would be waged "sans héros, sans noms propres; point d'individu en qui la gloire ait pu se localiser" ["without heroes and proper names, with no individual in whom glory could be concentrated"].[10] For La Mennais, however, the exalted masses needed a prophetic leader and that would be the pope. The papacy became in his vision the seat of prophecy, uniting a resurrected Christian Europe against the state and the bourgeoisie it served. Christianity would reclaim its spiritual life by championing the poor and oppressed.

La Mennais propagated these views in *L'Avenir* [*The Future*], a journal he founded in October 1830, three months after a Paris uprising nearly toppled the restored monarchy. Although never widely circulated, its influence quickly became powerful enough to be noticed. Hugo, Lamartine, Balzac, Vigny, and Michelet himself were among its contributors. La Mennais enjoyed a kind of miniature court of young and enthusiastic coworkers, two of whom, Henri Lacordaire and Charles de Montalembert, later played conspicuous roles in the Catholic liberalism which La Mennais seems virtually to have invented. In him, at least, that cause had its first martyr.

Rapt by his intense version of a Christian apocalypse, he had not reckoned that the papacy required diplomacy as well as prophecy, and no pope would likely respond well to an impetuous role casting and its implicit dictation from below. Besides, *L'Avenir's* attacks upon the Church establishment in France alienated its editor from any possible support there for his crusade against the state and the middle class. Rome received vigorous complaints about the insolent and dangerous populism La Mennais was promoting in the name of the faith. When, after a year, *L'Avenir* was forced to close due to poor financial management, he told subscribers he would go to Rome to appeal to Pope Gregory XVI.

Do prophets seek martyrdom? La Mennais, uncompromising and fervid, would have been a challenge for any pope, but Gregory XVI, of aristocratic lineage, a one-time professor of philosophy and a pontiff interested chiefly in theology, was beset by the very forces which La Mennais wanted to fuel with Christian zeal. There had been nationalist uprisings in Rome and in the papal territories; the pope put a lid on a boiling kettle, paying Austria and France for soldiers of occupation. If La Mennais had been inspired by the overthrow of the Bourbons in July 1830, the papacy was not. Gregory XVI received him politely and dodged discussion of *L'Avenir*. La Mennais did not know that by the time he arrived in Rome, the pope had received a report from theologians appointed by some French bishops. It concluded that La Mennais as early as his *Essai sur l'indifférence* had shown himself a libertarian, subscribing not to revelation but to universalist notions of individual conscience. Thomism alone might have persuaded Gregory that La Mennais was a dangerously modern man.

The encyclical *Mirari vos* (August 15, 1832) condemned La Mennais's presumption that Christendom needed renewal, as though Christian revelation could grow tired or stale, as though the Church itself "could be considered subject to defect or obscuration or other misfortune."[11] It attacked the implicit union La Mennais was forging with any revolutionary movement against state authorities, and it rejected his keystone proposition that church and state should be separated. This sharply worded document against virtually every idea that could be called liberal, modern, or progressive (including freedom of the press and of individual conscience), set the tone of the papacy well into the twentieth century, putting one pontiff after another on the defensive. The Syllabus of Errors, the Index, the doctrine of papal infallibility all variously express this rear-guard position against emergent ideologies. The Church at bay was far from able or willing to appreciate La Mennais's incendiary program, including his option for the poor.

Initially, he submitted. He even signed an act of submission, but within two years he published *Paroles d'un croyant*, one of the truly extraordinary documents of apocalyptic literature, if not of Christianity. A measure of its appeal came from its selling one hundred thousand copies; it was translated into a number of languages, including Flemish, Lamennais being particularly popular among Belgians struggling against Dutch rule.[12] Its prophetic, disjointed assertiveness exposes its weaknesses in argument and yet it makes clear the author's egalitarian bias against all established order. (He recast his name from the aristocratic La Mennais to Lamennais but neither appeared as the author of *Paroles*.) As we are all born equal before God, whose law of love and self-sacrifice precludes hierarchies, all kingships and other dominations must be ended so that a universal epoch of justice and unity can be realized. Lamennais directs his animus almost exclusively against secular powers but in one macabre passage he fantasizes a council of ghoulish rulers (they drink blood from skulls, as had happened in the Terror) enlisting clergy in a struggle to the death against Christ. Priests can be bribed into making the people wholly subservient to the state. Such was Lamennais's view of the Church under the Bourbons.

Paroles alternates between weird tableaux such as the vampiric eucharist and pious depictions of the oppressed—bereft, dispossessed families—which are meant to bring forth indignant tears. Chateaubriand, closing his *Mémoires*, complained that Lamennais had appropriated his language but not his ideas,[13] meaning, perhaps, that sublimity was no longer to be wondered at, but achieved by the insurgent poor. The most curious aspect of *Paroles* lies here, in its glowing vision of Christian harmonies established on earth and the vehement, wrathful calls to social and political leveling apparently necessary to achieve that vision. On one hand, Lamennais asserts that if only love could prevail, there would be no more servitude; on the other, he likens *liberté* to the kingdom of God, which only the violent can bear away. His apocalypticism fashions the impoverished into the image of Christ crucified and the ruling class into ministers of Satan.

The most startling of this book's assaults is directed at the military, at the French chivalric tradition of honor and what Lamennais scorns as *obéissance passive*, another instrument of oppression but one which can be converted to serve the poor. In a long strophic passage, with "Jeune soldat, où vas-tu?" ["Where are you going, young soldier?"] iterated fourteen times and answered with "Que tes armes soient bénies, jeune soldat!" ["May your weapons be blessed, young soldier!"], he conjures up his onward Christian soldiers for the end-time of justice.[14] It is not difficult to imagine how this invocation of a proletarian army confounded the entrenched officers of church and state, especially as it came from a prominent and influential ultramontanist now converted to the gospel of popular sovereignty. Had Lamennais not clothed his *Paroles* in the sanctifying rhetoric of brotherly love, he could have been dismissed as a mere apostate. Instead, he had made himself into a grotesque anomaly, a kind of Bolshevik St. Francis.

From the twenty-first century, we might recast *Mennaisisme*, as it came to be known, into terms long familiar to the debate on nationalism and colonialism. In state leadership and in the bourgeoisie it served, Lamennais decried what Sartre would call "systematic violence," an in-built structure of manipulation and oppression which could only be overcome by revolutionary violence. Lamennais *engagé* seems in that sense a precursor of Sartre, and like Sartre he had an immense influence upon the young generation of his age, George Sand within it. Further, the Church's censure of him is not unlike Camus's criticism of Sartre for an opportunistic alliance with movements that violated human dignity.

We need not look ahead to Marxism and its apologists in approaching Lamennais. His appeal to a *sens commun* exposes his substantial debt to Rousseau, who had mightily influenced his vagrant and, for a time, atheistic adolescence. But a weighty difference remains: Rousseau did not base his arguments upon Christian Scripture. Neither would Rousseau have ever imagined that the papacy could be the guiding light for political freedoms. Gregory XVI's rejection of Lamennais and his crusading *Avenir* explains in large part the absence of any churchly helmsman in *Paroles*. To Lamennais, the papacy had shown itself to be as corrupt as the priesthood in Bourbon France. That, too, is why the people themselves become the Christ figure in whom he foresees a resurrection from oppression. The work culminates in a Dantesque vision of luminous unity in God.[15]

For himself in *Paroles*, he cast the role of an exile wandering forever homeless. That was his fate after the pope denounced the book, "small in size, enormous in wickedness," in another encyclical, *Singulari vos*, issued June 25, 1834.[16] This Frenchman, he said, had "cloaked Catholic teaching in enticing verbal artifice, in order ultimately to oppose it and overthrow it." The pope seems to have been especially incensed that Lamennais wrote as though dispatched and inspired by God: "He twists the words of Holy Scripture in a bold and cunning manner in order to firmly establish his depraved ravings." *Paroles* could only promote anarchy by its calumnies and falsehoods. In sum, it was a prime specimen of the danger in giving any tether to individual conscience. Gregory concluded in the feeble hope that the prodigal might return submissively to the fold, but the fulminations of papal prose made that unlikely. Lamennais's supporters abandoned him rapidly.

He fell away from Catholicism but translated the Gospels, the *Imitatio Christi* (Thérèse read his translation avidly), and the *Commedia*. How he must have been quickened by Dante's savage words on Avignon's miscreant popes and on the wayward Church, caricatured in *Purgatorio* as the whore of French kings. He served in the French Assembly for two terms beginning in the convulsive year of 1848. It must have seemed that his time had come, but he did not distinguish himself—this prophet was eloquent on paper only—and after the coup of 1851, he withdrew into permanent obscurity. Gregory's successor, Pius IX, tried to coax him back into the Church but to no avail. As he had requested, Lamennais was buried in an anonymous pauper's grave, with no cross over it.

No one labored more assiduously than Lamennais to reconcile Christianity with democracy, to push the Church toward a candid dealing with social and political issues. He might be said to have invented the social or liberal Catholicism of modern activists, of all those who commit themselves to oppressed multitudes. Whether it is possible to reconcile the demand for rights with the call to bearing one's cross remains a debatable matter, even though the tag of Christian Democrat has long been sanctioned as something other than an oxymoron. But Christ did not overcome the world by running for office or leading a campaign of insurrection against the Caesars. He left the political establishment of his time wholly untouched, uncriticized, unchanged. The pope's charge in *Mirari vos* that Christians have always owed self-subordination to political authority is scripturally well based. Resist not evil. But what of the truth which is to make you free?

When Lamennais worked himself up into the anaphoric grievances of a prophet, he was standing much closer to Rousseau than to Jeremiah or even to the Johannine *Revelation*. Man was born free but is everywhere in chains: such could be the epitome of *Paroles* no less than of Jean-Jacques's *Discours sur l'origine et les fondements de l'inégalité parmi les hommes*. And like Rousseau, Lamennais seemed to be setting everything afire. (The pope called *Paroles* a "torch of treason.") It takes little imagination to assess his incendiarism from the pope's vantage. *Liberté* was a code word for license, if not chaos; a Pandora's box of subversions; 1793, again. The great Revolution had unleashed a furious, destructive hostility to the Church, and why should not any other revolution do the same?

Much was once made of Lamennais's catastrophic tone, that he defeated himself by his zealotry. Had he been temperate, controllable, more patient, he might have exerted a meliorative influence on the Church, even upon Pope Gregory. This seems an improbable, even anachronistic, view. Had he spoken, for example, the conciliatory language of *Gaudium et Spes*, of pastoral renewal and openness to the secular world, Lamennais would still not have been able to persuade the papacy to adopt a "progressive" policy if only because the non-Catholic society of that time would probably not have credited such a position. Gregory and every pope after him faced a turbulent world of anticlericalism and indifferentism, against which the ecclesia had no choice but to stand firm. It is one measure of the peculiar intensity of Lamennais's ultramontanism that he presumed the papacy could consign itself to the flood tides of the modern age and steer a sure course on behalf of the democracy which, under Robespierre and Saint-Just, had nearly destroyed the Church in France.

Here is one verdict on an extraordinary personality: "cet homme emporté, dont l'âme sembloit [sic] n'être qu'un assemblage de passions violentes que nourrissoit [sic] un orgueil sans bornes, se montra d'abord résolu à courber son front superbe sous l'autorité.... Mais lorsque ses erreurs eurent été proscrites à Rome...ne prenant désormais conseil que de ses sombres ressentiments, il changea tout à coup de langage, et, ne gardant plus de mesure, lança, dans sa fureur, anathème contre anathème et arbora l'étendard de la rébellion" ["this impassioned man, whose soul seemed only a gathering of violent passions nourished by boundless pride, at first showed himself resolved to bend his proud countenance before authority.... But when Rome had proscribed his errors,...he took only his dark resentments for counsel, wholly changed his language, and, observing no constraint, threw out in his fury anathema after anathema and planted the standard of rebellion"]. The subject of these remarks was Martin Luther. Their author was Félicité de La Mennais.[17]

It seems that Lamennais, had he not lost his belief in heaven, would have liked to spend his life doing good on earth. The present book is about someone else who lost heaven and who had precisely that idea of terrestrial beneficence, said so, and cast herself in the sterling lead role of Christian spirituality. "I shall be Love," she said. It was a kind of popular sovereignty which forced the Church's hand and enlisted her among the saints.

Like Lamennais, Thérèse broke from the static circle of convention and made her dynamic way into the recesses of a hard-won intuition. That kind of movement subverts by its inherent antinomian thrust. It makes a proleptic claim upon humanity by its exceptional and loving creativity.[18] The *réflexions* he appended to his translation of the Gospels stand as Lamennais's noblest work in that vein: unequivocal, incisive, exigent. What would Thérèse have made of them? She knew and treasured his translation of the *Imitatio Christi* with other *réflexions*. A work by Lamennais, that outcast?!? Too bad, she replied equably. The differences between him and her, these dauntless adventurers, are nonetheless marked, not least that Lamennais became programmatic and bitter. Thérèse, forever a daughter of the Church, had no program, and she knew that bitterness is a good tonic but a poor diet.

Renan and the *Libido Sciendi*

In the summer of 1863, Pope Pius IX issued an encyclical, *Quanto conficiamur maerore*. "With how much grief we are overwhelmed" not least because of "the corruption of morals so extensively increasing and promoted by irreligious and obscene writings." He might have been referring to one of the most devastating books ever written about Christianity, Ernest Renan's *Vie de Jésus*, published less than two months earlier. From 1846, his papacy's first year, Pius IX had castigated the modern world for its many errant isms: socialism, rationalism, indifferentism, latitudinarianism, and a year after *Quanto maerore*, he issued a summary of their falsehoods, the famous Syllabus of Errors. If we look within that engaging text for condemnation of Renan, we find it in the pope's decrying of human reason and of scientific progress in understanding religion and its dogmas.

Renan was one of the most accomplished philologists of nineteenth-century scholarship. He was decisively influenced by the positivistic dogma prevalent in his time, that knowledge is obtainable only within the demonstrable limits of the natural world. On that empirical base, Auguste Comte had erected what he called the religion of humanity, superseding theology and metaphysics. Taking this partisan view—truth counts only when measurable— Renan's reading of early Christian history via the New Testament sundered Jesus of Nazareth from Christ, the only begotten Son who proceeds from the Father. Although German Protestantism had produced scholars who tilled the soil around "the historical Jesus" long before Renan, his book remains of profound importance as a work composed within and effectually against the Catholic culture of France during and after the Second Empire. Its novelty was explosive: eight editions were issued within the first three months.

Like Chateaubriand, Renan came from deeply conservative Brittany and, also like him, he was answerable to a deeply pious mother. But his youthful apostasy grew and hardened, beginning in the seminary education which toward his life's end he affectionately recalls in his engaging autobiography. There he says of Lamennais that he exchanged one faith for another; leaving the Church naturally made this priest celebrant of another absolute: democracy.[19] Renan, although he left the Church, did so with not a drop of Lamennais's righteous vitriol, and his learning made him too much of an elitist ever to embrace multitudes unquestioningly. He, too, merely changed profound allegiances. The religion to which he transferred his credulous sensibility was science, the predominant faith of the mid-nineteenth century. Even so, he never stopped looking back to the religion which he did much to undermine. Indeed, he ventured to give spirituality a reformulation: "Car la foi absolue est incompatible avec l'histoire sincère. Mais l'amour va sans la foi.... Dieu s'était révélé avant Jésus, Dieu se révélera après lui" ["Surely absolute faith is incompatible with real history. But love proceeds without faith. ... God was revealed before Jesus and will be revealed after him"].[20]

Albert Schweitzer, his severest critic, charges him with insincerity, and why is little wonder.[21] Renan presents a Jesus he has unctuously aestheticized but does not believe in by any measure of faith. He purports to write in the scientific spirit of historicism, but he has simply discarded all the mystery and miracle of Christ—they are unprovable—and filled in his narrative with conjecture, which while entertaining is not consistently imposing. The emergent Jesus is soft, sentimentalized, deluded, and yet somehow indispensable to humanity. Renan might not have been the first to recast Jesus with the accommodating humanist tag of "great teacher," but that is about the best he can and wants to do. Shrewdly, Renan knew his audience. He did not write a scrupulously cautious, well-grounded (dry) academic work. Had he done so, it would never have reached that eighth edition nor even a second. Yet, the effect of his book's outraging the Church and its defenders was to discredit all genuinely scholarly effort in France toward historical reconstructions of Jesus and his time. Worthy biblical scholarship remained the almost exclusive province of German Protestants for generations.

That is not to dismiss Renan's interpretation altogether. He reads with at times bracingly candid eyes, drawing conclusions which rocked the piety of his day. For example, he asserts about Jesus: "Sa famille ne semble pas l'avoir aimé, et, par moments, on le trouve dur pour elle" ["His family seems not to have loved him and at times he is harsh toward it"], a remark which he undergirds with no fewer than seven citations from the four Gospels.[22] In effect, he was bidding his readers to undertake something they had never done before because it had been prohibited: reading the Scriptures for themselves. Interpretation was long the meat of Protestantism but fruit forbidden to Catholicism. Here was a scholar of intimidatingly high credentials, recently seated by Napoleon III in the chair of Hebrew at the Collège de France, subverting the shepherdly authority of priests.

It would be easy, even so, to overdraw the heuristic force of *Vie de Jésus*. Renan's readers of those eight brisk editions were not in the main genuine believers but rather, like himself, lapsed Catholics who had gone the secular way, many to the extremes of anticlericalism. The Church's direst foes usually have come from the once-docile ranks of embittered childhood and adolescence. Some, like Alfred de Musset, found themselves caught between heart and head, realizing it was now unfashionable to believe and yet unable to shed fully the trappings of faith and its not inconsiderable consolations.[23] The rigorously pious were warned off early with denunciations from the pulpit and higher. There were numerous early attacks upon Renan, but none of his foes could match his learning. Of those who wrote instantly against him, Schweitzer cites only the bishop of Orleans, the famous Dupanloup, as estimable.

Along with his chair in Hebrew, Renan held another trump. He had written *Vie de Jésus* while on the spot, in Palestine. It would be hard from our distance to measure the strength of this fact, that to the bourgeoisie of his day he had the double appeal of exoticism and authenticity. Chateaubriand knew that his own charm lay in his adventurism, inflated though much of it was and as it was expected to be: he had gone to the New World of *Atala*; he had nearly lost his life at the Niagara Falls where that melancholy story concludes. Renan had gone back toward Eden but had made of his journey something other than a romantic dreamscape: it was a scientific mission. French readers had long been familiar with travel literature on North Africa: Lamartine and Nerval wrote of Egypt (Chateaubriand had been there, too); Fromentin, of Algeria; Delacroix, of Morocco. Flaubert's disastrously bad historical fiction, *Salammbô*, was the product of his exuberant research in Tunisia. All of these writers fed the Gallic taste for an impressionism of the bizarre, the allure of a fantastic otherness sure to relieve, however fleetingly, the crushing ennui of life at home. Renan was different: he was disrupting the home itself and with the prestige of supposedly detached, disinterested scientific inquiry.

To smile at his scholarship is to risk condescension. He is confidently categorical, for example, about the limits of Jesus' learning. It derived at best, says this chair of Hebrew, from Hillel of fifty years before: their "aphorisms" match. Renan claims that Jesus did not likely know Greek, a matter still under dispute today, with some scholars confident that he could have learned it at the Greco-Roman resort town of Sepphoris, only three miles north of Nazareth. Gifted at scene painting, one of romanticism's fetishes, Renan somehow fails to depict a carpenter and his son with commissions among their cosmopolitan neighbors. On the other hand, he sometimes ventures into absurdity in trying to rationalize (dismiss) miracles: Lazarus was not raised from the dead. That would be too much for the age of skeptical science to swallow. No, he planned and performed the role of a dead man in order to spread Jesus' reputation as a wonder worker.

Renan's optic upon Jesus is complex and ever shifting. At times, it veers toward that of Lamennais, to whom he likens John the Baptist, "toujours irrité." The God of Jesus is not a punitive despot but "le Dieu de l'humanité." Jesus founded "la doctrine de la liberté des âmes...l'idée la plus révolutionnaire qui soit jamais éclose dans un cerveau humain" ["the doctrine of freedom of soul...the most revolutionary idea ever conceived by the human mind"], exactly the spiritual freedom Pius IX decried in the Syllabus. God is not to be proved by metaphysical argument, says Renan, because Jesus felt the divine within him, as Plato had before him; St. Paul and Augustine, after. That sounds almost digestible until one realizes what he is actually saying. Only passingly does the Church itself come in for swipes: "Jamais on n'a été moins prêtre que ne le fut Jésus, jamais plus ennemi des formes qui étouffent la religion sous prétexte de la protéger" ["Never was anyone less a priest than Jesus, never more inimical to the proprieties which stifle religion under the pretext of protecting it"].[24]

In his profile of Jesus, a recurrent number of giveaway epithets obtrudes: *charmant, sublime, doux, ravissant, délicieux.* Renan learned much from Chateaubriand and the taste he had created. For Jesus seems to be manifestly of his romantic stamp, an aesthete. Isolated from the exacting spirituality which speaks from every page of the Gospels, Jesus, no longer the Christ, becomes an admissible club member of the literate Second Empire bourgeoisie. It was a trick easy to turn and not for the last time, the refashioning of Christ into the terms of modern, sophisticated prejudice, a reduction to convenience and tacit dismissal. Much celebrated in salons later in his life, Renan once remarked that France wants to be flattered and to share its faults. In *Vie de Jésus*, he was rendering his subject according to that dictum: Jesus, the *cher maître*, negotiably noble, harmlessly inimitable, with all vestiges of the miraculous consigned to the bin of superstition and delusion.

The central tenets of the Christian faith, the Incarnation and the Resurrection, cannot figure here even as the inexplicable mysteries they are, because they belong to a prescientific antiquation. Renan dispatches altogether St. Matthew's scene with Christ risen standing before a woman who, according to *Mark* and *Luke*, had been possessed of seven demons. The facts will never emerge to confirm the resurrection of Jesus. All we are left with, Renan urges, is the powerful imagination of Mary Magdalene: "Pouvoir divin de l'amour! Moments sacrés où la passion d'une hallucinée donne au monde un Dieu ressuscité!" ["Divine power of love! Sacred moments when the passion of a hallucinating woman gives to the world a resurrected God!"].[25] By such legerdemain this professor of Semitic languages deftly reminded his readers that only the demonstrable realm of scientific investigation could be counted on for truth. Having lost the capacity for genuine, inner faith, Renan exalted the superstitious enlightenment of his age into the outer sort, one seeking ominous relief in the spread of complacency.

Renan's autobiography, an invaluable window onto the Church's intellectual life in midcentury France, shows how his use of reasoning, though flowered by rhetoric, not only served to confound the Gospel accounts but turned the medieval baggage of scholasticism inside out. All theological dogmas revealed by Scripture and authorized in councillary judgments had presumably been made demonstrable by and to reason. Revelation and church authority were thus proven. And so the Church was incensed—Renan was then a seminarian at Saint-Sulpice—when Lamennais told it to start anew, to begin not with reason, but with faith. How was that possible, since reason had for centuries been appointed the sole determinant of Christian truth?

It wasn't, and it remains to Renan's credit that he had recognized that fact long before he wrote *Vie de Jésus*. In 1848, he had declared abiding allegiance to the nostrums of his age: "C'est l'amour pur de la science qui m'a fait briser les liens de toute croyance révélée, et j'ai senti que, le jour où je me suis proclamé sans autre maître que la raison, j'ai posé la condition de la science" ["Pure love of science caused me to break the bonds of all revealed belief, and I felt that the day I proclaimed myself without any master save reason, I set out the terms of science"].[26] But for the Church, this new gospel, whether denominated as positivism or materialism, amounted to nothing other than atheism. The trouble was that the formidable scholarly authority of Renan, which he was careful not to parade before his popular readership, could not be matched by any learning within the ecclesiastical community. There was no such thing as biblical scholarship and "higher criticism" in France at that time.

It is instructive that when Renan's own master at Saint-Sulpice, Félix Dupanloup, a most prominent writer on behalf of Catholic education, wrote at length against his former student, his chosen audience was the piously concerned parents of impressionable young minds: *Avertissement à la jeunesse et aux pères de famille sur les attaques dirigées contra la religion par quelques écrivains de nos jours* [*Warning to Youth and the Fathers of Families about Attacks Directed against Religion by Some Writers of Today*]. At 125 pages, it was longer than a pamphlet but bore the compulsive gravity of one. Issued in precipitous response to *Vie de Jésus*, it makes no mention of Renan's bestseller, citing by ample quotes only Renan's *Études d'histoire religieuse* and his essays in the trendy *Revue des deux mondes*. Dupanloup charges him and the eminent medical encyclopedist Émile Littré (subsequently, editor of the great *Dictionnaire*) with *l'exégèse anti-chrétienne*. The incendiary post-Sulpician pronouncements come tumbling forth: faith stands in inverse proportion to mental vigor and intellectual cultivation. Faith is a strange malady which to the shame of civilization has not yet disappeared from humankind. No limit can be set to the human mind, as nothing is above man. God, providence, immortality are good old words, a bit heavy perhaps, which philosophy shall interpret in ever more refined ways. Dupanloup granted that, with Renan, negation was always well nuanced—a function of the protean self to which Renan himself admitted—but he also saw that this one-time seminarian was spreading his antitheism widely. *Vie de Jésus* was not constrained by the dry Teutonic pedantry on which it was built. It courted popular appeal and approbation.

Dupanloup knew his audience, too. He knew Renan could not be confronted on his own academic ground, only identified to the faithful as one of the false prophets in the age of ascendant sciences. Even so, Renan to the end of his life denied he wrote in a Voltairean spirit. He was aware that he could never shake off the Catholicism which had informed his early years, even when he had renounced it, and in that he was speaking for many contemporaries who might have presumed that they had become altogether modern and materialist. His enthrallment to the cult of reason closed him off to all that remains ineffable, to all that must remain forever mystery, beyond calculation, formulation, and control. His often-quoted *boutade* for the salons, that even God is possible, attests a poverty of which the Gospels do not speak. By that, Renan achieves a certain pathos even in acknowledging the void in him and in his age. Toward the end of his *Souvenirs* he remarks absurdly, "Le dogme de la grâce est le plus vrai des dogmes chrétiens" ["Grace is the truest of the Christian dogmas"], a concession that his unbelief, once professional and then fashionable, might have been helped.[27] Most poignant of all is his admission elsewhere that the direction which faith had given to his life persisted even when that faith had vanished. He speaks for the lapsed in all ages when he likens himself and them to animals whose brains have been removed and who yet go on making certain motions by force of instinct. That can go on only so long before attentuation is complete. We are living on the shadow of a shadow, he confesses, and what will those who come after us live on?[28]

A noble skepticism in the tradition of Pascal and Kant reached the end of its tether in Renan. Having lost Christian faith, he convinced himself that he was altogether reasonable in doing so. He knew that, a lost lamb, he had been joined by most of the herd. The shepherd must be permanently absent. Besides, did he not go on loving, or rather admiring, Jesus, the Mediterranean Jewish peasant? Was it not enough that that Jesus was anybody's great teacher?

Of our three Bretons, Renan stands closest to Thérèse. With the translated Gospels her daily companion, she longed for the skill to know their Greek, one of several languages Renan carried with magisterial insouciance. Likely awed by his learning, she would have matched him in wanting the truth. The terminus they both reached affords the apparent link. She, too, lost the assentive power of faith and knew unremitting darkness. At the close, she acknowledged as kin the company of those she called the "worst materialists." Yet, she did not amble through the void with uneasy rhetoric nor did she have the dubious benefit of a learning which could have propped her up by rationale, extenuation, and lofty excuses. She had no public to assuage or reassure in its barrenness. Writing a few stark pages, she fretted that she was expressing herself poorly, but in them she says much more than Renan did with many.

It is in that final text of hers with its searing and clairvoyant testimony that, one hundred years later, de Maistre's call for new Christian life was at last answered.

2

A Short Life in Brief

Il nous semblait voir en elle plutôt un ange qu'une créature humaine [We seemed to see in her an angel rather than a human being].
—"Le vrai caractère de Ste. Thérèse de
l'Enfant-Jésus," by her four natural sisters,
November 27, 1934, Archives du Carmel

Thérèse était touchée jusqu'aux larmes de ces marques de confiance
et d'amitié, mais elle répondait toujours qu'elle n'abandonnerait
pas son père vieux et malade dans ces circonstances aussi cruelles.
"Tu as raison, ma chère enfant," lui dit la comtesse, "tu remplis le
devoir d'une tendre et pieuse fille, Dieu te bénira. Demeure donc
auprès ton père, sois la consolation et la joie de ses vieux jours"
[Thérèse was moved to tears by these shows of trust and friendship but always replied that she would not leave her sick, old father
in such cruel circumstances. "You're right, my child," said the
countess, "you're fulfilling a tender, pious daughter's duty and God
will bless you. Stay then with your father and be the joy and consolation of his waning years"].
—Chanoine Schmidt, *La Guirlande de
Houblon*, a novel from the Martin
family's library

Eh! Qu'importent, après tout, des douleurs, des infortunes,
quand l'éternité nous appartient, quand nous pouvons conquérir le
ciel par la vertu! [Well, after all, what do pains and misfortunes

matter when eternity belongs to us, when we can conquer heaven by virtue!]

—Mme. Woilliez, *L'orpheline de Moscou; ou, La jeune institutrice*, a novel from the Martin family's library

The priest was telling the girls about hell and about their apparently more than favorable prospects of arriving there. It was even possible, he said, that one of them would die during the night. Twelve and thirteen years old, they were at a retreat before Communion, the first for some and possibly the last for one or another. In case anyone was drifting into boredom with his menace or into fantasy, imagining herself in her splendid Communion garb perhaps, he would rivet her attention with an image. As God hates mortal sin, picture a dove that has been trampled into the mud and can no longer fly. That is how a girl would be if caught in mortal sin, unable to lift her soul any longer to God.

Buoyed by these cheering words, they filed back to their rooms at the Benedictine school with the assignment to record their resolutions to live a pious life. What were they to write? That they would call on the Blessed Virgin to help? That they would do their best to curb their pride? One of them wrote down both of these resolves and added, "Je ne me découragerai pas" ["I will not be discouraged"].[1]

Her name was Marie-Françoise-Thérèse Martin. Millions know her only as Thérèse or the Little Flower. She was indeed so little that the foremost Catholic theologian of the last half-century, Karl Rahner, had no use for her. Pope Pius X (1903–1914) anticipated her sanctification when she had been dead for little more than a decade, calling her the greatest saint of modern times. Now she is called doctor of the Church.

And what did she call herself? A little grain of sand, a nothing, and the queen of France and of Navarre.

That last title came because, though she and her father, Louis, were bourgeois, he was her *cher petit roi*, her dear little king, and France was as good a kingdom as any to reign over and the only one that either of them knew, short of heaven. They lived in a democratic and republican age, however, and he lost his kingdom by losing all he had: his wife, his community, his daughter, and then his mind. She, for her part, lost him and then the prospect of heaven. Their sufferings give the keen and bitter edge to this story, which, as it concerns the fragility of love and its endurance of God's testing, is about a very dark grace.

When she was born in 1873, in the Norman town of Alençon, her father was well into his fiftieth year. He and his wife, Zélie, had lost four of their children. The five who survived were all girls, Thérèse being last, the *benjamine*. In 1877, Zélie died at forty-six of breast cancer but her profile remains, with her husband's, so vital to this story that she has earned a chapter for herself, chiefly because she was a writer. Beyond its own trauma, her death

FIGURE 2.1. "A monk astray in the world": Louis Martin in the last years before disaster. Copyright Archives du Carmel de Lisieux.

brought another one for her husband as he left the town in which he was deeply rooted and moved his daughters to Lisieux, some fifty miles to the north, where his wife's brother, Isidore Guérin, a pharmacist, lived with his wife and two young daughters.[2] It was tacitly understood in that time that no man, especially one so late in his life as Louis, could manage a family alone (see figure 2.1). Remarriage would have been unthinkable, and the Guérins provided indispensable psychological support for the bereaved Martin family. Isidore had, besides a conventional piety, some shrewd sense of financial management. Eighteen years younger than Louis, he became the guardian of the Martin girls.

Louis settled with his daughters, Marie, Pauline, Léonie, Céline, and Thérèse, into a house Isidore had found for them and which remains the most vivid entryway we have into the familial past, "Les Buissonnets." It is not a large house even by bourgeois standards of the time. The dining room and Louis's bedroom directly above it have the only ample dimensions, but the other rooms argue their coziness well, not least of all the smallest, which were on the top floor, known as the belvedere, where Louis had his study; the maid, her room; Pauline, a room for painting; and for all of them, a southwesterly view over Lisieux and its Cathedral of Saint-Pierre, where they were unfailingly attendant. There was even a crawlspace between two rooms, a kind of tunnel where someone could hide in the midst of a game. A large garden in the rear included a laundry house under whose shelter there was a swing for the younger girls. There, they staged little plays for the family and guests in summer.

The eldest daughters, Marie and Pauline, were educated at a Visitandine convent school in Le Mans, where their mother's only sister was a nun, Sr. Marie-Dosithée. They distinguished themselves well there: Marie and Pauline won book prizes for their scholastic achievements, thus setting a high standard that the younger sisters never were able to match. Marie had the early and inestimable privilege of being her father's favorite, as Pauline was her mother's. As in any family, especially a large one, the dynamics were not fixed, but gender was. While Marie's stubbornness earned her the sobriquet of *bohémienne* (gypsy) from Louis, Pauline showed herself to be the dutiful daughter of her mother, conscientious and complicit in Zélie's hope that her own frustrated intent in adolescence to enter a religious order could be vicariously realized.

Léonie, in the hazardous position of middle child, was sickly from the start and grew up with severe cases of eczema and neglect. When Zélie died, eight-year-old Céline vocally elected Marie, seventeen, as her new mother. Thérèse immediately chose Pauline, sixteen, for the same role. Hagiographies duly recount this pivotal episode but, following the saint's autobiographical account, they glide past the unspeakably wounded girl in the midst of that mourning.[3]

Léonie had to work out her sisters' strangely enduring blindness toward her. In the motherless home, she was the only one with a room of her own. She alone did not become a Carmelite, choosing instead the spirituality of St. François de Sales. In this story about suffering, love, and loss, about the spirituality of the hidden and forgotten, Léonie could be found competing with her sister for our attention. She has been given something of her due in the chapter on her mother, the one who finally discovered and in a sense redeemed her, at the last.

If, in her faltering and humiliated childhood, Léonie was first in discovering "the little way" famously associated with her sister, Céline provides another exception: she alone of the five girls was spirited and sociable, tough enough to have managed a secular life. Louis, who loved literature, recited poetry, and sang songs at home, his fingers tapping the rhythms on the dining table, had encouraged his daughters to pursue the arts, but Céline not only learned to paint, as did Pauline before her and Thérèse subsequently: she took up photography, a skill the French had once contested as an art but by the 1880s had come to regard as a manageable pastime for bourgeois ladies.

In the undeviatingly conventional Martin and Guérin households, the camera proclaimed some measure of independence and initiative. She was also the only sister to learn how to handle men, no mean accomplishment in a culture where women were kept subordinate in virtually every sphere. And she turned down marriage proposals.[4]

Those were years to come. Céline was too intelligent to perform as well as her older sisters in school. She had to face her gentle but exacting father with some mediocre grades from Notre-Dame-du-Pré, the Benedictine Abbey school in Lisieux where the dove had been trampled into the mud (the school, destroyed by Allied bombing during the Second World War, was rebuilt and now looks like an American junior high of the 1950s). Thérèse, eight, followed her there. Despite more than three years' difference between them, these sisters grew up closely together: they shared a room, played dolls together, read the same books.[5] In the hagiography, iterating Thérèse's own account, they sit many times together in early adolescence at the belvedere window of Les Buissonnets, looking out upon a nightscape, sharing reveries about Jesus, "le regard plongé dans le lointain" ["our gaze cast into the distance"] (A 48r), wrote Thérèse. Her romanticizing phrase puts the two girls closer at that moment to Lamartine, one of their father's favored poets, than to Augustine and Monica in the garden at Ostia, those being the saints with whom Thérèse is comparing Céline and herself.[6] (See figure 2.2.)

The life of any recollected family lives in its anecdotes. One not in Thérèse's autobiography came from Céline late in her nearly ninety years. In early adolescence, she had excited her younger sister with anticipation of a secret present. Thérèse's glee turned to instant dismay and tears when the present turned out to be a toy cap pistol. While this triviality says much about Céline—and did she have her own cap pistol?—it illustrates her sister's penchant for weeping at the slightest instance, not even nor usually a provocative one.[7] The difficulty was soon resolved by Louis, who, in the girls' presence, presented the pistol to a boy outside church awaiting his first Communion. The lad's delight was unbounded.

A keenly sensitive child, Thérèse resorted to the plangent throughout her life. She tells on herself, that she would not only weep over the smallest matters but that she would even weep for having wept. In her conventual life, when she was in charge of Carmelite novices, she would weep when one of them did. It was the outward measure of her vulnerability: she was in the main cosseted at home—a housemaid did all the cleaning, washing, and cooking—and thus she was rendered the more susceptible to the slighting and catty cruelty visited upon most children, especially girls *inter se*, at some time in their schooling. She never made a friend, let alone a lasting one, beyond her close-knit family. Away from Les Buissonnets, she played only with her cousin Marie Guérin, who was more than two years her senior. This self-confinement made it difficult for her to become fully aware of others, and

FIGURE 2.2. Céline at eleven, Thérèse at eight, a time of forbidden pink ribbons and a boat piloted alone on a troubled sea. Copyright Office Central de Lisieux.

only in the closing passages of her autobiography, confessing to the prioress, does she indicate how she had become aware of love for neighbor. In those final pages, it is almost as though she discovered the word *charité* and had just then integrated its full import into her perceptions.[8]

The French language draws a fine line between cherishing and pampering by supplying one word for both, *choyer*. Thérèse in maturing came to realize the deleterious effects of the family's solicitude, prompted though it was by anxieties about her sickliness and her inhibitions. Her confessor and retreat director, Abbé Domin, observed at the hearings held in 1910–1911 to consider her beatification: "elle était trop flattée, trop adulée par les membres de sa famille, et surtout par son père, qui semblait ne pas pouvoir se séparer d'elle, et l'appelait sans cesse 'ma petite reine.' J'estimais qu'on s'exposait à la rendre vaniteuse et pleine d'elle-même comme tant d'autres jeunes filles" ["she was too flattered, too adulated by her family, especially by her father, who seemed unable to be apart from her and incessantly called her 'my little queen.' I figured they were risking making her vain and full of herself like so many girls"].[9]

Although or because she was socially marginal in school, she did not mind being neglected by other students. In fact, they would cluster around her whenever she made up narratives, but that was too seldom to secure her any popularity. She did not seek out anyone to cling to in the exclusive desperation of the lonely—she had Céline and home—but she was keenly hurt when she began a friendship with another student which did not survive a short interval. From that crushing disappointment she infers in her autobiography the fleeting nature of all human relations, their incurable shallowness and vanity. Had sickness and sensitivity (and Céline's graduation) not sent her back home, had she been obliged to go through the full sequence of schooling years, she might have learned to accommodate mercurial behavior in others and to perceive it as immaturity. Her intensity of feeling and its attendant impatience precluded that ripening into acceptance. She had to learn the lesson later, not from children but from adults. They, Carmelites, became her most important teachers.

Like many bright youngsters who feel isolated in schools, she became noticeable to instructors. She was outspoken, also younger by a few years than most of the others in her class—placement in class by age is a modern fixation—but she made up that difference by the precocity Zélie had noticed early on. One of the Benedictines, Sr. St.-François de Sales, recalled some twenty-five years after the event Thérèse's asking her disconcerting questions about divine mercy and human freedom. At nine, she could not accept the convention that unbaptized infants are damned, and she wanted God to convert all sinners since it was in his power to do so.[10] Young, intelligent children often show themselves to be able philosophers and theologians, at least in posing questions. Thérèse's elementary concerns about justice and love begged for unequivocal and immediate responses, the sort which do not always nor convincingly come from adults (see figure 2.3).

One of the most arresting statements in her autobiography comes in characterization of her school years through a favored metaphor: "La pauvre petite fleur avait été habituée à plonger ses fragiles racines dans une *terre choisie*, faite exprès pour elle, aussi lui sembla-t-il bien dur de se voir au milieu de fleurs de toute espèce aux racines souvent bien peu délicates et d'être obligée de trouver dans une *terre commune* le suc nécessaire à sa subsistance!" ["The poor little flower had been used to setting her roots into a *chosen earth* made just for her; also, it seemed quite hard to see herself amid flowers of every sort with often coarse roots and to be obliged to find in *common ground* the sap necessary for her subsistence!"] (A 22r). The notion of apartness, here

FIGURE 2.3. Girls during recess at the Benedictine Abbey school in the time of Thérèse, whose account of her years there is not a happy one. Copyright Archives du Carmel de Lisieux.

elaborated into one of destiny and temporary displacement, points to a fundamental fact about Thérèse's way of seeing herself. In the confines of her world, one basically determined by walls, she used her quick and perceptive mind in a thoughtful way, by taking herself as the laboratory of her experience. She was experimental with her own realities, with an acuity in testing and observation that made her a perpetual commentator on her life. It seems amiss to call this procedure egotistical or egocentric because she did not expose herself to the milieux in which egotism necessarily functions. She remained by disposition apart, and even in Carmel she was criticized by some as aloof. Characterizing herself as a hothouse plant in need of special tending may sound snobbish but, again, a real snob needs other people for the snobbery to work. Thérèse's self-experimentation needed nothing more than a lone cell, and that she found.

Whence the flowers? Before her school years, Louis would take her out into the countryside on long walks to small villages with streams (they remain mercifully unspoiled) where he fished while she mused, gathered flowers, and likely started to raise to herself those weighty questions that bemused her Benedictine instructors. There is no record of conversations with her father on such lines, his only line being for trout, which he usually delivered to the houses of Lisieux's religious orders. He was, however, prompting in her something no less important than answers to possible queries: a keen love of the sensuous, from diminutive yet abundant flowers such as *pâquerettes* and *violettes*, still growing within Carmel's walls at Lisieux, to the vast expanses of clouds and skyscapes. She would have intuitively affirmed, I believe, Blake's perception of infinity in the palm of the hand, with the flower celestial and the eternal hour. This is to say that from the first and quite independent of dogmas, she was a religious person in her sensibility. She retained an eager receptivity to occasions of awe and wonder, which elicited from her an appreciable delight not least in very small phenomena. Nature was her first and greatest teacher in humility, and she instinctively turned to it when articulating her spirituality. Doctrine as such lagged so far behind in her awareness that if we called it secondary, that would be elevating it.

Why, if she was so responsive to the natural world, did she leave it for a cloister? First, she realized from the homes and families she knew that bourgeois domestic life imposed its own confinements, with outings a rather stiff, organized, Sunday afternoon affair. Few in her time had what we now think of as an environmental awareness, let alone a ready access to forests or to putatively salvific wilderness. Natural beauty was savored secondhand, through literary landscapes read aloud in family circles. Also, she knew from her sisters that Carmel was itself a garden, abundant in flowers, arbors, and bird life; both sanctuary and preserve, the only place where her Christian faith could thrive in paramountcy. And she had long sensed that she would have a short life. How would she ever have dreamed of marriage and motherhood?

She was beset with spells of sickness throughout her childhood and nothing was remarkable about most of them, though her loss of breath when running about with Céline in the Alençon days might have served as a portent. (It has been conjectured that she had asthma.) In an age prior to vaccinations, child mortality, especially in the infant years, was high. Having survived those odds, a normally healthy child when very sick would be sequestered for an indefinite period at home. Adolescent Marie was down for weeks when she came close to dying of typhoid. Confinement was imposed upon Thérèse for months when she fell sick not long after her tenth birthday. The psychogenic factor commonly adduced and hardly to be missed was that her adopted mother had just entered the Carmel at Lisieux. Pauline had not prepared her sister for this shock of separation, perhaps fearing importunate beggings and delayings. Inspired by saints' lives, Thérèse had nursed the fantasy of going with Pauline into a desert, an exalted version of running away from home. (Inspired by El Cid in her childhood, Teresa of Avila had hoped to go with her beloved brother to Islamic Spain so that they might both be martyred there *chez les Maures*.) Carmel decisively dashed the Martin sisters' runaway aspirations and Thérèse's fever was attended by bizarre behavior: convulsions and hallucinations.

As we shall return to this episode and to her final illness, I only remark here Thérèse's casting of her life into three periods, a kind of psychological chronology, with the middle one initiated by her mother's death and ended only by her entrance into Carmel. She characterizes herself in the prime of childhood as hypersensitive, withdrawn, unhappy, but her own accounts of these ten years indicate many times and occasions of joy (*joie*, an often iterated word in the chapters on her childhood) or at least relief from self. Her chief joy was being with her father in church on Sunday, a day and place which she regarded as an augury of heaven, with the promise of everlasting repose. She was likewise sustained by the rhythms of the liturgical year, the feast days, and the sacraments. Her first confession was as joyous an occasion as her first Communion. She had the normal childhood pleasures, too: her summer vacations in the countryside at nearby Saint-Ouen-le-Pin (the farm looks much as it did when she sketched its main house); less happily, at the resort beaches of Trouville and Deauville; and by the streams along Ouilly-le-Vicomte, where she sat as Louis was fishing.

She had been indulged from the first by her father and had to be disciplined by Pauline, to whom, according to Thérèse, he deferred, as she was in effect in Zélie's position. Raising her baby sister from the age of four, Pauline was discovering her own competence as a possible mother and homemaker, but then she would have had to find a man to match Louis, the paragon of fatherhood, and she never summoned the confidence or resolve to do so. She did not have to: Thérèse, after dying, became Pauline's creation. For her part, Thérèse had nothing of which to complain. She was neither abused nor neglected at home; she was not obliged to any physical labor; and if school was a miserable prison, it has always been so for any child alert and aware. Besides, when Céline accompanied her the ten minutes' walk downhill from home to the abbey school, they passed into St.-Désir, the working-class neighborhood of Lisieux. She could not have helped noticing children who were forever denied the bourgeois privileges she had, including school.

Perhaps most important, she had the close and constant companionship of Céline, to whom in her autobiography she gives praises rivaling in warmth only those given their father: "Je puis dire que *jamais* ma petite soeur chérie ne m'a fait de *peine*, mais qu'elle a été pour moi comme un rayon de soleil, me réjouissant et me consolant toujours" ["I can say that *never* has my dear little sister caused me *hurt* but she has been for me like a ray of the sun, delighting and consoling me"] (A 24r); and, in the ongoing imperfect tense, "nous n'étions pas blasées, notre âme dans toute sa fraîcheur s'épanouissait comme une fleur heureuse de recevoir la rosée du matin" ["we weren't bored and indifferent, our soul in all its freshness opened up like a flower happy to receive the morning's dew"] (A 24v). In the meringue of this rhetoric, the single soul she accords herself and her sister is noteworthy. She was to leave Céline, but Céline never left her.

What might be called her spiritual formation at home also came substantially from her sisters. Pauline gave her a little book she had composed in different colors of inks, with each day set for sacrifices and prayers before the most important of days, the first Communion, which she took on May 8, 1884. After writing each prayer, Pauline had left a space for Thérèse to record how often, in mantric fashion, she had said it. On March 2, a significantly early prayer, "Mon Jésus, faites que je ne sois plus orgueilleuse" ["My Jesus, make me no longer proud"], she said thirty times, but fifty times on March 13 she prayed to her guardian angel, "Gardez-moi sous votre aile dorée" ["Keep me under your golden wing"].

This engaging, fussily calligraphic little book[11] anticipates much of the language of Thérèse's own spirituality: "O Jésus rendez mon petit coeur brûlant d'amour" ["O Jesus, make my little heart burning with love] (thirty times on March 16); "Petit Jésus, je donnerais tout mon sang pour vous" ["Little Jesus, I would give all my blood for you"] (fifty times on March 29); "Petit Jésus, faites que je sois heureuse de souffrir quelque chose pour vous" ["Little Jesus, make me happy to suffer something for you"] (forty times on April 2). Pauline followed the floral conventions of spirituality in her time by giving each day a flower's name (églantine, violette, lys) and including standard metaphors: make my heart fragrant with virtues, come and rest in the calyx of my heart, etc. And amid all this sweetness came the somber prayer of March 14, when she asked Jesus thirty-five times, "Faites que je ne connaisse jamais la nuit du péché" ["Make me never know the night of sin"].[12]

Marie, effectively head of the house after Pauline's departure, taught Thérèse, who was also her godchild, the way to sainthood by performance of little daily tasks. In her Souvenirs intimes, recollections first set down in 1905 and reviewed in 1932, Pauline warmly praises Marie for her selfless devotion to tasks at home, a giving which allowed Pauline to prepare to leave home and enter a monastery. Marie, like Pauline, was for a time given the chance to try out a sort of motherhood, but Pauline had already been pledged to religious life by her mother. Marie had been bound in no such way and accordingly suffered sharp criticism from her Visitandine aunt.[13] Her bohemian air masked a restlessness which could find no surcease. One of her books, whose author identifies himself only as "A. B.," suggests why.

Les vacances d'une jeune fille chrétienne: Guide pratique pour bien passer le temps des vacances [A Young Christian Girl's Vacation: A Practical Guide for Passing the Time Well] appeared in 1878 from the Oudin press of Poitiers, which had printed the Carmelite Rule and Constitutions in 1865. In its first pages, Marie found what seem nowadays hilariously priggish cautions from A. B. about the hazards of reading books, meaning fiction. Louis read poetry, history, and biography but was not inclined to novels. Whenever Marie gave him one, he would put it aside with a polite smile. That she read them seems likely, but they had to be approved as proper reading. A. B. was warning her that too much reading would render her vain and pedantic or, worse, make her prefer dreaming to the active life: "elles ruinent ainsi lentement les forces de l'âme" ["that way they slowly destroy the soul's strength"]. "Résumons-nous: Jamais une jeune fille chrétienne et bien élevée n'ouvre un livre ou un journal sans la permission de son confesseur, de ses parents ou de ses maîtresses" ["In sum, never does a properly educated young Christian girl open a book or magazine without the permission of her confessor, her parents or her school mistresses"].[14]

Thérèse in her turn followed these prohibitions, usually. She also imbibed from her sisters the doctrine of self-sacrifice and suffering as the means to Christian perfection. Having known conventual life obliquely through their schooling at the Visitation in Le Mans, Marie and Pauline helped Thérèse to internalize daily living as a procedure by rules, with strict and regular accounting both to oneself and to authority, which was always female in domestic life. (Marie likely kept regular notice of Thérèse's entries in the Communion prayer book.) It may sound cheerless, but dutifulness was relieved by the close-knit, irreplaceable camaraderie which informed the Martin home. The girls had each other to depend upon. At school, Marie defended Pauline from bullying, and Céline did the same for Thérèse. They passed down to one another their school books. Pauline in her *Souvenirs* says she could not imagine how she survived her last year at the Visitation, when Marie was back at home, and Thérèse without Céline managed only four months at the abbey school.

Virtually a society unto themselves, the Martin girls had little incentive for forming real friendships on the outside. Indeed, in the church schooling of those days, close friendships between girls were not admitted. As A. B. admonished, "Telle jeune fille se sent un grand attrait pour telle autre: mêmes goûts, mêmes idées, mêmes habitudes, etc. Vous ne comprenez pas les motifs très-raisonnables qu'ont vos maîtresses de vous interdire ces sortes de liaisons, si souvent dangereuses à tant d'égards" ["One girl feels a great attraction to another: same tastes, same notions, same habits, etc. You don't understand the very reasonable grounds your teachers have for forbidding you such liaisons, so often dangerous ones in many ways"].[15]

In this feminine dynamic the anomalous nature of Louis's role becomes apparent. The Martin sisters were shaped by and for each other. Louis, no idler, worked chiefly outside the house: he tended the garden (not enthusiastically, according to Céline); fed the rabbits and chickens; cut, sawed, and piled the wood; gathered apples and made cider. Indoors was the maid's province. Louis's substantial time with his daughters came in abundant evening readings in piety and inspiration, most prominently Dom Gueranger's *L'année liturgique*. Louis might not have enjoyed novels for himself, but he read to his girls a sentimental and stridently moralistic one from the *Bibliothèque de la Jeunesse Chrétienne*: Mme. Woilliez's *L'orpheline de Moscou*. As one of Louis's sobriquets for Thérèse, "l'orpheline de la Beresina," comes from this story, it warrants brief summary.

Juliette and her mother, widow of a distinguished Russian officer, are living in Moscow when Napoleon invades. Fleeing amid refugees, they are separated when crossing the Beresina River. The bridge collapses, and Juliette's mother is swept away. Juliette is taken by a friendly couple as far as Paris where, after a carriage accident, she becomes governess to a baron's daughter, who has been spoiled by her frivolous, partying mother. Juliette reforms them both with pious resistance and not a few sermons. When the baron is wounded and captured by Russian troops during Napoleon's last campaign, Juliette manages to importune Czar Alexander to release him. After a delay, the baron returns to his home, having rescued from a prison none other than Juliette's long-lost mother. When the czar gives her her father's pension and generously compensates her mother for all the properties they lost in 1812, Juliette is set up for a life dispensing charity to grateful neighborhood peasants. "C'est ainsi que le vrai chrétien, quels que soient son âge et son sexe, exerce autour de lui une sorte de sacerdoce qui n'est jamais sans quelque heureux résultat" ["It is thus that the true Christian, of whatever age or sex, practices a kind of priesthood which is never without a happy result"].[16]

As Juliette at the story's beginning is already a ripe eighteen years old and by the end is reunited with her mother, it is not altogether clear why Louis and Thérèse after him made so much of the *orpheline*. Did Thérèse take inspiration from Juliette's unflagging shows of faith and works? Or did the story's bold message on the priesthood of all believers quicken a girl who knew she would never be able to serve formally as a priest or missionary? Did Thérèse ever ask why women were not priests?

There survives no record of any lively, informed discussions within the Martin household. As a devout churchgoer, Louis gave unquestioning deference to priests—"Le prêtre nous paraissait une quasi divinité" ["The priest seemed to us a kind of deity"], wrote Céline, reflecting an abiding convention[17]—and would not have dreamed of taking on himself the task of counseling his daughters to maturity in their religious life, which was life itself for the Martin family. Questioning, challenging, contesting—none of those postures would have been acceptable in that acquiescent time, least of all from young girls. Without a son for whom he could have played the heavy, authoritarian role, Louis remained a soft patriarch, a generous soul and revered as such throughout the parish community as at home, but he seems finally almost too mild. Céline recalled that he would try to settle fighting among the girls with the injunction "Douceur!" The gentleness was Louis himself.[18]

It is telling that he, a widower, regularly joined pilgrimages, which were attended overwhelmingly by women with tag-along husbands.[19] His gentlemanly comportment and his charitable nature argue themselves in this, that he would rationalize or otherwise excuse the faults of people he heard criticized or gossiped about. That habit goes some way to explain why his youngest daughter believed unswervingly in a loving and compassionate God.[20]

Yet, his grandfatherly age, retirement, and white beard set him tacitly on a periphery such as Thérèse in her sensitivity occupied: "un si *beau* Vieillard avec une si *petite fille*" ["such a *handsome* Old Man with such a *little girl*"] (A 17r) is her phrase for both of them observed at church, a tableau suggesting a shared isolation and vulnerability such as Dickens sentimentalized in Little Nell and her grandfather. Céline tells us that her father's real friendships remained back in Alençon, which suggests that his later years left him in a persistent dislocation. By marked contrast, Isidore, eighteen years his junior, was the one who held the reins, enjoyed playing the gruff, overbearing head of the house who terrified Thérèse with questions, and ran a town-center pharmacy which was a hub for Lisieux's clerical faction.

All of these facts inform the profile of the most important man (after her father) in Thérèse's earthly life, a tall, imposing, aristocratic presence so central to the Martin family itself that he deserves far more attention than he has been given. His role in it proves unhappy and mysterious though it hardly seemed either to anyone at the time. Born in 1843 in a Norman farmhouse, Almire Pichon became in his school years a brilliant student in philosophy yet longed for a life in the priesthood. At twenty, he became a Jesuit novice. Arguably, however, the most powerful influence upon his formation came from St. François de Sales, whose *Introduction à la vie dévote* was known in nineteenth-century France but whose message encouraging laity to prayer, trust in God, and affective love of Jesus could find no more zealous advocate than Pichon.

His priesthood was launched with a trauma. Shortly after his tertianship, he fell dangerously ill, and a young woman who admired him died within a month of offering her life to God for his recovery. Horrified at the notion that God would exact one life for another, he pledged to fight such a cruel and punitive misconception, which he mistakenly imputed to Jansenism, a heresy we shall look at within the discussion of Carmel.

He proved an energetic, persuasive communicator and quickly developed a reputation for giving uplifting retreats. Nowadays, he would probably be a television personality with an oceanic audience of devoted women, because he was exceptionally gifted in listening to women's complaints, problems, anxieties, their burdens of loneliness, inadequacy, helplessness, their longing to give and to receive affection. Sensitive to their primary need for self-confidence, he proved almost aggressively insistent that they accept the mystical love which was immediately before them in Jesus and their daily lives. Pichon conveyed an overwhelming combination of erudition and tenderness. He was authoritative and solicitous, convincing a communicant that he was listening specially to her, and such keen attentiveness put him immeasurably ahead of many priests (see figure 2.4).

Louis first met Fr. Pichon in Paris during the Easter Triduum 1883, a trip cut short by a telegram announcing Thérèse's sudden choreic convulsions.

FIGURE 2.4. Almire Pichon, S.J. All of the more than one hundred letters Thérèse wrote to him have been lost. Copyright Archives du Carmel de Lisieux and by courtesy of the Archives des Pères Jésuites.

She first met him months later, during an August visit to Alençon. When Louis asked her to thank Pichon for his prayers that she recover, she gave him the only kiss he ever received.[21] His singular involvement with the Martin family begins, however, with Marie, who heard him address an audience at the Lambert textile factory in Lisieux. After her first confession to him, she inundated him with letters, initially almost daily. She had found in Pichon someone who could give her the elemental self-assurance which would allow her to find her way. Unfortunately, she needed it in epistolary doses, but his responses, while hortatory, were also formulaic and cursory.

And yet, they have even now an unmistakable energy in their gentle imperatives. Here are some instances of Pichon's uplift, in some phrases of which we glimpse the mature spirituality of Marie's youngest sister: "Point de découragement! Supportez vos petits défauts avec résignation: ayons patience, dit St. François de Sales, d'être imparfaits" ["No discouragement! Put up with your little defects with resignation; as St. François de Sales says, let us be patient with being imperfect"]. "Vous malheureuse! Je vous défends de me dire jamais pareille chose, surtout de le penser. Gardez toutes vos faims dévorantes. Bienheureux, dit le divin Maître, les affamés et les altérés. Tout sera assouvi en Dieu. Un jour N.S. vous enivrera de son amour" ["You are miserable?! I forbid you ever to tell me such a thing, or even to think it. Preserve all your devouring hungers. Blessed, says the divine Master, are those who hunger and thirst. All will be assuaged in God. One day Our Lord will intoxicate you with his love"]. "Pourquoi votre âme m'-a-t-elle donné pleins pouvoirs pour commander? Pourquoi m'avez-vous inspiré cette confiance qui me permet de tout attendre de mon enfant, aidée de la grâce d'en haut?" ["Why has your soul given me such complete power of command? Why have you inspired in me this confidence which allows me to expect everything of my child, helped by grace from on high?"].[22]

It is not difficult to imagine the effect of such cascades upon a very young woman. If we ask how Louis figured in all of this, Marie would say that he did not really know her. To that, Pichon answered: "C'est par trop méchant de dire que votre père ne vous connaît pas. C'est vous qui le connaissez trop peu!" ["It's exceedingly wicked to say your father does not know you. It's you who know him too little!"].[23]

When Marie, having turned twenty-six, came severely close to spinsterhood, Pauline secretly wrote from Carmel to Pichon, who fitly nudged Marie into following her sister. He had been in Canada and on his return, Louis and Marie went to Calais to meet him only to learn after several frustrating days (they even crossed to Dover in search of him) that, the dates mistaken, he had already arrived in Paris. Six weeks later, on October 15, 1886, she entered Carmel with the name Pichon gave her, Marie du Sacré-Coeur.

Pichon's first letter to Thérèse came in response to one she wrote to him asking for his prayers for her first Communion. His extant fifteen letters to her over the following thirteen years have an iterative thinness about them, as do those to Marie, which number about a hundred: initially intense interest and encouragement but then rapid diminution as though with maturity a correspondent lost his interest or, to put it more charitably, he knew others were still in greater need of him. Besides, he was perpetually busy writing, having to write, the same sort of encouraging words to countless correspondents. At one point he admits to having about four hundred letters unanswered, and in Canada he was scheduled for as many as five retreats within a week and as many sermons within a day. Frequently on the road, exhausted, and with diminishing eyesight, he could hardly have sustained the unrelenting attention which exactly half of the Martin family required.

For Céline, too, came under his spell, wrote a vast number of letters to him, and destroyed all but fragments from a few of his toward her life's end— there are twenty-two extant. She was exceptional among the sisters in being flattered by his attention to her as his possible assistant in a Canadian lay order he was attempting to establish. He had shrewdly sensed her adventurousness and rather mischievously urged her to secrecy about his plans. They were divulged to Pauline only shortly—and significantly—after Louis died, and the response from Carmel was firm and precipitous so as to ensure Céline would join her sisters there. How the Martin Carmelites regarded Pichon at that time is not clear, but Thérèse in her autobiography reverently calls him *le Père*. An unwary reader might suppose she was speaking of Louis.

I suspect that what Marie, Céline, and Thérèse found most appealing about Pichon was something they intuitively loved in Louis, a certain femininity, even vulnerability. With a furtive longing to love and to be loved, Pichon implicitly spoke their language, one which most clerics in that time, authoritarian and perhaps misogynist, could neither hear nor speak. Pichon did them the immeasurable favor of refusing to play the conventional terrorist role of male dominance; he used his priestly office in the kindest way, ordering each to be confident that God loved her. He alone could not overcome the effects of a culture that obliged women to assume permanent postures of ignorance and inferiority; he was treating only the symptoms of this disease, chiefly, the ruinous lack of confidence, the dread of not being loved. His suppliants' need of masculine approbation made him an accomplice of the very disorder he was addressing. It is a piteous fact that he could administer to the Martin sisters only druglike exhortations, but his efforts were rewarded, in their way. These women seem to have loved him to the end of their lives.[24]

And Thérèse's letters? Toward her life's end, she said that she wrote to Pichon at least once a month during her years in Carmel: about 110 letters to him. There is a total of 266 extant letters from her, not one of them to Pichon. Apparently, he destroyed every one she wrote to him. As she is quoted as saying her whole self was in those letters, this loss is staggering, enough to prompt Msgr. André Combes, who long urged the publication of Thérèse's writings, to ask, "Le coupable pourrait-il espérer le moindre pardon?" ["Could such a culprit hope for forgiveness?"].[25] Even so, Pichon deserves some extenuation of any charge. Apart from the confessional nature of her letters, which in itself would have justified his destroying them, Pichon could not have foreseen the hearings for her sanctification more than a decade after her death. Prudent and discreet before the examiners, he did not exploit the exceptional personal knowledge that he had of her. Still, it remains teasingly likely that her vanished letters would have opened further to us the door to her recurrent darkness.

Of what else would she have written to him if not of her scruples? She had had the first serious bout with them for a year and a half after her second Communion, the one before which she had vowed not to be discouraged. We are left with pointless guessing about "ma vilaine maladie" ["my wicked illness"] (A 41v), as Marie was the only person with whom she shared this condition, and Marie was too cautious to reveal their precise nature during the beatification hearings. Did Thérèse feel the chill of atheism? Did she doubt her own salvation? Did heaven for the first time vanish from her consciousness and with it the hope, the long-held expectation of her family's reunion? On Marie's questionable instructions, she did not disclose anything but a list of negotiable sins to her confessor, gross offenses such as her girlish delight in some pink hair ribbons. Hence, this crucial subterranean phase of her preadolescent life remains closed. That Pichon continued to have influence on the Martin sisters well into their Carmel years attests to his extraordinary appeal, but it is impossible to determine the dynamic of the *confiance* which he had won and sustained in them.

Outwardly, Thérèse was burdened with such transient matters as her father's seven weeks' absence on a trip to Istanbul and her return to school without Céline, who was graduated in August 1885. An invaluable piece of writing by Thérèse dates from an October 1885 school assignment. As a *devoir de style*, or school composition exercise, it might seem artificial, but as she herself wrote of this time as one of scruples, this short, revelatory piece on her father's absence defies an ascription of fiction. Here is the first and by far the longest paragraph in full, with misspellings intact:

> Voilà déjà trois semaines que tu nous a quittées. Trois c'est bien long pour ta petite fille quand elle est séparée de toi. Si tu savais comme je désire que tu reviennes. Souvent je me représente t'on arrivée: tout le monde est content on se dépêche pour arriver à la gare on a peur de ne pas y arriver en temps, et pour en finir on arrive un quart-heure trop tôt, enfin le train arrive et nous t-embrassons, tu est bien portant nous sommes ravies. Mais plus souvent encore le tableau est noir, je me figure que tu est retardé et qu'au lieu de quinze jours que nous avons à attendre ce sera un mois où plus encors. Ou bien tu est malade parceque tu ne te soignes pas assez. Mon petite père chéri tu vas me dire que je ne suis pas raisonnable, que je me crée des chimères. C'est peut-être un peu vrai mais enfin que veux-tu puisque je suis faite comme celà, et je crois que je n'ai pas tout a fait tort car enfin ne peux-tu pas être retardé et puis avoue mon petit père que tu ne prends jamais assez de précaucion pour ne pas être malade; tu dis toujours tu dis qu'il n'y a pas de danger, mais il y a un proverbe qui dit: Aide-toi et le cil t'aidera; mais volà que je m'apperçois que je suis dans le chemin de te faire la morale mais pardonne-moi père chéri c'est la crainte qu'à ta petite fille que tu sois malade qui le fait parler ainsi.
>
> [Here it's already been three weeks since you left us. Three's really long for your little daughter when she's been separated from you. If you knew how I wish you'd come back. Often I imagine your

arrival: everybody's happy, rushes to get to the station and is afraid of not being on time and then gets there fifteen minutes early, the train finally comes and we hug you, you're fine and we're delighted. But more often still the image is black: I imagine you're late and instead of fifteen days we have to wait, it's a month or even more. Or you're sick because you don't take enough care of yourself. My little father, you'll tell me I'm unreasonable, I'm creating chimeras. That's maybe a bit true, but I'm made like that and I believe I'm not wholly mistaken. Indeed, couldn't you be late? And then I say, my dear little father, that you don't take enough precautions not to be sick. You always say, you say there's no danger, but there's a proverb that says, Help yourself and heaven will help you, but now I see I'm starting to moralize at you but forgive me, my dear father: it's the fear your little daughter has that you're ill which makes me talk this way.][26]

In her autobiography, she tells of a horrific incident which befell her when she was six or seven: from the maid's mansard, she was looking out onto the garden and saw near the washhouse a stooped veiled figure walking which she believed to be her father, then away in Alençon. She cried out for him, alarming her sisters and the maid. By the time they came, the figure had vanished up the walk. She records this bizarre event as a portent of what befell Louis years later, when he descended into mental and physical debility. This story finds its due in biographies, but the school exercise I have just quoted says far more about her anxieties regarding Louis: his absence, his longed-for and postponed return, her concern for his well-being, her admitted hypersensitivity, with the chimera perhaps pointing back to that mysterious figure in the garden. And the exercise itself serves as a portent of her own mature Christology: the spouse away indefinitely though needing her sustaining consolation, even while she is left in helpless waiting. The Song of Solomon is sung on the Via Dolorosa, but Christ himself has passed on, his yearning mourner left behind.

Late in the winter of 1886, Louis withdrew the queen from school because of her frequent headaches and resulting absences, not to mention her prolonged bout of spiritual darkness,[27] and thereafter she was tutored at a house she gently satirizes in her autobiography. It is entirely characteristic of Thérèse that she learned precious little from the books of Mme. Valentine Papinau, but she did learn how a girl's head could be turned. She was flattered with compliments by visitors to the tutor's house: her hair, her eyes—and what of those pink ribbons? She left pieces of them in her schoolbooks, where they remain to this day, alternating with *pâquerettes* and other little pressed flowers.

Mme. Papinau obliged Thérèse to continue with the *devoirs de style* and in them we have some minor but telling views on schooling in that time and how it informed Thérèse in particular. The extant *Cahiers scolaires* include lengthy poems she copied out, the beginning of her practice of long transcriptions. She also had dictation on historical themes and personalities and exercises on such snares as French homonyms, with some amusing gaffes.[28] Her spelling also contained some peculiar errors, as when she wrote of the "trihomphes" of Jeanne d'Arc. While it remains uncertain how many of her compositions are original, those listed as "sujet proposé" in her school text, the *Traité de narrations*, can safely be reckoned in that number.

The most charming of these celebrates the seven-year-old Teresa of Avila and her "piéte plus angelique qu'umainne." With her older brother (Rodrigo, but not named here), she would meditate on eternity. One day Teresa came upon the inspiration "que si ils pouvaient entrer tout de suite en possession du seul bien éternel et durable cela vaudrait beaucoup mieux" ["that if they could enter into possession of the one eternal and enduring good, that would be much better"]. The best way would be to "aller chercher la couronne du martyre chez les maures" ["go seek the crown of martyrdom among the moors"]. Figuring they could beg for alms on the way, Teresa took no provisions save a small cross, but as she departed from home wearing her *robe de princesse*, they were soon caught: "son frère qui n'avait pas tremblée à la pensée des suplices des maures se mit à pleurer devant le fouet paternel" ["her brother, who hadn't trembled at the thought of moorish torture, began to cry before the paternal whip"] and inculpated his sister, who boldly declared that martyrdom was her idea. "De sorte que toute la glore revint à cette héroïne de sept ans" ["So all the glory redounded to this seven-year-old heroine"]. It is noteworthy that the saintly life of her namesake taught the fourteen-year-old Thérèse the glory of intent, no matter how frustrated its goal.

Of all school exercises in that time, however, the most magnificent came not from Thérèse but from a sixteen-year-old Parisian girl who, we might suppose, inspired her, if not Marie, who had the text. It is included in *Les Vacances* with suitable praise from A. B. There for the first chronological time we catch glimpses of the little way, stated in such precisions it is as though Thérèse had been given yet another *devoir de style* to copy. At the risk of presenting Berthe Vosgelin's words as though they were a catechetical exercise, I note them without comment, with italics to indicate her own emphases in her prayer:

> Les plus *petites choses* sont encore bien au-dessus de mes forces,
> sans votre secours. . . . Rien n'est *petit* quand il s'agit de vous pro-
> uver notre amour. . . . Daignez m'accorder de marcher toujours d'un
> pas égal dans mon *petit chemin*, de mes *petits devoirs quotidiens* avec le
> même zèle, la même ardeur, la même exactitude, soit que j'aie l'âme
> joyeuse et pénétrée de votre grâce, soit que j'aie l'âme triste, sèche et
> abattue malgré moi. . . . il n'y faut rien changer sous prétexte de

grandes choses à exécuter [The very *littlest things* are yet beyond my strength without your help. . . . Nothing is *little* when it's a matter of our proving to you our love. . . . Grant that I walk always with a steady step on my *little way*, that of my *little daily duties* with the same eagerness, ardor and compunction, whether my soul be joyful and penetrated with your grace or gloomy, dried up and downcast in spite of myself. . . . there's no need to change anything about it on the pretext of carrying out *great deeds*].[29]

These were not abstract effusions: the eldest child of a rag-picker and a concierge, Berthe helped in raising her siblings. And she was keenly observant of suffering in the world immediately before her, remarking that in the hospice *de la Pitié* only a few paces from her family's door (near the Jardin des Plantes), there were hundreds of people "qui souffrent plus en une heure que je n'ai jamais souffert dans toute ma vie" ["who suffer more in an hour than I have ever suffered in all my life"].

Most striking of all in her essay is her explicit desire to spend her life "comme un petit ver de terre" ["like a little earthworm"] with grateful words that make her sound for all like a Carmelite novice: "je vous remercie, Seigneur Jésus, de m'accorder une vie obscure, cachée, inconnue à tous" ["I thank you, Lord Jesus, for granting me a life that is obscure, hidden, unknown to everyone"]. Until now, at least. A sister at Berthe's school recommended her for domestic service to a countess in the Panthéon quarter and, hired, she was not heard from again. To me it has been more than tempting to suppose that Marie or Pauline read Berthe's few pages to little Thérèse, that an older Thérèse read them to herself, there finding in an extraordinary and precocious acuity a sister with spiritual affinity to her and an uncanny anticipation of her own treasured *petitesse*.

At Les Buissonnets, an important change occurred: Thérèse took over for herself what had been Pauline's mansard in the belvedere for her attempted studying. It was her first *cellule*, a room to herself, if not her own. Likely there she started to read two books which were to have a lasting influence upon her. The first hardly needs introduction: the *Imitation of Christ*, which she knew in Lamennais' translation with his *réflexions* appended. She could quote it from memory in her teens, even when tested by book and chapter. In her writings, she quotes or paraphrases it nearly fifty times and alludes to it many more. Judging by their repeated citations, we find that her favorite passages concerned the vanity of learning and the preferability of remaining unknown, of being counted for nothing (I.2.3); the need to strip oneself of all self-esteem (II.11.4); the desirability of a love to which all things are possible and permitted (III.5.4); the necessity of unstinting charity toward others (III.49.7); and the brevity of earthly labor in preparation for eternal life with Christ (a *réflexion* on III.47).[30]

The notion of eternal recompense, drawn from 2 *Corinthians* 4:17, plays centrally in the other text which Thérèse took to heart in her adolescence, Abbé Charles Arminjon's *Fin du monde présent et mystères de la vie future* [*End of the Present World and Mysteries of the Future Life*], first published in 1881. This work and its celestial mercantilism will be discussed in the chapter on Thérèse as a writer. It would take her more years and much suffering to reach the close of the epistle in which St. Paul finds glory not in future recompenses but only in his present weaknesses.

Marie entered Carmel on October 15, 1886, thus depriving her youngest sister of counsel and maternal guidance. Thérèse's recollection of that time sustains a peculiar pathos. She writes that, with Marie gone, she could now turn only to her two brothers and two sisters in heaven. Dead in infancy, they had not known her sorts of scruples and were sure to have pity on her. Yet, as she owns, being the youngest child, she had also been the most beloved. She claims to have entered into a soothing colloquy with her celestial siblings, but gives no transcript, only this: "se trouvant à même de puiser dans les trésors Divins, ils devaient y prendre pour moi la *paix* et me montrer ainsi qu'au Ciel on sait encore aimer! La réponse ne se fit pas attendre, bientôt la paix vint inonder mon âme de ses flots délicieux et je compris que si j'étais aimée sur la terre, je l'étais aussi dans le Ciel" ["finding themselves drawing straight from Heaven's treasures, they ought to secure there *peace* for me and thus show me that in Heaven one still knows how to love! The answer wasn't long in coming, soon peace came inundating my soul with its delightful waves and I realized that if I was loved on earth, I was also loved in heaven"] (A 44r). While this statement seems to assert her faith and hope, it seems plaintive and even exacting: knowing herself loved, she needed even more assurance, peace, to still her anxiety.

To need to know that in heaven there is still something like earthly love is an odd craving for a Christian, especially as earth was conventionally conceived as a place of exile and worldly life was a source of contempt. The Christian's true home would be heaven. This passage reminds us that what we know about Thérèse's life comes almost wholly filtered through her spiritualization of it, that it begins and goes on as a record of divine mercies shown her, of which this episode is a manifest sign, and yet it is an ineradicable fact that she could affirm as true only what she embraced within her own temperament, what she learned experimentally. She does not make precise to us, nor to her sister, what sort of answer she received from their celestial family. All we can soundly infer is that no consolation lasted long, and she had to learn to do without any. She had to grow up.

She says she did so overnight when a weary Louis devastated her by remarking that he was tired of Christmas for children. She realized that she had to think of others, not herself, and later she did so by her solicitude for a man accused of murder. We meet him later. Christmas 1886 she herself signals as a conversion experience, her instant passage to adulthood or what she called a return in spirit to the expansiveness and affirmative joy of her childhood before her mother's death.

What we do not know is how attentive she was to her father's tiring, aging, and degeneration. On May 5, 1887, he suffered the first attack of hemiplegia. The paralysis proved mercifully transient but must have been unsettling: Louis's speech was temporarily impaired. Thérèse leaves no record of her awareness of this blow.[31] Between October 1886 and June 1887 there is no surviving letter; other than Pichon, no significant correspondent. Family business was transacted at the Guérin home or at the Carmel's grille where visitors spoke, so we are left in darkness about this time. The visits at Carmel pained Thérèse because, being youngest, she had no part in necessary discussions, which were limited by Carmel regulations to thirty minutes per week. She barely had time to greet Pauline when the hourglass stopped them both.

By the end of that May, she had asked her father's permission to enter Carmel, and he gave it. The connection between the hemiplegia and the request to enter Carmel argues itself powerfully from Thérèse's remembrance. On the episode of the veiled figure in the garden, she concluded: "Je ne pouvais pas même penser sans frémir que Papa *pouvait mourir*" ["I couldn't even think without trembling that Daddy *could die*"]. She then recalled how her father had once been on a ladder and warned her to stay clear of it lest he fall and crush her. Obstinately, she had then clung to the ladder, thinking: "Au moins si Papa tombe, je ne vais pas avoir la douleur de le voir mourir, puisque je vais mourir avec lui" ["At least if Daddy falls, I'll not have the grief of seeing him die, since I'll die with him"] (A 21r). This narrative takes on, as does so much in the first of her manuscripts, a parabolic force. Now, mortality had knocked on Louis's door, and she had heard it.

While her motivation to enter Carmel may be as unobjectionable as it is unequivocal—to save souls by prayer—Thérèse never explains her own impetuosity and why she could not wait until she came to a reasonably mature age. Nor is it clear why it had to be to the Lisieux Carmel that she applied. The supportive presence there of her two older, motherly sisters is as a determining factor discounted in pious biographies, but it seems overwhelmingly obvious that it was a powerful, if not definitive, incentive.[32]

And the other sisters? Léonie had spent six weeks with the Poor Clares of Alençon in the fall of 1886, then came home, and by late spring was looking to enter the Visitandine convent in Caen. Only Céline remained to take care of Louis, her own future unresolved, but Thérèse, closest to her, must have been anxiously aware that her sister, talented, attractive, in her eighteenth year, might well be leaving the house within a short time. We take Thérèse at her word. Of course, she could not bear the thought of her father's death without shuddering. She had lost one parent already, and Zélie's death had precipitated her into a ten-year period of hypersensitivity. What would Louis's death do to her, especially were she left alone to face it, the last of the Martin girls at home? He was now sixty-four, a much older number in those days than it is now, and must have had his own sense of a doom proximate, if not impending. His immediate assent to her request to enter Carmel and his continuous diplomacy on her behalf with churchmen was in a sense his tacit means of ensuring her future on the best possible terms. Louis, however much a St. Joseph, was also a businessman who understood the ledgers of life, that losses had to be anticipated and made up. From *his* perspective, Thérèse's audacious bid for Carmel was so sensible he might have thought of it himself, had she not been a mere fourteen and had she not come to him first. He knew that Céline was just enough older to be a mature and responsible caregiver and that Thérèse was not only too young but too fragile for such a task alone.

Writing of her request for his permission, she says that Louis initially demurred because of her age but that she made her case so well—she does not indicate her arguments—he soon conceded like an Old Testament patriarch with a blessing and thanks to God for asking of him his children. Her Christmas "conversion" episode now assumes its full significance: she needed to validate to herself that by it she had unequivocally passed beyond the recoiling from life which had marked her childhood since her mother's death. This validation justified her seeking out Carmel, beginning with her father's sanction only five months later. While the "conversion" joins her many other graces and establishes a tacit causality for entering Carmel,[33] the incontestably more weighty factor, her father's first stroke, makes its claim. Like any autobiographical account, this one must be read for what it does *not* say but what the known facts impose, and sometimes the silence becomes loud.

It seems curious, too, that Thérèse does not record the simple calendrical fact that after Louis agreed to her request, more than four months passed before she informed her guardian, Isidore, of her wish to enter Carmel. In short, she composes a dramatic sequence which obliterates the impertinence of time. Having won Louis, why would she not have turned straightaway to her uncle? His abrupt, interrogatory way had long been intimidating to her, and she might besides have intuited his resistance or been warned by her father to expect it. In the event, Isidore refused approval—she should wait until the requisite seventeenth birthday; what would people say?—and she languished under his objections for three days in a despondency which at twenty-two she recalled as a martyrdom. Her saying she felt alone and her citing Christ at Gethsemane would seem blasphemous were this passage not so funny: as we shall find in looking at her as a writer, her rhetoric could climb to melodramatic heights wildly disproportionate to the events which occasioned it. She had won support from Carmel itself, however, in the persons of Pauline and the prioress, Gonzague (Marie was opposed),[34] and

Louis's own permission now could be weighed. Isidore's authoritarian pose seems that of a man who enjoyed saying no and then, after a despotic interval, enjoyed even more a magnanimous yes.

After her uncle gave in to her, the first real and only sustained opposition came from the superior of Carmel, Jean-Baptiste Delatroëtte. In addition to Isidore's concern that proprieties be observed, there was a far more serious one which figured in the superior's reckoning. In the close-knit professional community of Lisieux, Delatroëtte knew from the Carmel's and the Martins' physician, Alexandre de Cornière, that Thérèse had a substantial medical history, necessitating lengthy absences from the Benedictine school. Had Louis and his daughter pondered the rigors of Carmel? Louis had been concerned about Pauline's entry because she had long suffered from migraines. How would the order's well-known austerities, the fastings, affect this delicate, not to say spoiled, child? The obituaries of France's Carmels, the *circulaires*, regularly reminded the sisters themselves of how hazardous Carmel might be for any but the robust applicant.[35] None of these cardinal facts appear in Thérèse's account because, while they might seem incontrovertible to readers, they were not pertinent to her writing of her progression in grace, the culmination of which came in Carmel.

Her straightforward account of the ecclesiastical resistance she had to face at Bayeux marks the first point in her story which could not be corroborated by any of her natural sisters. In her recollection, she was telling Pauline how well the *benjamine* could fare in the world of male authority and how her tears proved enormously valuable in bringing round Msgr. Hugonin: "Je vis bien qu'il était touché; me prenant par le cou, il appuyait ma tête sur son épaule et me faisait des caresses, comme jamais, paraît-il, personne n'en avait reçues de lui" ["I saw he was quite touched. Taking me by the neck he leaned my head on his shoulder and petted me as, it seems, he never did anyone else"] (A 55r). The bishop's primary concern was that she was needed at home: how could she desert her father? He was checked, however, by Louis's unstinting support, an exceptional show of parental backing in an age when, as we shall find in the Carmelites' histories, even pious and observant fathers could and often did mount stiff opposition to their daughters' entry into a convent.

Céline joined her and Louis on a jubilee trip to Rome, which began on November 4, 1887. What readers of the autobiography are not told is that Louis had secured tickets for that journey *before* the appeal was begun. Without that telling detail, one could infer the visit to Rome was planned as the last resort. Thérèse herself leaves that impression along with her unmistakable determination: "car j'étais résolue d'arriver à mes fins, je dis même que j'irais jusqu'au *Saint Père*" ["indeed I had resolved to get my way, I even said I'd go to the *Holy Father*"] (A 52r). Not only was the journey prompted by the well-advertised jubilee: it had been organized by the diocese of Coutances

as a demonstration of support for Pope Leo XIII at a time when anticlericalism in Italy was becoming feverishly demonstrative. The 195 pilgrims included 73 priests and members of eminent Norman families. The presence
of the Martins was a reminder to Abbé Révérony, the vicar-general who re-
presented the Bayeux diocese, that Louis was one of the most affluent middle-
class supporters of the Church.

Thérèse was surprised and dismayed when for the first time she saw
priests in worldly settings. She had known them only in the performance of
their offices, in their sermons and retreats. Now she saw them hobnobbing
with the affluent and aristocratic sorts, the royalist backbone of the Church's
strength. At the hotels she saw them every morning sipping hot chocolate
with people of landed names, *de* this and *de* that, and speaking of mundane
matters, joking, laughing. As a petite bourgeoise, she belonged to a class
envious of the anciently privileged, but she would never have been able to
follow her contemporary, Péguy, proud of his peasant stock, out of the Church
(1895) on the ground that the wealthy had hidden its mission. While it was
her strength to read and learn within her own experience, she could not go
beyond that experience to substantive social and economic perceptions. She
did not grow up with nor was she educated to such an inclination. That is one
reason that, with her acute affectivity, love figures centrally in her reality but
justice, humanly attempted, does not.

The itinerary began with Paris and a visit to Le Printemps, the fashionable department store, in which Thérèse found the one truly original symbol
of her Christology, an elevator. Here and now she was fleetingly exposed to
the bustling, gaudy, energetic world she had never seen but was already
pledged to leave behind in thorough contempt. Paris was not Lisieux. This
world belonged to Massenet and *Manon*, to Maupassant and *Fort comme la
mort*, to Zola denounced for the obscenity of *La Terre*; to Degas and his (nude)
Woman Standing in a Tub. These were the mundane, irremediably alien energies which Louis had fled many years before, to which Isidore had been
exposed as a student, at a time when Renan was in high notoriety for *Vie de
Jésus*. The Martins knew and wanted to know nothing of such a sensuous and
sensual stir, but they did know they were spiritually in a foreign land, even
though Paris afforded them Notre-Dame-des-Victoires, "un petit paradis terrestre" ["a little earthly paradise"], as Louis had once described it to his wife.[36]
In the trail of the Norman bluebloods, they also visited the Louvre, where
Thérèse, unless closely chaperoned, had the first occasion to see nudity pub-
licly displayed, and the Bourse (the Parisian stock exchange), where cupidity
got the same treatment.

The rail route amounted to what we would now call a cruise, with stops in
Lucerne and Milan (the Martin sisters climbed to the top of the porcupine
cathedral), then east to Venice and south to Loreto, site of the fabulously
transported house of the Holy Family. Strange, that in Bologna's rail station,

where Italian university students were gathered thick for greeting the pilgrims, Louis momentarily left his daughters to go fetch his (forgotten?) valise, and the twenty-nine-year-old Abbé Leconte of Lisieux's Saint-Pierre was apparently caught off guard; his "complaisance affectueuse" ["affectionate obligingness"] toward the Martin girls had perhaps already set tongues to wag.[37] Thérèse suffered the consternation of being lifted away from the train platform by an impetuous student (this was Italy, *certissimo*), who unloaded his baggage of flatteries. She was being carried off a good way ("bien loin déjà," recalled Céline) when "je lui lançai un tel regard qu'il me lâcha bientôt" ["I threw him such a look that he soon let me go"].[38] This incident, forbiddingly minor in itself, retains its interest because Thérèse told of it, "une petite aventure," in Carmel years later. Pauline, who had never had physical contact with young men, would have heard it one way; Céline, who danced with them, another. Thérèse herself had known only paternal and avuncular embraces. In one moment of fascinated horror, she entered physically the world celebrated in Solomon's Song and then left it forever.

The girls enjoyed an initiative and independence they would never know again, and they must have enjoyed taking coy advantage of men. At Loreto, they successfully importuned Leconte to give them their own Communion within the Nazarene house, rather than at the basilica's altar where Louis, sweetly conventional as always—Thérèse's phrase, "sa douceur ordinaire," seems a gentle mocking—knelt with everyone else. At Rome's Coliseum, the girls ignored the guide's solemn instructions and burrowed into forbidden passageways below ground and past a lot of rubble, seeking the dust consecrated by early Christian martyrs. As they vanished, Louis looked on, helpless, indulgent, and likely proud. Of his five daughters, these two let themselves go with an élan that supposedly only boys could show.

Their supreme challenge came at the Vatican six days later, November 20. Undoubtedly they had taken inspiration from the martyrs' crypts they had seen in the catacombs along the Via Appia. When they were received by Pope Leo XIII in the magnificent Sala dei Palafrenieri, three groups were formed for each diocese: first, women and children; then, clerics; last, laymen. Thérèse misremembered cardinals (only bishops were present) and records her father's papal blessing before her own, when in fact he was well behind her, and she could not have tarried to witness it. She credits Céline with prompting her to request from the pope her early admission to Carmel.

This frail man, seeming sickly at seventy-seven, had been pontiff for nearly ten years. Following the antimodern entrenchments of his predecessor, Pius IX (who dogmatized papal infallibility and the Immaculate Conception), Leo had had to be skillfully diplomatic toward the generally hostile and recently begotten parliamentary states of Western Europe: Germany, Italy, France. His recognition of the dignity of labor and the rights of working people to government protection from predacious capitalism remains a landmark in papal teachings: *Rerum Novarum* was four years distant. In this morning's audience from Avranches, Coutances, Bayeux, and Lisieux, he knew the Church had no adherents more devout. These families had borne martyrdoms in the Revolution, less than a century before. They had resisted successive waves of revolution (1830, 1848, 1871) and a vigorous republican anticlericalism. They had come to demonstrate their fealty in the face of Italian hostility to the Vatican. Rome itself was foreign territory to the papacy and its supporters.

The pope's Gospel recitation that morning would have been timely for Thérèse, had she known Latin: *Nolite timere, pusillus grex*: Do not fear, timid flock.[39] The pope was seated on a chair set upon a platform, so that pilgrims, on bowing and kissing his feet and hands, could receive his blessing. Révérony was standing beside him to introduce important people. Thérèse, not one of them, has left two accounts of her supplication, in Manuscript A and in a letter to Pauline which she wrote that evening (LT 36). In the latter, she describes Leo as "si vieux qu'on dirait qu'il est mort, je ne me le serais jamais figuré comme cela, il ne peut dire presque rien, c'est Mr. Révérony qui parle" ["so old you'd say he's dead, I'd never have imagined him like that, he can say almost nothing, Mr. Révérony did the talking"], which does not quite jibe with her narrative version. There, she presented her petition in words Pauline had written out for her in a letter: "Très Saint-Père, j'ai une grande grâce à vous demander!" ["Oh, Most Holy Father, I have a great favor to ask of you!"]. She would have liked to request that he allow her to enter Carmel at fifteen, but she was so overwhelmed with emotion that Révérony, vexed at her troubling the pope, had to explain her petition and that the superiors were considering the matter. In Manuscript A, she says that the pope in a kindly tone told her to do what they said and that she then replied, "Oh! Très Saint-Père, si vous disiez oui, tout le monde voudrait bien!" ["Oh, Most Holy Father, if you said yes, everyone would agree!"], but in LT 36 she says only that "j'aurais voulu pouvoir expliquer mon affaire mais il n'y a pas eu moyen. Le saint Père m'a dit simplement: Si le bon Dieu veut vous entrerez" ["I'd have liked to be able to explain my business but there was no way. The Holy Father simply told me, If the good Lord wills, you shall enter"]. She was then borne away forcefully by two zouaves, papal guards, with the embarrassed Révérony assisting.

The minor discrepancy in accounts points to the difference between an event in part blurred by emotion and the same event much later reconstructed into a dramatic exchange where Thérèse, a model of audacity, remains in control of herself. Pope Leo, said to be attentive to all petitions, would surely have remembered one in which his guards had to interfere, not to mention the suppliant, a fourteen-year-old girl who had taken him by the knees. (That point is corroborated by Céline, who had been waiting her turn but could not have heard the exchange.) Although Révérony subsequently showed himself agreeable to both Louis and Thérèse, even telling her at Cannes, just nine days later, "Nous ferons ce que nous pourrons, n'est-ce-pas?" ["We'll do what we can, right?"],[40] it seems possible that the pope himself facilitated the request.

Despite his vexation, Révérony emerges almost heroically from this story. He was attentive to Thérèse throughout the journey, noting her comportment and the impressions she made on others. He had shown himself indulgent toward her from the first but knew that his superiors would decide matters in which he was not even an official mediator, though as the bishop's representative in Rome his observations would be weighed. A curious anecdote informs his relations with this upstart girl. During the visit to Assisi, Thérèse somehow lost her belt and buckle, then lost time in retrieving them, and found that all the coaches had parted save the vicar-general's. She was sensible enough to ask him for a ride and he obliged, even though his coach was already "garnie des *messieurs* les plus distingués du pèlerinage" ["filled with the pilgrimage's most distinguished gentlemen"] (A 65v), one of whom gallantly took a seat by the driver. In that intimidating company, she was invited to speak of her hopes for Carmel, a clue that Révérony indeed looked kindly on her. It is a pity he did not testify at the *procès*; he died at fifty-five, only four years after the papal audience. The infirm, seemingly dead pope died in 1903, at ninety-three outliving his youthful suppliant by six years.

Without an immediate and unequivocal response, the only kind an adolescent could understand, Thérèse languished in anxiety, waiting for word from Bayeux. Louis promised her a trip to Jerusalem but she was weary of the world, even though she had shone in it and now knew that she could cope well enough in it. The dramatized fretting about admission to Carmel which she depicts in her autobiography had to do with precisely the attractiveness of the world, both the natural and the social. She learned that she could turn heads, be talked about, and hold her own amid stately gentlemen, no minor achievements for a fourteen-year-old girl. There was even a newspaper account of her meeting with Pope Leo, so that she was a celebrity of sorts back in Lisieux several days before December 2, when she returned there. She had grown in her intimate relationship with Céline by travel and by its liberating effects: both had a new sense of themselves and each other through the vast, adventurous whirl of Alpine heights and cosmopolitan venues: Venice, Naples, Pisa, Florence, Nice (staying at its Hôtel Beau Rivage, where Nietzsche lodged) in nearly a month's time.

Recovering from those exhilarating shocks, she wrote to Bishop Hugonin (Isidore polished the letter) and to the vicar-general, renewing her petition for Carmel. Christmas 1887 was especially trying for her because she was hoping to hear positively by then, the anniversary of her "conversion." When she did not, her disappointment wounded but it became unexpectedly more grievous when she was informed, on New Year's Day, that she was to be received into Carmel: not immediately but three months thence. Concerned about her sister's health, Pauline had urged Mère Gonzague to spare Thérèse the harshness of Lenten fasting. Had she not known that this sort of concern figured in the superior's resistance to her sister's application? At the same time, the imposed delay (Louis angrily blamed Pauline for it) helped the ever-resistant Delatroëtte to save some face, a diplomatic nicety of which Thérèse does not seem to have been appreciative nor perhaps even aware.

She entered Carmel on the calendrically late Feast of the Annunciation, April 9, 1888. For a change, everyone in her family but herself was in tears as she felt at last transported into that supernatural desert she had longed to reach with Pauline. She adds that she received the grace of entering under no illusions about the sacrifices immediately imposed upon her, meaning that she was to be treated for the first time in her life as a servant. She was humbled by her ineptitude in sweeping the dormitory, and she had to serve in the linen room under supervision. Gonzague criticized her unsparingly, spurred on perhaps by Delatroëtte's glacial disdain, voiced at the reception, of the Carmelites' indulgence in taking in a child. Even so, the first months were marked with festive occasions: Marie professed her vows and took the veil on May 23, the fiftieth anniversary of the Lisieux Carmel's foundation. Pichon preached on that occasion and gave a five-day retreat. Thérèse took him as her director, and he forthwith assured her that she had never committed a mortal sin.

Her account leading up to that extraordinary assertion deserves citation so as to restate the importance of this man in her life: "il croyait ma ferveur tout enfantine et ma voie bien douce. Mon entrevue avec le bon Père fut pour moi une consolation bien grande, mais voilée de larmes à cause de la difficulté que j'éprouvais à ouvrir mon âme. Je fis cependant une confession générale, comme jamais je n'en avais faite" ["he believed my fervor wholly that of a child and my way quite natural. My talk with the good Father was a great consolation for me but veiled in tears because of the trouble I had in opening my soul. Even so, I made a general confession such as I never had before"] (A 70r). He advised her, however, that if God abandoned her, she would become "un petit démon." More important, he told her to consider Jesus her superior and novice trainer.

In effect, Pichon implicitly subverted the harsh probative work of the Carmelite women by his mollifying and uplifting words. Nothing mattered more to Thérèse than the placation and thus the tacit approval of a male presence, human or divine. That procedure informed the gender game of the time, but it also figured within Thérèse's overly sensitive affectivity. Pichon's remark about devilry meant that if God left her, she would adhere to Satan with a devotion comparable to what she had once given to the divine. He accurately sensed the extremity of her fervor. Her need for masculine approval and acceptance, her need to please and to know she was not offending would remain unabated to her life's end.

By the summer of 1888, the full cost of Carmel to gentle King Louis was dramatically evident. Céline had received and rejected a marriage proposal the day her sister entered Carmel. Two months later, she told her father that she, too, wanted to enter Carmel, thereby confounding her own possibilities for a career as a painter. A week later, Louis left his home and roamed around in a paranoid hallucination. The medical evidence points to a gradually worsening condition: arteriosclerosis complicated by uremia. He suffered memory lapses, mood swings, giddiness, and something like panic attacks. Renal deterioration increased the possibility of cerebral edema.

Three days after his departure, Céline and Isidore recovered him at a post office in Le Havre. He had sent a telegram from there asking for money. He suffered two relapses on August 12 and November 2, the latter in Honfleur where he had gone with Céline to see Pichon off to his mission in Canada. During that time, Louis told her that he wanted to die, perhaps because his last earthly ambition, to live as a hermit, had been thwarted by his now-vigilant family and servants. Proverbially, the French regard old men as either wise or foolish, and Louis, Lear-like, was wavering precariously between the two positions.

Isidore was concerned about what Louis might recklessly do with his considerable fortune. At a mass late in 1888, the vicar of Saint-Pierre announced to the congregation that a subscription was going to be taken for the purchase of a new altar. After the service, Louis privately pledged the entire sum of 10,000 francs: the magnificent effect of his astounding generosity (not Isidore's assessment of this behavior) is still to be seen in the cathedral, with a plaque gratefully posted nearby.

In a letter as early as July 22, 1888, Céline reported unsparingly to her sister their father's pathetic reduction: "Il me semble maintenant si vieux, si usé. Si tu le voyais s'agenouiller tous les matins à la Table de Communion, il s'appuie, s'aide comme il peut, c'est à faire pleurer. J'ai le coeur déchiré, je me figure qu'il mourra bientôt, oh! je crois que j'en mourrais moi-même de chagrin. Cette pensée me poursuit, je le vois sans cesse à l'heure de l'agonie, mon âme est alors tellement accablée que je ne respire plus" ["He now seems to me so old, so spent. If you saw him kneeling every morning at the Communion table, supporting himself as best he can, it makes you weep. My heart is rent, I imagine he'll die soon, oh! I believe I'll die myself of grief. This thought haunts me, I keep seeing him in the hour of his agony, my soul so overwhelmed I can no longer breathe"] (LC 86). To that distress, Thérèse answered with no reference to Louis, only that Céline was, as Pauline had once called her in their intimate floral code, a "lis immortelle," an unfading and therefore stronger flower than the weak and mortal flower Thérèse herself was. That, she felt, was why Jesus had taken her first to Carmel. Only Céline was strong enough to manage the domestic woe. Thérèse in turn had become alarmed by a dream in which Pauline left her for heaven.

To Louis, she wrote a week later in the unreflected language they had always shared: he was still her king, even though now she was espoused to Jesus. Life itself was only vanity and loss, just as he had always told them. But she adds these definitive words: "Quand je pense à toi mon petit Père chéri, je pense naturellement au bon Dieu, car il me semble qu'il est impossible de voir quelqu'un de plus saint que toi sur la terre" ["When I think of you, my dear little Father, I naturally think of God, indeed it seems to me impossible to see anyone on earth more saintly than you"] (LT 58). Now, Louis had been changed from the Godlike patriarch to the afflicted Christlike figure broken in physical and psychological suffering. In her autobiography she says he became the sacrifice on the altar he had secured for the Church.

While it is impossible to determine psychogenic factors in her father's degeneration, it seems plausible that the successive loss of his daughters to Carmel overwhelmed him. He had been willing and complicit in their going and was indubitably proud to have made such sacrifices, but he could not have anticipated what the full cost to him would be. The encroaching helplessness and isolation so often attendant upon old age could not be assuaged by his financial resources. Another factor difficult to assess in its weight upon Louis was the virulence of anticlericalism. Leo XIII had worked to defuse it by encyclicals (*Nobilissima Gallorum gens* in 1884 and *Immortale Dei* in 1885) urging Catholics to regard their republican governments with forbearance. The Vatican saw accommodation as the readiest means for mitigating the excesses of the Church's opponents, but it did not reckon with local diehard antipathies and resentments. Many of the faithful were puzzled by what seemed papal tolerance given to programmatic enemies of the Christian faith, people they knew within their own secular communities. One measure of Louis Martin's apprehension of anticlericalism is that he offered Fr. Delatroëtte a hiding place at Les Buissonnets, as though the violent excesses of the Revolution might be reenacted at any time.[41]

Because of her father's uncertain health, Thérèse's entry from postulancy to the novitiate, normally a six-month interval, was postponed from November 1888 to January 1889. It is unfortunate, if not disastrous, that her letter to Louis dated January 8, two days before she took the habit, is the last one extant to him. All of her subsequent letters to him—and, to judge by the frequency in 1888, they were many—are lost. On becoming a novice, she signed her name for the first time "Soeur Thérèse de l'Enfant-Jésus de la Sainte-Face," conjoining the alpha and omega of her Christology, the Incarnation and the Crucifixion, the swaddling clothes and the shroud, the humbling of God to helpless infancy and the redemptive Passion. The cult of the Sainte Face, derived from the medieval legend of the "Veronica cloth," had been popular for over a generation, its image widely circulated by a layman, Charles Dupont of Tours, but Thérèse was realizing for herself its dire significance in her father's suffering.

Less than a month after attending her taking of the habit, Louis again became alternately excitable and languidly bedridden. Then, the hallucinations returned. Vivid remembrance of Prussians approaching Alençon in 1870 supplied convincing particulars: he could hear cannons and drums so he seized a revolver to protect himself and his daughters and would not be separated from them. Isidore managed through a friend to disarm him and then, with medical authorization, induced him to take a country ride, which ended twenty-fives miles to the west, at Bon Sauveur, the sanatorium in Caen. Before leaving Lisieux, Louis stopped under falling snow at the Carmel and handed Pauline some fish bait wrapped in a handkerchief.

A vast establishment, Bon Sauveur housed every sort of mentally disabled person, from the senile to the psychopathic. Unmanageable patients—and Louis at times became one—were strapped to their beds. Louis remained in his Carmel for three years and three months. He was released to the Guérins only when his legs were so enfeebled by strokes that he was no longer ambulatory and thus no longer a hazard to himself and others.

It is easy and pointless to blame Isidore for sequestering Louis, a move which brought the Martin family into calumny in Lisieux. It was gossiped that Thérèse's entry into Carmel had precipitated her father's breakdown. That noise inculpated Pauline as well since she had vigorously supported her sister's appeal. Céline and Léonie, alarmed and helpless before their father's bizarre behavior, could not have remonstrated with their uncle to keep Louis with them. Isidore had to consider their safety and Louis's own, and might Louis not wander off again? And what if, next time, he could not be found? Odd as it may seem, the protracted term in Bon Sauveur, an anguish for the family and a cross for Louis, Thérèse would later (in 1895) call "notre grande richesse" ["our great wealth"] and count it among the several signal graces of her life. Known in Lisieux as "le saint Patriarche," Mr. Martin had been reduced within hours by an affliction as thorough as Job's, and the family was kept subject to the scandal. While Pauline, Marie, and Thérèse were tormented by the chimeras of imagining their father's condition, they were at least sustained by a community which had known Louis as its benefactor many times over.[42] Their sisters were less fortunate.

For two months, Céline and Léonie boarded at a pension near the asylum so they could receive daily news of their father. Rules allowed them one visit weekly. Only a week before Louis was committed, Thérèse had written to Céline in terms which identified him with Christ on the Via Dolorosa, falling continually. But would he ever rise again? The three Carmelite Martins were wholly dependent upon Céline for word, and she was bleak in her reports, chiefly by remarking the *néant*, the vanity in all things.[43] The worst of it was that Louis was lucid much of the time. He told Sr. Costard, the nurse in charge, that he was there to overcome his pride. He wept when speaking of his daughters. Then, after six months of confinement, he was dispossessed.

When Isidore obliged him to sign over control of his property on July 18, 1889, Louis exclaimed that his children were abandoning him.

Writing "Je n'aurais pas cru qu'une si faible créature pût supporter une telle abondance de souffrances" ["I would never have believed such a weak creature could sustain such an abundance of suffering"] (LD, March 4, 1889), Céline could have been speaking of herself, as well as of Louis. Stunned by trauma to blank submissiveness, she longed for home and her sisters. For her part, Thérèse, putting on brave smiles to her spiritual sisters, attempted to exhort Céline and herself with reflections on what they were going through: sainthood requires absolute suffering; they must drink from the bitter chalice which Jesus was handing them; and now they were orphans.

In counterpoint to this schooling in Calvary, as Pichon styled it, the Guérins' May 1889 visit to Paris and the Exposition exposed cousin Marie to the Louvre's nudities. She wrote to Thérèse of the capital as a "véritable enfer" ["genuine hell"], insisted she felt most happy in church but admitted that she had been abstaining from Communion. Marie had much in common with her once-playmate cousin: younger sisters, sickly through childhood, they both suffered long bouts of scruples and aridity. On the superficially positive side, both were attractive and could have made a good match in the infernal regions. Neither, however, could have articulated an awareness of her own sexuality, the primordial pull of the body. They were of that generation of young women who informed de Beauvoir's indictment of marital initiation in Le deuxième sexe: profoundly ignorant of sexuality, of male urges, of copulation. We can only guess at how much they knew of their own menstruation.[44]

While Thérèse answered Marie's call for help with an insistence upon Communion, saying she herself had taken it even when she believed she had committed great sins (in those eighteen months after her first Communion), she was undergoing another spell of her own scruples but shared nothing with Marie. Thérèse's admonitions to Marie about spiritual backsliding—the Devil laughs, Jesus weeps—sound like pure Pichon, who was forbidding Thérèse to question her own state of grace. In the autumn of 1889, he characterizes her scruples as "vilaine défiance" ["base distrust"]: "Croyez obstinément que Jésus vous aime" ["Believe stubbornly that Jesus loves you"] (LC 117). In fine, Thérèse herself needed injunctions deeper than she had been giving to her cousin, a kind of autotherapy. Even Pichon, however, would not have heard from her about the vaguely (or not so vaguely) alluring world to which she and Marie were privy, but the plain fact that they remained a mystery to themselves as sexual creatures does not clearly define their scruples.

Obliquely, this issue is complicated during the next year when Thérèse begins reading San Juan de la Cruz and the Song of Songs. It is easy to overestimate the first of these, because she knew only the Llama de Amor Viva

[*Living Flame of Love*], the canticle, and a collection of maxims, which, as a disparate series of spiritual directives, occupies a world distant from the classical French genre of court society represented by La Rochefoucauld, Vauvenargues, and Rivarol. As the approaching tercentenary year of the saint's death, 1891, was bringing forth new editions of his works and renewed interest, she knew of but did not read the journey texts in which San Juan ascends Mount Carmel and passes through the *noche oscura*, the soul's dark night of initiation. She was standing on the tall peak of San Juan's passage without having gone with him through the valley of the profoundest shadow, yet she finally remained helpless in her own valley. Besides, San Juan's central text, *Subida del Monte Carmelo* [*Ascent of Mount Carmel*], was in her time commonly shunned in ignorant dismay, Carmelites themselves recoiling from its intimidating obscurity. As the *circulaires* show amply, many sisters suffered long bouts with scruples, aridity, indifference, desertlike bleakness within themselves, and felt no inclination to read such a daunting text. And why would those who did not suffer such burdens want to traverse an account of them?

The *Living Flame* proved valuable in telling Thérèse how spiritual directors may be suspect or errant and in furnishing abundant Old Testament references (Carmelites were allowed to read extensively only the New Testament), especially to the *Song of Songs*. In that erotic poem, read for generations as the mystical union of Christ and the soul, the beloved disappears after the union, and the awakened lover goes in search of him. The turmoil and darkness weighing upon Thérèse in the last years of her life find their most succinct formulation in those few verses.[45]

While her letters to Céline reveal at times a kind of anxious ardor, a feverish exclamatory drive of exhortation,[46] and yet constitute primary texts in her own spiritual maturation, her aridity persisted, becoming most bitter in retreats when she was forced into extended self-examination. Like many novices, she was especially fraught by her sense of unworthiness to take the veil, but the torment was compounded by the absence of the two men in her life: Pichon was in Canada and Louis in Caen. With Céline she launched the bootless hope of bringing their father from Bon Sauveur for the veil ceremony, but Isidore refused their plea, fearing Louis's comportment in public. September 24, 1890, brought the family close to public disaster as Thérèse and even Céline kept dissolving into tears, bringing sharp reproaches from Pauline—tears were useless!—and even from the venerable former prioress, Mère Geneviève.

Thérèse survived those first years in Carmel by reading San Juan de la Cruz for her own purposes. As early as July 1890, she inverted his notion, borrowed from the *Song*, that the human soul, sick in love for Christ, can be healed only in the presence of the beloved. For Thérèse, *Christ* is sick in love and thirsts for human hearts. Christ (Louis), the "suffering servant" prophesied in *Isaiah*, was distant and veiled, abandoned, to be comforted by the unflagging apostolic devotion of the Carmelite sister/daughter. She turned her scruples to advantage by reconciling herself to the weakness in her which they exposed and which St. Paul himself had acknowledged when he gloried in his infirmities (2 *Corinthians* 12:5).

With that delicate equipoise and missionary zeal she was able to carry on conventual life and daily tasks. She worked with Pauline in the refectory for two years (1889–1891), and she served in the sacristy (February 1891–February 1893). In her turn, she rang the bell for choir, a task which allowed her reading time prior to assembly, as there were texts available in the choir's anteroom. In her turn, she read aloud the sacred literature, inspirational texts, and *circulaires* assigned during the refectory hours. In all her years she remained at an ancillary level, or "seconde d'emploi," and when her three years in the novitiate were terminated, she chose to remain in that position, perhaps in deference to the implicit Carmelite understanding that only two natural sisters could be promoted to the choir.

That meant she never became a fully fledged Carmelite. She could not vote, and she remained unqualified for the important posts. She can be commended for her humility in this matter, but she was also deftly handling her part in the tense diplomacy she faced with Pauline and Gonzague, the latter allegedly possessive of authority. Pauline much later claimed that her first term as prioress was spent in tears. Only thirty-one, she had been preselected by old Mère Geneviève over several others who were older but for various reasons, small but definitive, were not to be reckoned: too humble (Sr. Marie-Philomène), too vague (Sr. Thérèse de Jésus), too pedantic (Sr. St.-Augustin), too ambitious (Sr. Marie de Jean-Baptiste). Old Geneviève saw in Pauline the steadfast and conscientious daughter of Zélie Martin, a model of filial devotion. When she became prioress, Pauline gave up her creative pastimes, the writing of poetry and plays for recreational hours.

In the Carmels of those years, it was not unusual for Carmelites to ask a sister with literary inclination to compose poems for them, usually in celebration of an anniversary or a feast day or on behalf of a particular devotion. Having written nothing in her first five conventual years, Thérèse's "gift" for the poetic would have been known only by her speech. In February 1893, she was importuned by the one sister she claims she so detested that she could hardly bear to be near her. In the hagiographies, Sr. Thérèse de St.-Augustin is usually drawn negatively out of unquestioning and unreflected deference to St. Thérèse, but to me she emerges as a Dickensian comic figure, overbearing and punctilious. She also stands as arguably the most important of the Lisieux Carmelites in this story because she challenged Thérèse on two vital counts: in inspiration and in charity. She also and alone received Thérèse's admission of losing heaven.

Here is Sr. St.-Augustin's own account of Thérèse's initiation into writing verse. I hope I am not alone in finding it amusing.

Un jour je lui demandai de composer un cantique sur notre sujet préféré (la dévotion à la Sainte Enfance).

"C'est impossible, me répondit-elle, je ne connais nullement la poésie."

"Qu'est-ce que cela fait, il n'est pas question de l'envoyer à l'Académie, il s'agit seulement de me faire plaisir et de satisfaire un désir de mon âme."

"J'hésite encore un peu parce que je ne sais pas si c'est la volonté du bon Dieu."

"Oh! Pour cela je vais vous donner un conseil. Avant de commencer, vous allez dire à Notre-Seigneur: 'Mon Dieu, si ce n'est pas votre volonté, je vous demande la grâce de ne pouvoir réussir, mais si cela doit procurer votre gloire, venez à mon aide.'"

[One day I asked her to compose a canticle on our favorite subject (a mutual devotion to the Infancy of Christ).

"That's impossible," she replied. "I don't know anything about poetry."

"So what, it's not being sent to the Academy, it's just to please me and satisfy a desire of my soul."

"I'm still hesitant a bit because I don't know if it's God's will."

"Oh, if that's it, let me advise you. Before starting, say to Our Savior: 'My God, if it's not your will, I ask you the grace of failing, but if it's to get you glory, then help me.'"][47]

From that exchange came the first of fifty-four poems within four and a half years, most of them occasioned by others but marked by Thérèse in an unobtrusively didactic way: she was writing for them but from herself. Of her epistolary style she once noted, "j'aime mieux laisser courir ma plume sous l'impression de mon coeur que de bien tourner mes phrases" ["I prefer to let my pen flow under the impression of my heart rather than to turn my phrases"] (LT 151), and on the same grounds we might be disposed to assess her poetic style as one highly derivative of a clichéd, threadbare, anachronistic romanticism. Even so, some of those poems speak vitally of her theology.

She was sometimes criticized for her painting and her writing as though she had come to Carmel chiefly to entertain herself, but one dramatic occasion proved her mettle. Thérèse, her sister Marie, and Sr. Aimée de Jésus served valiantly as the only ones who could stand, walk, and tend their sisters during the influenza epidemic which struck the Carmel in the winter of 1891–1892 and left three sisters dead in a week. France lost sixty thousand people.

Subsequent waves of influenza came early in 1893 and again in 1895, whose winter was unusually severe. Delatroëtte admitted that he had underestimated Carmel's youngest sister.

Thérèse's most important task in her nine years at Carmel came in training novices, a post requiring such maturity, patience, and insight that nothing could better attest the esteem in which she was held than in being assigned to it. Officially, Marie de Gonzague was the novice mistress after Pauline was elected prioress in February 1893; Thérèse was her assistant, known as *aide* or *auxiliare*, even though not herself qualified to leave the novitiate for another eight months. She retained that position three years later when Gonzague was reelected prioress after a bitterly prolonged series of ballots. Thérèse's four charges, with whom she met daily from 2:30 to 3 p.m. in the anteroom to her cell, included Sr. Marie de la Trinité, who wrote an extended memoir of her, and Céline, who entered Carmel in September 1894, even though Delatroëtte had stated that no more Martin sisters would be admitted. Pauline for her part complicated (compromised) her sister's de facto conduct of the novice training by having the novices report finally to herself, not to Gonzague.

Thérèse was likely unusual as a trainer of novices in welcoming their criticisms of her. As novices were permitted to say anything, they were also open conduits of gossip against herself and her sisters. She even shared with her novices the fact of her scruples, an extraordinary, not to say hazardous, confidence.[48] With these other young women, it might be said that she was trying out her "little way," insisting that they be able to imitate her in all things, hence her rejection of a novice's suggestion that it would be splendid if Thérèse, then being consumed by tuberculosis, were to die on a feast day. She herself had to be the pattern of littleness, cultivating the paradox of being exemplary by being unexceptional. She would allow the novices no grandstanding with penances and sackcloth, for example: sins, she said, were the occasion for joy, not tears, since they would glorify divine compassion. From the *circulaires* she had heard and read over her years in Carmel, she became alert to the physical and psychological hazards of mortifications, especially when indulged with girlish fervor. She even told the novices she had no spiritual director other than God, that she had learned nothing from books, even though—a happy contradiction—she frequently cited San Juan de la Cruz to them.[49]

Not least, perhaps, was her insistence upon the joyous countenance. This notion of *sourire*, the smile, requires some defense lest it be confused with an insipid agreeableness such as we commonly show to cameras nowadays. Is smiling not, after all, in sharpest contrast to the anguish recorded in the Sainte Face? Of course, it is. The theological point of the smile rests upon *confiance*, a trust in God's infinite mercy toward the most fallible soul. One could say that it was an outward sign of faith, hope, and love. Even so, *most* of the photos from the Lisieux Carmel do not provide such a sign, not even from Thérèse.[50] None of the Carmelites would have considered photography an enduring public record of themselves nor an accurate reflection of their spiritual dispositions. Yet Thérèse was even willing to violate regulations with her smiling: every evening upon retiring to their cells, she would smile at her neighbor, Sr. Marie-Philomène, thirty-five years her senior, a terribly shy and self-effacing woman who had passed through the novitiate with her.

One photo recorded a *sainte face* (see figure 2.5). Céline took it at Isidore's inherited country estate, "La Musse," near Evreux, on July 29, 1894. It was of her dead father. Lying gaunt and with his white beard frizzled, Louis embodied the popularized iconography of St. Joseph on his deathbed, except that Jesus was not present this time. I am told that Thérèse saw this photo. Happy though she was that her father was now secured by heaven, seeing that closing scene must have been painful, perhaps like the *circulaire* she and her sisters heard soon after Louis's passing: "Son père tomba malade peu après lui avoir donné son consentement; la famille eut la douleur de le perdre en très peu de temps. Dieu avait accepté le sacrifice qu'il avait fait de sa chère fille. Il voulut l'en recompenser dans le ciel" ["Her father fell ill soon after giving her his consent. The family had the grief of losing him in a very short time. God had accepted the sacrifice he had made of his dear daughter and wanted to recompense him

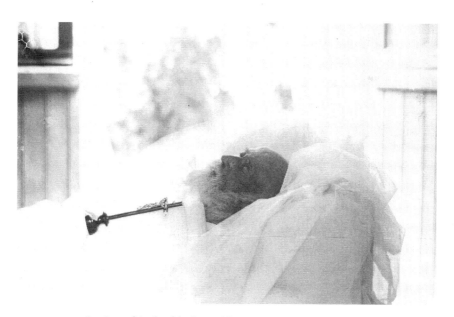

FIGURE 2.5. Louis on his deathbed at Isidore's estate, La Musse, July 29, 1894. The gauze, here folded back, protected the body from summer's flies. Copyright Archives du Carmel de Lisieux.

in heaven"].[51] As the Martin family had been gradually reconstituting itself within Carmel's walls—Thérèse had long been expecting Céline would join them and directly she had confirmation—it must have been clear that Louis, not any one of them, not even Céline, had been the sacrificial victim. Thérèse herself admitted as much in her petitionary poem/prayer to Louis, "Rappelle-toi qu'autrefois sur la terre Ton seul bonheur était de nous chérir" ["Remember that once on earth your sole joy was to cherish us"] (PN 8). In the end, did it matter that his sole and final joy was at La Musse where he could look out from his wheelchair upon the landscape and weep quietly?

His death brought Céline to a crisis: so long as Louis lived, she carried the burden of the dutiful and loving daughter. Pichon's years-old plan for her to join him in Canada was confounded by the far greater need of her expressed in Thérèse's letters during the summer of 1894. She was reminded that no earthly suitor, generally tagged as "creature," could satisfy her as Jesus could (and that included Pichon).[52] The paradoxical Christology of the thirsting savior, expounded in letters as early as 1889, was now directed to her, as though Jesus were the suitor. It is interesting that Céline, as though in her own defense, declared herself too dependent upon her younger sister. She needed apartness and her own cross to bear—an oblique expression, possibly, of her desire for family life. "Dieu fait à mon âme des appels étranges" ["God is making strange summons to my soul"] (LC 159), she pleaded. She had discovered her own maternal promptings in caring for Louis,[53] and she must have talked at length with her aunt and her wedded cousin Jeanne about the challenges of marriage and family life. On Louis's death, however, she had no suitors, and it was well known that she had turned down offers. Could she be sure there would be any others? She was now twenty-five. Thérèse in courting her reminded her of their parity in adolescence: they were one soul then and would be now, but in applying to Lisieux's Carmel, even stating her willingness to be a *converse* (a station wholly contrary to her temperament),[54] she was putting herself forever under her younger sister's tutelage. Céline was in fact admitted by sleight of hand as a *bienfaitrice*, the most marginal title,[55] but went through the full procedure of postulancy, novitiate, and vows and with full observance of the rules.

With her in September 1894 came her camera (by the exceptionally indulgent permission of Pauline, then prioress) and a lengthy series of Old Testament texts she had meticulously transcribed, including psalms and a full copy of the *Song of Songs*, which Thérèse had known only piecemeal from her readings of San Juan de la Cruz. The *Song*, with an I-Thou spirituality wholly unknown to the Gospels, became so fetching that Thérèse wanted to write a commentary on the poem, but Pauline forbade it, perhaps in the knowledge that such an effort had been undertaken only by the most lofty minds within the Church, Augustine and Guillaume de Sainte-Thierry, for example, but then there were also commentaries by Madre Teresa and the notorious quietist of just two centuries before, Mme. de Guyon.[56]

At the year's end, Pauline ordered Thérèse to write an autobiography, an endeavor initially meant solely for the Martin family. This undertaking occupied her through 1895. Whether she knew she was in effect writing her obituary remains unclear. In April of that year she confided to Sr. St. Augustine, "Je mourrai bientôt, je ne vous dis pas ce soit dans quelques mois, mais dans deux ou trois ans" ["I shall die soon, I don't mean in months but within two or three years"].[57] This judgment came not on physical but enigmatically spiritual grounds: "Je sens à tout ce qui se passe dans mon âme que mon exil est près de finir" ["I sense from everything that is happening within my soul that my exile is soon to end"].[58]

Likely with that presentiment, Thérèse composed on June 9, 1895, the most important of all her recorded prayers, the sacrificial offering of herself to God's compassionate love, *Offrande de moi-même comme Victime d'Holocauste à l'Amour Miséricordieux du Bon Dieu*. It came in response to a *circulaire* which had just arrived from the Carmel at Luçon (Vendée) where Sr. Anne-Marie de Jésus had left an *offrande* to divine justice. While Thérèse's view of an all-encompassing and merciful divine love has famously confounded the hoary tradition which rested on a punitive divine justice, the importance of Sr. Anne-Marie goes further. She had touched a nerve: "J'accepte les tourments intérieurs," she had said on her deathbed, "L'incertitude. Je n'ai pas assez de mérites; il faut en acquérir" ["I accept the inner torments. The uncertainty. I don't have enough merits; they must be gained"]. In her *offrande* she had sought to make reparation—a central theme in the vastly popular cult of the Sacred Heart—on behalf of the Church, the Holy Seat, France, and the bishop—all this, a standard inventory for an exceptional act. Sr. Anne-Marie had tried to live out sacrifice by extreme austerities such as prolonged vigils, hair shirts, nocturnal prostrations, the commonplace mortificatory procedures known to Carmel and to other orders. But there were two exceptional facts about her.

When she was a child of four, a painter had chosen her as the Virgin Mary being presented in the Temple. Inspired, he offered his sitter to God and put her under the Virgin's protection. No less momentous, her *offrande* to God was accepted: she died on Good Friday, chosen by Jesus, as the *circulaire* opens, "pour l'associer largement à sa douloureuse agonie" ["to share abundantly in his sorrowful agony"].[59] As Pichon had prompted Thérèse in the salvific power of affective love, Sr. Anne-Marie inspired her, perhaps by emulation, to sacrifice herself through it. Her own *offrande*, composed on the Feast of the Blessed Trinity, remains an eloquent compaction of her spirituality. Anyone who reads it attentively goes a good way toward meeting Thérèse.

As in many instances of *offrandes* recorded in the *circulaires*, this one was accepted. Thérèse's first coughing of blood, on Easter 1896, physically substantiated her premonition of an early death, or so she wrote in the summer of 1897, when it had become certain that she would not live much longer. Within those fifteen months she wrote from a private retreat the addendum to her autobiography known as Manuscript B, answering a request from her sister Marie to explain what she was calling her little way. In that brief work—it runs only ten folio pages—she expresses her long-frustrated desire to live in the male world of apostles and martyrs, to play something like the Jeanne d'Arc role which was as impossible for her as it was anachronistic. Yet, there was even as late as March 1897 the possibility that she could be sent to Indochina and the Carmel recently founded at Hanoi, there to realize at least the maleness of martyrdom.

Teresa of Avila had wanted Carmel's sisters to be as courageous as men. Some of them in going abroad to missions proved, as one Carmelite wittily put it, "courageuse et énergique comme Ste. Françoise-de-Chantal, douce et suave comme St. François de Sales" ["courageous and energetic like St. Françoise de Chantal, sweet and gentle like St. François de Sales"].[60] From the *circulaires* Thérèse learned of brave and exceptional women such as Mère St. Louis de Gonzague, who had had to wait for three years until her desire to save infidels was finally answered. Posted to Shanghai, she learned enough Chinese within three months to make herself understood. When the mission she organized burned down, she started another. When the Carmel community was alerted to the danger of attacks, the monsignor suggested to her that conversions would require martyrdoms and that Carmelites would be suitable. "Nous sommes toutes prêtes" ["We're all ready"], she replied equably.[61] Those words must have thrilled Thérèse with envy.

Some fears of (or hopes for) martyrdom abroad were more imaginary than real. At a Carmel in Bethlehem, Mère Marie du Mont Carmel had faced the general panic caused by rumors of an imminent massacre, the question being whose: "Tous les chrétiens allaient être massacrés le même jour. Les chrétiens avaient peur des turcs, les turcs craignaient les juifs et ces derniers redoutaient les chrétiens et les turcs. Aussitôt chacun s'enfuit" ["All the Christians were going to be massacred that very day. The Christians feared the Turks, the Turks feared the Jews, and the Jews feared the Christians and the Turks. Everybody scattered at once"].[62] A more subtle danger had awaited Mère Marie de la Croix, who left the Carmel of Angoulême and, after fifty-seven days at sea, founded one in Sydney. She feared attacks from neighboring Protestant heretics, but she soon won from them "une vénération profonde."[63]

The Vietnamese Carmels were of particular interest at Lisieux because it had founded Saigon's in 1861 and now the new Hanoi Carmel was seeking sisters. In the summer of 1896, the possibility of Pauline going to Saigon had been raised. The *circulaires* from there had been strangely uplifting: during an especially hot and rainy spell in 1889 three Carmelites had died within hours of each other, all of them native Vietnamese. That sufficed as proof to their prioress that "nos chères petites Annamites sont d'une constitution délicate, héritage d'une race débile, ce qui explique pourquoi les Français échappent aux épidémies plutôt que les indigènes" ["our dear little Vietnamese are of a delicate constitution, the heritage of a weak race, which explains why the French, rather than the natives, escape epidemics"].[64] Another Vietnamese Carmelite's death was explained thus: "Hélas, la mollesse du caractère oriental connaît peu les mâles énergies qu'exige le travail de la perfection" ["Alas, the softness of the oriental character scarcely knows the masculine energies requisite to the work of perfection"].[65] In fine, the hardy French colonial temperament was needed in Indochina.

Such considerations were not what Thérèse wanted or needed to know. Her motives were elsewhere and mixed at that: to save pagan souls, of course, but also to find martyrdom, if possible, or at least obscurity. As she came to savor the bitter over the sweet, she fancied that in an environment wholly different from the too-familiar one at Lisieux she could become anonymous. It was an odd turn to her search for a genuine humility, a littleness truly little because it would not be found and so could not be proclaimed. She got in lieu of that vanishing into a foreign mission the vicarious adventure with others in departure.

Thérèse was blessed with the adoption of two young missionary priests who became surrogates of the brothers lost to Zélie and Louis before she was born. In October 1895, Pauline, then prioress, entrusted to her sister a seminarian, Maurice Barthélemy-Bellière, a year younger than she, who was seeking to join the White Fathers, a missionary order working in Africa. The following May, Gonzague, reelected prioress, gave her Adolphe Roulland, just short of his ordination. He visited Carmel en route to Sichuan, a central-southwestern province of China. Both young men, of local provenance, had requested of the Lisieux Carmel that they be assigned a sister who would pray for their missions.

Bellière and Roulland were setting out to live in their way the unrealized life of Thérèse, the male career of apostle/missionary/martyr which she futilely longed to attain and presumably gave up hoping for when she composed Manuscript B. Her correspondence with Abbé Bellière (he was not ordained until 1904) has become well known, chiefly because, unlike Roulland, he was eloquently unsure of himself. She came to play for him as much a counseling as an intercessory role, but she did not live to learn of his missionary work, which ended early and unhappily. He died in Bon Sauveur at the age of thirty-three. To both men, she sent several of her poems. They exchanged significant dates in their lives, what she called "jours de grâces."

Roulland's reports from China include details of local violence and unrest of the sort which might well have seemed to Thérèse the guarantee of martyrdom. She was bold enough to tell him she hoped he would be killed and asked for a lock of his hair as a proleptic relic. From reading about the martyred priest Théophane Vénard, beheaded in Hanoi in 1861, she nursed a recessive hope of going there,[66] even though she knew her highly sensitive temperament would have made such an enterprise acutely difficult for her— immersing her, perhaps, in an environment as unfriendly, as mischievous as she had suffered at the Benedictine Abbey school. This, at least, is what she hints to us (Manuscript C 9v) after she has had to give up all hope of going to Asia. Perhaps she is evading the real reason she did not and could not go to Asia—her poor health—but the aside shows how experience, what she herself had tested and found true, remained her surest guide. The Lisieux Carmel, for all its confines and a few disagreeable sisters, was familial and sustaining. The abbey school had exposed her inability to endure an environment that lacked at least one of her sisters. Martyrdom apart, Roulland's letters take on a special valence in opening up to her the world a missionary had to face at its worst. On February 24, 1897, he wrote to her of the famine ravaging the area ·in which he was working. Beyond the usual threats of theft and murder, which faced him constantly, there was now brigandage and cannibalism. Parents unable to feed their children were selling them. He himself had barely survived a protracted bout of high fever. His self-assurance, robust good humor, and resolute faith had gotten him through a great deal of personal challenges—he was tonsured in Chinese fashion and was now learning the language—and the horrors he reports are the more effective for the dispassionate tone he gives them. He was providing Thérèse a perspective and focus which she in her secure and enclosed life could not have imagined nor sustained. It seems surprising that she said nothing to acknowledge the grotesque sufferings Roulland recorded, though she did thank him for the relic of hair. They belonged to another world, but beside them her confident assumptions of divine love and even of Christ's own suffering pale, and the talk of martyrdom seems an almost obtrusive instance of *amour propre*. Would her acute affectivity of love have been able experientially to bear the satanic world Roulland was reporting? That remains an open and a nagging question. She was only twenty-four when she died.

By her last summer, she was candidly sharing with her "brothers" the fact of her approaching death. Of the letters she wrote after she was placed in the Carmel's infirmary on July 8, 1897, one went to Roulland and four to Bellière. In June, she had composed the most important of all her writings, the breakthrough Manuscript C, which she addressed to Mère Gonzague, and continued talks with her sisters, chiefly Pauline, which were taken down in notes as early as April. These "entretiens," or conversations, together with Manuscript C attest to what some of the *circulaires* had already told her, though the medically astute might wish to contest it as a cliché: that with advancing illness came mental acuity, as though with the decline in one's physical well-being, one's perceptions grew toward a greater clarity.[67] She was under the urgency of time, now knowing from her own sisters, her novices, and others in the community that she had attained a perceptivity about religious life which could and should be shared with others beyond the walls. Abetted by Pauline, she was composing her own *circulaire.*

The conjunction of the tubercular onset and Thérèse's entry into a spiritual wilderness poses a conundrum in a later chapter. There we shall examine her medical history and the barbaric and pathetically inadequate measures taken against the illness which killed her on September 30, 1897.

3

On Her Mother

The Travails of Zélie Martin

Je me demande comment le cher Historien fera pour présenter ses deux héros de la souffrance sans éloigner les lecteurs du désir d'être "irréprochables dans leurs voies" puisqu'on y aboutit à une tel résultat! [I'm asking myself how the Historian will present his two heroic sufferers without alienating his readers from the desire to be "irreproachable like them" since that's what it comes to!]
—Céline Martin on her parents, *Notes préparatoires
à l'Histoire d'une famille*

[L]es succès de ce monde l'étouffent presque, c'est une vie d'agitation complète. . . . elle se tourmente déjà de ne pas voir de marques de vocation dans ses enfants [Worldly successes are almost suffocating her. It's a life of complete agitation. . . . she torments herself by not seeing any sign of a calling in her children].
—Sr. Marie-Dosithée to Isidore Guérin on their
sister Zélie, February 2, 1864

In the last weeks of her life, Thérèse imagined a sermon she might have given, had she been born worthy of priesthood. Among the *Derniers entretiens*, it is unusual for its length and assertive spontaneity. It reads as the fruit of a long time spent with the Gospels in an intuitive immediacy which set Thérèse proximate to the human subject of her sermon: not Jesus but his mother.

Thérèse had lived all her life within the cult of Mary. She and all her siblings had been given the name of Marie. She believed that Mary saved her from the mysterious illness of her childhood. She knew that her mother, dying of breast cancer, had gone to Lourdes, a pilgrimage site established only twenty-five years before, to seek the only remedy she believed possible: that which the Virgin alone could grant her. Possibly, Thérèse heard from her sister or from her uncle the chilling words her mother had penned in the last letter she wrote, to her brother Isidore: "Décidément, la Sainte Vierge ne veut pas me guérir" ["Obviously, the Blessed Virgin does not want to cure me"].[1] For Thérèse over most of her life, for her family, and for Catholics in their time, the iconographic Mary, however sustaining to the devout in their many needs, was a celestially regal figure. Since Chartres, she had held court as the Queen of Heaven, centered in that splendor of a rose window, even as she was centered in the amphitheatrical seating of Dante's paradise. Mary was the majestically perfect mother.

When Dante last sees his beloved Beatrice, she, though clear to his miraculously telescopic vision, sits at a stellar remove from him. Thérèse found herself in something like the poet's vantage when looking at the heavenly Queen: an image clearly seen by mind and heart, yet remote from earthly life. When we exalt someone, the sublimity in that effort comes at a cost, a cost neither of credibility nor even of accessibility but of a negotiably human engagement. Mary rendered on high becomes unreal as far as she is inimitable. It is easy to forget that a maternal figure of infinite consolatory power once needed solace herself.

In an almost debunking manner not distant from Renan's, Thérèse's sermon took on a story, or rather a hagiographic implantation foreign to Scriptures, which she had known from childhood, that Mary as a child of three went to the Jewish Temple to offer her "sentiments brûlants d'amour et tout à fait extraordinaires" ["burning and wholly exceptional feelings of love"].[2] Perhaps, remarks Thérèse dryly, she went simply out of obedience to her parents. And when, early in St. Matthew's account, Simeon predicted to Mary the sword's piercing of her heart, how could she, newly a mother, have been able to envision at that time the suffering of Christ? Thérèse says it was a generalized remark, which cuts the ground from its prophetic force. A sermon on Mary would have to address her real life, not the fictive "vie supposée." To make her imitable, to stress her virtues, would mean to appreciate Mary's having lived not within the Christian faith and therefore having been puzzled at the things spoken of Jesus when he was yet a child. (She even had to suffer—Thérèse knew yet did not include this Gospel fact—her son's rebuke when he called those anonymously assembled before him his mothers, sisters, brothers.) Mary is more mother than queen, and to say that in her glory she eclipses the saints' as the sun precludes the light of the stars is, Thérèse urges, absurd because a mother would not obscure the brilliance of her own children. Then the would-be sermon reaches its *envoi*: "Qui sait si quelque âme n'irait pas même jusqu'à sentir alors un certain éloignement pour une créature tellement supérieure et ne se dirait pas: 'Si c'est cela, autant aller

briller comme on pourra dans un petit coin!' " ["Who knows if some soul
would not even go so far as to feel a kind of distance from such a superior
creature and say, 'If that's the way it is, one might as well go shine as one can
in a little corner!'"].

Thérèse is great for having been small. One of the largest structures in Europe,
and the largest ever constructed in a woman's name, commemorates this
smallness. Her story, however, begins in Alençon, capital of Normandy's Orne
district, in a small house opposite the prefecture on the Rue de Saint-Blaise
(then no. 36, now no. 50), where she arrived as the ninth child of Zélie and
Louis Martin. She came on January 2, 1873, in the wake of what the French call
étrennes, or New Year's Day gifts, and her mother, then forty-two, knew that
Thérèse would be her last child, the last blessing she would have the patience
and stamina to endure.

Thérèse's parents lie vaulted behind that vast stone tribute to her on the
hilltop of Lisieux. Both, venerated on March 26, 1994, will one day become
saints. Veneration, not as procedure but as impulse, comes easy because we who
are human almost instinctively crave purification of life's sordidness and inadequacy, and so we designate some among us who have conspicuously overcome
such limits, be they called heroes or saints. On that count, Thérèse had nothing
in her life to endure and survive: her parents had prepared a kind of sacred
ground for her by their rigorously pious lives: devout to the church, devoted to
the children. Yet, even those lives admit nuances. They were not marmoreal,
fortunately, but we need no ledger of negatives for either Zélie or Louis in order
to find them human on the terms Thérèse set for Mary, a fretful and bemused
mother. Finding them human does not controvert what Thérèse herself wrote to
her missionary "brother," Maurice Bellière, two months before her death: "Le
bon Dieu m'a donné un père et une mère plus dignes du Ciel que de la terre"
["God gave me parents more worthy of heaven than of earth"].[3] It would be
difficult to imagine a deeper tribute from any child to any parent.

While this chapter is given primarily to Mme. Martin, because it was she
who, I believe, anticipated much of Thérèse's own spirituality, both parents
deserve a profile, however brief. How were they shaped, hurt, and warped into
the human condition by their cares? We shall first look back at Louis before
Lisieux.

Of solid provincial bourgeois stock, Louis, eight years his wife's senior, was
born (1823) into the great historical vacuum known as the Restoration, a void
filled by pecuniary energies and schemes of the ascendant commercial class
profiled in the novels of Balzac. Stendhal called it an age of moral asphyxia.
Ecclesiastical France had survived the revolution which produced a sea change
in human consciousness. And, though profoundly compromised, Catholicism
also survived the colossus whom that revolution had finally begotten. It had

rendered unto this Caesar what it was not Caesar's to claim. Napoleon had left in his wake a vast number of immeasurably lesser (save in ambition) men who were condemned to the reality that all the glory of France was due to him. "Ce souvenir fatal nous empêchera à jamais d'être heureux!" ["This fateful memory will keep us from ever being happy!"], exclaims Stendhal's Julien Sorel, who is peculiarly beset by "l'idée napoléonienne," that one's greatest feats must be achieved by one's thirtieth year.[4] The compass of everyone's latitude for world conquest had been shrunk miserably.

These melancholy facts were passed on, in their way, to Louis Martin. His father had served as a soldier in Napoleon's armies—in Belgium, Prussia, and Poland. He also participated in the Hundred Days but from the royalist side. Thus, the essential contradiction of a believing generation informed the Martin household: loyalty to the emperor who had humiliated two popes, demoted the church, and compromised the priesthood by civic oaths; subsequently, an unqualified support for the debilitated forces of reaction. The common denominator in such a turnabout is obvious, an unquestioning obedience to established power. Born into the post-imperial age, Louis internalized the asceticism of a soldier but had no campaign.

At twenty, he pursued not the red of the military but the black of the clergy. If he had been disappointed to have come into the world after Waterloo, he was disappointed anew when, setting out from Strasbourg, he arrived on foot at the hermitage of St. Bernard in Switzerland. He was promptly refused admission on the sobering grounds that he was ignorant of Latin, the Church's mother tongue and then the staple of any education worthy of the name. It is difficult to believe that he would have been so naive not to have anticipated a fact as obvious as it was insuperable; it seems likely that he had not consulted with any church official to discuss his decision to enter the monastic life. He would have been reminded about the Latin, at least. As he was not someone who acted on a whim, it must have been an acute diffidence or humility which held him back from sharing his hopes with a priest. Reaching the monastery's doors (at nearly 2,500 meters' altitude, well over 8,000 feet) required courage as well as physical exertion. Back home, he tried to learn Latin and then gave up. His carefully kept notebooks indicate that between October 1845 and January 1847, he was buying classical texts and paying a tutor, but there is no record of when nor why he stopped. Anyone undertaking a foreign language quickly finds out to what degree it comes with some ease, if at all, and Louis must have sensed, or feared, he did not have sufficient aptitude for Latin to keep going. His disappointment in knowing he would never enter an order painfully informed the rest of his life.

What we know of him might argue a dreamy man, one more disposed to reverie and solitude than to the bruising bustle of normal life, but the other emergent and recurrent need of his life was wandering, the very opposite of reclusion. He grew up not on Stendhal and Balzac but on the intoxicating spiritualities of Chateaubriand and the early Lamartine which created a kind of Christian aesthetic, transforming the natural world into theistic tableaux. Having been born in Bordeaux but into a family which moved first to Normandy and then to Alsace and then back, Louis learned to love to roam.

Pichon's view of Louis, that he was "un religieux égaré dans le monde" ["a monk astray in the world"] seems apt but does not quite explain the roving.[5] Louis had as well a penchant for setting himself apart: at Alençon he bought a wind tower at whose top he established a room for reading. There he stored equipment for his other regularly observed withdrawal, fishing. Perhaps he would have been at home only within the Ordre des Chanoines Réguliers de Saint-Augustin high in those Swiss Alps, a place which would have enforced upon him community and a stationary world.

At twenty-four and needing a profession, Louis turned to another form of asceticism, watch making, a fastidious and solitary pursuit. He had started its apprenticeship in Rennes and pursued it in Paris during the heady days of yet another revolution, one which carded the aristocracy from the capitals of Europe. When the Habsburgs were fleeing Vienna, Metternich told them not to fear the future because the barricade makers—students, professors, journalists—were fighting ideas, not things. He was right. The revolutions of 1848 all proved abortive. Yet, Catholicism itself was not wholly within the camp of reaction and had come partly of age since 1789 and 1830. As we have found, no one attested more eloquently to the capacity of a fervent Christian to embrace the modern, democratized world than Félicité Lamennais, but Louis was not so bold as to endorse the views of someone fallen under papal censure. At heart a provincial and a royalist, he never dared to challenge authority. To the extent that he had any political view, it would likely have been Montalembert's, that socialism aimed not to overthrow the institutional church only but the very stanchions of order: religion, property, and family.

We know almost nothing of how Louis fared in Paris during his two or three years there. Whether he was then disposed to or even aware of the reformist voices within the Church, such as Frederic Ozanam's, remains a pointless question. The Martin family biographer, Stéphane-Joseph Piat, records an anecdote that begs for focus and detail. Louis was invited to join a club of philanthropists dedicated to charitable works but discovered that it was in fact "une société secrète," meaning almost certainly a guild of Freemasons. Piat's gloss on this obscure affair comes to "ce sont les oeuvres de ténèbres qui recherchent les ténèbres" ["shady doings seek shadows"],[6] a strange note from a book written during the French underground's resistance to the Nazi occupation.

Another remark concerns that murky period in Louis's life, this from his wife. When Isidore was sporting his youth in the capital, pursuing studies in medicine, and looking about for a wife, Zélie wrote to him, fretful on all vague counts.[7] He was about to turn twenty-two. Louis had passed on his admonitions about the terrors of Parisian life: "il me dit que tu seras en butte à des tentations auxquelles tu ne résisteras pas, parce que tu n'as pas assez de piété. Il me raconte ce qu'il a éprouvé lui-même, et ce qu'il lui a fallu de courage pour sortir victorieux de tous ces combats. Si tu savais par quelles épreuves il a passé. . . . Je t'en conjure, mon cher Isidore, fais comme lui; prie, et tu ne te laisseras pas entraîner par le torrent. Si tu succombes une fois, tu es perdu. Il n'y a que le premier pas qui coûte, dans cette voie du mal comme dans celle du bien; après tu seras entraine par le courant" ["He tells me you'll be exposed to temptations you won't resist because you don't have enough piety. He related to me what tested him and that he'd needed courage to emerge victorious from all these combats. If you knew what tests he had passed. . . . I beg you, my dear Isidore, do like him: pray, and you won't let yourself be swept away by the torrent. If you give in once, you're lost. It's only the first step that counts on this path of evil, just as on the path of good; afterward, you'll be carried away by the current"].[8]

It seems unlikely that Zélie, in her anxiety about torrents and currents, was talking about such backwater activities as Freemasonry or other secret societies. Her concern was fixed solely and transparently upon the floodtides and swelling streams of sexuality. Her husband had emerged "victorious" from the siren songs of Parisian prostitutes. If we apply Thérèse's Mary-the-mother criterion, we might assume Louis had simply passed them by. "If you knew what tests he had passed" sounds monitory but teasingly blurry. Why she could not tell Isidore the vivid, salvific details is clear: in those days of a propriety remote to us now, Louis would not have offended her ears with particulars. Besides, a distance between husband and wife was scrupulously maintained. At the time of this letter, they had been married four years and had two children. In writing to her brother, Louis is identified solely as "my husband," "mon mari." That is how he was almost invariably mentioned even to her kin and to the end of her life, fifteen years later. That was the convention.

Zélie's fleeting words on the lurid life Louis eluded in Paris do not point to the common knowledge which gave her advice more than prudish edginess: the profile of syphilis was so high there that, as Flaubert hyperbolized, virtually everyone had the disease in some form. Syphilis thrived in a society where marriage was so constraining that adultery and prostitution were accepted as outlets. (The real scandal of Madame Bovary was not the adultery of its eponymous heroine but that the story occurs in a province, the station of respectability; there would have been no story had Flaubert set it in Paris.) The literary trials of Flaubert and of Baudelaire (both of them syphilitic and facing the same prosecutor) were triumphs of hypocrisy. Physicians and those they were training, such as Isidore, knew the prevalence of venereal diseases, not all of which were deadly. Leukorrhea, according to an estimate in 1865, affected as much as 80 percent of urban women.[9] Zélie's fearful cautions about the torrents of evil had, in medical fact, a sound pathological basis.

So Louis retreated to the known safety of the provinces. In watch making he made a name for himself in Alençon. He set up his shop on the Rue du Pont-Neuf, next to the bridge itself. The building continues to house a horologer. He did not marry until he had reached half of his biblical years, long enough to be reputed an irretrievable bachelor. His horror of sexuality, tinged with the remembrance of those women of Parisian streets, would have kept him in that solitary state, had he been left to himself. He was not. His mother, Marie-Anne-Fannie Martin, had borne five children, all but one of whom had lived through childhood, but he, the third, was in 1858 the sole survivor. It was in her maternal interest and in the Martins' that Louis be fruitful and multiply. It is alleged that she scolded him about his celibacy. Whether he remonstrated or not, she took the initiative, realizing that she needed an ally in a prospective wife. Too set in his solitary way, Louis could not be budged on his own. She found help in Azélie-Marie Guérin, at twenty-seven an accomplished lace maker.

The mystifying account is that Zélie, as she was known, chanced to pass Louis on a bridge in town and when she did, "une voix intérieure lui murmurait en secret: 'C'est celui-là que j'ai préparé pour toi'" ["an inner voice secretly murmured to her, 'He's the one I've prepared for you'"].[10] This pious overlay, the very stuff of hagiography, does not becloud the fact that, from the vantage of commercial bourgeois interests—money mattering far more in that day to the French marriage than did love of any sort—the match was shrewdly made. Both had a steady professional income; they could afford to raise a family. Further, and no small consideration, both were from the same class.

And both were devout Catholics. During the Second Empire and far beyond, domestic differences over religion played a substantial role in marital unhappiness. An anticlerical husband would not have been alone in taking offense at a pious wife, for women took their troubles and their confidences to priests; husbands tended to be distant, uncommunicative, bored, and perhaps resentful of a cleric's ascendance over their wives. Married men had mistresses and prostitutes. Women had the Church and the matriarchal hold over their progeny.

Louis and Zélie had no such tensions to negotiate. Steadfast and dependable, they had strictly defined spheres of interest and action: he, the clocks and fishing; she, lace and begetting. That his mother had prompted the union, if not the murmuring voice, argues that it was not one of passionate attraction—passion having little to do with domestic economy in those days, not to mention future stability—but of sense. His mother, then nearly sixty, would not be around to care for Louis all his life. But what of Zélie and her expectations?

Every life is prodigious in shadows. We cannot altogether penetrate them, fortunately. It is well, though, to sustain a sense of their obscurity, as a life in full light would daunt credibility. We do not know how deeply the disappointment over his rejection from the monastic life bore upon Louis, and even had he told himself or others (and with them, us) in writing, the telling would have been partial: not the feelings but a statement of them, and only at a particular time, the moment of his writing. The disappointment articulated to his wife would have been put differently from that given to a traveling companion on one of his trips from home—the priest, for example, who went with him to Turkey.

Strangely, in his book on Thérèse, *Histoire d'une Mission*, Hans Urs von Balthasar remarks that we know much more of Louis than we do of his wife. The opposite is patently the case, if only because she left fifteen years of correspondence (1863–1877), running to some 430 pages (see figure 3.1). Louis read, could recite long stretches of favorite poetry, but seldom wrote.[11] His wife's letters deserve attention not only because Zélie was the mother of

FIGURE 3.1. Zélie Martin, ca. 1875. A Third Order Franciscan, a lace maker, a devoted wife, a strict but loving mother, she saw and accepted God's will in every joy and woe. Copyright Archives du Carmel de Lisieux.

Thérèse and not because of any literary merit—they pretend to none—but as an intimate profile of a provincial household at whose vital center a loving mother and careful businesswoman labored with diligence and dedication. It implicates no less than three circles of women: Zélie, her housemaids, her five daughters, and the wet nurses; Zélie and her flock of lace makers, whose work she supervised and coordinated; Zélie and her closest family members: her sister Marie-Louise (here known as Sr. Marie-Dosithée) in the Visitandine convent at Le Mans; Pauline, who was in school there; and her sister-in-law, Céline Guérin, the only other mother among the correspondents.

Thérèse's mother's letters to her sister have been lost. Either they were destroyed by Sr. Marie-Dosithée at once, being confidential, or about the time of her death in 1877. We know from what has survived that Zélie, often exhausted and apprehensive over her children and her business, sometimes regretted she had not been able to take the veil, as her sister had. We know, too, that within the first year of her marriage she made several trips to Le Mans, seeking comfort and consolation.

She had had the awkward fortune of growing up as a middle child, more than two years younger than Marie-Louise, and nine years senior to Isidore, a distance which allowed her to become a kind of mother to him. There is a cryptic reminiscence from her which she shared with him: "Il faut renoncer à tout; je n'ai jamais eu de plaisir dans ma vie, non, jamais ce qui s'appelle plaisir. Mon enfance, ma jeunesse ont été tristes comme un linceul, car, si ma mère te gâtait, pour moi, tu le sais, elle était trop sévère; elle, pourtant si bonne, ne savait pas me prendre, aussi j'ai beaucoup souffert du coeur" ["One must renounce everything. I have never had pleasure in my life, no, never what is called pleasure. My childhood, my adolescence were as sorrowful as a funeral shroud; in fact, if my mother spoiled you, she was, as you know, too harsh toward me; even though so good, she didn't know how to deal with me and I suffered greatly in my heart"].[12] Marie-Louise had the advantages of the eldest child, and Isidore had the breezy benefit of being the youngest and the only boy, doubly spoiled.[13] Zélie's silent adversity informed her deeply and prepared her to be a mother perhaps more loving than her own was able to be, but she showed to her own middle child some of the severity she herself had endured from the unhappy middle position.

Her mother died in 1859. Her father spent his last years, fussy and helpless, within the Martin home in Alençon, at the house he himself had purchased. Like the elder Martin, Zélie's father had served in the Emperor's armies. During the Restoration, he worked in the gendarmerie, or local police force, at Saint-Artois, a small town just west of Alençon.[14] Although he had purchased what was to become the Martin house, by the time his daughters came of age, Isidore père did not have an income sufficient to provide a dowry. Besides, young Isidore's education had to be funded, a consideration closed to girls and young women until lycées were opened for their professional development over a generation later, in the 1880s. Marie-Louise settled her part of the financial problem in going to Le Mans. Zélie hoped to become a sister of charity. Her mother took her for an interview with the superior at Alençon's *hôtel-Dieu*, or community hospital, run by the sisters of St. Vincent de Paul.

It proved an unhappy experience. The superior rejected her without specification. Biographers pass on the vague speculation that Zélie's health might have been an issue, but they raise, too, the hagiographical presumption that the superior might have intuited (the murmuring inner voice?) that this young woman's true calling was motherhood; she was destined to beget a saint. Whether that presumption stretches the matter is of no importance. What did matter was Zélie's disappointment, perhaps even keener than Louis's over the hermitage, in that she had the example of her sister before her and there was no explicit ground for her rejection, as Latin became for Louis. As the Guérin girls had grown up in the close way of loving sisters, Zélie had no envy to overcome, but she did have to face the fact that, denied bridehood with Christ, she might have to reconcile herself to the second-class status of Catholic women, motherhood. Apparently no one sought to court her, and with her twenties advancing she was resigning herself to spinsterhood at home, the third option, and lowest in social esteem, for women in her time.

She undertook to learn lace making, enrolling in an *école dentellière* in order to master this extraordinarily complex, demanding craft. Like the meeting with Louis on the bridge, the choice of a profession allegedly came from an inner voice telling her what direction to take. She learned so well that she was able at just twenty-two to set herself up as a "fabricante de Point d'Alençon," working in her father's home. Given the responsibilities of that position, it was a daring step for such a young woman to take. She knew nothing about running a business and had no initial capital. It argues the resolve, focus, and determination of full maturity, but daring often conceals some desperation. Perhaps Zélie's disappointment over St. Vincent de Paul gave her a goading, but the alternative of working under a boss had already exposed her to unwelcome importunities.

Handmade lace had been Alençon's pride for centuries, a phenomenally local success which began with Marguerite of Lorraine, grandmother of Henri IV. She had taken up embroidery as a pastime and gave her works to monasteries and churches. In 1664, Jean-Baptiste Colbert, minister of state to Louis XIV, with his eye upon both trade and technology, brought to France thirty Venetian craftspeople in lace who set up their industry in various towns in the north. Unlike Colbert's ventures into silks, glass, and the production of mirrors, lace making proved a failure almost everywhere but settled permanently in Sens and Alençon.

The details of this craft involved as many as nine different stitches which had to be joined in turn by nine lace makers, each specializing in her own *point.* They worked in their own homes, then entrusted their work to an *assembleuse* who had to join all the pieces together so as to render a pattern without one thread loose. Zélie, as *fabricante*, secured a clientele, assigned and oversaw the works. She used tulle, a fine silk on a spool, to repair almost invisible rends. (In the house at Alençon, visitors can see still on her work-table the tiny scissors she used to remove those idle threads.) She was thus faced with an exceptionally difficult task: the completion of a delicate product for finicky customers and, to that end, the coordination of a corps of hired women for whose efforts she alone was responsible.

Her correspondence records randomly the fortunes of this industry, which, in an age of rapid technological advances, was becoming anachronistic: the lace, an aristocratic vestment in a democratic age, was exorbitantly expensive because every piece was handmade. Marguerite of Lorraine had not had to work on commission, meet precipitous deadlines, and risk rejection of her efforts from fastidious buyers. Neither did she have to bother herself with the turns of a national economy nor the effects of war and political upheaval upon her work.

Point d'Alençon, for all of its exquisite appeal, an appeal now sequestered to the city's museum of lace making, pulls as an undertow in Zélie's correspondence. It bore with almost literal force upon her health: frequent headaches and sleeplessness were concomitants of an ungrateful craft. Her response to the ebb and flow of work was ambivalent: when it was slowing down, she was relieved but left in worry about how long the slump would go on; when commissions picked up, she was assured of a renewed income but was harried to complete the work by an appointed time that seems to the reader cruelly short. She would even pass on in letters to her relatives the dimensions of material for which she was suddenly accountable. Of her 217 extant letters, not one was sent to any business nor customer. That is a pity, as we can surmise she wrote some, even though Louis ran errands for her as far as Paris.[15]

Marriage, then as now, was substantially a business to be run. It was expensive to raise a child but devout Catholics raised several, if they could, so each partner was necessarily a financial contributor. Savings and a secure income were alike indispensable to the running of a family. At the time of her engagement, Zélie had 5,000 francs from her father and 7,000 from her savings. Louis had a house, his pavilion, and 22,000 francs. By the Napoleonic Code, a husband controlled his wife's finances and income, but nothing in Zélie's correspondence indicates this condition, even tacitly. Rather than living subordinate to Louis, she seems independent of him. She even speaks of her business in the strict isolation of the first person singular, conveying no sense of teamwork with the women busy tatting in their homes.

Biographers note that the courtship of Louis and Zélie lasted only three months, but that is to judge from later standards when a lengthy time was set to ensure that two young people were not subject to romantic caprices. Louis and Zélie were neither young nor capricious; both were established professionally. Moreover, in their day, the engaged were generally older. What surprises is that initially they did not intend to have children.

Louis took the initiative in suggesting that he and Zélie live more as brother and sister than as husband and wife. In his hand there is some writing, copied from or summarizing a printed statement, that speaks of the sacrament of marriage as a bond separate from consummation. Mary and Joseph's provided the saintly model of this higher sort of union, one imitated by many saints as it also pointed to Christ's mystical wedding with the Church. Living with his parents as she did, Zélie must have felt more an adopted daughter than a daughter-in-law. What prompted Louis to this novel approach to marriage was not only piety, surely, but, if we may draw again on Thérèse's down-to-earth perspective, a fearful ignorance of feminine sexuality. His attraction to the monastic life had been predicated not on a renunciation of the womanly but on an avoidance of it altogether. In an age when the genders were schooled separately, with no education about sexuality, such apprehensions were virtually encoded in all behaviors. Relaxed, accepting postures necessary for genuine affection, physical and otherwise, were not there for newly wedded couples.

Simone de Beauvoir's now-classic *Le deuxième sexe* chronicles amply and in horrendous detail the shock which a young woman had suddenly to face on her wedding night, being virtually assaulted by a man to whom she had entrusted her life and future. Now she was an object, exposed and degraded, subject to demands she could never have imagined, let alone understood. The husband would quite likely have had sexual relations with other young women, prostitutes or otherwise, but the virginal bride had no such preparation. Zélie was burdened with that total ignorance and it is well to keep her perspective in mind, but she did not have a forward and demanding bridegroom to fear. De Beauvoir, whose testimony comes from a later but hardly more enlightened generation, does not discuss the apprehensions of the virginal male, the chaste, ascetic man who had had no sexual life and had sealed himself off from it, as Louis had. His writing down the ecclesiastical position on marriage as a sacrament (which it had not been in the first several centuries of Christianity) rationalized his dread into piety.

How costly it was for Zélie to have lived on these restrictive terms in an alien household no one knows. Her confidences went to her sister in letters and visits. She likely had her own ignorant aversion to sexuality. Yet she had married in the expectation of being a mother, consecrating her children to God, as the Bible's Hannah had in wishing for a son. Perhaps that orientation to childbearing dissuaded Louis from a disdain or fear of sexuality, but in the event only a priest was able to settle the matter by indicating that marriage was meant for procreation.

The first child was conceived in May 1859, ten months after the wedding. By the sequence of nine children born within thirteen years and including the months of pregnancy and of postnatal recovery—nursing was not prolonged in those days—Zélie menstruated perhaps no more than a dozen times in the course of her marriage and until her last child, Thérèse. The childbearing became itself a release and a relief from a sexual contact which was kept strictly functional. To say that sexual passion was not present in no way denigrates a marriage which was rock solid in what counted for the Martins, a mutual respect. The aversion to sexual activity for anything other than the creation of children may seem to some nowadays a quaint fussiness, but given the prevalence of venereal disorders in that time, marriage and its constraints had the semblance of a safe haven.

The absence of what we would call physical affection in marriages came from the mutually agreed distance between the genders. That distance brought with it more than a semblance of equality, although the Church, seeking to maintain the woman's role as home provider and mother, discouraged her independence. The same sort of prejudice could be found in its foes, the republicans, as well as in other faiths, such as Protestantism and Judaism. Yet, Catholic social reformers, taking inspiration from earlier writers, such as Bishop Fénelon, had articulated a case for the educational advancement of women. It would be easy to dismiss this position as functionalist, rather than genuinely libertarian, but it did recognize the substantial role women could play through their education. As to separatism, with its spheres of influence and discrete world of chores, not all feminists would condemn a life spent essentially apart from men. Neither Zélie nor Louis were aspirant to an economic station or social status higher than their own. Their businesses were maintained only to insure financial stability for the family and the future of their children. In that prudence they might have been following the cautionary wisdom of the day which warned that ambition was hazardous to one's health, but they were fortified primarily with the injunctions of their faith, which argued the corrupting power of Mammon and the follies of building expectations in a world so fleeting and insecure. One stay against economic uncertainty was the sale of one's business at a propitious time in the nation's economy or in anticipation of harder times: Louis sold his jewelry store and retired comfortably. Zélie nursed furtive hopes of doing likewise but did not live to carry them out.

In 1873, when Thérèse was born, Zélie, then forty-two, knew with reasonable certainty that she had borne her last child. The oldest of her five surviving children, Marie, was then only twelve. Raising five girls meant provision not only for their education in convent schools but for possible dowries. By her own disappointment at St. Vincent de Paul, she knew that, while a religious order might receive some of them, it was far from certain that they could all be so securely placed. Neither was marriage an inevitable alternative. She herself had had to deal with a creeping spinsterhood. Much of her worrying over her middle child transparently derives not from the incidentals of Léonie's contrariness but from a concern about what would ever become of her: too unruly to be compliant with the exigencies of a conventual life, too unstable to make a wife. Zélie might have wondered at times whether any of her daughters would find herself enmeshed, as she had become, in commercial life.

Of the 217 letters published in Zélie's *Correspondance familiale*, the greatest number (185) went to Lisieux and the home of her brother, Isidore. They were addressed mostly to Céline, his wife, yet both correspondents (we have only Zélie's half of the letters) could offer sympathy to her in her cares because each shared something of them: Isidore as an anxious entrepreneur and Céline as a mother. The common factors of business and childrearing were struggle and anxiety. Zélie, bearing both these burdens, found an outlet in writing.[16]

In her study of Thérèse, Dorothy Day marveled over the time Zélie, so busy throughout the waking hours, gave to her correspondence. She was sometimes writing late into the night, but the letters present themselves as a kind of comfort, an unburdening as well as a show of solicitude toward her brother and his own young family. Thérèse once remarked that when you think of someone you love, you are praying for that person. Zélie's letters might be called prayers on two hands: her deep worry, such as those she shared with her sister-in-law about Léonie, make poignant reading. When Céline lost her only son, stillborn, Zélie could address the only person within the family who now knew what she herself had been through in losing two infant sons within two years. At times, she seems to be consoling or reminding herself while addressing her correspondent, and the comfort which comes to the fore would find expression frequently in Thérèse's own writings: God gives you only as much as you can bear. The iteration of that view emerges from the letters like a mantra.

Complementing it is the caveat that there can be no lasting prosperity on this earth, and one should even fear its appearance as a cheat: "C'est mauvais signe quand tout prospère. Dieu l'a voulu ainsi dans sa sagesse, pour nous faire souvenir que la terre n'est pas notre vraie patrie" ["It's a bad sign when all is going well. God in his wisdom has willed it thus, to make us remember that the earth is not our true country"].[17] The occasion of that remark was the hideous accidental death of a couple who had recently had a magnificent home built. The woman had been claiming that she had reached the height of good fortune: health, wealth, and no children to unsettle her tranquillity. Zélie quotes the woman's boasts, but it remains unclear whether she heard them directly, or through gossip, or merely attributed them imprecisely. She remarks that these views were known to "everyone." On the alert to this Niobe

FIGURE 3.2. The house on the Rue de Saint-Blaise, Alençon, where Thérèse was born on January 2, 1873. Zélie worked on her lace by the windows on the ground floor. Copyright Archives du Carmel de Lisieux.

sentiment, she added that she had learned to tremble whenever she felt happy.

The negative side of her social perspective is a disdain for the fripperies of Alençon's leading or would-be leading ladies and their conspicuous airs. Zélie was by her own accounts a withdrawn person. She enjoyed working at home alone, by the window seat (see figure 3.2). She seems neither to have had nor to have desired what we would call even a normal social life: she had precious little time for such diversions. Resolute, she was quietly so and not obstreperous. She had no inclination to emulate women who liked to show themselves off with sartorial vanities. Why, then, did such vanities gain her notice at all? At best, they seem idle amusements for what she called "mon existence si laborieuse et monotone" ["my so tiring and monotonous existence"].[18]

On the occasion of that phrase, she revealed to Isidore the vicissitudes of her lace business, its tense and costly, uncontrollable rhythm: "j'ai bien des soucis que d'autres femmes n'ont pas dans ma situation. C'est ce coquin de Point d'Alençon qui me rend la vie dure: quand j'ai trop de commandes, je suis une esclave du pire esclavage; quand il ne va pas et que je m'en vois pour vingt mille francs sur les bras à moi coûtant, et des ouvrières que j'ai eu tant de peine à trouver qu'il faut renvoyer chez d'autres fabricants, il y a un peu sujet de se tourmenter, aussi j'en ai des cauchemars! Enfin, que faire? Il faut bien se résigner et prendre son parti de cela le plus bravement possible" ["I have troubles that other women don't have in my situation. It's this roguish Point d'Alençon which is making my life hard. When I have too many orders, I am a slave of the worst sort of slavery; when it's not going and I see myself stuck with it at the cost of 20,000 francs, I have so much trouble finding workers that I have to pass it to other fabricants. It's a torment and I'm even having nightmares about it. Well, what's to be done? Might as well resign yourself and do your part as resolutely as possible"].

She told her brother that, were it not for her husband and the children, she would go anywhere with him and tend house for him. When he set up a pharmacy in Lisieux, she thought it was a farewell forever in this life: "car, jamais dans ma pauvre vie, qui, je crois, ne sera pas de longue durée, je n'aurai le temps d'aller te voir. . . . et quand je désirerai te voir, je regarderai ton portrait, ce qui est une bien pauvre consolation" ["indeed, never in my wretched life, which, I believe, won't be a long one, will I have the time to come and see you. . . . and when I desire to see you, I'll look at your portrait, a very poor consolation"]. These odd, gloomy accents from a wife and mother suggest that happiness and even well-being had become dream realms for her. Nothing indicates that Louis was at all a cold man, but the distances of propriety which both observed meant that Zélie was starved of the natural affections and their expression which she had been able to develop for both her sister and her baby brother. It is difficult, given Zélie's letters, to overcome the impression of her acute isolation, dispelled only once and toward the end when she retrieved her lost lamb. When this mother of four girls, three months' pregnant, writes that she's not gay-hearted—"je n'ai pas le coeur bien gai"[19]—she is not speaking of an afternoon's mood.

The other men in her life were, if not a vexation, not entirely a help, either. She fretted over Isidore until he found and married, in September 1866, a woman she realized was suitable. Having missed the marriage because she was close to term with her fifth baby and wanting to visit for two weeks in Lisieux, she faced Louis's remonstrance; he could not manage with four young girls alone. Their infant brother had been given to a wet nurse. Zélie longed for relief but conceded that the children and her work precluded any leave. She also had to attend to her aged father, who lived and complained close by. She, the child whom neither mother nor father preferred (so she felt and so it was true for her), had to take care of him.

The bitter root of the matter was that her business, in earning her some money, was exacting from her dearly: "C'est au prix de ma vie, car je crois qu'il abrège mes jours et, si le bon Dieu ne me protège pas d'une manière particulière, il me semble que je ne vivrai pas longtemps. Je m'en consolerais facilement si je n'avais pas d'enfants à élever, je saluerais la mort avec joie" ["It's at the cost of my life; in fact, I believe it's cutting short my days, and if the good Lord doesn't protect me in some special way, it seems to me I won't last long. I could easily console myself: if I didn't have children, I would welcome death joyfully"].[20] Her sister at Le Mans was storing up treasures for herself in heaven, while she was forced to lick the earth, as Pascal would say, "me donnant une peine extrême pour amasser de l'or que je n'emporterai pas et que je ne désire pas emporter" ["giving myself extreme affliction to amass gold which I'm not bearing away and don't want to bear away"]. Having a baby boy at last consoled her greatly; she did not remember to caution herself when prematurely exclaiming that now her fortune was made. Now, if she could only attain heaven with her "dear Louis" (a rare instance of his name) and see her children as saints there, "tous bien mieux placés que moi" ["all of them better stationed than I"], she would not ask more.[21] Yet even that wish is cautiously expressed: "[p]ourvu que j'arrive au Paradis" ["provided I reach Heaven"]. This is a canny businesswoman speaking.

Between October 1864 and August 1870, Zélie gave birth to five children. One, Céline, survived. The first lost was her first son, Joseph-Louis, who died at five months on February 14, 1867. In the correspondence there is no record of this death nor of Zélie's feelings about losing him. When, many years after her death, her daughters at Carmel asked their uncle for her letters to him and their aunt, Isidore held back and then destroyed those he felt too intimate to share with anyone, even within the family. While it is tasteless to obtrude upon anyone's grief, we can still deplore the loss of the letter or letters Zélie sent while mourning: she was used to pouring out her fears, anxieties, hopes, and now she was faced for the first time with the worst suffering a woman could sustain. And the loss of her only boy—she now had four daughters—compounded the bitterness. Marie and Pauline, then six and five, later claimed that Zélie fantasized about her son's life as a priest, even to one day making for him an alb from her lace. It would have been her first labor of love over Point d'Alençon.

How did she articulate her anguish when he died? Did she say to Isidore and his new wife what she might not have dared to say to a confessing priest? Joseph-Louis came as the child upon whom she had been primed by her own mother to lavish a special affection, that reserved by any mother for a male child, female ones being only versions of herself. Her mother had doted on Isidore and now it would have been her turn to indulge, something her temperament did not otherwise permit her. Did the baby now love her from heaven? she wondered. Would he recognize her there? Such questions she put to her sister.[22]

By year's end, when she had given birth to a second boy, Joseph-Jean-Baptiste, she was at once in fear for his life: incessant crying, the wet nurse unwilling to take him to her home lest he die there. We shall look closer at the sociology of wet nursing in midcentury France and at infant mortality when we examine Thérèse's medical history; for now, it is enough to note that the death of infants was commonplace. Zélie, cautious with all the wariness of someone deeply hurt in life, was not morbid in her anxiety over the second Joseph.

The baby survived the first week and was removed to a farm just west of Semallé, where the wet nurse, Rosalie ("Rose") Taillé, lived. Zélie, however, could not master a subterranean apprehension: "car je crains sans cesse depuis qu'il m'est arrivé malheur pour son petit frère. Cependant, je crois que le bon Dieu me laissera celui-là" ["I'm in fact unceasingly afraid since his little brother came to grief. Nonetheless, I believe the good Lord will leave me this one"].[23]

He did not. Rose, with a peasant's immitigable fatalism, foretold the child's death early on, and as he grew, his resemblance to his brother, noted by their mother, only increased her dread that he too would vanish. Zélie fancied that St. Joseph, patron of those in doubt or anxious over dying, had sent her a second son after she had, in effect, given him the first: she offered the saint a novena and believed she had conceived immediately after it had been finished. "Tu vas peut-être rire de ce que je t'écris là," she wrote to Isidore, "mais moi je n'en ris pas, je prends cela à la lettre" ["Maybe you're going to laugh at what I've written but I don't. I'm taking it literally"].[24] In May, Joseph developed bronchitis. A vesicatory, or plaster, was applied between his shoulders, with a scalding that caused a blister from which blood, presumably bad, could be released. Zélie walked the eight kilometers (nearly five miles) twice daily, early in the morning and in mid-evening, to see him at Rose's farm. In July she brought him home. Rose had become burdened with care for her mother, but Zélie now had to contend with suddenly increased commissions for her lace trade and with her father in a rapid decline. He would cough to near suffocation. She had to force-feed him. The baby, suffering toward the end from enteritis, would vomit whatever he was given: "cela arrache le coeur de voir un petit être tant souffrir.... Quand tu recevras cette lettre, il sera probablement mort" ["It tears your heart to see a little being suffer so much.... By the time you receive this letter, he'll likely be dead"].[25]

From little Joseph-Jean-Baptiste's godmother, his sister Pauline, comes this early remembrance: "Quand on le mettait de matin dans le grand lit de nos parents, je montais sur le pied du lit et là j'exécutais des danses, qui faisait rire le petit à gorge deployée. J'entends encore le joli petit rire perlé qui me ravissait. Oh, que je l'aimais! Que j'eus de peine quand Maman ouvrant la porte de ma chambre me dit, le matin du 24 août, 1868, 'Ton petit frère est mort' " ["When he was put in our parents' big bed, I'd climb onto the foot of it and do some dances which made the little one laugh open-throated. I still hear the happy little pearl-like laughter which delighted me. Oh, how I loved him!

And how hurt I was when Mama, opening my bedroom door, told me, the morning of August 24, 1868, 'Your little brother is dead' "].[26]

Zélie's father died ten days later. Her view on this second suffering is recorded. The physical agony of the child attended by the mother's helpless grief had been so great that she could only wish for his deliverance. That wish was granted. Death came as itself a consolation. She had the same response to her father's death; she was at once brokenhearted and relieved. When she went to the grave site four days later, the sorrow for her lost men—father and infant sons—rendered her incapable of prayer. To her sister-in-law, she spoke of an apparent indifference: "ïl me semblait que n'importe quels malheurs me trouveraient maintenant insensible" ["It seemed to me that any sort of affliction would now find me void of feeling"].[27]

What surprises the reader is the absence of any word either to her brother, Isidore, or about her husband, Louis; they, too had suffered a loss, albeit for each only half of hers. She seems to have been both muted and sealed off by her anguish. It is strange to read her tribute to her father written to Céline Guérin: "Si vous saviez, ma chère soeur, combien j'aimais mon père! Il était toujours avec moi, je ne l'avais jamais quitté, il me rendait toujours tous les services qu'il pouvait" ["If you knew, my dear sister, how much I loved my father! He was always with me; I never left him; he gave me all the help he could"].[28] Zélie sketches in a few phrases the politics of the dead, that they are at once irretrievable and demandingly proximate. But she does more: her leaning toward hyperbole—combien, toujours, toujours—bespeaks present helplessness, isolation, perhaps some vestige of guilt, and an unwitting view of Louis, the steady, solid, and not effusive spouse. Zélie's exclamation of closeness to the elder Isidore would have seemed more fitting for a husband. In a culture where people were expected to constrain their emotions to the point of impassivity, death offered the one, the first and last, occasion to express feelings. Again, the vital life of letter writing abetted her. Numb though she had become to prayer, she was still able to pick up her pen. By the convention of that time, a wife would have read to her husband any letter she received. Still, it is odd that Zélie sent none to Isidore. We can infer as much not from Isidore's possible suppression but from Zélie's telling Céline that she was having fifty masses said for her parents. If Isidore wanted more, she says tersely, he would have to arrange that with her.

Her grief abiding, however subdued, Zélie reaccustomed herself to minor woes: headaches, toothaches, sleeplessness, difficulties in getting a reliable maid. Writing to Isidore of blood rushes during her seventh pregnancy, she says people have told her she won't have long to live, but she observes mordantly that she doesn't have the time to die. Two months before Céline was born, Zélie expressed to her sister-in-law her dread that the new baby would pass like the other two. "Quand les malheurs sont arrivés, je me résigne assez bien, mais la crainte est pour moi un supplice. Ce matin, pendant la messe, j'avais des idées si noires à ce propos, que j'en étais toute bouleversée. Le mieux est de remettre toutes choses entre les mains du bon Dieu et d'attendre les évenements dans le calme et l'abandon à sa volonté. C'est ce que je vais *m'efforcer* de faire" ["When afflictions come, I resign myself quite well, but fear is a torment for me. This morning at mass I had such black thoughts I was completely overwhelmed by them. It's best to leave all things in the good Lord's hands and await events in calm and abandon to his will. That's what I'm going to *force* myself to do"].[29]

Although she knew that fear torments worse than reality, she burdened herself with feverish misgivings in the first week of nursing Céline, the child she had presumed would be her last and so hoped would be a boy. Would this child, too, be taken from her? She was not consistently able to "force" herself into a posture of faith. In the autumn of 1869, Hélène, her fourth born, and Léonie came down with measles, then a life-menacing disease, and Zélie grew anxious over the health of her sister at Le Mans, who reported downturns in her own health with joyful anticipations of death—hardly comforting news for Zélie.

The new year, 1870, began auspiciously with two pregnancies, Zélie's eighth and Céline Guérin's second. Both were due in August. "nous aurons chacune un petit garçon, du moins je l'espère" ["we'll each have a little boy, at least I hope so"].[30] Mme. Guérin had given birth to a daughter, her first child, two years before. The first trimester did not go well for Zélie: despite recurrent fever, she rose early as always, even went to hear Capuchins who were giving a mission, and kept at her lace without remission. She worried about finding an adequate wet nurse, Rose not always being available. If only she could afford to keep a wet nurse within her own home, but it was already crowded enough: "ce n'est pas la paresse qui m'empêche de nourrir mes enfants, car je ne crains pas ma peine" ["it's not laziness which keeps me from nursing my babies; truly I don't fear my pain"]. She remarks to Céline the envy a common female acquaintance felt toward Mme. Guérin in her second pregnancy. That came from a woman unable to bear children, it seemed, who had rationalized that she preferred to lead a life of pleasure rather than to become a slave by having an indefinite number of children. The happiest people, concluded Zélie, are simply those who are the least unhappy, and she iterated to Isidore's wife the counsel she had given repeatedly to herself, "se préparer d'avance à porter sa croix le plus courageusement possible" ["to prepare oneself in advance to bear one's cross as bravely as possible"].

Ten days later, her five-year-old daughter, Hélène, died in her arms. The doctor had diagnosed congested lungs as the cause of a fever and prescribed only bouillon, but after the child took it, her suffering became more intense. Zélie, in passing her grim news to Isidore and Céline, does not spare herself the record of Hélène's few words in her last night: "Ma pauvre petite mère qui a pleuré!...Si je le mange, vas-tu mieux me l'aimer?...Oui, tout à l'heure, je vais être guérie, oui, tout de suite" ["My poor little mother's been crying!...If I eat, will you love me better?...Yes, right now, I'm going to get well, yes, at once"].[31] Zélie had something new with which to torment herself: she feared she had given Hélène too much to eat, including roast meat in wine, and had thus weakened her. With this remorse came the horror of losing a child well past infancy's hazards. From now on, she would fear for her children's lives at any age, and any sign of sickliness entailed dread, irrational yet grounded in the vivid savagery of suffering.

She wrote that she found Hélène more beautiful in death than in life. She would allow no one to touch the body and dressed it herself in the funeral shroud. Seeking consolation, she had the added pain of reading Isidore's astoundingly callous reproach of her for not giving Hélène sufficient medical care. She answered that she had seen her older girls weather the diseases of infancy and so she had no longer feared them.

Amid this grieving, Sr. Marie-Dosithée reproached Isidore for having troubled Zélie with an unnecessary guilt. She observed that the child's illness had not even been diagnosed. It is now conjectured that Hélène died of leukemia;[32] nothing could have saved her. Zélie was anguished by uncertainty, even extending it to the belief that her own recurrent fever and lassitude—she was now in her middle trimester—augured a death like Hélène's. She in fact longed for it because she wanted to see her child again; only the needs of her other children distracted her into an equipoise of desiderated death and necessary life. Her sister told her that God would perhaps even grant her "le grand saint que tu as tant désiré pour sa gloire" ["the great saint you have so much wanted for his glory"].[33] Neither could have guessed.

The thought of the lost child's celestial status offered scant relief for her mother, who felt condemned to recall a child who, unlike her infant brothers, had grown and developed a winning personality. Meanwhile, Zélie did not fail to remark the predilection of her youngest daughter, Céline, for her father. Her own favorite, Pauline, was now away, boarding at convent school with Marie in Le Mans. The school's students came from la haute société; Marie and Pauline were admitted through the influence of their aunt.

That latter fact reflects the Martins' reasonably secure means. Louis at forty-seven sold his shop to his nephew, son of his sister Anne-Françoise Leriche (who had died in 1853), and retired. He was now at leisure while his wife was left not only in her own world of exacting work but with her maternal charges, including a fifth child on the way. Louis had stationery made for himself with "Fabricant de Point d'Alençon" ["Manufacturer of Alençon Lace"] at its head, as the Napoleonic Code allowed him to arrogate his wife's title to himself. In fact, Louis did involve himself in lace design and as a skilled watchmaker he enjoyed the piquage, or needlepoint tracing, of lace patterns onto a green-tinted parchment but he did so at a leisure his wife did not enjoy. Retired, he could take trips, many of them inclusive of lace orders, but journeys of any sort would have been extravagance for Zélie. She alone carried the burden of worries over business and the children. Did his things-will-work-out response to her frettings ever appear cavalier? Céline tells us that her parents spoke to each other chiefly in pious platitudes about the next world and this one, so precarious and full of miseries, and about the wretchedness of France and hope for its relief from the Third Republic.[34]

When the eighth child, Mélanie-Thérèse, came on August 16, 1870, Zélie tried for four days to nurse her but had to forfeit her to a wet nurse. The correspondence from this time on is instructive. Letters go primarily to Céline Guérin, adopted sister in their shared motherhood. Céline's second daughter was born a week after Mélanie-Thérèse. A closing remark says much about how they were bound to one another by the singular intimacy of letters, even though they kept using the formal *vous*: "Adieu, ma chère Soeur, écrivez-moi le plus tôt possible, cela me fait tant de plaisir d'avoir de vos nouvelles! Isidore pourrait bien le faire, mais il est comme mon mari, très paresseux pour écrire. J'ai beau le prier, c'est comme si je ne disais rien" ["Goodbye, my dear Sister, write me as soon as possible. Your news gives me so much pleasure! Isidore could certainly do so, but he's like my husband, very lazy about writing. I've begged him to and it's as though I'd said nothing"].[35] While no vitriol taints these words, it is clear why Zélie made an epistolary friendship first with Céline Guérin and later with Pauline. What little pleasure she got in the adult world came primarily from other women, those in whom she could confide freely and trust to understand her burdens and needs. Her dismissal of her brother and husband suggests an offhanded boys-will-be-boys excusing, rather than a complaint. In short, Zélie delimited her own world and made it female.

Perhaps because he had chastised her about Hélène's death, Zélie sent Isidore details on Mélanie's, blaming the wet nurse for negligence. The doctor himself had spoken of counting the baby's ribs. She vowed that she would never again let a child go to a wet nurse's home, and no longer did the prized gender matter. "je ne désire pas un petit garçon, mais une petite Thérèse, qui lui ressemble" ["I don't want a little boy, just a little Thérèse who will look like this one"].[36] Only to her sister-in-law did she pour out her sorrow: "A chaque nouveau deuil, pour moi, il me semble toujours aimer l'enfant que je perds, plus que les autres. Celle-là était gentille comme un bouquet, puis il n'y avait que moi qui la soignais. Oh! Je voudrais mourir aussi! Je suis tout à fait fatiguée depuis deux jours; je n'ai pour ainsi dire rien mangé et j'ai été debout toute la nuit, dans des angoisses mortelles" ["At every bereavement, it seems to me that I love more than the others the baby I'm losing. This one was as pretty as a bouquet and, besides, only I took care of her. Oh, I would like to die, too! I've been completely exhausted for two days, have eaten virtually nothing and was up the whole night in mortal anguish"].[37] Her words to Céline Guérin mark the absence of any consolation. Zélie knew there was none. What could be said to a mother who had seen four of her children die within as many years? Only another mother who had sustained similar loss would know what to say, if anything.

From Le Mans on All Saints' Day, Sr. Marie-Dosithée urged her to consider that the infantile dead, as celestial souls, had special power in the heavenly court and loved their mothers more than other children. What comfort that brought Zélie is beyond measure. All that she expressed was fathoms down in bitterness. She dignified raw hurt by not seeking the familiar anodynes of faith. This time she did not "force" herself into consolatory beliefs. Her wish to die was not cast as a wish to join her celestial children; it was a plea that she be relieved of suffering their loss. The next child, Thérèse, who would spare her mother loss though not worry, once told Pauline that she had to bite her lips so as not to blaspheme. Might her mother have known what that meant? That death had etched itself implacably into her is clear from her untypically sardonic words to Isidore on her little daughter Céline's thinness: "Pour me consoler, plusiers personnes ont dit à la bonne que Céline ne sera pas longtemps en vie!" ["By way of consoling me, several people have told the maid that Céline doesn't have long to live!"].

Amid domestic desolation came war. France had already suffered its two major military defeats, at Sedan and Metz, and now only the Army of the Loire was trying to contain the enemy. The Prussians advanced through Normandy in November 1870, moving toward Alençon in the third week. Panicky citizens rushed to hide valuables from pillagers. Town authorities resolved to attempt a defense—a quixotic gesture in the face of 20,000 men—and Louis regretted being too old to serve as a sharpshooter. When Le Mans was threatened, Zélie was relieved to learn from her sister that as the enemy did not enter convents, people were sending their children into them for safety. The Visitandines were themselves besieged by the poor, the ill, all those displaced by the war. When they demurred to the civil authorities that they were stretched to capacity, the sick were left along the convent's walls so that the sisters had to take them in. Zélie reports the rumor that the municipality, anticlerical, was punishing the religious by these exactions, but even the wealthy were obliged to house wounded soldiers. Smallpox spread.

By mid-January, after the Loire army suffered a crushing defeat, the enemy had come literally to Alençon's gates. The prefect, directly across the street from the Martins' house, wanted to defend the town and proposed detonation of its bridges. French troops reeling in retreat streamed through the town. Zélie wrote to Céline Guérin of their mutilations and the futility of resistance before an enemy with black flags and with death's heads on its helmets. "Comment se fait-il que tout le monde ne reconnaisse pas que cette guerre est un châtiment?" ["How is it that no one acknowledges that this war is a punishment?"].[38] That notion, however, made audible rounds. From

Croisset, in the same province, Flaubert wrote to George Sand, "Les phrases toutes faites ne manquent pas: 'La France se relèvera! Il ne faut pas désespérer! C'est un châtiment salutaire, nous étions vraiment trop immoraux!' etc. Oh! Eternelle blague!" ["Ready-made phrases aren't lacking: 'France will revive! No need to despair! It's a salutary punishment, we were too immoral!' etc. What everlasting humbug!"] (November 27, 1870).[39]

Flaubert feared the war would end the revolution resumed by the removal of Napoleon III. Now, he groaned, everyone would become utilitarian, American, and Catholic. Zélie's fears were more concrete: how could she quarter the nine German soldiers billeted by a chalk scrawl on the door to her house? She did not complain; other residences had as many as twenty-five. The Martins occupied the upper floor, and Zélie found that the Prussians' only vice was gluttony. Food scarcities came with the occupation.

Louis sank into a depression, neither eating nor sleeping, but Zélie, having twice suffered far worse within the year, reported herself alone in being without tears. Indeed, she managed well, even with the hungry Prussians, and remembered to thank Mme. Guérin for sending the usual excess of New Year's Day étrennes. An armistice was concluded on January 28.

The war left France staggering in military ignominy. With the ancestral glory of the first Napoleon's time now obscured, Louis's patriotic gloom was widely shared. Zélie for her part attended to the economic realities, that acute uncertainty came with the defeat: people were declining to pay bills. What she nowhere remarks in her wartime letters and the sensational aftermath were two momentous events from Paris: the creation of the Third Republic on September 4, 1870, and the aborted life of the Commune, that rag-tag experiment which, while derivative of the Revolution, was without a Robespierre or Babeuf. It held out for fewer than three months, March–May 1871, and ended against a wall at Père-Lachaise. Thanks to Marx, who wrote about it, the Commune is now generally viewed not as the last of the great French uprisings but as the first of the modern socialist revolutions, a miniature of 1917.

For the Martins, however, all that mattered was the fate of the Church in the maelstrom of sudden political change. Zélie remarks the Commune's sensational firing-squad executions of sixty-four Parisian priests and the archbishop of Paris. The Communards contrived their version of the Terror. She notes the event with suitable horror but does not condemn nor expatiate; she does not even mention the Communards as such. How would she have reacted to the radical leftists' proposed association of producers in which men and women would be equals? And what would she have said of the 25,000 Parisians slaughtered when the national guard destroyed the Commune, a number greater than the military losses at Sedan or Metz? Did she ever learn that working women, burdened by children as she was, had been in the forefront of the revolt, having endured the long wintry Prussian siege of the capital and having had their starving share in the Parisian diet of horses and rats? Those facts would not have mitigated the grief which she felt for the massacred prelates. Besides, the fundamental issue of class warfare (never was the phrase so apt as in Paris that spring) remained a matter too distant from the provincial bourgeois world in which she had always lived. She was never obliged to choose between the propertied class, to which the Church hierarchy clung, and the working class, to which she implicitly belonged.

The Martins' political hopes were anchored in restoration of the monarchy. A letter to the Guérins (October 27, 1873) registers unease that the comte du Chambord, the would-be king Henri V, might subscribe to republicanism in exchange for a throne. (Having expressed his preference for a flag with the *fleur-de-lys* rather than the revolutionary *tricolore*, he lost a royal opportunity.) Beyond such minor notes, Zélie remained immune to the apocalypticism common to credulous people in that age.[40] A huge, red comet, Isidore told her, was reported to be nearing the earth: would it be the world's end? That was news on All Saints' Day (November 1, 1873), so she warned Marie and Pauline that they should try to earn sainthood. She herself longed to become a saint.

Zélie was sure that France would eventually be punished for its anti-clericalism. Pope Pius IX was still a self-proclaimed prisoner in the Vatican, his papal states not yet returned—nor would they ever be. "Je sais qu'à un temps donné et que Dieu seul connaît, il arrivera certainement de grandes catastrophes, que notre pays a bien méritées, mais cela peut n'être que dans plusieurs années" ["I know that at a given time which God alone knows, great catastrophes are bound to come which our poor country has quite deserved, but that can only happen several years from now"].[41]

The miscellany of politics aside, the Martins in their financial worries open a wider window upon the fretting of their time. Isidore had annexed to his pharmacy in Lisieux a hardware store and needed money to sustain the costs of this expansion. Zélie could offer him no help because Louis had taken a substantial loss in his stock investments (railroads and real estate), selling after a fall of over a third of the value of his portfolios. Zélie hoped that in financial ruin, which her pessimism foresaw, she could sustain the family on her lace-making commissions: "nous recevons des lettres de tous côtés pour des mariages, et il y a—et il y aura—toujours des riches" ["we're getting letters from all directions for marriages, and there are rich people—and there will always be"].[42]

She had long been fortified by her tendency to anticipate the worst: "Car j'ai remarqué que c'est toujours le contraire de ce que je pense qui arrive; aussi, je me défie de moi et de mes idées, surtout quand les choses ont de l'importance" ["In fact, I've observed that what happens is always the opposite of what I thought; besides, I distrust myself and my views, particularly in important matters"],[43] which should have told her that God might not visit catastrophes on France. Abetting her cautionary disposition was the conviction she did not abandon even when she lost her children, that God never weighs more than can be borne. On that count, she was inclined to remonstrate with Louis: "J'ai vu bien des fois mon mari se tourmenter à ce sujet.... je lui disais: 'N'aie pas peur, le bon Dieu est avec nous'" ["So many times I've seen my husband torment himself over this subject.... I've told him, 'Don't be afraid. God is with us'"].[44]

Louis's other concern, however, was about Mammon: "ce qui taquine le plus mon mari, c'est d'avoir les fonds à ne rien faire" ["what plagues my husband increasingly is having stocks that are not producing"].[45] Zélie having pressed him over the summer to sell inert stocks, he had no sooner done so than they began to rise; in effect, they could have saved themselves 1,200 francs.[46] The shares to which she refers came from Crédit Foncier, a mortgage bank established in 1852, which invested in urban renewals. During the Second Empire, it had financed Baron Haussmann's ambitious reconstructions of Paris. Louis's income now depended upon the continual, if not continuous, prosperity of a venture in rebuilding the capital he had fled in fear twenty years before. Zélie identifies the other company only as "Chemin de fer," which likely refers to Crédit Mobilier, a company built mostly on the expansive railway industry.[47]

Faith and finance merged in a singular way when Zélie, reading the stock market news, discovered that bonds were being floated on behalf of the pope. Pius IX had been dispossessed of his papal states when the war with Prussia called home the French troops defending those properties from Italian republicans. This investment genuinely depended on a faith she had no trouble in summoning. Returns would be excellent, she told Isidore, "parce que je crois fermement au triomphe prochain et au rétablissement du Saint-Père dans ses Etats" ["for I firmly believe in the coming triumph and restoration of the Holy Father to his States"].[48] The pope died a "prisoner" within the Vatican seven years later. Whether Louis invested in the "obligations Pontificales" is not certain.

Piat errantly claims: "La fortune acquise par un travail acharné fut de surcroît favorisée par d'heureux placements, sans que M. Martin se soit laissé tenter par les grossissements faciles de la spéculation" ["The wealth acquired by earnings from work was supplemented by fortunate investments, without Mr. Martin letting himself be tempted by the easy growth spurts of speculation"].[49] Louis was a small-scale investor who, like everyone whirled by capitalist enterprise, wanted his money to grow and was upset when it did not. His shares were not consistently fortunate. Zélie witnesses to an elementary fact which does not fit into Piat's hagiography but remained a daily datum of the Martins' financing. Piat labors to combat a prejudice that, as the family was financially secure in the main, Thérèse was spared the duress of poverty, as though that were some sort of demerit. There is no need to minimize the Martins' fiscal hardheadedness. However saintly, they remained shrewd and calculating. Their businesses internalized in them a sense of credits and debits. When Zélie's father was buried, she wrote to Isidore that she would gladly assume the paternal burdens of purgatory just to see him happy in heaven. Piat quotes that remark but excludes her ensuing complaint that her father's cemetery cross, "pour laquelle nous avons payé plus cher" ["for which we've paid more"], was less beautiful than that for her second Joseph: "C'est de l'argent perdu" ["It's money lost"].[50] Such a blunt reckoning was as much a part of Zélie as her piety.

Her attitude toward material prosperity comes to a small bundle of contradictions. On the one hand, she insisted to her brother that whatever gains we achieve are not owing to our own efforts: "çe n'est ni à tes capacités, ni à ton intelligence que tu dois ta réussite, mais à Dieu seul, comme moi, avec mon Point d'Alençon" ["it's neither to your capacities nor to your intelligence that you owe your success but to God alone, just as with me and my Point d'Alençon"].[51] but she also regarded the work from which her own success came as the meanest of drudgeries, "l'esclavage le plus complet," giving her no rest. Had God willed her to an endless Egyptian bondage? On the other hand, she looked to a secure stock investment and believed she found it in the papal future. Even so, "il est certain que la prosperité constante éloigne de Dieu. Jamais il n'a conduit ses élus par ce chemin-là, ils ont, auparavant, passé par le creuset de la souffrance, pour se purifier" ["it's certain that continual prosperity alienates us from God. He has never led his elect along that road; they have previously passed through the crucible of suffering in order to purify themselves"].

What, then, of prosperity on any terms? When Isidore became anxious about his pharmacy, Zélie wrote that she bothered herself only about little woes and resigned herself before the big ones, but her prescription for this pharmacist was better focused than any counsel to resignation: he had to observe the sabbath and keep his shop closed for business, even as Louis had with his *horlogerie*, even though it meant some loss to competition. "Tous les fidèles observateurs du jour du Seigneur, parfaits ou imparfaits, réussissent dans leurs entreprises et enfin, par un moyen ou par un autre, ils deviennent riches. . . . On obtient les grâces que l'on désire, mais à condition d'observer scrupuleusement les lois de l'Eglise pour le dimanche" ["All faithful observers of the Lord's day, perfect or not, succeed in their undertakings and in the end, by one means or another, they become wealthy. . . . You get the graces you desire but on condition of your observing scrupulously the Church's laws about Sundays"].[52] It is difficult to know whether this pharisaism was meant solely to bring Isidore in line with Louis or whether Zélie in fact believed she had a formula for becoming wealthy. What was the point of becoming prosperous if, as she often averred, life was essentially a trial assigned us by God, and a brief one? She had an appreciably critical eye turned on the shallowness of modish life exhibited in Alençon's *belles dames*, and she knew material wealth had no intrinsic value, so how could it be counted as a divine payoff for righteous observance of Sundays, with the shops' doors closed?

In their strict observance of proprieties on behalf of the Church, the Martins seem more Jewish than Christian. Beyond temperament and its behaviors, however, we always find economics. What registers here is the difference in dates: Zélie's 1872 letters were conditioned by the adversities following the war, including economic uncertainty, while those only a few years later suggest the will-o'-the-wisp of recovery for newly republican France. People become anxious about becoming wealthy only when wealth seems within reach and they see or fear others' success. That seems to have been Isidore's care, and one which his Visitandine sister denounced.[53] And *riche* remained a relative term for the Martins and Guérins. Neither couple would have presumed possible nor even desirable an elevation into the *haute bourgeoisie* of unearned, mannered leisure. A snugness free of debts and worries would suffice. The issue remains, however, not one of ledgers but of attitude and assumptions governing it.

Zélie's perspective on spiritual well-being was better focused because it integrated suffering into a divine politics of final, rather than temporal (or temporary) reward. This earthly life could only be short, painful, full of vanities; one's true life would begin beyond this one. The temptations of life are to be resisted and its trials borne. As her remarks from 1872 on earthly wealth indicate, such happiness in this life would prove a snare, and adversity was desirable as a sign of divine testing and thus of divine favor.

An instance came when the Guérins lost their first and only son, for whom Zélie was to have been godmother. She wrote two letters of equal length to each of the parents. To Isidore, she remarked her incapacity to weep and reminded him not to murmur against God: "le Maître peut nous laisser, pour notre bien, souffrir tant et plus, mais jamais son secours et sa grâce ne nous feront défaut" ["God can allow us, for our good, to suffer so much and more but his help and his grace will never be lacking to us"].[54] Yet, she blamed the doctor for the baby's being stillborn and wondered if he had allowed the fetus to be baptized. In fine, while accepting suffering from God, she was inclined to bitterness toward the unwitting agent of that suffering. She shared a prejudice common to her age, a resentment and distrust toward physicians, who were then ascendant in prestige: one felt abjectly helpless before them, and their words could seem fickle, cruelly deceptive, yet incontrovertible. They were paid prophets on matters of life and death, but their sibylline pronouncements were not always accurate. Even Flaubert, who came from a family of doctors, admitted to a prejudice against them. We find it later in Thérèse.

For all her brooding and anxiety, Zélie kept an almost Roman matronly hardiness unrecognizable to our own age, but it would be unfair to depict her in mourning clothes merely. She was not a lugubrious wretch, keen though her suffering and losses were. She enjoyed many treasured moments with her daughters and exercised a mother's permissible vanity in celebrating them in her correspondence as they grew. She makes brief but close observations, warmly affectionate and indulgently humorous, about their personalities, their idiosyncrasies, and their varieties of intelligence. Although we have studio portraits of the girls, Zélie's concise and comparative descriptions give us far better profiles.

The Guérins, especially Céline, were the natural recipients of Zélie's notes about her growing girls. Not only were their own two daughters, Jeanne and Marie, neatly sequenced among Léonie and Céline and Thérèse; these girls were the Martin sisters' only real cousins. The cousins naturally enjoyed the stimulation of their all-girl company, and visits to Lisieux were steadily arranged.

Zélie for years would regularly at every New Year chide Aunt Céline for spoiling Marie, Pauline, and then the others with *étrennes*. These are gently insistent protests over the disruptions of routine: she delighted in her children's glee over toys but was sensitive to the privileging and selfishness that sneak in with gifts. She had strict and decided views about and against anything which could turn her daughters' heads: sartorial vanity, the dressing up of a child in the latest fashions, was costly, and she saw the cumulative effect of such distractions in the society women of Alençon who gave parties and determined the course of town gossip. The only passages in her letters which hint of spite are about these women of social pretense and rank. They are valuable in reminding us that Zélie did not wear a halo; she had to live through and resist the bustling hollowness of the bourgeoisie's upward mobility, as meretricious in the Second Empire and the Third Republic as at any time before or since.

She describes to Céline Guérin a masked ball reported to her by someone who attended, and the tone turns biting: "C'était magnifique, admirable, sans pareil! Depuis qu'Alençon existe, on n'avait jamais vu cela" ["It was magnificent, wondrous, unparalleled! The town has not seen the like since it was founded"].[55] She describes a matron who, dressed up as La Folie, squeezed herself into a sari and became ridiculous before the more richly appareled ladies. The ball ran until 5 a.m., ending with a lavish dinner. A pity, Zélie concludes, to have gone to so much effort and expense to make oneself look ridiculous. That might well have been her summary impression of the town's ladies of fashion.

Alert to immunize her daughters from such foolishness, she was attentive to the possibility that any of them, evincing intelligence, would be flattered and encouraged toward presumptuousness and pride. She had a sharp ear for the shallowness of praise and its harmfulness. Her own childhood having been wounded by the absence of maternal warmth and approval, she knew such withholding had negative effects and did not make her own girls victims, and yet her feelings point to the thrift she instinctively practiced in her business and household management. Chary of fortune, she was careful with resources. Excess or presumption invited nemesis. Moreover, her culture and times did not encourage girls as it did boys. Had she been able to rear a son, would she not have lavished upon him the bounty of solicitudes given her brother, Isidore?

Let us look back to the girls. At the Martin house in Alençon, visitors entering the living room see a small glass case full of Marie's prize books from the convent school at Le Mans. Marie pleased her parents by such achievements, but she was by temper, according to Zélie, at once too wild and too shy to follow her mother's example and marry. When she was just thirteen, typhoid fever kept her near death for weeks. Her parents tended her night and day, and Louis even walked eighteen miles in a day, making a pilgrimage to Chaumont on her behalf. Marie's delirious groaning drove him to distraction. As she began to recover, he spoiled her by indulging her every wish, even when it was contrary to Zélie's.

The two eldest sisters provide instructive contrasts. For Marie, Zélie had become a negative model because of the constant drudgery she sustained in raising children and working at the lace. Marie owned to her the fear that more little sisters would come. She had resolved to become an old maid. Faced with the choice of marriage, convent, or spinsterhood, the hardy Pauline rejected all three options, so Zélie told Isidore.[56] Early on, however, she showed signs of emulating her mother: diligent at school, she took prizes even though she was the youngest in her class, but there was both an intelligence and discipline in her which marked her off from Marie. Louis, disappointed in not having a son, masculinized her as "petit Paulin," and she was indeed masculine in the way that Zélie herself had been in resolving upon a career. Pauline chose Carmel early; Marie, late and only with prodding.

It is tempting to read people's adult lives back into adolescence or even earlier, but Zélie's steady, even devout correspondence with Pauline coopted her. Any parent at some time is likely to play this game, ensnaring the child's attentiveness and peculiar loyalty either to secure sympathy or support or an invisible vote in the family's politics. How could Pauline have resisted her mother's wish that she achieve what Zélie had not, entrance into an order? And being schooled close to her aunt provided a positive contrast to Zélie's careworn life, even though Pauline chaffed at her aunt's spying upon her from a staircase to make sure she did not lose time to idle chatting with other students. Pauline once recalled that, when still "toute petite" she was told that in heaven virgins alone follow Jesus about, he being a spotless lamb there. Zélie added that they would be crowned with white roses and sing what no one else could. Married people would have only red roses in their crowns. "Et je m'écriai: 'Oh! Maman, je ne me marierai jamais, pour ne pas avoir une couronne rouge dans le ciel!' " ["And I exclaimed, 'Oh, Mama, I will never marry so as not to have a red crown in heaven!' "].[57]

Pauline also had at the age of five the sort of vision which Carmelite prioresses could take as a celestial sign that a young woman was called to the order. She dreamed of her guardian angel, white and winged, escorting her along a path of dense foliage onto a deserted plain where Christ was on the cross. The angel made her kneel before it and then disappeared: "Je trouve que ce rêve est une image de ma vie sous bien des rapports" ["I find that this dream is an image of my life on several counts"]. And she had as well a vision of the Virgin—not a dream but real, she would insist—leaning over her bed: "Sans rien me dire, Elle fit passer dans mon coeur des sentiments de pureté d'une douceur inexprimable" ["Without saying anything, She made feelings of an inexpressibly sweet purity pass into my heart"].[58] That vision was spoiled, however, when Hélène, to whom she confided the experience, mocked her with laughing and questions.

Zélie did not have to go far in urging conventual life upon her, but serious consideration of entry into an order presupposed a maturity beyond adolescence even though one was still in it. It was exceptional and demanding, no matter one's toughness of temperament. Pauline came to it in a circuitous route. When her mother died, she assumed the maternal role for Thérèse and with it achieved something that Zélie had not even imagined, the satisfaction of being a virgin mother with the still open possibility of becoming a religious. She was spared childbirth's pangs and the fearful years of infancy which had cost her mother dearly while her own future lay open: limited, experimental responsibilities. She even had the luxury of an older sister who could (and did) assume the maternal role whenever she herself wished to choose differently. In little Thérèse, she had a willfully precocious charge, one whose demandingness might well have encouraged Pauline toward Carmel, but more imposingly Alençon and Le Mans had trained Pauline for a life exclusively among women in varied balances of power and dutifulness. The only man she knew closely had given her a kind of vote of confidence by calling her "little Paul," a tacit recognition that she could manage among women in a commanding, masculine way. In sum, Pauline overcame the disappointments of her parents' lives: she became a nun and, as prioress, assumed the dominant, quasi-military role of which Louis had only dreamed.

The only counterpoint within the Martin family came from its rebellious third child, Léonie. She suffered by the scholastic achievements of her elder sisters but perhaps much more by their temperamental agreeableness: Marie, sweet of heart; Pauline, intelligent and yet obedient. Like countless children before older siblings, Léonie had to define herself against them and, at a distance of six and ten years in age, against her lively and promising younger sisters as well. Sickliness set her even further apart. Her mother's written assessments of her border upon harshness and even cruelty, however unwitting. Mother and daughter had been spiraling downward in a closed circle of resentment and failure, each helpless toward the other. Léonie, if not mentally slow, was slow to learn. Sending her at age ten to her aunt at Le Mans was, Zélie presumed, a waste of money but Sr. Marie-Dosithée perceived that this child would only keep wilting under tacit or explicit disapprovals of her and her shortcomings, and so she encouraged Léonie gently with shows of confidence. All the child wanted to do was to please. That is clear from a letter her observant aunt wrote to the Guérins (February 8, 1874), but Zélie remained ignorant of its contents and its wisdom for a good while.[59]

She had hoped the Visitandines would be able to transform Léonie's personality, not reckoning her own central role in its shaping. The school in part furthered Léonie's unhappiness by giving her a social outlet for it in rambunctiousness. Her mother characterized her behavior as "une dissipation sans pareille.... j'espère contre toute espérance. Enfin, je n'ai plus de foi qu'en un miracle pour changer cette nature. Plus je la vois difficile, plus je me persuade que le bon Dieu ne permettra pas qu'elle reste ainsi. Je prierai tant qu'il se laissera fléchir" ["foolish conduct beyond compare.... I'm hoping against hope. Well, my only hope of changing her disposition is a miracle. The more difficult I see her, the more convinced I am that God won't let her stay that way. I'll pray till he lets himself be moved to pity"].[60]

Zélie herself had to be moved. This letter to Mme. Guérin makes transparent, apart from a helpless vexation, her own stubbornness, a quality inherited by her youngest daughter, "très intelligente...belle...gracieuse," who so persistently distracted her from lace that she had to work until late into the evening. Such was Thérèse at eighteen months.

Léonie had to be sent home from Le Mans and was tutored by two elderly women who passed themselves off as nuns. When they were exposed and Zélie learned that they had abused another child in their supposed care, she went to the police and secured the child's removal only to learn later that the child was back on the fraudulent premises and much under their wing. This tragicomic episode, recorded at length in her letters, shows that this generous and loving woman had only to direct such good-hearted resolve in Léonie's direction.

It would be no exaggeration to claim that Pauline sustained Zélie in her last years, or rather the Pauline she longed for and who had to be away at school. At only fourteen, her daughter was reading this from her mother: "mon affection pour toi va croissant de jour en jour, tu es ma joie et mon bonheur. Enfin, il faut que je me raisonne et que je ne pousse pas trop loin mon amour, car si le bon Dieu allait te prendre avec lui, qu'est-ce que je deviendrais?" ["my feelings for you grow daily, you are my joy and my happiness. Well, I have to be reasonable and not push my love too far. If the good Lord were to take you with him, what would become of me?"].[61] And Pauline's Aunt Céline read this: "Pauline est toujours mon 'Benjamin'; je ne l'aime que trop, mais je ne puis m'en empêcher, elle est si exquise" ["Pauline is forever my favorite; I love her only too much, but I just can't help it, she is so exquisite"].[62]

Pauline, tormented by migraines as Zélie had been in her own adolescence, labored more or less successfully to make the honor roll so as to please her parents. Yet it was not scholastic performances to stroke parental pride which mattered to Zélie: "Ma Pauline chérie, toi, tu es ma vraie amie, tu me donnes le courage de supporter la vie avec patience" ["My dear Pauline, you, you're my true friend. You give me the courage to sustain my life with patience"].[63] By then, Marie had left school in Le Mans and had returned to Alençon, helping her mother to tend the younger girls, but she remained restive and simply amused her mother with protestations against marriage, a display Pauline never had to make.

Zélie even told Pauline of her desire for a simple life alone in a garret, forgetful of the world. "Aussi, je ne fais que rêver cloître et solitude. Je ne sais pas vraiment, avec les idées que j'ai, comment ce n'était pas ma vocation, ou de rester vieille fille, ou de m'enfermer dans un couvent. Je voudrais maintenant vivre très vieille, pour me retirer dans la solitude, quand tous mes enfants seront élevés" ["Besides, I dream only of the cloister and solitude. I really don't know how, with my views, it wasn't my vocation to remain an old maid or to close myself up in a convent. I would like now to live to old age and withdraw into solitude, once all my children are grown"].[64]

These confessional accents belong to a lonely woman. What, then, of Louis? Why was *he* not a friend to her and why did *he* not give that vital courage Zélie drew from Pauline? Why does Zélie speak only of herself in her future? Did she presume that, Louis being older, she would outlive him? No, she had remarked many times (not to Pauline) that she did not expect to live long. In strict and conservative milieux, roles remain tightly defined and unquestioningly performed, and none more so than those determined by gender. Zélie, with true feminine instinct, knew that finally only women know how to sympathize with women.

Her appropriation of Pauline as a confidante came naturally to her; she had had an intimate life with her older sister and recast it to the daughter perhaps closest in temperament to her. Louis, in calling his daughter "petit Paulin," was acknowledging or imposing a maleness on her which put her at some distance from him.[65] Marie and Céline were allowed to dote on him, furthering their own femininity and a vital confidence in it. The "Paulin" tag, by contrast, might have worked to diminish Pauline's confidence in herself as a woman and to predispose her for conventual life. Family dynamics go unwritten, but they remain powerful, all the more so beneath surfaces. It is not altogether surprising that Pauline early assumed at Carmel the title of prioress. A prioress is in effect the *fabricante* of the convent. But the saddest of little facts in Pauline's story comes from the day she walked out of her family's home for the last time. On the way to Carmel, Isidore, not her father, escorted her by the arm. Louis came behind, walking with Marie.

The intensity of devotion within the Martins' small circuit of feminine relations—Zélie, Pauline, the aunts—would be matched in the next generation at the Carmel. Léonie might have entered that circle, had her mother not died. What she herself called an odious childhood registers as a minority report on the hallowed Martin family history and thus earns its own attention. That wretchedness briefly turned into a singular, almost miraculous concord.

Léonie, in her acute loneliness within her large family, an isolation made keener by Hélène's death in 1870, turned to the family's maid, Louise Marais, who served in the house for nearly a dozen years until the Martins moved to Lisieux in the fall of 1877. In her mid-twenties, Louise, too old to be big sister and too young to pass as a surrogate mother, played the despot and ordered her about, subverting the parental authority. It was an almost penal form of attention, but attention nonetheless.[66] How could Léonie not know that she was hopelessly defeated by her sisters' success in pleasing their mother as she could not, that Pauline was to Zélie "un baume pour mon coeur" ["a balm to my heart"][67] while Marie's shows of piety compensated for her sartorial silliness and socializing, which even so her mother excused. It seems embarrassing if not prurient to read Léonie's pathetic efforts to win her mother's affection: "M'aimes-tu, Maman? Je ne te désobéirai plus" ["Do you love me, Mama? I won't disobey you any more"].

Zélie's concern for her was compounded by anxieties over her own health, as she began to feel the cancer at work in her breast, and over her sister at Le Mans, dying of tuberculosis. Zélie had hoped conventual life would straighten out Léonie but conceded to Céline Guérin that it needed a miracle: "car la pauvre enfant est couverte de défauts comme d'un manteau. On ne sait par où la prendre" ["indeed, the poor child is covered with faults as by a coat. One doesn't know how to get hold of her"].[68] Those last words were precisely the ones she had once used to describe to Isidore their mother's problem with Zélie's own adolescence. She now assumed her mother's role of frustration and censure, as though to exorcise a ghost.

When Zélie finally broke through the closed circuit of her daughter's deference to the maid, Léonie had learned that it was not difficult to please her mother, and they lavished attention upon one another. The breakthrough marked perhaps the only happy time in Léonie's young life, as though a profound psychological abscess had been lanced. What confers poignancy upon this rebirth (for both of them) was Zélie's increasingly urgent sense that she had to live on for the sake of this lost lamb now retrieved, but the cancer proceeded on its merciless course.

Toward the end of 1876, the tumor was producing numbness in her side. She had turned to Isidore for remedies—one measure of her helpless ignorance—but learned from a doctor that the only recourse, a doubtful one, would be an operation. As he could make no promises of a successful outcome, she rejected the option, fearing she would not be able to recover from it, that it would advance her death. It is usually argued that she had waited too long, the consultation came too late, but that seems a convenient retrospective judgment which biographers pass on to one another, even though it is prompted by one of the physicians with whom she had talked and the only one she trusted, Alphonse Notta, who practiced in Lisieux. As she reported to Louis, "[Il] trouve très regrettable que, dès le début, on n'ait pas fait l'operation, mais à présent il est trop tard. Cependant, il a l'air de dire que je puis aller très longtemps comme cela" ["[He] finds it very regrettable that there wasn't an operation from the start, but now it's too late. Still, he seems to say I can go on a very long while like this"].[69] She may have trusted Notta on Isidore's recommendation but also he gave her some hope, either from a bedside manner or out of ignorance of what was happening. She told Pauline that she could live maybe another fifteen or twenty years. If that seems bizarrely presumptuous, it helps to note that doctors in that age were sufficiently ignorant (or cautious) that they did not prognosticate. Before 1895, they did not have X rays to trace the progression of a tumor or to detect its metastasis.

Zélie had lived with discomfort in her breast for many years. The cancer set a new and rapid course which even therapy as we know it would perhaps not arrest. Dr. Notta would have been hard put to identify "le début." Just when a mastectomy would have been indicated and whether it would have been effectual, it is impossible to say. Zélie was even deceived by the sudden cessation of pains in her side, which gave her the illusion that perhaps she was cured. And her helplessness was not conditioned by fearful procrastination; it was essentially a function of her faith: at no time did she give up the certainty which had guided her entire life, that its course was determined by God. If it was the divine will that she live, then she would live. If it was her time to die, she knew Marie was old enough to replace her as caretaker of the children, and she could count on the Guérins to help Louis. A sensible businesswoman, she examined the family ledgers with both consolation and acceptance. And God was the only physician Mme. Martin fully trusted.

In tandem with such acceptance ran the belief that suffering in this life would advance the soul's purification and thus reduce the amount of time it would have to spend in purgatory. As her sister was languishing in the last weeks of her life, Zélie took what seems a macabre relief: "le bon Dieu fait bien tout ce qu'il fait" ["God does well all that he does"],[70] meaning that Sr. Marie-Dosithée's terminal tuberculosis was removing imperfections she would otherwise have to expiate later. Suffering was a way of settling accounts for one's failings in life, a reduction of debits which implicitly stored up credits for the next world. This bookkeeping mentality of Zélie and the commercial class informed Catholicism then as to a degree it does still.

The cardinal difference between the ecclesiastic and mercantile worlds was that one could not consult the ledgers of the spirit. There was no checking and clearing of its accounts in this world. That is why Zélie felt that the longer she suffered and the more painfully, the more likely she was to please the Virgin and secure a miraculous cure, but she could not be certain. Faith and prayer being her lifelong avenues through adversity, resorting to a physician meant going down an unknown byway, a hazardous detour along which words heard were far more mysterious than any within the language of the Church and the speaker could seem a sinister magician, antagonist to the fatherly, ever-reliable, if exacting parish priest. It is not difficult to understand these distinctions: physicians seem to control us through the arcana of our own bodies, of which we remain for the greater part helplessly ignorant; priests maintain access to the celestial, a realm never experienced but about which faith gives imposing certainties. It is no wonder that Zélie, dismayed by one doctor, bemused by another, went to the Virgin's pool, where millions yearly still gather. Only someone securely within Zélie's spirituality could understand her telling Céline Guérin, as the cancer spread and a tumor grew on her neck, that God had spared her of any fear: "je suis tranquille, je me trouve presque heureuse, je ne changerais pas mon sort pour n'importe lequel" ["I'm calm, I find myself almost happy, and I wouldn't change my lot for any other"].[71] She knew that were she to die she would be useful to her family as an intercessory agent in heaven, even as her sister was soon to become.

While she looked—could look—only to Lourdes for a cure, she admitted that she was more disposed to resignation than to hope, "moi qui vois tout en noir" ["I who see black in everything"].[72] To a degree such remarks amount to self-caricature, with perhaps a helpful trace of self-mockery. When she herself was dying, Thérèse heard from Pauline of their mother's penchant for exaggeration, the kind of dramatizing not foreign to lonely women. Even so, the last months of Zélie's life assumed a peculiar drama in which her sister and Léonie were centrally cast. Sr. Marie-Dosithée, dying, would serve from her celestial station to help Léonie find her way. Léonie for her part wrote to her aunt to pray that God secure her a religious vocation.

It makes a piteous story. Zélie, to help Léonie control her bad moods, had her put a nut into a drawer every time she had a "victory"—this girl was in her fourteenth year—and when Léonie was so successful that she ran out of nuts, Zélie cut the cork of a wine bottle into serviceable pieces. Sr. Marie-Dosithée's death on February 24, 1877, recast the family dynamics: she had exited with serenity and a "sweet" agony, according to the Mother Superior, and she would now be a protective spirit but could no longer help Zélie with advice and the possibility of the Visitandines' door opening yet again for Léonie. Zélie, losing this indispensable help, expressly denominated Pauline her aunt's successor as saint: "j'en ai l'espoir, mais pourtant, elle était bien meilleure que toi à ton âge" ["that's what I'm hoping even though she was much better than you at your age"].[73] In the same letter, Zélie recounted to her the misery and anxiety both she and Louis had suffered in the first year of their married life, before they realized that happiness for them both lay only in and through having children.

Zélie was presuming heavily upon her fifteen-year-old and had not thought to consider Pauline's viewpoint, not to mention her feelings. Was it a consolatory fantasy for Zélie? Not only had she herself been denied the opportunity to become a saint like her sister, but she was troubled with an incorrigible child and so needed a perfect one. Pauline would make up for Léonie. It hardly helped Pauline that she reported to her mother a dream in which Sr. Marie-Dosithée appeared to her niece from heaven and spoke. Zélie could hardly let go of this "vision," even as the Mother Superior at Le Mans was making sure Pauline did not feel privileged by what was only a dream. Pauline was disturbed by her mother's call to perfection and said so. Zélie backed off, begged her not to torment herself, and conceded a lifetime would be needed to reach sainthood. Pauline's letter, later destroyed, must have assumed an assertive tone, for Zélie next added to her frets the possibility that Pauline would not be so good at home as at convent school.

Would Mama please stop talking, stop asking about the dream? It is no wonder that Pauline, despite unrelenting migraines, did not wish to return home but asked to continue at Le Mans. Zélie tried to assure her that she need not keep winning school prizes. Heavy though school was, Pauline knew it was easier to be on her best behavior there than at home behaving impeccably, playing the saint before her hapless sister, and telling over and over about her aunt's oneiric visitation.

And Léonie? At the time of her aunt's death, she had been "toujours une croix bien lourde à porter" ["always a quite heavy cross to bear"],[74] but the turnaround came when Zélie discovered, through Marie's overhearing, the maid's "caractère violent," her "brutalité" toward Léonie, and intervened. Léonie quickly learned—this time, without nuts—to please Zélie by anticipating her wishes in daily matters, showed a four-year-old's joyous rowdiness (according to her mother, whose then four-year-old was the exuberant Thérèse), and so changed that Zélie came to feel indispensable to her. Léonie would not leave her side and confided to her the most secret thoughts. Believing that at last God was penetrating this young heart, Zélie now wanted to survive for the sake of her recovered daughter. She attributed the radical change in Léonie to her dead aunt's prayers but attributed to God the maid's brutish mistreatment as the precipitant which released Léonie from years of hidden bondage.

Zélie wanted confirmation of her illness from a physician before leaving Alençon for Lourdes in case she received a miraculous cure, but Louis objected. She did, however, visit a doctor (discreetly unnamed) only a week before she took the long trip south. He told her a surgical procedure was no longer efficacious. This time, she was offended by apparent indifference as he attempted to fob her off with another prescription (the previous one she had burned, unread), and when she asked concerning the tumor whether "ce serait bientôt percé" ["it would soon burst"], she got no answer. Apparently she had all along presumed it was an abscess which could have been lanced; she had not been rightly informed.[75] Better, the doctor conceded, if it burst, for then the illness would pass. "J'ai repris, 'Oui, quand je serai morte.'... J'eprouve une si grande repulsion pour la dureté de cet homme, que je ne saurais l'exprimer" ["I replied, 'Yes, when I'm dead.' . . . I feel such a great repulsion for the hard-heartedness of this man, I can hardly express it"].[76]

The pilgrimage to Lourdes began from Angers on June 18, with Marie, Pauline, and Léonie accompanying their mother. She knew the trip was financially as well as physically costly but believed the Virgin appreciated the family's sacrifices. Understandably, like thousands before her and millions to come, Zélie hoped to be cured, but for once Pauline weighed down upon her, saying a cure would come only if hope amounted to certitude. Like one of the afflicted in the New Testament stories, Zélie would have to bring a healing faith. She knew it was not in her character to be sanguine and looked to Pauline to be so in her stead. "Maman comptait sur mes prières surtout pour obtenir sa guérison. C'est incroyable comme elle avait confiance en moi et comme elle m'aimait! Mais je ne fus guère fervente pendant le voyage, et je vis bien qu'elle était deçue" ["Mama counted on my prayers for her cure. It's incredible what confidence she had in me and how she loved me! But I wasn't sufficiently fervent during the trip and I realized how disappointed she was"].[77]

The journey proved exhausting physically and psychologically. Zélie braved the chilling waters of the Lourdes pool no fewer than four times, fully clothed. During the first, "dans un état complet d'anéantissement" ["in a state of complete prostration"], she felt herself choking and withdrew but at the last, shortly before leaving for home, she stayed in the water up to her shoulders for fifteen minutes, "espérant toujours que la Sainte Vierge allait me guérir" ["always hoping the Blessed Virgin was going to cure me"]. As long as she remained in the cold immobilizing water she felt no pain, but on her withdrawal, the sharp pains resumed. At the pool's gate, her daughters were waiting anxiously: "Maman, es-tu guérie?" ["Mama, are you cured?"].[78]

Despite or perhaps because of her suffering, she observed others who came and left with their afflictions. For all those palpably uncured, she would have adduced the same explanation that she gave herself, that God was testing her still further. Her return to Alençon entailed the additional suffering of becoming a kind of exhibit to local society, and she would have preferred to hide. Even those who had advised her to take the pilgrimage now showed cynical grimaces. Did she genuinely believe, they wondered, that she would be cured?

Her account of Lourdes, one of the lengthiest in her correspondence, was sent to the Guérins on June 24, 1877. The mood is tranquil and resigned: "Hélas! La Sainte Vierge nous a dit, comme à Bernadette, 'Je vous rendrai heureux, non pas en ce monde, mais en l'autre'" ["Alas! The Blessed Virgin has told us as she told Bernadette, 'I shall make you happy, not in this world but in the other'"]. For her family, she bravely assumed a cheerful face, apparently disconcerting Louis with the good spirits that belonged to the cure both of them realized was not to come. To Pauline she wrote, contrary to her words to Isidore, that she was not bothered by the incredulity of the townsfolk; she continued to hope for a cure and that hope was only growing. At night she would dream of Lourdes and miraculous cures, but the pain from the tumor in her neck became so great that she feared she would cry out during mass. She told Céline Guérin that the attacks were so violent that Louis and Marie believed that the Virgin did wish to cure her, otherwise she would not allow the pains to occur at once; besides, they had commenced only with the pilgrimage. This news she did not share with Pauline.

Was she dissembling for the sake of the daughter who had hoped for her mother's cure and had left Lourdes in unspoken dismay? Zélie did her best to comfort Pauline for a devastating disappointment that bordered hazardously on disillusionment. How could someone so young have assimilated the resignation which Zélie over a lifetime, with many deaths around her, had long learned to sustain? As to Pauline's future, her mother advised her not to hope for earthly joys because she was sure to be deceived, "et si je n'espérais pas celles du ciel, je me trouverais bien malheureuse" ["and if I didn't hope for heavenly ones, I would be quite wretched"].[79] That motif, familiar to Pauline throughout her young life, had been enforced by Zélie's loss of four children, her exacting craft, and the self-confinements of her fearful disposition. The survival of five daughters somehow did not compensate her. Their assumptions of convent life ratified their mother's outlook on life. Pauline, first to enter Carmel, was not only pleasing her mother by pursuing the saintly life Zélie had missed; she was acquiescing to the view that no other life on earth, no marriage, no spinsterhood, could bring any real, lasting joy.

The bottled Lourdes water Zélie had bought she applied to herself and to Léonie's eczema. She wrote to Pauline what was to be her final estimate of this forlorn child: "Elle est moins privilégiée que vous des dons de la nature, mais, malgré cela, elle a un coeur qui demande à aimer et à être aimé et il n'y a qu'une mère qui puisse lui témoigner à tout instant, l'affection dont elle est avide, et la suivre d'assez près pour lui faire du bien" ["She is less privileged than the rest of you in natural gifts, but despite that she has a heart which asks to love and be loved and only a mother can give to her at every moment the affection she craves and attend her closely enough to do her good"].[80]

By mid-July, when her mother could no longer dress or undress herself unaided, Léonie was praying that she would die in her mother's place. Pauline wished to suffer for her, only to have her mother reproach her with the reminder that suffering was reducing her time in purgatory, where she figured she would spend about one hundred years. To the Guérins, she confided her growing sense that the Virgin did not wish to cure her, so that her only recourse was to resign herself and to take profit from present pain. With sturdy business acumen, she put it this way: "J'aurai double profit, je souffrirai moins en me résignant et je ferai une partie de mon Purgatoire sur la terre" ["I'll derive a twofold profit: I'll suffer less by resigning myself and I'll spend part of my Purgatory on earth"].[81] With that last phrase, she gave a cue to her youngest daughter, who read these words a generation later.

The protracted, atrocious manner of her dying anticipated that of Thérèse twenty years later. Weeks before her death, there were bouts of pain so acute that she and her family must have thought (and hoped) the end had come. The siege brought spikes of suffering, primarily from the pains in her neck. To Isidore, she wrote of crying out to him in the belief that only he could give her solace: "J'ai souffert, pendant vingt-quatre heures, plus que je n'avais souffert pendant toute ma vie, aussi ces heures se sont-elles passés à gémir et à crier. J'implorais tous les saints du Ciel, les unes après les autres, personne me répondait!" ["I've suffered over the last twenty-four hours more than I've suffered in all my life. Those hours were passed in groans and cries. I implored all the saints of Heaven, one after the other, and none answered me"].[82] She sat upright in bed, her rosary in her hands, and prayed constantly; the slightest movement was excruciating. Louis and Marie attended helplessly.

She mentions a doctor's arrival and his prescription of what must have been an opiate but in that day, as even now, there was little understanding of pain management: the proper dosages of drugs for controlling the pain; the suitability of the analgesic; the patient's own involvement, which gives a semblance of control. She was assisted by nursing nuns, but they could do little, serving primarily to relieve the tremendous psychological weight upon the Martin family.

In a letter to the Guérins, Marie attested to her mother's patience and resignation but what begs emphasis is Zélie's awareness within two weeks of her death that "Décidément, la Sainte Vierge ne veut pas me guérir" ["Obviously, the Blessed Virgin does not want to cure me"].[83] None of the saints nor even Mary herself, called upon in anguished iteration, had responded. Zélie's own response to this void accords with Marie's report to Isidore and Céline. She was resigned to God's will, as she saw it, that she rest "elsewhere" than on the earth. She began that rest on August 28, 1877.

She died having passed from hope of a cure to accepting there would be none. From at least two weeks before the end, she was without hope and her *envoi* about resting elsewhere is cryptic enough. How could purgatory be worse than what she had suffered? How can it be insignificant that she said nothing of heaven but rather left Isidore, as she leaves us, with the impenetrable eloquence of silence? When the family was gathered round her bed two days before her death, she was no longer able to speak and could barely open her lips but, according to Piat, when the Guérins visited her the next day, she fixed upon Isidore's wife "un regard profond et suppliant qui voulait dire tout l'espoir qu'elle mettait en elle et sa reconnaissance infinie" ["a deep and beseeching look which told of all the hope she had in her as well as her infinite gratitude"].[84] Whether that was what she was saying is uncertain but can be left as fitting to the life she had known with Isidore's wife through their letters. Mme. Guérin was losing a confidante, a correspondent, a sister in suffering.

Whatever the consolations of faith attending Zélie in the last days, it is arguably better to insist upon the extreme bitterness of what Piat called "le calvaire d'une maman."[85] Subsumed in that bitterness are her own words on the Virgin but also the ineffable weight of acceptance. Zélie's life, her letters, and the testimony about her left to her children and the Guérins for Thérèse's edification form what might be called the pre-life of Thérèse. Zélie provides some of the motifs which would shape her daughter's life and spirit, as though the mother were rehearsing for her daughter. Like most mothers, Zélie was a model of hard work and endurance. There is nothing original there, nor in her commonplace that no burden imposed on the believer is beyond the believer's strength. Concomitant to that view is the assumption that suffering is a divine test, and the greater that suffering, the more is the soul elevated by a kind of divine attention. That is why Zélie could tell others and herself that the more the disease ravaged her, the more she hoped for its cure. In later years and for her benefit, Thérèse's sisters hallowed their mother's strengths with anecdotes.

They might also have shared stories of her fears as a businesswoman, as a mother, that she had a wariness bordering upon distrust of doctors. That, too, was common to her times and was even exploited in literature by writers such as the Goncourts and Flaubert. Zélie mentions hearing a priest rail against the medical profession (March 26, 1876), and she herself blamed the Guérins' doctor for the death of her nephew and godson. She had been abjectly dependent upon doctors, but none saved three of her babies nor even Hélène at five. She remained in the dark about the cancer which consumed her. In a secularizing age, she clung tenaciously to the suasions of faith, pitting the divine realm against the medical community. It is not incidental that she recorded of the last physician she visited that he believed in nothing. An uneasy standoff occurred between Thérèse and Dr. Alexandre de Cornière in the last months of her life. For both mother and daughter, terminal illness became integral to spirituality and determined the character of their *abandon*.

Zélie was a caregiver, with a ripe maternal solicitude for the outcast. Her brave and finally legal intervention for an abused child, her feeding of beggars, but most wonderfully her retrieval of Léonie, would provide an example, if not explicit inspiration, for Thérèse, who within Carmel had not only the maternal load of training novices but undertook on her own to approach and deal with a few Carmelites who were standoffish or unsociable. Deeply experienced, Pauline in turn was a mother to Thérèse in the politics of the Carmel.

Zélie continued posthumously as mother to Thérèse through the stories Thérèse heard and the saved letters she read while writing her first manuscript. Eerily, the summoning of resolve in being on one's own joins mother and daughter. Zélie did not experience, or at least did not record, an eclipse of her faith nor even the temptations against it which Thérèse underwent, but both suffered acute spiritual isolation. No saint answered Zélie's entreaties. How could she not have felt forsaken by God? A *calvaire*, indeed. On her own, Thérèse, feeling heaven sealed from her, found the earth needed her witness to its not being shut out by God.

4

How They Paved the Little Way

Carmel and Carmelites in the Time of Thérèse

Oh! Qu'ils sont agiles les pieds de cette héroïne de quinze ans! Oh! Qu'il est joyeux le coeur qui voit enfin ses rêves réalisés! [Oh! How agile the feet of this fifteen-year-old! Oh! How joyous the heart seeing its dreams realized at last!]

> —*Circulaire* of Sr Saint Stanislaus, Saint-Flour, February 7, 1891

Mener une vie humble, cachée, inconnue, vivre pour Dieu seul, voilà ce qui m'est destiné et ce qui me réjouit [To lead a humble, hidden, unknown life, to live for God alone, there, that's my destiny and my rejoicing].

> —*Circulaire* of Sr Euphrasie du Saint-Sacrement, Tours, August 23, 1888

Aimer et souffrir fut l'aspiration de son grand coeur; ce fut aussi sa devise chérie qu'elle écrivit en ces termes à la suite de la formule de ses voeux: VIVRE D'AMOUR, VIVRE DE CROIX, MOURIR D'AMOUR, MOURIR SUR LA CROIX [To love and suffer was her great heart's aspiration. It was also her cherished motto which she wrote in the following terms immediately after taking her vows: TO LIVE FROM LOVE, TO LIVE FROM THE CROSS, TO DIE FROM LOVE, TO DIE ON THE CROSS].

> —*Circulaire* of Mère Anne-Victoire de la Nativité, Beaune, March 27, 1890

Devenir une petite Épouse de Jésus, bien, bien petite, bien aimante, toute livrée à ses bons plaisirs, c'est toute mon ambition [To become a little spouse of Jesus, really, really little, really loving, wholly delivered to his good pleasures, that is my exclusive ambition].

—*Circulaire* of Sr Clémence du Sacré-Coeur, Metz,
August 16, 1893

Les peines intérieures les plus cuisantes assaillirent son âme: ténèbres, désolations, sécheresses, tentations . . . Ce martyre intérieur dura plusieurs années: c'était une agonie, une mort, prélude nécessaire de la vie d'union intime avec Notre Seigneur [The most bitter inner pains assaulted her soul: darknesses, desolations, aridities, temptations. . . . This internal martyrdom went on for several years: it was an agony, a death and necessary prelude to the life of intimate union with Our Savior].

—*Circulaire* of Sr Marie de Jésus, Douai,
October 25, 1893

J'ai les mains vides, mais j'espère dans les mérites de Notre Seigneur. Loin de moi la pensée de me proposer pour modèle, je sais trop combien ma vie a été défectueuse [I have empty hands, but I hope in the merits of Our Lord. Far from me the thought of proposing myself as a model, I know only too well how faulty my life has been].

—*Circulaire* of Mère Thérèse de Jésus, Castres,
March 2, 1892

Je m'abandonne à la très grande, à l'ineffable miséricorde de mon Dieu! [I am letting myself go to the very great, the ineffable compassion of my God!]

—*Circulaire* of Sr Aimée de Jésus, Bayonne,
April 2, 1894

Pour cette âme droite, tout était grâce [For this virtuous soul, all was grace].

—*Circulaire* of Sr. Anne-Marie-Joseph
de la Nativité, Blois, November 30, 1888

It is a singular sociology: two to three generations of women are espoused to the same man, whom they meet only in images and in prayer. They, by their pledge to him, are pledged to a life with each other. They are closely confined, as in a prison, and remain so till death. Visitors are received only at a grille and for only thirty minutes—a week. For all but family members, a dark curtain is drawn between the interlocutors, and there is always another sister, known as a *tierce*, attendant to the conversation. The only men with whom these women are directly in contact are their confessor priest and their physician, who also has to use the grille. They sleep apart in spartanly furnished rooms. They pray, sing, eat together. They work singly and collectively.

Such was the conventual life of Carmel a century ago, one few of us would find inviting. It remains even today a life void of status, possessions, sensuality, relentlessly unglamorous and repetitive. At its center is a collective ethic almost wholly at odds with our modern attention to the psychology of the individual. The nostrums of growth, of progress, of all sorts of liberties and rights, mean nothing within a convent's walls. This life requires a rigor akin to the military in its discipline but there is little movement within ranks: one enters as a novice, may become subsequently a trainer of novices, and one or another assumes the weightiest office, that of prioress, for a term of three years, once renewable.

The monastic life, whether in its masculine or feminine form, will likely continue to fascinate the secular world by its sheer and pertinacious otherness and by its successive claim upon whole epochs long vanished, in fine, its medieval and static assurance of order, with the lasting perquisites of solitude and peace.[1] Proust says that the wonderful thing about other people's happiness is that we can believe in it, and so we of the noisy, hurried world can believe in the peace of the cloistered life, knowing that that peace is one thing which, by God's mercy, cannot be accessed from a Web site. Neither is it available from some mail order catalog. But there is more: outsiders to the monastic or conventual life feel a peculiar deference to all within because those within have had the stamina to exercise a power scarcely known nowadays, that of abstinence. As one's own worldly unworthiness becomes a self-accusation, it seems to follow, or so one might hope, that those disciplined to piety and righteousness and self-removed from secular harms have, in gospel terms, overcome the world. They are saints.

In this regard, there is an instructive story about Thérèse and her posthumous reputation. The notion of moving her toward beatification and canonization occurred first, it is alleged, to a Scotsman, Thomas Nimmo Taylor, who when visiting Lisieux within a few years after Thérèse's death, shared the idea with its then-prioress, Marie de Gonzague. Shouldn't Thérèse be made a saint? Oh, but in that case, Gonzague told him, you would have to canonize so many Carmelites!

This response is not amiss. It was an early assumption within the Discalced Carmel that strict, faithful compliance with the Rule and the Constitution of the Order would bring a sister at her life's end to a saintly perfection, a bypassing of purgatory. Thérèse herself believed that the venerable octogenarian Mère Geneviève, cofounder of the Lisieux Carmel, had attained that perfection by her serene simplicity. In Carmel's lore the prioress Béatrix de la Conception was famous for her injunction, "Soyons saintes!" ["Let us be saints!"] and urged that the way to that end was in the faithful accomplishment of little things.[2] Thérèse did not invent the *petitesse* for which she is famous.

Mère Gonzague shrewdly demurred before Taylor, because she knew her sisters well, not only from the tradition but from news about them as posted from other Carmels. This chapter examines the discipline of Carmelite spirituality from its inception and then moves to the formative texts as all the sisters lived them: in Lisieux, in France, and as far as Saigon and Shanghai. Word of these distant Carmelites came from their death notices, known as *circulaires*, some more of which we shall examine toward the chapter's end.

Carmel from Its Beginnings

Before approaching these Carmelites, it is helpful to review briefly where their order had come from. Lisieux's Carmel will then tell us much about how a convent was run.

The Order of Our Lady of Mount Carmel was founded in the 1150s, a good two generations before the orders of Saints Francis and Dominic. Unlike them, it had no imposing nor visionary personality at its head, but it did claim a particular fealty to the prophet Elijah, who from Mount Carmel (today, the site of Israel's Haifa University) contested with the priests of Baal. It is for his suffering and lone service to God, however, that he is revered. The Primitive Rule, established in 1209 by Albert, patriarch of Jerusalem, and confirmed with alterations by Pope Innocent IV in 1248, prescribed a rigorous asceticism, but, as happened subsequently with the Franciscan and Dominican houses, there was a rapid degeneration, abetted by the black plague and halted only by the creation of a Mitigated Rule. The first order of Carmelite sisters began in 1452, but the Discalced, or sandal-wearing, Carmel was initiated in 1567 by Teresa de Avila in an attempt to restore the order's original simplicity and to promote the contemplative life. It is known as the Teresian Reform.

What might be called a golden age for the Church itself came with her and her confidant and friend, Juan de la Cruz (John of the Cross), another Carmelite, who assisted her in her reforms and with her set down a robust and eloquent mystical theology. Their mysticisms emerged independently of the Church's earlier mystical traditions, such as the Augustinian and the Victorine. Juan de la Cruz was trained only in Thomist scholasticism while Teresa, albeit aristocratic, had no training to speak of, even though in her autobiography she deftly overplays her womanly ignorance and feigns simplemindedness. *Mysticism* means in the Greek an "initiation into the divine." A mystic has been granted access to or revelation of God's secrets. It is an essential part of its meaning, however, that mystical experience may be prepared for but cannot be sought. One might only become disposed to it by prayer and contemplation, actively passive but passive still. This supreme grace cannot be coopted by human will nor by guidebook learning. Some people claim that—or, more modestly, ask whether—Thérèse of Lisieux was a mystic. In experiential terms, the answer comes close to no.[3] She made no explicit claim to nor did she articulate any *unio mystica* or visitation. Besides, she lived in an age that was wary of fervor and visions. Within Carmel itself, illuminism was suspect. In textual terms, however, the answer could well be yes, if her writings and her attested remarks form the basis for the *theologia amoris* she created.[4] Her vivid and intense affectivity, her untiring ability to recreate Jesus within the terms of her emotional needs, give the reader a lively sense of the divine spouse ever before her, even when he is absent. With her as with the Spanish mothers, the phrase *life in Christ* is literal, not rhetorical. Her mysticism does not rest upon the extravagance of an event—a vision, an ecstasy, a levitation—but upon an abiding disposition to intimacy with Christ. As Jesus attests in the Johannine Gospel that there are many rooms in the divine house, there are many mysticisms as well, and the classical versions of them play no part in the present story.

It would be captious in any case to deny Thérèse as *writer* a place in succession to the great Spanish Carmelites, whose reformed order was introduced into France by Teresa's own assistant, Aña de Jesús, in 1604, more than twenty years after Teresa's death. The surviving sisters and Juan de la Cruz warmly received the idea of carrying the Teresian Carmel into France when it was proposed by Jean de Quintanadoine de Brétigny (he had a Spanish father but his mother was Norman) in 1585. The Spanish fathers, however, were jealous of their authority and opposed expansion of the order, even by foundations of monks. Quintanadoine was able to bring them around only through the courage and persistence of Mme. Barbe Acarie, a Parisian salon hostess and friend to a number of Parisian ecclesiasts interested in mystical theology. They included François de Sales and Pierre de Bérulle. When she first read Teresa's writings, Mme. Acarie was unmoved, but then she had a series of visions in which Teresa told her to bring the Discalced Carmel into France. Her eloquence won over her skeptical friends, who, to confound the Spanish hierarchy, applied to the Holy See and got permission not only to establish Carmel houses but also to bring Spanish prioresses for guidance.

After the first house, the Carmel of the Incarnation in Paris, begun by Aña with seven young French novices, others followed in steady succession: Dijon, Amiens, Poitiers, Rouen, Bordeaux, Besançon, all within ten years. By 1644, France had fifty-five Carmels. These pale summary phrases cannot convey the enterprise and endurance of that first generation under its extraordinary prioresses, all but one of whom moved on to found Carmels beyond France.[5] The Spanish mothers, while moving into unknown and (literally) virgin territory ruled by the heretical King Henri IV, had to resist attempts from French ecclesiastics to alter Teresa's Constitution, and they were uneasy with the neo-Platonic leanings of their foremost director, Bérulle. A tough lot, they were also subject to the dangerous enthusiasm associated with Spanish women in orders during that time. Teresa's autobiography had been ordered in part so that she could defend herself against charges of illuminism.

One of the most lively Spanish mothers, Aña de San Bartolomeo, left an autobiography of her formation under Teresa. She writes that her zeal to save souls was so intense that her confessor admonished her that it was demonic, but Teresa shrugged off his warning with advice to Aña that confessors had not understood her, either. A kind of bulimic of fervid visions, Aña saw Christ and the Trinity, as well as eternity. Her trancelike behavior brought doctors who, bewildered, applied tormenting plasters. Barely recovered, she was assigned to work in an infirmary and while tending the sick, she had a visitation from Elijah and Elisha, who roundly denounced her incompetence as a nurse. Realizing her best efforts were very imperfect, she wrote, "Bien que j'accomplisse ces travaux avec tout de fautes, il m'y consolat et il me paraissait que tout était amour de Dieu. . . . qu'il aimait mon âme, il m'envoyait quelques traverses afin que je connaisse mon amour-propre et que les ferveurs soient modérées" ["Although I performed these tasks with lots of mistakes, it consoled me and it seemed that all was God's love. . . . as God loved my soul, he sent me some adversities so I'd know my pride and that my fervors might be tempered"].[6] Three hundred years later, she herself appeared with Aña de Jesús to Thérèse—in a dream.

The Carmel in seventeenth-century France was distinguished by Marguerite de Beaune, who furthered the Carmelite devotion to the Infant Jesus and who used a phrase popularly associated with Thérèse, "la petite voie," the little way. The most substantial developments in Catholic spirituality during that century did not come from Carmel, but they would exert powerful sway over the Church for generations to come, not least in the turbulent time of Thérèse, and thus they deserve attention here. Very roughly speaking, we might characterize them as a contest between justice and love or as a contest between the human desire for purity and the human need for accommodation.

The first of these brings a skeleton from the closet of Catholicism. Named for a bishop of Ypres, Jansenism held that the human will is irremediably perverse. It also subscribed to predestination: all hangs upon God's justice and nothing upon God's compassionate love. This stringent view of divinity made the narrow way to heaven even narrower and consigned most of humanity to damnation. Although denounced from Rome as heretical, Jansenism spoke (and still speaks) deeply and directly to the need some Christians have always felt for a clearly demarcated righteousness over and against the world: the elect are those few who follow Christ and will be assumed on the latter day, as the sorry, soiled, and vast lot of sinners will pass into hell.[7] It did not bother Jansenists that they put a tight clamp upon God's love, as though God, having sent his only begotten Son into the world out of love for it, knew all along that it was mostly a wasted effort. Their mistake was to confuse an extreme rigidity with purity and to make any sort of charitable community impossible to realize. While Jansenism affords a ghastly grandeur and does in its way enforce a sober, uncompromising view of the sacramental life, its disdain of those for whom Christ came, taught, and healed gives it a pharisaic cast.[8]

To leave the matter there would amount to unfair simplification. Although, as a heresy, it has usually had a "bad press," Jansenism's subterranean appeal even into recent times needs probing. There is far more to it than the "sublime misanthropy" Voltaire found in its greatest exponent, Pascal. Perhaps its cardinal strength is that it rests squarely, in almost Protestant fashion, upon Scripture. Squarely, but selectively. Consider two passages about divine justice against sinners in *Matthew* 13: first, tares and wheat are bound together for the harvest day, when the tares shall be burnt (24–30, 36–43); then, the heavenly kingdom is a fishing net that gathers up the good and the bad alike; angels will cast the bad into a fiery furnace where "there shall be wailing and gnashing of teeth" (47–50). These grim, daunting tableaux confound the smilingly modern view of God as love and nothing but. Jansenism makes hay (or tares) out of the Gospels' own choreography of a coming hellfire. The assignment of salvation to the pure and very few (including oneself, of course) presumes percentages which are never made explicit in the New Testament, though *Revelation* 13 and 14 suggest that the damned, those who receive "the mark of the beast," will form a comfortable plurality.

Perhaps most fearsome about Jansenism is its punitive urge, so readily playing into the hands of those who deprecate Christianity. It amounts to a caricature of Christian faith by its radically uncharitable need to condemn the world, and yet any modern inclination to disown the radical division between Christ and the world flies in the face of the apocalypticism which informs much of Christ's preaching. He does condemn the religious establishment of his day, the Pharisees and scribes, he condemns Capernaum, the very town he lived in, and he condemns a whole generation.

In counterpoise to Jansenism's vindictive and (worse) thoroughly humorless need for a privileging justice from God, the "humanisme dévot" of François de Sales promoted a spirituality of sweetness and joy, "une amoureuse, simple et permanente attention aux choses divines" ["a loving, simple, and abiding attention to divine things"].[9] Privy to the Carmelite mysticism of Spain, François, a Genevan prelate, promoted a way to perfection through prayer accessible to laity, chiefly women, who were his correspondents. His most substantial achievement for the Counter-Reformation (now called the Reform) was coauthored with a woman, Jeanne de Chantal: the founding of the Visitandine order in 1610. Their "oraison de repos," the silent turning of love to God, without imagination's props and without words, attained the serenity known only to cloistered life. Indeed, the Visitation served initially in public charity, as its founder had wished, before becoming wholly contemplative. It was notably less austere than preceding orders. For the laity, the influence of François de Sales became widespread for many generations as priests in retreats drew from his treatise, *Introduction à la vie* devoté (1609), and his *Traité de l'amour de Dieu* (1616) for passages sure to assuage lay anxieties and self-condemnations.

Complementing the Salesian doctrine was the work of Pierre de Bérulle, the most imposing of the French Carmel's three overseers in its first generation. His emphasis upon reverent simplicity over intellectual subtleties opened an immeasurable avenue onto the immanence of God. Rather than seek vainly to know God, the devout soul should lose itself in the divine: we belong to God, he argued, not by our conceptions of the divine but by its hidden operations within our lives. Here was mysticism with a difference: free from the baroque exhibitionism of private visions, it was innate to the life of every believer and yet hidden.[10]

The notion that God is loving and accessible lies as much at the center of the Gospels as any certainty of hellfire. It is the very substance of Christ's mission, but it has needed iteration and accent throughout the Church's history. The peculiar drama of modern French history, however, is that the pull of Jansenism has been reinforced by the republicanism which issued from 1789. A society insistently secular becomes insistently unredeemable. It invites Jansenism's darkness upon itself. To pious believers, God became angry at France for its subversions of the faith, and reparations by the faithful became necessary, hence the cult of the Sacred Heart, the popularity of which peaked after the disastrous war with Prussia and the violent spring of the Commune.

The Carmel of Lisieux

I began by speaking of a sociology of Carmel, but there can be none in any conventional sense and for a reason which, though obvious, deserves noting. A sociologist would have an open and accessible field of materials and people with whom to work but Carmel could admit nothing of that sort. The women within were walled in, without access to the world which they had, after all, solemnly taken vows to leave behind.[11] Only very rarely, as during the Revolution and during the Allied bombings in the summer of 1944 did an entire sisterhood physically depart Carmel. Neither could anyone pass the grate and settle among them to study their daily ways. Archival materials such as the *circulaire* issued on the death of a Carmelite and circulated among Carmel convents are hermetically sealed within the language and strictures of the Christian faith. The same is true of the writings of Thérèse; not one line of them is uninformed by the Catholicism which shaped her language, its diction and semantic weight.

The women at Lisieux's Carmel in the generation of Thérèse have become well profiled because of her and her natural sister Céline, who became Sr. Geneviève. Céline brought her camera into the convent when she entered it in August 1894 and took numerous group photos—nine seconds of stiffness, please!—which depict the women variously working or posing. We know about some of them as more than cameos thanks to the series of hearings held by Church officials for Thérèse's beatification and canonization; several testified on her behalf, only one of them admittedly unenthusiastically. Only one, Sr. Marie de la Trinité, left extensive notes on her life as a novice under the guidance of Thérèse. There have been biographical portraits, hagiographical in tone, of the three other Martin sisters at Carmel. A fifth member of the family, Marie Guérin, made up the so-called clan Martin, a substantial minority in a convent of only two dozen sisters.

The convenience of Céline's camera points to the mighty sway of class, which carried over into Carmel. The Martin family was well off, if not securely affluent, but some of the Carmelites had come from relatively poor circumstances, including orphanages, and occasionally felt some resentment of both the Martin numbers and their social status. Even though in Carmel all were equally poor, there were donations from without. Louis, unstinting with flowers and fish, was known as Christ's postman. A sister of rural background, Aimée de Jesus, was openly critical of the "petit bourgeois" Martins and their devotion to roses; she insisted that potatoes be planted instead of good-for-nothing rose bushes. She also spoke out against the admission of Céline, the fourth Martin, remarking that Carmel needed nurses and menders, not artists. Céline for her part much later observed that her natural sisters were among "primitives."

Most of the Lisieux Carmelites in the mid- to late nineteenth century came from the towns, villages, and hamlets of the Calvados district. They came from pious and practicing families, deeply conservative, unobstreperous. Several had lost one or both parents and grew up in conventual schools. Few were well educated and one was so apparently dim that Céline not so charitably spoke of Sr. Saint-Raphaël du Coeur de Marie as "dépourvue d'intelligence à un degré rare" ["short of brains to an unusual degree"].[12] None, save Sr. Anne du Sacré-Coeur from Macao, had traveled far from home. Some had never seen the sea, less than twenty miles north of Lisieux. Thérèse and Céline were exceptional in having visited Rome and seen the pope; their father could afford a jubilee pilgrimage to Rome.

Among the few of an aristocratic background was the prioress, Marie de Gonzague, who oversaw the completion of Carmel, which had begun in 1838. Gonzague's family included in its lineage a cardinal, an archbishop, several ambassadors, a chamberlain to François I, and some distinguished in military services. The fourth of seven children (like Louis, she outlived all her siblings), she was educated at the Visitandine school in Caen and entered the Lisieux Carmel in 1860, only months before it founded the first Carmel in Indochina at what is now Ho Chi Minh City. Gonzague, one of eight then in the novitiate, offered herself as one of the four founding sisters but was held back by her superior, M. l'Abbé Cagniard.[13]

Adventures aplenty—not the life a Carmelite sought—awaited her. She became *sous-prieure* (assistant prioress) in 1866 at the age of thirty-two. In that year, the Lisieux Carmel was called upon by the bishop of Coutances to establish a Carmel there, and two years later it reestablished one in Caen which had dated from 1616 but had been closed by the Revolution. Typhoid and smallpox hit the community in 1869 and 1870, but there were no deaths. When, in September 1870, the Prussians brought the war with France to Lisieux, Delatroëtte, recently appointed Carmel's superior, allowed seven sisters, including Gonzague, to leave the convent. They reentered the following March.

First elected prioress in 1874, Gonzague was soon required to show she had an innate talent for wielding authority. When the Carmel was flooded after sudden and violent rains in July 1876, she got her family to finance the restoration (the flood had left the ground floor several feet deep in mud) and final extension of the monastery. She also turned to friends in the regional nobility and even other Carmels for contributions. After she was gratefully reelected prioress in 1877, she had to face municipal authorities ordering the exhumation of all nine of the sisters who had been buried on convent grounds.[14] Someone had noticed that, since the Franco-Prussian War, the Carmel had neglected to seek authorization for intramural interment. The municipal officers, in a fit of *égalité* and *fraternité*, drew back only when it was agreed that all Carmelites would now be buried in the public cemetery.[15]

Gonzague's example shows how a prioress had to be not only a model of a mother disciplined and disciplining in love. She had to exercise a shrewd sense of finances. Madre Teresa had enjoined prioresses to avoid debts and even mortgages, but there was no training manual to assist. An invaluable document of Carmel's fiscal life late in the nineteenth century, its *Registre des Recettes et Dépenses Générales*, indicates how carefully the budget had to be kept.[16] Steady income came from "pensions" given monthly by postulants and novices, but also (apparently voluntarily) by choir sisters.[17] The annual pension from Indochina's Sr. Anne du Sacré-Coeur was 1,000 francs in 1884, and every year 133 francs came from Mère Geneviève, with an average of 300–400 francs from other sisters. Thérèse's cousin Sr. Marie de l'Eucharistie brought an annual pension of 1,000 francs in 1896 and 1,400 in the next year. A dowry, or *dot*, came with each sister entering the novitiate but was kept as a deposit until she died: Sr. Marie-Philomène returned to Carmel in 1886 with a *dot* of 6,000 francs. Thérèse's sister Marie brought 8,000 in 1888, and Thérèse's own, listed in 1890, was 10,000. Money a sister inherited would be deposited in Carmel by a lawyer. Parish contributions, gathered by the curé of St. Vincent de Paul, reached 7,000 francs in 1885 and 9,000 in 1886.

Gonzague also invested in stocks, including the ill-fated Panama venture of Ferdinand de Lesseps. For that company, 491 francs are listed for 1887 and 1,556 francs in 1888, with half of a *dot* from that year (10,000 francs) also going to Panama. The 1889 ledger records the plunge to a chilling 175 francs gained from liquidation after de Lesseps's business collapsed in mismanagement and malaria. Gonzague was fortunate to find an especially generous friend in the marquise de Briges, who gave the Carmel nearly 50,000 francs during 1889–1891. Other investments included railroads (the northern and *midi* lines); the utility company Gaz et Eau, which brought electrical lines to Lisieux in 1897; and the most ballyhooed enterprise after Panama, listed by the *dépositaire* (keeper of records) simply as "les Russes," a government-backed scheme to finance Russian industrial development when France realized Russia was its surest ally against Germany. (The Third Republic's bourgeoisie substantially financed the trans-Siberian railway, not knowing that it was meant to help the Russian army protect Mongolia from Japan.) "Les Russes" got the other 10,000 francs from that *dot*.[18] A considerably smaller income for Carmel derived from the sales of painted images, ornaments, and miniatures, those "ouvrages" which steadily occupied Pauline in her first Carmelite years.

Donations which only Carmel could have received included a harmonium when Céline entered in 1894. Uncle Isidore gave books to the library (the deluxe Wallon on Jeanne d'Arc, for instance) and paid for badly needed bells from the foundry at Villedieu. He also purchased a second plot for Carmelites in the public cemetery.[19] In 1895, a Mme. Boucher gave 2,000 francs, with the agreement that four hundred masses were to be said after her death. And both Gonzague and Pauline ran small lotteries with other Carmels.

Expenditures beyond food and pharmaceuticals for the infirmary went substantially to construction and maintenance projects: the replacement of glass in the chapel, for instance, or the rebuilding of the tower (next to the *maison des tourières*) when it threatened to collapse. Gonzague also had to pay Carmel's chaplain and confessor, Abbé Louis Youf, whose annual income rose with the economy, from 700 francs in 1884 to as high as 900 in 1893, only to be drastically reduced when Pauline became prioress, to 525. She brought annual expenditures down by well over a third in her first term.[20]

Although Thérèse loved her and esteemed her highly, Gonzague, according to the testimony of several sisters, could be an imperious and capricious woman, jealous of her power and sometimes harsh in its exercise. She would impose orders at a whim and then forget them, and the sisters were not long in forgetting them as well. Only Thérèse, it has been piously claimed, was obedient enough to absorb them into her daily discipline.

Disgruntlement about Gonzague's apparent caprices, aired at the 1910 hearings for the beatification of Thérèse (Gonzague died of cancer in 1904), serves to call up an indispensable condition of conventual life, *obéissance*, an internalized deference to authority manifested in submissive acts. A famous anecdote within Carmel illustrates it: the prioress Aña de Jesús once ordered sisters at a convent in Salamanca to carry a large load of stones from one place to another and then back to the first site. When one of them complained about performing this useless labor, Aña replied that it was meant to teach that in religious life obedience does not require justification.[21] Orders might have been orders, but some gave them better than did others, and while Gonzague was scored for erratic behavior, her sisters recognized her organizational abilities and forceful personality, both of these being functions of class to a degree, and for all her seeming unpopularity (she was known as "the wolf" to at least one novice), she was elected prioress nine times, serving in that office for twenty-seven years.

It is standardly claimed that Gonzague had a peculiarly edged relationship with Pauline, Sr. Agnès, who was elected prioress from 1893 to 1896 at the express wish of Mère Geneviève. Those who have written lives of Thérèse are hard put not to take sides, and Gonzague is sometimes depicted in adversarial tones. However, a few weighty facts reveal that the conflict between Gonzague and Pauline has been overdrawn (see figure 4.1). Having served four terms as prioress, having literally built up the Carmel, and having brought in most of its novices and sisters, Gonzague had difficulty yielding her authority and demonstrable competence, but she knew she was constitutionally limited, and Pauline (or someone else) had to succeed her. In the unusually contested election of 1896, *both* women were humiliated: Pauline

FIGURE 4.1. The two prioresses in Thérèse's nine years at Carmel, Mère Gonzague (*left*) and Mère Agnès (Pauline), whose antagonisms toward one another have likely been exaggerated. Copyright Archives du Carmel de Lisieux.

by not being given the second term which attested confidence in her, and Gonzague, in having to endure other contenders. She felt she had been betrayed by ingrates. Pauline was not in that dark number: she knew that the admission to Carmel of herself, her sisters, and their cousin Marie had been chiefly Gonzague's doing. If Gonzague achieved a strong maternal dominion over Thérèse and thus stood in rivalry with Pauline, Pauline had had a comparable closeness with old Mère Geneviève. Besides, Pauline learned with lots of tears what a burden Gonzague had had to endure. Naturally, she would have smarted under Gonzague's moody censure but Gonzague, elected as recorder of the budget, also had the burden of noting that Pauline handled the Carmel's finances so tightly that it could only have seemed a criticism of her. No writer on Thérèse and Lisieux has previously observed finances as a ground for grief and bad feelings, but the numbers are eloquent. Even so, both numbers and words become mute before actions: when Gonzague was dying of cancer, Pauline and her natural sisters were sitting by her bedside.[22]

Some complaints about Gonzague are so trifling as to amuse: that she once promised Communion (not a daily sacrament when Thérèse was living) to a sister for having caught a rat; that she fed her cat calf's liver and sugared milk (neither on the Carmelites' diet); and once when during the strictly observed silent hour the cat was missing, she dispatched the novices to fetch it from a roof. An abbé at the hearings remarked that it was sad that souls seeking to find simplicity at Carmel were obliged to play politics. Pauline might have answered in some later words: "je continuais à aimer quand même Mère Marie de Gonzague, qui dans ses bon moments était réellement très aimable. Elle était pieuse et d'une grande franchise, avec une certaine candeur qui avait des charmes!" ["I went on loving Mère Gonzague even so, who in her good moments was really very kind. She was pious and very straightforward, with a certain charming candor!"].[23]

It might help to recast putative differences along generational lines. There were in effect three generations of sisters at Lisieux, which can be divided, somewhat arbitrarily, into the following periods: the first, composed of those who were part of the initial life of the Carmel or were born before the Second Empire, i.e., 1851; the second, those of the Second Empire, i.e., up to 1870; and the third, those of the Third Republic. Thérèse, then, had two generations of mothers in Gonzague and Pauline. As to Jansenism, it would have been familiar to, if not demonstrably predominant among the older sisters, while the corrective of a theology of love, which Thérèse did not invent, informed the younger. Such a symmetry, however, proves too neat.

Indeed, Thérèse was once criticized by one of the eldest, Sr. Fébronie, who had entered Carmel in 1842, for weighing too much upon God's mercy and not enough upon God's justice. And another, Sr. Saint-Jean-Baptiste du Coeur de Jésus, fifty at the time of Thérèse's death, Thérèse herself identified as "l'image de la sévérité du bon Dieu" ["the image of the good Lord's harshness"] (LT 230), for that sister, too, believed that Thérèse's theology of mercy shortchanged divine justice. Pauline herself, while not reasonably charged with Jansenism, was undoubtedly affected by, if not preoccupied with, divine justice as it was the orientation in which Louis was strictly raised. Further, much that Thérèse said and wrote about divine love seemed to bemuse her sister. Pauline's biographer, Jean Vinatier, urges that Pauline became a disciple of her younger sister, that she was in effect converted to a spirituality she had never entertained. And yet, decades after Thérèse's death, Pauline suffered fears of death and a void, much like that of Mme. de Croissy, the old prioress in Bernanos' *Dialogues des Carmélites*, whose terrifying death scene trenchantly depicts Jansenism's morbid legacy. Even so, the profile of Jansenist gloom might well be exaggerated in any one sister's instance. It lay in the murky depths where spirituality and sensibility were one, difficult if not impossible to retrieve.

Within every Carmelite portrait, literal or photographic, we might ask: is this sister burdened by notions of predestination and of irremediable damnation, or is she moving like many of the bourgeoisie toward what one historian of Catholic France has called a "soft devotion," an assurance of heaven?[24] In the nineteenth century, the family substantially replaced the church as the center of faith. To some extent, that was a class issue: the great Parisian cemeteries—Père Lachaise, Montmartre, Montparnasse—are monuments to the bourgeois accommodation of death in family tombs. The conservative or Jansenist strain would have persisted not only, as I have suggested, in age but in class, among the rural and less affluent. The Carmelites of and before the time of Thérèse came, however, from devout homes and had been shaped toward Carmel by spiritual directors. Some, having spent many deepening years in convent schools, were not truly contemporary to their age but rather were informed by the strictures of much earlier times.

It is commonly argued, with little heed to Salesian doctrine, that Thérèse with her "petite voie" confounded the Jansenist heritage, displacing its perverse justice with the message of divine love and the accessibility of any soul, lay or religious, to God. Her first audience for this message was the women in Céline's photos. What, then, do we make of the spiritual families of the convents, the enforced sisterhood and motherhood? It is a very mixed and mysterious bag. Even if we had all the Lisieux necrologies, we would remain at a substantial distance from the inner selves. We have only one: *Histoire d'une âme.*

Let us look at the sisterhood at work in the photos: perhaps the best one catches a dozen of them, a little less than half of the community, gathering hay (see figure 4.2). It is not quite "candid"; almost all of the sisters have ceased working (there were nearly five hours in each day given to work, two in the morning, three in the afternoon) and have been told to look ahead for the

FIGURE 4.2. Carmelites haying. Thérèse, at the center, carries her pitchfork, while Gonzague and Marie des Anges lean on theirs. These tools became devilish in Thérèse's recreational play *The Triumph of Humility*. Copyright Office Central de Lisieux.

required nine seconds. Only one is caught in motion, Thérèse entering the scene with pitchfork aloft. Most intriguing is a white-veiled sister to the left of Thérèse, Marie-Madeleine du Saint-Sacrement, who was four years older than Thérèse and under her governance in the novitiate. Even though the Totum edition of Thérèse's works indicate more references to her than to any other sister in the Carmel save Gonzague and the three natural sisters, she maintains only a minor profile in the literature about Thérèse.

Here is one assessment of her: Marie-Madeleine was "a very sullen and withdrawn character [who] [r]efused to confide in Thérèse: Feeling that Thérèse saw through her and could read her thoughts, she avoided the [novice] meetings. As for Thérèse, she never lost patience with her novice, but still loved her in a disinterested manner."[25] That qualifying clause adverts to the problem of what was called at the time "natural affection," the tendency, altogether human, to become drawn to someone in particular and develop exclusive amity or simply dependence. Thérèse herself had to overcome such feelings toward Gonzague, a second mother, barely two years younger than Zélie.

Marie-Madeleine testified during the beatification hearing[26] that Thérèse held a disconcerting power over her, a penetrating psychological sway, something akin to mesmerism. That says only that she *felt* such a power. Perhaps she would have savored the abbé's criticism[27] that this Carmel's lives were not founded on simplicity. She had not likely entered the convent under the assumption that she would feel dominated and controlled by someone younger than herself.

Some Carmelites came and left in peculiar circumstances. One of the most unusual was a widow who had lost her three children in infancy. One left after an episode of mental derangement which put her in Bon Sauveur in Caen, where Louis spent three years. Another had to leave after developing severe psychological problems long manifest in sudden, violent mood changes. Another, Sr. Anne du Sacré-Coeur, of Chinese-Portuguese origin, had lived at the Carmel in Saigon and eventually returned there. Her presence undoubtedly fed Thérèse's longings for missionary work in Vietnam.

What we know of these women, chiefly from Thérèse, confounds the notion that the convent was simply an institutional device for controlling women. It was also "a place for female agency where women could and did create religious and social meaning. Closed doors may have locked women in, but they also locked men out."[28] They were substantially on their own, enjoying an unparalleled space unto themselves, an artifice of family with mothers and sisters, sustained in routines of prayer, penance, and mutual devotion, with the special cohesion that comes only from camaraderie and genuine companionship.

It is inviting to consider Thérèse's writings as in a sense a distillation of those lives, as though her "petite voie" were implicitly their fashioning, their way. She had to some impalpable degree derived it from her exchanges with them. Most of the poetry she wrote was commissioned by the sisters for special occasions, such as an anniversary or an investiture. Her autobiographical manuscripts were written in three parts for three sisters. Not least, the photographs by Céline all come in situ, from the enclosed communal life each sister shared with two dozen other women. There may be much to suppose from Gonzague's riposte about the many Carmelite saints unrecognized, the truly little. Two genuinely humble and self-effacing women in Lisieux's Carmel will go unidentified, save that they are in the group profile taken in 1901, four years after the death of their celebrity (see figure 4.3). For Thérèse became an anomaly, magnified by fame because she insisted on her littleness to the point of its nothingness.

That contrast poses an essential difference within the Lisieux Carmel: Thérèse became its voice, its record through her writings and the *obiter dicta* conscientiously gathered (or, at least, recalled) by her natural sisters. Some of the other sisters' profiles, the *circulaires*, are quite brief (the usual length was four pages) because the deceased had expressly wished that nothing be said of them after their deaths. Gonzague was one of these, but Pauline, writing as prioress, gave her four pages anyway, and she buried their differences with charity. Thérèse, aware of this tradition of self-effacement even among the saints, noted that Teresa of Avila, like other writing saints, had enriched the Church by her "sublimes révélations" (C 2v). What sort of saint, then, was

FIGURE 4.3. The Carmelites of Lisieux in 1901, four years after Thérèse's death. Céline stands to the left of her sister's first portrait. Copyright Archives du Carmel de Lisieux.

the more pleasing to God, the obscure or the scribal? Both, answered Thérèse, as they were each following the Holy Spirit in their way.

What matters finally about these brides of Christ remains unspoken, at a recessive distance from both curiosity and probing. They lived, finally, an invisible life of the spirit, both solitary and collective. It is useful to recall from the Gospel accounts, especially *Mark*'s, that Christ's most devoted and loyal following was that of women. Carmelites were Marthas and Marys, hard working in daily chores but also pledged to contemplation for the greater part.

The *circulaires* of Lisieux's sisters who survived Thérèse almost invariably include some mention of her. That is because Pauline wrote them and because Thérèse had so rapidly assumed luminary status both within and without the houses of Carmel that her sisters were wont to recollect something about her even though only nine of them (including her three natural sisters and all of her novices) were called to the hearings for her beatification. In such a small community, to which each sister was a daily contributor, how could they have remained unaffected by her? Let us, however, remove her from stage center for awhile and put her back into the position she held within Carmel until her death, the years when she was no more prominent than anyone else and Carmel had not been stricken by fame. Let her recede and in a sense disappear so that others may pass by. This will be a recreation of sorts for outsiders, so they may find that much commonly associated with Thérèse she owed to the wider community of Carmel and to its traditions.

Lisieux's Carmel owes its origin to one at Pont-Audemer, twenty-five miles northeast. It had been suppressed during the Revolution and reestablished in 1803 with the government's stipulation that it found a boarding school, even though the Carmelite order was not pedagogic. Two sisters from an affluent family named Gosselin boarded there and decided on maturity to use their domestic wealth to found a convent. As that Carmel was then at capacity, the Gosselins could not become postulants but could live in the order as benefactresses under special vows. And so they did.

When, late in 1835, the bishop of Bayeux received their application, he chose Lisieux as the new Carmel site and assigned a superior to recruit sisters from the Carmel at Poitiers, where the Gosselins were asked to make a novitiate. They entered there in April 1837 and became Srs. Thérèse de St. Joseph and Marie de la Croix. Marie's piety proved costly: after pledging her soul to the cult of the Immaculate Conception, she became irremediably fearful that she had forfeited her salvation and would be consigned to purgatory, forever. She spent the last thirty-three years of her life unhinged and in bed, requiring at least an hour's daily attendance from the prioress toward the end.

On March 16, 1838, during a night of hard rain, the Gosselins and two other novices arrived in Lisieux by a public stagecoach with two Poitiers nuns: the new Carmel's prioress, Sr. Elisabeth de St. Louis, and the subprioress and mistress of novices, Sr. Geneviève de Sainte Thérèse. For five months, they lived in the improvised furnishings of a thatched house, with the chapel, choir, dormitory, and prioress's cell (less than tiny) walled within two garrets. They attracted little notice from the townsfolk, but the vicar who came to say mass fell to tremulous whispers as though he and the sisters were first-generation Christians in the catacombs. It is alleged that the Carmelites, unafraid, sang the offices in full voices.

They needed such hardiness. They faced destitution from the start, as few subjects admitted to the order had dowries and those brought were scant. The chaplain of the Collège de Lisieux, Abbé Gauthier, and the superior, Fr. Sauvage, had to roam far, soliciting funds to keep this Carmel alive, as it was the only conventual order in Lisieux, meaning that it was not self-sustaining.[29] Carmel literally did nothing to attract attention (or calumny) to itself other than to take up its final residence in the center of town, on the then Rue de Livarot.

Financial exigencies meant that construction proceeded slowly. The chapel was built in 1845, but the first wing of the red-brick convent was not begun until 1858. The July 1876 flood which inundated the Carmel with mud forced Gonzague to solicit help from relatives to restore and expand until the cloister reached a neat symmetry of chapel, two wings, and an enclosing wall, with a granite crucifix at the courtyard's center. It was this completed, now-historic Carmel which the four Martin sisters knew to the end of their lives.

Because the first prioress, Mère Elisabeth, died only four years after establishing the Lisieux Carmel, her successor, Mère Geneviève, who lived to eighty-six, is considered its true *fondatrice*. She was born Claire-Marie-Radegonde Bertrand and came from Poitiers. At three, it is said, she started reading the *Imitatio Christi*, and at seventeen, she had the first of many visitations in her long life, a voice which she wisely never characterized other than as friendly. When the room in which she was praying fell away, she had no idea where she was: "Plongée dans une lumière et une joie ineffables, j'entendais une voix si mélodieuse que toutes les harmonies d'ici-bas n'en peuvent donner l'idée" ["Plunged into inexpressible joy and light, I heard a voice so melodious that all the world's harmonies cannot give an idea of it"].[30] The voice told her to become a spouse of Christ, and she chose the Poitiers Carmel, but her shrewd father had already received from the prioress there a pledge that Claire would not be taken from him, so she did not enter until he was dead and she was twenty-four, in 1830.

Meanwhile, her spiritual director, Père de la Rochemonteix, tested her with reproaches and humiliations. After entering the Carmel and while completing her novitiate, she attended a retreat given by Rochemonteix which terrified her so well it convinced her she was damned. Only after the next day's Eucharist could she ask Christ why he had sent her such a storm. Her monitory voice replied that it was from love and to spare her ten years in purgatory.

She likely told this story many times to many sisters over the decades. She also told about her love for a long-dead prioress, Aimée de Jésus, but cautioned against the tendency novices had to become emotionally dependent upon a motherly figure: "j'y suis venue pour Dieu qui ne me manquera jamais; ainsi je serai toujours heureuse" ["I came here for God, who shall never fail me; in that way I shall always be happy"].[31] Mère Geneviève was articulating a central tenet of Carmelite and indeed of Christian life, that the delights of this world, including friendship, are shallow and deceptive because they are transient and occasion self-ruin. Life poses a series of cheats and snares. Protesting it and resisting them, Christianity thirsts for the absolute which is God.

A secular respondent might answer that life inevitably entails mistakes and disappointments, some of them ugly, bitter, painful, but that one simply goes on, that maturity involves acceptance of and adjustment to failings in others and oneself. A Christian might rejoin that it is the self which is at issue, that its pursuit of the disastrously illusory can be checked only when the self (selfishness) is overcome. The crucial difference for the Carmelites was that they were cloistered, and disastrous turns would affect the entire community. There was no convenient physical escape and no space, physical or otherwise, for rationalizing, denying, and self-excusing—the resorts of ordinary life. Disciplined, dedicated attention to one's shortcomings—the constitutional terms are "coulpe" and "faute"—and their correction was paramount. In the best light, a charity to oneself had to be practiced on behalf of all others.

The surest avenue to overcoming self lay in mortification, making self die. In this matter, another of Mère Geneviève's stories is illuminating. She taught the particular conjunction between suffering and love and how the one feeds from the other: to a sister who caused her a great deal of distress, she showed so many kindnesses in return that this sister eventually admitted herself vanquished by such charity. Mère Geneviève: "je n'agissais pas pour me vaincre, mais vraiment par affection; depuis que cette chère Soeur m'avait fait de la peine, je l'aimais davantage" ["I didn't respond in order to overcome myself but truly out of affection; as this dear sister had caused me pain, I loved her the more"].[32]

The clichéd assumption about masochism falls away here because there is no physical pain for physical pleasure, no sexual *frisson*. Indeed, addressing a prioress who grew stinging nettles so that they might make self-flagellation more bitter, Mère Geneviève cautioned about corporal penances altogether: "sans une grande prudence et un grand discernement, tout cela n'est que vanité et nourrit l'amour-propre" ["without a great deal of caution and discernment, all that amounts to vanity and nourishes self-love"].[33] She preferred less dramatic gestures and won the love of sisters by a Hebraic laying of hands upon their heads. As the Rule stipulated that no prioress could serve more than two consecutive terms, a total of six years, she was reelected as often as possible and was spared the priorate only when, at eighty, she was becoming too infirm from edema to stand up.

Mère Geneviève remains central to any account of Thérèse because this old woman was more than beloved by her and by all: in remarks from and about her, she provides a kind of prescriptive summa for Carmelite life in her time, including vital words which anticipate Thérèse's own lexical way. Gonzague, who had a unique perspective in succeeding her as prioress, found her "si *cachée*, si obéissante qu'on l'eût prise plutôt pour une novice que pour une ancienne Prieure et Fondatrice" ["so *hidden*, so obedient that one would have taken her for a novice rather than for an elderly prioress and foundress"].[34] When she characterizes Geneviève's simple confidence in God, it is as though the foundress had preempted the life story of this book's subject: "Une telle âme devait aller à Dieu par la voie de la *confiance* filiale, elle n'avait point d'autres rapports avec Lui que ceux d'un enfant avec le plus tendre des Pères" ["Such a soul must have gone to God by the way of childlike *trust*, her relationship to him was none other than that of a child with the most tender of Fathers"].[35] In short, the little way.

In her last years she became crippled, the edema in her extremities so grotesque that fingers and toes rotted off. She remained, even so, amiable and attentive to others and so grateful for the least solicitude that, as Gonzague puts it, one never approached her bed without feeling closer to God. But Mère

Geneviève herself was assailed with forebodings. On the sixtieth anniversary of her entering Carmel, she told the community from her bed: "Les plus grandes souffrances ne sont rien, mais ne pas voir Dieu! Être privée de Dieu!" ["The greatest sufferings are nothing, but not to see God! to be bereft of God!"]. She imagined herself plunged into fire but said that such torments were not so terrible as losing God. On the day before her death, she exclaimed that Christ had abandoned her, "moi qui vous disais toujours, In Te Domine Speravi!" ["I, who always said to you, In You Lord I have hoped!"].[36] A novice tried to convince her that her saintliness was such that she would be spared purgatory, a notion vouchsafed in the Constitution for all Carmelites who faithfully adhered to the Rule. It must have been dauntingly edifying to the novice, that for all the prescripts and regulations, what counted in the end was the expressive power of a person reduced to helplessness. Gonzague wrote at the end of the circulaire: "Elle était si humble! Si cachée! Elle a tant aimé et tant souffert!" ["She was so humble! So hidden! She loved so much and suffered so much!"].[37]

When she died, the Carmelites, unsure whether she would be permitted inhumation within the convent, had the attendant physician, Dr. de Cornière, remove her heart and preserve it in formaldehyde. It lies in a reliquary in the choir. After three weeks, burial of her remains in the chapel's sanctuary was authorized. So revered was Mère Geneviève that her casket was displayed for eight days and her obituary appeared in the town newspaper. For a good while after her death, the Carmelites were expecting miracles to be attested at the grave site. None came.

Still, Mère Geneviève remained the model of a living saint for the community. Quite in her shadow for fourteen years as the assistant, or sous-prieure, Sr. Fébronie de la Sainte-Enfance has the shortest of all obituary notices among the Carmelite circulaires. That is because she died during the influenza epidemic which struck the community in the winter of 1891–1892 and left even the prioress, Gonzague, too weak to write at length on the departed. Gonzague characterized her as "une âme véritablement intérieure, aimant la vie solitaire et cachée en Dieu" ["a genuinely interior soul, loving the solitary life that is hidden in God"], a remark which suggests the influence of the Imitatio Christi on conventual life at the time.[38] Fébronie once told a novice too timid to say anything of substance concerning her spiritual life that she should not have anything to say. And why? the diffident girl wondered. "Parce que votre âme est extrêmement simple, mais quand vous serez parfaite, vous serez encore plus simple, plus on s'approche du Bon Dieu, plus on se simplifie" ["Because your soul is extremely simple, but when you shall be perfect, you'll be even more simple; the closer one gets to God, the more one is made simple"].[39] This remark, altogether in keeping with the Carmelites' Constitution, serves as a foil to self-assertion, to any grandiloquent making much of self. Obscure, truly hidden lives are not advertised as saintly, and yet they are the very ones which serve, necessarily remotely, as exemplary of the perfection which the Carmel sisters were seeking. Unfortunately, the novice whom Sr. Fébronie was addressing became exceptionally adept at self-expression and self-depiction—not the surest avenue of humility.

Here was the quickest route ever taken at Carmel: another claimed by the epidemic, Sr. Madeleine de St.-Sacrament, was found dead in her cell bed, fully dressed as though expecting the departure. Gonzague, still weak, wrote that the community was devastated to lose someone so indefatigably devoted to it, but Sr. Madeleine had left a standard written request that nothing good be said of her and that prayers be said for souls in purgatory. Remarkably, given Gonzague's *circulaire* tribute, Sr. Madeleine asked the community forgiveness for all the trouble she had caused it "par mon mauvais caractère, mon orgueil, par mes manques de douceur, de charité, de régularité et de silence" ["by my wicked character, my pride, my lack of gentleness, charity, observance of the Rule, and silence"].[40] What eulogy could match that statement?

There is no point, however, in hallowing, glamorizing, or otherwise commending lives some of which were, even by the charitable claims in *circulaires*, nondescript. One sister, for example, who lived to eighty-three, was commended chiefly for her assiduity in caring for the poultry, or what might be called little daily tasks. Another, the bookish Sr. Saint-Jean de la Croix, proved a virtual isolate but followed all the rules with a perfect punctuality. When she spoke, it was chiefly through the mediation of one of the authors she had been reading. Rarely expansive, she once asked a novice to write a poem for her, and the resulting text, addressed to Christ and entitled "Comment je veux aimer" ["How I wish to love"], is so alive with solicitudes— *réjouir, charmer, consoler*—that it seems more fitly addressed to the recessive Sr. Saint-Jean than to Christ.[41] Its fervor glows in pointed contrast to the stern, prohibitive look from this sister past Céline's camera. She reminds us that one of the most frequent words in the Carmelites' argot was *cacher*, to remain withdrawn from the world and secreted within the heart of Christ, but the full sense of that hiddenness remains forever elusive, as it must.

Unabrasive, obedient, conscientiously adherent to what was expected of them, would these women have fared differently in a secular world of routine and of dutiful, unquestioning deference to male predominance? If the question seems cruel, the *circulaire* of Sr. Saint-Jean says straightforwardly that her entering Carmel was not by a calling, "une vocation d'attrait."[42] Conversely, one could argue that Carmel's conventual life was the only one they could have sustained; life in the larger, uncharitable world would have become unbearable for them. And yet, they had to be rigorously prepared for this life within walls.

Some might have felt keenly, at least for awhile, the pull of marital life or been embittered by the absence of its prospects. Marie du Sacré-Coeur was well on her way to old maidenhood when, at twenty-six, she was finally goaded into Carmel by Pichon. In the photos, Marie always seems a bit distracted, day-dreamy, and out of place. There remains no record of her ever having been courted but her sister Céline was. She alone of the Martin sisters knew directly the susceptibilities which might have taken her into marriage, even though, with her artistic ambitions, she might also have had an independent professional life.

There is an amusing series of photographs taken by her of a July 1894 outing at her uncle Isidore's chateau, La Musse, near Evreux. Entitled "Voyage excentrique aux Cordillères des Andes" and with quatrains composed for each scene by a novice of the Redemptorist order, Joseph de Cornière (son of the Carmel's physician), it includes Isidore's daughters, Jeanne and Marie (soon, Sr. Marie de l'Eucharistie), and son-in-law, Dr. Francis La Néele. The men armed with rifles, the party members pretend they are going through an Andean jungle. (Joseph had spent his novitiate in Chile.) In one photo, the rifles are aimed at an imaginary panther, Jeanne is recoiling in mock terror, Marie sounds a hunting horn, but the one dog available, Thérèse's spaniel, Tom, is already squatting indifferently before an imperturbable Céline. In another, trout fishing at a bridge, Céline smiles in coy amusement at the amiable Francis, as the unworldly Joseph looks down in blank awkwardness (see figure 4.4). It is a contrived bourgeois amalgam of leisurely poses, a somewhat labored pastime before the world of radios, automobiles, and cinema, but it makes clear that Céline, unlike all her sisters, could have found her way through the wicked world of the opposing sex.

She has left us this admission: "J'aurais désiré aimer et être aimée, la famille avait pour moi beaucoup d'attraits, mais surtout ce que j'estimais le plus c'était l'amour conjugal, il me semblait que cet amour était le dernier mot de deux coeurs unis. L'amour paternel et maternel me semblait idéal aussi, mais je pensais que les enfants étaient destinés à quitter les parents et avoir eux-mêmes d'autres affections et c'est à cause de sa stabilité que l'amour de l'époux et de l'épouse me paraissait supérieur" ["I would have liked to love and be loved. Family for me had lots of attractions, but what I especially esteemed was conjugal love. It seemed to me this love was the apex of two united hearts. Paternal and maternal love seemed ideal, too, but I figured children were bound to leave their parents and have their own ties and it's because of its stability that the love of spouses seemed to me superior"].[43]

Alone of the Martins, Céline knew that now old-fashioned virtue, renunciation.

After the postulant or entry term of six months, all sisters were obliged to undergo four years of training as novices, no matter at what age they entered. The minimal age was seventeen. They were assigned to a *maîtresse*, appointed by the prioress and running a term concurrent with hers, who was charged

FIGURE 4.4. The worldly life left behind: July 1894 at La Musse. Marie Guérin points out fish for Céline to shoot as Dr. Francis La Néele steadies her arm. His wife, Jeanne, waits with a net, while seminarian Joseph de Cornière, son of Carmel's physician, stands at the right. Copyright Archives du Carmel de Lisieux.

with maturing in them "la foi, la perfection, et la confiance en Dieu seul" ["faith, perfection, and reliance upon God alone"].[44] They wore white veils in order to be distinguished from the sisters of the choir, who wore black ones and recited the offices in Latin.[45]

One of the most beloved mistresses of novices, Sr. Marie des Anges, served nine years. Like Gonzague, she came from the aristocracy, her father a count and her home a chateau. As a first child, she was rejected by her father, who had wanted a son, and she grew up with a marked sense of unworthiness. She had left her family for Carmel reluctantly and only with help from her spiritual director, a Franciscan. Having suffered doubts about her faith throughout adolescence and having been challenged by natural affections and jealousies, she was sensitive to the needs of her novitiate charges and to the snares along their way. Her reminiscent self-characterizations suggest a painful awareness of limits: "J'étais certainement la plus incapable, la moins enrichie de ces dons et de ces charmes qui attirent, et que je voyais briller dans mes soeurs" ["I was undoubtedly the least competent and the least endowed with the gifts and charms which attract and which I saw shining in my sisters"]. As her time of youthful doubts convinced her that only fear of God forced her to practice religious virtues, once within Carmel she was subject to spells of bitter remorse: "je compris que j'étais coupable de tout, même des pires choses, sans la grâce" ["I realized I was guilty of everything, even the worst things, without grace"]. She managed to get through her profession of vows only because God had, as she put it, cast his eyes upon her *petitesse*.[46]

Particularly engaging in this profile is her version of the little way. To a novice with doubts and miseries she wrote: "Puisse la divine souffrance être l'élément de toute votre vie, plongez-vous dans cet océan sans fond, qu'il vous engloutisse comme Jésus, là seulement est la vie et la bonheur. Aimez toujours à être petite, si petite que le regard de Jésus tout seul puisse vous découvrir! . . Soyez pleine de confiance que le bon Jésus fera tout. . . . Jésus vous aime d'une tendresse de prédilection, payez-le en retour, et soyez heureuse d'aimer Jésus en souffrant pour Jésus!" ["That the divine suffering may be the substance of your entire life, plunge into this bottomless ocean that it may engulf you as it did Jesus, and there alone is life and happiness. Love always to be small, so small that only Jesus' sight can discover you! . . . Be full of confidence that Jesus will do everything. . . . Jesus loves you with a tender predilection, pay him in return for it, and be happy to love Jesus by suffering for him!"].[47] Smallness, confidence, unbounded love in gratitude to Christ—Sr. Marie forgot to mention only the little daily tasks.

These urgings, however, did not suffice for the distraught novice. And so her *maîtresse* wrote a second letter to her, addressing a disquieted conscience denominated only as *misère* in the response. The novice was worried that Jesus was not pleased with her. Sr. Marie took misery's inconsequence to its exponential terminus, arguing that it was a grace: "N'être rien, ne se sentir rien et surtout s'aimer rien, pour ne trouver tout qu'en Jésus, et par conséquent n'avoir d'appui qu'en Lui seul, quelle sécurité, quelle joie pour l'âme qui l'aime vraiment. Nous ne sommes rien mais Jésus est tout, nous n'avons rien, mais il a tout! Nous ne pouvons rien, mais lui peut tout et pour tout si nous sommes bien convaincues que nous, nous ne pouvons rien!" ["To be nothing, feel nothing, and especially love nothing, to find everything only in Jesus and so to have no stay save in him alone, what security, what joy for the soul which truly loves him. We're nothing but Jesus is everything, we've nothing but he has everything! We can do nothing but he can do all and for all if we're rightly convinced that we, we can do nothing!"].[48] This injunction to embrace one's nothingness bordered hard upon the doctrine known as quietism, which taught the total subordination of the will to God. Fortunately, Sr. Marie had also encouraged her charge toward love as a response to divine love, and so left her feeling not completely pointless and ineffectual.

In fact, Marie des Anges had written nothing original about nothing. She had almost certainly taken inspiration and notes from Pichon's retreat given at the Carmel in October 1887. He in turn had quoted Gaston de Sonis, a general who commanded papal zouaves under the banner of the Sacred Heart during the war with Prussia. De Sonis had died just two months before the retreat and left among his papers a final prayer: "Mon Dieu, me voici devant vous, pauvre, petit, dénué de tout. Je ne suis rien. Je n'ai rien. Je ne puis rien. Anéantissez-moi de plus en plus" ["My God, here I am before you: poor, small, denuded of everything. I am nothing, have nothing, can do nothing. Annihilate me more and more"].[49] Margaret de Beaune's little way here becomes a tiny or infinitesimal way, and we are left wondering how nothingness can be reduced. The point, however, is that Sr. Marie was part of a nearly consensual view about *rien*: Pichon had preached on it and everyone at the retreat would have taken the lesson to meditate upon, a lesson far more savory than hellfire sermons preached in retreats theretofore. But the notion that God is everything and we are nothing can be found as far back as Bérulle, who in his turn could have drawn it from San Juan de la Cruz or a sixteenth-century French translation of the *Imitatio Christi*.[50] It had long been a commonplace of Christian spirituality.

The Formative Texts of Carmelite Spirituality When Thérèse Entered the Carmel

Every sister had to know four definitive texts for her life within Carmel: the Constitutions, including the Rule, which guided her within the Teresian Reform; the *Papier d'exaction*, which set out the regulations of daily conventual life; the *Direction spirituelle*, which assisted her inner development; and Madre Teresa's *Camino de Perfección*. All of these readings were complementary: the Constitution served chiefly to root the Gallic sisterhood within its Hispanic tradition and what might be called its penal code; the *Papier* helped them to sustain the disciplines that were requisite each day; the *Direction* attended to their end goal, perfection of soul; and Teresa abided in maternal wisdom. Hence, a certain dynamism of past, present, and future. Each text had to be internalized in spirit and letter so as to preclude the first of faults, ignorance of the rules. The sisters also had access to a library of devotional readings, but these four books give us the definitive profile of Carmelite spirituality.

The foundational edition known to Thérèse was printed in 1865 and entitled *Règle primitive et Constitutions des Religieuses de l'Ordre de Notre-Dame du Mont-Carmel selon la réformation de Sainte-Thérèse pour les monastères de son Ordre en France*. Formidable as that sounds, it was less than five inches tall and less than three wide. Thirty-seven introductory pages established the Hispanic origins, papal guidance, and French history of the Discalced Order. The Constitution proper runs to twenty chapters and fewer than two hundred pages.

The *Règle* profiled the tasks of the prioress and the mistress of novices, the community's two chief officers, the latter so important that the prioress could assume the title herself, if she deemed no one else fit for it. The novices' mistress was enjoined to help them to break their own wills. Put positively, "sa charge est de nourrir des âmes en lesquelles Dieu puisse demeurer" ["her responsibility is to nourish souls in which God can dwell"].[51] Another officer, the *zélatrice*, seems little more than a spy upon sororal imperfections, which she observed and reported to the prioress, but faults were looked upon like symptoms of a disease which needed vigilant tending and efficient cure. Humiliation and mortification were prescribed as efficient ways of overcoming the natural self. In Thérèse's time, the post of *zélatrice* was alternated weekly (Pauline abolished it after she was appointed prioress for life by Pope Pius XI in 1923) and served the very busy prioress, but the abundance of possible "faults" the Constitution itemized and ranked according to gravity would have kept even the most remiss of sisters on her toes. The enumeration occupies sixty pages and makes the most engaging reading because it profiles what could go wrong within the tight politics of the convent. The Carmelite community knew that obedience in seemingly small matters was indispensable because they implicated far greater ones.

A weekly meeting, known as *le Chapitre*, was held in which each sister accused herself or another of infractions. The prioress meted out punishments in a charitable and equitable manner, according to the offender's intent and previous record. If that sounds like a criminal justice system, it was mitigated by the tacit intent of sustaining and developing the spiritual well-being of everyone in the community. Laxness or indulgence of weaknesses could harm inner and outer discipline irreversibly. One's accuser, then, was performing a charitable mission, helping in the correction of a fault before it became habitual.

The offenses ranged from light to very serious. Of the former, speaking idly, eating or drinking without permission (beyond the refectory), laughing or causing laughter during the chanting of offices, even singing off key were punished by imposed silence or penitential prayers. Moderate offenses included late arrival at or absence from the chanting, speaking out of line, raising one's voice when accused or otherwise contesting an accusation, and refusing to forgive one's offender. Disciplinary action was reserved to the prioress but could also be delegated.

Grave offenses were measured in three degrees. Speaking injuriously to a sister or reproaching her to cause shame, lying, defending one's fault, violating fasts, entering another sister's cell at any time without leave from the prioress—these transgressions were punished by isolating the offender at the refectory: she would have bread and water either at the end of the dining table or in the very center of the hall. Worse than those actions could bring as many as forty days of bread and water as well as privation of a voice in the *Chapitre* and of any assigned functions, such as work in the infirmary, linen room, or kitchen. Faults of that sort included irreverence toward the prioress, striking another sister, sowing discord, or attempting contact with people outside the community. Accused of any such thing, the sister would be expected to prostrate herself at once, beg forgiveness, expose her shoulders, and receive disciplinary action from the prioress,[52] which likely meant sequestration in a cell. The Constitution mentions excommunication (and even imprisonment) for the weightiest offenses: apostasy, incorrigibility (the refusal of penance), shows of violence, sensuality, or "crimes qui au monde mériteraient la mort" ("crimes which in the outer world deserve the death penalty").[53] I find most intriguing under this rubric the offense of owning property: anyone thus discovered or confessing ranked with apóstates and lesbians, and if a sister were found after her death to have owned property, she would be denied ecclesiastical burial.

A host of infractions not specified under the list of *coulpes* would have challenged the discretion and judgment of both the prioress and novice mistress. Here are two attested examples: during a retreat, a sister who had been in Carmel for seven years was discovered thumbing a fashion magazine (where on earth did she find it?).[54] The same sister, when her natural sister's profession of vows was being delayed by the prioress, made an issue of it after Sr. Aimée de Jésus observed that the prioress had every right to pose such a test: "Il s'agit d'un genre d'épreuves qu'on ne doit pas donner!" ["It's a matter of tests which one ought not to give!"] was the emotional retort. The first offense might well be called trivial, but the second was not: it was implicitly challenging the authority of the prioress. Sowing discord? The issue cannot be pressed because the offender in both these instances has always been held up for unblemished behavior and unswerving adherence to the rules. Her name was Sr. Thérèse de l'Enfant-Jésus de la Sainte-Face.[55]

When she acknowledged late in her life that she had not been an exemplary sister, one wonders what infractions of the *Papier d'exaction* she might have committed. (The edition of this text she used was issued in 1889, the year she took the habit, following nine months as a postulant.) *Exaction* signifies here not imposition but conscientious application and punctuality in carrying out instructions. Central to all of these for Carmel was silence, both exterior and interior. The *Papier*'s injunction to be "seule avec le Seul" ["alone with the Alone"]—the phrase hints at Bérulle's neo-Platonism—could not be followed amid the distractions of ordinary life. Sustained silence, interior and exterior, we in this age, enthralled by incessant mechanical noises and violence, cannot easily comprehend, but for the Carmelites it was the essence of prayer: by hushing self, one invited God to enter into self. Massillon characterized prayer as "le canal des grâces," the conduit of graces, but we might liken it to the arterial system: anyone would panic to be told arteries were 75 percent blocked and auguring a heart attack. Prayer through silence was and remains the Carmelites' vital circulatory system.

So rigorous was this injunction to silence, ideally, that the Carmel employed a kind of sign language to further, economically and charitably, *l'esprit érémitique*. It was an ancient and gentle custom in this order that if a sister began to speak superfluously, her interlocutor would prostrate herself, then the chatterer would do the same, and finally both would rise together in silence. A sister coming upon two idle talkers would prostrate herself before them; they would get her message. Places where talking of any sort was forbidden included the dormitory, refectory, cloisters, choirs, chapters, and garden. That left very little space apart from the recreation room, where the sisters spent two hours daily together, with the admissible luxury of a fireplace, the convent's only heated room. Even there, it was deemed charitable to listen rather than to talk. Gossip, including worldly news, was proscribed, even though at Lisieux's Carmel, the prioress Gonzague purveyed such information with pleasure and did not go unheard, most of the Carmelites being of local provenance.

Gonzague's behavior reminds us that these sisters were French, and the first rule of being French is to violate the overabundance of legalistic details and prescriptions the government weighs upon secular life. The difference is that this community was under the yoke of Christ, not that of a loveless, tax-exacting bureaucracy, and everyone was a close example for others to follow, to learn from, even to correct. If they did not love one another, they were reminded that they were to try to do so.

Even as she had prescribed *alpargates*, a Spanish sandal quieter than the usual, leathery sort, Teresa of Avila left a sequence of signs for minimizing noise. The sign signifying the prioress was a finger's touch on the brow; for the mistress of novices, a finger by the veil's border; for an urgent permission, one kissed the prioress's scapular; to request that someone approach, the hand was raised with thumb and forefinger joined at the tip. The library was signaled by folding the hands together and opening them. Lowering one's brow onto both open hands referred to the infirmary. The laundry was meant by both hands in a scrubbing motion. The doctor was indicated by a finger on the pulse and the gardener by the motion of raking.

.And they worked. The Rule told them that those who did not, would not eat. Laundering was a collective effort and one allowing conversation. It furnishes the occasion for two of Céline's best photographs. Each sister had to clean her cell every Wednesday and Saturday, but four sisters, known as *converses*, were responsible for meals and housekeeping. Even beyond physical exertions, all of the sisters were at work simply observing the exactions. They were enjoined to take on tasks repugnant to them (an arachnophobe, for example, was obliged to sweep dark recesses) even as at the refectory they were supposed to take ample helpings of foods they did not like and lesser ones of those they did. These very small, yet telling examples of self-mortification reminded them that they had not chosen Carmel for comfort and convenience.

The *Papier* told them to walk so softly as not to be heard; to keep their hands under their scapular unless carrying something (which, if broken, one would have to carry with its pieces tied round the neck); not to complain of minor unpleasantnesses such as winter's cold and summer's heat, lassitude or illness. Finally, bringing us back to Céline's camera, there was the claim of poverty, that sisters would not have nor desire for their own use anything not strictly necessary. Fortunately for us, Pauline as prioress allowed the camera and all its accessories, and there is no record of anyone's objection to this supremely bourgeois appurtenance.[56]

We are missing the ringing purity of Carmel, its bells. The *Papier*'s austerity yields briefly to a simple charm as we read its descriptions of the tintinnabulations (clangs!) reminding sisters of the day's schedule. These were not an alarm but a summons, and sisters had to attend to this precise chiming as though hearing God's own voice, as Aña de San Bartolomeo delightfully put it. The daily schedule was strictly appointed; each sister had to proceed according to it, and that meant listening. For example, three short double soundings of the bell signified gathering in the chapter. Not every sounding was collective. Near the bell outside of the choir, there was a list of all the sisters, with a sequence of strokes marked for each name, a kind of code which, while possibly disturbing everyone in summoning one person, meant that at every sound, each listened attentively. At three o'clock every afternoon, the Passion was recalled by a bell which prostrated everyone in the community, no matter where she was. The infirmary's bell, hung outside its entrance, had a sequence for emergencies, including one calling everyone to the bedside of a dying sister. There was even a bell within the recreation hour: the prioress sounded a *sonnette* whenever she needed to interrupt the talking and laughing.[57]

Punctuality regarding the bells exemplified those seemingly small things to which one had to be attentive. It extended as well to the refectory, where sisters ate with their eyes constantly lowered, without turning their heads or looking at others, including the sister who was serving. Latecomers were obliged to prostrate themselves in the middle of the hall until the presiding sister signaled them to rise. It was also here that sisters practiced mortifications for such things as oversleeping—they rose at 4:45 a.m.—which entailed wearing one's pillow suspended from one's neck. Mortifications, always voluntary, might prompt a miscreant to kiss the feet of all her sisters and then the scapular of the prioress.

Latecoming could disrupt the refectory readings, which were continuous (see figure 4.5). In our culture, where talking is much more valued than listening, even as noise is more valued than silence, it is hard to imagine any sustained concentration of ears during a meal, but so it was at Carmel twice daily. (What we would call breakfast amounted to a thick soup at 8 a.m., eaten standing and without readings. During fasts and vigils, there was no meal at that time.) During the first repast (at 11 a.m., except in summer, when it was at 10 a.m., 11:30 through Lent), passages from the Constitutions were read,

FIGURE 4.5. The refectory at the Carmel of Lisieux, where *circulaires* and saints' lives were read aloud. Copyright Archives du Carmel de Lisieux.

then saints' lives, and the *circulaires* of the recently deceased. Pauline introduced to Gonzague a book much read in the Martin home, Dom Guéranger's *L'année liturgique*, which was then read on the eves of festival days. Except for fish, which was inexpensive, the Carmelite diet was vegetarian. At the second, simpler meal, soup and a vegetable were served or, during fasts, bread and fruit from 6:00 p.m. to 6:45. Martyrologies and lives of the desert fathers were read as well as passages from the *Imitatio Christi*, the *Breviaire Romain*, and the life of Madre Teresa.

In hygienic matters, the *Papier* affords some surprises. A sister had to wash her hands every morning but her face at least once a week; she brushed her teeth at least twice a week and asked leave once every two months to cut her hair. There were no mirrors to feed vanity; one learned literally to see oneself as others did.[58] When anticlericalism became more than usually menacing, the sisters started to grow their hair longer in anticipation of a precipitous and enforced move back into the world, as had happened during the Revolution. Thérèse wore a wig for her performance as Jeanne d'Arc (January 1895), but by the time she died, her long hair was her own. In 1794, the expelled sisters of Compiègne had grown their hair out, only to have it cut once more, before they were beheaded.

The glory of the *Papier* lies not so much in its strictures as in one hundred pages of appended remarks about and from the Spanish Carmelites, that hardy generation of founding mothers who formed the vital link to St. Teresa herself. We read of their discerning balance of gravity and gaiety: "les dévotions sombres et alambiquées n'étaient de leur goût" ["brooding and convoluted devotions were not to their taste"], that they did not tolerate ill humor, boredom, or lethargy and least of all "les craintes serviles et scrupuleuses, ainsi que ces tristes obscurités qui retardent la perfection de tant d'âmes" ["base and worrisome fears as well as these gloomy darknesses which slow down the perfection of so many souls"].[59] They did not find the French souls so tough as the Spanish but that did not deter them from shrewd counsel.

This comes from Aña de San Bartolomeo: "Tenez pour assuré que les personnes du monde souffrent davantage faisant leur volonté, que vous ne faites renonçant à la vôtre. Songez à la condition où vous vous trouveriez si vous étiez assujetties à un homme dur et de fâcheuse humeur" ["Take it for certain that people in the world suffer more in doing their will than you do in renouncing yours. Imagine the situation you'd find yourself in if you were subjected to a harsh and wicked-humored man"]. Telling her sisters in Christ that "nous sommes entre ses créatures les plus infidèles et les plus méconnaissantes" ["we're among his most disloyal and most stubbornly proud creatures"], she adds, "Que de fois, en effet, nous parlons de religion! Et cependant je ne sais si nous connaissons bien ce que c'est" ["So often we talk about religion, and yet I don't know if we're truly aware of what it is"].[60]

From Isabella de los Angeles we read of charity subsuming every other virtue. All the world's evils, she wrote, come from the absence of love for others. Nor did she underestimate the costs of charity. The ethics discussed in her notes furnish a prolegomenon to Thérèse's Manuscript C with its account of her efforts for the marginal and rejected within the Carmel at Lisieux. No matter the outward semblance of a neighbor, says Isabella, "il a une âme en laquelle Dieu habite, et peut-être même que celui qui nous semble le plus imparfait et négligent, est verteux devant Dieu; ainsi il est très dangereux de juger des actions d'autrui, et l'on s'y trompe très souvent, pensant que la vertu est vice, et que ce qui est imperfection est vertu" ["he has a soul in which God dwells, and maybe even he who seems to us most imperfect and remiss is virtuous before God; so, it's very dangerous to judge another's actions and one is often deceived in thinking that virtue is vice and that what is imperfection is virtue"].[61]

No less abundant are monitions by prayers and *sentences* (from the Latin *sententiae*, signifying judgments), which constitute much of the third formative text, *Direction spirituelle pour s'occuper saintement avec Dieu à l'usage des Novices de l'ordre de Notre Dame du Mont Carmel* [*Spiritual Direction for Saintly Occupation with God, To Be Used by Novices in the Order of Our Lady of Mount Carmel*], published in Poitiers in 1869. They include the great mystical lights of the Reform, Teresa and San Juan de la Cruz, both of whom strike minatory notes bound to humble and intimidate or, to put it positively, to encourage the conventual soul in mortifications. Teresa, for example, urges that while bewailing one's past life and the lukewarmness of one's present, one should live in fear by pondering what one lacks on the way to heaven. Juan warns against the presumption that penances ensure one's perfection because such spiritual ripening comes not in virtues the soul knows but in those which God alone knows, "une chose cachée et secrète" ["a hidden, secret matter"]. The only satisfaction one can find lies in a blessed nothingness: "O heureux néant!"[62] It is easy to see from these virtual no-win prescriptions—mortify yourself to sanctification but remember that God's ways are not ours so everything is presumption—why many sisters lived in acute, even punitive anxiety about their unworthiness and their souls' destiny beyond death. It is not fair to fault Jansenism alone for bleakness. It is also clear why the physics of Christian love as set down by François de Sales performed the charitable rescue of souls (both lay and religious) fixed upon their ineligibility for a blessed life in God.

And the cross? As Christ's life was one of self-humbling, with humiliation, contempt, and tormenting death visited upon him, the Body of Christ can fare no better, at least for those vowed to an imitation of Christ. It can be only an austere life of renunciation and continuous self-denial. To outsiders, Christian conventual life seems a kind of death watch kept upon the self, sustained by prayer, both contemplative and intercessory; by the ritualistic binding with God through Communion and confession; and by perpetual examination of one's inevitable failings within community, the exterior "coulpes" addressed by Carmelites in their weekly chapter. The light through the clouds comes only in words of love and on love, but even that love is sacrificial and exacting. It comes not as an impulse nor a passion but as a command.

The *Direction* walks us through the austerities of the death watch, hour by hour: a Carmelite's day. It cues the novice with prayers from her first waking moment, as when dressing herself with the *toque*, the white cover under her veil: "Pensez que cette blancheur vous représente la pureté de conscience que vous devez avoir pour plaire à Dieu" ["Think that this whiteness represents the purity of conscience you must have in order to please God"]. In choir, she is enjoined to pray a heartfelt adoration of God even as she is "abîmée au plus profond de mon néant" ["sunk in the depths of my nothingness"], where Juan found that mystery of happiness. Seeking forgiveness for sins, the novice asks the grace of dying rather than ever to displease God.

Then, François de Sales arrives for the sequences of mental prayer: preparation, meditation, resolution. He suggests that the novice prepare herself as the prodigal son did before his father, with "défiance de soi-même et confiance en Dieu" ["distrust of self, reliance upon God"]. Meditating on the horror of sin and "our" wicked inclinations and passions which hinder "our" advancement, the novice dwells compassionately and with "l'abandon de soi-même" ["a giving up of self"] upon the sorrows of Christ. The most uplifting notes come here, at the resolution. In the Salesian view, this act is coefficient with grace itself in securing gifts from God, provided it be performed with humility and *confiance*. Even so, the genuinely humble soul will ask for grace to carry out the resolve, and for that asking, de Sales urges that the novice speak to God "par un colloque amoureux" ["by a lover's talk"]. When faced with spiritual dryness, that inability to affirm God's presence, bear with its pains, recognize your unworthiness, and trouble yourself no further. A shrewd man, de Sales.

The sequences of each day according to the *Direction* provide a singular equipoise between abjection and fervor, between self-abasement in contrition and exaltations. For choir at 6 a.m., for example, a sister prayed for purification of her heart of all that might displease God: "Ayez compassion de ma pauvre âme languissant et pleine d'imperfections. . . . je me trouve si pleine de péchés, si négligente en votre service et si froide en votre amour" ["Have compassion on my poor soul, languishing and full of imperfections. . . . I find myself so full of sins, so negligent in your service and so cold in love for you"], and yet this same miserable soul would be praying within the same hour for infidel nations, heretics, schismatics, and, not least, "plusieurs mauvais chrétiens qui vivent dans l'oubli de leur salut" ["many bad Christians who live forgetful of their salvation"].[63] At *matins* and *lauds*, beginning at 9 p.m., she was called to imagine herself before God's throne, chanting in the midst of countless angels and saints but when prostrated for some *coulpe* earlier in the day, she was to imagine herself deserving to be trampled under foot as an enemy of God.

No one could sustain such psychological tensions without escaping into a salvific (in its way) routine of motions or into some sort of madness. It is a relief to read that Madre Teresa did not want outbursts of laughter during the recreational hours; they were unseemly and disorderly, but at least they occurred. Every Carmelite, as a sinner aspiring to become a saint, was certain to be human along the way. The point against undue levity was that joking usually comes at another person's expense, a sin against charity. More likely was the other extreme, a melancholy or despondency which isolated its victim and implicitly injured the community. Among any Carmel's women at least a few were bound to be withdrawn, moody, and marginalized.

The metabolism, as it were, of recognizing one's imperfections and resolving to overcome them, on the one hand, and striving toward saintly perfection, on the other, each process necessarily abetted by grace—all of that defines the Christian itinerary, generally. In Carmel as in other orders, it simply and unequivocally subsumed all of a life. Life itself became ritual, stylized, free of the innumerable distractions, pulls, and grinding vulgarities of the extramural world, a distillation toward sanctity. The mewed-up life Thérèse knew has changed since Vatican II—sisters can leave Carmel for such things as voting and medical appointments—but the definitive coherence and discipline abide.

If the scale of faults was much reduced in comparison with secular living, awareness of them was immeasurably intensified. Besides, the requisite contempt for oneself could extend indefinitely into the soul's recesses. A sister would remain in her own eyes a sinner to the end; only others' eyes could see her lovingly, as the Carmelites of Lisieux did their Mère Geneviève. The *Direction* mercifully reminds its novice reader that Christ's disciples themselves had earned reproaches from their master: "Ils se contentaient de porter paisiblement cet état d'imperfection et de s'humilier profondément dans la vue de tant de faiblesses" ["They made do to bear calmly this state of imperfection and to humble themselves deeply in view of so many weaknesses"].[64]

Such mitigations restrained the urge some novices felt to mortify themselves in excess. A nostrum told the Carmel that God heals the very wounds he inflicts, but some novices, driven by adolescent exuberance, took that wounding upon some initiative of their own. Prioresses and mistresses had to be vigilant about tendencies to an indulgence that might nowadays be considered worthy of clinical attention. In raising this issue, we pass beyond the formative texts to another group of writings which, as a composite, offers the best profile of how Carmelite life was lived.

What the *Circulaires* Said

That composite is the *circulaire*, the death notice as biography which a prioress wrote and sent to all other Carmels upon a sister's demise. As a genre, it goes back to the medieval "rouleau des morts" ["roll of deceased"] sent from a monastery to others within the order, announcing a friar's death and asking for prayers on his behalf. Before the eighteenth century, it amounted to little more than a memento, but thereafter it included appreciative notes on the virtues of the departed. The *circulaire* depicted the sister's calling into religious life, usually signaled by a visitation or a miracle; then, her conduct within Carmel, including offices held and particular devotions; finally, how, through illness, she came to face death. Hence, there emerges a certain procedural uniformity. Pious phrases about the perfume of a sister's life, flower imagery being drawn from the *Song of Songs*, tended toward iteration because this writing was based upon itself as model.

As a Carmelite's life was by disposition and prescript a hidden one (no birth name was indicated), there would seem to be little to say, but some prioresses found inspiration for more than conventional portraiture. Even those sisters who had asked for no notice were accorded something: was it fair to deny others information and the occasion to mourn? Some *circulaires* ran to no more than two pages; others to as many as forty, especially when the subject had been a *fondatrice*, the organizer of a new Carmel, or a long-lived prioress. They became generational histories etched in reverent, even affectionate gratitude. A prioress at the Nantes Carmel took a year and a half to write a ninety-six-page tribute to her predecessor, Mère Agathe de Jésus, replete with extensive quotations. From this example, the Martin sisters might well have taken inspiration in making Thérèse's writings into her *circulaire*.

These death bulletins, averaging about forty each year, prove valuable first in getting us beyond Thérèse so that we glimpse Carmelites without cultish glamour, truly obscure, not trumpeted lives, yet it is they who take us back to Lisieux and the Carmel refectory where the *circulaires* were read. After the reading, each was available in the convent's library, and the more fetching ones would have been discussed in the recreational hours. Implicitly hortatory, the *circulaire* was also occasion to deal justly with the deceased subject's hardships, such as adversities in her childhood or difficulties in her adjusting to the Carmel's stringency. In such tenebrous passages, the subject comes to singular life but also to death: not a few Carmelites died young.

Vital statistics, were they available, could not be weighed against Carmel's asceticism because postulants had to show themselves of good physical constitution before acceptance. Mortality in Carmel was likely no greater than in the outer world. Still, physical (and mental) disorders could be hidden, even from the postulant herself. When parents objected to their daughter's request to enter Carmel, one very real concern was health: the young girl was either already considered sickly or deemed not strong enough to endure the legendary severities of Carmelite life, including fasts and unheated rooms.[65] By the Church's own rules, Thérèse was not permitted to fast until she was twenty-one, after six years in Carmel.

Some illnesses were indubitably psychogenic, based on traumas suffered in childhood. Chief among these would be the loss of a parent, especially the mother. Carmelites almost invariably came from thoroughly religious families, with the mother a model of piety as well as fertility. Spiritual directors would usually identify among several children in the home the girl exceptionally disposed to conventual life. She would be noticeably prayerful, withdrawn, and, if from bourgeois circumstances, charitable toward the poor. Some early sign of recoiling from the world—an indisposition to play ordinary childhood games—was desiderated. Totally absent from the prioress's account was any indication that the sister had sought to escape such circumstances as a marital prospect or some other variety of male harassment. A generalized horror of secular life, an almost instinctive recoil from its cheats sufficed. Curiously, the positive example of family life had not imposed itself. At convent school—the more affluent were tutored at home—the girls had learned much about communal rigors and experienced a protective exclusivity.

Most important for the director and the postulant was some indication of a literal calling: a voice heard in prayer, during an office, or altogether unexpectedly elsewhere. Thérèse could have adduced any number of significant moments or signs, Pranzini the murderer furnishing the most dramatic. This kind of summons is what Marie Martin never received; Pichon's prodding does not quite count, but what did count was her Visitandine education, Pauline's support, and the welcoming Gonzague. The three Martin Carmelites were given a splendid example of a calling in the very first of the *circulaires* Thérèse heard, shortly after its publication on April 10, 1888.

Sr. Saint-Gabriel of Toulon's Carmel had died at age twenty-six, after six years in the order. At nine, she had felt an invisible hand at church pulling her toward the altar and had asked who was leading her. "C'est moi," she heard. She became notably compassionate toward the elderly and infirm sisters. She often deprived herself of sleep in meditating on the Passion, her soul "pénétrée du desir d'alléger les douleurs du Coeur de Jésus" ["penetrated with the desire to relieve the sufferings of Jesus' Heart"], and she won from a retreat director this estimate passed to the prioress: "Vous avez une vraie petite sainte que peut-être vous ne connaissez pas, car elle prend un grand soin de se cacher" ["You have a true little saint you maybe don't know about since she takes great care to hide herself"]. The novitiate had been hard for her because she was weighed down with a sense of her unworthiness. The prioress attributed the pensiveness of Sr. Saint-Gabriel to the disease, unspecified, which wasted her away, but she noted that this young woman was unfailingly cheerful in the recreations. Facing death, she had said: "Mon plus grand sacrifice en quittant la terre est de ne plus voir cette belle nature qui m'a fait tant de bien à l'âme. Que de choses les moindres brins d'herbe m'ont apprises!" ["My greatest sacrifice in leaving the earth is no longer seeing this beautiful nature which has done so much good to my soul. What things the least blades of grass have taught me!"].[66]

Simplicity, humility, charity, littleness, joy—all of the theresian ingredients are anticipated in this four-page account. Perhaps if in dying Sr. Saint-Gabriel had been ordered to write of her life, it would have been an account as appealing, as eloquent as the great Carmelite autobiographies. But the Toulon prioress could not have given that order. Sr. Saint-Gabriel was illiterate.

In these necrologies, certain phrases of approbation recur to virtual formulae. Prioresses reading each other's reports developed a convention, yet each sister as subject challenged the prioress's charitable skill in drawing a genuinely informed portrait: the Carmelite ideal had been set down in the formative texts and at its heart was the disciplined obscuration of self, a lesson in the life lived toward spiritual perfection. Diseases had prominence as exceptional occasions when that process was measured by the victim's words, her suffering, her exemplum for others in an inspirational conformity. What we call personality or individuality would not have counted for anything. The convincing particulars of the unusual, like those instructive blades of grass for Sr. Saint-Gabriel, lie inconspicuously in the report.

The subjects for their part tended toward conformable word and practice as well. Here is one who covered the ground unusually well: Sr. Euphrasie du Saint-Sacrement, who died in the Tours Carmel after thirty-five years within it. From a devout family, she early showed signs of gravity by not being disposed to play with others. Her parents had taught her that she belonged to God—no need, then, for a voice calling—and Carmel had been for her "un paradis terrestre." Her only reported defect was excessive charity as she laughed with the happy and wept with the sad. Her quoted words are textbook perfect: "Mener une vie humble, cachée, inconnue, vivre pour Dieu seul, voilà ce qui m'est destiné et ce qui me réjouit. . . . Que l'on est heureux de n'être rien" ["To lead a lowly, hidden, unknown life, to live for God alone, that's my fate and what delights me. . . . How happy one is to be nothing"]. As today a young woman is complimented on her beautiful eyes, in Carmel it was "un sourire céleste," a heavenly smile illuminating the face, as it did this sister's. She savored humiliations as tests, remaining calm and serene throughout: "La confiance en Dieu était sa vertu favorite" ["Trust in God was her favorite virtue"]; "j'aime Dieu de tout mon coeur, je m'efforce de lui plaire, et puis tout est fini, je vais mon petit chemin" ["I love God with my whole heart and compel myself to please him, and then all is done and I go my little way"]. She was even able to sustain the inevitable spells of dryness with equanimity and good humor: "Je sens profondément ma misère, je ne suis qu'une bien pauvre petite créature, mais puisque la bonté de Dieu me tolère ainsi, pourquoi ne me supporterais-je pas moi-même?" ["I'm deeply aware of my wretchedness. I'm only a poor little creature, but since God's goodness puts up with me, why should I not put up with myself?"]. And last, the flawless charity shown, of all places, on her deathbed. Asked if she were suffering, she returned the question, "Mais vous-même, ma soeur, vous?" ["But what about yourself, my sister, what about you?"].[67]

This Carmelite by her conduct and words seems generically right, a summa in the flesh of what Madre Teresa would have expected—flawless to the point of becoming dull. She is opaque in her goodness, even making the most of those worrisome scruples. Most important, however, especially for novices listening to her story over the plate of vegetables and cheese, was the lesson that the little Carmelite way to perfection could be realized. Sr. Euphrasie's life had become a sermon in itself, the only one she was ever allowed to preach.

To a young Carmelite in 1888, not the least engaging part of a *circulaire* would have been those passages which compel the attention of a lay reader even today, the story of how the girl survived her early years in the outer world and finally came in from its storms of pointlessness. Some faced such forbidding circumstances that moving almost always alone against them attests to their courage and tenacity, yet the salient qualities which the Carmel would have looked for in an applicant, known as a subject, would have been the very ones likely to keep the girl at home: humility, chiefly, and submissiveness to authority. If a girl had to show herself obstinate and determined to leave home and enter a convent, what was to happen to the obstinacy and determination once she was within the cloister?

Prioresses proved deft in their explanations of conduct based upon the subjects' own stories told in recreations. A girl who had to defy her parents won commendation; she was, after all, giving herself to God. What was parental objection, sometimes fierce and unyielding, if the girl had been given a divine summons? Some parents would insist upon a year's waiting, only to have to argue the matter anew: "Ce consentement, hélas! lui fut énergiquement refusé. Mais cette âme généreuse ne devait s'arrêter devant aucun obstacle. A celui-ci elle opposa ses prières et ses larmes et enfin sa volonté inébranlable" ["Consent, alas, was vigorously refused. But this generous soul wasn't going to be stopped by any obstacle. Against it she opposed her prayers, her tears and her unvanquishable will"].[68] To the end of her life, Sr. Thérèse de Saint-Joseph of the Albi Carmel had to combat this willfulness, but she did it with wit. Whenever reproached for one of her imperfections, she would say to the prioress, "Voilà, ma Mère, un fruit de mon jardin!" ["There you are, my Mother, a fruit from my garden!"].

Some sisters had a calling early in their lives, sometimes at an altar or in a moment of prayer. An unusual summons had come for Sr. Magdeleine-de-Jésus of Bordeaux, who, at five, while making doll clothes, suddenly felt herself "comme investie et envahie par une présence de Dieu qu'elle n'aurait pas su définir alors, mais qui lui faisait comprendre qu'elle était aimée d'une manière ineffable et infinie" ["as though empowered, invaded by a divine presence she'd not have been able to define at the time but which made her realize that she was ineffably, infinitely loved"].[69] Others made less spectacular claims. Once asked the secret of her calling, a sister who even in recreations remained quiet recalled Christ's parable of the banquet where the guests made excuses not to come and so the host called in people from the street: "C'est parmi ceux-là que le bon Dieu rencontra mon âme" ["It's among such as those that the good Lord will find my soul"].[70] For unobstreperousness, it would be hard to beat that.

Most of the future Carmelites were directed toward Carmel by heedful priests serving in retreats or as spiritual directors. These clerics had to be supremely tactful before resistant parents. The girl who showed herself meditatively withdrawn at an early age seemed convent bound to a priest, but to her parents she seemed fated for spinsterhood: they would expect her to remain at home, unmarried and indefinitely waiting, as the euphemism went, to close their eyes. Many entered Carmel only when one or both parents had died, some subjects entering at forty or older, but age was presumed to work against them: these older women had to overcome the worldly ways to which they had long grown accustomed. Adolescent subjects were immature but finally docile. The *circulaires* do not, of course, record the numbers of women who failed to remain in Carmel.[71] Lisieux's novice sister Marie-Philomène left its Carmel when her mother was dying, only to be told at the deathbed that she could have done her mother much more good by praying for her in the convent. She was allowed to return to Carmel only after nine years.[72]

Those least likely to reach saintly perfection easily were noted for their shows of independence, impetuosity, or, as was noted of Niort's Sr. Elizabeth de Jésus, "une fierté peu commune" ["a singular pride"]. To a screaming show of childhood stubbornness, her father had warned her that God would come and put the family in hell, to which she replied that she would shut the door on God's fingers. When her pious sister told her that eternal blessedness meant looking forever at God, Elizabeth said she would be bored of that within half an hour.[73] When a bishop was summoned to the house to hear of such outrages, he surprised the family by saying that this little devil would one day become an angel. Stories like this were fetched up at recreation hours for everyone's amusement and edification: the greater the youthful pride, the greater the triumph in the sister's overcoming it. Some sisters, however, died before ripened: "le travail intérieur nous semblait loin d'être complet" ["the interior effort seemed to us far from complete"], a prioress at Rheims wrote of an acutely sensitive sister dying at twenty-seven, so feverish she could not be induced to kiss a crucifix.[74]

A prioress might have felt some joyful reassurance when reporting that her deceased sister had spent a life free of scruples and dryness—Madre Teresa referred to such untroubled women as saintly simple—and such testimony is eloquent in its way: "On parle toujours de peines intérieures, d'épreuves, qu'est-ce donc que tout cela? Il y a quelque temps je pensais à mes péchés, j'étais touchée jusqu' aux larmes. Est-ce là une peine intérieure?" ["There's always talk about inner pains and trials, what's it all about? Some time ago I thought about my sins and was moved to tears. Is that an inner pain?"].[75] Too many stories, however, record times of doubt or indifference for such spells to be reckoned abnormal. Besides, saints' lives were replete with them: St. Vincent de Paul for many years carried a written copy of the Credo with him because he could *not* believe in God.

The *circulaires* suggest a pronounced ambivalence about spiritual testings. On one hand, an upright, rule-bound sister would walk straight upward to God. The Rule and Constitutions pledged the way of perfection, including exemption from purgatory. A sister having followed that way "ne connaissait pas ces retours qui naissent des susceptibilités d'un amour-propre blessé" ["didn't know these reflections born of susceptibilities in one's wounded self-esteem"].[76] On the other hand, what of God's rigors "dont la jalousie se fait parfois vivement sentir aux âmes les plus fidèles et les plus saintes" ["whose jealousy makes itself felt sometimes in the most faithful and saintly souls"]? A Carmelite celebrating her golden anniversary (*noces d'or*) was asked by a sister who had known much testing whether she was using the unique occasion to think back on her sins. "Ma bonne Soeur, je pense à l'amour, je m'occupe de l'amour, tout est là!" ["My dear Sister, I think about love, I busy myself with it, that's all!"].[77] Even as there were two outward classes of sisters, those of the choir and of the *converses,* so there were two spiritual classes, those with "susceptibilities" and those without. It would have been a testing in itself for a sister burdened with indefinite spells of doubt and indifference to be keeping daily company with cheerful, confident sisters, apparently rock-solid in their faith.

One sister, a prioress, admitted to having spent five years in the darkness of unbelief. Another was bold enough to revile God as a bad husband. No wonder you have so few friends, Madre Teresa had allegedly remarked in a prayer. Some sisters were able to take consolation from the dictum that a testing such as unbelief was a sign of divine favors to come. But the more imposing testimony comes from those facing unresolved tensions, of which the notes left by a prioress in Montpellier afford an instance. Her life was a mélange of dullness and joy, light and shadow, with God variously attracting and repelling her: "Il m'appelle, je réponds et il se tait. Mon Dieu, soyez béni si dans cette nuit je vous glorifie plus que dans la lumière. Laissez-y mon âme tant qu'il vous plaira: pourvu que je vous aime et que je ne vous offense pas, voilà tout mon désir" ["He calls, I answer and he's silent. My God, be blessed if in this night I glorify you more than in the light. Leave my soul there so long as it please you, provided I love you and give you no offense; that's all I desire"]. Most admirable in this prioress was her way of heeding the community's needs, even though her own would seem to have been the more acute. She assiduously promoted "l'esprit d'enfance religieuse découlant du mystère de la crèche" ["the spirit of religious childhood derived from the mystery of the cradle"] and enjoined her sisters: "Devenez de petites enfants, délicieuses de simplicité et de docilité" ["Become little children, lovely in simplicity and meekness"].[78] Such a double life of inner conflict and outward joy, with exhortations to the community from someone who could not meet the tests herself, was more than occasional to every generation at any Carmel.

The culmination of every *circulaire* was its account of the subject's illness and death. In some instances, most of the notice amounted to little more: not a summing up of a life but a profile of how well the subject entered eternal life, usually after a prolonged and painful illness. All of Carmelite life had been an anticipation of that end time, and it had been prepared by mortifications. At this crucial juncture, all of the community would participate with vigils, prayers, and presence. At its close, each *circulaire* suggests a group portrait.

Given secular culture's highly advertised preoccupation with the body, futilely trying to make it fit and immortal, the notion of reducing the body to unfitness unto death seems willfully perverse. Perhaps our rash curiosity ascribes morbidity to mortification, so it is well to consider the substantial range of what the term could and did signify. There were five classes: first, assumption of all daily pains and inconveniences in the performance of duties; second, self-denial or self-sacrifice (asked by Céline why, unlike most other men, he never smoked cigars, Louis spoke of his abstinence as a mortification); third, patience to endure sickness and such unpleasantness as extremes of weather; fourth, repression of sexual impulses and of idle curiosity; fifth, penitence of the flesh by fasting, hair shirts,[79] prostrations, and night vigils. Of all these, chiefly the last tends to arouse our prurient attention. Fasting came regularly in Lent, but would be taken to extremes at other times, especially by eager novices seeking to convince themselves that they could meet the austerities of Carmel.[80]

After reading more than four hundred *circulaires*, I would estimate that corporal self-punishment was far more an exception than a rule. We could fashion a caricature from the prioress in Besançon who made herself a kind of prima donna of tortures and would show novices what she called her treasury, "véritable arsenal de son invention pour se mortifier toujours davantage" ["a veritable arsenal of her own devising to mortify herself more and more"]. She could become eloquent in telling them of her choice of martyrdom, to be devoured by horrific beasts: "ce gros ours, ce tigre, se jeter sur moi, mettre leurs pattes sur mes épaules et me mettre en lambeaux" ["some huge bear or tiger on me, with its claws on my shoulders, tearing me to tatters"].[81]

For another prioress, mortification meant chiefly denying oneself all sensuous enjoyments, which presumably could have included delicious attacks by bears and tigers. Privation, she said, was as central to prayer as prayer was to perfection: what was the point of becoming a Carmelite unless one lived for self-denial? She applied this view to the strictures on obedience: for a novice to enjoy performing obligations was hazardous, and it would be better to feel repugnance toward everything expected of her. Such alienation, she argued, was nearer to true spiritual perfection because one never acts more purely for God than when against herself. A hair shirt, in sum, need not be physical.[82]

Novices or any others who took mortification too earnestly would be ordered by an attentive prioress to desist. It was not in the interest of a Carmel that any of its sisters make herself ill by all-night vigils or excessive fastings. Incidence of illness was high enough from the severities of weather and deadly epidemics, such as influenza. In fact, novices approaching their first Lent were obliged to eat a lot of carbohydrates.[83] It was costly to support the ill because they were expected to eat meat to sustain what strength they had, and meat was much more expensive than the fish served weekly.[84]

Although *circulaires* usually reported an illness's progress until the patient's death, few prioresses specified what the malady was. They would not likely have known because the physicians themselves, always given an unquestioning professional deference, would not or could not specify. The high profile of tuberculosis, called phthisis in that time, gave it a noticeable identity, and some prioresses were bold enough to mention it. In many instances, a disease would progress rapidly, confounding the doctor's estimate and distressing the community.

For some sisters, the fear of death and of God's judgment came from an immitigable sense of personal imperfections and unworthiness, as though they had failed (as they must have believed they had) to live up to the Rule's confident urgings to sainthood. Some faced a lifetime of dread at the thought of falling into hell. One sister admitted she had been kept awake at night in fright at the prospect of her body's corruption in the tomb.[85] A prioress in Lourdes, who had told her community that death was a foyer "où nous sommes attendues et reçues par le meilleur et le plus tendre des pères, la plus douce et la plus aimable des mères" ["where we're awaited and received by the best and most tender of fathers and the sweetest and most loving of mothers"] herself gave way to fear on her deathbed: "Quelle obscurité! Quelles ténèbres! Quelles angoisses m'environnent! Mon Dieu! Pourquoi les approches de la mort me font-elles ainsi frissonner, moi qui l'ai toujours désirée?" ["What darkness! What shadows! What anguish surrounds me! My God, why does the approach of death make me shudder, I who have always desired it?"].[86] Such imaginative, not to say imaginary, dread was fed in part by the notion of a requisite saintliness, that "il faut être si pur pour paraître devant le Dieu trois fois Saint, qui trouve des taches dans ses anges mêmes" ["it is necessary to be so pure to appear before the thrice Holy God, who sees stains in angels themselves"], and few could pass that muster.[87]

Many on their deathbeds felt the *épreuve* of abandonment, but what could that forsakenness be other than an *imitatio Christi*? It was possible, even charitable, to construe all of the psychological torments of those facing death as species of mortification. Of one sister who had feared the day of judgment most of her life, the prioress wrote: "Cette souffrance était une permission divine, une action purifiante, qui en même temps augmentait ses mérites" ["This suffering came by divine permission, a purifying which at the same time increased her merits"].[88] True merit came hidden in a sister's conviction that she had none, and the horror in feeling bereft of God put her in closest proximity to the cross.

Paradox dictated, then, that a happy death should be most feared, but if the torments of fear marked one legitimate way into the next world, a resilient trust marked another: "La piété de ma Soeur Louise était tendre et affectueuse, elle allait à Notre Seigneur avec une grande confiance et un abandon tout filial" ["The piety of my Sister Louise was tender and affectionate. She went to Our Lord with a great confidence and a completely childlike abandon"].[89] While some sisters were graced with such fearlessness, all would have known the sustenance of their community, that they had lived lives which, however imperfect, worked in prayer and toward charity. They had formed both a family and a team, and the infirmary bell when sounded with the sequence announcing an imminent death summoned the community, as entire as a family or team, to the dying sister's bed. The approach of death brought a solicitude not readily found at a deathbed in normal family life, with all its generational tensions and politics (not to mention the will). "Que je suis heureuse de mourir dans une communauté où règne l'union, la charité, l'esprit de la famille" ["How happy I am to die in a community where accord, charity, and the spirit of family reign"][90] was a statement that could have been attested many times over.

Not infrequently a kind of seraphic composure in the dead women would be remarked. No matter the prolonged illness or infirmity, upon death the corpse reportedly showed no trace of suffering, only "une sérénité toute céleste" ["a wholly celestial serenity"].[91] Of a sister who had suffered a strange and atrocious disease over eight years, it was written: "Un air de béatitude et un doux sourire répandus sur sa physionomie nous donnaient l'heureuse conviction qu'elle avait reçu un accueil favorable du Souverain Juge" ["A look of blessedness and a sweet smile spread over her face gave us the happy conviction she had gotten a favorable reception from the Sovereign Judge"].[92]

Such hallowing language might seem suspect to some in the outer, hardened world, but that impression is best resisted. These writings, even apart from their period flavor, offer not sentimental effusions but testimony about the preparation of an entire life. The culminating hours, a time when death became a delivery, a birth and not a termination, also occasioned singing, and a dying sister's candid eloquence was carefully recorded for the *circulaire*. It comes as little wonder that one, dying at forty-six and asked if she wanted to go to heaven, answered, "Je serais heureuse de rester avec mes bonnes Mères et mes Soeurs, mais que la volonté de Dieu soit faite" ["I would be happy to stay with my good Mothers and Sisters, but may God's will be done"].[93]

If every Carmel was a family, the greater Carmel, the communities in France and abroad, formed the larger one, and the *circulaires* continually reminded every family of it. I believe that Sr. Thérèse de l'Enfant-Jésus de la Sainte-Face learned richly from them. It could well be claimed that her spirituality owes much to these dead and to the prioresses who wrote of them. If these sisters did not expressly shape her, she found in many of them something of and for herself. It is no detraction from her greatness to note that they, too, were aware, each of them, of the soul's littleness. If it appears that Thérèse achieved a kind of synthesis of their teachings by her writing, she left much that remains experientially her own. But let us admit that it is their lives, not hers, which have remained the truly hidden.

Here are a few final testimonies which offer complement and counter-point to Thérèse. Of Sr. Véronique de la Croix, the prioress in Tours wrote, "la vertu, pour être héroïque, n'a pas besoin d'être éclatante. Notre bien chère soeur fut une de ces âmes simples et droites qui s'enveloppent d'humilité et d'amour" ["virtue doesn't need to be flashy to be heroic. Our dear sister was one of these simple, dignified souls wrapped in humility and love"].[94] Thérèse, because she was a writer, was not and could not be one of Madre Teresa's saintly simple souls like Sr. Véronique. The model of self-effacement which the prioress holds up here—and every Carmel had some—poses a troubling question: does not genuine humility and genuine love preclude the first person singular from spiritual grammar?

About union with Christ, Le Dorat's Sr. Saint-Elie, who died at thirty, said, "Mon impuissance est absolue. Je tâche de disparaître pour le laisser faire.... c'est le seul rôle qui me convienne toujours" ["My helplessness is total. I'm trying to disappear so that he can act.... it's the only role that's always right for me"].[95] The trope of the role taken or chosen is commonplace to a life lived in ritual, because shared spirituality involves a kind of theater: Christ, by the synoptic accounts, acts out the old prophets' words as though his life had been scripted for him. Here, Sr. Saint-Elie anticipates Thérèse in the brilliant notion of a performative disappearance. In a poem on the eucharistic mystery, Thérèse considers the soul vanishing into the transubstantiating wine, sacrificing itself so that Christ's love has, as Sr. Saint-Elie put it, its *laisser faire*.[96] When dying, Sr. Saint-Elie said, "Si Dieu m'offrait la santé, je ne l'accepterais plus, parce que c'est mon sacrifice qu'Il veut" ["If God offered me health, I'd no longer accept it, because it's my sacrifice that He wants"]. Almost a Thérèse before Thérèse.

And in anticipation of Thérèse's last manuscript, Mère Aimée de Jésus in Cahors uttered one remark which deserves weighing with it: "Je voudrais, si c'était possible, en faire part à tous les malheureux, et si, dans le nombre, il s'en trouvait qui m'eussent fait de la peine, c'est à ceux là que je l'offrirai de préférence" ["Were it possible, I'd like to join all the wretched and if in that number there were found those who had hurt me, I'd prefer to be with them"].[97] Perhaps only a long life would suffice to reach such charitable perception and yet it adumbrates Thérèse's gospel of the table of ungrateful sinners and convinced unbelievers where, in her last months, she finally situated herself, a world apart from the Carmelites' Rule and Constitutions.

Srs. Véronique, Saint-Elie, Aimée, and hundreds of other sisters of Carmel remain obscure and forgotten, true noncelebrities, even as many of them expressly desired. In life they attempted to disappear into their communities, and some would, I hope, gently object even to their brief profiles in these pages. They leave Thérèse a kind of monstrous anomaly, a nothing like them but yet one to whom a gigantic basilica was erected. Their merit, if I may be permitted that awkward word, does not simply lie in their chosen obscurity nor in their having suffered, in not a few instances, *épreuves* deep, dark, and years long. Some individually challenge Thérèse in depth of insight and thus provide ancillary readings to the corpus of her doctorate.

Why did she not develop this lesson on how moral suffering could be diminished? "[E]lle avait appris, disait-elle, à regarder Jésus comme sa Mère. Une Mère!" ["She said that she'd learned to look upon Jesus as her Mother. A Mother!"].[98] The surprised prioress of Poitiers did not know that this insight put Sr. Marie-Joseph into the company of the great medieval mystics, such as Julian of Norwich, and after them François de Sales.[99] Drawing upon *Isaiah* 66:12–13, Thérèse consoled herself with a maternally sustaining God the Father but never accorded that femininity to Christ.[100]

The disastrous and pharisaical payoff psychology that Arminjon promoted fell away from Thérèse perhaps only when she lost heaven, but that deepening, the growing up from celestial mercantilism could have been abetted as early as the spring of 1891, when she was given these retreat notes from Agen: "Se sanctifier pour sauver son âme, cela est permis, oui, mais cela est mercenaire. Purifier, simplifier son âme pour la rapprocher de Lui, parce que cela le glorifie, c'est là servir Dieu pour Lui!" ["To sanctify oneself in order to save one's soul, that's permitted, yes, but it is mercenary. To purify and simplify one's soul to bring it closer to God because it glorifies Him, that is to serve God for Himself!"].[101]

One of the cardinal word concepts in theresian spirituality, *confiance*, had arguably its finest, most succinct formulation from a sister at Saint Chaumont: " 'Quand on ne veut que Lui, qu'importe où il veut être trouvé, à Nazareth, au Thabor, à Gethsemani? Il y est également quand je le cherche, dans les mystères et dans la grâce du moment, je suis sûre de ne pas le manquer.' Notre bien-aimée soeur ne connut jamais les préoccupations de perfection personnelle: elle allait à Dieu, voyant tout venir de Lui, allant de tout à Lui" [" 'If you want only Jesus, what does it matter where he wishes to be found: at Nazareth, on Mount Tabor, at Gethsemane? It doesn't matter when I seek him, in the mysteries and in the grace of the moment, I am sure not to miss him.' Our well-beloved sister never knew the preoccupations of personal perfection: she went to God, seeing all things coming from Him and going to Him"].[102] Many *circulaires* characterized their subjects as dwellers in Gethsemane's garden of the agony rather than on the (highly suspected) illuminists' mount of the transfiguration: suffering, yes; ecstatic vision, no. One of Thérèse's revelatory insights came in her fusing, even as her name bade her, Nazareth with Gethsemane, the twofold imitation of Christ in a trusting, childlike submission to God within unrelenting darkness. The experience was hers and what she perceived from it, but perhaps the cue came as a mustard seed from Saint Chaumont.

Finally, a cautionary word from the Carmel of Lectoure, far within the Midi-Pyréneés. Sr. Marie du Saint-Sacrement had come there all the way from Bretagne, "où la foi est encore si vive et si pure" ["where faith is still so alive and so pure"], and must have made a substantial impression upon the community for the prioress to have remarked the loss of Sr. Marie's retreat notes and other writings: "elle avait eu soin de tout brûler, dans la crainte qu'on ne pensât qu'elle avait pratiqué tout cela" ["she had taken care to burn it all in the fear that we'd think she had practiced it"].[103]

In this identity of humility and charity, those hidden Carmelites stand as one with Thérèse. Preceding her, they were her teachers; striking affinities between the *circulaires* and her writings say that she listened and learned. It is one of her hidden charities that she spoke for them, even as she forged her own singular way toward God.

5

Thérèse Writes Her Self

[A]insi, m'abaissant jusque dans les profondeurs de mon néant je m'élevai si haut que je pus atteindre mon but [So, lowering myself into the depths of my nothingness, I raised myself so high that I could achieve my goal].

—Manuscript B (3v)

[M]on chant sera d'autant plus mélodieux que les épines seront longes et piquantes [My song shall be all the more melodious as the thorns shall be long and prickling].

— Manuscript B (4v)

Jean Starobinski has suggested that there are basically two kinds of writing about oneself: the elegiac, which looks back upon a happy life with disillusion or regret, and the picaresque, which achieves the reverse, a life recovered from past upheavals and arrived to a mature wholeness. Rousseau's autobiography is predominantly elegiac, Augustine's, picaresque. The autobiography of Thérèse eludes both of these broad categories chiefly because she did not live long enough nor have an experience of the world sufficiently varied to have irretrievably lost one peace or attained another.

In her first manuscript, she opens a luminous window upon a connection between her childhood and the adolescence she completed at Carmel. Succeeding its fairytale aspect of isolation and escape, a variant of Cinderella's story, comes the salvific arrival. She is describing the usual Thursday afternoons off from school when she was obliged to play with the Guérin girls and their cousins on their mother's side: "Il fallait jouer non pas avec ma Céline, ce qui plaisait quand j'étais *toute seule avec elle*, mais avec mes petites cousines et les petites Maudelonde, c'était pour moi une vraie peine, ne sachant pas jouer comme les autres enfants, je n'étais pas une compagne agréable, cependant je faisais de mon mieux pour imiter les autres sans y réussir et je m'ennuyais beaucoup, surtout quand il faillait passer toute une après-midi à *danser* des *quadrilles*. La seule chose qui me plaisait c'était d'aller au *jardin* de *l'étoile*, alors j'étais la première partout, cueillant les fleurs à profusion et sachant trouver les plus jolies j'excitais l'envie de mes petites compagnes" ["I had to play not with Céline alone—I was happy when *entirely alone with her*—but with my little cousins and the Maudelonde girls. It was a real pain for me. Not knowing how to play with the other children, I wasn't an enjoyable companion, yet I did my best to copy them (but) without success and I got very annoyed, especially when a whole afternoon had to be spent *dancing quadrilles*. The only thing I liked was going to the *star garden* (the civic park next to the cathedral) where I arrived the first. Gathering the flowers in profusion and knowing how to find the prettiest I stirred the envy of my little companions"] (A 23r). The difference from fairytale scenarios is that Thérèse portrays no wickedness in anyone else. She charges herself with awkwardness and misfitting, an outsider without recriminations. The collectivity of the dance underscores her isolation but is relieved by the visit to the park, where she thrives in both the gathering of flowers and the admiration of the other girls. At last, she got one thing right and so much better than anyone else.

This passage plays effectively as parable for her conventual life: the ungainly girl who was not up to the chores the prioress assigned and who could not keep awake in morning prayers and yet had within her a certain gemlike gift she could impart to others.

In essentials, her account of herself in Manuscript A at first seems almost static, but no life escapes some woundings early on. Thérèse's mother's death and her loss of Pauline to Carmel devastated an acutely impressionable child. She was, besides, tormented by sickness and haunted from the age of seven by that spectral figure which she took to be premonitory of her father dead.

Zélie, Pauline, and the youngest of five sisters: the first of Thérèse's autobiographical manuscripts is very much a women's story, reminding us that while autobiography has many faces, perhaps no greater distinction can be made than that between men and women writing their lives. From men, we can expect a record of outward achievements, some profile in public and usually with momentous events in the background; there is a concomitant tendency to defend (excuse) one's conduct. Rousseau's sometimes grotesque leaps to self-exoneration mark an impulse in extremis which probably most male autobiographers feel. Vanity alone could do the prompting. Living and working within a civic arena (the very image is of contest), men naturally feel the need to defend themselves, especially in defeat. It is easy to whine over or rationalize failure or even to mask it as some sort of triumph, as Cardinal de Retz did in his account of the Fronde. Wholly exceptional is the deprecation of one's achievements, notably of a career, and with that a forceful diminution of self before an incontestably higher power: no one since Augustine has so eloquently (he could not forget his rhetorical flair) addressed himself not only to his readers but first to God, the final arbiter for any gathering of men. The first autobiography in Western literature is a model of self-humbling which few men since have followed convincingly.

Far different is the arena in which women have worked and written, in the main, an interior one, and most especially one of spiritual dynamism. Margery Kempe, the first autobiographer in English, Julian of Norwich, Teresa of Avila stand as exemplary recorders of their lives as a sequence of visions rather than of deeds. Although Teresa was a thoroughly shrewd administrator and a familiar of aristocrats, her self-account circles around the mystically summoned Christ, the savior whom Margery Kempe boldly denominated "very modir." Women writing in the Christian tradition have had a double interiority: sequestered socially and economically, they have further cultivated the meditative life of self-examination and penance, of imagination and what Mother Julian called "shewyngs."

Although she had spent a third of her life in Carmel, Manuscript A shows Thérèse's sustained awareness of the world without. Even before entering it, she had a missionary sense of retrieval, beginning with the famous Pranzini case. Her one, long journey beyond France gave her a vivid, informed sense of the world in both its *grandeurs et misères*. She entertained in adolescence some fantasies of male callings, priestly and martial. They were reinforced at Carmel by stories of the "male courage" of exemplary sisters.[1] She dispassionately wrote of herself as a prisoner of Carmel. It is telling that her sovereign wish to perform posthumously some good on earth implies a rejection of any possible enclosure in a celestial company. It may be called her supreme *imitatio Christi*, an engagement of the sick and ever-needy world, as though that celestial company of the righteous might manage without her, whereas in truth the heavenly residence, though not its company, vanished from her consciousness. In sum, she writes as one ready to assume the self of public performance associated almost entirely with men. Although promoted as a saint of submissiveness by the performance of little and obscure deeds, the salient fact about Thérèse is that she presents herself as a very keen activist and on a grand, unlimited scale.

Stylizing her life by writing it, Thérèse came to a sense of singular mission as most certainly she could not and would not have without that effort. As all autobiographers must, she edited a life into a narrative coherence that conferred upon its sequences a seeming inevitability. Her storytelling imposes portentous meanings upon events and even upon sayings which at the time of utterance they perhaps did not sustain. Her hagiographers and biographers alike have little choice but to follow her editing trail; what she says mattered is what matters to them.

To take an example from her lore, recorded by Zélie and iterated countless times by the older sisters: at the slight age of three, when obliged with her sister Céline to choose among some scraps of cloth for making doll clothes, she resolved the difficulty of a final selection by exclaiming, "Je choisis tout!" ["I choose everything!"]. This kind of child wit, at once ingenuous and mischievous, is familiar to the parents of any half-alert and reasonably expressive youngster. It is remarked and remembered simply for its humor, but Thérèse interpreted this incident as a portent of her will's destiny: she did not choose to return merely to Normandy nor to France nor to Europe. She chose all—the earth.

If enthusiasts are drawn ineluctably to a scenario of a saintly life signaled as though by a divine choreographer or scriptwriter, it is because the scriptwriter was Thérèse herself. Nothing constrained her to tell the "I choose everything" story except to make it part of her self-portrait. She was writing more than "was I not a clever child, then?" She was saying that such a child was integral—she was choosing to make that child integral—to the self who was writing sometime in 1895. Thérèse was creating in such instances a meaning and, by writing, *the* meaning of her own life as she saw it at that moment. Selecting the "I choose everything" was a self-reconstructing act, what Paul Ricoeur would call a "configuration of a prefiguration."

She affords this commentary on that story: "Mon Dieu, je choisis tout. Je ne veux pas être une sainte à moitié, cela ne me fait pas peur de souffrir pour vous, je ne crains pas qu'une chose c'est de garder ma volonté, prenez-la, car 'Je choisis tout' ce que vous voulez!" ["My God, I choose everything. I don't want to be a saint by half; that doesn't make me afraid to suffer for you, I fear only one thing and that is to preserve my will, take it, for 'I choose everything' that you will"] (A 10v). By her commentary, she provides God as reader, the agent of Ricoeur's refiguration, the way she would like that choosing to be accepted. In addressing God, she follows Augustine's turning of a life and its account into a prayer. All three of her autobiographical texts might be called prayers: first of thanksgiving, so far as she sees her life as a concatenation of graces, but also of supplication, even as grace gave her the strength to acknowledge her abiding weakness. As to her insistence upon *tout*, we shall find it again and again: everything. Like Rousseau, Thérèse could not mediate between everything and nothing. That is the extremism of *audace*, a peremptory boldness acknowledged even by her most devout admirers.

She thus resolves brilliantly a number of challenges. Any autobiographer faces the task of making the life to be told into something engaging and yet must do so at the risk of immodesty. Thérèse had to be ordered by her prioress to write her life; she could not have undertaken to do so on her own. Christian humility precludes such a purposeful lingering over oneself. Further, her life had been sheltered and in the main uneventful, void of interest to ordinary readers. But this twenty-two-year-old woman had no ordinary readers. As far as she knew, her only readers would be her natural sisters, beginning with Pauline, who, more than eleven years her senior, knew her story in many particulars better than did Thérèse herself.[2] What not even Pauline could know was how Thérèse would take an incident of family lore and employ it as a plea to God for suffering everything according to the divine will. The terms of her commentary are couched transparently in terms of Gethsemane: "Not my will but thy will be done."

Emulous of Christ, she does not ask whether it is possible for her to avoid suffering. In part that may be because in each of her three texts, she was in effect addressing Christ: Manuscript A to Pauline, who as prioress was by Carmel's convention the Christ figure within the community, as Gonzague was, once again, when Thérèse was nearing death and wrote Manuscript C. Manuscript B, framed in letters to Marie, is expressly love's letter to Christ, repeatedly addressed as *Mon Bien-Aimé* and *Mon Jésus*. It is Thérèse's Song of Songs, composed on her last retreat, as perhaps she intuited it would be, a yearly occasion which had usually troubled her with scruples but which, in this final instance, produced one of the masterworks of Christian confessional literature.

Thérèse, then, like Augustine, involves God directly in the proceedings of her life. The standard issues of autobiography, such as winning the reader's trust, maintaining the reader's interest, presenting the self in a winningly likable portrait or at least a credible one, are all vanity and void. She had no need to convince Pauline of anything, nor to induce her to a favorable estimate. She needed only to recreate herself in words. In such an endeavor, she had no difficulty because she had been a gifted storyteller from her school days. That talent and ingenuousness, the apparent transparency of her account, figure in the early popularity of her story. She had nothing to plead, to hide, to excuse. She wrote with effortless candor.

Why, then, the writing at all? Because Thérèse, by the time she commenced her autobiography, in January 1895, had already established herself as a kind of writer in residence at the Lisieux Carmel: she had composed fifteen poems for various occasions, such as feast days or the investiture of novices. Some were written on request. Only one did she write for herself, addressed to Louis after he died. These verses, seldom rising above the banal, cannot be taken seriously as literature, nor were they so taken then—she was wont to make mistakes in syntax—but they indicate that Thérèse had some rhetorical panache. She had also composed, in January 1894, the first of two dramas about Jeanne d'Arc. Pope Leo XIII had proclaimed the veneration of Jeanne, and a festival in her honor was appointed for May 8 of that year.

The occasion prompting her autobiography was not in any of those efforts, however. It came casually as she was telling stories about her childhood to her natural sisters. Marie, appreciating Thérèse's narrative gift, with its penchant for mimicry (she had been known at home as a *coquine*, or imp), urged that she write the story of her childhood. She could do so only by the order of her Mother Superior, Pauline at that time. The order was given. Nothing momentous was presumed to come from the effort; it would be a self-portrait of a young Carmelite, a *souvenir d'enfance* in which the only weighty event, spiritually considered, would be the first Communion. Pauline herself did not reckon it important; when Thérèse gave it to her in January 1896, she put it under lock and key and left it unread until she ended her term as prioress two months later. That might have been the end of what Thérèse had entitled *Histoire printanière d'une petite fleur blanche écrite par elle-même et dédiée à la Révérende Mère Agnès de Jésus* [*The Springtime Story of a Little White Flower Written by Herself and Dedicated to the Reverend Mother Agnes of Jesus*].

A more imposing reason for her writing lay within Thérèse's own history, that she had succeeded in gaining admission to Carmel when she was only fourteen years old. The record of her importunities in braving the solidly male ecclesiastical establishment, from Bayeux to the Vatican, would have sufficed to make her story exceptional. A decided girl, as Pauline knew, and yet that crucial and dramatic episode in her life did not ostensibly figure in anyone's mind when Marie urged, Pauline ordered, and Thérèse accepted the writing of her life.

From family to school to convent, Thérèse had outwardly led a life which admitted no deviation from an exclusively self-referential world. Save for one notorious incident, one which scandalized Thérèse, we have little sense that she was living in a time when anticlericalism was thriving and the Church was at bay. Yet, staunch Third Republicans were in the main merely hostile to Catholicism; they never posed to it any genuine and substantial danger. They satisfied themselves with some mean-spirited legislation and their prejudices. Far different was the time of Teresa of Avila, who undertook to write her autobiography under orders from the general of the Inquisition: he knew that by her so doing, she would probably save her very life from the charge of enthusiasm (demonic possession). Thérèse had the misfortune not to live in one of the great ages of faith, with all their attendant glory of hazard unto martyrdom.[3]

For all that, or because of it, she had to supply some drama in her writing and put herself at its center. It came fortuitously, in a sensational crime. On July 13, 1887, Henri Pranzini was found guilty and sentenced to death for murdering two women and a girl in Paris on March 17. The case became a tabloid success because Pranzini, a dashing young man of thirty (he was born in Alexandria), had won the hearts of society women, who turned out in large numbers to attend the trial. He had been adept in getting money from women subject to his charms and managed to exert a spell on yet more women in the courtroom. It was an irresistible temptation, to see a gigolo at last being punished and yet to be pitied, to be despised for all his perfidies and yet adored. This steamy sexual politics, the eroticism of the guillotine, could hardly have been in the mind of an adolescent who had no idea of sexuality, including her own, beyond Marie's vague enlightenments about menstruation.

Why and how did Thérèse, then fourteen, become engaged in this sensation? The answer comes from the Christmas "conversion" she had undergone in December 1886, when she had been forced to grow out of her infantilism or, as she puts it, to retrieve the strength of soul she had lost at her mother's death. Now, Jesus being content with "ma *bonne volonté* qui jamais ne me fit défaut" ["my *good will* which had never failed me"] (A 45v), she was ready to be a fisher of souls : "Je sentis en un mot la *charité* entrer dans mon coeur, le besoin de m'oublier pour faire plaisir et depuis lors je fus heureuse!" ["In a word I felt *charity* enter my heart, the need to forget myself in order to please and after that I was happy!"]. Yet, not quite: on seeing an image of Christ thirsting on the cross, "Je voulais donner à boire à mon Bien-Aimé et je me sentais moi-même dévorée de la *soif* des âmes" ["I wanted to give a drink to my Beloved and I felt that I myself was devoured by a *thirst* for *souls*"] (see figure 5.1).

The Pranzini case immediately ensues in Thérèse's chronicle, but his trial and condemnation came six months after that fateful Christmas. She writes that she had heard of him but does not specify where (from Uncle Isidore? at Mme. Papinau's?). Finally, on September 1, the day following his execution, she read Louis's Catholic newspaper, *La Croix*,[4] and learned of the trial at its denouement. "*Tout* portait à croire qu'il mourrait dans l'impénitence. Je voulus à *tout prix* l'empêcher de tomber en enfer, afin d'y parvenir j'employai *tous les moyens* imaginables: sentant que moi-même je ne pouvais rien, j'offris au Bon Dieu *tous les mérites* infinis de Notre Seigneur" ["*Everything* led to the belief he would die impenitent. I wanted at *all costs* to keep him from falling into hell, and to succeed I employed *all means* imaginable; feeling that of myself I could do nothing, I offered to God *all* the infinite merits of Our Lord"] (A 45v–46r).

Soon, Pranzini became "mon pécheur" ("my sinner") but when he was guillotined on August 31, he became something much more. Thérèse read that directly before the execution, he made a dramatic gesture. In her remembrance, forgetful that·the newspaper indicated that the condemned man's hands were tied behind his back, Thérèse colors the moment: "tout à coup, saisi d'une inspiration subite, il se retourne, saisit un *Crucifix* que lui présentait le prêtre et *baise* par *trois fois* ses *plaies sacrées*!" ["immediately,

FIGURE 5.1. Thérèse looking confident at fourteen, an Enfant de Marie and
with the Christmas "conversion" of 1886 behind her. Copyright Office
Central de Lisieux.

seized by a sudden inspiration, he turned, seized a *Crucifix* which the priest
offered him and *kissed* his *sacred wounds!*"] (A 46r). To her febrile imagination,
nothing could more soundly prove the efficacy of her prayer and the need
of consolation, which she admits that she felt for herself. She was convinced
that she had been instrumental in saving Pranzini from hellfire. That rescue
served to substantiate her conversion's calling to save wayward souls. Pranzini
was the first to benefit from this missionary zeal. Accordingly, he became
"mon premier enfant" ("my first child").

　　Pranzini became pivotal in her interpretation of her life and the direction
she believed she was divinely destined to take. No matter that any number of
other people might also have been praying for Pranzini; no matter that perhaps
he was not impenitent but was merely reported so by the popular press for its

delighted readership; no matter that even lapsed or unbelieving men were known, as though by reflex or by deference, to kiss a crucifix before their execution (as Dostoevsky observed at one arranged for him and fellow conspirators against czarism): she was convinced that her intercessory efforts were the cause of Pranzini's kissing that crucifix. In his own way, he had chosen all.

It would be gratuitous and unfair to object that this impressionable girl, profoundly moved by the image of Christ suffering a slow and horrible death, did not take a less imaginative and more humane avenue to individuate herself, the consideration that possibly, the trial's course notwithstanding, Pranzini died an innocent man. The newspapers were reporting the efforts of many society women to secure a presidential pardon, which was refused. They even besieged the prison with their husbands and carriages. Their motivation was that Pranzini, unbeknown to Thérèse, had protested his innocence from first to last, and a man gifted in extorting money from women would have had scant motives for killing some, when there would always be others. Even with his guilt presumed, however, Thérèse's involvement in his story implicates her in the obscene and anachronistic procedure which Camus, seventy years after Pranzini's death, called "une chirurgie grossière" ["a crude surgery"].[5]

Two generations before this case, Hugo, in prefacing his extraordinary fictive chronicle *Le dernier jour d'un condamné* [*The Last Day of a Condemned Man*], noted that France was living in a desacralized age. It could no longer be maintained that in taking a criminal's life, capital punishment was delivering his soul to a higher judgment. "Mais quelle espérance mettez-vous ... sur l'échafaud maintenant que la grosse foule ne croit plus ... maintenant que les petits enfants se moquent de Dieu?" ["But what hope do you put now in the scaffold when the enormous crowd no longer believes ... now that little children make fun of God?"].[6] Camus, a nonbeliever, wondered how people who put at the center of their faith the victim of a judicial error could not show themselves at least reticent in the face of a legal killing. With these powerfully humane and eloquent witnesses on either side of her history, Thérèse's adolescent solicitude for Pranzini seems touching yet oblique, if not impertinent, and her rejoicing in his putative salvation notwithstanding, her role in the case reminds us of how the Church sanctimoniously abetted the state which despised it, each an accomplice to the other's hypocrisy (see figure 5.2).

It is curious that her missionary work began with a crime, even as crime figured centrally in the two other spiritual self-portraits I have mentioned. For Augustine, it was the theft of a pear; for Rousseau, the theft of a hair ribbon. These petty acts directly implicated those men in their youth, but for the adolescent Thérèse to implicate herself in a criminal's fate, she had only to read the newspaper.

Adverting to Augustine is not entirely amiss. Thérèse herself does it when she describes evening conversations with her sister Céline in the belvedere,

FIGURE 5.2. Her "first child," Henri Pranzini, a petty thief convicted of murder and guillotined on August 31, 1887. Courtesy of the Service de l'Identité judiciaire, Police de Paris.

the top floor of their home, when they were, respectively, thirteen and sixteen: "Le regard plongé dans le lointain, nous considérions la blanche lune s'elevant doucement derrière les grands arbres . . les reflets argentés . . le souffle léger de la brise du soir . . *tout* élevait nos âmes vers le Ciel. . . Je ne sais si je me trompe, mais il me semble que l'épanchement de nos âmes ressemblait à celui de Ste. Monique avec son fils lorsqu'au port d'Ostie ils restaient perdus dans l'extase à la vue des merveilles du Créateur!" ["Our watching plunged into the distance, we looked at the pale moon rising gently behind the large trees . . . the silvery reflections . . . the light breeze as evening broke . . . *everything* raised us toward Heaven. . . I don't know if I'm mistaken, but it seems to me that the outpouring of our souls' confidences was like that of St. Monica with her son when at the port of Ostia they were lost in ecstasy at the sight of the Creator's marvels"] (A 48r; see figure 5.3).

She is indeed mistaken, in part. In Augustine's account, all the impressions of sense were to be stilled in order that he and his mother might contemplate divinity; the sensory world was not a conduit but a virtual obstacle. Granting that, however, we would miss Thérèse's strategic point. First, she gently promotes Monica and makes no explicit mention of Augustine. Then, she asserts that she and Céline had received a grace equal to that vouchsafed to the saints, Monica and Augustine, that in her observing the sensory world with Céline, God was manifesting himself to their souls. To transcendence, she poses immanence. Well and good. Her conclusion,

FIGURE 5.3. Les Buissonnets, the Martin family's home in Lisieux, as it appeared in their time. In the belvedere on the top, Thérèse and Céline played dolls and took inspirations. Copyright Archives du Carmel de Lisieux.

nonetheless, is jolting: "Le doute n'était pas possible, déjà la Foi et l'Espérance n'étaient plus nécessaires, l'*amour* nous faisait trouver sur la terre Celui que nous cherchions" ["Doubt was no longer possible, already Faith and Hope were no longer necessary, *love* made us find on earth Him whom we were seeking"] (A 48r). Having thus established that this loving was a grace such as was, by her estimate, accorded to the great saints, she concludes with the Canticle of Solomon: "L'ayant trouvé seul, Il nous avait donné son baiser, afin qu'à l'avenir personne ne puisse nous mépriser" ["Having found him alone, He gave us his kiss so that in future no one could despise us"].[7]

It is a remarkably bold passage, pointing to Thérèse's confident notion that accessibility to the divine is possible for anyone and is not the exclusive preserve of severe saints, levitated mystics or the supereducated. God is apprehensible by the works of the earth and can be savored there, in and through them. Rather unsettling, however, is her conclusion that not only does the magnificence of nature argue to human senses the existence of God; we find clear and adequate proof of God's presence in nature and therefore, we have only to love God here. Nature obviates not only doubts about God's existence but the very need for faith and hope. They are *unnecessary.*

The all-sufficiency of love enunciated here marks for the first time the singular path of Thérèse's strenuous and exacting theology. It becomes not, as it is in the sequence given by St. Paul, the greatest of the three Christian virtues; it is left standing as the only one, the others being dispensable. Here, already, early in 1895, Thérèse is on her way toward the spiritual void which would empty her of any belief in heaven. It is commonly assumed that her "dark night" occupied only the closing eighteen months of her life, but this passage suggests it was in process well before that period. Shrewdly, she ret-rojects her claim upon love into a quasi-mystifying moment of her childhood, so that we might wonder whether already in *that* time she was letting go of faith in faith and hope in hope. She never, however, let go of her love for love.

The allusion to Augustine opens another window, this one onto the cultivation of Thérèse as a mystic. Many years after her death, her sister was to assert that the belvedere experience was far more exalted than Thérèse herself indicates, that "pendant des heures de consolation céleste . . nous quittions en quelque sorte la terre pour la vie éternelle" ["during the hours of heavenly comfort . . . we after a fashion left earth for the life eternal"]. Céline could recall Thérèse pressing her hands with tears in her eyes: "c'était l'extase de saint Augustin et de sainte Monique à Ostie" ["it was the ecstasy of Saint Augustine and of Saint Monica at Ostie"].[8] Céline goes to excess precisely where Thérèse herself had stepped cautiously, where in fact, as simple com-parison would show, the incidents were incommensurable. Equation of the experience of two girls in early adolescence with the best-known rhetorical ascent in Christian spiritual writing seems absurd and delusory, and prime evidence of the peculiar vanity in the sororal project of promoting Thérèse as someone other than her own writing argues she was.

The key to Thérèse's notion of love lies in her seeing Christmas 1886 as a breakthrough to a new voluntarism in which Christ proved "more compas-. sionate" to her than even to his disciples by having effected in her a desire to be a fisher of souls and to convert sinners: "Je sentis en un mot la charité entrer dans mon coeur, le besoin de m'oublier pour faire plaisir et depuis lors je fus heureuse" ["I felt in a word charity enter my heart, the need to forget myself in order to please and after that I was happy"] (A 45v). Much of the appeal of Thérèse's account for her readers lies in what many autobiographers are not inclined to include, something trivial and out of the way and from daily experi-ence, but unlike most such writers, she was writing at an exceptionally young age and was thus forced to create significance chiefly from childhood and adoles-cence. The Christmas story weighs heavily beyond its triviality because Thérèse interprets it so portentously as a conversion, then describes her assignment as fisher of souls, and concludes that in "ma bonne volonté qui jamais ne me fit défaut" ["my good will which never failed me"] (A 45v), she had become happy at last, released from the anxieties and tears of a motherless childhood.

Only from this context can we make sense of her appropriation of Pranzini as "my first child." She had passed from childhood to a spiritual motherhood. What she could not have noticed was that nothing better indicated that she was still in childhood than her desire to please, which, with her ignorance of sexuality and its claims upon normal human life, kept her in what used to be called arrested development. The male presences she had elected to please were at an infinite remove: God and the decapitated murderer, even though both were vividly before her imagination.

How does her conversion set her apart from the Augustinian perspective? According to Augustine's way, conversion begins by taking oneself out of the sensuous world, freeing oneself from its sundry and mischievous appeals. Metaphorically, one turns from darkness to a neo-Platonic light, from the transient and deceptive world of phenomena to the abiding being of the transcendent. By the intensity of one's inner vision, one might hope to attain a *unio mystica*, an absorption into God. The theresian conversion might be characterized as an acute solicitude toward other people, marked by that adolescent desire to please. Most emphatically, it is focused upon people in present life. This perspective was developed during her middle period when, motherless, she would use her *chapelet de pratiques* to keep a record of good deeds performed by denial of herself and gratification of others.[9] Because, apart from her family, there were few human contacts for her, she could construe the solicitude for others chiefly only in terms of self-denial. The notion of a mutual sharing, of equity, was foreign to her: she could be a child or a mother but not yet a partner.

Thérèse's attention to others in this world was not this-worldly. Although cosseted by a home life which included the sartorial vanities for girls, she early resisted any real susceptibility to the blandishments of this world, to the hollow flatteries of prestige, wealth, even ordinary pleasures. Her parents' views on such matters, with many monitory passages left for her to read in Zélie's letters, instilled and enforced this recoiling. She betrays in one striking, almost caustic passage a bourgeois contempt toward the well-to-do, a disdain submerged in biblical rectitudes about the pointlessness of earthly delights and desires. Concerning what she calls her "entry into the world" on a visit to her hometown of Alençon, where at age ten she was pampered and petted by family friends and acquaintances, her long golden curls winning special praise, she writes: "les amis que nous y avions étaient trop mondains, ils savaient trop allier les joies de la terre avec le service du Bon Dieu. Ils ne pensaient pas assez à la mort et cependant la mort est venue visiter un grand nombre de personnes que j'ai connues, jeunes, riches et heureuses!!! J'aime à retourner par la pensée aux lieux enchanteurs où elles ont vécu, à me demander où elles sont, ce qui leur revient des châteaux et des parcs où je les ai vues jouir des commodités de la vie?" ["the friends we had there were too worldly; they knew too well how to combine the earth's joys with service to the Good Lord. They didn't think enough about death and yet death came to visit a great number of people I knew there who were young, rich, and happy!!! I love to return in my mind to the enchanting places where they lived and to ask myself where they are, what they're realizing from their chateaux and parks where I saw them enjoying life's conveniences?"] (A 32v).

While this passage is mercifully free of malice—she does not mention by name any of the "great number" of people overtaken by death and in effect punished for not appreciating the spiritual vacuity of their lives—it is difficult to miss in her remarks a kind of grim glee that those who seemed to have been battening on the world's delights came to premature grief. And is it incidental that in the last sentence she refers only to young *women*, a point lost in English translations? Young, affluent, happy women. For a moment, Thérèse's world intersects with Proust's. We have almost caught a glimpse of his Albertine and other *jeunes filles en fleurs*.

Admitting the limits of her own experience, Thérèse is strikingly confident—as how could she afford not to be?—that she has made the only possible choice: "Sans avoir bu à la coupe empoisonnée de l'amour trop ardent des créatures, je sens que je ne puis me tromper, j'ai vu tant d'âmes séduites par cette fausse lumière, voler comme de pauvres papillons et se brûler les ailes" ["Without having drunk from the poisoned cup of excessive love for creatures, I feel that I can't be deceived; I've seen so many souls seduced by this false light, flying like butterflies and burning their wings"] (A 38v). This avowal betrays Thérèse's failure or her unwillingness to consider to what a "creaturely" but not excessive love would have come. How could her own parents' example, hardly a creaturely sort of affection, have failed to register itself? In her pronounced devotion to her father, her "little king," did she presume that no other man on this earth could possibly rival him in piety and propriety, in sheer worthiness as both a husband and a father?

Economics, or what George Orwell called the "class racket," inevitably obtrudes, and the Martin girls were familiar with it from their schools, where some children came from the nobility. Thérèse's sister Marie had suffered from an emotional attachment to a young schoolmate, pretty and rich, whom she could not hope to emulate. This painful example likely reinforced Thérèse's apprehensions and her subsequent disdain.

In Thérèse's accents—"I *love*" to ask about the deserted chateaux—we might detect what Nietzsche believed to be the salient feature of Christianity's adherents, a *ressentiment* toward those who conspicuously enjoy life or triumph in it by the conventional standards of success and power, and with that *ressentiment* an inversion of the will to power, the exaltation of a slave ethic in which the wretched are vouched a final hegemony over those who have proven themselves earthly masters. The difference is that in Thérèse's account, the comeuppance is not celestial but earthly, so that the pious soul can savor the lesson and feel justified by it. It seems a sentiment unworthy of genuine charity, and we wonder how Thérèse would have felt to contemplate the prospect of former schoolmates who went on to marry and thrive with loving children and husbands, as in fact her mother, for all the adversities, managed to do. To assume that the abundant joys of this earth are all shallow and worthless is to forget that having created the world, God saw that it was very good. To assume an either-or, that one can either serve God or enjoy life, is to pose a punitive, not to say monstrous, ethic. It is pointless to pretend that Thérèse was somehow immune to the prejudices, social and religious, in which she was raised. By a happy irony, toward her life's close she came to a singular affirmation of this world as the ground upon which she would serve God to the end of time: what had long seemed her exile became her home.

The disposition to deprecate earthly joys complements the monastic urge, which can be credited or rationalized only by being made exclusive and implicitly triumphant: not merely the right choice but as it were the only one. Thérèse was well prompted to this end by her sisters Pauline and Marie, from within the Carmel, where they were in effect establishing a new home for her. Pauline even admitted her sensitivity to the criticism that Thérèse was entering Carmel because her sisters were drawing her there. How well prepared she was we find in her letters en route to Rome during the jubilee pilgrimage of November 1887. Of her first trip to Paris, where she toured with her father and Céline the obligatory venues (the Tuileries and the Louvre, l'Etoile and the Palais Royal), she wrote to Pauline and Marie just what they wanted to read: "nous avons vu de très belles choses à Paris mais *tout* cela n'est pas le bonheur. Céline va vous dire, si elle veut, les merveilles de Paris, pour moi je vais seulement vous dire que je pense bien souvent à vous, les belles choses de Paris ne captivent pas du tout mon coeur" ["we've seen very beautiful things in Paris but *all that* is not happiness. Céline will tell you, if she wants, about the wonders of Paris; for my part I'll only tell you that I'm thinking quite often of you. The beauties of Paris do not captivate my heart"] (LT 30, November 6, 1887).

She does not extend such a criticism to Rome, it being the city sacred to Catholicism but otherwise a monument to human vanity and evanescence in all its Caesarean dilapidation. Besides, Rome was the seat of famous Christian martyrdoms. Thérèse was thrilled by the catacombs along the Appian Way, and Saints Agnes and Cecilia had long been exemplary virgin martyrs, favorites within the Martin family of sisters.

How Pauline would have loved to join them! One of her cherished books in childhood was Cardinal Wiseman's sententious novel *Fabiola*, a chronicle of Christians persecuted under Diocletian in the early fourth century A.D. The fiction centers on St. Agnes, who underwent burning and, when that did not work, decapitation but retained her purity to the end.[10] Thérèse was more drawn to Cecilia, the model of a virginal wife to a pious husband, the couple Louis might have had in mind when marrying Zélie. The deeper attraction comes to the fore in the first manuscript: "Sa vie n'a pas été autre chose qu'un chant mélodieux au milieu même des plus grandes épreuves" ["Her life was nothing but a melodious song in the very midst of the greatest tests"] (A 61v) and hence a hortatory life. Thérèse already knew some greatest tests of her own, especially in the time of Bon Sauveur, and was struggling to attune her life sweetly to them. In a sense, the autobiographical writings are her way of melodious song, a counterpoint to immitigable bitterness.

As though to cauterize herself against all possible worldly attractions and temptations, Thérèse subsequent to her first Communion developed an eagerness for suffering accompanied by "l'intime assurance que Jésus me réservait un grand nombre de croix, je me sentis inondée de consolations si grandes que je les regarde comme une des grâces les plus grandes de ma vie. La souffrance devint mon attrait, elle avait des charmes qui me ravissaient sans les bien connaître" ["the intimate assurance that Jesus was keeping for me a great number of crosses; I felt myself inundated with such great consolations that I consider them one of the greatest mercies of my life. Suffering became attractive to me, having charms which ravished me without my knowing them well"] (A 36r).

To moderns, such sentiments seem macabre or masochistic, but it is helpful to underscore why this cult of suffering was so keen for Thérèse and so pervasive in historical Christianity. Spiritually considered, the assumption of suffering was a divinely sent means for overcoming the ego and its suasions. Christ himself urged his followers to take up each his own cross (Matthew 10:38). This cross bearing, by an active rather than inert receptivity to suffering, proves a genuine imitatio Christi. It is the one command by which Christ indicated a believer could become like him, however imperfectly. As the Greeks of old knew, suffering can be a ready means to a heightened awareness, to understandings not gained by a life untested and recumbent. A man of sorrows and acquainted with grief is also a man of exceptional, dearly won perceptions into reality. Adversity, inner or outer, much like Dr. Johnson's prospect of hanging on the morrow, concentrates the mind wonderfully. If, as we have noticed, the message of suffering substantiated or vindicated for Thérèse her childhood's scorn of the world's benefits, it also ratified her choice of a celibate life devoted to prayer and penance. It seems fair to say that both prayer and penance gain depth and focus primarily by their nexus with calamities, no matter the scale.

The option of suffering, the decided preference of it over comfort, figures prominently in one of the major texts of Thérèse's spiritual maturity, the Imitatio Christi, a composite work of several generations and authors but commonly attributed to the fifteenth-century ascetic Thomas of Kempen (in southern Germany). This exacting text on cloistered life argues the paradox that true inner peace is found only by daily dying to the self, but it also posits that life is so thoroughly signposted with afflictions that one can hardly avoid them; the point is to be sure not to, but rather to embrace them and to make them seem sweet. If misery pervades the world, then it could be assumed that the world's temptations will have far less force than Thérèse seems to give them, but she does so because she was aware of something neither the composers of the *Imitatio* nor Thomas in Kempen had to overcome, the bourgeois ambience of ease, of tidiness and possessions, of convenience and status, and the ascendance of that very Proustian commodity, *snobisme*, a very broad game board of earthly delights and hazards. Far better to play the one game she knew she could win: as the *Imitatio* soberly argues, many if not most believers yearn for the comfort Christ might bring but few yearn for his cross. Very few love Christ for his sake, not their own. The *Imitatio* then adds this strategic caveat: to assume a cross is not within human capacity; one must trust that God will confer the power to sustain suffering. Hence, a true imitation of Christ is God assisted. That collusion illumines in part the appeal of suffering in Thérèse's mind: suffering implicates God.

Far more imposing, however, would have been this claim upon her sensibility: "Et nonnunquam in tantum confortatur ex affectu tribulationis et adversitatis, ob amorem conformitatis crucis Christi, ut se sine dolore et tribulatione esse non vellet: quoniam tanto se acceptiorem Deo credit, quanto plura et graviora pro eo perferre potuerit" ["And sometimes one is so strengthened by a desire for suffering and adversity, out of love for conformity to Christ's cross, as to wish not to be free from pain and suffering: since one believes that the more affliction one has been able to bear for God's sake, and the heavier to endure, the more acceptable will one be in God's sight"]. No passage in the *Imitatio* spoke so tellingly to Thérèse, for nothing mattered to her so forcefully as her own desire—or need—to please, and God, in the familiar person of Christ (she speaks of him almost always familiarly, as Jesus), was an inexhaustible recipient of her endeavor to do so.

The *Imitatio Christi* was an especially popular book in Thérèse's time, as it gave forceful aid to many Catholics in the midst of Third Republican indifference and occasional hostility. Almost wholly forgotten now save by Thérèse's adolescent enthusiasm for it is another book which informed her attention to suffering, *Fin du monde présent et mystères de la vie future* ["The end of this world and mysteries of the life to come"], a series of lectures given in Chambéry (the neighborhood of Rousseau's adolescence) in 1881 by Abbé Charles Arminjon (1824–1885). Thérèse's father was given a copy by his daughters, and she read it in May and June 1887, "une de plus grandes grâces de ma vie . . et l'impression que j'en ressentais est trop intime et trop douce pour que je puisse la rendre" ["one of my life's greatest blessings . . and the impression I felt from it is too intimate and sweet for me to express"] (A 47v).

In fact she does indicate why she felt blessed in this reading: *Fin du monde* taught her of the eternal compensation God's faithful would receive in exchange for the sacrifices they would make in this life. A favorite single line from the abbé, part of an extended passage Thérèse copied into her school notebook, has a grateful God speaking to the faithful in-gathered to heaven, "Maintenant mon tour," or "Now, it's my turn." It is at last time for their reward.

It is well that Thérèse explains this book's appeal to her, because it leaves a mixed impression today. It is emphatically a periodic document, its author keen to set out, beside ecclesiastical dogmas on such matters as where purgatory is located, his awareness of modern scientific thought. He cites the work of the astronomer Alexander Herschel, for example, but then assails "la science" for combating what he calls "man's hope and glorious destiny" in the heavens. The book also emits the noxious fumes of anti-Semitism, a half-generation before Drumont and Dreyfus focused the energies of this kind of reactionary sentiment. Adverting to "the question" already being discussed in Germany, Arminjon sums it up: "il s'agit des progrès et de l'influence toujours croissante du judaïsme, qui constitue à l'heure actuelle une menace pour la civilisation, pour la sécurité et l'existence des peuples chrétiens" ["it concerns the progress and ever growing influence of Judaism, which at the present time constitutes a menace for civilization, for the security and existence of Christian peoples"].[11] He attacks modern liberalism for sentimentality and false egalitarianism in contributing to the Jewish ascendancy. Even assimilated Jews, converts to Christianity, win his scorn, since they are merely status seekers and job hunters whose money goes covertly to enrich the coffers of synagogues, not churches. We learn that the Antichrist, imminently expected, will be a Jew; a sure sign of his approach will be the rise of Freemasonry, etc. Fortunately, these unsavory pages seem to have passed one young reader's notice altogether.

Beside the dark fact of this prejudice, a poignant one. The lengthy passage Thérèse wrote out from *Fin du monde* is a miniature dialogue in which God speaks of imbibing the faithful now in heaven with his own divinity so that they become divine themselves—the serpent's bribe in Eden, "Ye shall be as gods," seems to have slipped from the abbé's remembrance—while Christ asks that they lose themselves in the sea of his brilliance, disappearing in a beatitude where the sense of an everlasting bliss is left them. That Thérèse copied out this rhetoric says much. It is as though she needed assurance or reassurance, or was she merely taken with the parataxis of heavenly blessings it displays? What matters is that she eventually lost the surety of whatever heaven she did have in her mind, heart, and schoolbook memory. If it was the abbé's sort of heaven, with surely no Jews or Freemasons admissible, perhaps the loss was a fortunate one.

Even so stale and embarrassingly dated a work as *Fin du monde* (Dorothy Day said she would have liked to read it) can teach us something about its enthusiast. A veteran of many retreats and conferences, Arminjon had a shrewd awareness of people's vanity and the minutest foibles. It is not his dismissal of the usual inadmissible delights and pleasures of life, the disappointed attachments to people, to power, to status, which captures attention in these "conférences"—that slighting is altogether de rigueur among religious. Nor his depiction of the wonders of purgatory with its hour of flames a greater torture than a thousand years of any pain on the surface of this earth—that is mere hyperbole. Nor his closing exhortations to suffering as the basis for ineffable joys in the next world. Rather, it is the abbé's noting that even the purest or most saintly joys in this one are not free from a certain complacency and egotistical satisfaction. Thus, true saints have always felt a disquiet in the midst of their own happiness and prosperity; wholly precious and honest pleasures are both enervating and corrupting because they tend to distract one from the thought of God. It can hardly be wondered, given this untender and hairshirt view, that Thérèse would have found only virtue in suffering.

Suffering and the wish for it were not idle abstractions for her. Well before she could have matured to an *imitatio Christi*, she had the example of her mother. Unlike her mother, Thérèse had not suffered the adversities of parental life nor the cares of an occupation; because she had secured the community of Carmel so early, she had to await unimaginable trials for herself. The first came with her father's confinement to a sanatorium for more than three years. When writing her first manuscript, she did not realize that a second would soon come with overwhelming gravity.

It may be helpful to distinguish Thérèse's desire for suffering as the means of an *imitatio Christi* from the mortifications to which she had been subjecting herself since childhood. When preparing for her first Communion, in the spring of 1884, she managed within those sixty-eight Lenten days 1,949 acts "of sacrifice and of virtue." As to prayers, she took inspiration from a preparatory book which Pauline had given her along with one-line invocations addressed to "Little Jesus," proclaiming love for him, asking for simplicity, and pride's humbling. By the end of Lent, she had reached the astounding number of 2,773 repetitions.

In her autobiography Thérèse credits her eldest sister, Marie, then still at home, with the inspiration which, in the recounting, adumbrates the "little way." "Marie me parlait encore des richesses immortelles qu'il est facile d'amasser chaque jour, du malheur de passer sans vouloir se donner le peine de tendre la main pour les prendre, puis elle m'indiquait le moyen d'être sainte par la fidélité aux plus petites choses, elle me donna la petite feuille, 'Du renoncement,' que je méditais avec délices" ["Marie spoke to me of the undying riches it's easy to amass every day, of the misery of spending (the day) without wanting to make the effort to stretch out one's hand to take them. Then she showed me the way to be a saint by fidelity to the smallest things and she gave me a little pamphlet, 'On Renunciation,' which I pondered with delight"] (A 33r).

While it cannot be gainsaid that such practices as Thérèse pursued with such avidity were of substantial help to an eleven-year-old child in forming pious habits, it can also not be denied that a semblance of pharisaism lurked in such practices. In the trying time of retreats, Thérèse importuned priests—the Jesuits Pichon and Laurent Blino, the Franciscan Père Alexis—to affirm that she had lived a life without any grave sin, that her faults were innocuous, that she could realize Christ's injunction to become perfect. And her little faults? In testimony for her sister's beatification, Céline presented a seamless image of Thérèse's life at home, but the correspondence indicates that Thérèse, for all that she lived a very happy, warmly sustaining life at home, was as subject as any child to petulance and fussing. In a teasing mood, Pauline addressed her as "mademoiselle la trembleuse, mademoiselle la fiévreuse" ["Little miss fraidy cat, little miss excitable"] (LC 10 April 1–2, 1883). Thérèse herself admits that in the time after Pauline entered Carmel, she became unbearably touchy.

The family correspondence around the time of Thérèse's quest to enter Carmel enlightens us on many particulars. We learn what a substantial role her sisters played, including Pauline providing her with a script for the papal audience she was anticipating. Gonzague, then prioress, was warmly encouraging, even though the superior of Carmel, Delatroëtte, was obstinately and more than once outspokenly opposed to Thérèse's entry. Her father had not only accompanied her to Bayeux to see the bishop, Msgr. Hugonin; he subtly importuned the vicar-general, Révérony, who had led the French pilgrims on the jubilee. As anyone can avouch who has spent a few weeks with strangers or mere acquaintances on tour, particular bonds are formed and formalities become relaxed. Louis Martin took shrewd advantage of the vicar-general, the official whose injunctions to silence before the pope were flouted by Thérèse. Even the ancient Mère Geneviève became involved, pressing Delatroëtte in the presence of the community for Thérèse's admission before Christmas. On him, of course, would have weighed all the responsibility had Thérèse embarrassed the Carmel with a failure to sustain its rigors. Possibly, Delatroëtte was familiar with her much older sister Léonie's repeated failures to enter a convent and stay there.[12]

The fascinating point in Thérèse's account comes in her response to the initial rebuff from her uncle, Isidore. She likens the ensuing three days of anguish, the weather cooperating with rainstorms, to his parents' searching three days for young Jesus (Luke 2:41–50), then to Jesus' own agony at Gethsemane. She speaks of her soul's dark night and of the feeling that God had abandoned her. This pulling out of the allusive stops should be taken with a discriminating measure, not of salt but of sense. She had hardly been abandoned; her father had supported her warmly; she knew she had the support of Pauline and the Carmel, if not of Marie, and her uncle was not an unreasonable man. We are reading an account of adolescent despair, without a doubt intensely felt, but on the order of a girl's chasmic disappointment in not being asked to the senior prom. At no time was she being denied Carmel; she was being denied what seemed to the reasonable a premature admission. No one seemed to have asked her why she could not wait and why she had to apply to Lisieux's Carmel rather than to another. Further, in pressing the matter, she was upstaging her older sister Céline, not to say abandoning her to care for Louis alone. Most trenchant of all was a caveat in Madre Teresa's manual for her spiritual daughters, *Camino de Perfección*,[13] warning against familial attachments. Characteristic of the teen years, the vantage of Thérèse shows the intentional maturity of an adult and the willful obstinacy of a child. She was used to getting her way from gentle Louis, "my little king," but now she was facing a succession of apparently unswayable men: her uncle, the superior of Carmel, the bishop of Bayeux, and his vicar-general.

Had she been able to read them a bit better, she would have realized how all of them—Delatroëtte excepted—were malleable. When her uncle suddenly relented and told her she was the little flower God wanted to pick, she knew from his choice of words that her father had had his way with his wife's brother.[14] And before introducing her to the bishop, the vicar-general likened her embarrassed tears to diamonds. Used to a never-questioned obedience and deference from adults and children, these men were caught off guard by an urgent fourteen-year-old girl and her thoroughly complicit father.

While this Bayeux-to-Rome story entices us to imagine Thérèse's own recounting of it in Carmel—it must have amused the sisters, natural and spiritual, to know that a girl barely into her teens had braved the austere male establishment, a David and Goliath story of sorts—what we have in the correspondence during the time of Thérèse's waiting after her return from Rome is invaluable. It shows us the degree to which her natural sisters, particularly Pauline, informed Thérèse's view of herself and of her subsequent mission. Not the least engaging aspect of the letters written in the fall of 1887 is their diction.

The whole push toward Thérèse's dramatically early acceptance into Carmel was predicated not simply on her stubbornly adolescent resolve to secure it but on the tacit agreement of everyone else concerned that she was mature enough to sustain the Carmelite regimen once she was admitted. The risk of an embarrassment was substantial, and Delatroëtte cannot fairly be blamed for weighing it decisively against Thérèse. She was not going on as a student at a convent school; she was asking to be admitted to a society of mature women. How could she presume that she was fit to be counted one of them?

Here, when compared with the hundreds of *circulaires* and their stories of the way to Carmel, Thérèse's stands unique. Because of her very young age and the presence of two sisters already *intra muros*, she was challenging ecclesiastical authority and Carmel's own tradition. We have noted in the *circulaires* that parents were frequently the antagonists of their daughters' resolve because of concerns for their health and Carmel's austerities; the parish priest or a retreat director would be the young women's defendant. Isidore's demurring apart, Thérèse stood in a position diametric to that norm: she had her family in aid of her, and Louis's support was unequivocal, even diplomatic. She had allies in Carmelites who had known her since Pauline's entrance in October 1882. She was opposed or at least hindered by the Church hierarchy, and Madre Teresa herself would perhaps have rejected her petition. The Spanish mothers of the early French Carmels had found the young women of France much too soft, and here was a capital case of indulgence. Surely, Teresa would have been aghast at Pauline's coaxing solicitudes.

What strikes us in both Pauline's and Marie's letters to her is the infantilizing language. Pauline, not Thérèse, set rolling the famous "little ball" image we find as a characterization of Thérèse in her relation to the child Jesus.[15] In a letter of November 9, 1887, Pauline fantasizes that Jesus as an infant is already inclined to weep for love, desiring all souls to turn to him. His mother, in order to placate him, gives him a ball to play with on which is written "Thérésita of the child Jesus."[16] (The diminutive was the coinage of the prioress Gonzague.) From then on, Pauline would address her sister as "little toy of Jesus."

Thérèse as the youngest child had long been known to the family as *benjamine*, named for the last and most favored child of the biblical Jacob. She was also known as "coquine," but Céline, too, had been an imp. Pauline had earlier written to Thérèse that she was a ripe fruit for Jesus to pick and in the same letter likens her to the beloved disciple in the Johannine Gospel, one privileged by close proximity to Jesus. She also referred to Thérèse, but only once, as a lily (October 30, 1887).

The ball imagery comes to predominate and takes some peculiar turns as Pauline imagines Jesus himself has made his little ball roll all the way to Rome (November 10, 1887). She shared her fancies with Marie, who writes to Thérèse that the infant Jesus is not asleep in his cradle but cherishing his "very much loved little toy" (November 11, 1887). As though to contain these childish conceits or at least to give them point, Thérèse herself acknowledged that Jesus had only to roll the ball wherever he chose, meaning that she was becoming resigned to the possibility that her request would prove vain, that all would in any case depend upon the divine will—that conceded, even as she was prepared to wager all on an appearance before the pope.

After Pope Leo had given an equivocal answer to Thérèse's request, Marie chose to read his "if God wills it" as an encouragement, but Pauline, who had been in a retreat on the topic of suffering, chose to run away with the ball. With an intimation of her little sister's grief over the failure to secure the pope's definitive assent, she creates a dialogue in which Jesus is called upon by an unidentified interlocutor to explain why he has pierced the ball so that it no longer bounces. Jesus answers that making holes in it brought forth breezes to caress his blond non-Semitic curls, and on making a bigger hole he found the ball was filled only with love for him and wanted to suffer for him. Thereafter he will repair the holes with kisses, confident that whenever he pierces it again, the ball will proclaim to him its "je vous aime." In that same letter, November 23, 1887, Pauline confidently asserted that in the divine willing that Thérèse suffer for love of Jesus, she was destined to become a great saint. While it is inexact to suppose that from this time on she became the object of Pauline's promotion, Pauline regarded her sister in an already exalted, sanctifying manner. Pauline had been primed to take over the promotional role because Zélie had laid it upon her: a daughter would become a saint in her mother's stead. And Thérèse was Pauline's daughter by adoption.

Thérèse's narrative of her time in Rome after the papal reception resumes the motif of divine abandonment sounded in her account of Isidore's refusal: she felt the silence and absence of Jesus. The autobiographical manuscript at this point suggests that Thérèse was writing her memoir in part from the perspective of her sisters in Carmel, as though their letters of exhortation during the autumn of 1887 were at hand. She must have imprinted them firmly in her memory, and they must have served her like amulets against despair. She could now only construe Pope Leo's words as an indication of a divine will: "les dernières paroles du Saint Père auraient dû me consoler" ["the closing words of the Holy Father should have comforted me"] (A 64r), exactly what Marie had written to her, but instead, she writes, she had to resign herself to whatever Jesus chose to do with his little ball, even to casting it upon the ground, kicking it, *piercing* it: "en un mot, je voulais amuser le petit Jésus, lui faire plaisir, je voulais me livrer à ses caprices enfantins" ["in a word, I wanted to amuse little Jesus, give him pleasure, deliver myself to his childlike whims"] (A 64r; see figure 5.4).

When she characterizes herself according to Pauline's appellation, as Jesus' "petit jouet," she adds that when she was in Rome he pierced his little ball, wanting to see what was inside it, then fell asleep and dreamed of playing with it—all this, an almost verbatim recasting of Pauline's bizarre script. Behind this rather tiresomely childish talk, however, there is more at work with the little toy. *Jouet* plays in French upon two meanings: it is both a toy and a kind of pawn, the object of delight and of malice. Rousseau used this word in speaking of himself as a laughingstock. Thérèse does not conjure up wicked behavior from anyone, but she makes herself something with which Jesus might for the while enjoy engaging but as likely as not will neglect once it's been shunted to a corner. This motif of discarding, of Christ's abandonment of her, returned in the last dark months of her life. Her last manuscript speaks much of God and far less of Jesus.

FIGURE 5.4. The Sala dei Palafrenieri in the Vatican, where Pope Leo XIII received Louis, Céline, Thérèse, and other jubilee pilgrims from Normandy on November 20, 1887. Copyright Conway Library, Courtauld Institute of Art.

When, following her return to Lisieux, she waited daily for some word from the monsignor and it did not come before Christmas, she writes of Jesus' sleeping still: "Il laissa par terre sa petite balle, sans même jeter sur elle un seul regard" ["He left his little ball on the ground without even noticing it"] (A 67v). Here she plays on the sense of *par terre*, which suggests ruination. The reduction of Jesus to an infant had been Pauline's way not only of making Thérèse's anxiety less severe but of making Jesus less culpable for neglecting her. It would be difficult to become angry or resentful of an infant for neglecting one's wishes. One could even forgive an infant for not knowing what he was doing in piercing the ball. Indeed, forgiveness was not ever an issue for Thérèse since in matters of divine will there could only be her submission and compliance.

The "jouet," then, sufficed amply for the two aspects of her character and even of her Carmelite name: she was the toy of the baby Jesus, but she was ready to be an object neglected and ignored by God, to suffer the abandonment she read on "the holy face" of the Veronica cloth. The childlike simplicity of her little way is matched by the predisposition to suffer. She was to wager all upon the caveat "Except ye be as little children, ye cannot enter the kingdom of God" (*Matthew* 18:3), but she knew that a deeply experienced awareness of spiritual adversity could alone sustain her Christian faith. In sum, she was reconciling the two polar injunctions of Christianity, its alpha and omega: be like a child and carry your cross.

In her correspondence, Pauline had inculcated her own gospel of suffering, telling Thérèse that she, Thérèse, had been born for it, that there could be only a cross for her because one could be certain of nothing else in life. That had been Zélie's message, often iterated. The infant Jesus himself sends only crosses to those who love him, Pauline claims, so that sanctity becomes a synonym for suffering. Jesus wants not our pleasure but his own by our self-denials (LC 64, 69: November 20 and 25, 1887). In fact, these somber accents came not only from Pauline but from Père Pichon, who held the retreat Pauline attended in October 1887. From him, Pauline took verbatim and passed on to her sister the encouragement that one's hours of desperation are God's hours, that one's hopelessness is a time of trial. That vital qualification effectively removes the charge, not uncommon among some laity, of masochism in religious asceticism: Pauline herself had already advised Thérèse that one should not suffer just for the sake of suffering as that would "ruin the sauce" (LC 52).

Thérèse, in reflecting upon her protracted wait, concludes that her anguish was a sign of God's testing. The New Testament itself, she records, afforded examples of how faithful people were sorely tried before they were accorded a miracle: Lazarus was allowed to die, leaving his sisters to grieve for him, Christ having delayed to come because he knew it was an occasion for his own glorification (*John* 11:21–27). Christ's mother at the wedding in Cana was frustrated in requesting her son's help to furnish the wedding couple more wine, his "hour" not having come to manifest his miraculous powers (*John* 2:1–10). But the wine was supplied, and Lazarus was raised. Is it incidental that Thérèse chose two stories about women denied their wishes? Or that in each narrative, the denial is in effect a delay and one almost immediately resolved, whereas for her, the bitter waiting had lasted months?

Recalling the imposed delay, her extended "exile," Thérèse rationalizes her disappointment as an occasion for her growth in *abandon*, or spiritual surrender, to the divine will as read in Pauline's decision. (It remains unclear why Gonzague, who had supported Thérèse all along, did not override Pauline's position.) Her account of how she spent the three months remaining to her life among laity is instructive: she insists that all those efforts were not mortifications in the sense of penances, because she was aware of none in herself. She would leave such practices, she adds mordantly, to "belles âmes" who have busied themselves that way their whole life. Rather than count up ways to make herself suffer, a routine in which she found Céline adept, she would let herself be wrapped in cotton and fattened like a little bird, a simile to which she returned often, even to the final vision of her spiritual journey.

For Thérèse, mortification meant the breaking of the will, a calculated program of restraint in which she would not seek to have the last word, would perform services for others but without presuming such acts worthy of anything, and would sit without supporting her back. The point of this simple regimen, what she called the exercise of nothings, is its prolepsis, that she is in effect recording her life after she entered Carmel but as though she had become a Carmelite *de iure* in her father's house. She went some way to prepare herself. Now without schooling or tutoring, she spent much of her time reading inspirational literature, chiefly two volumes of *Petites Fleurs.*

Each was composed of three series. The first volume dates from 1887. Thérèse was likely reading it during and subsequent to her Roman days: a bookmark within it shows a likeness of Pope Leo. The second volume, issued in 1888, bears evidence that only the first two series were read. Thérèse had not finished the book by April 9, when she entered Carmel.

These books offered her an abundance of spiritual insights and injunctions from such masters as Juan de la Cruz, Marguerite-Marie Alacoque, Bossuet, and Msgr. Gay. The gentle and penetrating wisdom of François de Sales told her that God is content with little by seeing that we do not have much; that God's love, while shown to faith and prepared through hope, is given only to our reciprocal love; that it is better to be weak than strong because God lets the strong walk but carries the weak. This book reminds us of how Salesian Thérèse was in this time and how François de Sales stands perhaps closer to her than does even Juan de la Cruz.[17]

From Juan, her master of darkness, she learned now to consider hope as the absence of possession and love as the absence of feeling: "Que Jésus crucifié vous suffise seul" ["Let the crucified Jesus alone suffice you"].[18] These injunctions gave her a foretaste of the Spanish mystic who would occupy much of her reading two years later, when she was seventeen and making her way through Juan's Canticle and his *Llama de amor viva (Living Flame of Love).*

One of the *Petites Fleurs* authors most instructive—by anticipation—about Thérèse herself is Frederick William Faber (1814–1863), an expansively popular early Victorian homilist and inspirational writer whose works were widely translated. In distinguishing three ways of loving Christ, he identifies the mystical elevation of a newly created state as passive love. He calls effective love the practice of continual mortifications, but it is affective love which prompts us "à répandre avec *confiance* notre âme devant Dieu ... à nous *abandonner* chacun tout entier entre ses mains avec la tranquille insouciance d'un enfant" ["to open our soul with *trust* before God ... to *yield* our whole self into his hands with the calm insouciance of a child"]. This is Thérèse to the vivid life. So, too, his notion of fervor as something hidden, like God, not seeking grand occasions but able rather "persévérer dans les choses ordinaires et peu dignes de remarque" ["to persevere in ordinary, unremarkable things"] with the alluring codicil that such was the fervor of the desert fathers and the ancient convents. No less important is his celebration of "les petites choses," little things which require a passive heroism but also a purer motive than the performance of the great.[19] One difference: Faber was talking about glory, not love.

Before we enter Carmel with her, it may be helpful to observe that the unsettling image of the child Jesus capriciously abusing his toy, Thérèse, was not the only picture of consolation which she shared with her sisters. A far deeper and more imposing one was of a small boat in which Jesus was sleeping. Its power derives from an incident in Scripture, *Mark* 4:36–41, when Jesus, having preached, crosses the Sea of Galilee in a boat, accompanied by his disciples. He sleeps as a storm comes on, and the disciples, fearing a capsize, wake him and he calms the storm, then reproaches them for their lack of faith.

The boat at hazard had been with Thérèse from childhood, when she was read a short story in a children's book called *La Tirelire aux Histoires*. Given the importance which Céline later attached to the story, a glance at it here seems justified.[20] Living by the sea, Marie, a spoiled child whose father has been away in the Indies, watches ships pass. Her mother reads her stories, and Marie falls asleep as a setting sun casts a brilliant golden trail over the darkening sea. The luminous path reappears in a dream, and she is suddenly transported to the helm of a ship with no one aboard but herself. She must navigate alone. A light breeze fills the sails, but then the air grows cold and winds churn the waves. Terrified, she recalls that her mother, once when ill, had bidden her to pray, and the prayer had prompted her mother's recovery, and so when in the Lord's Prayer Marie says "deliver us from evil," the boat reenters the golden path, and she arrives at an enchanted land, only to awaken when she steps onto the flowery shore. This moral fable, a compaction of adventure, helplessness, and humble recourse to divine protection, provided Thérèse with her own boat for the journey across the Sea of Galilee. Its analogue to the Markan passage needs no remarking. The narrative in all its oneiric power had impressed itself upon Thérèse by speaking directly to her temperament, not to mention the apt particulars of a sometimes absent father and an ailing mother.

When she was sustaining a dejected wait after her meeting with Pope Leo, Pauline wrote to console her that Jesus appeared to be sleeping in her little boat. She adds a line from the Solomonic canticle, "Ego dormio, et cor meum vigilat" ["I am sleeping, and (but) my heart is awake"] (*Canticum canticorum*, 5:2). (Those words in the Vulgate are assigned to the bride, not to the groom.) Their sister Marie had cited this passage in one of her own letters to Thérèse two weeks before. In effect, as each of the sisters supposed, Jesus was testing Thérèse's faith. She did not need to awaken him.

Like Thérèse's other favored imagery—flowers and birds, chiefly—the effectiveness of the boat image lies in its universality. It is immediate, unadorned, accessible. The metaphor of life as a boat is one of the most ancient—Augustine uses it at length in *De beata vita*—but the Martin sisters knew it in a variant by Lamartine, one of their father's favorite poets, who in "Réflexion" writes, "Le temps est ton navire et non pas ta demeure" ["Time is your vessel, not your dwelling place"].[21] Surpassing the toy ball imagery, the trope of the boat argues its furtive way into the darkness of Thérèse's last eighteen months, when she was waiting and kept waiting for Christ to awaken.

The Markan image informs our understanding of Thérèse's little way of unconditional love and acceptance of the divine will because it addresses the contingencies which challenge pursuance of that way: the storm and its buffeting waves countered by the mysterious presence of the divine. The image has the eloquence of simplicity and can be grasped and integrated into anyone's life, whereas the toy ball presents an almost cruelly capricious deity before whom it would be difficult for many to imagine themselves as objects of sport. With the ball, acceptance of the divine will means a receptivity to suffering which Jesus has permitted and hence imposed, even as that suffering joins one with him. It is the very condition for that joining.

Like the ball, the boat was tossed around in the Martin sisters' correspondence.[22] Curiously, they omitted the central role which the sudden storm plays in the gospel account. Céline, for example, wrote post-Rome that the process of furthering Thérèse's cause was at rest and all seemed asleep, not only Jesus. He was allowing the boat to rock gently on the waves, but its passengers had as yet no view of port. It was late, they were getting cold, and he should be roused. Four months later, only a few weeks before entering Carmel, Thérèse wrote to Pauline of Carmel's "rivage béni," or blessed shore, but the image is one of frustration rather than of hazard: "Ma petite nacelle a bien du mal à arriver au port, depuis longtemps j'aperçois le rivage et toujours je m'en trouve éloignée; mais c'est Jesus qui guide mon petit navire, et je suis sûre que le jour où il le voudra il pourra le faire aborder heureusement au port" ["My little wherry is having a hard time reaching port. For a long time I've been seeing the shore and I find myself always kept at a distance from it, but it's Jesus who's guiding my little boat, and I'm certain that the day he wants, he'll be able to make it happily reach port"] (LT 43.a). This image summons the mature, itinerant Jesus, the Christ of Scripture, rather than the doll/child Jesus invoked from nowhere in the Gospels but as from a nursery of the Martin sisters' fancy.

Many turns in the correspondence hint that Thérèse was becoming much older than her sisters presumed or even allowed, as though they needed to go on coddling the child they had always known, while she was effectively moving ahead of them. That subtle disjunction might in part tell why she was so attracted to Mère Gonzague, who had no such familial politics and knew how to be exigent, even to the point of seeming arbitrary and unfair. But the *benjamine* position Thérèse had always held before Marie, Pauline, and Céline informed even the writing of her story. It was, after all, meant as little more than a family entertainment. In composing for this quite limited circuit of readers—which extended to the Guérins, of course—Thérèse was obliged to speak the language they expected of her. The very narrative imposed this indulgence: she was writing of many episodes which they had talked about innumerable times in the colloquial terms of a family lexicon exclusive to every home. In Manuscript B, written eight months after A, and with C at another nine months' distance, she reveals (as do the letters of that time, LT 196 and 197) the sober self hidden beneath the erstwhile babying and cooing.

It is wrongheaded to accuse Thérèse, as some have, of infantilism. She was trying to escape it at work in her sisters' blandishments, even as she was wittingly participating in their common lexical games. The youngest of five (of seven, if we count the Guérin girls), she had all the more impetus to catch up. Within a very few years and by the crucible of suffering, she not only caught up but left them all behind, so that at her death they were as bereft as orphans.

The "Springtime Story," or what we less elegantly call Manuscript A, concludes with a brief narrative (fifteen sheets) of Thérèse's life after she entered Carmel on April 9, 1887. The only momentous events upon which she touches within the more than eight years up to the time of her writing were the death of Mère Geneviève (December 5, 1891); the influenza epidemic which came two months later; and Céline's long desiderated entry into Carmel (September 14, 1894).

The first of these seems the most important. Mère Geneviève had supported Thérèse's application. She had been at Lisieux for more than fifty years, elected prioress for five terms, and, while generally venerated as the "saint" of the Carmel, she became a kind of grandmotherly figure to Thérèse as well as a foil to Gonzague, who was almost thirty years younger. She had performed the same role for Pauline, who confided much to her.

Grandparents, without the requisites of discipline, can pamper and spoil children, tacitly working to undo the perceived severities of their own children, the parents. Mère Geneviève did nothing of this sort. In no way would she have intended nor effected subversion of the prioress, having herself carried the burden of that office and understood its difficulties. Further, although she speaks reverently of the foundress, Thérèse was disposed rather to Gonzague, the maternal figure, who had warmly encouraged her toward Carmel. But Gonzague knew the hazard of attachment, of developing preferential ties. There could be nothing so privative and exclusive as friendships in Carmel. Accordingly, Gonzague, prioress on Thérèse's entry, had resolved from the first to be unremittingly exacting of her new charge; she criticized her regularly for the least faults and omissions. She knew well that she would be subject to criticism from her superiors (not to mention grousing within the sisterhood itself) if Thérèse were pampered because of her adolescence, and Thérèse, looking back to her first years at Carmel, commends Gonzague for making sure that the latest Martin sister did not become a kind of pet or plaything (Thérèse uses the word *joujou*, a child's version of *jouet*, the toy of Jesus). Thérèse, the youngest and accordingly the most assertive of five children, had been used all her life to getting her way at home. She likely wheedled and cajoled her father with a precocious adroitness and he, a gentle man and loving father, lapped it up. She had had two caring mothers in her eldest sisters and in Céline, a close companion in the school trenches, a confidante and friend despite more than three years between them. She knew that her will (or willfulness) needed curbing, and Gonzague was, wittingly or not, an auxiliary to that end. The harsh criticisms of Gonzague sometimes seen in print are to no point when we consider that Thérèse herself appreciated her—and loved her, too.

Thérèse did not need Mère Geneviève for disciplining her will but for the model of serenity which elderliness and spiritual equilibrium at the age of eighty-five could alone afford. It is quite arguably from her that Thérèse began to discover her own little way, for she describes this ancient woman as a saint invaluable because she was not remote and inimitable but of "vertus cachées et ordinaires" ["hidden and ordinary virtues"] (A 78r). When talking to her, Mère Geneviève gave Thérèse the impression that Jesus was speaking and acting through her, and it is striking that toward the end of her narrative, Thérèse, while expressly denying that she herself had heard anything from Jesus, says: "je sens qu'Il est en moi, à chaque instant, Il me guide, m'inspire ce que je dois dire ou faire" ["I feel He's in me, at every moment, inspiring me to what I must say or do"] (A 83v), as though she had internalized her perception of Mère Geneviève and had herself become a model of that same Christ-in-me, the hortatory image familiar to all Christians from St. Paul (*Galatians* 2:20). Thérèse called it a "sainthood without illusions," the only true kind for her, and she wanted to attain it.[23]

Mère Geneviève's was the first death which Thérèse witnessed. She recounts that at the precise moment of what she calls the old woman's birth into heaven, " la naissance au Ciel," she herself was filled with an ineffable joy and fervor, as though the dead "saint" were sharing something of the lasting happiness vouchsafed in Arminjon's raptures on the celestial life. Thérèse had convinced herself that this gentle, all-understanding old woman was so saintly that she would bypass purgatory altogether. An exemplary good death, then, was, with humble and obscure virtues so quietly demonstrated, another of Mère Geneviève's contributions to Thérèse's education in Carmel. We learn first from this tender, briefly recounted relationship that the evolution of Thérèse's perceptions and what is construed to be her theology were in part the work of the community in which she lived, not all of whose members were so charitable toward her as Mère Geneviève. It is much to her credit that

Thérèse had the wit and the charity to learn as much from the not so loving as from those who were close to her.

If Mère Geneviève heartened her by example, she was buoyed even further by Père Pichon, who during a term of preaching at Carmel in May 1888, heard Thérèse's postulant confession and assured her that she had never committed a mortal sin. He has been criticized for the forwardness of this assurance, and Thérèse's need for it seems to have betrayed pride itself. What matters, however, is that she remembered and recounted it to her sister Pauline, for the record, as it were. What she did not record is her exchange with another priest, the Jesuit Laurent Blino, who preached a retreat at Lisieux some time in 1888. When she told him of her ambition to become a saint, he scolded her roundly for her presumption and told her to get on with addressing her spiritual errors, thus making small daily progress. But in her impetuosity she stood firm, citing Christ's injunction to be perfect. It seems to have been a difference about tempo, with Blino's *largo* at unharmonious odds with Thérèse's *presto vivace*. The remonstration of a spirited, not to say ambitious, fifteen-year-old girl could hardly have sat well with the nearly fifty-year-old priest who was likely unused to such boldness and tenacity in expression.

She fared far better with the Franciscan priest Alexis Prou, who gave a retreat in October 1891. She admits in her writing that preached retreats had always been more difficult for her than solitary ones. At the hearings in 1915 Pauline explained why: "la servante de Dieu cherchait toujours quelqu'un d'autorisé qui lui dise, 'Avancez en pleine mer, et jetez vos filets.' Elle trouva cet envoyé de Dieu dans la personne du R. P. Alexis" ["the servant of God always looked for someone in a position of authority who would say to her, 'Set out to sea and cast your nets.' She found this envoy of God in the person of Reverend Father Alexis"].[24] She felt her soul dilated, because Fr. Prou had understood her as though reading her like a book, but what she treasured was not so much that perceptivity as his assurance that she had not offended God, that God was indeed pleased with her.

Having observed Thérèse's conventual scorn for life's secular felicities, we turn to one of the most peculiar passages in her first manuscript, the wedding invitation she wrote upon her impending marriage to Jesus.

It had been prompted by the wedding in October 1890 of her cousin Jeanne Guérin to the physician Francis La Néele, who had a practice in Caen, twenty-five miles west of Lisieux. The announcement inspired a triumphalist invitation to her own nuptials: the All-Mighty Father and the glorious Virgin and Queen of the celestial court want to make you a part of the marriage of their august Son, Jesus, King of Kings, to Thérèse Martin, princess of realms endowed by her spouse's childhood and Passion. A variant invitation read that her father, Louis, proprietor and master of the signories of suffering and humiliation, and her mother, lady of honor in heaven's court, were marrying their daughter to Jesus, the Word and second Person of the Trinity.

This outlandish *rodomontade* apart, the pull of normal wedded life emerges when Thérèse confesses the terror she felt on learning that Céline was going to dance at the wedding reception of a distant relative, Henry Maudelonde, one of the men who had proposed to her.[25] That reception was on April 20, 1892. Thérèse tearfully prayed that Céline would be incapacitated so that she could not manage on the dance floor. This prayer was heard, and the evening proved a disaster for Céline—or rather for her beau. Had the evening gone well for them both, we might be without the substantial photo gallery of the Lisieux Carmel.

This fretful attention to her sister argues concretely that despite Thérèse's own claims, based on *Matthew* 19:29, that God rewards a hundredfold those who have abandoned all things for the love of God, she herself could not let go of her family. She was resolved that Céline would join her, Marie, and Pauline at the Carmel.[26] Thérèse later said that she could not understand the contempt of some saints for their families, but Christ himself uttered unequivocal words in such contempt (*Matthew* 12:48–50; *Luke* 14:26; *Mark* 12:25).

Thérèse was an attentive and insightful reader of the New Testament (she refers to St. Matthew alone more than 160 times in her writings, though many citations or allusions are used repeatedly), but like every other Christian who reads Scripture she had some favorite passages and perhaps a blind spot for others which proved hard to digest, such as those just cited, or were simply of less interest. She generally ignores the miraculous healings. The one time she cites *Matthew* 12:48–50, she edits it substantially, in her poem celebrating the Virgin, "Pourquoi je t'aime, ô Marie!" Christ's antifamilial views are a caution against the deceptive and delusory ties of preferential love, the very kind of earthiness Thérèse was warned—and warning herself—against, and yet it would be nonsense to contend that in Carmel she left her natural sisters behind and embraced a spiritual sisterhood. Céline's several photographic studies of her sisters and cousin point to the perdurance of "le clan Martin." Yet, it seems captious to find any fault in the well-established bonds of affection which Thérèse and her three sisters enjoyed. It would have been labored and ill advised for them to have created a distance from one another for the sake of the other women in Carmel. In the Johannine beloved disciple, Christ himself shows a preferential love, as also for Peter and the sons of Zebedee, for Martha and Mary of Bethany. Madre Teresa did well to inveigh against family bonds because she knew, too, that they are in most instances ineradicable. She herself kept a warmly affectionate bond with her niece in Carmel, Teresita, and with all her brothers.

Did Thérèse need her family in order to cope with the trials of faith besetting her? It is impossible to determine. She admits toward the close of

Manuscript A that early on within the convent she was prey to doubts about her worthiness, a not unusual experience for many young women, especially on the eve of taking vows and passing from the novitiate. While finding life at Carmel as agreeably arduous as she had expected, "le démon m'inspirait l'assurance qu'elle n'était pas faite pour moi, que je tromperais les supérieures en avançant dans une voie où je n'étais pas appelée" ["the devil created in me the certainty that this life was not made for me, that I deceived my superiors in proceeding on a path where I was not called"] (A 76r). She was subject to dryness, *la sécheresse*, an absence of religious fervor or of feeling altogether. The fear of remaining in indifference or apathy must have been disconcerting, if not terrifying, to so sensitive and readily anxious a girl as Thérèse then was—to be sequestered only to learn that one was a fraud—and it could have been meager consolation to Thérèse to know that this condition of apathy was hardly unfamiliar to the saints, including Teresa of Avila. It could weigh heavily even upon the mature, as Thérèse's sister Pauline attested in her memoirs: for several years (long after the death of Thérèse), she was faced with "une espèce de vide affreux" and "tentations de frayeurs de l'avenir" ["a kind of frightening emptiness" and "temptations to dread the future"].[27] But a Christian life cannot be lived without trials and temptations, since Christ himself had to face them. It is, moreover, a commonplace of spiritual life that the more one progresses in sanctity, the greater the trials become. The magnitude and duration of Thérèse's darkness might well serve as an index of the acuity and depth she had reached in her particular itinerary.

At that time, Jesus, it seemed to Thérèse, was asleep *comme toujours* in her little skiff. At this point in her narrative, she makes the perplexing assertion that Jesus will not awaken before she has entered eternity. She notes other bases of her wretchedness, that God seemed to be discontented with her (after Prou?), that she was even driven to question whether there was a heaven. She would resolve that question in a final negative. Rather than despairing, she was able to meet the spiritual darkness as a challenge willed by God, a test which while clearly calling for a substantial resilience of her soul also paradoxically enforced the sense of her own nullity.

In her letter of September 1896 to Marie, which opens Manuscript B and answers Marie's request for enlightenment about a retreat which Thérèse had just made, Thérèse writes in koanlike fashion that her only consolation was to have no consolations on earth. Perhaps she was remembering Madre Teresa's caveat about consolation, that it might well be satanic. In Manuscript A (36v), she had taken inspiration from the *Imitatio Christi* to ask that Jesus change all consolations into the bitterness she had come to recognize as a kind of truth serum. He had done so, but Thérèse did not share the cup with Marie. She reserved bitterness to herself as her chief epistemological tool to help her toward the Christian way things are.

This central portion of her autobiography is significant, however, in revealing her escape from the encompassing fantasies of choosing everything and reconciling herself to the passive role of a victim of divine love. Although written for her sister, Manuscript B is addressed to Jesus, whom she apostrophizes repeatedly, even though (or because?) she presumed him to be asleep to her needs. It was, she noted in passing, their sixth anniversary together.

For a long while before that time, she had nursed the ambition to be a missionary, one who would by some very special grace be able to cover all times and all spaces of the earth, enlightening souls as the prophets had. She had wished to become one of the doctors of the church. She had wanted to be a martyr and suffer all the torments known to Christian witnesses unto death: flagellation and crucifixion, boiling oil, beheading, the stake. Here, although alluding to her favorite female martyrs, such as Saints Agnes and Cecilia and, of course, Jeanne d'Arc, she was virtually replicating a passage appended to the *Papier d'exaction* from Père Jérôme Gratien's *Dilucidario de verdadero spiritu*, which records a recreation among Carmelite brothers who would talk of how they wished to become martyrs: "I would like to be decapitated for Jesus Christ," and then all the others would intone, "Me, too." Another would say, "I would like to be sawed in two for Jesus," and another "Me, too," and on it went.[28]

Eventually, she realized that all these hyperbolical desires were infantile. She claims that she learned from St. Francis of Assisi the humility to accept not becoming a priest, as though her inevitable, involuntary limit by gender and Francis's voluntary self-abasement were commensurate. What was left, then? From St. Paul's discourse on Christian love (1 *Corinthians* 13) she saw that all spiritual vocations would be void without love and that she would gain all-sufficient promotion if she became a willing, sacrificial victim of this love. Thus, instead of being all things to all souls in need—crusader, priest, missionary, martyr—she would identify herself with the love which subsumed all vocations and which embraced all times and places: "dans le Coeur de l'Église, ma Mère, je serai l'Amour. ... ainsi je serai *tout* ... ainsi mon rêve sera réalisé!!!" ["in the Heart of the Church, my Mother, I will be Love ... that way I will be *all* ... that way my dream will be realized!!!"] (B 3v; see figure 5.5).

Having put aside the desire to be all things to all souls, she ends by restating her longing (or need) to be everything, now through identification with divine love. Her ploy is to present herself as a child, weak yet petulant. A parent can deny a child nothing, she argues, and the Church, being her mother, in effect must accede to this insistent child's wish. She adroitly leaves all claims of glory to angels and saints, asking only to suffer for love but also to play in it by casting flowers. It is curious that her peremptory "I shall be Love in the Heart of the Church" is so often iterated, given that it is textually superseded by the yet more strident self-affirmation "moi, je suis l'ENFANT de l'Église" ["me, I'm the CHILD of the Church"] (4r).

FIGURE 5.5. Maurice Bellière in Africa. The first of Thérèse's spiritual brothers, this missionary, priest, martyr of the White Friars died at Bon Sauveur sanatorium in Caen in his thirty-third year. Copyright Archives du Carmel de Lisieux and by courtesy of the Archives des Pères Blancs d'Afrique.

There is an engaging two-sidedness to her ripened sense of a singular mission: suffering and playing. First, she presents herself as a sacrificial victim posed at a strategic moment, it would seem, in the life of Catholicism: "Pour satisfaire la Justice Divine il fallait des victimes parfaites, mais à la loi de crainte a succédé la loi d'Amour, et l'Amour m'a choisie pour holocauste, moi, faible et imparfaite créature" ["To satisfy divine justice perfect victims used to be required but the law of Love has succeeded that of fear and Love has chosen me for a holocaust, me, a weak and imperfect creature"] (B 3v).

Despite the explicit Old Testament resonances about perfect sacrifice, Thérèse's identification of the old order with the law of fear argues that she had in mind the implacability of divine justice. Love is her counter to a quaking fear begotten not by a cruelly exacting God but by a cruelly exacting notion of God, a manmade spiritual terrorism.

For her, justice must be understood within love and subsumed by it, as in the story of the prodigal son and his family. Her citations show this was one of Thérèse's favorite stories, because its justice, dissolving into love, lies both in the prodigal's recognition of his own nothingness and in his father's conciliatory words to the brother who has difficulty accepting the extravagant love shown to his no-good brother. It is that extravagant love which Thérèse, in all her irrepressible affectivity, found as her way to position herself centrally now within the Church. Manuscript B reads in a sense like a homecoming—she had been prodigal with hopeless desires of impossible roles—and that is how it argues kinship with the prodigal's parable. The centripetal pull in each is about reconciliation through loss of fantastic selves. We need not labor the irony that within the ambit of the prodigal's story, she had already identified herself, the Carmelite faithful to rules, with the dutiful, workaday brother (A 84r). Fundamentally, though, she knew herself one with the prodigal in all his weakness. In the godly father, all-patient, all-suffering, all-loving, who else would she have recognized other than her own little king? But Louis was gone, and as though to absorb his loss fully and finally she stood in his stead. Empirically, however, her weakness and helplessness, central motifs in B, appointed her as child in the heart of the Church.

She was not alone in that leaning toward a beneficent and loving deity. Some of the old hellfire views of God and heavenly justice lingered late into the nineteenth-century Church, but they had become anachronistic and distasteful to people who savored neither the image of their lost loved ones undergoing eternal punishment nor that prospect for themselves. In the earlier discussion of Carmelites, I noted that the architecture of Parisian tombs in the mid- to late nineteenth century exemplified a "soft devotion." They abound to this day in bas-reliefs profiling both grief and hope and a special need for sentimental assurance about heaven. We find that need pronounced, too, in the lyric, contemplative serenity of Gabriel Fauré's *Requiem* (1888), which dispensed with any shuddering over a day of judgment such as in Berlioz's (1830), just two generations before. Berlioz's grand-scale *Dies Irae*, its theatricality characterized by the composer himself as a "shocking magnificence," calls up the fearfulness Thérèse set herself to vanquish. Fauré knew his Third Republican audience, many of them believers still, and he saw fit to omit the horrific suggestivity of a *Rex tremendae majestatis* and even the wailing of a *Lachrymosa*. Thérèse's theology, though it possesses a dark aspect, dispenses altogether with the hoary old terrors, and that explains to a great extent her appeal, both in and beyond her generation. The gentle supplications of Fauré's *Pie Jesu, Domine* offer a musical complement to theresian spirituality.

While such masterworks as these requiems are accessible references for us today, the undertow of intimidation is perhaps less easy to retrieve—not that we need it. Thérèse faced it within the Carmel.[29] Pauline herself was inclined to stress Thérèse's sacrifice of her sufferings over Thérèse's own emphasis on God's compassionate love. Pauline's attention to a traditional notion of sainthood argues a certain blindness to her sister's breakthrough into a spirituality of benevolence, rather than of wrath. The *circulaires*, in their turn, successively reminded Thérèse that for some Carmelites, being a nothing was tantamount to deserving hell.[30] They read at times like cautionary tales about a path she could not follow, and Manuscript B might well be taken in part as a riposte to their sometimes fiery and livid pronouncements.

Why, then, had Thérèse cast herself as a victim in her bold, not to say precipitous *offrande* of June 1895, "holocaust" meaning that the offered sacrifice, herself, would be burned up? It implies that by standing in the stead of others she was placating or appeasing a god of angry exactions, precisely the deity she was psychologically incapable of accepting or even imagining. In her estimate, though, the reverse was true: she was assuming the Christlike role par excellence. Offering oneself as a victim proclaims a total concession to the divine will. As that will was itself Christ's sacrificial love, only a reciprocal love can enter the furnace of divine love. At the same time, as a voluntary gesture, it reads as a capital instance of her *audace*, a preemptive statement to God: now it is your turn, and do what you will. Thérèse's initiative took her sisters aback for its temerity. It was the same note she sounded fifteen months later, when composing Manuscript B, with the decision to cast herself as Love in the Church.

The other side of her mission involves her playing in the divine love. In the *offrande* Thérèse fancies herself casting flowers before the throne of Christ and singing in a silvery voice a canticle of love. Trivial though these gestures must be, and so she insists they are, she brings the ecclesiastical hierarchy itself into a choreography, with the Church Triumphant passing on her petals to the Church Militant. For all the protestations of her littleness, the tableau in which she sets herself seems grandiose.[31] The casting of flowers provides yet another link between the *offrande* and Manuscript B, since the helpless child of the church in that September of 1896 can accomplish no great acts: the only proof of the child's love comes in casting flowers and scenting the divine throne with them—and not forgetting the thorns among those flowers.

The abiding appeal of Thérèse's playfulness lies partly in rich mythic associations of which she was not fully aware: the young virgin gathering flowers could be a Persephone or Europa, the eternal feminine in its inviolate adolescence. She figures as well as an emblem of fertility and bounty. Thérèse's rose petals do not fall so triflingly as she supposed; they are metonymous for spring, beauty, life's primal and fleeting promise. Condensed into the simplicity of this image lie literary profiles such as Dante's mysterious maiden Matelda who, singing and gathering flowers in the *Commedia*'s terrestrial paradise, conveys the poet to Beatrice. From Thérèse's own time, we can adduce the pastels of Puvis de Chavannes, the painter who chronicled on the Pantheon's murals in Paris the story of another salvific figure, St. Geneviève, delivering the city from perdition early in its Christian history. That story had been familiar to Thérèse from her schoolbooks and the *Tirelire aux Histoires*.[32] It seems fitting that Thérèse *aux roses* is known throughout the world from her sister Céline's patently Marian portrait, one without the invaluable thorns, a stylization at remarkable odds to the photographic studies.

Manuscript B remains the most accessible of the three autobiographical accounts because it succinctly presents so much, if not the substance, of theresian spirituality. It is free of the anecdotal byways so abundant in A and affords only a few hints of the severe deliquescence of C. In B, Thérèse says that the smallest souls (us) can reach the top of the spiritual itinerary's mountain because Jesus asks of them only acceptance and gratitude, not great acts. One can do many little things profitably by love. Her final entry asks Jesus to recruit lots of little souls and make them, like her, victims of his love.

Strangely, these messages of uplift and consolation, including the one to herself about her centrality within the Church, seem confounded in her prefatory letter to Marie, where she rejects the very thought of consolation. Within B she relates her dream of the Spanish mother, Aña de Jesús, come to assure her (to *re*assure her) that she is pleasing to God, but introduces the account by saying that pretty dreams are not for her. She prefers and accepts the time of testing. That testing finds expression in B's most pregnant image, that of a small bird, with wings too weak and wet to fly, seeking by the mediation of male powers (her spiritual brothers Bellière and Roulland) the power to fly to the divine sun. The fiendish vultures will not snare this bird, but the wait will be indefinite. Closing B, Thérèse opens a window onto C.[33]

For all the revelatory tones of breakthrough in B, had she genuinely overcome the anxieties beclouding so many earlier retreats? From being Love at the Church's center, to its child, she concludes with imagery of helplessness and isolation. The only relief the reader can draw, as Thérèse herself seems to have drawn it, lies in a wondrous optic, that this tiny bird fixes its sight, as though with an eagle's eye, upon the solar Love: "Avec un audacieux abandon, il veut rester à fixer son Divin Soleil; rien ne saurait l'effrayer, ni le vent ni la pluie et si de sombres nuages viennent à cacher l'Astre d'Amour, le petit oiseau ne change pas de place" ["With bold resignation, it wants to remain fixed upon its Divine Sun; nothing will frighten it, neither the wind nor the rain, and if dark clouds are coming to eclipse astral love, the little bird is not moving"] (5r). More: she welcomes tempest and clouds and the obscuring of what she calls the invisible light hidden to her faith. "C'est alors le moment de la *joie parfaite* pour le *pauvre petit être* faible" ["That's the moment of *perfect joy* for the *poor little weakling*"] (5r).

With Luke's parable of the prodigal son, that celebration of resolute vision closes the frame in which B is set. Having discarded impossible ambitions for glory, she had, like the prodigal, spent herself and come to herself, a wretched, lowly, helpless self. But rather than cower or weep, she turns herself toward the redemptive solar light. At that point, however, remaining inert, she assumes the stance of the prodigal's father, who is able to see his son returning when the prodigal is still a great way off, too distant to be identified. Only the father perceived that it was he, because he sees with all-suffering love, even as he had when allowing his son to go play the wastrel. Thérèse can see the divinely invisible light, no matter how great the darkness gathered in her.

In B, she performs in her fashion the three male roles of Luke's most beautiful story: loyalist, prodigal, patient lover. Yet, this manuscript leaves, for all its élan and exuberance, an unsettling irresolution. Within its own terms, would the tiny bird at last take wing and fly to its Dantesque home in the sun?[34] No, that voluntarist finale she did not expect. She hoped that Christ, "Aigle Adoré," the Beloved Eagle, would come for her and bear her off into the burning abyss of divine love. But C puts her in her place, loving in a way she had never imagined.

FIGURE 5.6. Thérèse's second spiritual brother, Adolphe Roulland, spent fourteen years in China's Sechuan Province. Copyright Archives du Carmel de Lisieux and by courtesy of the Missions étrangères de Paris.

Manuscript C, the third and final portion of Thérèse's autobiography, was composed over a few weeks, from June 3 into the first week of July 1897. Although, like A and B, it ends with the definitive and conclusive word of her spiritual lexicon, *amour*, it remained unfinished. She had intended to write something about her two missionary brothers (see figure 5.6). During that time, the spitting of blood became so frequent that she had to be consigned to the infirmary. She notes in passing the frequent interruptions, however kindly meant, to her writing, those obtrusions in part accounting for the fragmentary, episodic character of the text. The addressee is Gonzague, reelected prioress in March of the previous year. It had been a difficult contest, and shortcomings of charity between Gonzague and Pauline might have surfaced, yet they in no way inform Thérèse's own feelings about the prioress unless we construe expressions of thankfulness as mere diplomacy. That would be captious and misleading: Gonzague became indispensable to Thérèse in finding the little way of humility, as Manuscript C makes clear.

When Pauline was elected prioress in February 1893, Thérèse was immediately appointed to oversee the spiritual formation of novices. She was then a bare twenty years old and had taken the veil herself only two and a half years before (September 1890). On her reelection, Gonzague confirmed Thérèse in the role of *maîtresse auxiliaire* to the novices, while reserving the primary title to herself—an unusual, not to say disruptive, proceeding. In effect, Thérèse could at any time be suspended from her working with the novices; the provisional arrangement remained unpredictable, given Gonzague's inconsistent temperament.

Yet, only through Gonzague's steady hammering upon her failings had Thérèse come to the conclusion that she herself was "un pauvre petit néant, rien de plus" ["a poor little nullity, nothing more"] (C 2r). The imminence of death—she was given extreme unction on July 30, 1897—gave her an eerie abandon, a carefreeness bracing in its frankness and, mercifully, not without humor: if God, she writes, makes her seem to be better than she is (a saint?), that does not concern her. God can do as he wishes. Her ambitiousness remains, even so, unabated. Father Blino, the Jesuit who had reproached her for aspirations to saintly perfection, might as well have been silent. Here, now, to Gonzague she iterates the cardinal point she had made to Pauline in Manuscript A, that God instills in one desires which only God can satisfy. The corollary is that God shall satisfy them, else why would he have created them? Her craving for sainthood would be granted despite her keenly acknowledged nothingness, her *petitesse*. Too imperfect to achieve saintliness and too near death even to try to overcome her imperfections, she resorts to a stroke—and an image—of genius: "je veux chercher le moyen d'aller au Ciel par une petite voie bien droite, bien courte, une petite voie toute nouvelle" ["I want to seek the means of going to Heaven by a quite direct, short, entirely new little way"]

(C 4r). Rather than proceeding on the arduous stairway to heaven, she would take the elevator.

The elevating agency would be the arms of Jesus lifting her in all her littleness. In a phrase, she dismisses all the nostrums about growth in an age of expansive industry and technology. In order to ascend on the elevator, she has no need to grow but must instead remain little, even become ever littler. In the humility of her incredible shrinking self, she provides a telling variant on Christ's emblem of the mustard seed of faith.

Manuscript C stands apart not only as a final statement but as one written literally at fever pitch. Thérèse knew she was dying and that death might well be imminent. When she had composed B, in September 1896, she was still entertaining hopes of going to a sister Carmel in Vietnam. Now, in June 1897, she knew she had perhaps weeks, perhaps days to live. She became so debilitated by fever and lack of nutrition, being unable to digest most of what was given her, that she could barely climb the stairs to her room. By the time she was finally borne to the infirmary, it had been taking all of her refractory energy and upward of half an hour to undress herself. That harrowing gives to C its particular acuity and depth: one might rightly call it a miraculous document, not only for its definitive substance but for the fact that its author marshaled the strength to write at all: thirty-seven pages within a month to A's eighty-four pages over a year when she was still in reasonably good health.

Outwardly, C seems to say little: she reports her ongoing darkness now reaching new depths, and she passes on to Gonzague some reflections on what she has understood from her Carmelite sisters, chiefly the not-so-pleasant ones, about charity. Her training of novices had made her the best sort of teacher, one who knew how to go on learning, and this final letter to Christ in the person of the prioress tells Gonzague things which in her own way and by decades of experience she already knew but was reminded of afresh: themes with theresian variations.[35] An unfathomable night and some minuscule lights of charity: the significance of C lies in the conjunction between its two seemingly disparate parts.

A prolegomenon to its study falls chronologically halfway between B and C. In B, Thérèse had drawn a trajectory of her illusions, her masculinizing dreams of spiritual adventure far from the confines of Lisieux and of Carmel. She did not let them go. On February 2, 1897, she wrote what might be called her one love poem to a man, Fr. Théophane Vénard, who on that very day thirty-six years before had been beheaded (after five whacks) in Hanoi. In the previous November, she had been reading and copying passages from a volume of his life and letters.[36]

In Vénard, she perceived a kind of transposed version of herself: not only a missionary priest who had fulfilled the logic of that post by ending a martyr, he poeticized in Thérèse's own terms. The Eucharist, he had written, was poetry itself, "l'exquise et fine fleur de toute poésie" ["the exquisite, delicate flower of all poetry"].[37] The night before his execution, he had filled his wooden cage with flowers and had written in farewell to his family that his lopped-off head would be like a spring flower that God, the master gardener, would gather for his pleasure. All souls were such flowers, he added, even the virginal lily and the humble violet. Reading such fragrant rhetoric, Thérèse might have recalled Louis in the garden of Les Buissonnets, plucking the flower in token of her departure.

Now, toward journey's end, she had in Vénard her realized self. She kept a lithograph of him pinned to the curtain of her infirmary bed. In her celebration, "À Théophane Vénard," *he* becomes the virginal lily plucked at thirty-one, yet as well the soldier of Christ coming by sword and fire,[38] *igne ac ferro*, terms borrowed from the Roman siege of enemy camps. Martyrdom forms both the alpha and the omega of a mission, as Thérèse closes her seven stanzas of praise with the entreaty that Vénard descend to her on her dying day so that she can join his missionary cortège. Thérèse is giving to Vénard, this other self, the role she had seen in and given to Christ, her Solomonic spouse. The difference lies in the missionary destiny for which Vénard had provided a dramatic cue: she wishes to join him so that they can fly together to "cette plage infidèle/Qui fut l'objet de ton ardent amour" ["this faithless shore which was the goal of your burning love"]. There, her own feeble love and consecrated sufferings will fulfill her mission, to make God loved.

By his exemplary life and death and no less by his writings, Vénard had vividly affirmed her intuited certainty that "le Bon Dieu ne saurait inspirer des désirs irréalisables, je puis donc malgré ma petitesse aspirer à la sainteté" ["God wouldn't prompt unrealizable desires, so I can aspire to sainthood despite my littleness"] (C 2v). That interior revelation counted among the graces which she had sung in Manuscript A. The oxymoronic conjunction of their power and gentleness expressly figured in a poem she wrote the next month, on March 25, 1897, for the profession of vows by her cousin Sr. Marie de l'Eucharistie, but it is Thérèse's particular alteration of biblical language which most deserves our remarking for that occasion and leads us to C.[39]

"Mes Armes" draws upon *Ephesians* 6:11–17, a passage quoted in the Carmelite Rule's exhortations. Paul's metaphoric assumption of military hardware for fighting the devil includes the cuirass of justice (righteousness, in the KJV), but as justice was connotatively difficult for Thérèse to negotiate, she substitutes obedience. Paul's sword of the Holy Spirit signifies not the word of God but chastity. And in celebrating poverty as the first sacrifice imposed on a Carmelite novice, Thérèse has enlisted the three obligatory pledges into conventual life.[40] Her truly singular deviation from St. Paul's text (and from its citation in the Carmel's Rule) comes with the buckler or shield that wards off demonic weaponry. She does not arm herself with the saint's "bouclier de la foi" but with "le Bouclier de mon coeur." Not faith but her own heart shall protect Marie—one of the most audacious emendations Thérèse made.

In C, she reveals her discovery and landing on a shore far larger than any Vénard had come to. But first she collapses all of the voluntarism of missionary effort and combat: "le Bon Dieu n'a besoin de personne (encore moins d'elle que des autres) pour faire du bien sur la terre" ["God doesn't need anyone (her even less than others) to accomplish good on earth"] (C 3v). With that, she claims that the greatest of graces she has received lies in realizing both her littleness and her ineffectuality. Then she proceeds to the dark grace, the truly greatest of her life, which took both faith and hope from her.

After first coughing up blood, during Holy Week of 1896, she had rejoiced with faith and hope of going soon to heaven. At that time, however, Jesus made her aware (*sentir* signifies more than *feel*) that some souls had truly lost the precious gift of faith. She adds that they had done so by abusing grace. She had not, but Jesus was allowing "que mon âme fût envahie des plus épaisses ténèbres et que la pensée du Ciel si douce pour moi ne soit plus qu'un sujet de combat et de tourment" ["that my soul be invaded by the thickest shadows and that the thought of Heaven, so sweet for me, be nothing more than the occasion of struggle and torment"] (C 5v). Although telling Gonzague that her narrative abounds in confused, ill-expressed words, she conveys the weight of her dark grace with apt and unequivocal images: a thick fog, a tunnel, and, most harrowing, "un mur qui s'élève jusqu'aux cieux et couvre le firmament étoilé" ["a wall which has been raised up to the sky, covering the starry vault"] (C 7v). She has been sealed off from the heavenly host, the communion of saints, her deceased family, all.

She likens her story to a fairy tale turned into a prayer, one that comes from the most striking of all the images in her writings, with herself in the third person. She is seated at a table of bitterness, amid sinners, eating the bread of grief ["le pain de la douleur"], not to rise till God permits. "Mais aussi ne peut-elle pas dire en son nom, au nom de ses frères: Ayez pitié de nous Seigneur, car nous sommes de pauvres pécheurs! ... Oh! Seigneur, renvoyez-nous justifiés" ["But can she not also say in her name and in the name of her brothers, 'Have pity on us, Lord, truly we are poor sinners! ... Oh, Lord, release us justified'"]. In assuming the contrition of *Luke*'s publican (18:13), she abases herself to the lowest possible degree, hoping thereby to be exalted, eventually. Including other sinners, she charitably assumes that they, too, may prove contrite, perhaps in eating the bitter bread of their ingratitude to God or of their otherwise loveless lives.[41]

With this collectivity, Thérèse sounds the communitarian note which predominates in C. If with B she had discovered a role for herself in the Church, with C she has discovered the meaning of charity. She admits as much to Gonzague. It sounds odd, given that in B she had identified herself with Love at the centripetal point of the Church, but she now leaves that vast and blurry tableau behind and proceeds to a far more convincing setting, a series of small-scale scenes in which she has to sustain the shortcomings of other sisters and to learn how not to be dismayed by their weaknesses: the grating mannerisms of Sr. Saint-Augustin; the ailing petulance of Sr. Saint-Pierre; Sr. Saint-Joseph, who seldom failed to splash Thérèse in the face with cold, dirty water off the laundry basin; Sr. Marie de Jésus, clicking her teeth during prayer.

These staggeringly trivial examples profile the many abiding challenges of living in a community with people one would not naturally choose as friends. Thérèse puts these instances to work, showing how they obliged her to realize her own weaknesses: impatience, vexation, aversion. Facing and accepting those weaknesses keeps her from grandstanding in a Lady Bountiful way about others' faults. She mentions an episode with the infirm Sr. Saint-Pierre. Accompanying her plaintive groaning from the choir one dark winter evening, Thérèse heard party music beyond the walls. She imagined a bright, festive gathering, and the contrast with her own immediate lot struck her with gratitude: "Pour jouir mille ans des fêtes mondaines, je n'aurais donné les dix minutes employées à remplir mon humble office de charité" ["To enjoy worldly parties for a thousand years, I would not have given those ten minutes in fulfilling my lowly obligation to charity"] (C 30r). It is small wonder that her novices found her severe.

Reflecting on sisters who gave her difficulties by simply being themselves, she remarks Christ as an artist whose work lies deep within every soul. (Some *circulaires* had spoken of Christ as sculptor.) When she discusses her novices and how on her own she could not have read deep down into their spiritual needs, she returns to the trope: she and Gonzague after her are but Christ's brushes; she, the smaller one for sketching the novices' formation. Again, she delights in her weaknesses as a reliable gauge of her smallness. She knew that whatever good the novices drew from her injunctions and example would not be due to her.

She makes two vital admissions: that, as San Juan de la Cruz had told her, there are more differences among souls than among faces, and no one sure way of access to them: "on sent que faire du bien c'est chose aussi impossible sans le secours du bon Dieu que de faire briller le soleil dans la nuit. ... On sent qu'il faut absolument oublier ses goûts, ses conceptions personnelles et guider les âmes par le chemin que Jésus leur a tracé, sans essayer de les faire marcher par sa propre voie" ["one realizes benefaction is as impossible without God's help as making the sun shine in the night... It's absolutely necessary to forget one's tastes and personal views and guide them by the way Jesus has marked out, without making them tread one's own path"] (22v–23r). Thus, she outstrips her own "entirely new little way" of humility, seeing that it is not inevitably accessible nor even desirable for others. For her young and impressionable novices, yes, she felt her own low bar setting was necessary lest they take premature and presumptuous urges too far or, conversely, be daunted by what seemed immeasurably beyond their reach, but the older sisters taught her how even one's cruelties are crosses one has to bear.

Then, she admits her trouble in formal prayer, especially in saying the chaplet. When she arrives at her own notion of prayer, the expressivity of her temperament shows itself paramount. Discarding the fine phrases of prayer found in books, she says she speaks with childlike ingenuousness: "Pour moi la prière, c'est un élan du coeur, c'est un simple regard jeté vers le Ciel, c'est un cri de reconnaissance et d'amour au sein de l'épreuve comme au sein de la joie; enfin c'est quelque chose de grand, de surnaturel qui me dilate l'âme et m'unit à Jésus" ["For me, prayer's an ardor of the heart, a simple look thrown toward Heaven, a cry of gratitude and of love in the bosom of testing as in the bosom of joy; something grand and transcendent which expands my soul and unites me to Jesus"] (25r–v).

She had one desire so strong that surely God would not have put it there had it not been meant for realization: her mission to save souls, great criminal souls like Pranzini, who had launched her on her way to Carmel. Such a mission she could accomplish within Carmel's walls. But she had also looked outward, to Indochina. In seeking a foreign mission, she said she wanted poverty, absence of indulgence, and exile of the heart (10r). Not that she would or could be good for anything, since she knew that she knew nothing of the world, but she would hope only to accomplish God's will.

Did she ever realize that she had attained her mission? Probably, since that realization seems to inform the serenity, despite intermittent physical torments, which gives the predominant tone to the last summer's conversations. Jesus had sent her on that mission, to the table of sinners where she would be eating the bitter bread until the breaking of the seventh seal and the seventh sounding of the brass. Had she been able to resume her writing, she would have told Gonzague of the special grace of having two spiritual brothers, Roulland and Bellière, but we need regret nothing of the way in which C closes, ending like A and B on the note of love, yet one of far higher valence than can be found in those earlier texts. At the last, she is identified with three of the New Testament's best-known sinners, all culled from *Luke*: the publican observed by a self-satisfied Pharisee; the woman who washes and anoints Christ's feet; and the prodigal son, with whom she finally finds a kinship she could not affirm in his stuffy, law-abiding brother.

What do they all have in common? Like Thérèse, they are extremists: the publican, so wretched he cannot even lift his eyes in praying; the prodigal, so wretched he believes himself fit only to be a common laborer in his father's house; and the once much sinful woman, who weeps quietly, uttering no word. They are all deeply penitent. In a sentimental mood, Thérèse says she has been seduced by the woman's example and imitates "son amoureuse audace qui charme le Coeur de Jésus" ["her loving boldness which charms Jesus' Heart"] (36v). But charm has nothing to do with the New Testament—Thérèse is speaking in her time's idiom—while the relation to love and forgiveness has everything. It is a point deserving attention in a discussion of her theology, beside the audacious claim which closes C, that were she to commit the greatest crimes, she would tearfully turn to Christ, seeking forgiveness.

Why, then, did she say she would be sitting till time's end at the table of sinners? If she felt an affinity with the prodigal, the publican, and the weeping woman, was it in the Gospel-based assumption that she could love greatly only if forgiven greatly, that by remission of her seeming sin in letting go of heaven she would feel keenest gratitude? Such questions as these await a discussion of her theology. Some of her other writings lead in that same direction.

6

On Her Theatricality

Plays and Poetry

The first duty in life is to be as artificial as possible. What the second duty is no one has yet discovered.

—Oscar Wilde, *Phrases and Philosophies for the Use of the Young*

Ces pauvres poésies vous révéleront non pas ce que je suis, mais ce que je voudrais et devrais être [These poor poems will show you not what I am but what I would like to be and should be].

—Thérèse to Maurice Bellière, February 24, 1897

Among her writings, Thérèse's plays, or *récréations pieuses* as they were known within Carmel, occupy a peculiar position of neglect. Her other works, the prayers and poems, the letters, the autobiography foremost—all have been translated and long circulated. The plays remain far behind as virtual closet dramas, composed ad hoc for feast days full of rejoicing. It is a strange and unhelpful neglect; unhelpful, because the plays open to us, no less than do the poems, valuable windows onto Thérèse's spirituality; strange, because in them we have a concrete and lively idea of the communal physics of Carmel and how its sisters—its prisoners, Thérèse might have said—lifted themselves from routine through an inspired, if generally mediocre pen. On those feast days, they relaxed, they enjoyed, they learned, they even laughed.

This chapter examines first the plays and then the poetry.

As literature, the plays might be judged as negligible as the poetry. We do not, however, read these brief, inspirational dramas (the longest runs only twenty-five sheets) with the expectation we would bring to Hugo and *Hernani*, to de Musset and *Lorenzaccio*, to Rostand and *Cyrano de Bergerac*, no more than in Thérèse's verse we would expect to find a Verlaine or a Mallarmé. They engage us first and last because Thérèse wrote them; also, because they were joyous occasions, when the sacred silences were broken into song, an emotive release the force of which we can only guess at when imagining lives wrapped in the dignity of quiet and of self-constraint. Also, in the plays we twice find the heroine to whose model she aspired with the piteous urge of emulation, Jeanne d'Arc.

No less important, the plays serve as the outward and formal sign of Thérèse's lifelong penchant for theatricality, by which I mean her reading of life as a drama, her casting of those close to her into roles, with herself tacitly the director as well as chief actor. Theatricality here does not mean fakery or insincerity. Rather, it signifies a stylized control of one's life, a shaping of it into the coherence which might become art, a higher consistency such as Christian rites and sacraments themselves present. The Eucharist serves believers not least as enactment. All of Thérèse's writings reflect a dramatic contemporaneity, and none was composed from the safe elevation and distance of age. She did not live long enough to attain the seasoned repose and equanimity which can come only by looking back, *hors de combat*.

A not-so-sympathetic Carmelite, Soeur Aimée de Jésus, once complained that the Martins were "trop artistes." She might have been referring to the scripts which Thérèse furnished on eight occasions between January 1894 and February 1897. It might have been a complaint about the way the Martins had grown up.

Louis was perhaps chiefly responsible. I have noted that he loved to recite favorite poetry, and his girls grew up familiar with his renditions of Chateaubriand and Lamartine. He handed out the sobriquets: Marie was "mon diamant bien-aimé"; Pauline, "ma perle fine"; and, of course, there was "ma petite Reine." He was also a convincing mimic, a gift which Thérèse inherited and practiced within Carmel's walls. Mimicry in the Martins' domestic instances was not mockery; one often mimics people of whom one is very fond. It serves as a temporary appropriation and fleeting portraiture of another person and argues an ear exceptionally alert for tone and nuance. Anyone who has given attention to Thérèse of Lisieux, whether in adoration or in critical sobriety or even in both, has likely longed to know the sound of her voice. Without that knowledge, we in an elementary sense do not know her at all.

Her father recognized and encouraged his daughters' interest in art and would have afforded them professional training had not Carmel exerted its centripetal pull. There was, however, the hazard of unlikelihood for a young woman in the world of the arts, and it would have meant, in the end, a term in the abominated capital whence Louis had long before fled in dismay and revulsion. Especially Céline cultivated her hand and if the paintings in the

family's dining rooms in Alençon and Lisieux serve as evidence of her promise, she might have been trained toward a competence greater than her extant
ghastly, all-too-period pieces on religious subjects indicate. When torn between Pichon and Carmel, between marital prospects and a career in painting,
Céline had a small Parisian flat already rented for her by Louis. Strangely,
her lasting achievement, by which we owe her our deepest gratitude, lies in a
medium she did not recognize as at all artistic: her photography. We may
regret not having Thérèse's voice, but we have caught her eye.

Thérèse began her mature life as a writer as George Sand had, in the writing
of plays strictly meant for conventual performance. She debuted first, however,
as a performer in a play by Pauline, *Sainte Agnès*, taking the title part in a fête for
Mère Gonzague on June 21, 1888. This fabled young martyr of early Christian
lore had long fascinated Pauline, not only from the breviary, but from Cardinal
Wiseman's vastly popular Victorian novel *Fabiola*, which depicted pious Christian girls under brutish Roman sway. Before the threat of the choleric prefect's
fire and sword, Agnès said that nothing would make her renounce Jesus.
Imagine the ardor with which fifteen-year-old Thérèse declaimed such lines
as these: "J'ai sucé de sa bouche le lait et le miel, et mes joues sont teintes
et ornées de son sang" ["I've sucked milk and honey from his mouth, and my
cheeks are tinged and rouged with his blood"].[1] This debut role enacting the
exquisite fantasy of martyrdom and glory must have given Thérèse a lively sense
of drama as an expressive medium, but she did not compose anything of her
own in this genre until the winter of 1893, her twentieth year.

In composing her plays, she was carrying out the expressed intent of the
founder of the Discalced Order, Teresa of Avila, who saw that the exacting life
of prayer within the sequestering walls of a convent would be psychologically
trying for the sisters. They needed some release. Besides, while the church
calendar supplied predictability, the fêtes' dramas were original and unique,
not usually intended for revivals.[2] They convey the particularity of the spontaneous, lost to all but our imaginative engagement with them despite the
listlessness of the printed text. Like Thérèse's poetry, many passages became
songs, set to well-known arias; Ambroise Thomas's *Mignon*, a now almost-
forgotten opera, doing service along with Gounod (that dreadful *Soldiers' Cho-
rus*), Verdi (the witch's third-act narrative in *Trovatore*), and many other, now
totally obscure composers. The sheet music for piano, now piled high in the
Carmel archives,[3] came from the Guérins' parlor, where both Jeanne and Marie
had exhibited their charming and accomplished voices.[4]

Covertly, her plays offered Thérèse the unusual opportunity to convey to her
fellow sisters her understanding of not only Carmelite but Christian spirituality
tout court. In three of her plays, *La Mission de Jeanne d'Arc* (January 1894), *Les
Anges à la Crèche de Jésus* (October 1894), and *Jésus à Béthanie* (July 1895), she
took on the Jansenist fear of damnation, that dread of God's justice which
haunted many Christians both within and without monastic walls. In these

dramas, she portrays three conversions of fear into love, thus giving it a primacy unwonted to others but so natural to herself as to be indispensable. Freedom from fear was the implicit but necessary corollary to the joy and self-giving which informed her entire life, yet it is easy to miss or underrate. In a rudimentary fashion, these plays presented to her sisters what became for her the central certainty that a weak and helpless soul (and whose is not?) need only show trust, confiance, in God's merciful love. That presupposed not only a power within the human soul which they were not likely to credit but an unqualified compassion in God which was no less of a challenge for them to accept. It could not have been easy for any of the sisters to shake off the weighty and afflictive sense that the unworthiness they properly felt in themselves was tantamount to damnation. Madre Teresa herself had seasoned her Vida with the iterated conviction that she deserved hell, even though she remains unhelpfully blurry about the vices she believed should take her there. Thérèse proved entirely immune to such morbidity,[5] but while her message of trust in God's love, a kind of gratitude, may seem to our modern disposition both healthy and uplifting, to at least some of her sister Carmelites it likely smacked of heresy. Perverse? Shocking? Who was this girl to be telling them such things?

In the first of those plays, Thérèse cast herself as the adolescent Jeanne of Domremy, a girl subject to voices. It would be as fair to say that she cast Jeanne as Thérèse because the girl's temperament, so diminutive that it is caché, reveals her author's. The play itself remains adolescent, chiefly because Thérèse evinces no psychological interest in the Jeanne beset by inner voices which could as well be demonic (psychotic) as angelic. In this trite version, no room is left for ambiguity nor for any real characterization. Jeanne moves from apprehension to acceptance once she is visited by St. Catherine of Alexandria, a famous fourth-century martyr responsible for many conversions, and St. Margaret of Antioch, another virgin and martyr of the same century.[6] St. Michael, the guardian of France, initially intimidates her by his overbearing masculinity but with the saintly women to sustain her, she accepts the mission to relieve the invested Orleans and bring glory to France.

The martial accent proves mercifully subdued in this version; Thérèse's complicity with the French imperial mission via the Church came to the fore later. Here the dramatic weight, what little there is, falls upon the celestial promise that Jeanne is bound for an early death, as her saints and she herself were, but for all that this Jeanne is told, she could presume that death would come in battle. In this innocuous fantasy of enablement, Jeanne is far too passive to be of any dramatic substance. The passivity derives not merely from her unreflected acquiescence to the saints; it rests in her notion of martyrdom as a glorious means of assumption into heaven.

In preparing her play, Thérèse consulted Henri Wallon's biography of Jeanne (a gift from Isidore to the Carmel), which was published in 1876 in a deluxe edition, abundant in illuminated prints and lithographs. Pope Pius IX wrote a commendatory letter to Wallon, included in this printing, thus sealing Wallon's version of Jeanne as the one upon which all pious readers could depend. Wallon's work rested upon the thorough documentary research published from 1841 to 1849 (five volumes) by Jules Quicherat for the Société de l'Histoire de France. (Translations of the Latin and archaic French required another twenty years.) Since that time, the Jeanne cult had grown apace in two lively directions: for nationalists, like Lamartine, she was a tragic heroine, a figure of what has been called romantic humanism, shorn of all theistic constructs. For the Church and its adherents, she was above all a martyr.[7] In 1869, the bishop of Orleans, Msgr. Dupanloup, opened the campaign for her canonization.

It was, however, the humiliating defeat of France in the war with Prussia which gave a steady impetus to the Jeanne cults, secular and sacred. The German wresting of Alsace and Jeanne's own Lorraine meant that French national pride had to bear an open wound. The Germans were viewed with hatred and contumely as the successors to the English, who had claimed French soil centuries before. Nationalists could ignore Jeanne's celestial visitations and batten on her well-documented jingoism. Having centered her interest primarily upon Jeanne's will to martyrdom once she had received the call, Thérèse gives only *en passant* attention to the clamor for driving the enemy from France. She carried little of the freight of chauvinist or nationalist suasions. Her patriotism remained unreflected but mercifully unheated.

It is instructive to note what Thérèse took from Wallon and what she left out. On Jeanne's "voices," Wallon comments that mysticism was not characteristic of her native Lorraine and besides "ses révélations nettes et précises n'ont rien de commun avec les vagues épanchements des illuminés de son temps" ["her revelations, distinct and precise, have nothing in common with the obscure effusions of inspired people in her age"].[8] Asked how she knew the apparitions were of St. Catherine and St. Margaret, the historical Jeanne had answered, "Par la manière dont elles me saluent" ["By the way they greeted me"], but Thérèse's St. Catherine identifies herself. Thérèse's most curious, even prophetic digression from the historical record comes in the denouement of the saints' visit. Jeanne had testified that when they were leaving her, she wept, longing for them to take her with them, but Thérèse's Jeanne says in answer to their summons that to win heaven, she is willing to go to the ends of the earth and pour out all her blood. That extreme urge finds resonance in Thérèse's desire to fulfill the vocation of a warrior and martyr, accomplishing "toutes les oeuvres les plus héroïques" (B 2v). Was reflection upon another adolescent's abandonment too painful for Thérèse to ponder, let alone portray?

There can only be guessing about how deeply Thérèse might have meditated on the intimacy of Jeanne's visions, which are the very stuff of the first play. The historical Jeanne, when asked at her trial if she had embraced the saints whom she had alleged to have seen with her physical eye, had claimed to have thrown her arms around their necks. Thérèse discreetly omitted such flamboyance: it was behavior hardly proper to a trainer of novices! Unfortunately, it is in such missed particulars that the humanity of Jeanne comes through to us today. The judges were fascinated with the rings taken from her when she was captured, as those rings were, or so they presumed, instruments of her witchery. She admitted that she had touched St. Catherine with one of them. And where had she touched her? "Vous n'en aurez chose," she coyly rejoined: "You'll not find out."[9]

In Thérèse's second and much longer play on her, *Jeanne d'Arc accomplissant sa mission* (January 1895), martyrdom is realized. Having relieved Orleans on behalf of a compromised, not to say spineless Charles (no battles, save for offstage exclamations in the third scene) and having seen him crowned at Rheims, she is imprisoned by the English, just as her voices had foretold. Far more important for Thérèse is Jeanne's preparation for martyrdom by her saints and then her apotheosis, carried out here to suitably operatic length. To fault Thérèse, though, for adherence to such exalting tableaux would be idle. She was presenting what her Carmelite sisters expected and what privately fascinated her: the allure of martyrdom.

The Jeanne plays belong to the time of her unripened spirituality, when she was still dependent upon models for emulation. She had not yet crossed the fault line which would put her decisively on her own. Only when Thérèse lost the expectation of heaven and of any conduit to it could she shift from a conventional, programmatic passivity to her own singular initiative. The value of these banal early productions lies precisely in their providing the measure of that rapid maturity into her own true voice. The one striking aspect of the Jeanne productions can be found in the first of the photographs Céline took of her sister about the time of the second play. Thérèse, dressed in cerulean blue with gold sequins and with a dark wig that helps us forget she was blonde, stands with her left hand holding the standard of Jesus (*Jhesus* in the lettering) as her right holds, quite listlessly, a wooden sword. It is a pose far more contemplative than martial. In that season, she was writing her first autobiographical manuscript, reliving daily her childhood and her slow, painful coming of age, but this is the first photograph to suggest someone much older than her then twenty-two years. In its detachment and gravity, it belongs with the mature portraits of June 1897.

We miss in both presentations of Jeanne the commendable performance (to take that word in either sense) recorded of her in the famous trial: her shrewd ripostes, canny silences, and seeming confidence in the face of interrogators. Jeanne's offhandedness about St. Michael deserves note: she said she had not seen his crown nor noticed his clothes. Asked if he was naked, she said, "Do you think our Lord Jesus had nothing to dress him in?" And did he have hair? "Why should he have cut it off?" It is a pity that Thérèse omits the trial sequence altogether, but she did so perhaps in recalling her own embarrassment and subsequent shame when interrogated informally at Carmel about her vision of the smiling Virgin. (At that time, she was only ten years old; Jeanne's visions first came when she was thirteen.) Also, including the trial would have meant iteration of the charge of heresy, and Thérèse wants a whitewashed Jeanne who in the first play is already pledged to fight heresy.[10] That, as perhaps she did not know, sounded an anachronistic note: however hateful the English invaders, they were still loyal to Rome. Besides, it was Cauchon, England's lackey and Jeanne's chief interrogator and tormenter, who had pronounced *her* an apostate. What did Thérèse think when she and her family entered the Virgin's chapel at Lisieux's Saint Pierre, where Cauchon is buried?

Jeanne d'Arc is popularly known by cinematographic depictions, of which there have been perhaps too many. Two alone are worthy of notice here because they bid for informative contrast with the theresian: first, the Carl Dreyer version of 1927, *La Passion de Jeanne d'Arc* (long vanished till a pristine print was recovered in 1981 from a Norwegian sanatorium's closet), with the immortal Melle Falconetti keeping her tear ducts ever open before her grotesquely aged, pugnacious, and hypocritical judges; second, the Robert Bresson version of 1962, *Procès de Jeanne d'Arc*, in which the convincingly adolescent and virtually anonymous Jeanne (Florence Carrez, truly *cachée*) is subjected to an eerily dispassionate (genuinely Bressonian) juridical hostility. Thérèse misses, or simply ignores, the two vivid aspects of the Jeanne legend which these filmmakers capture splendidly: her suffering before a harsh and uncomprehending ecclesiastical authority and her extreme aloneness (Falconetti gets at least some comfort from the angelic Artaud as Jean Massieu) and vulnerability as a girl (Carrez, a sullen adolescent) barely reaching womanhood.

Thérèse, it seems, was too attentive to this story's beginning and end, the hiddenness of an obscure life and the apotheosis in which not dreams but visions come true. She neglected the proceeding which connected the obscurity and triumph: chiefly, the trial. Before her darkness, Thérèse did not live in a truly adversarial world, one of savagery and enmities, and that prompts one to wonder, did she truly grasp that men were bent upon destroying Jeanne?

Of the execution itself, Dreyer settled for sheer horror, with Jeanne's body appallingly conflagrated into ash, and Bresson for mystery, as Jeanne disappears literally in smoke. Both seem disposed to nullify the glory attendant to the legend. It could be charged that the interpretations from Dreyer and Bresson reflect the punitive masculine world which tormented and condemned Jeanne. Neither of these cineastes was interested in just what mattered to Thérèse, the visionary life and the martyr's glory it promised. If they are too earthbound, she is too heavenbound for most modern tastes, which is to say that people are happy to accept the hackneyed "woman warrior" mold, here historically realized for once, but are bemused by the essential and elusive matter of whether there is a divinity shaping human fate.

Not that Thérèse was ignorant of masculine politics: she had had her own firsthand experience of unsympathetic, not to say inquisitorial men in her attempts to reach Carmel at age fourteen. She had in effect undergone her own *procès*, and that experience, though she survived it, might have left enough of a negative impress upon her, despite its felicitous outcome, that she did not want to summon any suggestion of it by presenting Jeanne under interrogation. How could she forget the peevishness of the Carmel's superior, Delatroëtte, who had consistently opposed her entry and embarrassed the Carmelites with his scorn when she was admitted?

Although radically incomplete, Thérèse's Jeanne conforms to the figure shaped by Wallon. Keen to the modern contention over her, which he characterized as "la lutte de l'inspiration contre l'autorité, du libre génie gaulois contre le clergé romain" ["the struggle of inspiration against authority, of free Gallic genius against the Roman clergy"], he contended that Jeanne was not significant as a liberator of France. The English would have been driven out sooner or later. Her mission plays a secondary role: "Ce qui est merveilleux dans cette histoire, c'est Jeanne, c'est ce qu'elle dit d'elle-même, quand on connaît par toute sa vie la fermeté de son intelligence et la simplicité de son coeur" ["What's marvelous in this story is Jeanne, what she says of herself, when one knows from her entire life the steadfastness of her intelligence and the simplicity of her heart"].[11] It is an odd pity that Thérèse, similarly endowed, failed to do justice to the first of these marvels and only sketched in the second when depicting her martyr saint.[12]

Most of Thérèse's other *récréations pieuses* were composed for the Christmas season and center upon the nativity in novel ways. In a dialogue in verse, *Les Anges à la Crèche*, written for Christmas 1894, the infant Jesus is visited not by shepherds nor magi but by the angels of his destiny, among them those of the Eucharist, the Resurrection, and the Last Judgment. The theme of divine hiddenness, *le Dieu caché* but also *la vie cachée en Dieu* (Carmelites hide their lives in God), became especially important in Thérèse's perception even as far as Manuscript C and here becomes pronounced: divinity is reduced to the small and helpless humanity of an infant and thus adored. However, omitting the peace and goodwill bromide of greeting cards, the balm so soothing to our vanity, the angels dwell upon ingratitude. Ours. This Dostoyevskian motif, that God is not loved (St. Francis had said that Love is not loved), is no less fundamental to Thérèse and a bracing tonic to those who see her as a mere dispenser of flowers. The fact of human selfishness justifies the presence of the angel of judgment, a horrific vindicator of the Jansenist persuasion.

This exterminating angel of retribution would have been the inevitable, not to say welcome presence for not a few of the Carmelites assembled that

Christmas day. Their Christology had been centered upon their own mortificatory exercises to appease a divine wrath, to suffer in turn as Christ had, for a sinfully distracted world. Suffering assumed for the salvation of souls (and the renunciation of self) had been the traditional Carmelite way. Now, Thérèse imports into this tense little drama her own indisposition to extraordinary mortifications. The infant Jesus himself disarms the angel of apocalyptic vengeance by proclaiming his mission of a compassionate, redemptive love. At the play's close, this dire and brooding angel, poised with sword to dispatch all ingrates, is both demoted—it is for Christ to judge the world—and converted to Christ's "ineffable *amour.*" The angels are left hapless, wishing they too could become humble infantile creatures. Such was Thérèse's shrewd elixir gently administered to sisters who, in presuming to save others by chastening themselves, were also subtly subjecting themselves to the pharisaical pride whispering to them that they, the blessed, were working for sinners. This play served obliquely to introduce the Carmelites at Lisieux to what became the indispensable complement of theresian *confiance*: remaining lowly, *rester petite*, or becoming such, *se faire petite*.

Best of the plays centered on Jesus is the one in which he has no speaking part, *La Fuite en Égypte*, composed in celebration of Pauline's third year as prioress and performed in January 1896. This play proved exceptional in an unhappy way, as Pauline abruptly broke it off in mid-performance,[13] devastating Thérèse—an action that became for Pauline years later a source of anguished regret. Because Thérèse invested herself in convincing characterizations of nonsaintly people and gave her story some psychological tensions, she succeeded here even as she had failed in her Jeanne plays. This drama, second in length only to *Jeanne d'Arc accomplissant sa mission*, stands alone among the eight as one which, with imaginative attention, could be brought to a secular performance.

In brief, Thérèse traces the flight of Joseph and Mary into Egypt, barely mentioned in *Matthew* 2:13–14, and tells how they are received in Egypt by a woman, Susanna, whose husband, Abramin, heads a small band of brigands. Their infant son suffers from leprosy. When Susanna gives Mary water to cleanse the baby Jesus, Mary gives the water back to her with the assurance that, if Susanna will only believe, this water will cure her child. Departing from Scripture, this story affords the very first miracle wrought by Christ. Mary and Joseph serve as not only the pious models of parenthood, like Zélie and Louis, but exegetes of the Jewish Scriptures, fully confident in their son's divinity and his mission. Fortunately, Thérèse does not shape them from plaster and remembers to afford some humor. Joseph complains that he had to receive the news of Herod's menace from an angel: why couldn't the baby have told us himself? Why must I be heaven's messenger for transmitting orders? Having just completed Manuscript A, Thérèse was disposed to see the Holy Family in the same earthy tones with which she had portrayed her own.

Here, Joseph wriggles in mild discomfort with his appointment as heaven's stooge. We can almost hear the sisters chuckling.

Then comes a note not otherwise heard in any of Thérèse's writings, the unrest begotten of class tensions. Joseph is a struggling day laborer and Abramin, a thief who rationalizes stealing from the wealthy: what else are the poor to do? Susanna warns Mary that Egypt is more impoverished than Judea. A certain gruff realism in the husbands provides a foil to their wives' calm submissiveness. Abramin, witnessing Jesus' miraculous power in the healing of his son, wonders why this deity did not spare the innocents massacred by Herod's soldiers and kill the evil tetrarch himself. Susanna for her part gains depth as a woman who longs for a god unknown to her, one who can cure her child and redeem her husband from his pointless criminality. She has no use for all the jewelry he has purloined and would rather be poor. (It is she who has that aria, somewhat abridged, from *Trovatore*.) Even after the meeting with Joseph and Mary, it seems that her husband, momentarily dazed with reverence, will resume his thievish ways. Their son, it is hinted, shall rejoin Christ at the very end of their lives, becoming the penitent thief promised paradise toward the close of *Luke* (23:39–43).

Few of Thérèse's writings reflect so economically her familiarity with the Gospels. This play affords exactly fifty allusions to them all (except *Mark*) as well as to the Jewish Scriptures. Yet more important are their imaginative interweaving into intimate tableaux of convincingly real people. If Mary and Joseph turn a bit pedantic in their prophetic awareness of their infant son's mission and destiny, that failing can be readily excused. Later, Thérèse grew beyond the characterization of Mary presented here and gave her a portrait from life which was far more credible.

La Fuite en Égypte assumes a poignant significance if we regard it as Thérèse's last articulation of an unequivocal confidence before the vaulting off of an afterlife and the rolling in of a fog sequestered her from Carmel, from her own history, and from the conventions of hope and faith itself. The epiphanic angel at the play's close provides an ironic *envoi* to what would soon become Thérèse's untroubled past:

> Oh, quel instant, quel bonheur sans mélange,
> Quand les élus paraissant glorieux,
> De leur amour recevront en échange,
> L'éternité pour aimer dans les Cieux

["Oh, what a moment, what happiness beyond dilution, when the elect appear in glory and shall receive in exchange for their love an eternity for loving in the Heavens"].

Of the eight plays, the most engaging in the circumstances of its composition is undoubtedly *Le Triomphe de l'Humilité*, performed on Saturday, June 20,

1896. It was the first of only two which Thérèse composed after the onset of her Easter darkness in that year. But she intended it chiefly as an occasion for reconciliation, coming only three months after the tensely protracted electoral process by which Gonzague was reinstalled as prioress. The Carmel had been split in two and wounds had perhaps run deep and were slow to heal. Gonzague was embittered by the realization that she was not so loved as she had believed (or so she construed the vote), and in the first four ballots Pauline, too, was rejected as she did not receive the needed three-fourths of the vote, and so, as the rules prescribed, her name could not be on the fifth.

Thérèse's message pleads that a union of hearts, "cette douce gaîté," can be achieved only when each person becomes small with humility. Here we find the social dimension of the little way, prescribed in the midst of an unhappy and riven community. While from an outsider's perspective, the electoral divisiveness seems overwhelmingly petty, the community members had to struggle to get past it. It had not yet done so months later, and the play was meant to help them.

It proves exceptional on another count, as Thérèse cast herself and two of her novices, her cousin Marie (Sr. Marie de l'Eucharistie) and the difficult Sr. Marie-Madeleine as themselves. In the first scene, they discuss the impropriety of wishing for visions. San Juan de la Cruz had inveighed against the desire for revelations as a venial sin (*Maxima* 34; *Carmel* II.21, III.30), to which Sr. Marie de l'Eucharistie replies, "C'est une faute. ... Je n'en savais rien. ... Eh bien! Pourtant je les désire aussi" ["It's a fault? I didn't know that. ... Oh, well, I want them anyway"]. Thérèse adroitly recalls to her charges that the blessed are those who believe without seeing, and so they settle for hearing but cannot presume to bring down heavenly strains. Instead, they shall hear voices from hell, introduced by St. Michael.

The play was performed, like the others, in the recreation hall with a screen before which the three performers were seated. On cue, the demonic voices came from behind the screen, accompanied by the sound of chains dragging and the projection of the convent's pitchforks. Lucifer, Beelzebub, and Asmodeus, suitably fractious, immediately accuse one another of delinquencies in ruining souls. Beelzebub complains that he would prefer to spend his hell on earth, a canny twist anticipating Thérèse's most famous words, spoken to Pauline a year later.[14] He blames Asmodeus for having lost a fiancée named Diana Vaughan.

Lucifer organizes an expedition against Carmel because it is under the protection of his mortal enemy, the Virgin Mary. When the Carmelite novices cry out for help, St. Michael appears in order to rout the fiends. He speaks in rhymed couplets in answer to Lucifer's prosaic vaunts. Finally, weighing poverty, chastity, and obedience against the satanic virtues of pride, autonomy, and willfulness, St. Michael prevails by adding humility, whose model is

Mary, into the balance. An angelic refrain at the close enjoins the novices to remain forever little for Jesus, their spouse.

At this point, Diana Vaughan claims a lengthy digressive background. She became a *cause célèbre* for embattled Catholicism in the second generation of the anticlerical Third Republic. A memoir published under her name chronicled a young Franco-American girl's initiation into and deliverance from a satanic cult said to be practiced by Freemasonry. *La Croix* had taken up her cause and in the issue of May 8, 1895, had asked for prayers for her conversion through Jeanne d'Arc, whom Pope Leo XIII had proclaimed venerable the previous year. Within a month, the conversion had been effected.

In the midst of this fantastic and sensationalized affair, some sober and cautious people became doubtful about Vaughan, but the seeding ground had been well prepared and covered another issue, anti-Semitism. A book by Georges Romain, *Le péril franc-maçon et le péril juif* (1891), pressed the connection. A memoir published in a monthly serial (begun in 1892) under the pseudonym of Dr. Bataille, *Le diable au XIXe siècle* (*The Devil in the 19th Century*), purported to expose Freemasonry's satanic cults whose secret laboratories prepared drugs and poisons. The Vatican itself left no doubt as to the intended victims. The *Osservatore romano* claimed that Freemasonry was the weapon Judaism was using to destroy Christianity and bring on the earthly reign of Satan.[15]

The *satanisme* imputed to Freemasonry had no basis save that this movement had been born of the Enlightenment and carried its impetus into the nineteenth century. It had been condemned as early as 1738 by Pope Clement XII for its indifference to religion and the state. This censure rested firmly upon the fact that Masons subscribed to deism and in their way contributed to the ideological pretensions to reason during the French Revolution. Early in the Third Republic, the esteemed Msgr. Dupanloup exposed the Masonic subversion at book length, listing its program for such incendiary goals as universal suffrage, abolition of capital punishment, the rights of labor, and reduction of war budgets. The latest attack had come from Pope Leo XIII in *Humanum genus* (1884), where Freemasonry was denounced for its secrecy and, far worse, for its subversion of Christianity under a feigned tolerance of all religions. The Masonic support for separation of church and state meant the destruction of both, said the pope. He equated Freemasonry not with Jews, however, but with the Italian republicanism which had powerfully subverted papal influence.

At the time of Thérèse's play, France's most famous Jew, Captain Alfred Dreyfus, framed for treason, was serving his second year of life imprisonment on Devil's Island. He had been condemned by the army, whose officer corps was solidly Catholic. Unlike Diana Vaughan, Dreyfus split the nation in two, and while the ignominy of his trial, the spectacle of Esterhazy's court-martial acquittal, Dreyfus's retrial, Zola's *J'accuse*, and the exculpation still exert their fascination as historical events, the word *dreyfusard*, if not its antonym, is still found in the Larousse. The Dreyfus trial played as the foremost drama of the acutely histrionic and sensationalized time in which Diana Vaughan emerged.

Whether we like it or not, Thérèse's play belongs to this epoch rampant with fear, hatred, and presumed conspiracies. Yet, she remains at a charitable remove, protected as though by Carmel's very walls from the virulent polemics of that time, as her uncle Isidore did not. He took up the royalist rightist cause of conservative Catholics by becoming an amateur polemicist, contributing articles to a local newspaper, *Le Normand*, with attacks on Freemasons and Jews.

The Lisieux Carmel for its part became enthusiastic about the conversion of Diana Vaughan, and Thérèse herself received permission to write to her. She included a photo Céline had taken of them both from the production of the second play on Jeanne d'Arc. She in turn received not only an acknowledgment but also a copy of a eucharistic novena which Diana Vaughan had composed. Pope Leo XIII himself had read it, and Thérèse copied lengthy portions of it. But by year's end, skepticism was gaining the upper hand in the Church, and Rome began an inquest. When Diana Vaughan published an attack upon the skeptical commissioner in charge of the inquest, Msgr. Lazzareschi, Thérèse was shocked, according to Pauline's testimony at the *procès ordinaire*: "Ce n'est pas possible que cela vienne du bon Dieu" ["It's impossible that that came from God"]. But Thérèse herself knew what it meant to be subjected to devilish voices and might well have been indulgent in a way the other Carmelites were not.

All doubts were removed, however, on April 19, 1897, the announced day for a press conference with Diana Vaughan in Paris. In a hall packed with more than four hundred people, the image of Thérèse and Céline as Jeanne d'Arc and St. Catherine was projected onto a wall. A bald, white-bearded man named Léo Taxil revealed that the converted Diana Vaughan was his own invention (the real Vaughan was only his typist), along with the memoirs and the novena published under her name. Shocked as the Carmelites were, Thérèse had been doubly humiliated, by her show of trust and by the public exposure of herself playing Jeanne d'Arc. Her response was mute but unequivocal: according to Pauline, Thérèse cast the letter from Diana/Taxil onto the convent's manure heap, and she (or someone subsequently?) drew heavy lines through the delicate references to Diana Vaughan, quondam fiancée of Asmodeus.

This peculiar episode in Thérèse's life deserves particular attention because it forms, as it were, a test case. She had long known and practiced humility through humiliation. Gonzague had dispensed that humbling regularly through the first years. Now, however, it had come from a world which Thérèse had acknowledged only in prayerful pity: the world of her adopted criminal-penitent, Pranzini, the world of the renegade Carmelite priest, Father Hyacinthe Loyson, who rejected papal infallibility and argued that priests had the right to marry, a presumption on which he acted. She had prayed for these spectacular strays, both well profiled in the sensational press, and yet she had not put up her guard when Diana Vaughan, similarly hooplahed, came to her awareness. Here was yet another celebrity soul in need of rescue, but Diana Vaughan's conversion, unlike Pranzini's, did not mark a denouement. It was Taxil, not Thérèse, who assigned the roles and gave her, in her unwitting good will, that of a dupe. All the nonsense about satanism within Freemasonry had also been his invention. That he could have played so long and so well upon the credulities of so many Catholics, even the pope, makes l'affaire Taxil a splendid case study in collective susceptibility.

In this incident, she came close to a true *imitatio Christi*, in all the bitterness of a jeering. The *Imitatio* itself, from which she drew in much of her writing, counseled her to tolerate the faults of others since, as it told her, she had plenty of her own for others to endure (I.16.2). Besides, the truly patient person does not dwell on someone who is putting her to the test but remains "indifférent sur les créatures" and aware that all that is contrary to oneself comes from God (III.19.3). All that is well and good, but Taxil's assault was the more sinister for being unexpected and gratuitous. He mocked her from out of nowhere. Was she able finally to embrace the hoaxer Taxil as she had embraced Pranzini? It is a commonplace for Christians that one cannot love God more than one loves the person one loves least. Taxil deserved her contempt but did he receive her prayerful love?

We do not know. Pauline testified at the first *procès* that Thérèse said nothing about the hoax after it was revealed. Taxil's scheme and Thérèse's unwitting involvement in it furnish a substantial caveat to biographers and theologians alike: in the absence of evidence on the matter of her forgiveness of and private solicitude toward Taxil, we are reminded of how little we finally know about Thérèse, how little we can say with an absolute confidence. My own view is this: God's compassionate love is so fundamental, so axiomatic to Thérèse's spirituality, and her own loving in response is so powerful that it would have been difficult for her, if she indeed became embittered toward Taxil, to have remained so. She had never met him. She was surely wise enough to perceive that his deceitfulness, while darker and deeper than the sins of Pranzini and Loyson, had the pathos of all sin. For all his buffoonery, or because of it, he invited compassion. A heart-hardened Thérèse seems too anomalous to be conjured.

Less than two months separate Taxil's press conference and her writing to Gonzague that she had found a place for herself at the table of sinners. They were those she called "materialists of the worst sort." She knew she would find Taxil there.

Thérèse's poetry has received so far two modern English translations, yet neither, for whatever its merits, helps to promote her as a writer. It is difficult to assume that any but the most indiscriminate reader could manage to make a steady way through them, because they are plagued by a very dated aesthetic, already two generations old when Thérèse was writing.[16] It belongs to the very conservative Catholic sensibility of the young, pre-reformist Lamartine, whose *Méditations poétiques* (1820) were among Louis's favorite readings and recitations. Further, they tend to be iterative in both diction and substance, and only rarely did she sustain the register of images toward an imaginative coherence.

She had not so much a limited range of expressivity as a limited range of intent, yet it would be captious to fault her for not being *as poet* a prima donna like Gerard Manley Hopkins, S.J. She was writing both as a Carmelite and for other Carmelites, and that was all. It would not have occurred to her to forge nor to wrench language into her own terms nor to make it a medium of some special way of seeing the world. She did not have the masculine need to advertise or otherwise enlarge an ego by turns of rhetoric. She did not even have the self-pity requisite to being a poet. What matters is that her verse coheres with the Thérèse we know in everything else she wrote.

All of her poems might better be called prayers of thanksgiving, a succession of gratitudes for graces, a kind of verse autobiography, even though many of them were occasional works which her sisters, natural and spiritual, requested for anniversaries or feast days. Celebration, however, is not infrequently limned with entreaty. Thanking God, we cannot let pass the urge to importune as well. Sometimes, the prioress, whose permission was necessary in any case, would simply order the writing for an occasion. Thérèse composed those poems and set them to *mélodies* of the day, even as San Juan de la Cruz had used popular *canciones* of his time. Like the *récréations pieuses*, they realized a one-time, collective performance: everyone was able to sing the composition because the meter conformed to a well-known song or an operatic aria they had heard at home or had sung in their convent schools.

It bears emphasis that the daily offices of Carmel were declaimed, not sung; there was not even a harmonium in the convent. The sublimity of Ambrosian or Gregorian chant, vulgarized by a modern secular culture which mistakes it for some form of soothing, had been known to these sisters in their parish churches but not in the convent. Music, rare for them, was treasured. Singing poems such as Thérèse's gave them a distinctive occasion for joyful release. Some of the sisters, notable among them Sr. Marie de St. Joseph and Sr. Marie de l'Eucharistie, had especially lovely voices. Thérèse's own singing voice was, it is said, wholly undistinguished.

Because of their contingent sharing, their communal enactment, the poem-songs had a festive air. None of them would nor could be fretted with mortifying lamentation or a deep penitential, psalmic force. But neither did Thérèse write such downbeat verses spontaneously for herself. The minor keys she sounded only in the privatives of *petitesse* and *faiblesse* or in the adumbrations of those spiritual trials, including the great and final one, which must be counted as yet more graces. Jesus had sent them. When other sisters confided their darknesses or drynesses to her, she transposed those notes with a sure hand and exquisite tact.

While, in the plays, Thérèse was fully herself as writer and hence covertly as teacher, in the requested or intended verses she was writing under instructions as to what another sister wanted to hear as, for example, in regard to her special devotion or favorite saint. Obliquely, sometimes transparently, Thérèse comes through as though she had merged with the sister whom she was serving. She was not so much obtruding upon another's person as voicing what they shared in temperament and understanding. That holds patently for her natural sisters—four poems each for Marie and Pauline, seven for Céline—and for Sr. Marie de l'Eucharistie, their cousin, but it also obtains in the poems, eight out of fifty-four of which Thérèse wrote for the novice who enjoyed elective affinities with her, Sr. Marie de la Trinité.[17]

In this discussion, we shall move from the periphery to the center, from some of the poems Thérèse wrote for those not so close to her; then, some poems for those who were; and finally, those she wrote for herself. Such an approach violates chronology but affords another sort of coherence. First, however, some background notes: how Thérèse wrote, how she saw herself in writing, and to whom she was indebted.

With characteristic charity and no little hyperbole, Sr. Marie des Anges, in profiling each of her sisters to other Carmels, had characterized Pauline as "Poète enchanteur, auquel les anges ont prêté leur lyre pour nous faire entendre les échos du ciel" ["an enchanting poet (masculine), to whom the angels have afforded their lyre so we can hear heaven's echoes"].[18] Deferring to her sister/mother, Thérèse was not beyond emulation. Her admission (A 81r) that in observing Pauline's writing and painting, she had thought, "je serais heureuse de savoir exprimer mes pensées en vers et de faire aussi du bien aux âmes" ["I'd be happy to know how to express my thoughts in verse and also to benefit souls"], suggests an apologia for her own writing of verse. Perhaps Pauline had been unfair in trying initially to discourage her from that effort.[19] After the importunity of Sr. Saint-Augustin (January 1893), the communal response to Thérèse as poet was slow and intermittent but finally enthusiastic enough to indicate she had not fallen short of her hopes.

When, on May 27, 1897, Pauline spoke with Thérèse about the *circulaire* which both of them knew would soon be written, they might have discussed inclusion of some of Thérèse's poetry. *Circulaires* only rarely quoted a sister's verse and such efforts were found only posthumously. By that May, Thérèse had written her last and most important poem, a celebration of the Virgin Mary as an earthly, accessible woman. In the event, Pauline included no fewer than twenty-five of the poems, nearly half, as a supplement to *Histoire d'une âme*.

If the poem on Mary as well as others Thérèse wrote spontaneously for herself can be accorded preference, that is not to detract from those she wrote *à la demande* or *à l'intention*. Those poems complement the spontaneous ones in a vital way: she told Maurice Bellière that the eighteen poems she sent to him in February 1897 revealed "non pas ce que je suis, mais ce que je voudrais et devrais être" ["not who I am but who I would like to be and ought to be"] (LT 220). Of these, only two had she written without occasion, "Vivre d'Amour" and "À mes petits Frères du Ciel." Almost all the others were addressed to her natural family: to Marie and Pauline, women to whom she deferred since they were, in her self-humbling estimate, eagles to her swallow, lilies to her *pâquerette* (B 5r); to Céline and cousin Marie, for whom she was *compagne* in the novitiate, far advanced in Carmelite life yet self-convicted of inadequacy in its pursuit.

She was in all the poems variously like every Christian, both a shepherd and a sheep; in Carmelite terms, both Martha and Mary, serving her sisters, praying with and for them. She writes poems as both novice and de facto as *maîtresse*. Each of those sisters, no matter their rank, could savor the hortatory tensions Thérèse revealed to Bellière, the Carmelite ethos of spiritual completion and one's frailty and susceptibility in seeking to attain that completion. Thérèse's caveat to Bellière was, in fine, normative. Her writing marked the artifice of desideration, what she wished for herself and all her sisters, even as she learned to affirm imperfection in all its weakness. And why not? Madre Teresa herself, before laying out her *Camino de Perfección*, had made plaintively clear in her autobiography that she spent her whole life falling down, straying, needing God to pick her up again.

It may prove most helpful, then, to read Thérèse's poems as prayers which indefinably range between petition and benediction, between the sometimes implicit, sometimes explicit and supplicatory *faiblesse* of being a Carmelite and the paradoxical gratitude of *confiance*, the trusting that grace alone sustains the soul in its weakness and draws it on. Perhaps, Thérèse regarded her poems as psalmic. The fact that poetry in itself amounts, as Yeats once observed, to fakery, to rhetorical showmanship, would not have occurred to her at all.

Thérèse wrote verse under the mildly adverse circumstance of daily physical exhaustion. Her only writing time fell in a late hour of every day, from 8 p.m. until 9, when concentration would have required more than usual effort. I suspect that she was composing a great deal in her head through the day, silently, in snatches, perhaps over the laundry or even in the recreational hours, editing the while (see figure 6.1). When she was composing in her head for another sister, she might well have spoken with her to engage in coediting. She did not have the leisure of writing and recasting, but when she finally sat down on her stool and took up her *écritoire*, a wooden frame about the size of a

FIGURE 6.1. The laundry at the Carmel of Lisieux, where Sr. Saint
Joseph splashed Thérèse in the face with dirty water. Copyright Archives du
Carmel de Lisieux.

metropolitan phone directory, she likely knew what she wanted to set down.
She might well have memorized some of the poems in toto, so that she was in
effect copying them under the single light of her lamp. Pauline, *enchanteur*,
later corrected the prosody and syntax and sealed the whole with her own
diction in sometimes excessive degrees, and not always to a poem's better-
ment. It was her versions which for generations passed as Thérèse's own.

When this poetry is denominated (or dismissed) as *lamartinienne*, a
narrow ambit is meant. The subjects are love, with God and nature as the go-
betweens. Superficially, that gives us the profile of the early Restoration's
most celebrated young poet; his *Méditations poétiques* reached its ninth edition
within three years, an unparalleled triumph. But the tag may be formal as
well. Untrained, Thérèse confined herself to the predictable measures of
couplets, alexandrine or octosyllabic. She submitted as readily and unquestioningly to received forms as she had to the Rule and the *Papier d'exaction*.

But those poetic forms and even the beat of the musical settings were sub-ordinate to her message. This regimental fixity into which she poured no small measure of her *audace*—new wine in old skins—does not immediately jar, but it does subject her obliquely to Rimbaud's charge against Lamartine himself, that he had been strangled by those outmoded meters. How much more, then, was Thérèse in an age when poetry became the elixir of its own music. The emblems of her *épreuve*, the great spiritual darkness of the fog, the tunnel, the *néant*—all seem far more suitable to the calculated obscurities of *symbolisme* than to the faded Byronic posturing of Romanticism.

That is not, however, altogether fair to Lamartine. His *Méditations* are not pious exercises. They are spiked with blasphemous arraignments of a cruel God who makes sport of human suffering, consigning a helpless and bewildered humanity to wretchedness and despair. In "L'homme," one of the most bracing of the *Méditations*, he anticipates a deeper than theresian darkness: humanity is a living toy, "un jouet vivant" of a tormenting deity, much as Thérèse had once fashioned herself a ball kicked, pricked, or rolled aside by the infant Jesus. A kind of Karamazov, Lamartine claims that humanity's only crime is epistemological: being human, we long to know, but God, all sufficient, remains silent in eternity.

Lamartine relieves his reader of this metaphysical gloom only intermittently and not without ironic bite. In "La Providence à l'Homme," an ostensible answer to the soul's disquietudes, comes a divine pledge that all apparent evils under which humanity groans will be changed to virtues. All nature obeys the celestial order, proclaims this Jansenist God; only humanity revolts: "Mais ma vengeance paternelle/Confondra ce doute infidèle/Dans l'abîme de ma bonté" ["But my fatherly vengeance shall confound this disloyal doubt in the abyss of my goodness"].[20] Not for us an auspicious universe.

I have drawn Lamartine into the discussion because his plaintiff's posturing before *le Dieu caché* makes him spiritually akin to Thérèse. They occupy the same world, finally, even though she declines to complain or sue. Lamartine groped toward a theodicy; Thérèse saved herself the effort of doing so, because the Carmelite ethic of assuming Christ's suffering—one she embraced with joyous affirmation—sufficed her to the end. What did love have to do with indignation, not to mention the whine of self-commiseration, when it affirmed the very condition upon which that indignation was focused, exile from God? Even Lamartine's ontology of the human, "un atome oublié sur les bords du néant" ["an atom forgotten on the margins of nothingness"] (from "L'Homme") could be ratified as a workable definition any Carmelite might have given of herself. Thérèse expressly embraced the atom's limit. Barely had she turned sixteen when she told Pauline that she, a little grain of sand, wanted to become "un atome visible seulement aux yeux de Jésus" ["an atom only Jesus could see"] (LT 74).[21] Was not God everything, and the itty-bitty self a nothing?

The paradoxical ontology of nonentity takes a curious turn in a couple of the poems Thérèse wrote for the perhaps least congenial of all her sisters, Sr. Saint-Vincent-de-Paul, who was more than thirty years her senior. Like other *converses* profiled in the *circulaires*, she prided herself on her learning, a kind of defensive reaction, possibly, to her working-class status. She could intimidate others, including Thérèse, with her tart tongue—"fine et maligne" ["keen and sly"], as Céline later characterized it—and she sang impromptu with a disconcerting boom. Two facts set her in a less adversarial posture: at the age of seven, she had watched both her parents die of typhoid within forty-eight hours. She and her younger brother were raised by Visitandines, in whose school she served in adolescence to younger students so well that on her death, Lisieux received numerous testimonials from some gratefully reminiscent charges. To Céline's camera, she usually shows a wry contentment.

As she had a special devotion to the Eucharist, she instructed Thérèse to make it central in the verse. In the first two of four poems for her,[22] Thérèse plays on the atomic topos: in each, the atom is a soul awaiting Jesus in the host. Rather weirdly, it seeks first to lodge in the ciborium, the vessel holding eucharistic wafers. In the second, more coherent poem, the atom is a grain of dust pursuing the Carmelite ethos of forgottenness, silence, the world's scorn, and the mission to pray for and save souls. The assured littleness of being a nobody runs concurrent with a joy in being fired and self-consumed in love's tabernacle.

The two later efforts indicate that Thérèse's own maturing ran in tandem with her productivity even on behalf of someone so distant to her sensibility as Sr. Saint-Vincent-de-Paul. In the third, "Mes Désirs" ["My Desires"], the Eucharist by union becomes a permanent divine presence; the altar, a new Calvary where Christ's blood continues to flow for the soul. Now, dust and atoms aside, that soul is a pure, fermented grain chosen to become a host so that Christ will live in it. In the poem's bold closing, Christ is asked to transform the soul into himself. The notion that the soul might lose its identity remained alien to Thérèse, so we are left to guess at discussions she might have had with Sr. Saint-Vincent-de-Paul on this matter. That she could entertain and articulate another sister's spirituality does not signify that she made it her own.

Even more mysterious is the fourth poem, "Mon Ciel à Moi!" ["My Very Own Heaven!"], the only one composed for this sister during Thérèse's darkness. Only in this of all her poems did she write of an "épreuve de la foi," a phrase warranting supposition that Sr. Saint-Vincent-de-Paul was having one of her own and shared the fact. (And did she not know of Thérèse's?) Unusual, too, is the soul's claim, its "heaven," to impart Christ's graces and his divine fire "sur les âmes/Sur l'Eglise ma mère et sur toutes mes soeurs" ["upon souls, upon the Church my mother and upon all my sisters"]. Thérèse would not have recoiled from such language, but it is clearly not her own, no more than the references to the Spiritus Sanctus and to *abandon* in response to the testing of faith: "voilà ma seule loi" ["That's my only law"]. Law in any context was wholly foreign to the calm urgency and spontaneity of her temperament.

If Sr. Saint-Vincent-de-Paul posed a challenging personality as well as a generational distance to Thérèse, the sister for whom she wrote the largest number of poems, eight, was at another extreme, a kind of other self. This was Sr. Marie de la Trinité.[23] Only twenty months younger than Thérèse, she had been admitted at seventeen to the Carmel de la rue de Messine, one of two Parisian Carmels, but was obliged to leave because of illness, with the proviso of readmission only when she reached twenty-one. Lisieux had gotten word that this Carmel had an adolescent much like Thérèse, and the two became bonded even before meeting. After convalescence in her native Normandy, Sr. Marie de la Trinité was admitted to Lisieux during Pauline's priorate.

Thérèse the *benjamine* had at last a younger sister for whom she could play Pauline's role of exacting and loving overseer. For her part, Sr. Marie de la Trinité brought a sunny disposition, if also a naughty one. In the photos, she looks variously coy, amused, and serenely happy, perhaps much the way she had felt in her preconventual life, when she had enjoyed sneaking out of her parents' home and entertaining herself at shops and fairs. She was the only sister ever to show Céline's camera the full teeth of a grin, twice.

In sharp contrast, Thérèse's three older charges in the novitiate brought pronounced psychological issues: Céline had entered with renunciations and faced an instructor who had always been her junior. The naturally withdrawn Sr. Marie-Madeleine could not overcome an acute diffidence. And Sr. Marthe de Jésus, more than seven years senior to Thérèse and like Sr. Saint-Vincent-de-Paul scarred by orphanhood, tried her with fits of aggression, jealousy, and a willful clinging to Gonzague. Thérèse knew that a radiant impishness in Sr. Marie de la Trinité needed some curbing, but her faults must have seemed minor beside the ones the other novices bore. Yet, in guiding all four young women, Thérèse was herself guided—to the breakthrough realization of the soul's abiding imperfection. With their unwitting help, she controverted the Carmelite ethic of perfectibility and set her own weak, little self as the sufficient mark by which they could securely take their own measure (see figure 6.2).

As Sr. Marie de la Trinité was by her very immaturity the most docile of them, Thérèse's eight poems for her convey a transparent didacticism, "lessons" of simplicity the others would have resisted. "Rester petite," to remain little,[24] a central formulation in theresian spirituality, appears in the first (December 18, 1894), along with a psalmic plea to the Virgin to hide this little lamb under her mantle. It was a favorite image among Carmelites. Even so, this effort is warped by meliorist accents about merit and growth in virtue,

FIGURE 6.2. Thérèse with the novices she guided (*left to right*): Sr. Marie of the Trinity, Sr. Marie Madeleine (kneeling), Sr. Martha of Jesus, Sr. Geneviève (Céline). Gonzague and Pauline are in the window. Copyright Office Central de Lisieux.

scales which would finally fall away from Thérèse's eyes but which reflect the reward psychology common to the age. It is amusing that she uses the language of commerce itself.

In "Mon Ciel ici-bas!" ["My Heaven down here!"], composed for the twenty-first birthday of Sr. Marie de la Trinité (August 12, 1895), Thérèse discloses her debt to San Juan de la Cruz and his notion that by the divine union of love the soul takes on the semblance of Christ. In contemplating the Veronica cloth on which Jesus left the image of his suffering countenance, Thérèse seeks to hide her littleness, as though she could pass mystically within the holy face. Imprinted with that semblance of *douceur*, she—Marie, Thérèse—can, like Jesus, attract souls. For a brief moment, she was writing of her destiny.

The Marie poems, if I may call them such, take on a severe ripening in the time of Thérèse's entry into her final darkness. Reverting to the cult of the Eucharist, "Qu'il nous est doux de chanter ce jour radieux" ["How sweet for us to sing this radiant day!"], on the day of Marie de la Trinité's professed vows, Thérèse celebrates the Carmelite peace of daily self-immolation. In the closing quatrain, the convent itself becomes the ciborium, *mystérieux ciboire*, into which the prioress has placed the hosts: the professed sisters. Thérèse is fond of such baroque imagery, but she never spins it out into the conceits of so-called metaphysical poetry. It is a passing *grotesquerie* as though to startle into reflection. While the sisters did not then enjoy daily Communion, they were themselves the daily host.

The day of that poem's genesis, April 30, 1896, was extraordinary, not only for the photo Céline took to commemorate the profession of Marie de la Trinité. It was the day Thérèse produced a second and far weightier poem, a verse paraphrase of a passage from the *Llama Viva de Amor* [*The Living Flame of Love*] by San Juan de la Cruz. She told Marie that when she read that passage, it had taken her breath away, as it showed her precisely what her darkness meant and how to see it, even as it was starting.

Using both inner and outer suffering to extreme degrees, says San Juan's doctrine, God brings souls to perfection by deifying them in union with infinite wisdom. The formula for living in exilic darkness was an inconsolable yet consuming love for God, which would transform the soul into that very love: as pledged in "Qu'il nous est doux," one's soul would become a host. But what had truly fetched Thérèse, and as long before as the summer of 1893,[25] was San Juan's luminous assertion that love takes profit from both the good and the bad in the self: "du bien, du mal qu'il trouve en moi" is her straight recasting of San Juan. There, Thérèse found warrant for the soul's acceptance of its every failing and weakness, and left "du mal" (could it be evil?) to lie unchurned in its own semantic depths. Yet more: this notion of God's making use of one's credits and debits, as it were, allowed her to play freely at what she called Love's bank, without the least concern of what might be in her account or how her shares might be faring. "Je ne m'occupe pas des coups de bourse" ["I don't care about market indices"] she had quite equably told Céline.[26] What would her thrifty parents have said to that?

In her memoir, Marie de la Trinité remarks not only San Juan's influence on Thérèse as *compagne* but her own high-strung sensitivities. Like Thérèse, she had an acute need to love and to be loved and was susceptible to the world's enticements. She had remained a child, seeking monastic life as a way to resolve tensions. Just before entering the Messine Carmel, she had asked her father to indulge her with a ride on a merry-go-round. Thérèse addresses that weakness of temper in the final poem for her, untitled, in May 1897. As far as it could have been addressed to every sister who properly considered herself a poor little nothing, without virtues and loving Christ alone, this poem seems an unremarkable verse valedictory to the Carmel itself. But it also takes up Sr. Marie de la Trinité's devotion to the protectress Virgin, Notre

Dame du Perpétuel Secours. It was she, writes Thérèse, who had saved Marie in her childhood and adolescence from falling from the "précipices" of worldly devotions. If there is a subtext here, "un petit agneau loin de la bergerie ... jouant au bord des précipices," the lamb far from the fold playing near the edge was Thérèse herself, now the lost but far from infantile creature that only the Shepherd himself could—and would, surely?—retrieve. Behind the immature antics of Sr. Marie de la Trinité, fondly recounted in the recreational hours, stands Thérèse, the shepherdess playing at her own cliff's edge, an image of hazardous insouciance (recall the banking trope) that would have ravished Nietzsche. Manuscript C was only a few weeks away from her pen.

In her instructive celebration of young Marie de la Trinité as the lily that would not droop into the mud of worldliness, Thérèse in her own fate recalls another image, this from Dante, of the light bearer in the dark, who safely guides someone coming behind the lantern but cannot himself see the way securely.

Sr. Marie de la Trinité was a child to be raised up. How far different was Sr. Geneviève, an adult who had tasted fleetingly the pleasures at those "précipices" and had nearly fallen down from them. Thérèse could not confound those attractions; she could only turn her sister toward the Carmel's lights while Céline was still to a degree distracted by the memory of secular ones. Even when Céline was still "in the world" and Louis alive, Thérèse had been tugging at her, fantasizing that if she did choose marriage, that most dire of life routes, she could still remain pure, a suffering virgin like Saint Cecilia, who had persuaded her pagan husband, Valerian, to leave their marriage unconsummated. She had even managed to convert him, said the legend popularized in Wiseman's *Fabiola*, that chunky homiletic fiction Pauline had especially treasured in her adolescence.

Once within Carmel's walls, Céline quickly felt unhappy and bored. During her six months of postulancy, she was painting figurines instead of grand tableaux, and her assigned work in the *roberie* was tedious. She must not have been shy about complaining because the poem Thérèse wrote to assuage her restiveness enjoined a silence tactfully identified with the refusal of consolations, pretty thoughts, and special favors. A Carmelite forgets her own hurts and finds the adequacy of silence for loving God. It was likely an acrid tonic for Céline to swallow, especially in remembrance of all those talkative times she had enjoyed with her little sister in the belvedere. Now she was being dressed down gently, obliquely, but firmly.

Of an entirely different tone was the calmly elevated "Chant de Reconnaissance" ["Song of Thanksgiving"], which Thérèse wrote for Céline's entry into the novitiate (February 5, 1895). The key lines in its decasyllabic quatrains, "Je viens chanter l'inexprimable grâce/D'avoir souffert ... d'avoir porté la Croix" ["I'm going to sing the inexpressible grace of having suffered ... and borne the Cross"], could have been written for any sister who had already lived at some length in Carmel but in fact pointed to the bitter years Céline had sustained with Louis. Ironically, it was that filial suffering in the outer world which had helped Céline, like many other older postulants of Carmels, to reach a worldly seasoning that the Carmel had to render unsavory.

Toward that end, Thérèse composed one of the most inspired and in-volved of all her writings, "Le Cantique de Céline" ["The Canticle of Céline"], a verse biography with a kaleidoscopic profile of her *vita nuova* in Carmel.[27] Although she gives the first eighteen of the poem's fifty-five strophes to Cé-line's childhood and youth and another thirteen to her cross-bearing years with Louis, the heuristic momentum begins only in Céline's detachment from the world, at the thirty-second strophe. The dogma from San Juan de la Cruz which Thérèse had shared with her three years before (LT 135) was that whoever has Jesus has all things. Ergo, in Carmel, Céline had all the abun-dance and profusion of the natural world which she and her sisters had loved with taxonomic thoroughness in their adolescence. But while in San Juan, the claim to have in the Beloved "the murmurs of amorous zephyrs" meant, according to his own commentary, that the soul became privy to divine virtues, in Thérèse the splendors of nature carry no signification beyond themselves.

> En toi, Jésus, j'ai toutes choses
> J'ai les blés, les fleurs demi-closes
> Myosotis, bouton d'or, belles roses
> Du blanc muguet j'ai la fraîcheur
> L'odeur!

["In you, Jesus, I've all things, I've the grain, the half-closed flowers, Forget-me-not, buttercup, fair roses, from lilies of the valley I've the fresh fragrance!"]

Thérèse could think and write in metaphor, but she was averse to recasting the realm of experience to a symbolic code. The flowers she denominated in this strophe were vividly present to her consciousness and remained themselves, not stand-ins for an abstract rapture. If that concedes a persistent banality in her poems, it also underscores how firmly rooted she was in the sensuous and immediate as the seedbed of her expressive élan. Her poems neither need nor invite much explication nor lengthy commentary. A Car-melite's life was to be hidden and obscure but not her words.

Thérèse's rootedness in this world's perceptive life comes home even better in her most lengthy poem for Céline, a gently powerful scolding en-titled "Rappelle-toi!" ["Remember!"]. Céline had been in the novitiate only eight months when she asked Thérèse to compose a lengthy poem recalling to Jesus the sacrifices she had made for him in entering Carmel. Shouldn't he be grateful? (See figure 6.3.) The response came in thirty-three strophes (not an

FIGURE 6.3. Thérèse's most vigorously didactic poems were to Céline (*left*), who could have pursued marriage or a career in painting. Léonie sits crocheting, with almost empty hands. Note the identical dresses. Ca. 1894. Copyright Archives du Carmel de Lisieux.

idle number), sequenced with four decasyllables, two alexandrines, and two hexasyllables, closing with the mantric tetra, Rappelle-toi![28] But the recollections the poem calls upon Jesus to summon are about his own life in love and sacrifice, followed by a heady summons to match them. The importunate Céline in first person is given the effacement due a contemplative, longing for inundation in the divine source.

Céline's true station is assigned, but it is Thérèse's as well:

> Rappelle-toi qu'enfant de la lumière
> Souvent j'oublie de bien servir mon Roi.
> Oh! prends pitié de ma grande misère
> Dans ton amour, Jésus, pardonne-moi
> Aux affaires du Ciel daigne me rendre habile
> Montre-moi les secrets cachés dans l'Evangile

Ah! que ce Livre d'or
Est mon plus cher trésor
Rappelle-toi.

["Remember that as a child of light I often forget to serve my King well. Oh, in your love take pity on my great wretchedness, Jesus, forgive me and make me fit for Heaven's ways, show me the secrets hidden in the Gospel. Oh, that this Book of gold is my dearest treasure, remember."] Thérèse condenses here the complements of an initiate's unworthiness and a longing for revelation of secrets, as though the obverse of humility's lowly coin might be an "open sesame."

If the reprobation of Céline seems unfair, it proves wondrously mild compared to the penitential language so abundant in the *Vida* of Madre Teresa. There, in caustic iterations, the soul is castigated at times as evil and base, worthless and deserving of hell. Thérèse is altogether sparing of such terms, relying instead on the ontological insufficiency of the soul's littleness and weakness, the inescapable helplessness any honest person must face amid what Teresa called "esta farsa de esta vida tan mal concertada" ["the farce of this disordered life"].[29] It was to set that life in order that Christ came, says this poem, and only by divine love can it be accomplished. The soul's task is to sustain its humility in order to receive that love and then to offer it anew.

What then of the "hidden secrets" of the Gospels? Not knowing Latin, Thérèse did not have access to the literal sense of the psalmody she had before her in the two daily hours of prayer and during choral office.[30] Such were the limits of education for women, a generic chasm between them and men in sacred orders. Much of Thérèse's famous *audace* is fueled by simple uncertainties which her will to truth wanted to penetrate: only an informed grasp of sacred texts would have satisfied her, not a dry pedantic learning—nothing could have been more remote to her than that—but a familiarity of access such as she enjoyed in her keen and loving knowledge of flowers. Without any real education, she tried all the more urgently to find her intuitive way.

There was another, no less negative goad: she knew she lacked the steady revelations of the great saints. To take the same monitory example, Teresa's *Vida* overflows with God's light castings, and holy figures, even the recent dead, appear to support her and to provide timely advice. Although, unlike San Juan de la Cruz, without scholastic training, Teresa had, like him, lived rich in visionary sustenance. Thérèse remained grounded. All her flights in poetry she herself generates, and none becomes mystical testimony in the old Baroque way of the masters.

One tactical way to bring the soul's measliness to the recondite treasury of divine love was through Scripture itself. Thérèse profiles Céline as a kind of prodigal like *Luke*'s because her weaknesses, the tugs of career or of marriage or even that Canadian stint for Pichon, threatened to impose on her the kind of waste and loss the prodigal son had to overcome. Now, if Céline calls Jesus to remembrance, he will respond to her much like the prodigal's father, himself so prodigal in celebrating his son's return. At the same time, conventual life bade a model Carmelite to regard herself as the prodigal's brother, ever sustained and obedient. Although she conveniently ignores the bitterness and anger of that dutiful son, Thérèse made of the prodigal son parable the exemplary story of conversion and central to her theology.

Seeking the treasured knowledge, Thérèse had been finding it, or so this poem suggests. If the Johannine figure known as the Beloved Disciple was privy to Christ's secrets, so too was she as Christ's spouse, a role which allowed her an exclusive claim on his heart.[31] This assurance afforded what might be called an adult access to Jesus, the completion of a familiarity, the soul secured by practicing the childlike virtues of simplicity and trust.[32] On professing vows, Céline would become a spouse. She could not remain child-little but would have to learn to become so, *devenir petite*, and Thérèse had the expedient which would best suit Céline's lively temperament: fire.

"Rappelle-toi" covertly enlists Céline in Thérèse's own project, the blazing *offrande* she had made only four months before: to imitate Christ by dying for love. She presents the sweating blood of Christ at Gethsemane as a dew of love fecundating virginal (Carmelite) flowers, which will in their turn "enfanter un grand nombre de coeurs" ["beget a great number of hearts"].[33] By this mystical parthenogenesis, the Carmelite enacts an *imitatio Mariae*. She will give her mystical children to Christ by making him loved through her own burning love and martyrdom.

This condescension—to use the word in its old sense—is complex. Thérèse imbricates Christ's thirsting upon the cross and his offer of living water at the Samarian well (John 4:6–10). His real thirst was one of sacrificial love for souls. Thérèse in effect recapitulates for Céline her *offrande* by wanting to share this divine ardor: the more burned by the divine flame, the more she will thirst to render souls to Christ. The promise of living water is subtly transposed into the bride herself as she is Christ's "vivant sanctuaire" ["living sanctuary"] and, recalling the poems for Sr. Saint-Vincent-de-Paul, his ciborium. Here, the poem gives resonance to one of the most inspired, most audacious, and most beautiful passages in Manuscript A (48v), where she writes of the Incarnation as Christ's finding "un autre Ciel qui lui est infiniment plus cher que le premier, le Ciel de notre âme, faite à son image, le temple vivant de l'adorable Trinité" ["another Heaven infinitely more dear to him than the first, the Heaven of our soul, made in his image, the living temple of the adored Trinity"].

Oddly, after such flights, Thérèse closes her poem with caveats. It is as though a symphony, reaching majestic resolutions of a theme, were suddenly to trail off *pianissimo* into a minor key. Desolation, oblivion, the nothingness of sleep succeed transfiguration. If Christ is absent, all the flowers shall wither—a turn upon Madre Teresa's gardening metaphor in the *Vida*. The desire to console Christ for the forgetfulness of sinners reminds us that she and Céline have been implicated in that forgetfulness (strophe 12). And when, finally, she asks to share Christ's sleep through life's storm, thus confounding her own longing for fiery consummation, it is to achieve simply "une paix profonde" ["a deep peace"]. That may have been the message Céline had needed most, all along.

Although Thérèse is discernibly at work in all of the poems she wrote for the sisters, the nine she wrote spontaneously for herself must claim the due of their particular vim. All but three of them she wrote during the last nine months of her life, giving these verses an urgency of culmination not found concurrently elsewhere—in her letters, for example—but they serve chiefly as gauges of her spirituality within a closing darkness. The brightest of all these lights shines at the end.

Her best known poem, "Vivre d'Amour" ["Living by Love"], came during the Lenten season of 1895. Céline rated it "king" of all the poems, but that estimate may be challenged. As Manuscript A (3r) indicates, Thérèse early in 1895 was writing not merely her reflections on the graces God accorded her but on trials which she had survived, implying that the storm was over: "je puis jeter un regard sur le passé, mon âme s'est mûrie dans le creuset des épreuves extérieures et intérieures" ["I can cast a glance upon the past, my soul has been ripened in the crucible of outer and inner testing"]. While that reckoning cannot be called complacent, it was mistaken, nonetheless. She was to be ripened far deeper than she could ever have imagined.

As the Spiritus Sanctus moves around, Thérèse recalled the *circulaire* of a prioress in Beaune, Sr. Anne-Victoire, who died in March 1890. Her *devise*, or motto, had been "Vivre d'Amour, Vivre de Croix, Mourir d'Amour, Mourir sur la Croix" ["Living by Love, Living by the Cross, Dying by Love, Dying on the Cross"]. Perhaps those bannerlike words had been iterated within the Lisieux Carmel over the five years' interval. In the event, they made their impress upon Thérèse, and she composed a catechism of what living by Christian love signifies.[34] To climb Calvary rather than to pitch a tent on Mount Tabor, to give without measure and without seeking reward, to banish fear and morbid dwelling on past failings, to sew peace and joy in all hearts (a Franciscan accent), to seek forgiveness for sinners—these precisions of devotion and sacrifice preponderate, leaving only two strophes for death by love, a cry for "un bien doux martyre" ["a very sweet martyrdom"] in Love's consuming flame.

While her *audace* emerges in the trope of divine fire annihilating in an instant "mes péchés" (in a penitential time, she could not avoid the gravity of "sin," an otherwise rare word in her lexicon), she attains the nobility of a final detachment from self—"Ah! sans compter je donne étant bien sûre/Que lorsqu'on aime, on ne calcule pas!" ["Oh, I'm giving without reckon, being certain/That when you love, you do not tabulate!"]—from the *mercantilisme* of heavenly remuneration: "Mon Dieu sera ma Grande Récompense/Je ne veux point posséder d'autres biens" ["My God will be my Big Payoff/I want to possess no other goods"]. In her very disclaimer of a ledgers-and-accounts settlement, she employs language redolent of its scheming, but she has made it unequivocally clear that she is free at last from the baleful suasions of Arminjon. In theresian spirituality, anticipations of compensation in the next world mean as much as consolations prefiguring them in this one, which is to say they mean nothing at all. A soul seeking to be wholly fired by love for God does not ask, What's in it for me?[35]

The stanzas on love-death carry, then, as high a valence as the many on living love which precede them, and not least in Thérèse's having tucked into the first of them a rare notion of dreaming that she would die of love. She asked Jesus to realize that dream, and he did.

Far inferior in substance though scarcely less inspired was a poem Thérèse wrote within two weeks of meeting her second spiritual brother, Roulland, who stopped at Lisieux on July 3, 1896, en route to China. Before sailing on August 2, he received a dozen of her poems transcribed, the last of which attests a rekindling of her missionary fantasies, now realized vicariously. "À Notre-Dame des Victoires" ["To Our Lady of Victories"] addresses the Virgin as queen of apostles and martyrs, her station as overseeing the evangelization of infidels and the conversion of sinners. Its triumphalist tone celebrates Roulland's glory—she capitalizes him into *Lui*—a reflection of which shines upon her as his sister. So powerfully did she feel that, as Vénard had been in Vietnam, Roulland might well be martyred in China as to make that possibility desired and concluded. In its eerie way, the poem serves as prolegomenon to Manuscript B and the abandonment of the futile wish she had nourished to pursue such a high drama for herself.

Of far greater import is "À Mes Petits Frères du Ciel" ["To My Little Brothers in Heaven"], an apostrophe to her dead siblings. None of them had she known but all of them she had heard about from Louis and her older sisters throughout her childhood. Before the redaction of Manuscript A, she read Zélie's poignant letters about caring for them desperately and losing them. They had long been angels in her mind. Zélie and Louis had joined them, and they were all awaiting her. When the first hemoptysis foretold her death, her rejoicing came in the prospect of her union with this greater than half of the Martin family. It is revealing that the poem is not addressed to her parents as well, a fact which underscores the essential quality of the infants, their immortal innocence, that they had been truly weak, little, helpless, and did not live to pass into the darkness Thérèse had reached. Theirs was a genuine, unblemished *enfance*. Like them, with nothing of her own to claim, she could await everything, *tout*, from God. Her propensity for referring to herself as "bébé" to Pauline was not so much baby talk to indulge her older mother/sister as it was a kind of ontological imperative, as though she were reminding herself: I have been and must remain a very small child.[36] This poem, dated December 28, 1896, has a dramatic backdrop. When Thérèse completed it, the other sisters at the *récréation* wanted to sing it that evening. Gonzague agreed but then rounded on Pauline (not on Thérèse), saying she was unhappy about verses set for the community to sing. It could only sustain one's pride. Years later, Pauline recalled being downcast but Thérèse was not, "sa mort étant trop prochaine pour se laisser troubler de quoi que ce soit" ["her death being too near to let her be bothered by anything whatever"] (NPPA, notes on "Humilité").

The poem was completed three days after Thérèse's last Christmas.[37] The breviary's reading for that day was about the massacre of the innocents, the first victims for Christ, flowers of martyrdom harvested by persecution, as the text put it. And so she wrote of her departed sisters and brothers, too, as harvested ("moissonnés"), not by tormentors but by God at their life's dawn, yet it is the massacre of Herod's infant boys which was doubtless in her mind in entitling the poem "To My Little Brothers." It did not matter that two of the four little Martins were girls. Hélène and Mélanie-Thérèse were also answering the Carmelite call to be masculine, a promotion of sorts, but were they not all cherubs now, anyway?

By using the breviary's text as an oblique rationale for this poem, Thérèse was overcoming the traditional antifamilial postures of many saints' lives, accounts which had bemused, if not dismayed her. The hagiographies had those holy men and women fleeing from their kin as they were fleeing the world; in some instances, the family was itself the world they were rejecting for a higher calling.[38] Thérèse, in entering the stringent life of Carmel, had given up a comfortable bourgeois security and the warm emotional suste-nance of her family, but as that family was severally refigured within con-ventual life, she cannot be said to have fled it entirely. That she had gone out of her way to keep a distance from Pauline in her first Carmelite years—so effectively that Gonzague once reproached her for lack of charity—only un-derscores the strength of an attachment that was never broken and would be resumed ever stronger in the last months. She had, however, longed to realize the tremendous spiritual challenge of a supreme hiddenness and obscurity in an Indochinese Carmel—a surrogate for missionary life, whether in Saigon or Hanoi—but by December 1896, she knew that that aspiration was bootless. It is doubtful she could have long survived, if at all, the physical stresses of a voyage. That Christmas, she knew she would remain with her natural sisters to the end. To a degree, "À Mes Petits Frères du Ciel" reflects this familial enclosure and juxtaposes it to the heavenly realm.

The unearthliness of the departed Martin children receives an iterative and ironic emphasis: they have attained glory without effort; their budlike souls have opened to the sun of divine love; they form the cortege of the lamb: "Les trésors des Elus, leurs palmes, leurs couronnes/Tout est à vous/Dans la Sainte Patrie, Enfants, vos riches trônes/Sont leurs genoux" ["The treasures of the Elect, their palms and crowns are all yours, Children, in the Celestial Country, your precious thrones on their knees"]. Besides, they are privy to supernatural wisdom, with God instructing them in how he makes the winds to blow and flowers to grow, things which "Ici-bas nul génie ne sait" ["no genius here on earth knows"]. Such are the apocalyptic strains of the poem, drawn substantially from *Revelation* 14, a text which reminded Thérèse that heaven would be peopled only by the faultlessly virginal.

No matter that she depicts her brothers and sisters as scamps (*lutins*) as she and Céline had once been, playing about and charming God himself with their infantile audacity, even daring to caress the face of Christ. This poem leaves unmistakable marks of bitterness because Thérèse feels keenly her distance from these truly blessed infants, all so effortlessly secured forever. They had never learned to know "nos amères tristesses" ["our harsh sorrows"]. The bite comes, however, from the spiritual imperatives of living itself, here on terra firma.

Thérèse makes this point in an exceptional Christmas Eve letter to Céline, just four days before she completed "À Mes Petits Frères du Ciel." Céline had been downcast by what she admitted to be outbursts (*sorties*) against her sisters, uncontrolled moments of an impetuous pride.[39] Rather than instruct her through the admonitions of a *compagne*, Thérèse writes as though she were an amanuensis of the Virgin. Knowing Céline's distress, Mary declines to console her because she herself knows the cost of suffering: "si tu savais combien mon âme a été plongée dans l'amertume lorsque je voyais mon tendre époux St. Joseph revenir tristement vers moi sans avoir trouvé d'hôtellerie" ["if you knew how my soul was steeped in bitterness when I saw my husband, St. Joseph, returning sadly to me without having found an inn"] (LT 211). While the griefs of Mary and of Joseph, her *amertume* and his *tristesse*, offset the bliss of the little Martins, what matters in the message to Céline is that adversity should be desired. Why? Because Jesus himself wishes it. "Il aime mieux te voir heurter dans la nuit les pierres du chemin que marcher en plein jour sur une route émaillée de fleurs qui pourraient retarder ta marche" ["He prefers to see you stumbling in the night over the stones of the way rather than to walk in the plain light of day on a path carpeted with flowers that could slow down your steps"].

Not for the only time, Thérèse prefers and even prescribes bitterness in place of sweetness, the necessity for struggle against complacency, the darkness which helps one toward poverty of spirit as a counter to the garish light in which one can pretend to be a somebody. Of the three signposts of the Carmelites' itinerary (where they experienced Jesus), Bethlehem, Tabor, and Gethsemane, two are tableaux of darkness, vulnerability, and helplessness. Céline's contest with her pride was just what she should have been undertaking.

And yet Thérèse knew that even with more than two years of Carmel now behind her, Céline, still a novice, needed the uplift of a happy ending.[40] Mary seeks to assure her: "Un jour tu viendras avec ta Thérèse dans le beau Ciel, tu prendras place sur les genoux de mon Jésus bien-aimé et moi je te prendrai aussi dans mes bras et je te comblerai de caresses" ["One day you'll come with your Thérèse into the beauty of Heaven and take your place on the knees of my beloved Jesus and I'll take you as well into my arms and cover you with caresses"] (LT 211). For all the poverty of spirit they have sought in this earthly life, they shall be rewarded even as their departed sisters and brothers had been—all, finally, in the lap of Jesus. Fortified as she herself was in her own bitterness, and almost ruthlessly responsive to it as the avenue to truth, Thérèse was shrewd enough to mitigate it, as here in the Savior's lap, with the consolation of a soppy infantilism.

In the poem to her siblings, however, Thérèse can say only how she *wants* to attain on earth their sacred incorruptibility: "Ah! daignez m'obtenir les vertus de l'enfance./Votre candeur,/Votre abandon parfait, votre aimable innocence/ Charment mon coeur" ["Oh, grant me to obtain the virtues of childhood. Your ingenuousness, your perfect trust, your lovely innocence becharm my heart"]. The supplicatory tone of the poem provides a gentle but marked difference to the forthright declarative tone of the Virgin's letter to Céline.

Five months later, Thérèse remarked to Pauline that the holy innocents were not little children in heaven: "ils auront seulement les charmes in-définissable de l'enfance. On se les représente 'enfants,' parce que nous avons besoin d'images pour comprendre les choses spirituelles" ["they'll merely have the indefinable charms of childhood. They're depicted as children be-cause we need images to understand spiritual matters"].[41] That meant as well, presumably, that the lap is also and only an image. The severely unappealing sub-Raphaelesque paintings of little angels which Céline and Thérèse herself produced, efforts very much of the period, remain solely there. But Thérèse could not help spinning out images. When, in May 1897, Pauline asked her whether she hoped to join the holy innocents, Thérèse answered yes! "S'ils veulent, je serai leur petit page, je tiendrai leurs petites queues" ["If they want, I'll be their little page and carry their little tails"]. With only a few months to live and on so solemn a business as final things, she did not lose her sense of humor. Her equanimous wit punctuates her last summer's conversations at redemptive intervals.[42]

In the previous chapter, I noted that Thérèse's verse celebration of the mar-tyred (and now Saint) Théophane Vénard has its own special exuberance, as though they were twins of an exclamatory joy and had somehow shared their *épreuves*. This martyr's death at thirty-one sealed for her a discriminating affinity, signaled by her addressing him in the poem by his baptismal name, a freedom she could never have exercised with Roulland and Bellière. Vénard had savored "le bonheur de souffrir," a happiness not through suffering but in its very midst, when he was preparing himself for decapitation. Like the four little "brothers," he was a virginal flower God had gathered; like them, he was a *lys*, the lily which Thérèse consistently identified with souls she regarded as superior in virtue to her own.

Just as she wanted to join the phalanx of celestial innocents, so she wanted to bring up the rear of Vénard's "cortège éternal," but in both his and the "little brothers" poems, her very wanting betrays an undertow of frustration and anxiety. The difference is that the poem for Vénard holds within it a telltale trace of the fantastic brio of ambition which she had presumably laid to rest in Manuscript B, at the point where she became a rather sedentary Love in and for the Church. Vénard's missionary devotion and his gruesome, glorious end now rekindled the Thérèse who wanted to be a warrior, a Jeanne. That vigorous activism comports oddly, if at all, with the recumbence of the lilies gathered by God, both the children and Théophane. By not ever identifying herself as a lily, Thérèse implicitly left to herself another role, one as yet undefined and perhaps unclear in her own mind, but we catch a glimpse of it in the poem's fifth stanza. There, she asks Vénard to furnish her with his weapons on behalf of sinners: "Je veux pour eux ne cessant pas la guerre / Prendre d'assaut le Royaume de Dieu. Car le Seigneur apporta sur la terre / Non pas la paix, mais le Glaive et le Feu!" ["For them I wish incessant war, to take by storm the kingdom of God. Indeed, the Lord brought upon the earth not peace but fire and sword"]. The storming of heaven derives from one of the most ambiguous passages of the Gospels, *Matthew* 11:12, where Christ speaks of the violent seizing the heavenly kingdom. Some interpreters weigh substantially upon the brutality of the verb (ἁρπάοσυζιν in the Greek, *rapiunt* in the Vulgate) with its connotation of laying waste. They assume that it refers to those who murderously opposed Jesus even as they opposed John the Baptist, to whom Jesus refers in the preceding verse. As John had just suffered martyrdom, it would seem fitting that Thérèse in extolling Vénard would have understood 11:12 in that way, but clearly she did not. For her, the taking of heaven by force has a peculiarly charming allure, which she justifies brilliantly by adding that Jesus himself was violent, casting apocalyptic fire upon the earth (*Luke* 12:49) and bringing not peace but a havoc-raising sword into families (*Matthew* 10:34). Besides, *she*, not the sinners, is carrying out the assault upon heaven. Doing so, she in effect is imitating Christ in his extraordinary ferocity.

Whatever the merits of this poem—outwardly, they may be few—it presents in a few lines evidence of how sage and innovative Thérèse is as an exegete of the Gospels. Unadorned by formal learning and training, she shapes her reading of Scripture with an intuitive verve. Only she, I believe, goes so far as to suggest that Christ himself is in the company of the violent,[43] is indeed (with John?) their exemplar. This is a stunningly original gloss.

No less important, if it does not make an overt, proleptic move toward Manuscript C and the table of sinners, the development of this passage seems to point in that direction. In asking for Vénard's armory, Thérèse writes, "je voudrais ici-bas / Lutter, souffrir à l'ombre de tes palmes" ["I would like to struggle, to suffer in the shadow of your martyr crown"],[44] which, as a kind of somber tableau, prepares us for the suddenness of the assault upon the kingdom. It is also revealing that Thérèse came to that Matthean phrase on violence after first writing about the sinners, "Pour les sauver, ne cessant pas la guerre Je veux ravir le royaume de Dieu" ["to save them by warring without cease I want to ravish the kingdom of God"].[45] In dropping those words, she was leaving behind two crucial notions, that of saving sinners and thereby of delighting heaven. In remembering who she was rather than who she wanted to be, her tactics became bold, if not desperate. Her reassumption of the warrior posture is no longer meant to vanquish paganism on a distant shore but to champion its adherents: she is armed to storm heaven, not the seats and altars of idols.[46] (See figure 6.4.)

Then, she reverts to the supine flower image, telling Vénard that she too wants to be plucked by God and fly with other souls in the martyr's wake. Just as in the Virgin's letter to Céline, Thérèse no sooner sets a bold course in images than she palliates it with a bland and sunny alternative, one that reeks of conventional uplift. Initially it seems as though she were recoiling from the implications of her own daring, but it might be accurate to assume that she is having it both ways: she is both the warrior woman and the innocent flower, both the soul eager to achieve great things by which to please God (even if heaven be shaken by her coming!) and the innocuous pageboy bringing up the celestial rear.

Yet it is that fifth stanza which lingers beyond the conclusive glory. Jeanne d'Arc proved too fetching to be put aside with any assurance that she would stay there. Besides, she complemented the sweet, effete Vénard perfectly. He had no need to storm heaven; his martyrdom would trumpet him straight up into it. But Thérèse needed siege engines to carry out the most amazing of stratagems, laying hands upon heaven so as to surrender herself and become the prisoner of Jesus. Thus, and not for the first time, she reconciles the desiderata of an imperative will and the ontology of a nobody. A mighty child, Merton called her.

Late in the spring of 1897, Thérèse wrote two more apostrophic poems. The shorter of these, in five alexandrine quatrains, she addressed to Jeanne d'Arc. Now, as she felt her own mortal life drawing to its end, she was able to see the passion of Jeanne in the only way that ever imposed itself upon her, by her own experience: not of the stake but of prison's isolation and darkness. She at last

FIGURE 6.4. The martyr and now saint Théophane Vénard, whose picture Thérèse kept pinned to the curtain of her infirmary bed. Copyright
Archives du Carmel de Lisieux and by courtesy of the Missions étrangères
de Paris.

could see that Jeanne's true greatness lay in having to drink from the bitter
cup, in being bereft of all human solicitude, betrayed. The anaphoric expression of that desolation lies at the poem's center: "Pas un de tes amis ne prit part
à tes peines/Pas un ne s'avança pour essuyer tes pleurs" ["Not one of your
friends shared in your pain/Not one came forth to wipe your tears"]. The motif
of the friends' desertion (but before this, the play's Jeanne had had only saints
to help her)[47] puts her securely in the company of Christ betrayed in Gethsemane by his feckless disciples running off, but the oxymoronic discovery that
Jeanne's glory was "au fond d'un noir cachot" ["at the bottom of a black cell"]
suggests that Thérèse is in Jeanne's company, at last.[48] These lines on a very
gloomy splendor were just weeks, perhaps only days from Manuscript C's
depiction of Thérèse's own dark cell, what she called the "tunnel." She concludes this poem with the nervy claim that Christ came to humanity seeking
betrayal (a novel reading of *Philippians* 2:8), but what counts is the spiritual
bonding which she here and finally achieves with her beloved heroine.

The most substantial of all Thérèse's poems, in depth if not in length, was
the last she wrote, a summa of her spiritual life. Her writings are so much of a

piece that it might seem arbitrary to isolate one small portion of them but if someone were to anthologize Thérèse enthusiastically, this poem could well stand alone as the consummate expression in verse of who she became in the swift ripening of her last months. I believe that "Pourquoi je t'aime, ô Marie!" ["Why I love you, Mary"] bears juxtaposition with Manuscript C as a fair and final measure of its author.

A sufficient profile of the Virgin Mary in Thérèse's life would require a lengthy exposition, much of which could be prompted by Manuscript A. Only a few hallmarks can be indicated here. At the Benedictine abbey school, Thérèse absorbed the Marian cult in daily meditated recitation of the rosary, and on Sunday she observed "le Petit Office de la Sainte Vierge" ["The Little Office of the Holy Virgin"]. She participated in all the Marian feast days, including processions, singing, and the ornamentation of altars.[49] Mary delivered her from the torments of a mysterious illness in her tenth year, during the spring of 1883. In the next year, she became a member of the Confrérie du Rosaire de la Très Sainte Vierge, which recited the rosary once a week and attended mass for deceased members.[50] When she was thirteen, Thérèse became an aspirant to the Enfants de Marie at the school, and in the following year she was received, though by then she had left the abbey and was under private tutelage.[51] Most important of all was Thérèse's entry into a spiritual community and life over which Mary was tutelary, l'Ordre de Notre-Dame du Mont-Carmel.

Facing a statue of Mary, she knelt and prayed before undertaking to compose her first manuscript. Within that text's abundance of references to Mary, Thérèse writes (73r) that Carmelites feel the sufferings of Christ in cherishing him as Mary did. His sufferings pierced her heart. But from the first, even before Christ's coming, Mary exemplified the Carmelite ethos of a humility that, being so, could only be hidden.[52] In her poem of thanksgiving to Mary, however, Thérèse gives that humility an astonishing turn, saying that Mary preferred her chastity to the motherhood of God incarnate.[53] It was that very lowliness which ravished (one of Thérèse's favorite verbs) God, so that she drew into her heart the divine Trinity of love.

Lest this portrait seem too ethereal, it is driven by Thérèse's desire to strip down the image of Mary to the gospel facts, without pious embellishments and myth making. She is not denying the glory of Mary, but she is rejecting much that has been made of her. By mid-spring, Thérèse had dropped all of her reading save the New Testament, though she would resume favorite passages of San Juan de la Cruz while she was in the infirmary. Like the early hermits of Mount Carmel, she saw the Mary of the gospel narratives very much as though Mary were the first Carmelite, leading a chosen life of suffering and obscurity. At the same historical time, in her littleness, Mary contained the all of Jesus, an oceanic love, and as Mary is her spiritual mother, Thérèse makes the same claim of the divine treasure within her own small frame, the host of the Last Supper. To the imitation of Christ succeeds an *imitatio Mariae*, the purport of which lies in Mary's suffering as a mortal, proximate to those Thérèse denominates as Christ's brother sinners of incalculable number: "de ses frères pécheurs bien grand sera le nombre."

Here is the poem's first nexus with Manuscript C and the table of bitterness. Thérèse had already claimed her own kinship with those brother sinners in an earlier poem,[54] but now she implicates Mary herself in that bitterness, the experience of a helpless distance from Jesus. The gospel incident to which she alludes is his disappearance, at age twelve, from his parents' returning to Nazareth when he stayed behind in Jerusalem and spoke with the elders in the Temple (*Luke* 2:41–52). Having underscored how dutifully submissive a son he had been, Thérèse now understands the significance of his absence for both Mary and herself: "Mère, ton doux Enfant veut que tu sois l'exemple/De l'âme qui Le cherche en la nuit de la foi" ["Mary, your gentle Child wants you to be the exemplary soul that seeks him in the night of faith"]. This is a truly original reading: even as Jesus permitted the darkness to descend upon Thérèse, he had wanted his mother to be desperate, "plongée dans la nuit, dans l'angoisse du coeur" ["plunged into the night, into the heart's anguish"], that there she would discover that "souffrir en aimant, c'est le plus pur bonheur" ["to suffer in loving is the purest happiness"]. That perception, one which is almost too difficult for most of us to imagine, let alone affirm,[55] is hardly warranted by the narrative itself, when Mary scolds young Jesus for causing her and Joseph intense mental grief. The difference between a distraught mother and a convented sister, a young woman of twenty-four who was both physically and spiritually tormented, might best be explained by noting that Thérèse's distance from Jesus has its analogue in the Solomonic story of the lover's mysterious departure (*Song of Songs* 3:1, 6:1), an absence now understood to have no apparent closure. At the table of bitterness and stationed at the furthest remove from Jesus, as though on a precipice's edge, she is pledged to wait indefinitely.

Not searching for Jesus marks the culmination of Thérèse's *abandon*, the only possible answer to the *épreuve de l'amour*. In this *attente de Dieu*, a phrase which belongs to her rather than to Simone Weil, with whom it is associated,[56] Thérèse's purest happiness is in *knowing* that Jesus first exemplified for us the suffering of love and that he willed it for her, as for Mary. The true predicate of love is not some sort of fulfillment but an intense longing, so acute as to bring pain: "une amère tristesse/Comme un vaste océan vient inonder ton coeur" ["a bitter sorrow like a vast ocean inundates your heart"]. Thérèse's notion of purest happiness remains substantially epistemological and can best be approached that way: love arrives not merely at a deeply felt truth but a divine one. What greater joy could a Christian experience than the knowledge that the cross borne is one willed by divine love?

Mary is also exemplary of the humility with which suffering must be sustained. She walked the common road without desire for miracles, raptures, ecstasies—a democrat like Thérèse, in short. Anyone can follow her because she was down to earth, which is the old, first sense of the word *humilis*. Everything in Thérèse's hermeneutics of Mary hangs upon that unassuming lowliness, and with it she takes on some passages in the Gospels which present, if not a troubled, then a wrinkled view of Jesus' family life. Regarding Jesus' rebuke of his importunate mother (*Matthew* 12:46–50), when he identifies his anonymous listeners as his true family in carrying out his will, Thérèse claims that Mary accepted her son's disowning her and rejoiced in his love for others. She loves in turn as Jesus loves, consenting to be at a distance from him for their anonymous, faceless sake.

In that distancing, she becomes a "refuge des pécheurs," a phrase weighty with implications for Manuscript C. Would Mary, "restant exilée" ["remaining in exile"], be found at the table of bitterness, for example? It is clear that she has at least become Thérèse's refuge in the darkness: after Jesus leaves us, he gives us to Mary: "*Aimer c'est tout donner et se donner soi-même,* Tu voulus le prouver en restant notre appui" ["*To love means to give all, including oneself,* You wished to prove that in remaining our support"].[57] Manuscript C, then, depicts both Thérèse's *imitatio Christi* and her *imitatio Mariae*: she sits down to banquet with sinners in an all-giving love. This suffering of love provides the common denominator of mother and son, signifying that the *imitationes* are synonymous in and through Thérèse's perspective. "Pourquoi je t'aime, ô Marie!" serves as the indispensable ancilla—Mary's own title in the Magnificat—to Manuscript C. While all of Thérèse's writings can be found complementary to one another, the link between her final verse and her final prose provides occasion to consider the keen maturation and costly depths this very young and excruciated woman attained.

If that seems too bleak a note on which to end, the poem offers a reprise of Manuscript B and its maternal lap, as Thérèse, sustained by her remembrance of Mary at the sickbed, calls upon her to smile upon her once again. The closing, twenty-fifth stanza makes a startlingly confident stride toward the heaven from which she had felt herself sealed off: "Avec toi j'ai souffert et je veux maintenant/Chanter sur tes genoux, Marie, pourquoi je t'aime/Et redire à jamais que je suis ton enfant!" ["I have suffered with you and now I want to sing upon your knees, Mary, why I love you and say forever anew that I am your child"]. The poignant undercurrent in these lines is the more marked for Thérèse's never having written "dark sonnets" à la Gerard Manley Hopkins. There never comes from her pen the whining, despondent self-pity which her terrible isolation would have amply justified. "Rester petite," the two words which remain indelibly the emblem of her life, precluded such all-too-human theatrics.

A jarring note from a minor key does sound, however. It is so seemingly uncharacteristic of Thérèse that we might almost presume Pauline had inserted it in the midst of their discussions of poems to be published posthumously. Toward the close (stanza 23), Thérèse likens Mary to a priest at the altar offering up Christ to appease divine justice. How could that image possibly find conformity with Thérèse's leitmotif of love, which determines the course of the entire poem in the person of Mary?

Fortunately, Thérèse herself explains in a letter to Roulland dated May 9, 1897. He had been concerned that, were brigands in China to take his life, he in his unworthiness would be unfit for heaven and would have to depend upon Thérèse's prayers to wrest him from purgatory. He had written nothing expressly about divine justice, but Thérèse took the cue. Drawing upon Psalm 102 (103), she told him she was joyous and confident in God's justice because it is grounded in compassion for human weakness. "Etre juste, ce n'est pas seulement exercer la sévérité pour punir les coupables, c'est encore re-connaître les intentions droites et récompenser la vertu" ["To be just means not only practicing severity in punishing the guilty, but also to recognize good intentions and reward virtue"] (LT 226). The proper intentionality, she adds, is to acknowledge one's nothingness and give oneself over to God as would an infant. That is her version of perfection, one she knew to be far easier to attain than the kind she had read in saints' lives which, as she mock scandalously noted to Roulland, cracked her head and dried her heart.

Thérèse discreetly leaves aside the matter of severe punishments meted out to the guilty and the thornier question of doing evil with good intent. How to measure such "virtue" gone awry? But she also omits a cardinal phrase in the psalm, when God is likened to a father who has compassion for his children. This is a loving, Louis-like God until we reach the close: "ainsi le Seigneur a compassion de nous" ["so the Lord has compassion upon us"] and the passage restricts the number of children to "the ones fearing him."[58] As fear had nothing to do with Thérèse's deeply felt trust, "ma joie et ma con-fiance," it did not impress itself into her consciousness. She had never ex-perienced real fear of any man active within her life, and so she was experientially unequipped to deal with the terrorism which countless others of the faithful felt toward God. She gives it the nod in her last poem by imag-ining the priest's role of placation taken over by Mary, but that image admits the unsettling impression that Jesus has entrusted Mary to humanity because she is the necessary maternal mitigation of a possibly wrathful God the Fa-ther. Mary in place of the priests adroitly omits all but sacramental need of them, and the old fantasies left behind in Manuscript B are again confounded by a simple humble woman as intercessor. Only a darker view of God, however, warrants such intercession to begin with. Does a loving, compas-sionate father need a motherly adjutant to remind him that he has weak, little children?

The answer comes in Manuscript C's petition to God, where Thérèse has taken the place of solicitude which she had affirmed in Mary at the close of "Pourquoi je t'aime, ô Marie!" The passage, luminous with charity and insight, reads as her *imitatio Mariae* with the striking difference that Thérèse identifies herself with those for whom she is entreating: "Ayez pitié de nous Seigneur, car nous sommes de pauvres pécheurs! ... Oh! Seigneur, renvoyez-nous justifiés... Que tous ceux qui ne sont point éclairés du lumineux flambeau de la Foi le voient luire enfin!" ["Have mercy on us, Lord, for we are poor sinners! Oh! Lord, send us back justified.[59] ... May all those who have not been enlightened by the brilliant torch of Faith see it shine at the last!"] (C 6r).

Thérèse's little way of trust ends and begins in this cry, a plea searing in its economy of utterance and its universal compass, *de profundis clamavimus*. It is as though all of her life had been preparing her for the moment when she wrote those lines of supplication, which I have unfairly wrenched from their greater and necessary whole. But Thérèse herself did not see it in such grandiose narrative terms. She tells Gonzague, "ma petite histoire qui ressemblait à un conte de fée s'est tout à coup changée en prière" ["my little story which was like a fairytale suddenly changed into prayer"] (C 6r). And what else would she have wished?

7

Tubercular

[F]or affliction is a treasure, and scarce any man hath enough of it.
No man hath affliction enough that is not matured, and ripened
by it, and made fit for God by that affliction.

— John Donne, *Devotions upon Emergent Occasions,*
Meditation XVII

Borges has written of the thousand possible biographies of any one
person. One biography of Thérèse could dwell upon her patholo-
gies, the sicknesses which beset and determined her life in portentous
ways: enteritis, Sydenham's chorea, tuberculosis.

This chapter addresses these questions: what was the nature and
what the course of the diseases which afflicted her? What did French
medical practitioners in her time know about these diseases? How
did Thérèse respond to these diseases and make them integral to her
spirituality?

Her cult of suffering for love was substantially informed by the
enforced apartness which sickness brings, the frustration and helplessness in feeling set aside and left behind by the fit and healthy.
That sharp otherness holds dramatically true of her illnesses: the
months she spent at the age of ten, bedridden with a mysterious
physical and temperamental debility from which she believed only
the Virgin Mary delivered her; and tuberculosis, which coincided
with the spiritual darkness she experienced throughout the last
eighteen months of her life, when she struggled to hold onto Christ.

How far along the road to sainthood would she have come
had her life not been so deeply burdened by illness? She can be called

one of death's discoveries, her autobiographical manuscripts having been transposed into her necrology: she suffered long enough from tuberculosis to complete her own book-length obituary. One of her most engaging works she herself did not write, the obiter dicta known as *Derniers entretiens* and *Novissima verba*,[1] remarks she made—sometimes prompted by others' questions—which were sedulously noted by her sisters, chiefly Pauline, in the final weeks when she was too exhausted to hold a pen. That document shall be cited repeatedly within this chapter. It grew while death watched beside her amanuensis.

Immobilized and helpless, the afflicted can gain a heightened focus upon life's limits; it is a schooling of insight into our vanities, our mortality, our inconsequence. It may entail a ripening of consciousness such as John Donne records in his *Devotions upon Emergent Occasions*, the foremost meditation upon sickness and death in the English language. Donne anticipates Thérèse's perceptions, grounded as they both were in the certainty that they were facing death. (Donne recovered, however.) Suffering has supreme value because it does not lie and bids the sufferer not to either.

For Thérèse, suffering meant much more. In her notes on a retreat Pichon gave in the spring of 1889, she records that sainthood must be conquered at sword's point: "il faut *souffrir . . . il faut agoniser. . . .* Et moi je croyais qu'il ne fallait pas souffrir *petitement* et *misérablement*" ["it is necessary to *suffer, to agonize. . . .* As for me I've believed that one must not suffer *pettily* and *wretchedly*"].[2] Only a grand, brave, and generous scale of suffering would do. That notion jibed with her insistence that one cannot be a saint by half. For her, a central component of sainthood was extremity. Such absolutism, to recall her propensity for the allness of *tout*, signaled both a goal and a vital creative flexibility in reaching it. Setting the bar high gives time for initiative and resourcefulness. What Thérèse could not know, though she claimed its intimation, was that she would not have much time.

Wet-Nursing and Breast Cancer

Of the five Martin children who survived infancy, only Thérèse died young. The others lived well into old age; Pauline and Céline both died two months short of their ninetieth birthdays. Marie died in her eightieth year and Léonie at seventy-eight. We recall that between Léonie and Céline, three children were lost: a girl, Hélène, at five, suddenly and mysteriously, perhaps from leukemia; and two boys within their first year. An eighth child, Mélanie-Thérèse, died within two months. The boys died of erysipelas and bronchitis, both while in the care of a wet nurse with whom they were living, a few miles from Alençon. Mélanie-Thérèse died on the eve of the Franco-Prussian War. Unable to nurse her, Zélie had failed to find adequate care.

The Martin family was altogether typical of the French petite bourgeoisie in sending its infants out to wet nurses. This practice had the advantage of allowing women to go on working, if need be, or to beget more children, as a good Catholic family was expected to do. As conscientious Catholics, Louis and Zélie Martin would never have countenanced birth control measures, various kinds being available in the 1860s—Dr. Condom's device was known as *lettre anglaise*—nor apparently did they reflect much upon Zélie's stamina: nine children were born to her within fourteen years. They were likely unaware of a grim statistic, that the mortality rate for wet-nursed children, known as *nourrissons*, was over 50 percent; it was under 20 percent for children nursed by their mothers. Wet nurses were sometimes sustaining several children, including their own; some were negligent. The hazards of infection were not attended. But the Martins did not need statistics to be aware of the risks they were running. Zélie believed that she had lost Mélanie because of the wet nurse's incompetence and pledged she would never again consign a child to one.

She had nursed her first three infants only briefly. The hagiographical assumption has always been that her health gave out. That view appears to be inaccurate, if not unfounded. The likely reasons that she stopped nursing are manifold and have little to do with her health: she would not have become incapable of nursing further—there is no record of her suffering from mastitis—and she continued in full charge of the household and her lace-making business. In addition to her domestic and professional life, she was not only a devout attendant of church (the "working-class" mass had the family up every morning at 5:30) but a steady correspondent. One factor sometimes adduced in biographies can now be safely isolated from subsequent developments, that in childhood she had received a severe contusion to one of her breasts. That would not have interfered with her ability to nurse; besides, a mother can nurse with one breast. She had suffered pains in that breast, but they would not have been symptomatic of breast cancer, the tumor itself being painless—the very reason that early detection requires vigilance. Those pains were likely due to cysts which swelled with fluid. Breast cancer proceeds rapidly. Zélie contracted it years after the birth of Thérèse, who was four years and eight months old when her mother died.

A recently discovered photo of Zélie, undated but likely taken around 1875, shows a remarkably alert woman. The portrait of the long-suffering mother requires some focus: who could gainsay the anguish of a mother losing her children? The death of Hélène had been especially painful, as she had survived infancy, and her wasting away had no ostensible cause. As a Catholic, however, Zélie had the consolation of believing that the loss of her four children was divinely willed and that they had all become angels; she would see them again after her own death. Sometimes told it would have been better never to have given them birth, she said she could never appreciate such talk. At a time when child mortality was commonplace, there was a convention of parental grief and attendant solace (as in England: the etherealizing Dickens gives to Little Nell and Paul Dombey), which, since vaccinations and higher standards of hygiene, has long passed.

Zélie, tough in will and constitution, was as ignorant as her time. The story of Thérèse's first months is exemplary of that fact. She allegedly developed intestinal problems only two weeks after birth. It is assumed that she had enteritis from about January 17, when the symptoms were noted. On March 1, the baby was "très mal." Doctors in those days presumed that infantile enteritis was caused by ill-digested foods (Thérèse had not been eating), by fermentations due to bad hygienic conditions (the Martins kept a clean house), by premature weaning, or by badly regulated feeding times. If enteritis did figure, only the last factor seems a possible cause. The physician warned that only breast milk would save the baby. Zélie had tried nursing her but turned to bottle feeding out of the fear, completely unfounded, that her breast milk was insufficient. The bottle disrupted the milk flow and the timings. Zélie's saying it was impossible to make Thérèse return to breast feeding is understandable, but had that been so, a wet nurse would have been pointless. Zélie seems not to have known very much about her own body and about nursing.

In brief, the nursing dyad requires equilibrium between mother and infant. Most of the time, once the letdown of milk has occurred, the infant sucks normally. During the course of a year's nursing, however, there is invariably something like a growth spurt in the infant when more milk is demanded than the mother has been supplying. For a period of as much as seventy-two hours, the infant sucks in frustration because the milk supply has been exhausted. Naturally, the infant becomes exhausted from the vain effort, and the mother is subject to her own anxiety and frustration. At that time, physical and especially psychological support from others, especially the father, can be crucial. The increased milk supply will come, but patience and endurance are vital. Zélie, alone (the elder girls were all away at school), became fretful and desperate. It may even be that "enteritis" was a code word for the disruption of the dyad, the quite natural though uncomfortable period of readjustment.[3]

She resorted to a wet nurse, then. Even medical texts of the time prescribed, as the best hygienic condition, regularly timed feedings by a good wet nurse. Rosalie Taillé lived on a farm to the west of Semallé, in a hamlet nearly five miles outside of Alençon. (The small house, along the road but inaccessible, is still standing.) Zélie walked that distance early one morning to fetch her. Rosalie had wet-nursed the two Martin sons, and Zélie had trusted her. "La petite Rose" returned with her, stayed a few days, and agreed to take Thérèse back to Semallé. That willingness and her mother's saved the sickly infant, assuaging perhaps the guilt Zélie felt over the loss of Mélanie.

Baby Thérèse thrived in the countryside for thirteen months (see figure 7.1). In her first autobiographical text, Thérèse claims that the memories of

FIGURE 7.1. The farmhouse of Moïse and Rosalie Taillé, where Thérèse's life was saved and where she spent thirteen months of her infancy. Copyright Archives du Carmel de Lisieux.

her childhood were so keenly etched that what she was now recounting seemed to have happened only the day before. Ten years later, the Martin family came from Lisieux to Alençon for a visit of several weeks (August 20–September 30, 1883) and again in 1886, but there is no indication that they saw the Taillés during either time.

In her correspondence, Zélie records a visit that Rose made with the baby on a market day. While Rose was selling her goods, the baby was left at the Martin house and was passed among Zélie's lace makers. Thérèse accepted them to the extent that they were dressed like Rose. A bourgeoise who came to visit was rejected by the baby on sartorial grounds. Thérèse howled again when she was finally returned to her family, that understandable protest serving as the very first sign of a runtish willfulness. Her mother's joy and gratitude in this story of feminine bonds ends the first chapter in her life.

The depths of suffering, sacrifice, and endurance here are all feminine. What imposes itself, however obliquely, is the absence of Louis. Given that Mélanie had died within just two months of birth, why was *he* not available this time to make that long walk to Semallé? The answer, broadly sociological, is that nursing and rearing were women's work. Only women held the keys of life and death, as this episode demonstrates. Even had Louis, retired and at leisure, been at home, Zélie would have made that walk because only a mother's importunity would have convinced another woman. A Gospel passage resonates: Mary ran alone to Elizabeth, and it was Mary, not Joseph, who was told that a sword would pierce her heart. In literally vital matters, men tend not to count.

Dancing with the Saints

Illness had prompted separation from her first mother and came with Thérèse's separation from her second. Pauline entered Carmel in October 1882, at the age of twenty-one. When her sister was about to take vows in the spring of 1883, Thérèse, ten, became so strangely ill that she seems to have been registering an extraordinary protest over the loss of Pauline. Her own testimony spiritualizes the disease pointedly as a visit from the infernal: "Il est surprenant de voir combien mon esprit se développa au sein de la souffrance, il se développa à tel point que je ne tardai pas à tomber malade. La maladie dont je fus atteinte venait certainement du démon, furieux de votre entrée au Carmel il voulut se venger sur moi du tort que notre famille devait lui faire dans l'avenir" ["It's amazing to see how much my spirit grew in the bosom of suffering, to such a point that I wasn't slow in falling ill. The sickness I caught surely came from the devil, who was outraged by your entry into Carmel and wanted to take revenge on me for the harm our family was going to do him in the future"] (A 27r). She goes on to claim that "the sweet Queen of Heaven" was watching over her, smiled from on high, and caused the demonic storm to cease at the point when Thérèse was about to be overwhelmed.

This vivid little drama—a miniature apocalypse which suggests that perhaps Thérèse was already, at twenty-two, conceiving of her life as a saint's (devilish onslaughts being highly profiled in the Gospels and in saints' biographies)—was an attempt to explain what was almost certainly Sydenham's chorea, a nervous disorder named after a seventeenth-century physician known as "the English Hippocrates." Historically associated with holy figures, it is still variously designated in medical literature under their names: St. Anthony's, St. Guy's, St. Vitus' dance.

Sydenham's chorea has been identified in sequence with rheumatic fever. It has sometimes occurred subsequent to a streptococcal infection. It is a condition most common in the young, especially girls, between five and fifteen years old. Typical of its syndrome is an acute emotional lability, accompanied by choreic movements of the face, tongue, and extremities. Those motions are called dancelike but are often severe, irregular, and spasmodic. Involuntary and random, they can render the muscles so rigid as to seem paralytic. Because of the link with rheumatic fever, the chorea might be attended by myocardial and valvular damage. Years after her illness, Thérèse was accused of being shiftless in her chores (sweeping, for example) about the convent, but she may have suffered a debilitation of her heart dating from this childhood sickness, so that certain exertions would have fatigued her, even though the early convent photos show her looking robust.[4] (At the Carmel, she stood at 1 meter, 62, or just under 5'4", which was considered tall in that time.)

Recovery from Sydenham's chorea can take from one month to as much as four, but the emotional unsteadiness ("even actual mania" is possible)[5] may go on longer. It is little wonder that Thérèse (as well as her frightened family?) ascribed her sickness to a devilish agent. It is now known that a cerebral lesion is responsible for the chorea, but its location remains indeterminable.

During the Christmas season of 1882, Thérèse had been suffering bouts of headaches and insomnia. The fever, so low that Thérèse was initially able to continue with her schoolwork, began after Louis took Marie and Léonie to Paris, leaving the two younger sisters with the Guérins. There had been reminiscences about the children's mother which could only have upset the youngest child, making a beloved and prematurely lost presence seem the more remote, if not unreal. When her muscular spasms began, her aunt presumed them to be the effect of fever, but her condition was so extreme that Louis on his return believed "sa petite fille allait devenir folle ou bien qu'elle allait mourir" ["his little daughter would go mad or die"] (A 27v). In *Histoire d'une âme*, Pauline, drawing on her sisters' witnessing, writes this for Thérèse: "J'avais peur absolument de tout: mon lit me semblait entouré de précipices affreux: certains clous, fixés au mur de la chambre, prenaient à mes yeux l'image terrifiante de gros doigts noirs carbonisés, et me faisaient jeter des cris d'épouvante" ["I was absolutely frightened of everything: my bed seemed to be surrounded by dire precipices; some nails on the walls of the room assumed in my eyes the terrifying image of huge fingers burned black and caused me to cry out in astonishment"].[6] Pauline's precision indicates, as Thérèse's own does not, why Louis feared she was losing her mind.

At another point, her father having entered her room carrying his manteau, she suddenly exclaimed, "Oh! La grosse bête noire!" ["Oh, the big black beast!"]. Marie, the oldest daily witness, later testified: "Ses cris avaient quelque chose de surnaturel; il faut les avoir entendus, pour s'en faire une idée" ["Her cries had something supernatural about them; you would have had to hear them to get an idea"].[7] At times, Thérèse tried to jump from the balustrade of her bed or pound her head against its *parois*, and her sisters had to hold her down forcibly. Although Thérèse in writing claimed that she had at no time in this period lost her reason, at times she did not recognize members of her immediate family. Weakening of memory figures in the syndrome of chorea.

The attending physician, Alphonse-Henri Notta, concluded that nothing could be done: "La science est impuissante devant ces phénomènes"

["Science is helpless before such phenomena"].[8] That inconclusiveness left the door open to spiritualizing interpretations such as Thérèse's. Given, however, the medical texts consulted at that time, it is a wonder that the doctor did not pursue his passing hypothesis of St. Guy's dance, that is, chorea.

In F.-J. Collet's *Précis de pathologie interne*, a standard reference in the Third Republic, the nervous symptoms of chorea are set out: "Dans les formes graves de la chorée, il y a du délire, des hallucinations et même de la manie aiguë" ["In the serious instances of chorea, there is delirium, hallucinations and even acute mania"].[9] Notta said nothing further because he did not wish to alarm the family; death from complications was not rare in this disease. Even short of death, disturbing possibilities remained. Although the muscular spasms normally would be attenuated and then disappear altogether, "[l]'affection peut passer à l'état chronique, même généralisée: elle laisse souvent après elle un état mental bizarre" ["the disease can pass to a chronic, even generalized condition and often leaves behind it a bizarre mental state"].[10]

Thérèse herself admits only that she was subject to "des frayeurs très grandes de certaines choses" ["enormous dread of particular things"] and begged that during her convalescence no others beyond the family be allowed to visit her lest they be standing "autour de mon lit en rang d'oignons me regardant comme une bête curieuse" ["around my bed like a row of onions looking on me as a strange beast"] (A 29r), but she commends her sisters, charitably attentive to "une idiote" (A 29r) whom only their solicitous love kept them from fleeing.

During this domestic drama, Louis wrote to Paris (April 8, 1883) and had a novena said at Notre-Dame-des-Victoires for her cure. A month later, during Pentecost, she from her bed, with her three sisters joining, prayed to Bouchardon's statue of the Virgin Mary, about three feet in height, given to her father by a friend. She broke into tears when she saw it, classically contained like the Venus de Milo, smiling at her. From that moment, the desiderated miracle having occurred, she believed herself cured. None of her sisters shared this vision.

When Marie informed Pauline and the other Carmelites, they asked for details, not only embarrassing Thérèse but implicitly calling into question her veracity. That apparent skepticism was warranted, of course, and had the putative miracle been investigated by formal ecclesiastical procedures, she might have been made far more than unhappy, her vision and herself being challenged. On the other hand, the incalculably weighty example of another visionary girl, named Bernadette, imposed itself on both her and the Carmelites. Pilgrimages to Lourdes had commenced only a generation before. The risks of sensationalism and of embarrassment were too great to run. If any of the sisters, natural or Carmelite, remained dubious, she let the matter rest.

Realizing that she had not been wholly believed oppressed Thérèse from that time until her trip to Rome, when in Paris she stopped and found relief at

Notre-Dame-des-Victoires: "pendant quatre ans le souvenir de la grâce ineffable que j'avais reçue fut pour moi une vraie *peine d'âme"* ["for four years the
memory of that ineffable favor I had received was a true *pain in my soul"*] (A
30v). Made to feel, or rather believing she had been made to feel (not the same
thing) like a liar, she rationalized that she was paying for the miraculous cure
by grievous humiliation, a suffering which she tells us she willingly embraced.

One of her critical admirers, Hans Urs von Balthasar, has made much of
this episode. He argues that Thérèse's impetus to enter Carmel came chiefly
from the need to ratify her experience of the miraculous cure. Or to escape it:
at Carmel, she would secure the protective veil, the Rule, and silence, as well
as her natural sisters, but they indulged her. Balthasar suggests that with her
cultivated aversion to things sweet, bitterness being the concomitant of suffering, she grew weary of the sugary praises, the deference given her at
Carmel by the Martin sisters, and that her disdain extended to the image of
sainthood they promoted: "Le dégoût du mets sucré est au fond le dégoût
qu'elle éprouve devant la statue de plâtre de sa sainteté, sans cesse érigée
devant elle" ["The disgust before sugared foods is basically the disgust she felt
before the plaster statue of sainthood ceaselessly held up to her"].[11] In short,
her preadolescent need for acceptance was succeeded by an adult awareness of
flattery and the desire for truth.

Had she flattered herself in her account of the cure? No. Given the weird
and unexplained nervous affliction, she naturally imputed it to a demonic
source, and only a powerfully benign force could outweigh and "cure" her of
that affliction. Only a supernal good could cast out evil. That a chorea is
prompted by a brain lesion would have given her no illumination, as she could
still have presumed a demon had caused that lesion.

Given her thorough readings in the Gospels during her time at Carmel
and her self-comparison with characters such as Mary Magdalene, it is surprising that in discussing her illness she does not mention the medical sort of
miracles wrought by Christ, as for the daughter of Jairus or, more aptly, the
boy who tossed himself into fire and water, a possible instance of chorea
(*Mark* 9:22). Instead, and incongruously, she mentions only the "maladie" of
Lazarus: hers, like his, would serve to glorify God (A 28r). The choice of
Lazarus figures in a singular way; among many stories of exorcism, this one
alone involves resurrection. In effect, Thérèse implies that she was brought
back from a kind of death to life. Further, the attendance of the weeping
sisters, Martha and Mary, should not be discounted. They knew that only a
miracle performed by Jesus could deliver their brother back to them.

Christ sometimes tells the healed that it is their trust which has saved
them, but for Thérèse it was what Balthasar called a plaster sainthood, albeit a
Marian one. The incredulous may take refuge in the fact that the emotional
turmoil entailed in Sydenham's chorea generally lasts no more than four
months, and Thérèse's time had run. Psychiatric assumptions, that the illness

came in response to Pauline's leaving her for Carmel, meaning the loss of a second mother, might be overdressed. Thérèse had always been an acutely sensitive, impressionable child, and the departure of Pauline was deeply painful to her, but she still had her other sisters—Céline being her favorite—and Louis. Pauline, a short distance away, could be visited. It seems unlikely that she would have resorted even subconsciously to such extremes as her fearful visions and her poundings against the bed in protest over her sister's leaving home. The syndrome of Sydenham's chorea, including rheumatic fever, provides a less dramatic causality but also a more convincing one.

Were Her Doctors Competent?

In the second half of the nineteenth century, the consensually best treatment for tuberculosis was sanitary: rest and clean air in a relaxing, sustaining, closed environment. The Carmelites' daily schedule ran virtually counter to the regimen of a sanatorium: the sisters arose at 4:45 a.m. with prayers and mass before a breakfast of soup, taken standing, which came at 8.[12] During fasts such as Lent, there was no breakfast. Although there were recreational times and a noon siesta in the summer (none in winter), there were also about five hours of work daily, and retirement came late, at 11 p.m. The Carmelites were virtual vegetarians; they ate fish regularly but were allowed meat only when seriously ill. As religious, they did not enjoy the appurtenances of secular life found even among the lower classes: furniture and ample protection from cold or damp.[13] Complementing these outward rigors, however, were positive factors which it would be hard for a layperson to reckon justly because they appear abstract: a shared and pertinacious attention to another life, a collectivity of prayer and song, and not least, the unity of gender. On the mundane side once again, there was a healthy diet—lots of vegetables, fruits, and carbohydrates—and exceptional hygiene, laundering being a regular and shared task. Their habits, being woolen, were not boiled.

Although, unlike sanatoriums, the Carmel convent was not founded for the promotion of longevity, most of the sisters who dwelled there during Thérèse's time passed into old age. Of the thirty-two she knew, twenty-four reached their seventieth year or more, well beyond the life expectancy of their time. Only two others, both of her generation, contracted tuberculosis: an external sister, Marie-Antoinette, who died at thirty-three in November 1896, and Thérèse's cousin, Marie Guérin, Sr. Marie de l'Eucharistie, who died at thirty-four in April 1905. So an environmental causality cannot be claimed for the disease. Carmel neither helped nor hindered its development.

During most of Thérèse's years at Carmel, she enjoyed good health; at least, no important problems have been recorded. The first reference to a bronchopulmonary condition came on June 28, 1894. A few weeks later, on

July 17, Pauline noted in her *Cahiers verts* that her sister had a persistently sore throat which was being cauterized with silver nitrate. The assumption was that her throat was irritated by steam when she was washing the *vaisselle* in the kitchen and by dust when she was sweeping.

A more curious note came much later in a letter from her cousin Marie to her sister, Jeanne, Mme. La Néele, on October 21, 1895. Marie observed that Thérèse's voice had undergone a change. Dr. La Néele observed that it was nothing serious but that it could become so, and one day there would be no remedy.[14] These mystifying remarks point to the simple fact that without radiological precision, it is not altogether certain that Thérèse contracted tuberculosis. Another possibility is that she contracted a form of bronchial dilatation. X-raying had begun only in that year, 1895, and no one would have imported the machinery into a convent so as to identify a pulmonary disease.

What remains objectionable in the behavior of the chief physician, Alexandre de Cornière, then chief surgeon at the Lisieux hospital and Carmel's consultant, as well as of Dr. La Néele, concerns their apparent indifference to a standard medical practice since Koch's discovery of the tubercular bacillus in 1882: the examination of sputum. Their auscultations were perhaps inadequate because they could use their stethoscopes only through the oratory grille, but they failed to take the notes by which respiratory semiology was properly conducted. Had they done so, noting such indicators as cavitational breathing and rattling, which are signs of tuberculosis up to its final stage, they would not necessarily have cured Thérèse but might have spared her suffering from the outrageously primitive procedures common to a then unreflective French medical practice. The auscultations would have had to be regular and, in so foxy and unpredictable a disease as tuberculosis, would have offered a variety of evidence as to the intensity, rhythm, and quality of their patient's respiration. Unfortunately, de Cornière's extant notes indicate only prescriptions he made (filled by Isidore) and not for whom they were intended.

De Cornière and La Néele did not even, it seems, gather the standardly vital information on Thérèse's fever,[15] her weight loss,[16] and her pulse. As de Cornière was the Carmel's official physician, he carried the substantial responsibility. His negligence of professional diagnostic procedures can at best be called shabby, and no scruples about the fact that he was treating a religious can afford credible extenuation. It is no wonder that de Cornière never identified tuberculosis (La Néele did, toward the end) and that he simply threw at his patient the conventional apparatus for the treatment of symptoms in pulmonary as well as other diseases.

Compounding this unhappy picture was the progress toward death by another Carmelite, Sr. Marie-Antoinette, who first manifested tuberculosis early in 1895. She had a particular position within Carmel as its *tourière*, the noncloistered go-between who brought articles to the convent from the wider world. In the *circulaire*, Gonzague noted that in the late spring of 1895, "la maladie de poitrine dont elle était atteinte fît de tels progrès que notre dévoué docteur ne nous laissa plus aucun espoir" ["the pulmonary sickness which afflicted her made such progress that our devoted doctor did not leave us any hope"].[17] The fact that a Carmelite was already presumed fatally incurable of a lung disease should have put de Cornière and La Néele on their guard. Ironically, as Sr. Marie-Antoinette was pious, sweet in disposition, and discreet, "nous n'hésitâmes point à la recevoir malgré sa très faible santé" ["we did not hesitate to admit her (to Carmel) despite her very weak health"]. Whether their medical histories had predisposed them to tuberculosis is a question that can be posed about both Marie-Antoinette and Thérèse. It seems likely that de Cornière, observing the apparently rapid progress of Marie-Antoinette's sickness, misidentified it as miliary tuberculosis, then known as acute phthisis, which is much faster in its development than chronic tuberculosis. If so, surprised perhaps by Marie-Antoinette's holding onto life for the next year and a half, he may have been more cautious about a diagnosis of Thérèse.

The malady which was to kill Thérèse was not immediately evident when it came. Without heating, all of the Carmelite sisters were coughing in the winter months and into spring. For a long while after she first coughed up blood, Thérèse was able to conceal her condition from the community and even from Pauline, Marie, and Céline. It seems that she also minimized it to the doctors. In her childhood, when she was sick virtually every winter between 1877 and 1881, she would make what Pauline called "des efforts héroïques pour dominer son abattement parce que je lui disais que ce n'était rien" ["heroic efforts to control her debility because I told her it was nothing"].[18] By minimizing an illness, Pauline was concealing her own fears, or so she attested later. Thérèse herself wrote that she took the first hemoptysis as a portent of death and rejoiced in it, but no one else was so apprised for a long time. Sr. Marie de la Trinité recalled at the first *procès* that Dr. La Néele gave the first coughing of blood no importance because he could not examine Thérèse closely. Pauline thought that perhaps a small blood vessel had burst in her throat or even in her nose without her knowing it.[19] Insidiously, a first hemoptysis would usually be abundant and subsequent ones much less so until the disease had progressed over perhaps several months. An uninformed victim could be lulled into a false ease. Thérèse's claim to instant knowledge of what the hemoptysis meant rested in part upon what she had learned from *circulaires* but more profoundly upon an intuitive, one might venture to say, spiritual certitude.

A popular home guide to medicine early in the Third Republic, the *Manuel du Docteur Dehaut*, confirms that an initial hemoptysis was not in itself cause for alarm. More important than the blood loss, no matter the quantity, was what it signified, possibly the beginning of a severe pulmonary condition. *Dehaut* prescribed for the first hemoptysis total rest in a well-ventilated room and ingestion of cold water by teaspoon. It dismissed all syrups and pastes because they were treating only symptoms, and it identified two poisons which when carefully prepared served as possible remedies for grave pulmonary diseases, including tuberculosis: arsenic and phosphorus. The difficulty de Cornière would have faced in using such hazardous agents would have been obvious, that they would have required careful daily supervision and observation of the patient, a logistic not admissible at Carmel. Total rest in fresh air hardly comported with the asceticism of Carmel. It is not likely that Thérèse would have agreed so early to be sequestered from the communal life nor that the prioress would have allowed it. De Cornière, besides, could not have understood that here was a patient who was not looking to be cured.

De Cornière wins some extenuation in what otherwise looks like negligent treatment. He knew he could not insist upon such elementary matters as total bed rest nor could he have safely begun to prescribe the hypophosphites which *Dehaut* called "précisément les plus efficaces entre tous les remèdes capables de guérir la phtisie" ["precisely the most efficacious remedies capable of curing phthisis"].[20] Perhaps his experience at the Lisieux hospital had taught Carmel's physician some skepticism about such claims.

Complicating this tableau is the unquestioning trust the Carmelites placed in de Cornière and La Néele. The *circulaires* from all the prioresses indicate a unanimously high estimation of Carmel's physicians,[21] in part because these sisters were used to unswerving deference to male authority (a tautology for them) and also, in the instance of Thérèse, due to the sentimental loyalty of a familial connection, La Néele being the husband of her cousin Jeanne. Only with time did Thérèse have difficulties with de Cornière and never did she indicate distrust of La Néele. In a time when the medical profession enjoyed lofty prestige in France, no Carmelite was dubious about the procedures of men who, by all the evidence, were at best average practitioners.

Thérèse on the Rack

Thérèse lay in succession to countless thousands of tubercular patients. The disease figured in the nineteenth-century rather as AIDS did late in the twentieth, claiming people of all classes and many illustrious people whose biographies included at the terminus this "white death," at once a lurid and even glamorous fate. The ideology of high romanticism hallowed both love and death, so their conjunction was of special moment. Among the well-known victims of tuberculosis are the chroniclers of domestic love, the Brontë sisters; Alfred de Musset and Chopin, both of them lovers of George Sand;[22]

Keats and Shelley and Robert Louis Stevenson. Among other French victims, the Breton physician René Laënnec deserves a lasting profile as he invented the stethoscope, a major advance toward accuracy in diagnosis, and he wrote a definitive tract on auscultatory procedures (1819), which Thérèse's doctors should have known but seem not to have consulted.

The most famous tuberculosis victim in France, however, was Marie Duplessis, immortalized by the younger Dumas through *La dame aux camélias* and further, through Violetta in Verdi's *La Traviata*. In dying young, at twenty-three, and in explicit identification with flowers, Marie suggests a kind of secular Thérèse, but even more so in becoming a cultural icon: even as at churches and cathedrals throughout France, flowers are regularly placed before the statue of only one saint, so Marie Duplessis enjoys ever-renewed bouquets of camellias at her graveside in Montmartre. Young lovers are devoted not only to each other. As the votary of erotic love, Marie might be reckoned an anti-Thérèse, but they both knew that tuberculosis is without glamour.

There remains, nonetheless, "cette coquetterie de mort" ["this coquetry of death"], a phrase we find in a shrewd fictional sociology of tuberculosis in nineteenth-century France. It comes from the now mostly neglected and yet occasionally still despised Goncourt brothers, Jules and Edmond, in their *Renée Mauperin* (1864). The Goncourts had researched disease and dying among patients at the Hôpital de la Charité in Paris. They did not pretend to be medically informed, but they were intelligent observers, in fact, the best-known informants of their time. I have found in their consumptive heroine, Renée, a useful profile to set by the dying Thérèse.

What distinguishes Thérèse as a tubercular patient from almost every-one else who has left us a record of facing this illness is that she welcomed it. In the seeking of Christ, her attentiveness to suffering had suddenly been pointed to its apogee, its final sense. She had for years sensed that she would not live long and now that tacit awareness had found dramatic confirmation. Far more important, however, is the fact that this pulmonary affliction came concurrently with her maturing spirituality and perhaps informed it in recondite ways. The common denominators between them are *faiblesse, anéantissement, abandon*: weakness, a voiding of the self, acceptance. Thérèse herself might have intuited this juncture because in her mind every trial, including physical pain and its debilitating effects, came from God. Her diseased lungs were her schooling. Hence, her affliction, far from distracting her from her spiritual life, intensified it. She once admitted to feeling aversion toward her own body, a not unusual reaction in feminine adolescence, and when it was being ravaged she remarked: "Ça devient déjà squelette, v'là c'qui m'agrée" ["It's already becoming a skeleton. Fine with me"]. Then this, a week later, "Oh! Que j'éprouve de joie à me voir me détruire!" ["Oh, what joy I feel seeing myself destroyed!"].[23]

The cue came from the timing: she experienced her first coughing of blood during the night of Good Friday, April 4, 1896. No sooner had she laid down for the night than she felt a gurgle rising to her lips. As the lights had been extinguished for the night, she had to wait until dawn to be sure of what had happened.[24] This is how she described her night to Gonzague: "Je ne savais pas ce que c'était, mais je pensais que peut-être j'allais mourir et mon âme était inondée de joie" ["I didn't know what it was, but I thought that perhaps I was going to die and my soul was flooded with joy"] (C 4v–5r). Why such an outlandish response? "Ah! mon âme fut remplie d'une grande consolation, j'étais intimement persuadée que Jésus au jour anniversaire de sa mort voulait me faire entendre un premier appel. C'était comme un doux et lointain murmure qui m'annonçait l'arrivée de l'Époux" ["Oh, my soul was filled with a great consolation; I was intimately convinced that Jesus on the anniversary of his death wished to make me hear his first call. It was like a sweet and distant murmur announcing the Spouse's arrival"] (C 5r). That conjugal image at the close suggests *The Song of Songs*, but the more timely text comes from *Matthew* 25, the story of the virgins, wise and foolish, who slept while awaiting the bridegroom. The wise had oil for lamps and the foolish, of course, did not, and then the bridegroom appeared unexpectedly in the night.

This parable, which seems so quaint (how many virgins did the groom need?) and so cruel (the lazy virgins are locked out), finds apposition in that April night. Thérèse was forbidden from lighting the lamp to discover the bubbling flood emerging from within her and yet she felt ready to receive the Christ who, at this time, was on the cross, not yet risen. As another beloved text, the *Imitatio Christi*, had instructed her, "il faut être prêt à souffrir pour la vie éternelle tout ce qu'il y a de plus pénible" ["one must be ready to suffer for eternal life everything that is most painful"].[25] Now a ghastly ultimate in such suffering was at hand.

Here was a peculiar reversal, indeed, or so it appears to modern points of view. Some recent studies claim that people with religious convictions manage to sustain their terminal illnesses better than nonbelievers because such convictions give their lives meaning; they are or at least can be buoyed by hope and prayer, even though that hope is in search of more earthly life. Those without such an anchor are more likely to give way to death, either in despair or resignation. Thérèse was looking confidently deathward and beyond, sustained supremely by the faith she had up to that point carried unquestioningly through all of her twenty-three years.

It appears odd that she shared nothing about her discovery for a long time. It seems to me certain that in that time she reflected often on her mother's dying, as her family had recalled it to her. Learning she had cancer, Zélie, a woman of figures and facts, had told Louis and their girls immediately. In the damp often chilly climate—Normandy being one of the more pluvious areas of France—Thérèse's coughing would not have immediately signaled a grave condition. Her sister's invaluable photographs, besides, bear strange witness on this point, as only in the summer of 1897, within a few months of death, does Thérèse look drawn and exhausted. Contrary to what we would expect from emaciation, the patient's face did not show it until the very end: "il y a peu d'exceptions à cette règle" ["there are few exceptions to this rule"].[26]

That she concealed her sickness was in part a matter of her temperament. Like any other victims of terminal illness, tubercular patients could become on occasion highly irritable in their apartness from the everyday, resentful of the healthy and strong and of life itself. Like Dostoevsky's Ippolit Terentev, they could turn almost maniacally flighty, not to say rhetorically brilliant, as Terentev is before Myshkin.[27] (Dostoevsky had observed tuberculosis at close hand in his first and very high-strung wife.) "Le mal ne donnait point à Renée ces contrariétés d'humeur, ces brusqueries de volonté, cette irritabilité nerveuse qui met autour des malades un peu de leur souffrance dans le coeur de ceux qui les soignent . . . La vie s'épanchait d'elle sans qu'elle parût la retenir et faire effort pour l'arrêter.. . . Elle laissait la mort monter, comme un beau soir, sur son âme blanche" ["The sickness didn't give Renée the moody vexations, abrupt willfulness, and nervous irritability that sends around the sick a little of their suffering into the hearts of those tending them. . . . Life was unburdening itself of her without her seeming to hold it back or try to stop it. . . She let death ascend, like a beautiful evening, onto her white soul"].[28] The Goncourts' hallowing rhetoric indicates how tuberculosis could make its victims models of a decorum of acceptance, and it cannot be denied that Thérèse conforms to this scheme. But let the terms be precise: she accepted the disease and its pains as a grace. She made a profoundly Christian response to her illness.

The Goncourts could etherealize their Renée because in many, if not most, instances (including Sr. Marie-Dosithée's), tuberculosis was not particularly painful: "Des douleurs ou du malaise dans la poitrine existent dans la majorité de cas; mais il est rare que ces douleurs soient très fortes, et c'est ce qui explique, sans doute, la facilité avec laquelle les phtisiques font illusion sur la gravité de leur état" ["Pains and discomfort in the chest exist in the majority of cases, but rarely are the pains very pronounced, and that undoubtedly explains the ease with which the tubercular (patients) are deluded about the seriousness of their condition"].[29] While that might have been so, there were also cases of fierce pleuretic or neuralgic pains, and Thérèse suffered them.

Unlike the Goncourts' consumptive heroine, Thérèse enjoyed the inestimable benefit of not being cut off. She did not go to the convent's infirmary until July 8, 1897, fifteen months after she realized she was mortally ill and within three months of her death. While she did not lose community (and the invaluable sustenance of the Carmelite sisters), she did lose its *raison d'être*. The Easter season marked in her reckoning the beginning of her temptation against the faith. In the course of the next eighteen months, Thérèse only very rarely articulated her denial or loss of that faith. Pauline revealed to a Carmelite sister, Louise de Jésus (who lived at Lisieux from 1919 until her death in 1982), that Thérèse sometimes felt herself so violently assailed by "un esprit de blasphème" that she had to bite her lips so as not to utter impieties that seemed to be coming from her involuntarily.[30] Her admissions in Manuscript C to Gonzague, however, indicate that her feeling cut off from all awareness of heaven, her great fog, was not an involuntary incident but an ongoing burden of awareness. At no time does she ascribe that fog to demonic influences. Had she made open and ejaculatory statements against faith, she would have been subject to examination and possible expulsion from Carmel; others who proved psychologically unpredictable or unstable had been so dealt with. The question here is whether she was subject to some kind of hysteria, a recurrence of the mania and fear which possessed her in her tenth year: she had experienced from that trying time the conjunction of physical and psychological debilities and would quite understandably have been alarmed by their concurrence. Did her loss of faith come with the death notice she had received with hemoptysis?

She had been acquainted with death: she saw it come within her family, saw it descend upon old age, and rush in with an epidemic. Her own protracted dying had no serenity about it nor merciful suddenness. Tuberculosis revealed itself in a host of minor symptoms: lassitude, pallor but also a flushing of cheeks, night sweating, hoarseness in speech, rough coughing, low yet remittent fever. The tubercular bacillus formed a primary lesion by creating a mass which would expand while softening at the center in a process known as caseation. Tubercles varied in size from the dimensions of a lentil to those of a walnut. Two tendencies were possible: the tubercle might contract into a hard and fibrous nodule, into which the caseous matter would be absorbed; or the caseation would form a magma which could break out and spread. Once the lesion had formed a hardened nodule, the tubercular bacillus could go on living within it for years.

There is no way, then, to determine how long Thérèse was hosting the disease prior to the initial hemoptysis. As the bacillus was aerobic and needed oxygen to thrive, chronic pulmonary tuberculosis provided optimal conditions for eventual collapse of the bronchial wall and diffusion, a development known as cavitation. As the necrotic or caseous matter would be coughed up with the bacillus, contact with a patient could be deadly. The bacillus would also be coughed down into the digestive tract and take residence there: caseation could lead to gangrene. When pulmonary lesions became peripheral, they would affect the pleura and lead to tubercular pleurisy, a condition which made coughing an intense wracking and immitigable assault. Vomiting, diarrhea, severely labored breathing, the mortification of the intestinal tract (enteric necrosis)—in her last days Thérèse's abdomen was as tight as a drum. It is recorded that her breath stank, an indication of gangrene. No matter how ethereally listless a patient was for much of the journey, toward the end tuberculosis marked out a grisly pathway to death.

Not uncharacteristic of the syndrome of tuberculosis, however, was an eerie exhilaration, a heightened awareness attended by a sort of superior ease. The Goncourts depicted this higher station and its morality in their Renée Mauperin: "Elle lui parla de toutes les misères et de toutes les petitesses qui s'en vont de nous lorsque nous souffrons, des instincts d'ironie qu'on perd, du méchant rire qu'on dépouille, du plaisir qu'on ne prend plus aux petites peines des autres, de l'indulgence qui vient pour tout le monde" ["She spoke to him about all the wretchedness and pettiness that passes away from us when we suffer, of how we lose the inclination to irony, get free of wicked laughter and no longer take pleasure in other people's hurts, about the in-dulgence we feel toward everyone"].[31] Again, an ethic of suffering promises an otherwise unattainable illumination to life. Such moments can come to the mortally ill because diseases such as tuberculosis and cancer have an irreg-ular, lurching tempo: there are terrible days and some less terrible, like a sheet of music in which bars of rests are alternated with discordant sforzandi.

Concomitant with pain came a sharpened perceptivity: "l'intelligence semble quelquefois prendre une énergie et une acuité remarquables, au fur et à mesure que le terme fatal approche; l'imagination est surexcitée; il semble, en un mot, que l'âme s'affranchisse dans une certaine mesure du joug que le corps fait peser sur elle" ["the intelligence seems sometimes to take on a re-markable energy and acuity as the end draws near; the imagination is roused; it appears, in a word, that the soul to a certain extent frees itself from the yoke which the body has weighed upon it"].[32] How much Thérèse's ordinarily keen intelligence may have been whetted in the time of her late conversations with her sisters remains indeterminable, but the epistemological breakthroughs she set down in Manuscript C make an argument.

That is, however, to anticipate. For several weeks in the late spring and early summer of 1896, the condition was what physicians call clinically silent. Even the dry cough faded. That interim marked the end of what is called primary tuberculosis, unless, as is possible, Thérèse had been infected at some earlier time. If not, this period of calm or dormancy was awaiting reactivation to secondary tuberculosis. Warmer weather and fresh air might have been helping resistance to the infection, the rate of its progress being determined by the subtle balance between bacillar virulence and the body's constitution. Thérèse's correspondence with Léonie is especially valuable from the time of the first hemoptysis into this dormant phase as it shows how much Thérèse was willing to admit.

Léonie was not only the sole Martin sister who did not become a Carmelite; she was working toward a record number of disappointed attempts to enter religious life. In July 1895, she left the Visitandine convent in Caen, a third failure. For the next four years, she lived with the Guérins in Lisieux. Literally and figuratively an outsider, she wanted her sister to explain the cult of suffering which Thérèse, in a letter written only a week after the first bleeding, had grounded in an *imitatio Christi* taken from *Luke* 24:26. Léonie complains: "je ne comprends pas les personnes qui aiment cette vie de souffrance et de mort continuelle" ["I don't understand the people who love this life of suffering and ongoing death"], and as to matters of health, "je n'ai pas confiance en toi car tu me dis toujours que tu vas bien ou mieux et je n'en crois rien du tout" ["I don't trust you since you're always telling me you're doing fine or better and I don't believe any of it"] (LC 164). Thérèse answered only that she was no longer coughing but added that of course God could take her whenever he willed. The vague response was charitable and candid: short of reactivation, it would have been natural for a tubercular patient to feel virtually normal.

Three days later, on July 15, 1896, de Cornière examined her. According to Msgr. Laveille, Thérèse's official biographer after her canonization, de Cornière resorted to then-familiar devices for the treatment of respiratory disorders: suction cups, vesicatories, and the medieval-sounding "pointes de feu" (fiery needles), these serving presumably to prevent a recurrence of hemorrhaging. (Even de Cornière knew that a pulmonary lesion proximate to a pulmonary artery could bring on a fatal rupture.) Precise dates for all the treatments are lacking, but it is not hard to imagine the excruciations they brought. The *ventouse*, a glass cup rounded on its bottom, was warmed by a match-lit piece of cotton placed within it,[33] and then applied to the skin for five minutes; the skin was raised, turned violet by the afflux of blood, and incised, scarring the skin. The cup was then emptied. The vesicatory, or plaster, was another so-called revulsive, or *dépuratif*, for pleuretic diseases, including pneumonia and tuberculosis. In winter, the plaster would be heated by a fire before being applied (Thérèse was subjected to this procedure in early December 1896), and a napkin was folded over the plaster to keep it in place. The patient had to lie still for several hours, and if at any point the plaster was displaced, she would suffer terrible pain.

The blisters created for pulmonary illness were generally much larger than those created in the treatment of other diseases, the plasters being as much as three times the standard size of 9 × 12 centimeters. The assumption was that vesicatories purged the blood by removing "humors" present in the serous or clear fluid that came out with bleeding. The patient's skin was literally peeled away. As though such procedures were not enough, cauterization was another option. The *pointe de feu*, a steel lancet heated by fire until it glowed red, made a subcutaneous cut of 2 centimeters and spontaneously produced suppuration or pus formation; it was credited with changing the mixture of blood and "humors." In one session, witnessed by Céline, de Cornière made five hundred little jabs into Thérèse's back.[34]

These torturous applications, complacently supplied free of anesthetics, attest the well-meaning ineptitude of the medical establishment in France during the early Third Republic, but what startles the reader of texts such as Dr. Paul Labarthe's *Dictionnaire populaire de médecine usuelle* are the confident claims which justified de Cornière's procedures. Vesicatories enjoyed "les plus grands succès dans les affections morbides les plus variées" ["the greatest successes with the most varied sicknesses"], among them "phthisie pulmonaire," a malady which those fiery lancets "guérira ou ameliorera infalliblement" ["will cure or ameliorate unfailingly"].[35] The advent of a vaccine to prevent tuberculosis was French but a generation away, in the bacillus Calmette-Guérin, first widely employed after the 1914–1918 war. All that can be said about the plasters and lancets is that they caused their patient/victim pointless cutaneous suffering.

It is only fair to note that there was no clear consensus on the use of such treatments. *Dehaut*, for example, enthusiastic about hypophosphites, was dismissive of vesicatories and bleeding generally, perhaps chiefly because under the name of Dehaut there were large numbers of purgative pills for home use and the *Manuel* includes a fifty-page introduction to their application. Where did that leave the vesicatories? "L'emploi méthodique de la purgation nous a permis, depuis longtemps, d'abandonner presque entièrement l'usage de ces remèdes utiles, mais fort pénibles et fort désagréables" ["The methodical use of purgation has for a long time allowed us to abandon almost completely these useful but very painful and disagreeable remedies"].[36] Whether the Dehaut pharmaceuticals would have helped to "purify" Thérèse's blood may be doubted, but they would have not probably produced pains comparable to those occasioned by the bleeding devices Dr. de Cornière randomly employed.

The Coquetry of Death

On his initial visit, de Cornière disappointed Thérèse's hope of an early death by telling her she looked well. With the coughing subdued, there was no immediately apparent need of treatment. In mid-October 1896, she wrote upon order by her confessor, Père Godefroid Madelaine, a Credo. She did so in her own blood (not on the priest's order), pricked by a pin, and carried the Credo recorded in her little book of the Gospels[37] (see figure 7.2). Perhaps Madelaine told her about Saint Vincent de Paul carrying that text on his person (and in his blood?) throughout his own years of darkness.

Her relapse, the secondary phase of her tuberculosis, did not begin until the third week of November. When the coughing returned during that time, the prioress ordered Thérèse to use a foot warmer. The lesions of the primary infection had been reactivated. (In most secondary instances, they are located in the apex of the lung and are about 30 millimeters in diameter.) The vesicatory treatment in December must not have convinced Thérèse of its efficacy since in January she was alluding for the first time to an imminent death, in a

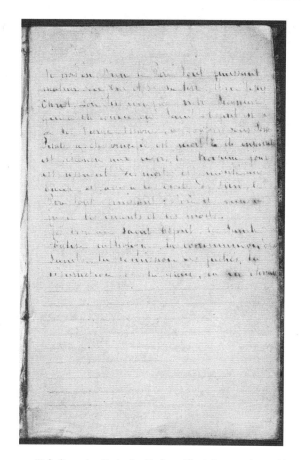

FIGURE 7.2. "I believe in God, the Father Almighty, maker of heaven and earth . . ." The Credo which Thérèse wrote in her own blood. Copyright Archives du Carmel de Lisieux.

letter to Pauline: "J'espère aller bientôt là-haut" ["I hope to go on high soon"] (LT 216), but her doubts were evident, "S'il y a un Ciel, il est pour moi" ["If there is a Heaven, it will be for me"]. That was her subjunctive variant on a line from Alexandre Soumet's *Jeanne d'Arc* (1825) which she had included in one of her Jeanne dramas. Her letter implies that she had already informed Pauline orally of her imminent death.

It was nine months away. During Lent 1897, with fevers coming in the afternoons, *pointes de feu* were put into her side. Despite her loss of appetite, de Cornière ordered that she be given double portions of fish and vegetables. As Gonzague obliged her to eat everything served, Thérèse complied but suffered yet more, this time from indigestion.

Her first written reference to her illness precedes by three months the writing of Manuscript C and comes in a brief, incoherent note to Isidore on

April 3, 1897. She mentions that she regularly has a fever in the night, about 3 a.m. The note was appended to a letter home written by Marie, whose correspondence provides a valuable record of Thérèse's consumption by the disease. On the next evening, Thérèse wrote to Pauline these cryptic words: "J'ai peur d'avoir fait de la peine à ma petite Mère, je l'aime pourtant! Oh oui! Mais je ne puis lui dire tout ce que je pense, il faut qu'elle le devine" ["I'm afraid I've hurt my little Mother whom I love even so, oh yes! But I can't tell her all I'm thinking. She has to guess it"] (LT 223).

That is the whole of her message, and a caveat to all biographers on how much their subjects might hide and might remain themselves hidden. Even Pauline, who in a maternal way knew her sister best, was left guessing: was Thérèse referring to her deadly illness, to her testing and the possibility of blaspheming, or was the occasion of her words an altogether trivial one? Although her fever was not being recorded, her coloration suggested it was high, and she could barely stand from exhaustion. Pauline claims that Thérèse even wanted to carry out the offices of the dead as the Carmelite Constitution prescribed: "Elle faisait cela avec tant de simplicité qu'on oubliait presque son héroïcité" ["She did that with such simplicity that one almost forgot her heroism"].[38]

Thérèse had learned to cherish silences, so much so that Pauline resorted to recording as much as she could of what her sister did say, beginning on April 6 with a yellow notebook later subsumed in the *Derniers entretiens*. It begins by commending Mary, sister of Martha, who was silent when accused of idling. While some of her remarks, especially on politics within Carmel, or "des combats contre les soeurs," as Thérèse dryly puts it, might owe much to her experience in training novices, her insightful detachment might owe as much to her being apart through sickness. Her insistence upon truth telling, upon the need to be sparing of consolations for others, suggests the shrewdness of someone raised above daily strife and pettiness. She had, besides, an equanimity, even humor about her illness, likening her coughing to the sound of a railroad engine arriving at a station (May 7) and the illness itself (which she does not identify as tuberculosis or phthisis) to a lottery ticket. As to death, "ce n'est pas un fantôme, un spectre horrible, comme on la représente sur les images" ["it's not a phantom, a terrible specter such as is shown in pictures"] (May 1) and besides, she claims, it was not death that was coming to fetch her. It was God.

Until the relapse in November 1896, she had entertained the hope of going to the Carmel founded (1895) in Hanoi by the one in Saigon, itself the offshoot of the Lisieux Carmel. In May, she still entertained hopes of going there but told Pauline she had no illusions about accomplishing anything. She claimed to have become indifferent to both life and death or was at least disappointed that death was showing itself tardy. She likened herself to a child to whom a cake has been promised but then withheld, then to a child whose parents were about to put her on a train—if she missed one departure, she would simply wait for the next.[39] It was the helpless recumbence of the patient, the enforced passivity, which begot these metaphors. Their frankness seems refreshingly distant from the infantile language she had exchanged with Pauline at the time of her awaiting another departure, to the Carmel ten years before, when Jesus had been toying with her.

Thérèse in Abandon

What did she feel about her medical treatments? "Je suis convaincue de l'inutilité des remèdes pour me guérir" ["I'm convinced that the remedies for curing me are useless"] (DE, May 21–26, 1897), but as she wished that they could be used for missionaries who were ill and without medical care, she was saying merely that her own cure was hopeless. De Cornière had unwittingly teased her with the prospect of death, one day giving her hope by his consternation and the next day speaking of her curing—that, as late as July 16 (LT 255). Such vacillation on his part, while understandable (every physician knows how capricious a disease can be), explains why in her *entretiens*, Thérèse sometimes believed her death would be coming soon and yet she would conjecture about what she might do when cured. On being subjected to *pointes de feu* a second time (in May), she consoled Pauline: "Ne vous faites pas de peine pour moi, j'en suis venue à ne plus pouvoir souffrir, parce que toute souffrance m'est douce" ["Don't be troubled about me. I've gotten to the point of no longer being able to suffer since all suffering is sweet to me"] (DE, May 29, 1897). Perhaps the lancets had been heated exceptionally well: "L'application du cautère actuel détermine une douleur excessivement vive, mais dont l'intensité est en raison inverse de la chaleur de l'instrument" ["Application of the cautery at present entails an extremely sharp pain but its intensity is in an inverse proportion to the heat of the instrument"].[40] As the *pointes* were applied to her sides, Thérèse could see the lancets and their incisions, but they were also applied to her back; the vesicatories, or cups, on her chest.

That Thérèse did not complain of such inflictions was altogether in character. Beyond the Carmelite ethos of suffering, she has left ample testimony to her receptivity to hardships, physical and otherwise. That she says nothing about her illness by name might seem surprising. Did she know that it was tuberculosis which was killing her? Her aunt had died from it. Did she even know that Sr. Marie-Antoinette, the *tourière*, had died from it? It seems improbable that she knew much at all: Dr. Cornière himself might have been under conventual restrictions and not allowed to impart his diagnosis. His late and vague promise of healing—"Vous voilà en voie de guérison" ["You're on your way to a cure"] (LT 255)—would have misled her only if she believed a cure possible. Blithe claims of cures by treatments such as *pointes de feu* which we read in Labarthe's *Dictionnaire populaire* come from blanketing tuberculosis under the rubric of less grave pulmonary disorders, a pleural inflammation due to rheumatic fever, for example.

Her only expressed view of de Cornière is an unhappy one but does not concern his professional competence. Although throughout June the illness had not progressed markedly (after an unspecified attack following Communion on June 4, she was put on a milk regimen to supplement her feeble diet), she had endured the doctor's ambiguous bedside manner, vacillating herself between a belief in her imminent death and an indifference about whether she lived or died. Early in July, de Cornière, with an astonishing lack of tact, spoke of a woman she knew who had died from a tumor he had been unable to diagnose. What a pity, he told Thérèse, that he had not been able to perform an autopsy. Whether talking to himself or too fatigued to notice the slip in professional decorum or misestimating the Carmelite detachment from secular life, he dismayed her: "C'est comme cela qu'on est indifférent les uns pour les autres sur la terre! Dirait-on la même chose s'il agissait d'une mère ou d'une soeur? Oh! Que je voudrais bien m'en aller de ce triste monde!" ["That's how indifferent people are toward each other on the earth. Would one say that about one's mother or sister? Oh, how I would like to take my leave of this sad world!"].[41] This painful episode recasts the question: if de Cornière was so indiscreet about another person's grave illness, how discreet was he toward Thérèse about her own?

This doctor also occasioned her mordant dismissal of bromides and little sayings, words of edification and uplift, such as Pauline once sought for him from her sister. Had he requested something? And was she surprised at Thérèse's response? "Ce n'est pas mon petit genre" ["That's not my little genre"], she demurred, on one of her worst days of sickness. "Que M. de Cornière pense ce qu'il voudra. Je n'aime que la simplicité, j'ai horreur de la feintise" ["Let de Cornière think as he likes. I love only simplicity and have a dread of feigning"].[42] And she teased him: when a mouse was found injured, she had it brought to her bedside and asked de Cornière to apply his stethoscope to the poor creature.

Like any other patient, Thérèse knew that her body's pains were not lying. Twice, on June 9 and 26, she mentioned distress in her side, which suggests the development of peripheral pulmonary lesions or the beginning of tubercular pleurisy. The last photo of her upright, in which she is kneeling with the images of the infant Jesus and the Veronica face, was taken on June 7, when she was near exhaustion. After two photographs, she urged Céline to make haste before she collapsed. By that time, she was having difficulty swallowing. Yet, most oddly, she was also feeling sufficiently better that she remarked only a day after one of her pleural bouts that she no longer understood her illness. She presumed that, had she only kept quiet, no one would have known she had become ill (May 18). By mid-June, her hope of death had been "used up," but it is difficult to accept straightforwardly such utterances as "je suis une petite fille guérie" ["I'm a little girl cured"] since they were perhaps defenses against the well-meaning but importunate visits she received while working on Manuscript C and its details on her spiritual testing. She might well have spoken of a condition she knew was not improving, but she tried to minimize others' fretting over her. She admitted to "une gêne extrême que j'éprouve quand on s'occupe de moi" ["a pronounced discomfort (or embarrassment) I feel when people fuss over me"].[43]

What was happening to her spiritually to some degree reflects the irregular and incalculable character of her illness. While she claimed she had no fear of her final struggle with the illness—the sisters were naturally curious about her attitude toward death and her equanimity so consolatory and disconcerting—she had reached a new turn with her testing against faith. In a moment charged with ambiguity, she told Pauline that she would be glad to quit the earth, she would die of joy, were it not for her testing.[44] How was this testing holding her to life? She was eager to be free of it through death, but her words suggest that she was somehow deepening her self-awareness in the experience of doubt. "J'accepte *tout* pour l'amour du bon Dieu, même *toutes* sortes de pensées extravagantes qui me viennent à l'esprit" ["I'm accepting *everything* for the love of the good Lord, even *all sorts* of extravagant thoughts which come into my mind"]. Possibly, she means here the walling up of heaven and the thick fog to which she referred only days afterward in her letter to Gonzague, but a week later she promises not to "break my head" with self-torments.

The testing became "quelque chose de suspendu" ["something suspended"] and there were no more snakes hissing in her ears. Her spirit remained subject to an undulation like that of the tuberculosis, and how she characterized her testing depended upon the day and the audience. Her rhetoric of allness now becomes a device of encompassing acceptance. She was learning to integrate doubt into faith, darkness (fog) into light. It is not known what she said to the Carmel chaplain, Abbé Louis Youf (who died at fifty-five, only a few days after Thérèse), when he advised her against her temptations, "Ne vous arrêtez pas à cela, c'est très dangereux" ["Don't stop there, it's very dangerous"], but she did pass on to Pauline her estimate of his urgings: they were hardly consoling but fortunately she was not affected by them: "je ne m'en impressionne pas."[45]

With her difficulty in swallowing, she became reconciled to the prospect of no longer receiving Communion. She did not need it, anyway, since "*Tout est grâce*" ["*Everything* is grace"] (DE, June 5). These words, a summa as only a lifetime's end could express, deserve the attention usually accorded to her pledge to spend her heaven doing good on earth. In becoming, like Dostoevsky, a child of both faith and doubt, she became a child of her age. What marks her singularly is that she learned not to struggle, not to be tossed between them in anguished irresolution but to sustain the contraries within herself.

With her reflections that June, both in Manuscript C and in the *Derniers entretiens*, she steps into the company of nonscholastic but truly modern theologians, writers such as William Blake and Simone Weil. "Joy and woe are woven fine, clothing for the soul divine," in Blake's *Auguries of Innocence*, complements the peculiar fusion of light and darkness in Thérèse's spirituality; if, that is, we honor her by taking that darkness in full seriousness. Blake's "Man was made for joy and woe" subsumes the theresian lesson that suffering must be embraced, not fled, if we are to savor genuine happiness: "And when this we rightly know, through the world we safely go."[46]

The extraordinary equanimity Thérèse achieved while enduring the spiked hand of a deadly disease can be integrated into her professed love of God and comprehended as its highest expression. Weil wrote that we attain a pure love of God when we can receive divine mercies and divine afflictions with equal thankfulness. This severe harmonizing of opposites, like Blake's, seems to be emerging in Thérèse's attitude toward her temptation against the faith. If not for this testing, she would gladly leave earth. In fact, she was savoring the testing. Pauline asked how she could want to die amid incessant temptations. "Ah! mais, je crois bien au Voleur! C'est sur le ciel que tout porte. Comme c'est étrange et incohérent!" ["Oh, but I really believe in the Thief! Everything is aimed at heaven. How odd and incoherent that is!"].[47]

Suffering Unperturbed

Tubercular patients sometimes manifested a peculiar exuberance, a gayness at apparent odds with the wracking of their bodies. It is as though the human body, pushed to the extreme of its own ruin, can find recompense within the narrowing compass of refractory means. It may be, however, that the tuberculosis itself provides this giddy relief through its toxins: mercy killing, indeed. Let us look at and listen to Thérèse in the precipitous decline of her last three months.

July began with a stark downturn. When able to walk, she could do so only by leaning against a wall. Pauline did not dare to take her arm in support. De Cornière's prescription of condensed milk, known as *lait maternisé*, became a torment. She wept at the sight of it. According to Sr. Marie de l' Eucharistie, de Cornière had decided, "Ce n'est pas la tuberculose, c'est un accident arrivé aux poumons, une vraie congestion pulmonaire" ["It's not tuberculosis but an injury to the lungs, a true pulmonary congestion"].[48] He ordered that Thérèse not stir, not move even to the infirmary until the right lung had cicatrized. His chief concern was her "grande faiblesse," and he told

Gonzague that the likelihood of Thérèse's survival was only one in fifty. If she could eat, he could prolong her life but a cure was impossible. If she could not digest the milk, he would give her only days.

Marie reported to her father how lamentation spread over the Carmel: "Te dire dans quel état est la Communauté, ce sont des larmes, des sanglots, des désolations de tous les côtés. . . . nous sommes brisées, atterrées et ne pouvons croire au malheur qui nous menace" ["To tell you in what state the community is in, there are tears, sobs, grief at every hand. . . . we are shattered, dismayed, and cannot believe the ordeal which is threatening us"].[49]

Despite (or with) her suffering, Thérèse insisted she was happy, and so there appears a peculiarly inverse accord between her mind and the ravaging disease, as though her physical decline ensured a spiritual robustness.[50] Pauline addressed the smiling Virgin in the hope that the hemoptysis would abate, but Thérèse confounded that hope by saying that for herself to be happy, the blood spitting would have to continue. As she grew weaker and more emaciated, she rejoiced. Joy itself, however, became suspect to her, no less than the sadness which she consistently struggled to deny or overcome; both were the cheats of fluctuation, unresolved, testing her patience. Even her joy in anticipating heaven, through an overheard and suggestive music one evening, was as fleeting as its chords. The brusque, irregular rhythms of her disease wearied her because she was still capable of being duped about her condition. As late as July 11, she was resigned to being ill for several months, leaving the outcome unstated, but on the day previous she claimed that de Cornière was deceived and she was not seriously ill. That was just two days after she was delivered to the infirmary, so weak she had to be carried.

Marie wrote to Mme. Guérin of how Thérèse was "la gaité même, faisant rire tous ceux qui l'approchent, parlant avec bonheur du voleur (le bon Dieu) qui va bientôt venir" ["cheer itself, making everyone who approached her laugh, speaking happily of the thief (the good Lord) who was going to come soon"] and of Thérèse's special consideration for Marie's still childless sister, Jeanne La Néele: "Je serai encore plus avec vous qu'avant, je ne vous quitterai pas, moi qui veillerai sur mon oncle, sur ma tante, sur ma petite Léonie, sur tous enfin, quand ils seront prêts à entrer au Ciel, j'irai bien vite à leur rencontre. Et puis pour ma petite Jeanne, la première chose que je ferai en entrant au Ciel, ce sera d'aller dans le grand magasin des petits Anges et puis je choisirai le plus gentil et je lui dirai: Toi, il faut que tu t'en ailles bien vite chez Mme La Néele pour faire sa joie et son bonheur" ["I'll be even more with you than before. I won't leave you. I'll watch over my uncle, my aunt, my little Léonie, over everyone. When they're ready to enter Heaven, I'll go quickly to meet them. And for my little Jeanne, the first thing I'll do on entering Heaven will be to go to the big shop of Angels and I'll pick out the nicest and say to him: You have to go very quickly to Mme. La Néele and make her joyous and happy"].[51]

It is not difficult to reconcile this inane and infantile talk with the dark, interior reality which Thérèse had been recording for Gonzague: she could not have shared that inner darkness with anyone, especially not as she was approaching death, and she knew what any number of dying people realize, that it is not the dying person but those being left behind who need reassurances. Her gaiety was kindly tailored to their weakness and their ingenuousness. It might be the tone of a mother shrewdly managing her anxious children with soothing words.

When Thérèse managed a couple of days without vomiting and diarrhea and de Cornière fatuously remarked, "Je suis vraiment content, il y a du mieux" ["I'm quite happy, it's better"], Marie told her father, "nous renaissons à l'espérance, non pas de la guérison puisque ce serait un miracle, mais de la conserver encore quelque temps. . . . elle ne souffre que de faiblesse, d'anéantissement" ["we're reborn in hope, not of a cure since that would be a miracle, but of keeping her for still some time. . . . she suffers only from weakness and exhaustion"].[52] If she was speaking for the other Carmelites, Marie's equanimous tone suggests that the sisters were not dependent upon de Cornière for cheering, hopeful words. Besides, Thérèse's own insouciant receptivity to death was itself preparing them. When, on July 20, Marie reported that Thérèse's hemoptyses were coming steadily as though "réglé comme papier à musique" ["measured like sheet music"] with a cup being filled with blood in fifteen minutes, de Cornière at last announced he had found several cavities in her right lung: "il dit bien lui même qu'elle est perdue à moins d'un grand miracle, ce qui fait jubiler notre petite malade" ["he says himself that she is lost short of a great miracle, and that makes our little invalid rejoice"].[53]

When told that death was drawing contractions on her face, Thérèse answered that soon she would be making only smiles. This minor observation imposes itself because Céline's photos show a seamless face. A medical thesis on Thérèse argues that absence of the furrows which tuberculosis puts on the brows and of the hollows it invariably makes on the cheeks in the last stage would suggest she was suffering from some other pulmonary ailment.[54] At the same time, her fading became experimentally what she called a dying of (or from) love, and she stressed that it was not the same thing as ecstasy or transport, the common baggage of mystical death. She played on the dual sense of éprouver, to test and to feel. God's will, she said, lay not in self-mortifications but in the sort of épreuve to which she was now subjected.

The testing was taking ever more grotesque turns: as the hemoptyses became more frequent and violent, Pauline admitted that she desired her sister's death so as not to see her suffer. Thérèse told her that suffering was what she herself liked about life. So now she was having her fill of it, literally: she was choking from the congestion of sputum. Twice it was feared that she would be suffocated. De Cornière prescribed what were called frictions, vigorous rubbings with a horsehair belt that produced an afflux of blood in the vicinity of an organ so as to decongest it. Thérèse said that she was being "étrillée," or brushed like a horse, and that it proved a treatment more painful than anything else. The spitting episodes became purgatorial. After one night's bout, on July 17, she said she would pass her heaven doing good on earth, but she did little good for de Cornière while she was still earthside.

He prescribed for her a foul elixir which was sweetened, not altogether successfully, to taste like currants. When he was about to depart for summer leave, she passed to her sisters what she called a souvenir, as though she would never see him again. (In fact, she did, in September.) "Faites-lui une image avec ces paroles: 'Ce que vous avez fait au plus petit des miens, c'est à moi qui vous l'avez fait' " ["Make him an image with these words, 'Inasmuch as ye have done it to the least of these my brethren, ye have done it unto me'"].[55] Thérèse had long had a casual way of importing the Gospels' characters or tableaux into her life (when her three natural sisters went to sleep while tending her, she referred to them as Peter, James, and John), but this instance, taken from *Matthew* 25, is exceptional for being, if not accusatory, ambiguous. (Christ was commending those who visit the sick, not those who attempt to heal them.) If she spoke it only in jest, it was cutting; if not in jest, it betrayed an unsettling bite. De Cornière had tortured her with treatments, appalled her with insensitivity, and even irritated her with a vague request for words of wisdom.

Apart from Francis La Néele, de Cornière was virtually the only layman Thérèse knew and had to deal with during her adult life. Her entire world had been determined by ecclesiastical company. Although resorting to the outmoded and tormenting procedures common to his day, de Cornière likely did so in good medical faith. I suspect (and it can only be a suspicion) that Thérèse's antipathy to him lay in the fact that like her, he was tossed about by her sickness, swaying (to her mind) between hope and doubt. He was not a fixed figure of identifiable convictions but a man of medical science, supposedly cautious, supposedly skeptical (his vacillating remarks put both these terms in question), and therefore disturbing. He was not a miracle worker, but she did not expect one. His trade was in suffering; he had a clinically informed familiarity with affliction and dying that was, as her repugnance toward him about the autopsy showed, earthily free of the sanctimony she invariably brought to such matters. He was a man to whom she could not respond in the posture of affectionate deference given her beloved ecclesiastical males (Louis, the pope, friendly prelates, God), and the terms of his authority were alien to her. In sum, although he was a Catholic (his first son became a priest) and also a friend of the ultramontanist Isidore, he was also a modern, secular man. Possibly some of the hurt she had suffered from Léo Taxil worked itself off against de Cornière, whose "remedies" were in their way another manipulation of her which required blind trust. With his blistering plasters, his fierce lancets, his scalding cups, not to mention the loathsome concoctions, did he not seem to be toying with her? Beside the men to whom she devoted herself in correspondence over her last year, her "spiritual brothers" Roulland and Bellière, this physician cuts a rather sorry profile. He is a contaminant threatening a sterilized field.

Another ground for her disdain of him comes from her disdain of herself as a human body, and it was her body, not her soul, which concerned de Cornière. She told Pauline—could it have been much of a revelation?—that "Toujours mon corps m'a gênée, je ne me trouvais pas à l'aise dedans . . . toute petite même, j'en avais honte" ["My body has always embarrassed me; I've never been at ease in it . . . even when small, I was ashamed of it"].[56] This sense of discomfort is hard to distinguish from the generic disgrace common to women in a culture implicitly disparaging the feminine and reducing it to the extremes of chastity or prostitution. Without any education about her sexuality, Thérèse in her menstruations was exposed to what Simone de Beauvoir called the horror of feeling dirty, mutilated, smelly, her period coming like a shameful disease. "Être féminine, c'est se montrer impotente, futile, passive, docile,"[57] says de Beauvoir: to be feminine is to show oneself helpless, useless, passive, tractable—the condition to which Thérèse had been reduced by sickness.

De Beauvoir, albeit no friend to saints, proves helpful at this juncture first because her own assumptions and her documentation for Le deuxième sexe were informed substantially by Thérèse's generation but also, and far more important, by her insider's view of French womanhood shaped from infancy by Catholicism. At times, she seems to be profiling Thérèse in particular, the I-choose-all Thérèse, as in her discussion of infantile imperialism: "La jeune fille veut tout recevoir parce qu'il y rien qui dépend d'elle" ["The young girl wants to get everything because nothing depends upon her"].[58] Feeling void and yet illimitable, the young woman wants to attain tout from the bosom of her nothingness: saintly women ask God to overwhelm the void of their being. Thérèse had filled that emptiness with her writings, coopting God in every one of them by her profession of love, her eagerness for suffering to win God's pleasure, but de Cornière was effectively casting her back into that primally feminine position of pointless inertia, enforcing upon her the unruly physical self she could not help being and which a deadly ailment kept telling her she was.

Within the theresian lexicon, souffrance occupies a forward position, but humiliation is not far behind, and her submissions perforce to de Cornière's treatments, sessions so desperate as to seem cruel, gave her ample cause for feeling debased, but that experience, too, could be placed under the hallowing rubric: "Ce qui fait notre humiliation au moment fait ensuite notre gloire même dès cette vie" ["What at the moment causes us humiliation afterward brings us glory even in this life"].[59] Even so, occasions came in which she lost patience and, by her own admission, became less than loving. She regretted those lapses keenly: one must be charitable to everybody, she said. I believe that her "souvenir" to de Cornière was one of those moments of vexation.

Thérèse's suffering continued in its dire unpredictability through August. The blood spitting and the spells of stifling which had become severe toward the end of July ceased on the fifth, but by then she was scarcely able to move. As her condition remained unchanged for ten days, she likened herself to Robinson Crusoe waiting on an island shore for her boat. On the fifteenth, she suffered acute pain in her left side and was wracked with coughing and a conspiracy of other pains through the rest of the month. In her tough way, she proved herself up to these agonies: she told her sister that she loved the pains because God had given them to her. Céline having taken over the infirmary and occupying a small bedroom next to hers, Thérèse prayed to the Virgin that she would not keep her sister awake with her coughing—she called it her hiccupping (hoqueté)—but added that she would love the Virgin more if the prayer went unanswered.

Sensible people might ask, why? Her illness seemed to invite her to cultivate a need for bottom-line truth, for what would present itself as unequivocal and not possibly a cheat. Perhaps the indeterminable tempo of her body's degeneration, leagued with her frustration in having to accept anything as God's will, contributed to this bizarre preference for whatever seemed true because unsparing. She said that the more the saints were deaf to her prayers (as they had been to Zélie's), the more she would love them because she did not want to see them nor to see God but to stay in her night of faith. She claimed to desire that station more than others desired one from which they could see God.

Oddly, this preference for truth meant an absence of answers, even consolatory ones, and is bound closely to her distrust of formulas and solutions. To Pauline at about this time, she spoke at length about the nature of her épreuves. She depicted a demonic temptation to believe "le raisonnement des pires matérialistes" ["the worst materialists' arguments"] concerning the progress of science: that science would eventually explain everything.[60] Her notion of science seems to derive from the positivism of Auguste Comte, the belief, bedecked as a philosophy, that observable facts and phenomena can be marshaled without concern for their ultimate origin or cause and shall someday attain a serviceable completion. Positivism several generations on continues to exert a kind of subliminal force in popular expectations about what science and especially its instrumental arm, technology, can achieve: prolongation of life, eradication of diseases, engineering of fetuses. Thérèse's apprehensiveness might still speak to those concerned that spirituality has been eclipsed by this demonstrably more powerful faith. Comte himself attempted to make humanité a kind of modern gospel, and Lamennais's passing from hoary reaction into rapture over democracy suggests the same will-o'-the-wisp. The exaltation of the masses went in tandem with the exaltation of fact. Democracy and science were the great levelers of tradition and superstition, including foremost the ecclesiastical and scriptural. Thérèse was not speaking to imaginary fears.

Without knowing it, however, she was doing service to the mystery of the inexplicable, the indemonstrable, the unprovable, even though to Pauline she could only lament: "Je veux faire du bien après ma mort, mais je ne pourrai pas! Ce sera comme pour Mère Geneviève: on s'attendait à lui voir faire des miracles et le silence complet s'est fait sur son tombeau" ["I want to do good on earth but won't be able to! It will be as for Mother Geneviève; it was expected that she'd be seen performing miracles and there was complete silence over her tomb"][61] (see figure 7.3). To believe Pauline's recollection, as the vivid reference to the venerable Geneviève bids, it seems that Thérèse suffered a lapse of memory in her otherwise formidable awareness of the Gospels: the blessed are those who believe without seeing and to those seeking a miraculous sign Christ gave none. Her fear that her beneficence would not be verified or, worse, would be ridiculed, seems to have been seeded in the

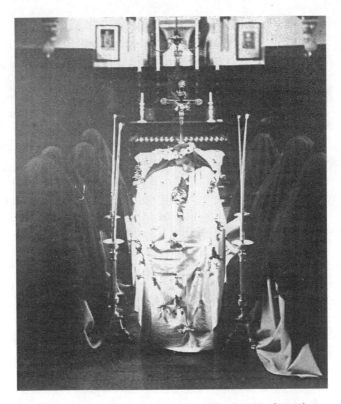

FIGURE 7.3. Thérèse's first real awareness of death came from the corpse of Mère Geneviève, here in the Carmel chapel in December 1891. Thérèse, almost nineteen, may be one of the taller of the veiled sisters flanking the casket. Copyright Archives du Carmel de Lisieux.

humiliating exposure by Léo Taxil but, in a positive sense, it accounts for her new denomination of herself: first, as not a great saint but a little one (August 4), then as a nothingness (August 8) and "une toute petite âme" ["a thoroughly small soul"] (August 9). She told Pauline she did not seek to reason with her demonic tests, but she did attempt to bury such temptations in her inner void. When her sister Marie noticed her glancing into the sky, she presumed that Thérèse was loving heaven but that presumption was deflated; she was looking merely at the sky: "l'autre m'est de plus en plus fermé" ["the other is more and more closed off to me"].[62]

The sure sign that God wanted her suffering came in the fact that de Cornière's dismal remedies only did her harm, but the tuberculosis, now advancing in its terminal phase, would not have responded to any treatment. Because of vomiting and exhaustion, she was afraid to take Communion; her last was on August 19, dedicated to the famous apostate Hyacinthe Loyson. She said that if asked to recount her pains, she would certainly suffocate. She grew tired even from listening to her three sisters gathered and pressing her with questions, and she grew speechless due to sputum in the larynx, a common event in the terminal phase of pulmonary tuberculosis.[63]

The only balm left to her now was sleep. Wakefulness meant an unremitting struggle against pain, a fact she expressed not in her usual directness but in a reversion to baby talk, which, given her situation, seems more bitter than coy: "Il n'y a plus rien que dodo [= dormir] pour bébé . . . tout, tout fait souffrir!" ["There's nothing for baby but beddy-bye . . . everything, everything is causing pain!"]. Thérèse had long lost her appetite and endured a virtual forced feeding even of liquids (in a rare moment on August 12, she spoke of wanting to eat chicken, chops, and tuna), but the caseation made digestion of anything difficult, if not impossible. Her excretions brought severe pain. When seated and coughing she felt as though she had been placed on spikes of iron. In a fearful moment, she asked that all external medicines in the infirmary be placed out of her reach (even though she could not walk to get them) lest she take them in desperation. Pauline's Cahiers verts, from which these remarks come,[64] state that had Thérèse not had faith, she would not have hesitated for a moment to commit suicide.

That testimony should be juxtaposed to this from Msgr. Laveille: "A chaque visite, le médecin témoignait à la Mère Prieure son admiration: 'Ah! Si vous saviez ce qu'elle endure! Jamais je n'ai vu souffrir autant avec une semblable expression de joie surnaturelle. C'est un ange!' " ["At each visit the doctor attested to the Prioress his admiration: 'Oh, if you knew what she's enduring! I've never seen such suffering with such an expression of supernatural joy. She's an angel!' "].[65] The witness is not de Cornière but La Néele, who saw Thérèse four times while de Cornière was on holiday.

Gangrene and supernatural joy perhaps jibe if mortification of her digestive system entailed some toxic release, possibly not unlike the exhilaration experienced in gradual starvation, and she was indeed starving. The milk regimen was ended on August 23. She experienced continual thirst but when she drank she found her thirst growing. With slakeless thirst came an excessive, even foamy salivation. Offered ice water, she said it was like pouring fire into her insides. Her tongue became so desiccated that Pauline likened it to a rasp or grater, a note at variance with tuberculosis generally, one diagnostic of which is a clean tongue.[66] With every breath, she suffered.

When Pauline exclaimed a platitude, how miserable it is to be ill, Thérèse insisted that it is not a miserable thing to die, and being afraid to die is ridiculous unless one has a spouse and children: "mais moi, qui n'ai rien!" ["but I who have nothing!"].[67] Macabre as it may seem, Pauline and other sisters were curious to know whether Thérèse would die on a feast day but August 6 (the Feast of the Transfiguration) and August 15 (that of the Assumption) passed without convenient drama. Thérèse told them it had never mattered to her whether she died on a feast day. That it did not matter whether she lived or died the next day came not from indifference but resignation. As God determined, she would accept. She contented herself that her prayers seemed to have been answered: on reading San Juan de la Cruz, she had asked that like this mystic, she too could be consumed by divine love. She did not delude herself into believing that that *consomption* spelled some sort of transport of celestial happiness. The prospect of going heavenward gave her calm, nothing more, and her pulmonary suffering with all that it had induced in the rest of her body she endured without consolation because she found she could do so without anxiety as well. "Une souffrance sans inquiétude" (her own words of August 29) resounds as the very word *inquiétude* (anxiety) had assumed since Baudelaire a metaphysical weight.[68] Thérèse's *épreuve* alone could have justified her use of this word, but it does not figure in her story with any lexical prominence.

A substantial change within the narrowing scope of her life occurred on August 28, when her infirmary bed was turned ninety degrees so that she now faced directly the statue of the Smiling Virgin and to her left was the window onto the garden. To the left of that light was Céline's painting *Le Christ à l'agonie*. No longer able to stretch or extend her hands, she joined them in anticipation of her death. She likened herself to the beaten man in *Luke's* parable of the Samaritan, half-alive, half-dead. While her frame was constantly thinning, her feet were distended by venous edema.

Had she been bedridden much longer, she might well have died of a pulmonary embolism, the edema serving to warn of a possible thrombosis in her legs, a risk run by patients immobilized in bed for lengthy periods. Another consequence of this confinement was the development of decubitus ulcers, more commonly known as bed sores. As though her skin had not been abused enough by the vesicatories and red-hot lancets, Thérèse had ischemic necrosis; already emaciated, she had too little subcutaneous fat to relieve the pressure on her vascular system. Her sacrum, or lower back, was especially vulnerable. While she was being gnawed within, the skin of her back was beginning to appear gangrenous, gradually rubbed down to expose connective tissues. The resultant ulcers were subject to infection and could have induced septicemia. In that time, there was no such thing as physiotherapy for terminally ill patients and Thérèse had reached a point of such debilitation that she could not have profited from the exercise of it. Intravenous feeding would have checked to some degree her emaciation, however, and that would have given her some strength to move in bed and sustain enough fat tissue to reduce the likelihood of bed sores. In the event, too weak to turn herself, she was subject to a kind of assault from the gentle hands of her sister Céline. Céline, and anyone else, pained her simply by touching her.

La Néele told her that she was so close to the end that she might die while turning in bed. As he was visiting her only four times and within the last two months of her life, his remarks were unsparingly frank. He sensed accurately that she preferred no equivocation. De Cornière, on the other hand, continued to vacillate; at least that is how she read his consternation on seeing her after he returned from his vacation. It is likely only he that she means in this plural: "Ils disent et dédisent!" ["They say and un-say!"].[69] She might not have told him that by this time even her weeping brought physical suffering.

La Néele occasioned a remark which shows how far Thérèse had come in her spirituality of acceptance. She did not care whether she lived or died, but after he had predicted for some unknown reason that she would have no death struggle, Pauline asked her whether she would choose to have one or not: "Je ne choisirais rien!" ["I would choose neither of them!"].[70] Although she said a week later that she seemed to be always in a death struggle, she had moved away from choice, from the assertive will altogether, to an almost serenely concessive one, an unwill due not only to the enforced recumbency of her illness but to what it had given to her most inwardly. She called it "une paix étonnante," an amazing peace.

De Cornière told Gonzague that till now he had never seen the face of a tubercular patient unaltered by pain—yet Céline says that even in August Thérèse was "pâle et défigurée par la souffrance" ["pale and disfigured by the suffering"][71]—but when he indirectly commended Thérèse for "héroïque patience," she scoffed: "C'est mentir! Je ne cesse de gémir, je soupire, je crie tout le temps: 'Oh! la la!' Et puis: 'Mon Dieu, je n'en puis plus! Ayez pitié de moi!' " ["That's a lie. I don't stop groaning, sighing, and crying out all the time, 'Oh, la la!' And then: 'My God, I can't go on! Have pity on me!' "].[72] After de Cornière's last visit, on September 24, she admitted to Pauline: "J'avais envie de dire à M. de Cornière: Je ris parce que vous n'avez tout de même pas pu m'empêcher d'aller au Ciel; mais, pour votre peine, quand j'y serai je vous empêchera d'y aller de si tôt" ["I felt like telling M. de Cornière, I'm smiling because you've all the same been unable to keep me from going heavenward, but for your pains, when I'm there, I'll keep you from arriving there very soon"]. She kept her word: he lived another twenty-five years and was over eighty when he died.

With shortness of breath came a raucous noise described by her sisters as a *râle*, but it was not yet a death rattle (a sound which comes only when the body shuts down with death). Her hands were trembling with fever and her face was bathed with sweat. It is amazing that on the last day of her life, September 30, 1897, she was able to sit up in her bed.

Pauline's descriptive notes on Thérèse's final appearance, after she had gasped out her love of God in an apostrophe, invite comparison of her with Teresa of Avila in the ecstasy depicted by Bernini: "Elle faisait certains beaux mouvements de tête, comme si Quelqu'un l'eût divinement blessée d'une flèche d'amour, puis retiré la flèche pour la blesser encore" ["Her head made some lovely motions, as if Someone had divinely wounded her with an arrow of love, then withdrawn the arrow to wound her again"].[73] Far more gripping than this transparently hagiographic, not to say derivative, account is the phenomenon of her sudden resurgence of strength in her last hours. After all of her pain, with her right lung gone and her left barely functioning, with her intestines turned to morbid cheese, she must have astounded her sisters by saying that she thought she wouldn't die yet, but had months or years still to live: "Voyez, ce que j'ai de force aujourd'hui! Non, je ne vais pas mourir!" ["See, what strength I've got today! No, I'm not going to die!"]. Anyone familiar with *La Traviata* will recall Violetta's ecstatic delusion of rebirth to life immediately before she dies.

To corroborate Pauline's hallowing record of Thérèse's death, we have Céline's last photo of her, taken as soon as she was girded with flowers (see figure 7.4). The composure is incontestable, but the serenity registers the effects of a common biological mechanism of death, the rush of adrenalin which brings vasoconstriction and an increased heart rate, even as blood flows away from inessential sites. This process amounts to the body's terminal gesture toward restoration of its normal physiological condition.

Thérèse's ethereal demise was not exceptional, or so the closing passage of *Renée Mauperin* suggests. It was based upon the Goncourts' numerous observations of tubercular deaths. "En quelques minutes, la maladie, les signes et l'anxiété de la souffrance s'étaient effacés sur la figure amaigrie de Renée. Une beauté d'extase et de suprême délivrance. . . . La douceur, la paix d'un ravissement était descendue sur elle. Un rêve semblait mollement renverser sa tête sur les oreillers. Ses yeux grands ouverts, tournés en haut, paraissaient s'emplir d'infini, son regard, peu à peu, prenait la fixité des choses éternelles" ["In a few minutes, the sickness, the signs and the anxiety of suffering had vanished from Renée's thinned face. A beautiful ecstasy, a final deliverance. . . The sweetness and peace of a ravishing came down upon her. A dream seemed to be gently turning back her head upon her pillows.

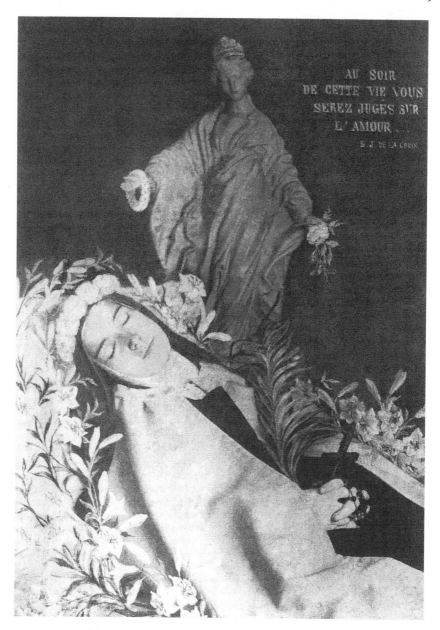

FIGURE 7.4. Thérèse on October 1, 1897. Copyright Office Central de Lisieux.

Her large eyes, open, turned on high, seemed filled with the infinite as her look gradually became fixed upon eternal things"].[74] All of this could have been recorded about Thérèse—and countless other victims of tuberculosis. Her signal difference from those others remains apparent in her perceptions and in the struggle which reduced her will to a kind of majestic nullity.

Like most other corpses, hers began to decompose almost immediately. The sometimes bruited view that Thérèse died "uncorrupted" or otherwise intact can only be dismissed as a hapless fiction, one that pays no regard to the medical and physiological facts about her last eighteen months. Suffering stripped her down to a bareness which affords final sense to the all, the *tout* she had offered of herself.

Upon her death, all of the fabrics on the infirmary bed were promptly burned.

8

Perfecta Caritas

Notes for a Theology of Thérèse

Je ne crois pas à la vie éternelle, il me semble après cette vie mortelle il n'y a plus rien…Tout a disparu pour moi, il ne me reste plus que l'amour [I don't believe in eternal life. It seems to me that after this mortal life, there's nothing more.…Everything has disappeared for me, and only love remains to me].

> —Cited by Sr. Thérèse de Saint-Augustin,
> *Souvenirs d'une sainte amitié,* 1898

[S]on langage n'était pas celui de la foi qui espère mais de l'amour qui possède [His language was not that of faith which hopes but of love which possesses].

> —To Mme. Guérin, July 20, 1895

Je ne suis réellement que ce que le bon Dieu pense de moi [I'm really only what the good Lord thinks of me].

> —Cited by Sr. Geneviève de la Sainte-Face,
> *Conseils et souvenirs,* 1952

L'Amour, voilà l'ineffable mystère qui t'exila du Céleste Séjour [Love, that's the ineffable mystery which keeps you in exile from the Heavenly Realm].

> —Thérèse de l'Enfant-Jésus de la Sainte-Face,
> *La Rosée Divine, ou Le Lait Virginal de Marie*

Among the Saints

Thérèse of Lisieux became a doctor of the church in the centenary year of her death, 1997. She stands with only two other women in this position: Teresa of Avila, so declared in 1970 with Catherine of Siena. Of men, there are thirty doctors. The criteria for this exalting appointment center upon writings that reflect profound learning and deep sanctity so as to instruct the faithful in every generation.

Within only a few years of her death, Thérèse had her share of acknowledged sanctity. Even the pope, Pius X, called her a saint. But profound learning? She could lay no claim to an education in patristics nor in systematic theology. She did not command Latin. Her formal learning had been limited, interrupted by sickness and terminated by her entry into Carmel. Neither could she claim initiation into reaches far greater than the human and intellectual: the mystical life with Christ. Teresa of Avila set down exuberant versions of that life in her autobiography. Neither had Thérèse received the several supernatural gifts granted to Catherine of Siena: a spiritual betrothal to Christ proclaimed to her by himself, levitations, miraculous healings, even a trancelike viewing of heaven, purgatory, and hell.

Thérèse not only did not have a mystical life of that sort; she expressly did not want its ecstasies and visions. She had an ironic disdain of "nos belles pensées, nos oeuvres éclatantes" ["our pretty thoughts, our flashy works"]. If Christ wanted those things, she says equably, he could get them from angels. "Il ne s'est fait la fleur des champs qu'afin de nous montrer combien il chérit la simplicité" ["He became the flower of the field only to show us how he cherishes simplicity"] (LT 141). Her little way virtually precluded the spectacles of mystical life because, while she knew that a mystical initiation might be fake, a real one was inaccessible to most people. Love for God does not require the eloquence of the intellectually embroidered Spanish masters, San Juan de la Cruz and the *fondatrice* herself, whom French theologians call "la grande Thérèse."

These cautions might suggest a certain anti-intellectualism, but they derive from Thérèse's own experiential world, nothing of which, including the smile from the Virgin's statue, finally imposes itself as mystical in the grand old Spanish way nor in any way. She was consistent in carrying over her nonmystical perspective into her training of novices: they should neither seek nor desire visions, and she cautioned them to expect no miraculous signs after her own death. She remembered the disappointing post mortem of Mère Geneviève.

It could be argued that the absence of mystical theater from her life, her ordinariness and obscurity, formed much of her sudden and extraordinary appeal. Is she not the saint of the average person, of the sort Vita Sackville-West snootily dismissed as "lowbrow"? If so, how can she then be measured into the company of such formidable minds as those of Augustine and Jerome, Chrysostom and Bede, Bernard of Clairvaux, Bonaventura and Thomas Aquinas? How can her name be summoned in any discussions of Teresa and Catherine? If Thérèse exerts a kind of democratic appeal, an accessibility which so plainly, if only partially, derives from the absence in her of the high aristocracy of ecclesiastical intellect, then what sort of learning has the Church found in her and left us to look for?[1]

Before examining Thérèse's stature as a theologian, or rather as someone from whom a theology can be derived (not the same thing), it might be helpful to consider the case made against sainthood altogether as an enterprise. A plaintiff in this regard, and one still modern after one hundred years, is William James, whose *Varieties of Religious Experience* weighs in heavily against the saintly exclusivity of devotion to God along with the attendant excruciations of asceticism. The neologism James provides us for this slanting is theopathy: one becomes literally crazy about God. His exemplar is the rigorously abstemious Jesuit St. Louis de Gonzaga, "a type of excess in purification," who forbade himself all contact with women and was uncomfortable even in the presence of his mother, to whom he sent letters as from a spiritual director to a novice. James scores Louis, who died at twenty-nine, for his indifference to the world and to issues of what James rather quaintly calls "social righteousness." In sum, the god of this youth was small. Characteristically gentlemanly in tone and judicious in assessments, James proves unsparing in this instance: "when the intellect, as in this Louis, is originally no larger than a pin's head, and cherishes ideas of God of corresponding smallness, the result, notwithstanding the heroism put forth, is on the whole repulsive.... better that a life should contract many a dirt-mark, than forfeit usefulness in its efforts to remain unspotted."[2]

Even though James recognizes the exemplary value of sainthood—"the saintly group of qualities is indispensable to the world's welfare" and "let us be saints, then, if we can"[3]—his skepticism about its intellectual value within the narrowness of theopathy should make us approach Thérèse with caution. Not that she was deficient in intelligence but that she used it within a strait channel. If that be so, then the formidable Spanish mystics cannot be reckoned any bit superior to Thérèse in their intellectual compass, no matter what "highbrow" ratings such people as Sackville-West might hand out to them.

Is that, however, a fair charge: a narrowly used mind? If, as Bonhoeffer insists,[4] one's love of God is indissolubly linked to one's love of the human species, so that it is impossible truly to claim either love without the other, then the theopathic Louis de Gonzaga remains the cautionary profile James saw: it is impossible to shun humanity or any portion of it (women) in pursuit of the divine. Where, then, does Thérèse stand? Was she a victim of theopathy? Her theology, if not her busy theologians, will tell and chiefly through the great dynamo of her affective life, *l'amour*.

Giving Her Self Up

Of the many avenues into a theology out of Thérèse, one of the most substantial, if inconspicuous, lies paved in a poem she wrote in May 1897. The title itself serves as a summing up, "L'Abandon est le fruit délicieux de l'Amour" ["*Abandon* Is Love's Delicious Fruit"]. *Abandon* in the theresian context does not denote abdication through lassitude or wearying of the will nor concession to the inevitable. Rather, it signals an affirmative acceptance of the divine will, the glad, even eager submission of a self-humbling soul to what is immeasurably greater than any human consequence.

When we speak of being resigned to the inevitable, to "fate," it often concerns something dire which has happened or is about to, such as a close relative's sudden death or the course of a terminal illness. There is no point in fighting an insuperable fact. Thérèse's attitude is nowhere proximate to this kind of resignation. As her poem reveals, *abandon* can properly be only the effect of recognizing divine love at work not least, in fact at times most vividly, in the midst of adversity. As an *imitatio Christi*, it takes impetus from Christ's words at Gethsemane, "Not my will but thine be done." Hence, the Latin word for *abandon*: *simplicitas*, a dissolution of willfulness in the self so as to live (or die) in conformity with the divine will.

Most striking in this poem, the guiding image unfolding from the first metaphor gives us the tree of divine love, its roots in the celestial life, so that the foliage and fruit are implicitly growing down into this world for our savoring.[5] The poet rejoices in its heavenly scent, a treasure to touch and to taste. Remarkably, for all that, it is the aftertaste which counts, but then she shifts the metaphor for *abandon* abruptly:

> Il me donne en ce monde
> Un océan de paix
> En cette paix profonde
> Je repose à jamais

["It gives me in this world an ocean of peace; in this profound peace, I rest forever"].

As I have noted, in other poems, Thérèse does not exert any deft and deepening control over her imagery. She wanders freely here, turning to the daisy opening before the sun whose heavenly ray causes a perfect *abandon* to be born in her soul.[6] The capacity for spiritual acceptance, including its affirmative joy in complicity with divine will, comes as a grace. *Abandon* betokens

God's working through the soul, and so it is at the furthest possible remove from the inertness it might superficially suggest.

What compels theological attention in this poem is its restrictive scope, not of images but of dramatic effect, that the *abandon* confers an everlasting peace *in this world alone*. The soul, in assuming *abandon*, countenances abandonment as well, Christ's desertion within this life, even though the soul has proclaimed its devoted and continuing love for him.

> Et si tu me délaisses
> O mon Divin Trésor
> Privée de tes caresses
> Je veux sourire encor.

["And if you desert me, O my Divine Treasure, bereft of your caresses, I want to smile still."] The "if" becomes a "when" in order for the soul to proclaim a trust in its own agency:

> Non, rien ne m'inquiète
> Rien ne peut me troubler
> Plus haut que l'alouette
> Mon âme sait voler.

["No, nothing disturbs me nor can trouble me. My soul knows how to fly higher than a lark."]

Such is the peculiar physics of Thérèse's sensibility, her perception and response to what she took to be the truth, that while she had long cultivated *abandon* as a supreme deference to the divine will and a ready acceptance of it, she sustained within her that confident thrust in her own will, an appropriative élan, which in her infancy had claimed everything. Like Rousseau, she occupied extremes and did not attempt the middle ground between them. Likely few other saints in the Church's history have plumbed so thoroughly as she the message Christ gave to his puzzled disciples, that the last shall be first.

Theresian humility, the unquestioning, almost supine posture before the greatest calamity of her life, the loss of heaven, fed ravenously on the Christian paradox of being last, so last that she was in effect destitute. She occupied the interior of the vault, was astray in the fog, and when she fed at the table of sinners she remembered to insert above her statement about it the word "seule," with no one else. *Abandon* entailed implicit abandonment, as her poem on its "delicious fruit" anticipates. Here she pushes herself to the limit of human endurance and credibility. A biblical analogue comes not from the New but the Old Testament, when Job says to God, "Though he slay me, yet will I trust in him."[7] And the voluntarist conclusion to that verse is Thérèse to the life: "but I will maintain mine own ways before him." So she does, assigning to herself the upsurgent lark's wings, as though she could fly into the heavens by her own power.

Perhaps the most engaging aspect of Thérèse's spirituality lies here, in this ongoing and unresolved tension between the noble acquiescence of *abandon*, a consummate loving toward God no matter what the cost to herself, and her never quite inactive voluntarism, a primal assertiveness of will which was integral to her character from the first years. It deeply informs her attitude toward Christ. Often, she seeks in him the sustaining comfort of the Solomonic spouse. She also seeks to hide herself away in him, matching his own hiddenness from the world's scorn with her infinitesimal self. She even imagines being so hidden that, although it would be impossible, God would not know her suffering, and she would be happy, still (C 7r). It would not matter if God did not know her benefactions came from her; her love would take such delight in pleasing him.[8] And yet, as though the history of self she recorded in Manuscript B was not quite finished, she also wants to face that world in the chivalric crusader/priest/martyr spirit she identified with Jeanne d'Arc: "Je veux t'aimer comme un petit enfant, Je veux lutter comme un guerrier vaillant" ["I want to love you as a tiny child, I want to fight like a valiant warrior"] (PN 36). In those two lines, the often-cited boldness, the *audace*, of her temperament is exquisitely condensed.

These opposites or contraries, the child and the unisexually worthy spouse, provide the dynamism in Thérèse's writings. They should not be rationalized, the one to the exclusion of the other, as though either could be suppressed by or subordinated to the other. Both served as active forces within her personality and thought, for even though her *abandon* may seem limp and passive, it is a continuously affirmative yielding to whatever God would bring, be it an indefinite living on in suffering, be it death on the morrow. It is a hidden, furtive responsiveness. On the other hand, had Thérèse lost her assertiveness, her confident urges to role casting for herself and others, she would have become unrecognizable to us and even, I suspect, to God.[9]

Clichéd though it may be, Thérèse's "Oui, je veux passer mon Ciel à faire du bien sur la terre" ["Yes, I want to spend my Heaven doing good on earth"][10] succinctly catches both the *abandon* and the voluntarist impulse which complements it. The latter is obvious: it will be *her* heaven, spent not among the blessed, not among her beloved family and all the saints but here, on terra firma. She makes the request to God, confident that her wish will be fulfilled as she has always believed that no wish for the good could be idle, coming as it does from a divine source. If she has a wish, God has planted it in her, and it was meant to be fulfilled.

Far less obvious is the *abandon*. Her choice of the oxymoronic earthly heaven as her own hereafter emerges as the terminus of her accepting the closing off of heaven. If she were not to regain the sense of heaven which had always been vividly intuitive to her and if that meant she was not certain nor confident of securing it, then, so be it; she would improvise with what God had left her, this sorry and beloved earth. In creedal terms, without the communion of saints and the celestial life known as the world to come, she would make do in the world she did know, one in whose suffering she had been schooled and with which she knew how to deal. In a moment worthy of Kierkegaard, she remarked that she could not imagine dwelling in heaven, a place without suffering, because it was inconceivable to her that she would then no longer be able to save souls. It is a telling remark, as she does not mention that heaven was sealed off to her, anyway.

Her strongest resource lay in her predisposition (a gene from Louis?) to look for the good in anyone and anything, rather than its opposite. She enjoined her novices to dwell upon the good in those sisters they found objectionable or reproachful. She applied herself thus to the closing off of heaven: "Si je n'ai que la pure souffrance, le ciel est tellement noir que je ne vois aucune éclaircie, eh bien! J'en fais ma joie. . . . j'en fais jabot . . . ! comme des épreuves de papa qui me rendent plus glorieuse qu'une reine" ["If I have only pure suffering and heaven is so black for me that I see no clearing of the clouds, oh well! I make of it my joy. . . . I preen, even as with Papa's trials, which make me more glorious than a queen"].[11]

Thérèse's *abandon*, in short, matured into a shrewd empiricism, a remarkable ripening of spirituality for someone dying so young and so dispossessed. There can be no point in minimizing or denying this extraordinarily resourceful gambit, the acceptance of a destiny few Christians would dare to countenance, the absence of heaven, in tandem with the trumping beneficence of her resolve to dwell among those well short of celestial bliss. That wretched company included the wicked, the blasphemers, the nonbelievers, sinners—all of whom she acknowledged as her brothers. Indeed, she could imagine herself as both their sister and as their unflaggingly loving mother. This position within suffering was, as she told Céline, vital to her because only suffering could make the soul truly childlike,[12] an emphasis which, incidentally, keeps Thérèse from the accusation of a rosy infantilism.

If Thérèse was to be denied the creedal substance of faith and the elementary predicates of hope, she still had within her the vibrant power which had animated her all her life, and that was love. Her acceptance of the vault attests her love of God; her taking on a mission to attend the suffering of others attests her love of humankind. In that attentiveness, she eludes the fatal charge of theopathy which James brought to the bar against St. Louis de Gonzaga.[13]

Doing without Hell, Purgatory, . . . and Heaven

Thérèse did not become indifferent to creedal faith and hope and certainly did not feel herself an infidel or hopeless but the vaulting and the fog brought her into a state of consciousness in which these virtues were not operant. The more she attempted to believe and to hope, the more vain did faith and hope become. She learned she could not will them. She tells us so explicitly, and dodging that primordial fact can only hinder the possibility of a judicious appreciation of her darkness and her coping.

This point demands iteration through her own words and their emphases to Mère Gonzague: "Lorsque je chante le bonheur du Ciel, l'éternelle possession de Dieu, je n'en ressens aucune joie, car je chante simplement ce que *je veux croire*. Parfois il est vrai, un petit rayon de soleil vient illuminer mes ténèbres, alors l'épreuve cesse *un instant*, mais ensuite le souvenir de ce rayon au lieu de me causer de la joie rend mes ténèbres plus épaisses encore" ["When I sing the happiness of Heaven, the eternal possession of God, I feel no joy in it. In fact, I'm simply singing what *I want to believe*. Sometimes, it's true, a little ray of sun comes to enlighten my shadows and then the testing stops *for a moment*, but then the memory of that ray instead of causing me joy makes my shadows even thicker"] (C 7v). It seems convenient for some commentators to suppose that wanting to believe is tantamount to believing, but Thérèse could not be more emphatic that that is not the case for her. She was being brought up against her own willing in this *épreuve* and tamed into a submission, a kind of *abandon* she had never experienced. What kept her going was her love of the truth. In time that love shaped an explicit preference for shadows over a light which she sensed was a will-o'-the-wisp. Once she accepted that her inherited and unreflected notion called heaven was a void, she let it drop.

Her equanimity in this central matter of faith and hope can only amaze believers and nonbelievers alike, because she did not attempt to contrive or imagine some other realm. When she told Sr. Saint-Augustin that she did not believe in heaven, she was not in despair nor in hysterics. She had learned to read God's testing of her. She could go on loving God even if all thought of heaven and its delights were taken from her. She had, besides, not believed in hell, either: it did not comport with her total assurance that God, inexhaustibly loving, would not consign his creatures to eternal torments. To believers who insisted upon the damnation of the wicked, she might have answered that they were limiting God's compassion. What, then, of divine justice à la Dante? For her, divine love was itself justice.

Unlike many sisters known to her in the *circulaires*, she did not dwell upon purgatory because it prompted fear and apprehension even among the most pious, a kind of recoiling from *confiance*, the trust in God's love. As though to countervail such dread, she showed in her writing and speaking a refreshing insouciance about purgatory, even to the wish that she could spring all of its souls (A 77; LT 74). Yet, she also took inspiration from Madre Teresa's saying she would remain in purgatory till time's end if her prayers could save a single soul (LT 221). As to her own occupancy there, Thérèse remained unperturbed, figuring that like Shadrach, Mishach, and Abednego, she would walk about in the flames but would also sing the canticle of love.[14] A definitive statement comes at the end of her first manuscript: "les âmes saintes peuvent seules y avoir accès, mais je sais que le Feu de l'Amour est plus sanctifiant que celui de purgatoire" ["only the saintly souls can have access to purgatory but I know that the Fire of Love is more sanctifying than that of purgatory"] (A 84v). Besides, purification belongs to this life. That was the point of her *offrande*, to be consumed by a divinely compassionate fire.

I suspect that Thérèse stopped crediting heaven for the same reason that she could never credit hell and purgatory, because they were all constructs of human projection, a kind of eschatological real estate imposed upon God. Hell was abhorrent to her because it was privative, a denial not of humanity but of divinity. So, too, heaven, because it was exclusive of those whom she took on with her sororal and maternal solicitude, the wicked and lost. Perhaps she learned to apply the logic of the last becoming first in a new way: not on a scale of humility, with the most humble getting the first seat, but on a moral scale. Those who love God least would have the furthest to go, would have to have eaten the bitterest bread. She stationed herself at their table for that particular eucharist. She ate the bread there but for her alone it did not taste of the bitterness which came in rejecting God's love.

So she came to perform a role which she had imagined for herself almost two years before: "Un soir ne sachant comment dire à Jésus que je l'aimais et combien je désirais qu'Il soit partout aimé et glorifiée, je pensais avec douleur qu'il ne pourrait jamais recevoir en enfer un seul acte d'amour, alors je dis au Bon Dieu que pour lui faire plaisir je consentirais bien à m'y voir plongée, afin qu'il soit aimé éternellement dans ce lieu de blasphème" ["One evening, not knowing how to tell Jesus that I loved him and wanted him to be everywhere loved and glorified, I thought with pain that he could never receive a single gesture of love in hell and then I told the Good Lord that to please him I'd consent to be plunged into it so that he'd be loved forever in this place of blasphemy"] (A 52r). What she did not know then but learned in her darkness was that hell is lived by many upon this earth, in this life. And she would join them.

Without Faith, without Hope

It is possible to argue from her own writing that stipulatory, creedal faith and hope were never so ripened in Thérèse as to matter to her as love did. It was love which bound her to her parents and siblings, and she exerted its affective power in creating the infantile Jesus for her childhood's favor. The predicates of faith she knew by catechismic rote but her immaturity did not assimilate them and make them her own in either childhood or adolescence. It is instructive that a retreat director told her to write out the Credo as a way of containing the suffering of her *épreuves*.[15] The reason that creeds did not weigh decisively with her is evident: she adhered steadfastly to the source from which they had been drawn, the Gospels, which in their incomparable narrative power retained an almost exclusive hold upon her attention. An inveterate storyteller herself, she found that the narrative power of the New Testament sufficed.

She applied the same economy to the tradition of saints' lives. As she had no interest in mystical visions and raptures, her little way to some degree confounds such extravagance. She had no interest in public shows of cult worship, preferring the intimate and small scale: not the ecclesial but the hymeneal. Consider this exclusivity, admitted to Céline: "Tu sais, moi je ne vois pas le Sacré Coeur comme tout le monde, je pense que le coeur de mon époux est à moi seul comme le mien est à lui seul et je lui parle alors dans la solitude de ce délicieux coeur à coeur" ["You know, me, I don't see the Sacred Heart as everybody else does, I think that my groom's heart is mine alone as mine is his alone and I speak to him then in the solitude of this savory heart to heart"] (LT 122). She so trusted her own spontaneity that she was not perturbed when, exhausted by cold sleepless nights, she dozed off in the midst of morning prayers. She was challenged by the mantra of the rosary, even admitting self-astonishment at her apparent lack of devotion in getting through it. Yet, toward the end, she was hopeful that Mary, her beloved mother, was content with her good intention.

In just a few lines closing her first manuscript, and before the onset of her testing, she almost collapses dogmatic tradition: "c'est par-dessus tout l'Évangile qui m'entretient pendant mes oraisons, en lui je trouve tout ce qui est nécessaire à ma pauvre petite âme ... Jésus n'a point besoin de livres ni de docteurs pour instruire les âmes, il enseigne sans bruit de paroles.... Jamais je ne l'ai entendu parler, mais je sens qu'Il est en moi, à chaque instant, Il me guide, m'inspire ce que je dois dire ou faire" ["it's above all the Gospel which engages me during my prayers; in it I find all that's necessary to my poor soul.... Jesus doesn't need books nor learned people to instruct souls, he teaches without the noise of words.... I've never heard him speak but I feel he's in me. At every moment he guides me, inspires me to what I must say or do"] (A 83v). In these startling words, for which the *Imitatio* itself had given her the cue,[16] the historical complex of creeds, council statements, theologies, and decrees seems to fade before a radical intimacy with Jesus. What else does or can Christianity mean but the person of Christ?

This intimacy, a kind of Christ-in-me such as that of which St. Paul writes, was the subjective or voluntarist side of faith, and it was to that that Thérèse gave primacy. This is Lutheran territory, but the difference between Luther and Thérèse lies in the absence of atonement in her thought and disposition. So intimate did she feel with Jesus, she did not sense the need for his reconciling power. Calvary meant for her not the sacrificial act of recon-ciliation with God (from whom she had never felt alienated) but the terminal suffering of her beloved, which she met with a sister's or mother's supremely feminine impulse to assuage and relieve suffering. The child whose toy she had long been was himself broken and abandoned at Calvary.

Neither the objective faith of creeds nor the subjective faith of self-investment in the atonement seem relevant to Thérèse. Her loving trust in Jesus was too deep to require either, but it warrants conjecture as to why conventional faith did not exert its hold upon her. In the creeds, Christ is set at a remove from "we believe." He entered history and shall come again to judge the living and the dead. His kingdom shall have no end. This Christ, even so, is transcendent. Thérèse's Christ, always Jesus, is immanent and abiding in her writing. We might even infer a certain impatience in her with the belief in a Second Coming since Jesus is always present to her. Faith and hope, like Sacred Heart processions, form collectivist expressions of need but love possesses the object of faith and hope, even when that object, Jesus, is absent. For Thérèse, that absence was signaled by her Gospel-based image of his sleeping in a boat during a storm; but it was her storm, her boat. None of the creedal props sustain the intimacy with Jesus which serves as her keynote, and the hiddenness of that intimacy precludes the communal setting, ex-pectation, and chanted responsiveness which the creeds provide.

Hope for its part is predicated upon distance. One is separated from what one wants or needs. Thérèse had always known the rhetoric of exile which predisposes the believer toward heaven, and she located its rewards, her parents, and her siblings within the postexilic realm. Heaven meant, as it does still for countless Christians, a family reunion. It had a vivid substance within the everlasting peace of the divine. When Thérèse came to sense the non-existence of heaven, she did not sink into depression or sullen grief, as almost anyone else would have. Ever resourceful, she affirmed the more vehemently her love as the apprehension of Jesus' earthly presence.

In her poem on *abandon* she underscores this now crucial centrality of love:

> En paix je veux attendre
> Doux Jésus, ton retour
> Et sans jamais suspendre
> Mes cantiques d'amour.

["In peace I want to await, sweet Jesus, your return and never stop even for a while my canticles of love."]

Those lines carry no apostrophe to Jesus, as though he were far away; it is clear that he remains immediate to her consciousness, held there by the Solomonic song. Thérèse had made the revolutionary discovery that love binds the divine to the soul, so that even the absence of the divine, the desertion of the soul by Christ himself, can be overcome.[17] Desire marks the presence of an absence. That is the supreme voluntarism of love, its unceasing re-creation of the beloved in the lover's consciousness. The mother of a dead child would not cease to love that child. In Thérèse's ripened love, the supernatural act of the Spirit working through her made her the agent of love for God, pure because uncircumscribed by the human needinesses of faith and hope. The pneumatological character of her *confiance*, an unshakable confidence which seems synonymous with her love, is worthy of theological pondering. Thérèse has been tagged a ruse of the Holy Spirit, perhaps because she has no business with systematics nor dogmatics but only with what Pope John Paul II called "living theology."

That she could even countenance a life without faith and hope is clear from the exclusive and positive construction she put upon love when she told Pauline of her Augustinian moment at the belvedere of Les Buissonnets, an ecstatic moment she had shared with Céline in the summer of 1887. At age fourteen, Thérèse imagined, so she writes, the earthly presence of Christ: "Le doute n'était pas possible, *déjà la Foi et l'Espérance n'étaient plus nécessaires, l'amour* nous faisait trouver sur la terre Celui que nous cherchions" ["Doubt was not possible, *Faith and Hope were no longer necessary, love* made us find on earth Him whom we were seeking"] (A 48r; my emphasis). Such earthboundness seems premonitory. At the time of writing that remembrance, Thérèse was only months away from the descent of spiritual night. But the accent in this passage is affirmative and revelatory: with the sense of Christ's presence here and now, faith and hope appear almost nugatory. At best, one might liken them to the booster stages of a rocket which, at a point rendering them unnecessary, fall away (are faith and hope to be found in heaven?), but it would be amiss to assume that they had ever had any real primacy before love in Thérèse's life. From her earliest years, the supreme vigor lay in her loving and in being loved. Put in that brightest of lights, faith and hope are simply but mightily outshone by love. That is where her audacity might well become nonnegotiable. Would it be best not to ponder it?

So Thérèse had revealed (or retrojected in her writing) an eclipse of faith and hope well before these mainstays of Christian life disappeared into the void where that vault was framed and that fog suspended. The sufficiency of love so confidently uttered from the belvedere and from adolescence was fiercely tested and found solid by the subtraction of heaven ten years later. Faced with Christ's apparent desertion, Thérèse's poetic voice nowhere indicates the language of faith and hope but abides in love's intuitive certainties. For proof on this matter, the Cerf concordance of her complete works shows that *foi* and *espérance* enjoy embarrassingly meager entries (57 and 38 times, respectively) compared with the overwhelming predominance of *amour* (756). Her diction tells us that love was not the keystone in her life's arch: it was the arch itself.

What to make of this disconcerting fact? People do not misplace faith or hope; they are taken away, usually by circumstances or perspectives not chosen but imposed. Those who are shattered by the death of someone close or staggered by some catastrophic event have been taken out of their faith, deprived of hope, or so they feel and thus they are. Anyone can adduce instances of such a falling off.[18] Others are overwhelmed by the lure of worldly indifference. Christ's parable of the four seedings covers this ground.

Thérèse's case is altogether her own: she was tested by long bouts of scruples from early adolescence, by the humbling loss of her father to an asylum, by a furtive and capricious disease, and tested most keenly during her last eighteen months. Her survival by a love so intense and assured as to endure without the sustenance of hope and the bolstering of faith could not possibly serve as normative. Neither would she ever have wanted it to become so, and yet *la petite voie* and *l'épreuve de l'amour*, the little way and the testing of love, are not only inseparable. They are identical.

Very few people come so tough. Paradoxically, although she is accessible to people in her earthbound, nonmystical, nonlevitational way, she is as remote from them by the austerities of her experience as if she had had visions and levitations. Thérèse with her roses of solicitous love is never depicted with the thorns of her suffering, the very condition by which her love thrived and grew. She treasured those thorns. The sharpest of them was the loss of heaven.

The Consolations of the Commentators

Even as the vaulting and the fog put her at an isolating remove from her Carmelite sisters, she continued to perform her office within the novitiate, not leaving the slightest intimation of the pervasive darkness within her. Manuscript C shows that Thérèse was *not* at the time of its writing afflicted with *sécheresse* or dryness, the absence of genuine religious fervor. It would be humanly impossible to be spiritually lively all or even most of the time. That even Thérèse herself had spells of dryness now and again is evident from her own hand. About the time of her father's breakdown and confinement, she wrote that "la sécheresse était mon pain quotidien" ["dryness was my daily bread"] (A 73v). Besides that spell, however, she admits that well before the onset of her tuberculosis she had been subject to doubting the existing of a celestial life. As far back as 1891, "J'avais alors de grandes épreuves intérieures de toutes sortes jusqu'à me demander parfois s'il y avait un Ciel" ["I had at the time great interior trials of all sorts to the point of asking myself sometimes if there was a Heaven"] (A 80v). The recurrences of this experience, however, indicate that she was able to recover herself, however fitfully, and to continue in faith and hope as well as in love.

All that granted, her writing suggests by the self-portraiture an ardent spirituality that knows how to overcome the self. We never catch her on the page having an off day of short temper or petulance. The act of writing seems to stand in as an act of faith. It becomes for her a means of self-assurance, albeit temporary, and a record of her steadfastness for others. On several poetic occasions, it is clear that she is writing more to herself than to the sister who had asked her for some verse. All of the poetry finally comes back to its author and is chiefly about her, even though certain overt statements about heaven, for example, are meant to uplift someone else. That is why her published apologists tend to give her darkness a bright lining, as though she had triumphed somehow and had vanquished it. They have been lulled into the very consolation which Thérèse was dispensing within the Carmel.

Their benevolent attempts to dress Thérèse in certifiably orthodox dress, to fit her upon the procrustean bed of piety, may be either out of a misplaced concern for the Church and Thérèse's legions of admirers—many of whom have known their own darkness—or, just as likely, out of an understandable hesitation to follow Thérèse into the darkness in which she ended her life.

Here, briefly, is a review of four chief commentators on Thérèse.

One of the foremost washers away is Jean-François Six, who poses one of the most adroit explanations of her testing time. His *Vie de Thérèse de Lisieux* (1975), though rambling and without an index, affords many useful passages on historical contexts and is abundant in insights. Six rightly claims that Thérèse's writings, especially her plays, were carrying to the Carmelite sisters the hidden and revolutionary message of God's loving compassion. He rightly claims that these sisters, had they learned of the depth of her darkness, would have likely presumed that she was rejected by God and thus damned. At the same time, he wishes to retain faith and hope for her. He asserts that her hope of heaven had simply been directed to earth, "c'est-à-dire non pas le souhait puéril d'une récompense plus tard, mais l'expérience de la foi sur terre, dès maintenant" ["that's to say it was not the childish wish for a payoff later on but the experience of faith on earth, from now"].[19] But it is exactly that reorientation which forms the other part of her revolutionary spirituality: it subtracts what for all conventional believers constitutes the whole impetus of faith and hope, namely, the celestial, supraterrestrial, and "puérile" payoff. It retains an intimate love of God and of humanity, which sets the high bar for Christian life.

Six correctly states that Thérèse discovered the otherness of materialism. In losing heaven, she could identify herself with nonbelievers and agnostics. She was delivered to the enveloping fog which they knew and had in some instances entered voluntarily, as did Renan, in willful unbelief. Six errs, however, in making the issue of belief and nonbelief purely voluntarist, that a human being has the power to deny or to affirm God according to will. Thérèse, it must be stressed, never reached the point of atheism or of agnosticism. Although heaven ceased to exist for her, she at no time expressly denied the existence of God and the immediacy of Christ in her life. But she also knew that one could not simply will a belief. Had it been so easy, she would have had no problem, but she learned that exertion on her part was bootless and she would fall back into a darkness made even more profound by her efforts. She knew the difference between will and grace; if she could not affirm heaven, could not profess faith, could not utter hope, it was because God had not given her the cue to do so, and she accepted that testing. Acceptance of the void was the greatest challenge to her love of God, and, as far as her writings and the *Derniers entretiens* tell, she met it.

Six is further mistaken when he tethers Thérèse to the view that human freedom to accept or to reject God constitutes human *grandeur*. He claims that the sometimes insistence of Christian faithful upon divine greatness and human smallness has prompted revolts which fashion the human to be great and the divine to be of no account, and that both extremes must be avoided. Well and good, but Thérèse's *petite voie* depended exactly upon that human littleness, insufficiency, and empty-handedness made totally deferential to God. No matter that she looked to divine love and spurned conventional notions of divine justice (hellfire and the like), God for her remained immeasurably great, and she never tried to exalt human wretchedness, languishing in indifference or atheism, into the Romantic mold of Promethean dignity or defiance.

Instead, she learned within her fog to consider spiritual strays as her kindred. She denominated herself their sister in characterizing her darkness with a prayer to Christ: "elle vous demande pardon pour ses frères, elle accepte de manger aussi longtemps que vous le voudrez le pain de la douleur et ne veut point se lever de cette table remplie d'amertume où mangent les pauvres pécheurs avant le jour que vous avez marqué" ["she asks of you forgiveness for her brothers, she agrees to eat for as long as you wish the bread of grief and she does not wish to rise from this table of bitterness where the poor sinners eat before the day you have appointed"] (C 6r).

Rather than glamorize atheism with fashionable posturing, she catches the despair in the "poor sinners" with whom she is eating by relating to Mère Gonzague a diabolical mockery, which she heard within herself: "tu rêves la possession *éternelle* du Créateur de toutes ces merveilles, tu crois sortir un jour des brouillards qui t'environnent, avance, avance, réjouis-toi de la mort qui te donnera non ce que tu espères, mais une nuit plus profonde encore, la nuit du néant" ["you're dreaming of the *everlasting* possession of the Creator of all these marvels, you believe you'll one day leave the fogs which surround you, advance, advance, rejoice in the death which will give you not what you hope for but a night still deeper yet, the night of nothingness"] (C 7v). Her confessor told her it was best that she not attempt to answer these voices.[20]

Instead, she drew upon Psalm 91 (92), rejoicing in divine works with the promise of glorying in them. Convinced that the darkness was God's work, that it had been appointed to her to suffer, she could affirm it. The *Imitatio* told her that all she was suffering, Christ was suffering with her, and if she could find that suffering sweet and love it for Christ's sake, she would find paradise on earth. That is the purport of what she wrote in a poem composed for Pauline:

> Lorsque le Ciel bleu devient sombre
> Et qu'il semble me délaisser
> Ma joie, c'est de rester dans l'ombre...
> J'aime autant la nuit que le jour

["When the blue Heaven darkens and seems to desert me, my joy is to remain in the shadows... I love the night as much as the day"] (PN 45, January 21, 1897). It remains a fearsome fact that Thérèse learned to welcome the void of faith and of hope. It is as well an indigestible fact.

Characteristic as well of a whitewashing approach is the discussion of Abbé Pierre Descouvemont, whose *Guide de Lecture* (1997) is a formidably comprehensive summary of Thérèse's thoughts and writings based on an ingathering of word frequencies. He notes her carrying on her person the Credo she wrote in her own blood on a page of her portable New Testament. Descouvemont takes that act as proof that she believed "de tout son coeur" ("with all her heart") in the existence of heaven. He seizes upon her admission to Mère Gonzague of having performed more acts of faith in the year since June 1896 than in all her previous life as more proof that she was "loin de douter" ["far from doubting"].[21] In fact, these actions, including the blood-writing, suggest the very opposite, that these were emergency measures meant to shore her up. Had she been secure in her faith and hope, she would not have needed such recourses. The little acts-of-faith recitation actually marks a recidivism to the pharisaical ledger keeping she had outgrown in her childhood, the difference now being that she could not possibly have assumed a pharisaic satisfaction because it was simply not there for her. Descouvemont is misled by the attempt, confounding it with a putative result.

He errs in assigning to her a conventional notion of hellfire, the Jansenist picnic for the damned: "Elle *croit*—sur la parole de Dieu, interprétée de façon authentique par l'Église—que l'enfer est un abîme dans lequel risquent de tomber tous les êtres humains, à commencer par elle-même" ["She *believes*—on the word of God, interpreted in authentic fashion by the Church—that hell is an abyss all human beings risk falling into, beginning with herself"].[22] That claim is highly dubious. No matter what she had been taught and had nominally accepted about damnation, Thérèse, as I have noted, implicitly rejected hell because it was incompatible with her exclusive attention to a loving God. The only abyss she recognized was one of love, and if she kept the imagery of a consuming fire, it was the conflagration not of punishment but of willing sacrifice. The abbé, mistaking her for gloomy sisters within her community and many other Carmels, has projected upon Thérèse a disfiguring orthodoxy which detracts from her luminous originality.

He makes a similar mistake with hope: "Elle *espère* de tout son coeur qu'en remettant sa liberté de créature fragile entre les mains de Jésus, son Sauveur, elle échappera à l'abîme" ["She *hopes* with all her heart that in entrusting the freedom of her fragile self to Jesus, her Savior, she will escape the abyss"].[23] This, too, strikes a false note. As the abbé concedes elsewhere in his *Guide*, the keynote of Thérèse's writing regarding Jesus is an ebullient confidence in their mutual love: his compassion, her devotion. If Thérèse conveys anything, it is a temerity which casts out the horrid scenario of the dark abyss by its almost sublime fearlessness. The abbé has scrounged around that abyss in order to find something he claims that she believed and hoped. These are not the proper predicates for someone who knew the future tense of love.

The abbé claims that Thérèse continued to believe in the existence of heaven by relying upon Christ's words, but Christ said that the kingdom of heaven is within oneself. It is not a spiritual roof garden. That inner kingdom seems to be what Thérèse affirms in one of the poems which make explicit her darkness. It was composed for one of her novices, Sr. Marie de la Trinité, when she took her vows on April 30, 1896, only a few weeks after the onset of Thérèse's continuous doubting. Its concessive tone must have startled the recipient:

> Je possède au moins sur la terre
> La vie Céleste de l'Amour . . .
> Mais par Amour je veux bien vivre
> Dans les Ténèbres de l'exil.

["At least on earth I possess the Celestial way of Love . . . But by Love I want to live in the Shadows of exile"] (PN 30, "Glose sur le Divin").

It should be clear by now that Thérèse's embrace of shadows, her love going to the extreme with suffering at its most extreme, was not masochism. Nothing could be more errant than attribution of such a psychopathology to her, appealing though that tactic might be to anyone seeking some point for detraction. Hers was never a love of suffering for its own sake. Neither, however, was it a means, as it was for Dostoevsky, of self-redemption, moral and spiritual, and thus both desirable and necessary, a kind of elective purgatory in this life.

Let us return for a moment to purgatory. No matter how firmly entrenched within Church doctrine since its invention by Augustine (*De Civitate Dei* XXI.13) and its formal profiling by the Council of Lyon (1274), it amounted to little more than an embarrassment for Thérèse. She gave it a nominal due but could not assimilate it to her intuitive grasp of a mercifully divine love. She was given signs that those she especially cherished, such as her father and the venerable Mère Geneviève, had upon their deaths skirted this sorrowful realm altogether. She remained at a vast remove from the most eminent Carmelite mystics, Teresa of Avila and San Juan de la Cruz (despite his substantial influence upon her understanding of love's suffering), because she was temperamentally and experientially alien to their purgative way of prayer, which required that one be acutely conscious of one's sins, acutely sorrowful for one's past, and acutely desirous of expiating all of one's offenses against God. Thérèse, not conscious of deep sins, could not grieve over a past nor seek to expiate for it. Suffering had been visited upon her by God's leave, not by a conscience riven with guilt or shame. Her very love of God could fairly be called a will bent upon pleasing God in advance, preemptively, and that is why her response to her own spiritual calamity is not only accepting but affirmative. She resolutely assumes a wholly concessive position, which is where her singular voluntarism and her no less singular *abandon* attain fruition, together as one.

The equipoise of those two forces within her are well depicted in our third reference. The Carmelite Emmanuel Renault has provided an excellent study, brief yet dense with allusions and insights, specifically on Thérèse's night of temptations. In *L'Épreuve de la foi: Le combat de Thérèse de Lisieux* (1974), he makes vital concessions about the limits to our understanding her within the dark tunnel. People who have been supremely tested set before us a final incomprehensibility; their suffering's profundity, recalling the Passion itself, leaves us with a humbling sense of mystery. Renault emphasizes that even (and especially) for the person undergoing that test there is mystery, an inscrutable politics with God, including the absence of God. Earthside in our own darkness, we who are engaged by the saintly can work only with the approximations of hypothesis. That concession, however, allows us to entertain the possibility that Thérèse lived finally more in doubt than in faith and hope, if in fact she had any hope and faith left. The imbalance would explain why she identified nonbelievers as her brothers. She had come to realize an existential community with people she had never known nor even seen: "des impies n'ayant pas la foi...pauvres incrédules" ["the impious having no faith...wretched unbelievers"] (C 6r, 5v). Thérèse perhaps makes the point best in comparing herself with St. Marguerite-Marie Alacoque, who had spoken of herself as a poor sinner, "pauvre pécheresse." What this saint had spoken in humility, wrote Thérèse to Bellière, she herself was "en *toute vérité*" (LT 224). Thérèse found that this recognition of sinfulness, the doubting of heaven, made her even more humble than before. In the company of atheists, materialists, spiritual desperadoes, she found that her little way had become even littler.

As to the possibility of love without faith—our key issue in this discussion—Renault asks whether a house can stand without a foundation. But we have only to turn to Thérèse again to find that she could make so tremendous a distinction as the following, less than two months before her death: "Oh! comme je sens que je me découragerais si je n'avais pas la foi! ou plutôt si je n'aimais pas le bon Dieu" ["Oh, how discouraged I'd be if I didn't have faith or rather if I didn't love God" (DE, August 4, 1897). A great deal weighs on how we interpret "or rather." To me, these little words are revelatory if taken to be concessive. A faith claim is what she could *not* seriously make. To have tried to make it would have been fraudulent and futile. Her craving for truth required a ruthless honesty about where the *épreuve* had led her.

Honesty and humility required each other. Thérèse gives perhaps the best formulation of her own littleness when in Manuscript C (2v) she compares the Church's saints to herself: they are as lofty mountains to a grain of sand under someone's passing foot. They have been exalted (by God), and she has been kept lower than low by her own inadequacy. Her point is that although alone, one is always helpless, that fragility must be experienced. Discussions of the little way invariably and rightly stress its humility but, ironic as it may seem, a covert triumphalism is left to be inferred unless the precariousness of that way is given its due.

Thérèse goes so far as to claim she is a nothing, but did this assertion serve as a stratagem for annihilating the sense of sin in her? Oddly, the reverse seems to be the intent. Her nothingness consisted in her having no merit, only imperfections. She says she rejoiced in them and was always eager to find new ones because they made her more dependent upon God. In this perception of spiritual poverty and helplessness, she boldly dismisses the usual claims of righteousness. As she wrote to Marie, in trying to explain what making oneself a sacrificial victim to divine love means, "plus on est faible, *sans désirs, ni vertus,* plus on est propre aux opérations de cet Amour consumant et transformant" ["the weaker one is, *with neither desires nor virtues,* the more one is fit for the workings of this consuming and transforming Love"] (LT 197, September 11, 1896; my emphasis). Being without desires and virtues seems unequivocally to signify the absence of the very perquisites of spiritual life, the comforts of faith and hope.

It might well be objected that Thérèse's *Acte d'Offrande* (June 9, 1895), in which she asked to become divine love's victim, was itself a gesture of faith and hope, but Thérèse herself, in the letter just cited, characterized the desire to please God as her "espérance aveugle," a blind rather than a creedal hope. As Fr. Renault concedes, her temerity in *abandon* came in giving her own immeasurable love to God without expectations of getting it back. To presume an outcome, a reward, was to betray the very notion of sacrifice.

It is on this point that the three Christian virtues part company. Contrary to the notion, promoted generations ago by the medievalist scholar Abbé

André Combes, that in Thérèse's inner life faith and hope enlighten love, and love perfected saves in turn faith and redeems hope—a convenient but too neat symmetry—Thérèse's extremity and exclusivity of love came from the extraordinary insight that one's imperfections, one's very sins ensure a dependence upon God such as righteousness cannot afford: "Oh! Que je suis heureuse de me voir imparfaite et d'avoir tant besoin de la miséricorde du bon Dieu" ["Oh, how happy I am to see myself imperfect and so much in need of God's mercy"].[24] The darkness within, the absence of faith and hope aimed heavenward, provided the fuel for transformation by divine love. As she put it in her poem "Glose sur le Divin":

> L'Amour, j'en ai l'expérience
> Du bien, du mal qu'il trouve en moi
> sait profiter (quelle puissance)
> Il transforme mon âme en soi.

["I have experience of Love's good, which knows how to profit from the evil in me (what power), transforming my soul into himself"] (PN 30, April 30, 1896). This insight marks her greatest debt to San Juan de la Cruz.

Perhaps the most scrupulous of Thérèse's modern interpreters is the Carmelite scholar Conrad de Meester. His study, *With Empty Hands: The Message of St. Thérèse of Lisieux* (2002), abounds with helpful insights and a courageous probing. (Unfortunately, it is the only one of the four books discussed here which has appeared in an English translation.) He suggests, for example, that the acute turmoil of her early adolescence was in part due to her total ignorance of her sexual self—a note rarely sounded by religious but probably obvious to most lay readers.[25] He also counters her own testimony about the blessing she and her natural sisters received in suffering their father's derangement. Louis's breakdown shook her faith: how could God afflict the man who had been most like God to her? But he leaves open the question of whether this disaster within the family prompted her to lose all sense of heaven.

De Meester exposes a curious flaw in Thérèse's understanding of love. It concerns Mary Magdalene. Thérèse cannot belie the gospel fact that a repentant soul loves God more deeply than an upright and pure one such as she had long presumed herself to be. Christ sought the lost lamb, not those securely within the fold; he came for sinners, not for the righteous. The synoptic narratives Thérèse loved should have reminded her of the generally unsavory company he kept. As we have just noted, however, Thérèse's embrace of her spiritual darkness included her acknowledged kinship with the impure and fallen, faceless though they remained for her.

To take de Meester's point further: she had entertained a sophistical notion of prevenient grace, that God had given her a greater blessing than Mary Magdalen's because he had kept her from falling into sin. As Urs von Balthasar has observed, that suggests, dangerously, that she presumed herself like Mary of the Immaculate Conception, with the difference that Mary was supremely humble by her naïveté, whereas Thérèse, reading the Bible to find her own place within it, was too reflective of and for herself even to approximate such humility.[26] Now, she knew herself desolate and impotent, delivered to an absurd darkness, keeping company with the desperate. She had used the old trope of the Carmel as a prison but now she was truly imprisoned. Strangely, in the midst of this torment, there was also peace. Her composure came from knowing experientially that, stripped of faith and hope, she could now be overwhelmed by God. Reduced to this bottom-line nothingness, her vision could not be clearer. Most important of all, from this vantage, with all desires gone save to love Jesus (A 82v), that love was the purest possible.

Most helpfully and in a post–Vatican II spirit, de Meester notes Thérèse's proximity to Luther in the assumption that adherence to Christ is all-sufficient. But Luther marked a radical departure from medieval tradition: instead of the conventional notion of faith as *assensus*, a nodding to creeds, he spoke of *fiducia*, a reliance upon Christ alone. The absence of the dogmatically conventional and the foregrounding of love, indeed, its sufficiency, denotes Thérèse and makes her virtually unique within Roman Catholicism. As for Luther, he cared little for love.

It is in discussing hope that, in my estimate, de Meester falters: "Perhaps a certain state of desperation is necessary in order to discover hope. True hope is found beyond the condition of dreaming."[27] That may be, but neither of these statements is pertinent to Thérèse. She never recorded a state of desperation, so we have little to indicate she had reached it. Had she in fact done so and had it become manifest, she would likely have had to leave Carmel. She knew as much. Neither, however, was she a dreamer. The quality of her reliance upon Christ was beyond hope itself. It was free from an invested expectation. She was content to stay within the shadows, to abide in darkness and leave all to God. There is no warrant for de Meester's resolution of the issue by assuming that Thérèse in dying was suddenly given the open door to a heaven of saints. "Hope had finally done its work" seems a forced, not to say desperate, conclusion, a peculiarly disingenuous note on which to end an otherwise admirably thoughtful presentation. Worse, in awarding her the celestial scenario, de Meester unwittingly threatens to trivialize the profundity of darkness which Thérèse endured. This concluding lurch into the hagiographic does little good and rings false, a tacked-on triumphalism.

These four assiduous, instructive, and faithful commentators are in a sense up against the rugged clear-sightedness which Thérèse achieved late in her life. Sometimes even she was surprised by the distance she had covered in this dark adventure: "Je suis tout étonnée en voyant ce que je vous ai écrit hier" ["I'm completely astonished at what I wrote yesterday"] (C 8r) could count for more than the one passage to which this admission refers.

Briefly, What the Darkness Was Not

From a secular perspective, it would be easy to presume that Thérèse's darkness indicated that she was suffering from depression. The image of the encircling fog proves powerfully suggestive of depression's brooding helplessness. This is a clinical issue and I am not competent to address it as such, but let us review quickly the symptoms generally associated with depression and weigh their applicability in the theresian context: loss of self-esteem; a sense of failure; lack of concentration; sleeplessness; trouble with memory; poor judgment; agitation, irritability, and anxiety; an inability to make decisions; dread of aloneness or of death; hopelessness and self-pity; a conviction of uselessness. This might not be a comprehensive list, nor would any of these symptoms suffice to indicate a chronic condition.

Amid all of these negations, save for sleeplessness (but it was induced by shivering), it would be difficult to find Thérèse. That is not to conclude she was not depressed but even to say she was would mean very little as she was intelligent enough to identify her own condition and to cope with it. She talked with her retreat director of her temptations against the faith and she wrote at perceptive length about the entailing darkness. She told Mère Gonzague that she feared to write further because she was risking blasphemy. She feared to offend God, and yet it seems regrettable that she did not go on writing.

What sustained her and in effect precluded most of the symptoms listed above was, I believe, her work with the novices. They obliged her mercifully to consider the well-being of someone other than herself. She seems to have thrived on the challenge which they put to her in part because they, and they alone, were the only people in her life for whom she was delegated as a kind of elder, a teacher, a spiritual guide. Her novices gave her a position in part maternal and in part older-sisterly, even though some of them, including Céline, were her seniors. In her daily performance of obligations to them, she could not readily have lost a sense of purpose. Needed, she had to be decisive, make insightful judgments, and minimize the novices' anxieties and irritabilities while hiding any of her own.

Most important of all, she was in a community prompted by loving camaraderie. The Carmelite ethos of continual, prayerful attention to the needs of others, to the sinful and lost, she learned to make particularly her own through her stationary position in darkness. It is not idle that she called herself the sister of sinners, but she had as well the incalculable boon of four family members close by and, at an epistolary reach, the two young men whom she fashioned her true brothers.

Perhaps the most powerful and preclusive antidote to depression was Thérèse's hard-won ability to deal with difficult people. She endured what she called "certains petits combats" ["certain little struggles"] which seem trivial if compared to her struggles in spiritual darkness and against the progressive ravaging of tuberculosis, but she makes much of them in Manuscript C. Their recounting would, she suggests, make Mère Gonzague smile: they concern, however, a very great effort of charity in seemingly small things. She learned by experiment to respond with loving acceptance to behavior in other sisters which she found almost unbearably disagreeable and irritating. A fetching instance concerns Sr. Marie de Jésus, like Sr. Marie-Philomène a self-deprecating soul but with the habit of clicking her fingernails on her teeth during evening prayer. Thérèse was stationed close enough to hear her, and the bothersome, relentless sound became a torment. The scraping of shells against one another is her image of it. Rather than confront Sr. Marie and hurt her with a reproach, even a gentle one, Thérèse resolved not only to accept the noise but to take joy in it, "au moins dans l'intime de l'âme" ["at least in the intimacy of my soul"], she adds, "comme s'il eût été un ravissant concert" ["as if it had been a ravishing concert"]. Thérèse concludes with a turn at once humorous and uplifting: "toute mon oraison (qui n'était pas celle de quiétude) se passait à offrir ce concert à Jésus" ["all my prayer (which wasn't one of quietude), turned to offering this concert to Jesus"] (C 30v).[28] A caveat in Carmelite regulations had told her that failure in little things leads to failure in big ones. She records here how imaginative charity in a little thing won through in that evening hour, an hour which always came, day after day after day, scraping the shells.

Thérèse's unsentimental and loving attention to life with its many foibles, each with a human face, preserved her from the melancholy, pessimism, and discouragement which denote depression.

Of the scarcely more than two dozen Carmelites at Lisieux, one remains extraordinary in her relationship to Thérèse because of the peculiar nature of the bond that developed between them during the darkness of spirit. This was a woman who had, according to Thérèse, "le talent de me déplaire en toutes choses: ses manières, ses paroles, son caractère me semblaient *très désagréables*" ["the ability to offend me in everything: her demeanor, her remarks, her personality seemed to me *very unpleasant*] (C 13v). Thérèse, italicizing this sister's effect upon her, was careful to put all the unpleasantness in the past tense. It was June 1897. She was not yet bedridden but was looking back upon a strange relationship as though it were history. It was not yet so.

She had taken the behavior of Sr. Saint-Augustin as a challenge. As she told Mère Gonzague, she had to overcome an "antipathie naturelle" and treat this woman, seventeen years her senior, as she would treat the person she loved most. She prayed thankfully for this woman's merits and virtues, hidden away, she writes without irony, by "Jésus l'Artiste." While attempting to do her services, Thérèse had to resist the temptation to tell her off. She took an

FIGURE 8.1. Thérèse disliked almost everything about Sr. Saint-Augustin, but it was she who launched Thérèse as a writer within Carmel and to her alone Thérèse admitted her loss of belief in heaven. Copyright Archives du Carmel de Lisieux.

injunction from the *Imitatio Christi* (III.44.1) that it is better to leave a person who has expressed an adverse opinion than to contest it with one's own. On occasion, Thérèse had to rush suddenly away from her in order to arrest an outburst. At other times she would force a kindly smile, a tactic that explains why Sr. Saint-Augustin never suspected the aversion Thérèse felt for her. At the *procès* some twenty years later, she deposited a lengthy memoir of what she called their blessed friendship (see figure 8.1).

All of these particulars, while central to any study of Thérèse's ethic, form only a backdrop to a dream which Sr. Saint-Augustin had and recounted in her memoir. It dated from January 1897. In a very dark room, Thérèse was asked to adorn herself before joining her father. Louis, dressed in red and gold, was near an "extremely black" door beyond which there was only light. When she told Thérèse her dream, Sr. Saint-Augustin received a dumbfounding response: "Je ne crois pas à la vie éternelle: il me semble qu'après cette vie mortelle il n'y a plus rien. Je ne puis vous exprimer les ténèbres dans lesquelles je suis plongée. Ce que vous venez de me raconter est exactement l'état de mon âme. La préparation qu'on me fait et surtout la porte noire est si bien l'image de ce qui se passe en moi. Vous n'avez vu que du rouge dans cette porte si sombre, c'est-à-dire que tout a disparu pour moi et qu'il ne me reste plus que l'amour" ["I don't believe in eternal life. It seems to me that after this mortal life there's nothing more. I can't tell you of the shadows in which I'm plunged. What you're telling me is precisely the state of my soul. The preparation I'm supposed to make and especially the dark door is the very image of what's happening in my soul. You've seen only red in this grim door, which means everything has disappeared for me and I'm left with only love"].[29]

Thérèse believed that only God could have revealed the state of her soul to Sr. Saint-Augustin. This sister's naïveté had not been able to penetrate Thérèse's dissembling smile; she never suspected the thorough antipathy behind it. Disagreeable as she was in Thérèse's eyes, she was not scored for malice or mischief, and it is unlikely she could have made up anything about her dream and the response it received. As to Louis, she had known him since 1877, the year she professed her vows. It does seem odd that she, of all the Carmelites, was the one to bear a clairvoyant dream record about Thérèse and to her. That argues eloquently the love she felt for and somehow from Thérèse. Here was something of that innerness of virtue Thérèse commended to Mère Gonzague.

Thérèse took some dreams as revelatory, prescient, and treasurable, and this was one of them, made all the more imposing because it had been vouched to someone she disliked but who had ingenuously cherished her. It provides a counterpoint to one of Thérèse's own dreams on May 10, 1896, a month after the darkness began. The Spanish Carmelite and companion of Teresa of Avila, Aña de Lobera, founder of the first Carmel in France (1604), appeared to her with two other sisters, veiled but casting a brilliant light. Thérèse dreamed that she asked Aña whether she had long to live and was told with a promise that God would soon fetch her. Upon another question, she was told that God was pleased with her. Aña, she writes to her sister Marie, caressed her more lovingly than the tenderest of mothers caresses her baby. The vast consolatory power of that dream gave Thérèse some respite from the darkness: "je croyais, je sentais qu'il y a un Ciel et que ce Ciel est peuplé d'âmes qui me chérissent, qui me regardent comme leur enfant" ["I believed, I felt there's a Heaven and that this Heaven is populated with souls who cherish me and look upon me as their child"] (B 2r–2v).

Nothing so tellingly conveys the power of Thérèse's darkness than that even such a blissful portent as she had received from Aña de Lobera, though Thérèse had happy recourse to it many times thereafter, failed to overcome the obscurity within herself. The dream related by Sr. Saint-Augustin reinforces that impression because Thérèse herself edited it in her response. She did *not* respond to the bright light which the dream reported to be behind the dark door. She does not even mention Louis, the only other person seen in the dream. In effect, she does not get beyond nor even to the dark door. She seems oblivious to the cue of hope which the dream narrative was affording, that on the other side of the darkness there would be light and the company she rejoiced to consider after the news from Aña. It seems that by the midwinter of 1897, she had passed beyond all likely or even possible retrieval of faith and hope in a celestial life.

Where can we look to identify a source corroborative of Thérèse's extraordinary love without faith and hope? In the Bible, of course. The magnificent hymn to spiritual love in St. Paul's first letter to Corinth's Christians stands almost as an argument unto itself for the all-sufficiency of love. Paul writes that it does not seek for itself and does not fall short. Immediately, however, we face a challenge for the theresian context: love believes in and hopes for all things. On her own testimony, Thérèse had been left *wanting* to believe and thus to hope. At no time does she write nor say that she was hoping for a return to her faith in eternal life. Instead, at its most positive and noble, love assumes an exclusive position in a passage where Thérèse alludes to 1 *Corinthians* 13.

It is helpful to note not only what she says there but what she, almost deliberately, does *not* say: "La Charité me donna la clef de ma vocation. . . . Je compris que l'Amour *seul* faisait agir les membres de l'Église. . . . Je compris que l'*Amour* renfermait toutes les Vocations, que l'Amour était tout, qu'il embrassait tous les temps et tous les lieux" ["Charity gave me the key to my calling. . . . I understood that Love *alone* caused the members of the Church to act. . . . I understood that *Love* subsumed all the Vocations, that Love was everything, that it embraced all times and places"] (B 3v). This reprise of ecclesiastical history seems a bit generous—to the point of being unreal unless by it Thérèse was claiming only that the Holy Spirit has acted through the Church's members from the beginning. Given the Church's all-too-human history, that claim seems dubious. It would have been convincing if in place of love she had recognized faith as the great historical engine of Christendom.

As the *Imitatio* observes, many people love Christ in their adversity and they love him, too, when they receive consolations, but when Christ hides himself they become depressed. "Mais ceux qui aiment Jésus pour Jésus, et non pour eux-mêmes, le bénissent dans toutes les tribulations et dans l'angoisse du coeur, comme dans les consolations les plus douces" ["But those who love Jesus for himself and not for themselves, bless him in all their tribulations and in their heart's anguish, as in the sweetest consolations"].[30] Thérèse refers to the *Imitatio* nearly fifty times in her writings, and although the passage just quoted is not among those references, it is plausible that she took it to heart as she started reading this book from her eleventh year. (It was a gift on her first Communion.) If there are few who truly love Christ, she would be confident to count herself among that small number, affirming him in her love not despite the darkness she was in but with it.

Another medieval text of stringent spirituality deserves mention here, even though Thérèse never read it. The *Theologia Germanica* puts her darkness into high relief, for in that book, hell is the condition of one's self-conviction, the abiding sense that one is damned, unworthy, lost. It is preferable to the uncertainty and indifference which marks ordinary life because it prepares the soul for God: it is contrition of heart taken to an extreme. But the darkness to which Thérèse submitted, the cutting off from heaven, was not a function of such a ghastly posture as the *Theologia* commends. At no time did she feel damned, lost, unworthy of grace and its rescue.

The *Theologia Germanica* nonetheless trenchantly affords the seeking soul an imitation of Christ *and* points the way to Thérèse's *abandon*. The soul, it claims, must dwell in hell because Christ himself was there, visiting it before he ascended into heaven. The soul which enters hell accepts it without resistance, feels uncomforted and unsaved, but it is from this condition only that the soul can be retrieved by God and taken to heaven. That is a strange twist to popular notions of what makes hell. It is an earthside hell, however, and one shaped by the soul's awareness of unworthiness. Yet more strange comes the admission that one can be discomfited in heaven, troubled and confused. We recall that for Thérèse the thought of heaven was troubling because she could not imagine a state without suffering and without solicitation for the needy. It deserves iteration that she found comfort in her shadows. The peace of Christ makes sense only if it is experienced in the midst of anguish, hardship, tribulations. Admirers of Thérèse who are dismayed by her affirmation of her darkness might construe her equanimity in that way. Thérèse can be understood, if at all, only in and through that darkness because that is where she had to endure and to be tested.

Christian theologians tend to center either upon the incarnation of Christ or upon his crucifixion and resurrection. Within the German tradition to which I have alluded, Meister Eckhart exemplifies the first tendency and Martin Luther the second. Readers of Thérèse are aware that she is securely within the first group. For her, the immanence of Jesus, his continuous presence in her life, remains distinct, not least when she sees him as a child for whom she can be sported like a toy. She lives to please him; that is the pith and moment of her love. Of course, she is also Thérèse de la Sainte Face, keenly attentive to the sufferings of Jesus, the emblem of which became the Turin shroud, photographed shortly after her death. While there is no substantial dwelling upon Calvary in Thérèse's mind and writing, the Via Dolorosa occupies her vividly: the contempt, abuse, rejection of Jesus occasion the fathomless hurt she would assuage. She could have grasped as her own Pascal's insight that Christ shall be in agony unto the end of time. A fortiori, she pays scant heed to the Resurrection.[31] Christ as Jesus remains intimately earthly. Her indefatigable affectivity feeds upon his immanence with what she called a possessive love.

That does not minimize the Passion, in which Christ's suffering reaches its acme. She felt with him in the garden at Gethsemane. Echoing the *Imitatio*, a letter to Céline (LT 165) enjoins her to remember that many serve Jesus when he consoles but few when he is in that garden: "Qui donc voudra servir Jésus pour Lui-même?...Ah! ce sera nous" ["Who then would wish to serve Jesus for himself?...Oh, we will!"] Thérèse puts the Passion narrative to imaginative use by recasting the story of Jeanne d'Arc with references to it and by bringing to the infant Jesus in his crèche the premonitory angel of the Sainte Face.

Thérèse's writing, in creating for the reader that sense of intimacy with Jesus, borders upon the mystical. In her closeness to Jesus, she speaks of him both as friend and lover, which argues something akin to what has been called (by Nathan Söderblum) a "personality mysticism," an experience of Christ in the midst of life here and now. That notion speaks far more for her than any "infinity mysticism" of absorption by a transcendent power, such as St. Paul's rapture into the third heaven.

A secular, skeptical view of this intimacy might fashion it the fantasy of a protracted adolescent sexuality, a fixation upon a male rescuer figure par excellence. Having known no brothers, no schoolboys, and no young men, Thérèse was supremely ill equipped to negotiate normal heterosexual life. That is not why she entered Carmel, however, and the ardent responsiveness she shows toward Christ shows she was mature in disposition, if not by experience. She had had only the adult models of her benevolent father and her less gentle but equally pious uncle: earthly versions of God the Father in love and justice, and both of them crucially positive models of accessibility. Much of her confidence toward God the Father and toward Jesus she owed to her close relations to those two older men, quite different in temperament from one another yet alike in their compliance toward her. Louis could deny her nothing, and Isidore required only a little time to be brought around.

With Jesus, she constructed for herself both inequity and parity: she the toy, humble and deferent, but then the eager lover. Her images of Jesus were mediated by the Gospels and the *Cantica* of Solomon, imported into Carmel by Céline. If for the Carmelite tradition, the story of Elijah, the ascetic and prophet, was and remains necessarily central, for Thérèse herself, who refers only a few times to Elijah, the *Song of Songs* was immeasurably more important. Among her writings are seventy-seven references to its eight brief chapters. Most iterate favorite passages such as the gently amorous "Open to me, my sister, my love, my dove, my undefiled" (5:2) and "The joints of thy thighs are like jewels" (7:1). This eroticism protests itself unobjectionably, as it has long been part and parcel of the Christian tradition, both in art and in literature. It asserts the capacity of the human temperament to respond with one's whole self, rather than with an arid, abstract, and too intellectualized or simply rhetorical affirmation of God.

The major issue raised here is the sundering of faith and hope from love. Is that possible? I believe that Thérèse's last years argue that it is. It is curious that Thomas Aquinas makes precisely this distinction. In the *Summa Theologica* (I–II q.65.a.5), he asks whether love can exist without hope and faith. Let us leap to his altogether expected conclusion: it cannot. He says we are oriented to God as the object of blessedness through faith and hope; also that faith and hope are the fruits of love and presuppose it. There is the rub. *Must*, to borrow his image, the radix or root of all virtue produce the branches of faith and hope?

The most intriguing portion of this discussion centers upon Christ, who did not, Aquinas concedes, have faith nor hope but only a *perfecta caritas*. "In loco fidei, habuit apertam visionem; et loco spei, plenam comprehensionem" ["In place of faith, he had expansive vision; in place of hope he had complete understanding"].[32] I would suggest that Thérèse, too, in her own imitation of Christ, attained an exceptional lucidity of vision and understanding, that even beyond death a Christian soul might be a ministering one. With imaginative and resourceful brilliance, she responded to what would have caused despair in most other believers by fashioning for herself a role she knew she could fulfill. It is an audacious variant upon Christ's pledge, "Lo, I am with you always, even unto the end of the world" (*Matthew* 28:20).

Thérèse, in her ever-distinctive way, departs from a strict imitation of Christ: on the cross he was just short of despair, crying out (in *Mark* and *Matthew*, at least) his forsakenness to God. In her fog and under the vault, Thérèse did not give in to despair. It remains unclear whether she ever felt abandoned by God. In her verse, she anticipates the possibility that Jesus, himself forsaken, shall forsake her, and yet her love proclaims a compelling power of expectation, that he will return to her.

She has played upon the Carmelite theme with her particular variations: prayer rendered to God on behalf of sinners and the willingness to suffer in their stead demonstrated the power of sanctity, the capacity (especially among women) to take up hardship. It was one avenue to power which was wide open for women throughout the Christian centuries. Thérèse extends that intercessory role into the post mortem by substituting the Carmelites' earthly mission into a transcendent perpetuity, one she alone will occupy. But earthside she has taken up residence among the sinners, makes herself one with them in their spiritual isolation. By claiming that nether position with them, she acknowledges the loss of the superior vantage of prayer and its benefits extended down to them. She in effect demotes herself from the Carmelite position—I shall suffer for poor you—and makes herself a kind of Magdalene.

Her Christology thus views Christ from the publican, rather than the pharisaic, position. That is why it is refreshingly free of dogma and any hint of intimidation. Knowing the Gospels closely, she intuited that one of the many avenues to Christ is not through faith and hope but instead through the helplessness (call it existential, if you will) which goes on without either. Christ came for the lost, not for the comfortably found. That is a paradox which conventional, unswervingly faithful believers must negotiate: there is the danger of hidden pride in their seeming advantage of belonging within the folds of faith and hope. How can faith be kept free from the contaminants of routine and how can hope be kept free from the pull of presumption? If darkness of spirit threatens despair, a light may be a devilish delusion. Teresa of Avila repeatedly expressed her concern about it. Christ's words against believers, those who cried out Lord! Lord! are almost too terrifying to read.

The Eagle Eye of Love

This interpretation may seem extreme and improbable. My answer would be that Thérèse was an extreme and improbable person. Under the press of time and illness, she fashioned a revolutionary ethic of love, one which subtracted, in part by neglect and in part by experience, the tenets of faith and the self-absorbing illusions of hope. Alone, she confounds the prejudice of many non-believers who charge that Christianity is motivated by self-interest, the promise of celestial immortality, or what George Orwell called "the Christian bribe." Without looking to heaven, since for her it had ceased to exist, Thérèse's love proves as hardy, as exigent as any could possibly be, in part because it was tried in the crucible of abysmal suffering, physical and psychological, a condition with which her imaginative resilience was able to contend and even to shape. Simone Weil once wrote that the genius of Christianity is not that it overcomes suffering but that it puts it to a transcendent use. That, it seems to me, is what Thérèse did with her darkness, the vault and the fog. By anyone's estimate, her example should stand as a tribute to human tenacity and resourcefulness against apparently insuperable odds. A Christian could and should maintain that it was by grace itself that she went on. Thérèse herself would have agreed.

Her significance lies right here: not merely in the little way of humility—anyone can make an injunction to that and it comes from the Beatitudes, anyway—nor in the strewing of roses, which came first from somebody else's witnessing about "pin-headed" St. Louis de Gonzaga, but in her challenge to us to heed what a keenly tested Christian love amounts to. Could any of us love God from utter darkness? Could any of us love from the cross, from Christ's own position of abandonment? Could any of us attain an ultimate disinterestedness of affirmation, a loving of God and others which does not entail, even covertly, a payoff for good behavior?

We all tend to be weak like the sparrow self which Thérèse imagined at the end of Manuscript B, and few of us have her eagle eye of love, her unflagging and insuperable affectivity, unbroken even in extreme adversity. Our challenge is to determine how far or even whether she can provide a model for the conjunction of revelation and human personality in situ, which is the concern of what is called fundamental theology. The issue is complicated because any interpretation of her life must be based upon her particular axis of Carmelite life and spirituality (the horizontal plane, so to speak) and the Gospels (the vertical). To neglect, to diminish, to slight either of these would warp any perspective on her out of all shape.

The table of sinners where she took residence is stationed along the axis described. It is a communitarian image and a sacramental one. Carmelites were edified during the refectory hour by readings in sacred and constitutional literature but some were also chastened there for their transgressions. Thérèse writes in Manuscript C that she alone will be eating the bitter bread. In the Gospels, the dining table is the seat of communion and instruction, and Jesus first faces opprobrium from scandalizing talk about his banquets. Making herself a sister to sinners of the worst sort, Thérèse sacralizes a somber scene by praying on their ungrateful behalf. She, loving among the treacherous and indifferent, seems to be sitting on their periphery, as one who does not belong, even as at the Last Supper, Judas, treacherous among the loving, does not belong.

Whether Thérèse ever thought of such symmetries is dubious. Among the Gospels' narratives which did matter to her, the story of the prodigal son was implicit throughout Manuscript B and explicit at the end of C. I believe it serves as a splendid analogue to her life and spirituality. Rather than live the righteous life of the prodigal's brother and claim Arminjon's "my turn" reward, she chooses to make the most of her darkness. She has the audacity to realize and to accept that from there she has a greater claim than any of justice: love, love for sinful neighbors which is turned to God. Her station with them seems wholly at odds with the Carmelite way to perfection; quite the reverse, it is the way of imperfection, static with *petitesse* and *faiblesse*, the two denominations of Thérèse's hard-won perceptions. But just as she knows that Jesus has allowed the darkness to descend upon her, she also knows that he has set her at the table of sinners. I like to think that her charity toward the cranky and difficult sisters of Carmel and her formation of her beloved novices also pointed that way. She learned to read in others some sufferings and anxieties which were not distant from those which had long beset her, and her experience of paradise lost opened to her the awareness of how others live in darkness, some even by conviction.

Thérèse had long wanted—as who among the sisters would not?—to attain the serene simplicity of Mère Geneviève. In that beloved old woman everyone had seen a visible saint. Her example might even have offered a consolation, the promise of a goal reached by a long life borne in piety. The *circulaires* abounded in comparable notes of uplift, especially in accounts of the elderly departed. Thérèse could have forgotten that only adversities would do. As Madre Teresa had been careful to note, consolations may be satanic and mislead.[33] One possible key to Thérèse's equanimity and acceptance of the bitter bread and the sinners' table is that they could offer only disconsolation. They reeked of the truth of suffering at its depths.

Pascal remarks that atheists should not be abused. They are wretched enough, he says, as they are. Thérèse, as though not content with that nor even with prayers for them, *accepts* herself in their company, which is to say that she accepts them. She could do so because although not fallen into atheism, she realized in her testing that she was acutely susceptible, ever ready to fall and thus akin to those who were in fact fallen, situated in a darkness they themselves could not identify. Her prayer for them serves for that identification. She was held from falling only by the intuited certainty of a prevenient grace, the final note she sounded in Manuscript C. Discovery of fallibility's terror is one measure of how far she had come from the deathbed of Mère Geneviève.

The gesture of a punitive eating is revealing: in the parable, the prodigal was so reduced by his own extravagance that "he would fain have filled his belly with the husks that the swine did eat" (*Luke* 15.16). Thérèse, herself starving toward death, did not need to be instructed on the prodigal's bitter bodily need, but she could appreciate the *audace* which took the young man from his father's house to the swilling of pigs. His prodigality is not so distant from her string of fantasies recorded in Manuscript B, her wanting to lose herself to inanition in mannish ways.

Closing B, she reconciled herself to the infinitely smaller ambit of humility, the little way of accomplishing little things: to being a child in the Church's bosom. Such was the alpha of her name, there reaching a matured end, an everlasting *enfance* Jesus warranted as the way to enter celestial life. But Manuscript B was insufficient and too narrow by its very ecclesiasticism. Thérèse was drawn on to ripening and completion in the omega of suffering which was the other half of her name. It required that she find a place *extra ecclesiam*, with the Pranzinis and the Taxils of this world.

· Again, *Luke*'s parable provides a gloss. The brother complains at the father's show of love for the prodigal but the prodigal makes no complaint about the brother. Ergo, love is superior to justice, and we sense the prodigal has gotten the better deal; hence, the brother's resentment seems entirely credible. The beauty in the story is that the father, too, is a prodigal (like son, like father) with his banquet, ring, and shoes. Seeing his son obscured by rags and at an infinite distance, this loving father is precisely Thérèse's God, all-compassionate, merciful, excusing. What is her prayer from the table of sinners other than a petitionary compassion, a seeking of God's mercy?

It could be said that Thérèse recasts the parable in her own terms, by staying in the distant land, at the pig sty (her table), where all is bitter. Her implicit *confiance* is that God will eventually call her, and that is how she complements the prodigal, who takes the little way of explicit *confiance* by returning home: he trusts his father will take him back, even in the lowliest station. Thérèse remains in lowly dependence upon the loving father, in self-submission and an unlimited trustfulness which seems alien, if not outrageous, to those of us who proceed by rules and make the stairway climb of dutifulness and effort. Tidy, rule-fitted lives do not countenance audacity. It puzzles, exasperates, challenges.

For all its beauty, *Luke*'s parable ends on an unresolved note of bitterness: the bitterness of loss and regret in one son passes before the bitterness of resentment in the other. In Thérèse's terms, the bitterness at the table goes on being savored but it does not poison the soul with contumely or blame. If it had, she could not have prayed for those at the table with her, those who in parabolic terms were spiritually dead. In joining them, Thérèse realized a central part of the *offrande* she had made in June 1895. There she had thanked God for passing her through the crucible of suffering, but now she was lying at its bottom. She had wanted to console God for the ingratitude of the wicked, but she had now come as a small, imperfect soul to kinship with them, not in the wickedness but in the weakness. She had asked that in the Eucharist God remain within her as in a tabernacle. Transformed into the host, God would transform her, the unworthy communicant, into the divine semblance of the suffering servant.

That meant she had to take the elevator deep down into a darkness she had not been able to compass in her earlier testings. It became her utmost *imitatio Christi*, the most severe mortification, beyond any imagined by Carmel or even by Madre Teresa. In her petitionary helplessness there at the table, she remains Sr. Thérèse de l'Enfant Jésus. In the eating of that bitter bread amid companions unsavory to her soul, she becomes Sr.—truly sister—Thérèse de la Sainte Face.

Living Theology

Pope John Paul's denomination seems what Thérèse herself would have called her journey, an *itinerarium cordis*, wholly experiential yet void of the operatics of medieval mysticism even while sustaining a daily one, the desire for God. This desire, itself most desirable (she is almost that Proustian), joins the soul by loving even to those who feel incapable of it, reject it, despise it. Without those sinners and their table, Thérèse would be safe for us, comforting, and carefully dead.

Keenly observant and probative, Thérèse was too intelligent to be an intellectual, that is, someone content with ideas per se and their spinning from and around our vanity. Rahner's disdain of her has its locus here, that she declines to fit into intellectualizing structures which put aside a more urgent business of life, a loving of God and others that requires another kind of thoughtfulness. She forms her own trajectory of Henri Bergson's *dynamique*, her writing being the true missionary work assigned her. A pathfinder, she tugs away from the holds and bars of the assumed, as when in her plays and poems she transparently seeks to free her sisters from the judiciary gloom associated with Jansenism. In modern terms, she seems to have served as a therapist for her Carmel, best qualified by keeping directly before her the awareness of her own final helplessness. Epistemologically, however, she is far from helpless; indeed, she seems clairvoyant. Her writing and counseling for compassionate love as the real wholeness of Christian life turns out neither impressionistic nor sentimental. It is too steadfast, too forge-tested to be either.

Her coherence lies in her witnessing to the underside of grace, to what is more than hidden from convenient and predictable view. The table of sinners and the bitter bread, her version of Bon Sauveur, provided her with the consummate grace, something completely unforeseeable over the early and maturing years of a life lovingly insulated within proprieties. Her life ends with this salutary arrest of our expectations, much like the closing of *Camino de Perfección*, when after lengthy hortatory strides with her sisters, Madre Teresa takes us by surprise, admitting she is not certain that she loves God.[34]

Disconcerting as it must be, the table of sinners provides the ground for Thérèse's ever-renewable mission. She becomes the saint of the dispossessed, of all who sit in darkness, including those who care to gloat in it. At the same time, she speaks to those within the folds of faith who feel deeply troubled and bereft of hope, who find themselves lacking the warmth and sustenance of faith. Thérèse is the saint of the hopeless, both within and without the Church. She is the saint of those who fear to acknowledge that their faith has been weakened or lost altogether. The roses and the statuary remain for those to whom they are vital signs of the little way of little doings, but neither roses nor statuary belong in that testing darkness where both the fallen and the fallible are found. Which includes most of us.

The Rest Being Silence

Among the monitions Pauline painted on the Carmel's white walls, one above the *dortoir*'s entrance said that silence is the language of angels. And of sisters: their Rule says sin takes its chief opportunity from words, so often idle, anyway: "Que chacun [*sic*] donc se fasse un poids et des balances pour ses paroles, et un frein pour sa bouche, afin que sa langue ne le fasse chanceler et tomber et que sa chute ne soit incurable à la mort" ["Let each make weight and balance for words, a bridle for the mouth, lest the tongue cause one to falter and fall and the falling be without remedy upon death"].[35] The Constitution proscribed speech among sisters save for occasions of encouraging one another in love of Jesus, their spouse, or of consoling one another when necessary, as under a temptation. It even expressed concern about shared working places as opportunities for breaking silence. Positively considered, silence furthered the Carmelites' supernatural prayer, Madre Teresa's *oración de quietud*, the will attaining peaceful union with God even as the understanding would go its wandering way.[36] Martha, troubled and talkative, importuned Jesus to get Mary to work (*Luke* 10:38–42). Mary kept a silent attendance.

Most important of all for Thérèse, silence provided the medium for both the imitation of Christ and nuptial intimacy with him. She had never been fully at ease with the two daily hours for psalmody, even claiming herself unfit to be reciting it, the Latin eluding her and her affective drive to articulation. Another discomfort attended her search through prayer books, but even the most beautiful of printed prayers did not furnish what mattered to her most, an unvarnished and child-simple spontaneity. The Lord's Prayer furnished exception: she took to heart Madre Teresa's injunction that one earnest and concentrated recitation of it surpassed any number of its procedural iterations. She found her own path, however, by a medium that Madre Teresa nowhere considered (nor would have allowed beyond retreat) and yet used substantially: in the silent speech of the pen. But is writing all that silent?

Céline once asked her what she was thinking during the divine Office and she answered that she fancied herself on a desert mountain alone with Jesus, telling him of her love in terms she herself did not understand but he, pleased, did. It is not certain that in this scenario she was speaking aloud, only that whatever was in her surely came out as "un élan du coeur" and "un cri de reconnaissance et d'amour" ["a heart leap" and "a cry of acknowledgment and of love"] (C 25r). That is what she wrote, but even writing as a thanksgiving remained an earthly pastime and posed insuperable limits: "car je sens mon impuissance à redire avec des paroles terrestres les secrets du Ciel" ["indeed, I sense my incapacity to relate in terrestrial words the secrets of Heaven"] (B iv). If, as she told Marie in that passage, Jesus wants our love, not our works, how is Thérèse's writing itself to be construed?

The writing occupies an uneasy ambiguity as the loving work, as proximate to Martha as to Mary. Jesus himself wrote nothing. In Thérèse's central legacy itself, then, there is no imitation of him. The very predicates of her spirituality, of Carmel's, meant silence: humility requires no utterance, nor does *abandon* ever profess or protest anything. Immolation of self, a daily practice Thérèse enjoined upon her novices and recorded in poems for them and other sisters,[37] implicitly canceled God's own gift out of Eden, speech. Even by the assertive, surrogate self, her pen.

Toward the end of her greatest writing, Manuscript C, Thérèse told Mère Gonzague that it would not pain her were Gonzague to use it for kindling, to burn it even before its author's eyes (C 33r). The prioress knew everything Thérèse could possibly say, even as Pauline had known the *Histoire printan-nière* before it passed into ink. It is a mercy that nothing Thérèse composed was burned, but it seems likely that she would have cast the same fiery permission on all her writings, even those which as occasional pieces had sustained or consoled the sisters to whom they were addressed. Sr. Saint-Vincent-de-Paul received four of her efforts in verse but said of her, according to Céline, "C'est une gentille petite soeur, mais que pourra-t-on dire d'elle après sa mort? Elle n'a rien fait" ["She's a nice little sister but what could one say of her after her death? She's done nothing"]. Thérèse would have concurred. For posterity, though, the greatest grace was in her obedience. Told to write, she wrote.

If, then, its lessons meditated, her writing could be marginalized into vanity, like some cunning dross of pride or a satanic consolation, where else can we seek Thérèse's silence? Finally, silence served within her darkness. She created a mantra-like prayer, her *Acte de foi*, proclaiming her readiness, with the help of grace, to shed all her blood in affirmation of her faith, yet she was sometimes so beset by the urge to blaspheme that she had to bite her lips hard.[38] Silence became literally decisive to her soul. In her sunken tableau, the sinners' table, her prayer is silent, her mouth taken with the chewing of the bread's bitterness.

That position, determined by Jesus, was itself a grace, a humility, a littleness as Elijah had heard it: the still, small voice. Not only silent, this tableau has never attained hagiographic portraiture, even though it is central in any approach to Thérèse's spirituality. The table of sinners remains hidden and, by tacit neglect or revulsion, strategically forgotten. It seems to mock the Last Supper. Had she listened all too well to the demonic voices proclaiming her nothingness? Not at all. As Thérèse conceived herself praying there as sister to those hostile or indifferent to Christ, even as she was still most ardently loving him, we might imagine her occupying the table's center. In the last pages to Mère Gonzague, she imagines herself in the place of Jesus at *John* 17, but discreetly omits these words of his: "I am not praying for the world."[39]

There, from Manuscript C, the direction of B is subtly reversed. In B, she had given up apostolic longings and in an overweening moment, studded with exclamation marks, she proclaimed herself a hypostatic Love at the Church's center, but in the end she realized she would become a much less demonstrative love *extra ecclesiam*, among those Christ came to redeem. It is as though in Manuscript B she had given herself an enormous chunk of marble called Love only to realize within the next nine ripening months that she would have to carve from it a love of much less ambitious bulk. At the dark table she is humbly and simply apostle and priest, martyr and teacher, all without her saying or even knowing so. Nowhere in all of her writings is her love so eloquent as in this darkness, where it is silent prayer, the Carmelite way. Had she never reached that table, Thérèse would have remained little, but she would also have much less to say to us.

The table of sinners, then, is her abiding station amid the spiritually derelict, the self-victims of what Aquinas called *infidelitas Dei, odium Dei, desperatio Dei,* company such as Thérèse could never have dreamed she would keep, certainly not to time's end. Here, only here, is where the real triumph of humility occurs, so rightly recondite that it goes unnoticed. That table becomes her Hanoi of obscurity and forgottenness where she at last reaches the true *abandon* of no titles for self: not martyr, not Love at a center, not anyone save a sister of other poor sinners. It is, finally, her bodhi tree, where she sits down exhausted after a long, restive journey of soul and heart, one of untiring articulations for love of Jesus, and now she is content to wait for his summons. In that darkness she prays that those of no faith may at last see its brilliant torch, but it is Manuscript C (6r) itself which is luminous, like one of those coruscating moments of sheerest light in Dante's *Purgatorio* when an angelic presence flashes by.

How far she came from futile concerns of role playing in B is best measured from this point in C through the small incidents in which she reports her epistemology of charity, her discovering Christ within some hapless, marginal sisters. These minor, almost chatty passages would be easy to slip by but they reveal that *charité* is the lexical key to C, repeated so frequently that we are caught short by her admission that her love for Christ amounts to not even a drop of dew in the ocean and that if she is to love him, she must borrow some of his love so as to give it back. This admission suffers in any translation into English, because Thérèse has replaced the intimate *tu* of Manuscript B with the distancing *vous.* That shows that she finally lost her need of a peremptory claim upon Jesus. This is the humblest of all her petitions.

The calm and lucid humanity in C brings us to the lasting and most beautiful of all her silences, which we owe to Céline and her Dorlot. In those photographic postures, Thérèse speaks the wordless language the Carmelites called angelic. Some sibylline, some sphinxlike, her gaze achieves at times a penetrative disarmament of the beholder. In these pictures, her life story seems to find a successive recapitulation, from the first scene at the Croix du Préau, chubby and cheerful (that one was not taken by Céline), to the ones shaded by approaching death. In the gesture which has become her iconic identity in countless chapels, the strewing of flowers, Thérèse, eyes caught closed, becomes pale and drawn, ghostly amid her novices. Taken between June 3 and June 8 of her final year, it is that somber portrait which seems apt, had we to choose one, to present her at the table, in darkness, among the lost. Evidence of her suffering, it prompts a shudder.

FIGURE 8.2. The second of three poses the feverish Thérèse made for Céline on June 7, 1897. Copyright Office Central de Lisieux.

The most fetching of all the photographs comes from the trio Céline took in June 1897, perhaps on the same day as the strewing of roses. The Martin sisters wanted a formal remembrance of their dying sister, and this series, posed with her kneeling, the images of her namesakes in either hand, offers striking variations. The first shows an uncharacteristically diffident face, almost recoiling. The third, after Céline's preparatory busyness, had brought their subject close to exhaustion. She urged Céline to hurry. A grieving fixity in the eyes argues a woman much older than twenty-four years.

The second, denominated in the archives as "La Languoureuse," seems far from the dullness or stagnation implicit in the tag (see figure 8.2). Helpfully, it carries a slight blur, as though to remind us that Thérèse eludes a final precision. Yet the face shows the warmth of her intelligent heart, her eyes incautiously glancing away.

These photos and others argue that a theology of silence from Thérèse can find secure integration into Pope John Paul's "living theology" because it requires a meditative reach into her affirmations of weakness, imperfection, littleness—the experiential ground by which she (and anyone else) could trust in divinely compassionate love. This theology humbles by *not* deepening understanding, by furthering acceptance of grace as mystery and the ineffables of grace as well as the mystery of suffering which binds God with humanity. It mercifully precludes bookish constructs which seek to net divinity, yet it is inextricably bound to the Gospels.

Perhaps nothing would be so misguided as an enthusiastic attempt to anthologize or select from Thérèse's writing, and fortunately that surgery is unnecessary. Her writing is all of a piece, with even the slightest of the poems contributing to the mosaic of her charitable regard for her sisters and to our sense of her. That regard informs the concluding scenes she records in C, which is her summa. Definitive though C is, however, it can be understood as such only by B, and both of them are efflorescent of A.

In B she includes "doctor" in the list of positions—warrior, priest, apostle, martyr—she would have liked to be able to assume in her longing to accomplish all things for Jesus, what she called "toutes les oeuvres héroïques" ["all the heroic works"] (B 2v). It is tempting to suppose that *docteur* figured as the least important to her so far as it was the least dramatic (heroic), with no uplift from battles, distant lands, martyrdom, nor even the sacramental life and preaching of a priest. It suggests a life achievement award.

That supposition gains force from the first pages of Manuscript A, in which she reflects on the mysteries of difference, that God created flowers of magnificent beauty but others of a smaller yet no less engaging beauty. She observes that were all souls of such resplendent worth as "des Saints docteurs qui ont illuminé l'Eglise" ["the learned Saints who have enlightened the Church"], God would not have had to descend to the lowly, the poor soul who had only natural law to follow, and "l'enfant qui ne sait rien et ne fait entendre que de faibles cris" ["the wholly ignorant child who can express only weak cries"] (A 3r). Certainly, Thérèse identified herself with such humble company, even to the end.

Is there any other saintly doctor whose teachings, wholly free of propositions and proofs, could be so elementary, yet so penetrating? And those teachings come most helpfully where they are least expected, in C *de profundis* as she sits at the table, then passes on to tell us about seeing Christ within the suffering of other souls. In such a twofold nexus of love for God and for other poor souls, Thérèse does not so much teach Christian doctrine as embody Christian life. She is not a *souffleur* of Christianity but someone who loves Christ and can see Christ in others. She can do so only in her weakness and littleness and that is what so oddly and surely proclaims her magnificence.

Probably most Christians who read her autobiography to the end would like to retrieve Thérèse as *compagne*, but because that is not possible save by grace, they can content themselves with being novices to her writing. They can delight in the anecdotal wealth of Manuscript A, the lyrical energy and consolatory purport of B, and then await the vast company of those whose only access to Thérèse comes from the helplessness she depicts in C.

Charitably, Thérèse forgets no one.

9

Inconclusions

[I]l est très dangereux de juger des actions d'autrui, et l'on s'y trompe très souvent pensant que la vertu est vice, et que ce qui est imperfection est vertu [It's very dangerous to judge another's actions. We're often deceived by thinking that virtue is vice and that what is imperfection is virtue].

—Isabelle des Anges, *Papier d'exaction*

Au soir de cette vie, je paraîtrai devant vous les mains vides, car je ne vous demande pas, Seigneur, de compter mes oeuvres [In this life's evening, I'll appear before you with empty hands. I don't ask you, Lord, to reckon my works].

—Sr. Thérèse de l'Enfant-Jésus de la Sainte-Face,
Prière 6

Ne parlez pas de mains vides, car le Coeur de Jésus est votre richesse, sa miséricorde, et non vos mérites, est le fondement de votre espérance [Stop talking about empty hands. The Heart of Jesus is our treasure and his compassion, not our merits, forms the basis of our hope].

—*Circulaire* of Sr. Anna du Très-Saint Sacrament,
Tarbes, July 26, 1894

Quand on lira ces lignes, j'aurai été jugée par Celui en qui je crois, en qui seul j'espère, et que j'ai toujours désiré d'aimer, malgré mes infidélités sans nombre. Ce qu'on dira ou écrira de moi importe donc peu en réalité [When these lines are read, I'll have been judged by Him in whom I believe, in whom alone I hope and whom I've always desired to love, despite my countless infidelities. What's said or written about me really matters very little].

—*Circulaire* of Mère Louise du Coeur de Jésus,
Paris, September 8, 1895

A character in a Chekhov story remarks on the happiness of being alone. The fallen angel, he says, likely betrayed God because he longed for solitude, about which the angels know nothing. Thérèse was no fallen angel, no rebel, but she did know the pleasures as well as the harms of solitude, even in Carmel. I take *solitude* here not in a physical sense but as the singularity which is both the cause and consequence of personality, something shaped by experience. While it is true that all of us are singular and there is no such thing as a normal nor an average person, some of us, to put an Orwellian turn on the matter, are more singular than others, and a few are most singular.

Three conditions defined Thérèse's apartness from the other Carmelites, including her natural sisters. The first of these was her particular intelligence, the exception of self manifested early on and remarked by her mother: the assertive ego of the *benjamine*; the precocity of learning, limited only in the bookish sense; the adeptness in storytelling and in such seemingly minor skills as mimicry, which is the gift of an observant, satiric mind; the imaginative, even audacious reading of Scripture. These suffice as outward signs of what became in her writing and talking the fully flourishing intellect, one which took on with a kind of bravura the task of interpreting Christianity to the Carmelites in a new and vital way.

The second was her writing itself. For Zélie, writing was a release from the daily tedium of her lace business and childrearing, a way of sustaining herself in sympathetic bonds. For Thérèse, it was almost the reverse. The autobiographical fragments are nothing if not a declaration of a liberated spirituality, traces of which were left behind for the well-meaning but likely bemused Pauline, Marie, and Mère Gonzague to ponder. In the poems requested by other Carmelites, Thérèse continued to speak primarily in her own voice. If each recipient had only left in turn some account of her reaction to these verses, we would have a substantial register of how apart Thérèse remained from them: except for the unusually sympathetic Sr. Marie de la Trinité and perhaps cousin Marie, she remained apart from the reach of their understanding, certainly not by any intention or calculation on her part but by insights which her pen in part discovered for her, so far as the writing was a process revelatory to its own creator. There were no mirrors in Carmel, but the pen served her in that reflective function, urging her to portray herself as she was and to imagine in counterpoint a perfected Carmelite self. Her caveat to Bellière on her seeming self and her real one reflects this distinction.

It remained one which even her natural sisters had difficulty in accepting as she became to them in the last months of her life a sibylline figure of substantially their own styling. With the protraction of her suffering through the summer of 1897, she took on the role played by many dying sisters in the *circulaires*, her words weighing with a kind of prophetic force. Those last months seem the final *récréation pieuse*, extended over summer days when, recumbent in her father's *voiture*, she and her energies became ever more attenuated.

Her dramas became interpretive enactments of an idiosyncratic progress in understanding Christ and the gospel of suffering which she was learning in her own terms, even while attempting to impart those terms to others. How far they can or should reflect the Carmelite tradition is not a matter I am qualified to address, but it deserves careful assessment. How can an exceptional person be representative of anything? And yet the Carmelites of Lisieux turned to Thérèse because she had assumed, quite without anyone's intending, the unofficial office of *auctor*, an advisor, a model, a harbinger, someone who in verse was capable of re-creating each of them on request. Nothing in the Rule nor in the Constitutions provided for such a vatic function. Reverent commentators follow her lead in speaking of her *audace*, but none of them locates its accomplice and facilitator, her pen.

Nothing goes so far toward autonomy as writing. It both expresses and furthers the solitariness of self. Thérèse was at home with it early on, but there is no evidence that she intended to become a writer per se. She might have intuited her gift from her correspondence, where she was free to exalt and bemoan and to supply the exclamation points of her sensibility. On the page, she, like her mother, enjoyed latitudes denied to a woman in the company of conventions and the conventional. Writing exerted a furtive appeal, it was a gamesome form of hiding which befitted a gamesome personality. Writers generally wish to communicate but they are not beyond a certain catch-me-if-you-can elusiveness, and Thérèse left her sisterly readers far behind her. She did not *wish* to leave them in the dark but she might have sensed it was almost impossible not to do so, at least for a while. Their incomprehension in part accounts for the aloofness with which at least one of the Carmelites charged her. A more intimate gauge of incomprehension Pauline registered in her many revisions of her sister's writings, a substantial abundance of small but subtle changes in diction which Thérèse's unquestioning and consistent deference to her sister does not seem always to justify. Thérèse gave absolute trust to Pauline's judgment, a trust proper in itself, but the real value of Pauline's revisions is that they supply a counter by which to assess what and who Thérèse was not.

There is a passage in her last manuscript where, in referring to Pauline, she could be writing of herself. She admits to having felt dismay in the summer of 1896 when it seemed that Pauline might be sent to Vietnam:

"je sentais . . . une grande tristesse dans mon coeur, je trouvais que son âme si sensible, si délicate n'était pas faite pour vivre au milieu d'âmes qui ne sauraient la comprendre" ["I felt . . . a great sorrow in my heart; I found that so sensitive and scrupulous a soul was not made to live in the midst of souls who would not understand it"] (C 9v). Could that not have been said of her own life within Carmel?

Yet it was part of her mission, as Manuscript C itself tells us, to understand those non-understanding souls with the sure epistemology of love, which meant seeing Christ within each sister, beginning with the more challenging among them. At Carmel, she made the logical conjunction of her own story, Manuscript B leading to Manuscript C: the centrality of love is found only in the depths of human foibles, as God is hidden in the obscurity of our own many weaknesses. Quite fittingly, Manuscript B's gradual ascent to the exclamatory role of her love in the Church's heart gives way to Manuscript C's diminuendo of very little tableaux of hurt and helplessness where that love is at work. The triumphant forte of one text finds its resolution in the lowly piano of its successor. Both are thoroughly Thérèse: the expressive burst and the unassuming, yet penetrating calm. These two faces of her style, the lyrical and the matter-of-fact, complement one another, rooted as they both are in this writer's reaching experientially for truth. The reaching stretched as far as her telling Sr. Saint-Augustin that she did not believe in heaven. That was neither a statement of nonfaith nor against faith, but a record of the immediacy of her consciousness. Wanting to affirm what she could not, she spoke in the most brutal terms of what she was experiencing. She did not perceive her *épreuve* as some sort of game which she knew she was bound to win. She had no experienced certainty that she would nor was she seeking any. When we consider the tubercular onslaught that accompanied the *épreuve*, her equanimity, almost palpable in the late writing, is so amazing as to seem supernatural.

It is a mercy to readers that Thérèse as writer had neither the training nor the inclination for the high artifices of rhetoric, for persuasion by oratorical concatenations. That is not to say she is a populist in style, only that in her gentle way she is the best of foils for the sublime Bossuet. Every citation I have given from her writings shows that whatever challenge she posed to her contemporary readers (and now to us) came from the nature of her perceptions, not from the language by which she expressed them. Her limpid style belongs within the tradition of classical French prose, blessedly free of opacity, pretentious language, and *snobisme*. It is transparent and gives ease of access. But what may be apparent may not be immediately comprehensible. We owe thanks to her sister Marie for prompting the writing of Manuscript B with a question that seems gratuitous to anyone raised in the Christian way of humility but which Marie felt needed explanation: what is the little way?

Thérèse's being drawn out in this instance to an expository length—Manuscript B is a ten-page letter—might have quickened her awareness of a skill she could have developed, had she lived. At the hearings, some sisters remarked that she would have become an exemplary prioress, and they were left to imagine the kind of *circulaire* tributes she would have written for them. How would she have weathered the ongoing fog? Would the vault finally have collapsed or would she have gone further in her identity with those cut off from heavenly promises?

Putting aside these bootless questions, we can be content that the Thérèse we know is her own best interpreter, especially as she was shaped by the great calamities which had their final onset in the Easter season of 1896. That point brings us to her third singularity, her afflictions both physical and psychological. Other Carmelites had sickened and died, but none during Thérèse's years at Carmel had endured the protracted torments to which tuberculosis subjected her. Nor had anyone else, as far as I know, entered and remained so long within what she called the "somber tunnel" of thick shadows where the little lights of faith and hope had been extinguished. Illness isolates acutely, and Thérèse profited, if that is the word, from her twofold isolation: when it did not beset her with terrible physical pain and (toward the end) a near suffocation, tuberculosis humiliated her with debility, yet she sharpened her already keen vision in the midst of her struggling. It is as though the sheer diminution of her energies forced from them a final and concentrated exertion. Over all her writings, Manuscript C stands as the most vital, a testament of vivid details of agapic devotion, what Blake called "minute particulars," in an inky-black night. Her last months begot a mysterious resilience. And beyond C come the delicious scraps from the table, those indispensable moments from Thérèse without her pen: *derniers entretiens*, last remarks over a summer of excruciated serenity.

With whatever small measure of caution and humility, we can best attempt to approach that perdurance—a word she would not have recognized regarding herself—through the one and steady source of her sustenance, the New Testament. This approach should not be confused with so-called proof texting. We need only identify passages in Scripture to which Thérèse herself was especially drawn and from which she took comfort—in the old sense of that word: strengthening, not soothing. We know as much from the frequency of citations she gives to them in her letters, verse, and autobiographical manuscripts.

Central among them comes *Galatians* 2:20: "I am crucified with Christ: nevertheless I live; yet not I, but Christ liveth in me: and the life which I now live in the flesh I live by the faith of the Son of God, who loved me, and gave himself for me." Thérèse refers to this passage in the vicinity of the tunnel just cited, but she had already used it in one of her most important poems, "Vivre d'Amour." There, she interprets St. Paul's message to signify that living on love is living on Christ's life. She asks Jesus, hidden in the sacramental host, to hide her from his other lovers: "il faut la solitude / un coeur à coeur qui dure nuit et jour/Ton seul regard fait ma béatitude/Je vis d'Amour" ["Solitude of heart to heart is needed, lasting night and day. Your look alone brings forth my blessedness. I live from Love"] (PN 17.3). Contrary to Paul's profession, however, Thérèse's makes Jesus and his love immediate rather than historical. Even more important, her own crucifixion, the twofold burden of disease and darkness, is not, as it might be charged against Paul, rhetorical: it is the very condition by which she enjoys that present solitude with her beloved.

Some of her favorite passages in *Matthew*[1] suppose her profound affinity with Jesus: her sharing of his yoke, her being least and thus closest to him, he the Solomonic bridegroom come at midnight for her. With that intimacy came a heightened sense of the world and its "materialist" nonbelievers. It is as though, sequestered within Carmel's walls, she had somehow learned wisdom from "the mammon of unrighteousness," even as Christ enjoined in *Luke* 16:8–9. At the same time, reaching out in cognitive and affective sympathy with sinners, for whom she now felt herself a sister, was she not also distancing herself from the ecclesiastical hierarchy? Had she not done so in claiming that Jesus alone was her spiritual advisor? Could she not lay claim to the gnosticlike arcana in Jesus' rejoicing prayer, thanking God "that thou hast hid these things from the wise and prudent, and hast revealed them unto babes" (*Luke* 10:21)? This passage deserves particular notice as the only one she cites in all three of her manuscripts. Subsuming this intimacy and initiation, the most poignantly human of all passages in the Christian narrative are words which she could justly have made her own, *Luke* 22:42, when Jesus prays that the cup of bitterness be removed from him.

Adversity intensified and ripened within her the radical intimacy with Jesus which she had enjoyed from the childhood years when she literally toyed around with him. By "radical," I mean that she was not much concerned with the once and future Christ, St. Paul's Galilean who once died out of love for him and who will come again to judge the living and the dead. Whole patches of Christian dogma and even Scripture she has left untouched: the temptations in the desert, the many miracles Jesus performs, the apocalypse. She mentions the transfiguration on Mount Tabor only to shift attention away from it.[2] Her Jesus remains forever to her consciousness within the little boat crossing the Sea of Galilee in *Mark*'s fourth chapter. If he seems to us peculiarly static, she puts him to the dynamic uses of her sensibility and stretches her reader's awareness by making Jesus all-sufficient. That fact is unequivocally clear in her bold, if not subversive, remark in Manuscript A (48v) that Jesus does not need books and expositors to instruct souls.

That said (by her), nothing would or could be further from the truth than to depict Thérèse as a heretic or apostate, certainly not in any programmatic sense. She would have recoiled in horror at the very words insofar as such denominations invoke separation, division, discord. Thérèse's whole impetus was precisely the opposite to all that. It was supremely unitive but it is so unto the furthest reaches of humanity, which is to say *catholic* in the first sense of that word.[3] The best index of that illimitable reach came in the first version of her *offrande*, where she wrote of her "désirs infinis" but was obliged by a cautious cleric to change her wording to the tame and manageable "désirs immenses," even though she was addressing an all-powerful God of boundless mercy. If she had been charged with imprudence about her trust in God's love, she would, I believe, have heartily acknowledged it was so, and she would also have seen that at the heart of so-called prudence is the supreme blasphemy toward God, which is lukewarmness. What is called her audacity is in sum a rejection of such tepidity of heart and soul. The simple proof of that fact comes in C where the loving heart of the Church finds its home amid souls struggling and pathetic in their own darkness. That is where Christ found them. It is there and with them that this book will close.

I began these chapters with the French Revolution and the challenge it had posed to the future of Christendom, the need for its rediscovery in some extraordinary way, as de Maistre had shrewdly foreseen. Neither Chateaubriand's aesthetic of faith, nor Lamennais's prophetlike calls for democratic justice, nor Renan's all-too-humanization of God (Jesus, the deluded Jewish peasant) sufficed to that end because they were in effect recasts of the revolutionary nostrums, *liberté, égalité, fraternité*. However vital such bromides might be to modern life, they are not in themselves sufficient. Free of any programmatic urges, Thérèse realized both by her sensibility and by her experience that humility, compassion, and love are far deeper energies and speak far more profoundly to the human condition.

The stringency in her love for God may be forbidding to some: the unwavering devotion to Christ despite the disappearance of heaven. Thérèse seems emphatically modern in the darkness from which at the close she comes to us. Tuberculosis and the sinners' table of bitterness indicate decisively that Thérèse's attention to suffering was not merely about some *idea* of suffering. Without those terrible afflictions, she could well be accused of a cozy rhetoric. As it is, her example, shaped in the cruelest of crucibles, proves radiant, and Christians can see it as a grace. She herself said she did not understand her darkness,[4] but she did know that Jesus had allowed it to come, and so it was for her a grace. No less paradoxical is her love of neighbor, that she sits down by godless sinners with whom she feels an unspoken affinity that might be construed as a mystical complement to the Virgin Mary's smiling upon her. Her company unto the end of time is not only with those who make pilgrimages to Lisieux (unless they come, as perhaps many do, in anguish and doubt) but with spiritual derelicts, including those professing the persistently fashionable notion that chance and meaninglessness are in charge, a dogma that began with Epicureanism, three centuries before Christ.[5] At the inglorious table, Thérèse adds the indispensable corollary of charity to St. Paul's text (1 *Thessalonians* 5:5) on the children of light and the children of darkness. However glowing or faint the light, its children must sit with those who do not have it and the darkness will be common, God being hidden within it. What distinguishes the table is that everyone at it is so terribly alone—Thérèse says she is eating alone—despite any appearance of community. How could there be, when God has been denied? This tableau recalls Dante's *Inferno*, where every damned soul is invincibly isolated, no matter how populous the company. That is what makes Thérèse's prayer so powerful. She utters it on behalf of those who would despise and reject both her and it.

As I have already remarked, Thérèse's urgent significance to the Church, this imperative into the obscurity of our secular age, points to her abiding pertinence to it. One of her less-heralded contributions is that she makes Nietzsche, foremost and fieriest of dissenters, accessible to Christians. Read by her tiny light in the dark, his rage against human paltriness is like a fever that keeps trying to reach its pitch and can break only into *petitesse* and the humbling acknowledgment that humankind cannot overcome itself. He knew, finally, that humanity in his time was too botched and bungled to justify his rhetorical inflations on its behalf.[6] Had he lived to see how that rhetoric could be warped to sinister ends, he might have felt the keenest repugnance. He believed that Pascal, had he lived, would have become an atheist. I would submit that Nietzsche, had he lived (sanely), might have become a Christian a second time. It is usually overlooked that his Zarathustran, leonine *Übermensch* ends redemptively as a child, innocently free of *ressentiment*. Thérèse's life of *confiance* is the surest antidote to the poisons of *ressentiment* which feed even some among the Church's faithful. Nietzsche's writings and those of Thérèse can be read in tandem.

The great contest of the twenty-first century finds empiricism set against transcendence; vulgarly put, science abetted by technological wizardry and demonstrable fact against religion and claims of faith. Distinctions usually come in terms pejorative to spirituality: the open against the closed, hypothesis against dogma, experiment against creed, the dynamic of progress against static reaction. There is nothing new in that, only that the stakes in an age of nuclear power and terrorism have become far greater than before. The fact that, for Christians, science serves not to eliminate but to deepen awe and reverence before mystery does not consistently register with those who care to dismiss or to degrade Christianity. Some, in the long train of Feuerbach, claim that we celebrate as divine what is in fact human, God being a projection of our own worth and virtues. Such Prometheanism, in the wake of Hitler, Stalin, Mao, and their miniature copies, seems obscenely anachronistic.[7]

In this darkness and confusion, Sr. Thérèse de l'Enfant Jésus de la Sainte Face has a Copernican role: she occupies the immanent world of fact while affirming the transcendent. Sitting with sinners, including those who do not see themselves as such nor even have a sense of what sin is, she confounds fanaticism and the cruelty which spurs it. By that sitting she fulfills in her singular little way Christ's injunction (*Matthew* 10:16) to be at once as gentle as a dove and as subtle as a serpent. Her *audace* here attains its uttermost expression in humility. Spurred by love rather than creed, she remains implicitly open to religions beyond Christianity, and yet because Christ, Jesus suffering in the garden and on the cross, is always at the center of her love, she can never be mistaken for someone who advertises Christianity even while diluting it in a kind of one-worldly embarrassment. Her exigent and confident love occupies a polar remove from the mishmash of today's fashionably vague religiosities, but she is a truly cosmopolitan figure. How could a Muslim reject her central message of unqualified trust in God? How close is her ontology of nothingness to the Buddhist's nirvana? I put these questions to suggest that both in her supreme affectivity and her *néant*, Thérèse is Christendom's foremost voice to non-Christian worlds. She is a missionary in a sense that even she did not realize, and of the best sort: one who by her own weakness and littleness does not play the one-up game, the we're-it legerdemain of the patronizing. Instead, even as she had stylized the beginning of her spiritual life as a choosing of all—that indomitable *tout*—she closed her life in the ripened awareness that the only *tout* she had was herself, a self not to choose but to give. That she did so with empty hands, as the phrase went, remains a merry little paradox.

In her lively, lyric advocacy of divine love against the very human conventions of punitive justice, she is especially vital because that punitive justice, a mask for aggression and chauvinistic hatreds, has made and will continue to make yet more comebacks in vengeful apocalypticism, whether purveyed in evangelical fantasies or in righteous jihads. Divine justice on our terms—that is an easy card to play and a deadly one. Science and its wonder-working technology cannot possibly deliver us from these passions. Only an informed spirituality can. Thérèse's exemplary charity must be not only democratized but internationalized.

Fortunately, in her, the Church has discovered perhaps its greatest of modern missionaries. After the Second World War, her reliquary began an itinerary which has since reached to lands half the earth's distance from Normandy. It has been seen, touched, revered by millions of people, many of whom have read little that she wrote[8] but who have been moved by the wish she uttered in that last summer, to spend her heaven doing good on earth. There is also the iconic appeal of the photos, occasions for what I have called a theology of silence. A transcultural phenomenon, witnessed again and again, Thérèse's many journeys into Asian and African nations have widened the way to the Southern Hemisphere as the future ground, perhaps the future home, for Christianity in this century.

If anything, even more auspicious is the shrine to Thérèse in a suburb of Cairo. There, Muslims come regularly to pray to the woman they know as Allah's daughter. In Arabic, she is known as "the little saint whose wishes Allah always grants." Only a few weeks before martial violence was visited upon the helpless people of Iraq, in March 2003, the remains of the daughter of Allah were in Baghdad. While en route to Christian communities in Lebanon, she was welcomed impromptu in many Muslim villages, with ever-hospitable and reverent people receiving her. This simple diplomacy, with Thérèse hidden and silent if not unknown, opens a luminous window onto the deadly antagonisms of cultures and faiths. In reviewing her much-desired apostolic titles in Manuscript B, Thérèse had not considered becoming a peacemaker, but the title does not fit awkwardly.

As though such a mission were not enough, Thérèse in her mute and eloquent manner, humble as it is, challenges the hubris of what Oswald Spengler called the Faustian age. Ongoing, it designates a time when more and more people would sit down to the table of sinners in the assumption that it was a ballroom banquet, a proud celebration of human achievements. We are back to the issue of how to read and live the immanence of life. It has sometimes been alleged against Thérèse that she remained ignorant of evil, and it must be admitted that the *belle epoche* in which she lived seems at an almost Edenic historical remove from us, this side of Hitler. It was a time ignorant of world wars, concentration camps, and genocidal ferocity. Whom did she expect to find at that table of sinners? an accuser might ask. Would she have sat down beside a Himmler or a Stalin? Could she have grasped evil doing at an exponential degree of efficiency? Where would one find the little way on a map that includes Treblinka, the gulags, the Cambodian killing fields? And what of the furtive, less-spectacular evils of our time, as when someone on a phone anonymously moves countless millions of dollars and ruins a far-distant economy where poor people work at wretched wages making things for our greater comfort? Could Thérèse have perceived such depravity? Are not all things pure to the pure?

These questions admit no ready answers. It can be said, however, that the little way of trust in God includes an unspoken but altogether salutary distrust of human sufficiencies. The path to barbarisms, military and commercial, while always there to take, will lead only to spiritual desolation. Pride in the technological engineering of life and death follows the same trajectory. How can that be doubted any longer?

Thérèse's exemplary weakness and littleness seem antimodern, naïve, and pointless against the onward Goliathan suasions of power, profit, subjugation, acquisition. And yet those and all avenues of assertion and domination prove cheerless and loveless to the individuals caught up within them. Thérèse does not speak to the dynamos of nation-states and institutions but to single human hearts, where the decisive sorts of dark behavior are found in their inception and miserable completion.[9] It is only there that her unflinching affirmation of Christian love and its divine mystery can be given heed. In her, love of God and of others comes not as some cheap, syrupy formula. It exacts suffering, one that transforms those who suffer because they are at the juncture of Christ's cross and humanity. If that now seems steep and impossible, Thérèse's writing and her life suggest otherwise.

Her little way of loving trust in God is lit by her little light of compassionate love for the rest of us, including those who might seem or are most unworthy. It is the only light by which we can safely find that way. Alternative ways and seeming lights prove too unspeakably bleak and dim even to contemplate. It remains a matter worth everyone's pondering that so momentous a view upon this life of ours could have come from a very young woman who knew herself to be little and weak.

Weak, little, a nothing.

Notes

CHAPTER ONE

1. Desecration of graves, for one: Chateaubriand was so haunted by the predations in the autumn of 1793 that forty years later he asked the municipality of Saint-Malo in Brittany to arrange for his burial on Le Grand-Bé, an island off the coast. Were he to die abroad, his remains were not to be touched for fifty years thereafter. He got his insular grave, without his name but with an unmistakable self-regarding inscription. See M. Regard in Jacques Roger, ed., *Histoire de la littérature française* (Paris: Armand Colin, 1970), II:664.

2. *Mémoires d'outre-tombe* (Paris: Librairie Générale Française, 1973), I:255.

3. "Condition de l'homme: Inconstance, ennui, inquiétude," in *Pensées* (Paris: Gallimard, 1936), 199.

4. *Mémoires d'outre-tombe*, I:292–293.

5. Quoted by Pierre Reboul in his introduction to *Génie du christianisme* (Paris: Flammarion, 1966), I:21.

6. In his *Souvenirs politiques*, cited by Reboul, ibid.

7. *Mémoires d'outre-tombe*, I:267.

8. F. de Lamennais, *Essai sur l'indifférence* (Paris: Garnier, 1859), I:21. La Mennais changed his name to Lamennais after 1834.

9. Ibid., 274–275.

10. Quoted in Claude Pichois, *De Chateaubriand à Baudelaire, 1820–1869* (Paris: Flammarion, 1996), 105.

11. www.papalencyclicals.net/Greg/16/g16mirar.htm.

12. Owen Chadwick, *A History of the Popes, 1830–1914* (Oxford: Clarendon, 1998), 16.

13. *Mémoires d'outre-tombe*, III:726.

14. *Paroles d'un croyant*, 3d ed. (Geneva: Les Marchands de Nouveautés, 1834), 62–64.

15. For a detailed and forceful criticism see Abbé Bautain's *Réponse d'un chrétien aux paroles d'un croyant* (Strasbourg: Février, 1834).

16. www.papalencyclicals.net/Greg/16/gsingu.htm.

17. *Essai sur l'indifférence*, I:142–143.

18. I borrow this notion from Henri Bergson's *Les deux sources de la morale et de la religion* in his *Oeuvres* (Paris: Presses universitaires de France, 1970).

19. *Souvenirs d'enfance et de jeunesse* (Paris: Flammarion, 1973), 133.

20. *Vie de Jésus*, edited by Jean Gaulmier (Paris: Gallimard, 1974), 107.

21. *The Quest of the Historical Jesus* (1906; rpt. New York: Macmillan, 1979), 191. See also Owen Chadwick, *The Secularization of the European Mind in the Nineteenth Century* (Cambridge: Cambridge University Press, 1975), 211–223.

22. *Vie de Jésus*, 138.

23. De Musset, "L'Espoir en Dieu": "Ma raison révoltée / Essaye en vain de croire et mon coeur de douter" ["My reason in rebellion tries vainly to believe and my heart to doubt"]. *Poésies complètes* (Paris: Gallimard, 1957), 343.

24. *Vie de Jésus*, 159, 170, 181, 194.

25. Ibid., 410.

26. *L'Avenir de la science: Extraits* (Paris: Larousse, 1954), 35.

27. *Souvenirs*, 213.

28. *Dialogues et fragments philosophiques* (Paris: Calmann Lévy, 1876), xix.

CHAPTER TWO

1. OC, 1201.

2. Marie to Louis Martin, November 16, 1877: "Oh! Oui, nous tâcherons d'être bien bonnes, de te rendre la vie bien douce pour te remercier du grand sacrifice que tu fais pour notre bonheur" ["Oh, yes, we'll try to be very good and give you a very sweet life in thanks for the great sacrifice you're making for our happiness"], in *VT* 56 (October 1974): 304.

3. Worse, many years later, in the ecclesiastical hearings for the beatification of her sister, Céline stated that, Marie having been chosen, Thérèse did not want Pauline to feel left out. The terrible wounding Léonie must have suffered at that moment seems to have occurred to none of the others. PA, 287–288.

4. I suspect that had her mother lived, Céline might have been more inclined toward marital life. The marriage of Zélie and Louis had been the work of his mother, and with three daughters already in Carmel, it would have been natural to hope for progeny.

5. At age four, Thérèse disclosed to Pauline her plan to join Céline in a convent. She, Thérèse, would be the Mère: "je mè promenerai toute la journée dans le cloîtrage, et puis j'irai avec Céline, ou jouera au sable et puis à là poupée" ["I'll walk about all day in the cloister and then I'll go with Céline and play in the sand or with dolls"]; CG I:96.

6. Manuscript A 48r. My characterization of their time as reverie rather than meditation is based upon Thérèse's own emphasis: "Oui, c'était bien *légèrement* que nous

suivions les traces de Jésus" ["Yes, it was quite *lightly* that we followed Jesus' steps"]. A somewhat more convincing allusion to Monica and Augustine at Ostia occurs in the *circulaire* of Sr. Madeleine de la Trinité, Carthage, September 8, 1893, 4, AC.

7. NPHF, 468. In his book, Piat tells this story but omits the crucial detail of the breakdown.

8. She uses the word twenty-nine times in her autobiographical manuscripts: once in A, twice in B, twenty-six times within twenty pages of C. In her letters, she speaks of charity only five times, three of them within the last year of her life.

9. PO, 532.

10. PO, 547.

11. A loving labor by Pauline who was otherwise kept busy in Carmel painting ornaments for sale.

12. This vital document is not at the Carmel Archives of Lisieux but on display in the showcase of Thérèse's bedroom at Les Buissonnets. I was grateful to be permitted to see a photocopy of it. It was reproduced many times not long after Thérèse's death.

13. "[T]u es médiocrement dévote" ["your devotion is mediocre"], and "tu es l'esclave de ton humeur, avec toutes ses bizarreries, tu te règles d'après tes caprices" ["you're the slave of your mood with all its whims, and you conduct yourself according to your caprices"]. Sr. Marie-Dosithée to Marie Martin, January 6, 1876, and February 20, 1876, in *VT* 48 (October 1972): 295, 297.

14. A. B., *Les vacances d'une jeune fille chrétienne: Guide pratique pour bien passer le temps des vacances* (Poitiers: Oudin, 1878), 13.

15. Ibid., 45.

16. Mme. Woilliez, *L'orpheline de Moscou* (Tours: Mame, 1852), 43. This remark about Juliette is made as she prays over dead troops after the battle of Borodino, but no happy result is recorded.

17. NPHF, 556.

18. Jacques Maître's mischievous *L'Orpheline de la Bérésina*, 297 and passim (see bibliography), presents Louis as weak and ineffectual (was that how he begot nine children?) before his wife and daughters, but it was a convention then and remains so even now that the household is the province of women. Fr. Pichon's characterization of him as *un religieux égaré dans le monde* (PO, 380), "out of place," is apt on more than one count: Louis would have been happily at home in a medieval monastery.

19. In the Bayeux-Lisieux diocese during the last third of the nineteenth century, only 10 to 14 percent of the communicants were male. See Srs. Marie de la Rédemption and Camille, "Horizons de Femmes à La Fin du XIXe Siècle à Lisieux: Le Bourgeoisie et le Carmel, Cadre de la Vie de Thérèse," in *Thérèse Carmélite*, edited by Dominique Poirot (Paris: Cerf, 2004), 37.

20. Like father, like daughter. Isidore's maid, who later became a Benedictine nun, said that Thérèse on hearing blasphemous language spoken by men of the working class remarked that they were more wretched than culpable and, besides, had far fewer *grâces* than her own family enjoyed. PO, 362.

21. Reported by L. Boncompain, S.J., *Un Directeur d'âmes: Le Père Almire Pichon* (Messager, 1921), 40.

22. Pichon to Marie Martin, May 19, 1882; September 1, 1882; September 30, 1882, in *VT* 62 (April 1976): 135, 145, 147.

23. Pichon to Marie Martin, December 14, 1882, in *VT* 65 (January 1977): 67.

24. Some may wish to presume an erotic bond in these relationships, but there is neither evidence nor likelihood of such a development, so such a presumption seems gratuitous. For young, diffident women like the Martin sisters, attention and encouragement were primary concerns. Affection would have come, if at all, a very distant third and eros was not even in the running.

25. R. P. Almire Pichon, S.J., *Retraite*, edited by Msgr. André Combes (Paris: Vrin, 1966), 12. "On reste stupéfait, indigné. Comment ne pas avoir senti le prix d'un tel trésor, la gravité d'une telle suppression?" ["One is left stupefied and outraged. How could he not have sensed the value of such a treasure, the seriousness of suppressing it?"]; "ce fut au Carmel que je lui ouvris mon âme" ["it was at Carmel that I started opening my heart to him"]; A 34v.

26. CG I:200–201.

27. Her sister Marie makes this point and says she in the maternal position agreed with Louis on the withdrawal. PO, 242.

28. For example, confusing *scène* (scene) with *cène* (supper) after the word *scène*, she writes, "Je viens d'être temoin d'une cène bien touchante" ["I witnessed a very touching supper"]; and for *cène*, "C'est pendant la Scène que Notre Seigneur institua l'Eucharistie" ["During the Last Scene Our Lord instituted the Eucharist"].

29. A. B., *Les vacances*, 136, 140. Subsequent quotations are from 137.

30. There is an abundance of other passages which are so pertinent to Thérèse's evolving spirituality that they read like signposts, e.g., that when you find suffering sweet, you have found paradise on earth (II.xii.11); that when grace leaves you, the only remedy is *abandon*.

31. On that day Marie wrote to him: "Pauvre père, que tu as d'ingrats enfants! C'est à qui te retiendra le plus longtemps sur cette terre de misères. Et au besoin tout le Carmel s'en mêlerait" ["Poor father, what ungrateful children you have! That's what will keep you for a long time on this wretched earth. And in case of need the whole Carmel will be meddling"], in *VT* 56 (October 1974): 307.

32. Thérèse herself says of Pauline at Carmel in 1885, "j'espérais la rejoindre bientôt et attendre avec elle le Ciel" ["I was hoping to rejoin her there and await Heaven with her"]; A 35v.

33. It may be that she took the notion of conversion from *circulaires* she had heard or read: Mère Agathe de Jésus, Nantes, had what she called a conversion when her older brother, to whom she was very close, left home to become a sulpicien, and not long after she, at eighteen, was told by her superior that she would become a Carmelite. *Circulaire* of June 2, 1894. Sr. Anna du Très-Saint Sacrament, Tarbes, had in adolescence become neglectful of piety until her confessor quickened in her what she called a conversion: she then went to the Carmel for a retreat but the prioress took her in for good. *Circulaire* of July 26, 1894.

34. Marie felt her little sister was too young for Carmel; she also feared the ensuing grief for Louis: "Car Thérèse était dans sa vie le vrai rayon du soleil" ["Indeed Thérèse was the true ray of sun in his life"]; PO, 243.

35. "[L]e Carmel était considéré et dépeint comme un tombeau où l'on devait s'ensevelir toute-vive" ["The Carmel was regarded and depicted as a tomb where one was supposed to be buried alive"] (*Circulaire* of Sr. Anne de Saint Michel [Saint-Flour],

June 1, 1894) reflects a popular view two generations before, during the time of Louis-Philippe, but it likely kept its force since parental opposition continued to be strong well into Thérèse's time.

36. *VT* 37 (January 1970): 36.

37. This young man intrigues by having disappeared altogether from the Martin chronicle. There is no subsequent word of him nor even a photo in the substantial Carmel Archive.

38. See OC, 1262, n. 258, which claims, "Elle s'est dégagée promptement en lui jetant un regard noir" ["She freed herself promptly by throwing him a black look"] which contrasts in tempo with Céline's account quoted in a note from Pauline, in the 1997 Cerf edition of *Histoire d'une âme: Manuscrits autobiographiques*, 303, n. 6.

39. Abbé Huet, *Journal du pèlerinage de Bayeux à Rome* (Caen: Chénel, 1887), 18. This vicar of Saint-Étienne in Caen notes, as does Thérèse, that the pilgrims had their first inclement weather on that morning, but she does not note and he does, that it also rained steadily through the next morning at Pompeii, clearing only in the afternoon. In her superstitious attention to the weather she would have been hard put to explain the second day's rain.

40. *Manuscrits autobiographiques*, facsimile edition of 1956 edited by Fr. François de Sainte-Marie and published by the Office Central de Lisieux, 44.

41. The Society of Jesus had been unhoused by government decree in 1880, but the Jesuits had grouped without incident or violence. The next major wave of bullying came in 1904 when all of the teaching orders were dispossessed of their schools and posts.

42. Some of the sisters were not so charitable about Louis during his illness.

43. The burden rested almost wholly upon her: Isidore had come into a substantial inheritance from his wife's relations (by French law it went to him, not to her), sold his pharmacy, and was busy moving house; Léonie had never been close to the other girls, who were now looking to Céline for candor.

44. At the hearings, Marie Martin spoke only in veiled terms on her instruction of Thérèse regarding monthly times.

45. Chapter 3:1–2: "By night on my bed I sought him whom my soul loveth; I sought him, but I found him not. I will rise now, and go about the city in the streets, and in the broad ways I will seek him whom my soul loveth; I sought him, but I found him not."

46. The letter of July 18, 1890, provides an exemplary excitement and confusion, as she struggles with the inadequacy of words to express "the most intimate depths of the soul."

47. Sr. Thérèse de Saint-Augustin, "Souvenirs d'une sainte amitié," 1–2, AC; reproduced in *VT* 99 (July 1985): 244–255. To this testimony should be appended Thérèse's rejection of a manual of versification shown her by a novice, Sr. Marie de la Trinité: "J'aime mieux ne pas connaître toutes ces règles: mes poésies sont un jet de coeur, une inspiration" ["I prefer not to know all the rules; my poems are a burst from the heart, an inspiration"]; (*Conseils et souvenirs* of Marie de la Trinité, 34, AC). These remarks are of a piece with her anti-intellectual resistance to discursive theology.

48. "Je ne voudrais même pas vous dire à quel point la nuit est noire dans mon âme, de crainte de vous faire partager mes tentations" ["I wouldn't want to tell you

to what degree the night is black in my soul, for fear of making you share my temptations"], *Carnet rouge*, 15, AC.

49. *Carnet rouge*, 18, 50, 46.

50. The camera's requisite nine seconds for a pose exacted a rather forced smile, anyway.

51. *Circulaire* of Mère Olympe du Sacré Coeur de Jésus, Pamiers, August 13, 1893. Louis's own view of his suffering came from the *Imitatio Christi*, II.ix.7, that one is not worthy to be raised to God without having suffered tribulation.

52. I believe that Pichon is meant in Thérèse's poem "Le Cantique de Céline," PN 18, strophe 11: "j'aimai la créature / Qui me paraissait être pure" ["I loved the creature that seemed pure to me"] even though it may also refer to one or another of her suitors. But how could any of them have seemed so pure as this priest? Note that PN 18 was written in April 1895, seven months after Céline entered Carmel.

53. She wrote to her adopted mother that she herself had become Louis's mother, LD, ca. July 20, 1893: "Mon cher petit Père est mon petit baby [*sic*]. . . . tu ne te figures pas, ma chère Marie, toute la tendresse que j'ai pour lui" ["My dear little Father is my little baby. . . . you can't imagine, my dear Marie, all the tenderness I have for him"]. It is interesting that she wrote this letter to the favorite daughter of Louis. It's a claim Marie could never have made: she had played without much personal satisfaction the maternal role at Les Buissonnets after her mother's death. Also, Céline was not writing this to Thérèse, for whom Louis was always in the spousal role, king to her queen. Only Céline was privileged with the virginal/maternal role that made Louis a child.

54. The *converse* was a domestic who wore the white veil of the novitiate even after making her profession of vows. She attended the choir but did not use the Latin breviary and would have had no vote in elections. Usually, a Carmel would have four sisters at this station. Those who in their pre-Carmelite life had once performed as maids were almost invariably *converses* in the cloister.

55. Communication from the Carmel at Lisieux.

56. Thanks to Bossuet, who had her imprisoned, Mme. de Guyon was for centuries under a cloud but it has been lifted in recent times, and comparing her highly emotive yet simple and accessible spirituality with Thérèse's would be a worthy topic for someone's graduate thesis. For a start, see Madame Guyon, *Le Moyen court* (Paris: Mercure de France, 2001), esp. 32: "Que [l'âme] n'y [à l'oraison] aille jamais pour avoir quelque chose de Dieu mais pour lui plaire et faire sa volonté" ["May the soul never go to prayer to get something from God but to please him and to do his will"]. And 56–57, "Des défauts."

57. "Souvenirs," VT 99 (July 1985): 249. By then, Thérèse had already written what would become her most celebrated poem, "Vivre d'Amour," concluding its penultimate strophe with "Mourir d'Amour. . . Car je le sens, mon exil va finir" ["To die of love. . . Indeed I sense my exile is coming to a close"]. As we shall note, "Vivre d'Amour, Mourir d'Amour" was inspired by an 1890 *circulaire* from Beaune.

58. In the manuscript, the phrase about exile is added in the margin.

59. *Circulaire* of Sr. Anne-Marie de Jésus, Luçon, May 30, 1895. The postmark from Luçon is dated June 7, which means that it would have arrived in Carmel probably no sooner than June 9. If we presume it was read that day in the refectory,

the composition of Thérèse's own *offrande* would seem to have taken instant inspiration. Sr. Anne-Marie's fortuitous, Good Friday death was of the sort to inspire awe—and just what Thérèse herself resisted: the spectacular occasion which would make someone exceptional.

60. *Circulaire* of Mère Thérèse de Marie, Lyon, July 16, 1894.

61. *Circulaire* of Mère St. Louis de Gonzague, Shanghai, September 10, 1891.

62. *Circulaire* of Mère Marie du Mont Carmel, March 25, 1895, Bethlehem. This Carmel had been founded by the Carmel of Pau but Marie came from Oloron's. No date for the panic is supplied in the *circulaire* but it occurred sometime during 1876.

63. *Circulaire* of Mère Marie de la Croix, February 14, 1891. It would likely have caught Thérèse's notice that Sr. Marie had been appointed mistress of novices as soon as she left the novitiate.

64. An extraordinary *circulaire*, inclusive for three Vietnamese sisters, two of them white veiled, June 8, 1889.

65. *Circulaire* of Sr. Marie du Mont Carmel (Maria Dinh), Saigon, May 2, 1892. This *circulaire* is unusual for identifying the secular name of the sister.

66. One of the Lisieux Carmelites, Anne du Sacré-Coeur, had come from the Saigon Carmel and returned there in July 1895.

67. "Sa présence d'esprit semblait même se développer à mesure que le physique baissait" ["Her presence of mind even seemed to advance as her outward appearance declined"] and "se manifestèrent les premiers symptômes de la maladie de poitrine qui devait nous l'envoler, en même temps l'état de son âme s'améliora sensiblement" ["as the first symptoms of the pulmonary illness which was to take her from us became apparent, the state of her soul at the same time markedly improved"]; *Circulaire* of Sr. Isabelle-des-Anges, Orleans, September 14, 1894.

CHAPTER THREE

1. CF, 433 (August 16, 1877).

2. *DE*, August 21, 1897.

3. CG II; LT 261 (July 26, 1897).

4. Stendhal (Henri Beyle), *Le rouge et le noir* (Paris: Éditions Garnier Frèrer, 1973), 89.

5. PO, 380.

6. R. P. Stéphane-Joseph Piat, *Histoire d'une famille* (Paris: Pierre Téqui, 1945), 24.

7. But not nearly so urgent as their sister Sr. Marie-Dosithée, who exclaimed: "te savoir seul à Paris! à ton âge, entouré de mauvais exemples, avec plus ou moins d'amour du plaisir et de l' indépendance je frémis continuellement sur ton sort" ["to know you're alone in Paris at your age, surrounded by bad examples, with more or less a love of pleasure and independance. I tremble continually over your fate"] (May 16, 1865), in *VT* 37 (January 1970): 46. By then, Isidore had already spent more than two years in what she called "cette Babylone moderne" (October 27, 1862), in *VT* 36 (October 1969): 194. She herself knew Paris by seeking commissions there when Zélie was first setting up in the lace-making business.

8. CF, 14 (January 1, 1863).

9. Theodore Zeldin, *France* (New York: Oxford University Press, 1977), I:303.

10. Piat, *Histoire d'une famille*, 33.

11. Apart from his few extant letters, a notebook with copies from his favorite reading, primarily romantic poets, dates from his youthful days in Rennes, where he was an apprentice to a watchmaker. These "Fragments littéraires" bear the date 1842, AC.

12. CF, 34 (November 7, 1865).

13. Sr. Marie-Dosithée to Isidore Guérin, August 6, 1865: "car certainement je n'éprouve ni pour Zélie ni pour mes nièces ce que j'éprouve pour mon cher poupon d'autrefois" ["I certainly don't feel for Zélie nor for my nieces what I feel for my dear one-time baby"], in *VT* 37 (January 1970): 48.

14. The parish church has in its chapel, dedicated to Thérèse, a proudly framed letter from Pauline on the hundredth anniversary (1931) of her mother's baptism there.

15. Louis maybe often said to her such words as these from October 8, 1863: "J'ai quelques commandes de la Compagnie Lyonnaise; encore une fois, ne te tourmente pas tant, nous arriverons, Dieu aidant, à faire une bonne petite maison" ["I've gotten some orders from Compagnie Lyonnaise. Once more, don't torment yourself so much. God helping, we'll succeed in making a good little home"], in *VT* 37 (January 1970): 36.

16. Céline does not explain the absence of Louis in his wife's letters to the Guérins: "car, on voyait bien que cette pauvre petite Mère, débordée ne lui faisait pas une assez large place dans sa correspondance, ce n'était bien sur pas par l'indifférence, car comme ils s'aimaient et comme leurs âmes étaient semblables!!!!" ["indeed, you notice that this poor little woman, stretched, didn't make much of a place for him in her letters, but it wasn't out of indifference [for] indeed they loved each other and their souls were so alike!!!!"]; NPHF, 194.

17. CF, 20 (March 28, 1864).

18. CF, 33 (November 7, 1865).

19. CF, 40 (April 22, 1866).

20. CF, 43 (December 23, 1866).

21. Thérèse noted, on the Virgin's relation to the saints, that a mother would never wish to outshine her children.

22. Or so we can infer from Sr. Marie-Dosithée's letter to Zélie, February 15, 1867, in *VT* 39 (July 1970): 161–162.

23. CF, 51 (January 2, 1868).

24. CF, 57 (March 23, 1868).

25. CF, 63–64 (August 23, 1868).

26. Pauline, *Souvenirs intimes*, 3, AC. N.B.: This is the pagination of the typescript version of the document in the Archives du Carmel. The notes date from March 2 to March 9, 1932. From Sr. Marie-Dosithée came this consolation for Zélie on August 25, 1868: "depuis ton enfance jusqu'à présent que de peines de tout genre n'as-tu pas souffertes! Mais la fin viendra et la mesure de ta joie sera celle de tes afflictions" ["from your childhood till now what pains of every kind have you not suffered! But their end will come and the measure of your joy will be that of your afflictions"], in *VT* 39 (July 1970): 174–175.

27. CF, 67–68 (September 7, 1868).

28. Ibid.

29. CF, 77–78 (February 28, 1869); my emphasis.

30. CF, 85–86 (February 12, 1870).

31. CF, 88 (February 24, 1870).

32. So I was told by the oblates at the Martin home in Alençon.

33. Sr. Marie-Dosithée to Zélie, February 23, 1870, in VT 41 (January 1871): 51.

34. NPHF, 194: "Je dis cela pour montrer leur union de pensée et de sentiment, en tout" ["I say that to indicate they were one in thought and feeling, in everything"]. She objected to Piat's contrasting their personalities, that Mme. Martin "si vivante, si spirituelle, si positive, apparaît en un relief puissant, tandis que M. Martin donne l'impression d'un caractère rêveur, un peu romantique et lamartinien" ["seemed so lively, intelligent, positive, in imposing relief, whereas Mr. Martin gives the impression of a dreamer, a bit romantic and poetic"]. Her mother, she goes on to insist, "rêvant aux choses de l'éternité, elle ne cédait en rien à Papa sous ce rapport" ["dreaming of eternal things, did not yield in anything to Papa in this regard"].

35. CF, 100 (August 23, 1870).

36. CF, 102–103 (October ?, 1870).

37. CF, 101 (October 8, 1870).

38. CF, 110 (January 17, 1871).

39. Flaubert to Sand, in Gustave Flaubert, *Correspondance*, edited by Bernard Masson and Jean Bruneau (Paris: Gallimard, 1998), 583.

40. According to her sister, September 17, 1871: "[les bons] me font l'effet des Apôtres que Notre Seigneur avait pris avec lui la nuit de la passion: ils dormaient . . . et les ennemis de Jésus ne dormaient pas ils s'agitaient comme des furies d'enfer" ["the good act like Our Lord's Apostles the night of the passion: they slept . . . and the enemies of Jesus weren't sleeping but busy like the furies of hell"], in VT 42 (April 1971): 109.

41. CF, 231 (April 29, 1875).

42. CF, 116 (May 29, 1871).

43. CF, 119 (September 5, 1871).

44. CF, 114 (May 5, 1871).

45. Ibid.

46. He once remarked to Céline about an investment, perhaps the Panama Canal venture, which was to lose him tens of thousands of francs: "Je ne vais pas suivre cela d'aussi près, c'est si facile de tomber dans la spéculation, dans l'agiotage" ["I'm not going to follow it closely, it's so easy to fall into speculating and gambling"]; NPHF, 4.

47. It passed into an irreversible decline due to an overextension of capital with much smaller returns than anticipated and an ill-based confidence in unending growth.

48. CF, 120 (September 5, 1871).

49. Piat, *Histoire d'une famille*, 55.

50. CF, 71 (November 1, 1868).

51. CF, 137 (July ?, 1872) and 132 (April 24, 1872).

52. CF, 244 (September 29, 1875).

53. Sr. Marie-Dosithée to Isidore Guérin, June 27, 1875: "à quoi donc te servirait de devenir si riche? Va tu n'en serais pas plus heureux, ni tes enfants non plus!" ["so what will be the point of your becoming so wealthy? You'll not be the happier for it nor will your children, either"], in VT 46 (April 1972): 141.

54. CF, 121 (October 1, 1871).

55. CF, 147 (March 9, 1873).

56. CF, 186 (November 29, 1873).

57. Pauline, *Souvenirs*, 1. Of the twenty pages of this document, this vivid childhood memory occurs on the first of them. In theresian style, we might call this incident Pauline's first grace.

58. Pauline, *Souvenirs*, 1–2.

59. VT 44 (October 1971): 243. The report on April 5, 1874, is negative. Her mother "avait tant de confiance que la douceur et la charité de la Visitation changeraient sa fille et maintenant cet espoir s'est évanoui" ["had so much confidence that the gentleness and charity of the Visitation would change her daughter and now this hope has vanished"]; ibid., 247.

60. CF, 196 (June 1, 1874).

61. CF, 244 (September 29, 1875).

62. CF, 253 (October 31, 1875). Did she know that Pauline herself was subject at school to such clinging or what was known as "affections exagérées," an excessive emotional attachment to teachers? "Oh mon Dieu, pourquoi ne vous ai-je pas uniquement aimé? Pourquoi me suis-je laissé couper et brûler les ailes, à cette flamme trompeuse de l'affection si vaine des créatures?" ["Oh, my God, why haven't I loved you alone? Why did I let my wings be clipped and burned by this deceitful flame of such pointless affection for people?"]; Pauline, *Souvenirs*, 5.

63. CF, 254 (November 7, 1875). In her *Souvenirs*, 7, Pauline recalls that she was bothered by such effusions from her mother because they made her feel how unworthy she was.

64. CF, 269 (January 16, 1876).

65. He did the same with Thérèse as queen, using the masculine: "mon petit Reinot."

66. Pauline's most vivid recollection of Louise came from a tickling on a bed. As the maid was busy with the child's feet, Zélie, hearing the laughter, broke in on them and reproached Louise: "Q'est-ce que vous faites?! Vous ne voyez donc pas le danger que court cette pauvre petite!" ["What are you doing?! You don't see then the danger this little one is running!"]; Pauline, *Souvenirs*, 3.

67. CF, 311–313 (October ?, 1876).

68. CF, 350 (January 21, 1877).

69. CF, 337 (December 24, 1876).

70. CF, 357 (February 13, 1877).

71. CF, 361 (February 20, 1877).

72. CF, 346 (January ?, 1877).

73. CF, 366 (March 4, 1877).

74. Ibid.

75. As early as February 4, 1877, Isidore advised her against the twenty-four-hour train trip as impractical. "Et si la tumeur est percée, penses-tu rester aussi longtemps

sans changer de linge et...les voisins, surtout si c'est en été? Pèse bien toutes ces considérations" ["And if the tumor bursts, do you imagine remaining a long while without changing clothes and...what of the other passengers, especially if it's summer? Weigh well these considerations"], in *VT* 54 (April 1974): 142.

76. CF, 406 (June 14, 1877).

77. Pauline, *Souvenirs*, 6.

78. Ibid. Her mother several times bathed Léonie's face in the grotto's waters. "Ce ne fut pas en vain, car Léonie est devenue une vraie sainte" ["It wasn't in vain, as Léonie has become a true saint"].

79. CF, 418 (June 25, 1877).

80. Ibid.

81. CF, 426 (July 15, 1877).

82. CF, 431 (July 27, 1877).

83. CF, 433 (August 16, 1877).

84. Piat, *Histoire d'une famille*, 191.

85. Piat, 167.

CHAPTER FOUR

1. Carmel's fathers are allowed to preach beyond the walls.

2. "Enseignements, Instructions et Avis de nos Mères Espagnoles," in *Le Papier d' exaction apporté en France par nos Mères Espagnoles* (Paris: Mersch, 1889), 57.

3. In *DE*, July 7, 1897, she recalls burning with love when making the *offrande* of June 1895: "J'ai compris alors ce que disent les saints de ces états qu'ils ont expérimentés si souvent" ["I understood then what saints say of these states they've so often experienced"].

4. Child of her age, she used the term "science of love."

5. See Anne-Elisabeth Steinmann, *Carmel vivant* (Paris: Editions Saint-Paul, 1963), 101ff.

6. Anne de Saint-Bartelemy, *Autobiographie*, translated by Pierre Séroult, O.C.D. (Ghent: Carmelitana, 1989), 73.

7. For a modern profile of this still irrepressible heresy, see Max Vilain, "Influence du Jansénisme et Thérèse de Lisieux," *VT* 75 (July 1979): 189–210. The pointed, penetrating citations from Julien Green are especially noteworthy. In more-recent times, the Jansenist sway (not named such) can best be measured by rollback opposition to the Second Vatican Council, including condemnation of Pope John XXIII and every subsequent pope, and bristling anti-Semitism.

8. Complementing Pascal and Sainte-Beuve's masterwork on Port Royal are two now-classic studies on Jansenism: Paul Bénichou, *Morales du grand siècle* (Paris: Gallimard, 1948), 121–218; and Lucien Goldmann's *Le Dieu caché* (Paris: Gallimard, 1959).

9. Jean-Pierre Joshua, *Seul avec Dieu: L'aventure mystique* (Paris: Gallimard, 1996), 101.

10. On Bérulle and "le Bérullisme" see Henri Bremond's *Histoire littéraire du sentiment religieux en France: La conquête mystique* (Paris: Bloud and Gay, 1921).

11. For a modern sociology of French conventual orders, see Catherine Baker's addictively fascinating study, *Les contemplatives: Des femmes entre elles* (Paris: Stock, 1979).

12. *Annales de Sainte Thérèse de Lisieux* 614 (June 1983): 4; cf. PO, 458, for Thérèse's remarks to an irritated novice on charitable patience toward this sister. Her lesson was that learning to regard another's infirmities with kindness will remove one's own unhappy displeasure at them. As to Sr. Saint-Raphaël, the disparagement seems overdrawn: she served on the prioress's building committee and as *sous-prieure*. She could not have been all that stupid.

13. See LT 221 and C 9v–10r.

14. The law forbidding inhumation within enclosures dates from June 1804. In 1842, when the *fondatrice*, Mère Élisabeth, died, the Lisieux community asked permission to bury her within Carmel; the mayor refused, but the departmental prefect overrode him. Other sisters were subsequently buried in the civic cemetery but exhumed and reburied within the convent when a mayor favorable to Carmel was elected. In 1887, the civic indulgence ended.

15. As of September 1884, the Carmelites of Rennes had to be interred in the civic cemetery, "l'autorisation pour notre cimetière ayant été refusée." *Livre des Soeurs défuntes*, Archives du Carmel, Rennes, n.d.; see entry for Sr. Pauline de St. Pierre. There is no record of obligatory exhumations. Most of the Carmelites in the Rennes Carmel at that time were buried in Gosselies, Belgium, during the long exile of 1901–1920.

16. This carefully written document was kept by a sister elected for a three-year term as *dépositaire*. For the years I consulted, Sr. Marie des Anges (also trainer of novices at the time) served in this capacity until 1893, when Gonzague was elected to it. When Gonzague again became prioress in 1896, Pauline was elected *dépositaire*.

17. According to the monthly *Registre* of the Carmel at Rennes, the prioress herself, Marie Thérèse de Jésus, gave 600 francs in January and 1,200 in April each year through the 1890s, with the 1,200 once given a month earlier than usual (March 1895) when the balance, *en caisse*, was down to only 75 francs. Other sisters' pensions ranged in the mid-100s as at Lisieux, but the annual *Registre* at Rennes shows that the Carmel budget there averaged less than half of Lisieux's during Gonzague's priorate, the number of sisters at Rennes being much smaller. There was no apparent stock investment at Rennes. Its *aumônier* was paid only 300 francs yearly at a time when Lisieux's was paid 850 (1890) and 900 (1891–1892).

18. See Gilbert Guilleminault and Yvonne Singer-Lecocq, "Le Mirage des emprunts russes," in *Le roman vrai de la IIIe et de la IVe République*, edited by Gilbert Guilleminault (Paris: Laffont, 1991), I:251–265. This volume includes an essay on Edouard Drumont's 1892 exposure of the Panama Canal company's briberies of government officials: Alain Colin-Simard and Jacques Robichon, "Le Scandale de Panamá" (I:201–227). I have been unable to trace another entry in the Carmelite budget: "les voitures de Paris."

19. The one purchased in 1887 was filled within ten years. Thérèse was the first Carmelite buried in the second plot.

20. The total expenditures for 1890, 1891, 1892 (Gonzague's term) were, respectively, 37,423 francs; 34,739; 38,728. In 1893, 1894, 1895 (Pauline's term), they

came, respectively, to 17,730; 21,633; 23,455. Pauline's cautious budgeting may well have been determined by the sharply declining balances in Gonzague's term: from 8,902 francs in 1890 to a mere 1,340 in 1892.

21. "Enseignements," *Le Papier d'exaction*, 55.

22. A discussion of the relations between Gonzague and Pauline might well start with the latter's early letters from Carmel to Marie, with words such as these on Gonzague: "j'ai raconté tout notre parloir à la Mère unique que tu connais, si tu savais comme ella comprend bien tout. Je l'aime de plus en plus. Je crois que son affection pour toi a encore redoublé la mienne" ["I've told all our conversation to the sole Mother you know. If you knew how she understands everything well. I am loving her more and more. I believe her affection for you has even redoubled my own"]; Pauline to Marie Martin, August 4?, 1885, in *VT* 64 (October 1976): 310.

23. Pauline, *Souvenirs intimes*, 9.

24. Thomas Kselman, *Death and the Afterlife in Modern France* (Princeton, N.J.: Princeton University Press, 1993).

25. *Saint Thérèse of Lisieux: Her Life, Times, and Teaching*, edited by Conrad de Meester (Washington, D.C.: ICS, 1997), 117.

26. PO, 476–482.

27. At the initial *procès* on the matter of Pauline v. Gonzague.

28. Ulrike Strasser, "Bones of Contention: Catholic Nuns Resist Their Enclosure," in Nancy Falk and Rita Gross, eds., *Unspoken Worlds: Women's Religious Lives* (Belmont, Calif.: Wadsworth, 2001), 208.

29. Matthew James Dowling, "The Evolution of a Modern Pilgrimage: Lisieux, 1897–1939" (unpublished dissertation, Yale University, 1995; UMI no. 9613971), ch. 1, passim. Notre Dame de la Providence ran a crèche for poor children; the Sisters of Mercy tended the sick; the Little Sisters of the Poor (est. 1855) housed two hundred elderly of both sexes; the Benedictines ran a school; and Notre Dame de la Miséricorde (est. 1873) housed up to two hundred young women, many of them prostitutes, thieves, or unwed mothers, who outraged the working class by taking in laundry and making undergarments at the lowest rates.

30. *La fondation du Carmel de Lisieux et sa fondatrice la Révérende Mère Geneviève de Ste. Thérèse* (Lisieux: Office Central de la Bse Thérèse, 1912), 38. No author is indicated but it was almost certainly Pauline, then prioress, who drew from memory and archival materials, including the *circulaire* of 1891, composed by Marie de Gonzague.

31. Ibid., 55. On natural affection's danger to the acutely sensitive Thérèse, see Emmanuel Renault, *Thérèse de Lisieux Carmélite: La règle, la liberté et l'amour* (Paris: Cerf, 1998), 51–53.

32. *La fondation*, 58.

33. Ibid., 56.

34. *Circulaire* of Mère Geneviève by Mère Marie de Gonzague, December 5, 1891, AC; my emphasis. In *La fondation*, 94, there is an anecdote about her late years when she was confined to the infirmary. The prioress is unnamed but it was obviously Gonzague who came in precipitously while a sister was reading to the invalid. "Ne vous occupez plus de rien dans la maison. Vous ne voyez pas ce qui se passe, et vos conseils tournent à mal" ["Don't busy yourself any longer with the house. You

don't see what's going on and your advice is turning out badly"]. The old woman thanked the prioress for the charity of her remarks and asked forgiveness, saying that when one has been a prioress, one goes on interfering in business not her concern.

35. *Circulaire*, 14; my emphasis.

36. Ibid., 18, 20. In the *circulaires* a great deal of narrative is given to the closing days of the subject, including physical sufferings, in order to provide a definitive profile of a good end. The account of Mère Geneviève's psychological torments toward the close is mitigated by descriptions of her smiling or her shedding of diamondlike tears: "son visage s'illumina d'une beauté céleste" ["her face shone with a heavenly beauty"], etc.

37. Ibid., 21. The same could well have been written of many others within the Carmel. That is not to detract from the subject of this laudation nor its sincerity.

38. *Circulaire* of Sr. Fébronie, January 6, 1892, AC. For the *Imitatio Christi*, see I.2.

39. Manuscript A 70v. The novice was, of course, Thérèse.

40. *Circulaire* of Sr. Madeleine, January 7, 1892, Archives du Carmel, 1–2. It was Thérèse who found her dead.

41. PN 41, one of the poems most doctored by Pauline. See *Poems of St. Thérèse de Lisieux*, translated by Alan Bancroft (London: HarperCollins, 1997), 138.

42. *Circulaire* on Sr. Saint-Jean de la Croix, September 3, 1906, 1. In a prayer to Thérèse found posthumously in her offices book, she had signed herself "Un tout petit rien" ["A thoroughly little nothing"], 2.

43. Quoted in the anonymously authored Carmel publication, *Le Père Pichon et la famille Martin jusqu'à la mort de Sainte Thérèse, 1882–1897* (Lisieux: Morière, 1968), 41–42.

44. *Règle primitive et constitutions des religieuses de l'Ordre de Notre Dame du Mont Carmel* (Poitiers: Henri Oudin, 1865), 94.

45. After their novitiate, a few sisters retained white veils and became *converses*, attending the choral offices but also serving for domestic labor such as cooking and housekeeping.

46. *Circulaire* on Sr. Marie des Anges, January 24, 1924, 1, 2, 4, 5. See also *Annales* 596 (November 1981): 12–13.

47. Letter of Sr. Marie des Anges to Thérèse, November 1889, LC 119; CG, I:509–510.

48. Letter of Sr. Marie des Anges to Thérèse, November 21, 1889, LC 120; CG, I:512.

49. The full text is quoted in CG, II:1170.

50. See *L'internelle consolacion* (1856; Kraus Reprint Neudeln, 1979), 59: "Souvienque vous, mon tresdoulx Dieu et Seigneur, que je ne suys rien, je n'ay rien, et ne puis rien."

51. *Règle*, 191.

52. I am assured that no such thing was ever witnessed in France's Carmels. Communication from the Carmel of Lisieux.

53. *Règle*, 247.

54. Answer: when painting images, Carmelites used magazines for their pictures of flowers, borders, and decorations. Communication from the Carmel of Lisieux.

55. For the first incident, see PO, 252. The testimony comes from Marie, who says that Thérèse excused herself by saying that in observing the world's vanity she was elevating her soul. That sounds charmingly disingenuous. The second incident is reported by Sr. Aimée in PO, 573, who says the response was emotional. Her testimony has the peculiar value of having been given "sans enthousiasme et sans attrait sensible."

56. "It aroused considerable interest on the part of the nuns, most of whom had never seen a camera before.... The iconography of the convent, rather meager until that point, became considerably enriched." *The Photo Album of St. Thérèse de Lisieux* (1962; rpt. Allen, Tex.: Christian Classics, 1997), 17.

57. The bells came from the famous foundry at Villedieu-les-Poêles, near Mont St.-Michel.

58. Most, if not all the Carmelites of late nineteenth-century Lisieux would have known the *Imitatio Christi*, including Lamennais's pointed words on charity toward others' failings: "Tournez vos regards sur vous-même, et voyez si vos frères [et vos soeurs!] n'ont rien à souffrir de vous." That injunction comes in his *réflexions* on I.16. There is no pagination in the 1873 edition which I have cited, one used by Thérèse herself.

59. *Le Papier d'exaction*, 47, 58.

60. Ibid., 68, 73, 75.

61. Ibid., 100.

62. *Direction spirituelle* (Poitiers: Oudin, 1869), 227 (no. 8), 240–241 (nos. 32, 37).

63. Ibid., 39, 40. Even as *Le Papier d'exaction* refers explicitly to the *Règle* and the *Constitution*, so this text refers to both of them and to the *Papier*.

64. *Direction spirituelle*, 168.

65. Even the homes of the well-off in this time were not well heated in all their rooms.

66. *Circulaire* of Sr. Marie de Saint-Gabriel, Toulon, April 10, 1888, 3, 4. The date given refers to the time of writing, not the date of death. Usually, there was an interval of only a few days, but occasional delays occurred because of especially heavy burdens on the prioress, as during the influenza epidemics of 1891, 1893, 1895, or an overbooking at the printer's.

67. *Circulaire* of Sr. Euphrasie du Saint-Sacrement, Tours, August 23, 1888, 2, 3.

68. *Circulaire* of Sr. Thérèse de Saint-Joseph, Albi, August 12, 1890, 2.

69. *Circulaire* of Sr. Magdeleine-de-Jésus, Bordeaux, July–August? 1890, 1.

70. *Circulaire* of Sr. Antoinette du Saint-Esprit, Albi, January 17, 1890. The parable comes from *Luke* 14:16–24.

71. The *Livre des soeurs défuntes* of the Carmel at Rennes lists over two generations only three sisters who left early, two of them, Sr. Marie Claire, twenty, and Sr. Marie de St. Charles, twenty-three, departing on the same day, June 8, 1869, the latter after just five months.

72. According to her *circulaire*, that term was imposed by the then-prioress, Mère Geneviève, but it was reduced to seven by Mère Gonzague.

73. *Circulaire* of Sr. Elizabeth de Jésus, Niort, November 19, 1893, 2.

74. *Circulaire* of Sr. Aimée de Jésus, Rheims, January–February? 1890, 2.

75. *Circulaire* of Sr. Louise de la Croix, Luçon, December 18, 1891, 4. This Breton's adolescence was marked by an interest in the cult of virginity. She went to several bookshops in Nantes looking for a book to learn what virginity was all about.

76. *Circulaire* of Sr. Thérèse de Jésus, Mangalore (India), December 10, 1894.

77. *Circulaire* of Sr. Emmanuel, Agen, March 27, 1894.

78. *Circulaire* of Mère Thérèse de Jésus, Montpellier, June 24, 1890.

79. They figured in the monthly budget of the Carmel at Rennes, which lists 34 francs for *cilices* in October 1891 and 22.80 in July 1894. It would seem they could be ordered individually, undoubtedly only by permission of the prioress.

80. The Rule prescribed fasting from September 14 until Easter.

81. *Circulaire* of Mère Thérèse de Saint-Augustin, Besançon, December 18, 1892. See also the *Circulaire* of Mère Saint-Jérôme, Tulle, July 9, 1885: "Notre Mère eût fait revivre les austérités des anchorites du désert *si on ne l'en avait l'empêchée*. Les cilices, les ceintures de fer, les longues disciplines auraient été le pain quotidien de son âme" ["Our Mother would have revived the austerities of the desert anchorites *if she had not been constrained*. Hair shirts, iron belts, lengthy watches would have been her soul's daily bread"]. Even a prioress would have been answerable for such behavior; no superior would have let it pass unnoticed.

82. *Circulaire* of Mère Agathe de Jésus, Nantes, June 2, 1894. She had died more than eighteen months before, on November 28, 1892. At an astounding ninety-six pages, this *circulaire* amounts to a book-length biography of its subject. It served the Martin sisters, I believe, as a precedent and perhaps an inspiration for their own lengthy narrative, Thérèse's autobiographical manuscripts.

83. That is why Céline and Thérèse Martin look bloated in their first Carmel photos.

84. The accounts book of the Lisieux Carmel, *Registre des Recettes et Dépenses Générales*, indicates for 1884 the following annual amounts in francs spent: milk, 494; fish, 590; eggs (which were alternated with fish at the midday meal), 528; cheese, 199; meat, 483; butter, 489; bread, 1,859. The annual heating bill, which referred only to the recreation room and the kitchen, came to only 190 francs for coal and 104 for wood.

85. *Circulaire* of Sr. Augustine de la Croix, Niort, March 6, 1893.

86. *Circulaire* of Mère Thérèse de Jésus, Lourdes, October 2, 1892.

87. *Circulaire* of Mère Thérèse de Jésus, Limoges, February 12, 1894.

88. *Circulaire* of Sr. Aimée de Jésus, Agen, February 2, 1895. To the contrary, a lifelong fear was sometimes resolved on a deathbed. One sister, long tormented by not feeling she had loved God, ended happily. " 'De quoi pouvons-nous nous inquiéter ayant un Dieu si bon?' C'était, en effet, le sentiment de la confiance qui, dans cette dernière journée, avait remplacé les craintes de la mort et des jugements de Dieu qui l'avaient tant fait souffrir pendant sa vie" [" 'What should bother us, having so good a God?' In effect the feeling of trust on her last day had replaced the fear of death and God's judgment which had made her suffer so much during her life"]; *Circulaire* of Sr. Marie de Saint-Joseph, Paris, June 13, 1893.

89. *Circulaire* of Sr. Marie du Coeur de Jésus, February 20, 1895, Abbeville. This notice is unusual for the singular possessive cited in the quotation.

90. *Circulaire* of Mère Thérèse de Jésus, Périgueux, January 10, 1893.

91. *Circulaire* of Mère Saint Coeur de Marie, Aurillac, July 14, 1888. She had come there from the Carmel at Montauban and served as both *fondatrice* (1858) and for twenty-seven years as prioress. As an adolescent, she had brought sweets to those hospitalized at Montauban's Hotel-Dieu, and she distributed food to the poor on feast days. After she established the Carmel at Aurillac, an Irish-American Protestant on visiting gave her 25,000 francs to build a proper chapel. As prioress, despite the Carmel's limited funds, she resumed the practice of charities to the sick and poor. On her death, the townspeople turned out in large numbers to pay respects at the grille and the chapel was packed for her funeral mass. Lisieux's *fondatrice*, Mère Geneviève, was accorded similar respect upon her death in December 1891.

92. *Circulaire* of Sr. Marie-Madeleine, Algiers, November 9, 1888.

93. *Circulaire* of Sr. Marie-Josephine, Bourges, May 11, 1893.

94. *Circulaire* of Sr. Véronique de la Croix, Tours, August 6, 1888.

95. *Circulaire* of Sr. Saint-Elie, Dorat, January 31, 1889.

96. PN 25, "Mes Désirs auprès de Jésus caché dans sa Prison d'Amour," was composed late in 1895 for the *converse* Sr. Saint-Vincent-de-Paul, whose barbed remarks she feared.

97. *Circulaire* of Mère Aimée de Jésus, Cahors, April 11, 1888. This notice would have been the second which Thérèse heard in the Carmel refectory.

98. *Circulaire* of Sr. Marie-Joseph, Poitiers, March 12, 1891. She was too fearful ever to profess vows and was made a *bienfaitrice*, esteemed as a model of charity and devotion who was always eager to show herself last.

99. See Jacques Maître, *L'Orpheline de la Bérésina* (Paris: Cerf, 1996), 50–55.

100. At the opening of both Manuscript B and Manuscript C she cites in conflation *Isaiah* 66:13 and 66:12. In the C citation she reveals her elevator image, which she identifies with Jesus' arms reaching down for her, but she then resumes for herself the maternal consolatory role of pleasing him. Implicitly she works to a parity with Jesus in that both must suffer and they console each other, but she is far more interested in the earthly work of consoling him, trying to please him by suffering, than in the celestial nonwork of being sustained or dandled by him.

101. *Circulaire* of Sr. Victime de Jésus, Agen, April 19, 1891.

102. *Circulaire* of Sr. Marie de l'Assomption, Saint Chaumont, November 30, 1892.

103. *Circulaire* of Sr. Marie du Saint-Sacrament, Lectoure, November 7, 1893.

CHAPTER FIVE

1. *Circulaires* of Sr. Marie-Véronique, December 11, 1891, Compiègne; Sr. Marie de Jésus-Hostie, January 15, 1893, Bayonne; Mère Louis de Gonzague, May 10, 1895, Le Mans. In her *Camino de Perfección*, ch. 7, Teresa of Avila enjoins her sisters to be so manly as to astonish men, an echo of 1 *Corinthians* 16:13.

2. Pauline testifies in the PO, 155, that "il n'y a rien dans le manuscrit que nous ne connussions par nos conversations intimes" ["there's nothing in the manuscript we didn't know by our intimate talks"], and Thérèse, she adds, had asked, "Que voulez-vous que j'écrive que vous ne sachiez déjà?" ["What do you want me to write that you don't know already?"].

3. The Third Republic's legislative persecution of religious orders, the notorious expulsions and dispossession, came only a few years after Thérèse's death, but there was never any real threat to the lives of priests and nuns.

4. It is amusing that, Louis having forbidden his girls the reading of any newspaper, Thérèse figured she was not disobeying him when she picked up *La Croix* and read the account of Pranzini's last moments. When she writes of "lisant les passages qui parlaient de Pranzini" ["reading passages that spoke of Pranzini"], she allows us to infer that she read more than one issue of *La Croix* as it was reporting the trial.

5. Albert Camus, *Réflexions sur la guillotine* (Paris: Gallimard, 2002), 153.

6. Victor Hugo, "Préface de 1832," in *Le dernier jour d'un condamné* (Paris: Gallimard, 2000), 49.

7. The dangling participle is of less interest than that Thérèse initially ended with "priser," "to size up."

8. Documentation du Carmel de Lisieux, quoted in Abbé Charles Arminjon, "Note Liminaire," in *Fin du monde présent et mystères de la vie future* (1881; rpt., Lisieux: Office Central du Carmel, 1964), ix–x.

9. Not to be confused with a rosary used when praying to the Virgin Mary. The little beads, called *perles mobiles*, could run on the cord, as on an abacus.

10. Pauline, *Souvenirs intimes*, 5: "Je m'enthousiasmai à cette lecture. Tous les portraits de héros et de vierges martyres me ravissaient" ["I was stirred by this reading. All the portraits of heroes and virgin martyrs ravished me"]. Her edition of *Fabiola* is in the Archives du Carmel.

11. Arminjon, *Fin du monde*, 66. It is unfortunate, not to say disastrous, that *Fin du monde* was reissued in 1964 by the Office Central de Lisieux and is identified in its introduction as an indispensable text for theresian studies.

12. Besides, he had had to face adverse publicity when another young Lexovien girl sought entry, attended by calumnies of Carmel from her father. The sting of this example was a sufficient caution.

13. See Teresa's injunctions against all kinds of attachment to people, including relatives, in chapters 8 and 9: "I do not know how much of the world we really leave when we say that we are leaving everything for God's sake, if we do not withdraw ourselves from the chief thing of all—namely, our kinsfolk." *The Way of Perfection*, translated by E. Allison Peers (Garden City, N.Y.: Doubleday, 1964), 85. All the Martin Carmelites knew of these strictures but passed them by with insouciance.

14. The diction might not suffice. Louis's relations with Isidore and Mme. Guérin remain obscure. Pauline probably exerted her substantial influence with her uncle on behalf of Thérèse. Besides, she was thoroughly familiar with flowery language, as her preconfirmation book for Thérèse documents amply.

15. She had taken it from a poem by Père Jean Léonard, a Cistercian abbot of Fontfroide.

16. Likely an allusion to the niece Teresita, born in 1563, who entered the Carmel at age twelve.

17. For an extended comparison, see Augustin Hemour in *VT* 3 (July 1935): 92–96; 4 (October 1935): 122–126; 2 (April 1936): 58–62. Their common denominators are simplicity, missionary zeal, and a down-to-earth accessibility to ordinary people.

18. *Petites fleurs; ou, Extraits de la doctrine et de la vie des saints et des auteurs approuvées*, 3d ed. (Paris: Au Monastère de la Visitation, 1887), I:50 (1st series).

19. Ibid., I:105–106 (my emphasis); and *Petites fleurs*, 3d ed. (1888), II:61–62 and 121 (4th series).

20. Mme. Louise S.W.-Belloc, *La tirelire aux Histoires* (Paris: Garnier, 1870), 248–252. Céline late in life wrote in the frontispiece of this edition that *Tirelire* was "le livre de lecture preféré de Sr. Thérèse de l'Enfant Jésus étant enfant. Le chapitre et l'image 'Le Sentier d'Or' l'avaient surtout frappée" ["the preferred children's book of Sr. Thérèse of the Child Jesus. The chapter and the picture of 'The Golden Path' especially struck her"].

21. *Oeuvres poétiques complètes* (Paris: Gallimard, 1963), 500.

22. For example, from Pauline to Louis, August 31 (or September 3), 1883, about a little drawing she had sent him: "C'est moi qui suis dans le petit bateau et c'est Jésus qui est mon Pilote, comment ne pas parvenir heureusement au port?" ["It's me in the little boat and it's Jesus who's the Pilot, how not to arrive happily at port?"], in *VT* 57 (January 1975): 61.

23. It was this old prioress who early on cautioned Pauline about her little sister's "excessive audacity," adding the injunction: "Surveillez-la" ["Keep an eye on her"]. *Carmel de Lisieux: La fondation du Carmel de Lisieux et sa fondatrice la Révérende Mère Geneviève de Ste-Thérèse* (Paris: Librairie St.-Paul, 1912), 88.

24. PA, 159.

25. Marie was once almost courted. In CF, 296, Zélie mentions to Céline Guérin hearing through maids' gossip of a young man "dont Mlle Martin ferait bien l'affaire" ["Mlle. Martin would make quite happy"], but Marie broke down in tears when she heard of this exchange. Her mother comments prophetically: "Je crois bien que jamais elle ne se mariera; elle n'a pourtant pas l'air d'avoir de vocation religieuse, et cependant, ce n'est pas une nature à rester seule" ["I'm quite sure she'll never marry though she doesn't seem to have a spiritual calling, and yet it's not in her nature to remain alone"].

26. Léonie's poor record in and out of other convents put her beyond consideration, yet it was this odd girl out who supplied Thérèse with the writing paper for her autobiography.

27. Quoted by Jean Vinatier, *Mère Agnès de Jésus* (Paris: Cerf, 1993), 160.

28. *Le Papier d'exaction*, 142. Gratien's work dates from 1608. Although not translated into French, it was widely used by the Spanish prioresses who were founding Carmels in France at that time, and its nineteenth chapter was translated for inclusion in the *Papier*.

29. From Sr. Febronie de la Sainte-Enfance, for example. And yet it was this same sister who advised her that the more a soul approaches God, the simpler it becomes, and it was the simplicity of a child which Thérèse was now recovering for herself. Thus, Sr. Fébronie made her contribution to "the little way."

30. *Circulaire* of Mère Anne-Victoire, Beaune, March 27, 1890: "Elle ne se regardait devant Dieu que comme un pur néant, digne de l'enfer" ["Before God she considered herself only a pure nothing, worthy of hell"].

31. In the iconographies after her death, however, she stands solitary, holding flowers (her favorite and inevitable roses) in chapels or casting them about, as in

propagandistic drawings during the Great War. See my article "Thérèse of Lisieux in the Trenches of the Great War, 'Je veux lutter comme un guerrier vaillant,'" in *Les Femmes et la Guerre*, edited by Françoise Lejeune (Nantes: Presses de CRINI, 2004), 141–151.

32. In the *Tirelire*, 273–276. From school we find Gustave Hubault's *Histoire de France à l'usage des écoles primaires* (Paris: Delagrave, 1881), which is signed in front, "Thérèse Martin, No. 20."

33. She ended Manuscript A with this musing about herself: "Peut-être la petite fleur sera[-t-elle] cueillie dans sa fraîcheur ou bien transplantée sur d'autres rivages" ["Maybe the little flower will be gathered in all its freshness or transplanted onto other shores"]. By the time of C, she knew the first condition was certain and within a few weeks she made the second her desideration, to do good on earth.

34. I refer to the first of Dante's dreams in *Purgatorio*, IX:13–33.

35. "[V]ous connaissez depuis longtemps ce que je pense et tous les événements un peu mémorables de ma vie, je ne saurais donc vous apprendre rien de nouveau" ["You've known a long while what I think and all the scarcely memorable events of my life, so I'd hardly have anything new to tell you"]; C 32v.

36. Vénard was indirectly the victim of French mercantilist inroads into Vietnam, which the French navy had abetted with force under Admiral Léonard Charner in the winter of 1860–1861. The violence of this *mission civilatrice* had been centered on Saigon and Tourane (now Danang), well to the south of Vénard's missionary circuit, but the mandarin who had him arrested interrogated him about the invasion as though he were one of its agents. Although caged, Vénard was treated kindly by his captors. He was even twice banqueted by the mandarin, and the jailer addressed him in the deferential language used only for royalty. Admiring his youth and bearing, some presumed he was a soothsayer, a physician, a prophet. He was told his life would be spared if he trampled upon his cross, and there was apparent dismay that he did not do so. In a final letter to his father, who had died at home eighteen months before, he wrote: "Depuis le grand-mandarin jusqu'au dernier des soldats, tous regrettent que la loi du royaume me condamne à la mort" ["From the great mandarin to the least of the soldiers, everyone is sorry the royal law is condemning me to death"]; *Vie et correspondance de J. Théophane Vénard*, 2d ed. (Poitiers: Oudin, 1865), 319.It is much to Vénard's credit that years before, in June 1857, he decried the adventurism of France's then foremost imperialist in Cochinchina, Louis Charles de Montigny, who used gunboat diplomacy on the pretext of defending missionaries from persecution: "Ces expéditions mesquines ne sont pas dignes de la France dont le cœur est si généreux. Si la France fait quelque chose devant le monde, elle doit le faire grandement, selon son caractère" ["These wicked forays are unworthy of generous-hearted France. If France acts before the world's eyes, it should act magnificently, according to its character"]. Cited by Etienne Vo Duc Hanh, *La place du Catholicisme dans les relations entre la France et le Viet-Nam de 1851 à 1870* (Leiden: Brill, 1969), 188.Vo Duc Hanh indicates (292) that it was not so much the military and mercantile French who brought Vénard to martyrdom as the Vietnamese converts to the Catholicism he preached. While the Vietnamese people and its government naturally resented the inroads of the affluent and powerful "Diables de l'Occident" [Western Devils], the conversions wrought far deeper grievances as they made natives into strangers within

their own country. Worst of all, with conversion, Vietnamese Christians ceased to honor their ancestors and abandoned veneration of the tutelary spirits of their communities and nation. For another discussion of the character of the French colonial experiment, see Milton Osborne, *The French Presence in Cochinchina and Cambodia: Rule and Response (1859–1905)* (Bangkok: White Lotus, 1997).

37. *Vie et correspondance de J.-Théophane Vénard* (Poitiers: Oudin, 1865), 116.

38. She conflates in just four lines three passages from the Gospels: the mysterious assault of the violent upon heaven (*Matthew* 11:12), Christ's sword image for the division he would be causing in families (*Matthew* 10:34), and his casting of fire upon the earth (*Luke* 12:49), a fire usually construed by biblical exegetes to be the eschatological Holy Spirit judging the world, but construed by Thérèse as Christ's own consuming love.

39. A bittersweet occasion: Céline's profession of vows (February 24, 1896) could have brought another poem from Thérèse, but Gonzague assigned the composition to Sr. Marie des Anges.

40. She brilliantly likens poverty to the ascesis of an athlete stripping down so that he can run better. That invokes yet another image from St. Paul, *1 Corinthians 9:24–26*.

41. This tableau, central to any discussion of Thérèse's spirituality, has a psalmic gravity. It seems initially a song of lamentation, of exile: she and the sinners around her have been made to eat the bread of tears (Psalm 80:6); they are nourished by the bread of sorrow (Psalm 127:2). However, if we shift from the eating to the table itself, we recall the table prepared in Psalm 23, in the presence of those who bring tribulation, even as Taxil did for Thérèse. Further, in Psalm 78:19, the disbelievers who openly scorn God ask in derision whether God will be able to furnish them a table in the desert; they do not trust in God's salvation of them and even after God has fed them, they persist in their sinning. It seems certain that Thérèse, a careful and diligent reader of the psalms, conflated images and occasions such as these when she wrote C 6r. It is integral to her charity that she does not dwell upon the sinfulness of the others at the table but seeks only their redemption.

CHAPTER SIX

1. *VT* 71 (July 1978): 235.

2. Although Pauline's *récréation* "Les vertus au berceau de Jésus," which she wrote for a performance in 1884, was reprised at Christmas 1893.

3. All of the music is reprinted with her settings in *Les musiques de Thérèse* (Paris: Cerf, 1997).

4. The Carmel archives include a wax cylinder of Jeanne ca. 1910 singing a cappella the setting of one of Thérèse's poems.

5. Thérèse early took inspiration from the *Imitatio* III.5.4, that love believes all is possible and permissible: "La *prudence humaine* au contraire tremble à chaque pas et n'ose pour ainsi dire poser le pied" ["*Human scruples* on the other hand tremble at every step and do not dare, so to speak, to take the first one"]; A 75v.

6. The Cerf edition mistakenly identifies her as St. Margaret, Queen of Scotland (1045–1093), perhaps because Margaret of Antioch, although engorged and disgorged

by a devilish dragon and although responsible for mass conversions of spectators when she survived torture by boiling cauldron, has been dismissed from the Church's calendar, that is, she no longer has a name day. The once-popular cults of both women have been suppressed.

7. Even though the court which condemned Jeanne had been ecclesiastical, its authority had been compromised by complicity with the English, and the Church made rapid strides to "rehabilitate" Jeanne—and itself—within a generation of her death.

8. Henri Wallon, *Jeanne d'Arc* (Paris: 1876), 32. The quotation following is found on 244.

9. Ibid., 271.

10. Another factor: there were not enough younger sisters to take all the parts. A courtroom scene would have been top-heavy in personae. As to heresy alleged against her, it figures in the condemnation pronounced by Cauchon, the bishop of Beauvais, in the eleventh scene.

11. Wallon, *Jeanne d'Arc*, 383, 386.

12. To extenuate, however: in January 1895, when she composed this play, Thérèse was spiritually far less mature than she became within the short space of a couple of years. Wallon, documenting the trial and Jeanne's rehabilitation, noted that she did not always understand her "voices" and her disorientation and uncertainty marked for her a kind of *épreuve* which Thérèse in her last year could well have sketched to an imposing depth.

13. Likely toward the end, the seventh scene, with a canticle of eight strophes of eight lines each. It is anticlimactic and draggy, as a modern production has demonstrated.

14. *DE*, July 17, 1897: "Oui, je veux passer mon Ciel à faire du bien sur la terre" ["Yes, I want to spend my heaven doing good upon the earth"].

15. Quoted in Jean-François Six, *Vie de Thérèse de Lisieux* (Paris: Seuil, 1975), 254.

16. Jean Guitton, "Sur sept paroles de Sainte Thérèse," *VT* (July 1954), 36, remarks on her being exposed to the nineteenth-century Romantic proclivity for putting religious feelings "dans le style, l'élan et le sublime qui était dans l'âme" ["in the style, impetus and beauty that was in one's soul"], but then makes the fantastic and absurd claim that "elle seule était sans mauvais goût et sans péché: car le style est toujours beau quand il est exact et quand il est vrai" ["She alone was free of bad taste and of sin: indeed, style is always beautiful when exact and truthful"]. This view washes over her keen awareness of the limits of expression and of her inadequacies in working within them. Let's speak not of bad taste but of threadbare conventions which she, limited in education, was content to use and which her audience within Carmel expected, anyway.

17. Thérèse was aware that some poems would be published with her *circulaire*, as is evident from her indications of passages for a publisher's italics, at the close of PN 51 and PN 54.

18. *Poésies* (NEC edition), 270.

19. In NPPA, her notes for the second *procès*, Pauline confessed that early on she had been unhappy about Thérèse's poetic composition, feeling and saying that she

could not succeed and giving her advice about technical matters only with considerable reluctance.

20. Alphonse de Lamartine, *Méditations poétiques* (Paris: Gallimard, 1981), 51–52.

21. In her strangest trope of all, in LT 95 (July–August 1889), she imagines becoming an atom Jesus hides on his face, where the atom would be free from the fear of sinning further. She had said in LT 74 that to be an atom means to be no longer occupied with self, as even a humble grain of sand might be.

22. Only the fourth, PN 32, can be precisely dated: June 7, 1896; the others fall somewhere during 1894 and late 1895.

23. She entered as Sr. Marie-Agnès de la Sainte-Face, but changed her name in the spring of 1896.

24. See LT 141, 154; Manuscript C 3r; RP 1.12v; PN 13.5, 31.4, 45.4, 54.6. "Rester petite" needs to be distinguished from "se faire petite," to make oneself little by humbling. Thérèse preferred to recognize that the soul is by its nature small and weak and therefore must aspire to be nothing more. One need not humble oneself if mindful that one is always lowly to begin with.

25. LT 142, to Céline, July 6, 1893. She cites the key passage again in Manuscript A 83r with this gloss: "on peut bien tomber, on peut commettre des infidélités, mais, l'amour sachant *tirer profit de tout*, a bien vite consumé *tout* ce qui peut déplaire à Jésus, ne laissant qu'une humble et profonde paix au fond du coeur" ["one can surely fall and commit infidelities but love, knowing how to *take profit from all things*, has rapidly consumed *everything* that can displease Jesus, leaving in the heart's core only a humble and profound peace"]. The emphases, including the balance-book phrase about profit, she owes to San Juan de la Cruz.

26. CS, 71.

27. Fifty-five strophes, with the following sequence: two octosyllabic lines, then a decasyllabic, followed by a third octosyllabic, concluding with a disyllabic "chute," which creates a kind of echo of the ultimate word in the preceding line.

28. She had employed this structure in the first poem she wrote for herself—also a "Rappelle-toi!"—a loving tribute addressed to Louis, who had died shortly before.

29. *Libro de la Vida*, edited by Dámaso Chicarro (Madrid: Cátedra, 2001), 238.

30. But as French, stepchild of Latin, has many words close to it, Thérèse intuited a great deal.

31. So she argued in LT 122 (October 14, 1890) to Céline about virgins and virginal hearts. There, too, she dismisses the populist cult of the Sacré Coeur: "le coeur de mon époux est à moi seule comme le mien est à lui seul" ["the heart of my spouse is mine alone as mine is his alone"].

32. Thérèse never cites Matthew 18:3, "Unless you *become* as little children."

33. On blood as dew, see Manuscript A (45v and 46v). A conceit as old as Homer, *Iliad*, XI:54.

34. This poem has fifteen strophes of seven decasyllables with a trailing tetrasyllable.

35. See Pri 8: the consuming fire of love is what she sought as a Carmelite. Concomitant with that love, its very essence, was the desire to make God known and loved.

36. *DE*, June 23, 1897.

37. This poem, dated December 28, 1896, has a dramatic backdrop. When Thérèse completed it, the other sisters at the *récréation* wanted to sing it that evening. Gonzague agreed but then rounded on Pauline (not on Thérèse!), saying she was unhappy about verses set for the community to sing. It could only sustain one's pride. Years later, Pauling recalled being downcast but Thérèse was not, "sa mort étant trop prochaine pour se laisser troubler de quoi que ce soit" ["her death being too near to let her be bothered by anything whatever"] (NPPA, notes on "Humilité").

38. St. Francis of Assisi and St. Clare were both runaways from their parental homes.

39. See OC, 1334, note to LT 209.

40. In her second letter to Bellière, December 26, 1897, she sounds the same chords: she cannot console him for the pain of giving up a still-beckoning life out in the world; she can only pray and suffer with him. But then she *does* console him with the heavenly recompense, "au centuple les joies si douces et si légitimes" ["the hundredfold sweet and rightly joys"] to be accorded him by Jesus for his sacrifices (LT 213).

41. *DE*, May 21–26, 1897, no. 9.

42. *DE*, May 27, 1897, no. 9: Thérèse remembered from her childhood a three-year-old neighbor at Les Buissonnets saying to her mother that she was being called by some other children and asking to be allowed out: "Y veulent de moi!" Now, on that day late in May, Thérèse said the little angels were calling her, "et moi je vous dis comme la petite fille: 'Laissez-moi donc partir, y veulent de moi!'" ["and like the little girl I'm saying to you, 'Let me go, they want me!' "].

43. On the assumption that zealots are the violent who bear away the kingdom, see Ulrich Luz, *Matthew 8–20: A Commentary*, translated by James E. Crouch (Minneapolis, Minn.: Fortress, 2001), 139–142. Beyond the theresian, the most striking reading I have found is St. Jerome's, that the violent are those of us who, lacking this heaven-besieging ability by our nature, acquire it by virtue. But not even this view includes Christ as exemplar.

44. A line which Pauline transformed into the passive "donner mon sang, mes larmes" ["to give my blood and tears"], which is the version used by Alan Bancroft in his translation of the poems.

45. That is the phrasing in her initial sketch. The margin contains the definitive version.

46. Thérèse mentions *Matthew* 11:12 in one other passage, to Bellière in November 1896 (LT 201) when she misquotes it by writing, "les violents seuls le ravissent." She claims she took Carmel's "kingdom" that way, an ironic trope as she describes herself as Jesus' prisoner there.

47. The desertion may bear a cryptic pointer to the Diana Vaughan affair. In *Le Triomphe de l'Humilité*, Thérèse, playing herself, had characterized Vaughan as "une nouvelle Jeanne d'Arc" (RP 7.1r). Thérèse might well have felt that she herself had betrayed Jeanne, however unwittingly, by championing the fraud. She had sent Taxil the photo of herself in costume for her second play about Jeanne. In PN 50, a mysterious stranger heaps sorrows upon Jeanne, as Taxil had heaped them upon Thérèse. The historic Jeanne had, by the way, a fair share of earthly supporters.

48. Thérèse was not isolated from her sisters psychologically or physically, but without question her spiritual darkness was exclusively her own. How could she have shared it?

49. Sr. Anne-Marie Roué, O.S.B., *Thérèse élève à l'Abbaye* (Paris: Médiaspaul, 1993), 136–137.

50. Then as now, recitation involved three chaplets in succession with meditation upon the mysteries, joyous, dolorous, and glorious. Pope John Paul II added luminous. Thérèse disclosed toward the end, *DE*, August 20, 1897, no. 16: "Quand on pense que j'ai eu tant de mal toute ma vie à dire mon chapelet!" ["To think I've had such trouble all my life in saying my chaplet"]. See also Manuscript C 25v, on her falling short of devotion in communal prayers and "la récitation du chapelet me coûte plus que de mettre un instrument de pénitence" ["recitation of the chaplet costs me more than applying an instrument of penitence"].

51. It was a mixed experience: her older sisters had all been received into this association, but it was customary to have a mentor, or *maîtresse amie*. Thérèse never got one. The tutoring had sequestered Thérèse and when she appeared twice weekly at the school on late afternoons, she felt ignored, if not shunned. She hovered quietly over her work, counting the moments till Louis came to fetch her. In A 40v, she candidly remarks how trying it was for her even to apply to become an *enfant* and that her only real friend was Jesus, as though she could not at that time feel friendship with his mother as well. The "ouvrage" to which she refers was the decorative needlework which any well-off young girl was supposed to master. For its stunning variety, see Thérèse de Dillmont, *Encyclopédie des Ouvrages de Dames* (Dornach, Alsace, n.d., but ca. 1890).

52. In a gay mood, she asks Mary to clear away the debris in her soul and to set up in it a vast tent "et puis j'invite tous les Saints et les Anges à venir faire un magnifique concert" ["and then I'm inviting all the saints and angels to come and have a magnificent concert there"]; A 80r. The deft theresian humor comes in asking Mary "l'orner de ses *propres* parures" ["to supply her *own* trimmings"].

53. The last of her prayers (and of her writing: September 8, 1897) is to Mary, that were she, Thérèse, the Queen of Heaven, and Mary were herself, she would want to be Thérèse so that Mary could be Queen of Heaven. It is a variant on Augustine's prayer to God with the same switch of predications. That prayer had possibly been read in the refectory on August 28, Augustine's feast day. Pauline could have brought it to Thérèse. But Thérèse had already been in the vicinity of this idea on her own and much earlier, in LT 137 (October 19, 1892), when she claimed to be happier than Mary since she has La Vierge for her mother, but Mary has no such mother to love.

54. "À mon Ange Gardien," PN 46: "Je veux pendant ma courte vie / Sauver mes frères les pécheurs" ["During my brief life I want to save my brother sinners"]. This poem, dated January 1897, marks a major advance in her spirituality. The next involved her dropping the mission of saving them.

55. She had taken it on inspiration from Vénard: "Le vrai bonheur est de souffrir. Et pour vivre il nous faut mourir" ["The true happiness is in suffering. And in order to live we must die"], which she quotes in LT 226 (May 26, 1897), to Roulland. While the second sentence is patently derived from the Gospels (*Mark* 8:35; *Matthew* 16:25; *Luke* 9:24), the first has a koanlike abruptness which Thérèse admitted was

beyond her: "Oh! que les pensées divines sont au-dessus des nôtres!" ["How divine thoughts are above our own!"].

56. I suspect—and now have no way to confirm—that the late Gustave Thibon, Weil's host and intellectual antagonist during her last years in France, met his contentious guest with armor supplied by Thérèse. During the 1930s, Thibon, a devout Catholic, contributed essays on Thérèse to *Études carmélitaines*. He surely knew that Thérèse in both her life and spirituality was the one sure foil to Weil and her relentless intellectual perturbations, her quixotic leftism, her would-be Christian cantankerousness. Weil ended her life imagining herself at the juncture of Christianity and all that is not Christianity. That was exactly Thérèse's position but not an imaginary one. Weil on the threshold of the Church would be forever looking into it; Thérèse, from the same vantage, is looking out.

57. *DE*, July 8, 1897: When she told Pauline that "les petits anges" (their siblings) were amusing themselves in hiding from her the light which would reveal her approaching end, Pauline asked if they had hidden Mary as well from her: "Non, la Sainte Vierge ne sera jamais cachée pour moi, car je l'aime trop" ["No, the Holy Virgin will never be hidden for me, I love her too much"]. But on August 8 comes this poignant word: "Je voudrais être sûre qu'elle m'aime, la Sainte Vierge" ["I would like to be sure she loves me, the Holy Virgin"].

58. In the Vulgate: "Misertus est Dominus timentibus se," a present perfect, which suggests a historical compassion ongoing to this moment—only?

59. These words call up the image of the prodigal going back home enlightened.

CHAPTER SEVEN

1. The *Novissima*, published in 1926, was an edition drawing on various materials which were critically re-presented in *Derniers entretiens*, first published in 1971.

2. OC, "Ecrits Divers," 1232.

3. There is a comparable case of another French child, born a generation later to a healthy twenty-year-old woman named Anne-Marie: "Les veilles et les soucis épuisèrent Anne-Marie, son lait tarit, on me mit en nourrice non loin de là et je m'appliquai, moi aussi, à mourir: d'entérite et peut-être de ressentiment" ["The vigils and cares exhausted Anne-Marie, her milk dried up, I was sent to a wet nurse nearby and set myself, me too, to dying: of enteritis and perhaps of resentment"]. That child grew up as cosseted as Thérèse. His name was Jean-Paul Sartre; see *Les mots* (Paris: Gallimard, 1964), 16.

4. Postulants and novices were obliged to eat a forearm's length of bread daily, hence the pudgy look of both Thérèse and Céline in their respective first photos at Carmel.

5. *Butterworth's Medical Dictionary*, ed. Macdonald Critchley, 2d ed. (Boston: Butterworths, 1978), 1642.

6. Notes to Manuscript A, 301; 46 in the 1911 edition.

7. PO, 241:311r.

8. PO, 241:311v.

9. F.-J. Collet, *Précis de pathologie interne*, 6th ed. (Paris: Octave Doin, 1910), I:400.

10. Ibid., 401.

11. Balthasar, *Thérèse de Lisieux: Histoire d'une mission*, 75 (see bibliography).

12. In rural areas, soup was the standard breakfast item in Thérèse's time: usually it was made of carrots, potatoes, and leeks all reduced in the cooking, with bread added for consistency.

13. Their summer robes were worn-down (*usagé*) versions of their winter ones, but they were allowed in winter to wear woolen stockings and *chausses*, and they had wool garments over their serge or muslin tunics as well.

14. See *DE*, 806.

15. "C'est là un fait capital dans l'histoire de la phthisis. La fièvre indique, à quelque degré qu'elle soit, que la maladie évolue; l'absence de fièvre montre qu'elle est stationnaire" ["There's a primary fact in the history of tuberculosis. Fever indicates, at whatever the temperature, that the illness is in process; absence of fever shows that it is stationary"]. J.-B. Fonssigraves, translator and annotator of W. H. Walshe, *Traité clinique des maladies de la poitrine* (Paris: Masson, 1870), 532 n.

16. Weight loss (*amaigrissement*) is a common symptom of tuberculosis due to loss of appetite, vomiting, diarrhea, and sweating. Fonssigraves, in Walshe, *Traité clinique des maladies*, 544 n, maintained that an important early sign of the disease in women was the thinning (*fonte*) of their breasts.

17. *Circulaire* of Sr. Marie-Antoinette, Lisieux, November 4, 1896.

18. Brigitte Bancillon, "Le dossier médical de Sainte Thérèse de Lisieux," unpublished doctoral thesis in medicine, Pierre-et-Marie-Curie Université, Paris, 1983, 16.

19. NPPA, 94; *DE*, 807, par. 2 and 3.

20. *Manuel de médecine, d'hygiène, de chirurgie et de pharmacie domestiques*, 18th ed. (Paris: Chez l'Auteur, 1891), 461.

21. Some characterizations from *circulaires* in the year Thérèse died: "Grâce aux soins intelligents de notre si dévoué Docteur, le mal sembla céder"; Sr. Elie du Sacré-Coeur, Castres, January 20, 1897. "Notre bon et dévoué Docteur"; Sr. Saint-Augustin, Poitiers, January 25, 1897. "Monsieur notre dévoué docteur nous tranquilisa"; Sr. Elisée de la Croix, Grenoble, February 28, 1897. "Monsieur notre Docteur, dont le dévouement inaltérable nous assure en toute occasion de sa bienveillante sollicitude"; Sr. Aimée de Jésus, Lectoure, April 6, 1897.

22. Her final lover, Alexandre Manceau, also died of tuberculosis, putting in doubt her reputation for sensual love: how could she have escaped contagion? Was she merely mother of them all?

23. *DE*, July 8, 1897, no. 6; July 14, 1897, no. 10.

24. She could have relit her cell's little lamp but, obedient to regulations, did not do so.

25. III:47, translated by Lamennais.

26. According to W. H. Walshe, *Traité clinique*, 544: "la face ne perd son embonpoint."

27. For a discussion of "phthisical insanity" induced by tubercular toxins, see D. G. Munro, *The Psycho-Pathology of Tuberculosis* (Oxford: Oxford University Press, 1926), 60: "exaggerated ideas of well-being" and "a strange access of buoyant and youthful spirits [that] so often accompanies the disease." Eric Wittkower, *A Psychiatrist*

Looks at Tuberculosis (London: National Association for the Prevention of Tuberculosis, 1955), 22, includes in the syndrome a forced cheerfulness and defiant jocularity and, in mitigating the disease's severity, "a carefree temperament, need for self-punishment, masochistic trends." I have been able to find no recent studies of the psychological factors in tuberculosis, which now ranks third, after malaria and AIDS, as the world's most deadly illness.

28. Goncourt, *Renée Mauperin* (Paris: Bibliothéque-Charpentier, 1920), 305–306.

29. Walshe, *Traité Clinique*, 531, but Fonssigraves takes vigorous issue with this claim in a note on the same page on which I have drawn above.

30. OC, 1456.

31. Goncourt, *Renée Mauperin*, 325.

32. Walshe, *Traité Clinique*, 540. These clinical remarks anticipate those mentioned in n. 27 above.

33. In secular, domestic environs of that time, the cup, used in France well into the twentieth century, was exposed to the flame of a lamp heated with alcohol.

34. CS, 172 (1973 edition).

35. Paul Labarthe, *Dictionnaire populaire de médecine usuelle* (Paris: Flammarion, n.d.), 1094, col. 2, and 364, col. 1.

36. *Manuel du Docteur Dehaut* (Paris: Chez l'Auteur, 1891), 666.

37. According to Pauline, PA, 151. See Manuscript C 7r: "je Lui dis être prête à verser jusqu'à la dernière goutte de mon sang pour confesser qu'il y a un Ciel" ["I tell (Jesus) I'm ready to spill the last drop of my blood to confess that there's a Heaven"].

38. *Cahiers verts*, 4–5.

39. *DE*, May 21 and June 9, 1897.

40. Labarthe, *Dictionnaire populaire*, 365, col. 1.

41. *DE*, July 3, 1897.

42. Both citations belong to *DE*, July 7, 1897.

43. *DE*, June 14 and June 30, 1897.

44. *DE*, May 21–26, 1897. Pauline notes that she was unsure of the exact date of this remark.

45. "J'accepte tout" comes from June 4, 1897; the other citations are from June 6.

46. Blake, *The Complete Poems*, edited by W. H. Stevenson (London: Longman, 1989), 590.

47. *DE*, July 3, 1897.

48. Sr. Marie de l'Eucharistie to Isidore Guérin, July 7, 1897, *DE*, 680.

49. Sr. Marie de l'Eucharistie to Isidore Guérin, July 8, 1897, *DE*, 682.

50. Given her hard-won maturity, it would be mistaken to say her spirit grew stronger, greater, higher; all the usual positives about progress fall amiss here.

51. Sr. Marie de l'Eucharistie to Mme. Guérin, July 10, 1897, *DE*, 689.

52. Sr. Marie de l'Eucharistie to Isidore, July 12, 1897, *DE*, 694.

53. Sr. Marie de l'Eucharistie to Isidore, July 20, 1897, *DE*, 715.

54. Bancillon, "Le dossier médical de Sainte Thérèse de Lisieux," 86.

55. *DE*, July 30, 1897.

56. Ibid.

57. Simone de Beauvoir, *Le deuxième sexe*, rev. ed. (Paris: Gallimard, 1976), 99.

58. Ibid., 131.

59. *DE*, July 29, 1897.

60. PA, 151, folio 376.

61. Pauline's NPPA, cited in OC, 1468.

62. *DE*, August 8, 1897.

63. The *Derniers entretiens* indicate that often she could utter only a few words and with effort. She often excused herself to her interlocutors, but that difficulty may have been due to pulmonary debilitation and attendant breathlessness rather than to laryngeal congestion.

64. They are cited in OC, 1104.a.

65. Laveille, *Sainte Thérèse de l'Enfant Jésus (1873–1897)* (Lisieux: Office Centrale, 1926), 384.

66. "[L]a langue propre," according to Bancillon, "Le dossier médical de Sainte Thérèse de Lisieux," 86.

67. *DE*, August 27, 1897.

68. Its highfalutin restlessness carried on into existentialism, a fashionable posture for intellectuals who had no inclination to Catholicism or any structured faith.

69. *DE*, September 10, 1897.

70. *DE*, September 14, 1897.

71. OC, 1158.

72. *DE*, September 20, 1897.

73. OC, 1145.

74. Goncourt, *Renée Mauperin*, 124.

CHAPTER EIGHT

1. Requirements for considering any appointment to the doctorate include (1) that it involve a canonized saint; (2) that there be a doctrine with something to say; (3) that there be disciples who apply this doctrine and read the saint's works. Clearly, the second and third criteria had been met by Thérèse even before she met the first. Pope Paul VI confounded prejudice in 1970 when he named the first women doctors, Teresa of Avila and Catherine of Siena.

2. *The Varieties of Religious Experience: A Study in Human Nature* (1902; rpt., New York: Modern Library, 1994), 387–388.

3. Ibid., 411.

4. Dietrich Bonhoeffer, "Die Struktur des verantwortlichen Lebens," in his *Ethik*, edited by Ilse Tödt et al. (Gütersloh: Kaiser, 1998), 256–289.

5. As Thérèse never read the *Commedia*, it is interesting that in *Purgatorio* (Canto XXII.130–135), Dante anticipates this bizarre inversion. (It had already been used by Albertus Magnus.) Thérèse's fruit, though, hangs for the picking, in plain contrast to the forbidden fruit of Eden as well as of Dante's purgatory.

6. Once more, the *Commedia*: the flower opening from night to the warming sun is Dante's image of the wayfarer's accepting the divine will which initiates his journey through hell, *Inferno* II.127–132.

7. *Job* 13.15; no matter that scholars have long recognized the vigorous defensiveness and attendant hopelessness in the Masoretic text. Thérèse herself cites this

passage in *DE*, July 7, 1897, no. 3, which she had likely read in one of her good conduct prize books awarded at the abbey on August 4, 1884: Abbé Chaudé's *La théologie des plantes ou histoire intime du monde végétal* (Paris: Société générale de librarie Catholique, 1882).

8. *DE*, May 9, 1897, no. 3.

9. Thérèse's central role at the Lisieux Carmel reflected this fusion of contraries: as *maîtresse auxiliaire au noviciat*, or assistant trainer of novices, she directly shaped the spirituality of her charges and served as a kind of maternal guide, and yet she chose to remain in the novitiate. She was never allowed to vote in the election of a prioress, an occasion reserved to the *capitulantes*.

10. *DE*, July 17, 1897.

11. *DE*, May 27, 1897, no. 6. A *jabot* was a lace cravat which dated from the seventeenth century. Thérèse would likely have seen some in her mother's workplace. Knotted and draped in a bow, it had the aspect of a frill, and puffing it up was a sign of ostentation.

12. LT 129, July 8, 1891; cf. A 81r.

13. Admirers of James and of Thérèse can only regret that, writing within only four years of her death, he had not taken notice of the *Histoire d'une âme* with her revelatory proclamation of her mission appended in Pauline's collection of the *Derniers entretiens*.

14. *DE*, July 8, 1897, no. 15.

15. The shortest of all her written prayers, Pri 19, reads: "Mon Dieu, avec le secours de votre grâce, je suis prête à verser tout mon sang pour affirmer ma foi" ["My God, with the aid of your grace, I'm ready to pour out all my blood to affirm my faith"].

16. I.iii, on tiring of reading and listening, the writer desires only Christ: "Que tous les docteurs se taisent...parlez-moi vous seul" ["Let all the learned be quiet...you alone speak to me"].

17. As she says in the bold apostrophe of "Vivre d'Amour": "O Trinité! vous êtes prisonnière de mon amour!" ["O Trinity! you are prisoner of my love!"]; PN 17.2.

18. It need not be permanent, of course. In fiction, Dostoevsky's Alyosha Karamazov is consternated by the swift putrefaction of his spiritual mentor's body, but he recovers himself. Dostoevsky was shaken by the sight of Holbein's painting *The Dead Christ* and its ghastly, nonconsolatory realism. Among Catholics of Thérèse's generation, Edward Elgar, the devout composer of three great oratorios, *The Kingdom*, *The Apostles*, *The Dream of Gerontius*, was so devastated by the First World War that he became an atheist and died one. For a history of losing Christian faith during the nineteenth century and after, see Angus Wilson, *God's Funeral* (New York: Ballantine, 2000).

19. Jean-François Six, *Vie de Thérèse de Lisieux* (Paris: Seuil, 1975), 264.

20. *Imitatio Christi*, III.6.3, enjoins the reader not to be troubled by phantoms.

21. Abbé Descouvemont, *Sainte Thérèse de Lisieux: Guide de lecture* (Paris: Cerf, 1997), 326, based on C 7r.

22. Ibid., 310.

23. Ibid.

24. *DE*, July 29, 1897, no. 3. It was a day extraordinarily rich in simple and penetrating words.

25. Conrad de Meester, *With Empty Hands*, 46 (adolescence), 32 (abandonment) (see bibliography).

26. Hans Urs von Balthasar, *Thérèse de Lisieux: Histoire d'une mission* (see bibliography), 276. He claims that Thérèse until nearly the end had no real understanding of original sin.

27. De Meester, *With Empty Hands*, 122, 142.

28. On her experience of quietude, see *DE*, July 11, 1897, no. 2. About a week in July 1889: "Il y avait comme un voile jeté pour moi sur toutes les choses de la terre.... J'étais entièrement cachée sous le voile de la Sainte Vierge" ["It was as though a veil had been thrown for me over all earthly things.... I was completely hidden under the mantle of the Blessed Virgin"].

29. Sr. Thérèse de Saint-Augustin, "Souvenirs d'une sainte amitié," *VT* (1985): 249.

30. II.ii.1; Lamennais's translation, the one used by Thérèse.

31. In her second *récréation pieuse*, *Les Anges à la Crèche*, an angel of the resurrection has the fewest lines. Thérèse remains this side of the cross because the suffering of Jesus is central to her spirituality.

32. Thomas Aquinas, *Summa Theologica* (Madrid: Biblioteca de Autores Cristianos, 1962), 2: 406–407.

33. In LT 197, Thérèse identifies the complacency attending consolations, "que l'on croit qu'ils sont *quelque chose de grand*" ["one believes they're *something substantial*"]. Besides, consolations would disturb the equipoise which Thérèse sought in her littleness and poverty, the condition in which the soul, unconsoled, would summon a totally blind hope in God's mercy.

34. "Y lo que no se puede sufrir, Señor, es no poder saber cierto que os amo, ni si son aceptos mes deseos delante de Vos" ["What is insufferable, Lord, is not knowing for certain that I love you and that my desires are acceptable to you"]; Teresa de Jesús, *Camino de Perfección* (Madrid: Espasa, 1997), 269.

35. *Règle Primitive d'Albert*, 65.

36. Teresa de Jésus, *Camino de Perfección*, 212–213.

37. See PN 21, "Cantique d'une âme" for Marie Guérin: "près de l'Eucharistie [Marie's special devotion] m'immoler en silence" ["to immolate myself by the Eucharist"]. PN 25, "Mes Désirs," she composed for Sr. Saint-Vincent-de-Paul, the sharp-tongued *converse* whom many sisters kept at a fearful distance. A piquant irony threatens to assert itself in the line "Je ne veux d'autre jouissance / Que de m'immoler chaque jour" ["I want no other pleasure than to immolate myself each day"]. And to her dear Sr. Marie de la Trinité, she cited Jesus' words on the greatest love, self-sacrifice: "Jésus en s'immolant Lui-Même / Nous a dit à son dernier jour" ["Jesus immolating Himself spoke to us on his last day"]; PN 29, "Qu'il nous est doux" ["How sweet he is to us"].

38. So Pauline reported to Sr. Louise de Jésus (in Carmel from 1919 to 1982), OC, 1456.

39. This is one of the most fascinating of her biblical citations, as she takes the place of Jesus. To begin with, here is her sequence of verses, with some internal

omissions, from John 17:4, 6, 7, 8, 9, 11, 13, 15, 16, 20, 24, 23. Most startling of all is her appropriation into the feminine: "que le monde connaisse que vous les avez aimés comme vous m'avez *aimée* moi-même" ["that the world know you have loved them as you have *loved* me"], which comes in verse 23.

CHAPTER NINE

1. Favorite by their iteration: 11:29, 20:23, 25:6 and 40. An in-depth study of how Thérèse interpreted Scriptures, sometimes rather deviously, is still desiderated.

2. Two significantly brief allusions: LT 142 and PN 17.4. Both are taken from the Markan account of that scene, 9:2–10.

3. Among the first pages of her autobiography, she writes of her wondering as a child about "le pauvre sauvage n'ayant pour se conduire que la loi naturelle" ["the poor savage having nothing to guide him except natural law"]; A 3r.

4. *DE*, May 21–26, 1897, no. 10.

5. Probably its best and most succinct formulation is from Velleius the Epicurean in Cicero's *Natura Deorum*, I.8–20. The argument gets high marks for sophistication and even higher ones for barrenness of heart.

6. Perhaps, like Dostoyevsky's Svidrigailov (*Crime and Punishment*), Nietzsche found that in the midst of incessant human mediocrity, a superman would be hard put to know what to do.

7. Marx, of course, played the same tune but Feuerbach scored it first. He had a very high and controversial profile from the time *Das Wesen des Altertums* [*The Essence of Christianity*] (Stuttgart: Reclam, 1969) first appeared, in 1841. He was of enormous import for Nietzsche, but this sentence would, I believe, have enthralled Thérèse: "Die christliche Religion ist so wenig eine übermenschliche, dass sie selbst die menschliche Schwachheit heiligt" ["Christianity is hardly a superhuman religion, since it itself consecrates human weakness"]; *Das Wesen*, I.6.117.

8. Before her reliquary reaches any point on its itinerary, the episcopal conference of the country of arrival makes the request for the stop and agrees to provide a nationwide pastoral program, making available her writings and teachings. Documentation that this process has been fulfilled must be sent to the Pèlerinage de Lisieux in order to finalize the visit.

9. For documentation, consider the wretched ends of the most infamous dictators of the twentieth century: Hitler, Stalin, Mao.

Annotated Bibliography

LIFE PORTRAITS

Chalon, Jean. *Thérèse of Lisieux: A Life of Love*, translated by Anne Collier Rehill. Ligouri, Mo.: Ligouri Publications, 1997.

A reverent, romanticized version of its subject, this book has the biographical essentials but is short on critical insight. It suffices, however, as an introduction.

Day, Dorothy. *Thérèse*. Springfield, Ill.: Templegate, 1991.

This book is not so much a biography as a commentary on the autobiographical manuscripts. As such, it is invaluable. Day's reflections are to the point and often insightful, refreshingly free of knee-jerk pieties. She will surprise the unwary, as for example by her not especially sympathetic estimate of Louis Martin. Besides, in recording how she first came to know Thérèse's writings, she is candid about her aversion to the autobiographies, a reaction common to many initial readers. She found the period style repellent, but she plodded on. This response is a worthy caution: whoever starts to feel put off by Thérèse should leap ahead, from Manuscript A to Manuscript C. Starting there, one sequence could be C-B-A-B-C. That, at least, is my recommendation.

Gaucher, Guy. *Histoire d'une vie: Thérèse Martin*. Paris: Cerf, 1997.

Msgr. Gaucher, a Carmel friar, has spent more than fifty years in theresian studies, and this biographical introduction is by far the best, and fortunately it is available in English translation as *Story of a Life* (San Francisco: Harper and Row, 1987). Drawing richly on archival sources, Gaucher, superior of the Lisieux Carmel until the fall of 2005, affords many details not found in other profiles, and he quotes generously. Not least, there are lots of period photographs.

Görres, Ida Friedericke. *The Hidden Face: A Study of Thérèse of Lisieux*. San Francisco, Calif.: Ignatius, 2003.

Excellently translated from the German by the well-known team of Richard and Clare Winston and first published in 1959, this book has long been the measure of all theresian biographies. It is psychologically probing and even-handed, especially commendable in profiling the dynamics of the Martin sisters in relation to Marie de Gonzague. Görres was the first to draw heavily upon the testimony of the hearings for Thérèse's beatification. Unfortunately, she skirts the central issue of Thérèse's final darkness, and her discussion is marred by occasional flights into a fulsome rhetoric of piety. The original text has abundant footnotes of a theological sort, with many patristic references.

Piat, Stéphane-Joseph. *Histoire d'une famille*. Paris: Pierre Téqui, 1945.

This book, whose English translation has been reissued in paperback, continues to serve as the best-known hagiographical portrait not only of Thérèse but of her immediate family, with an especially high regard for Louis. It provides, however, interest of its own as an *à rébours* mirror of piety and of antimodern prejudices. This book was written in the Vichy years; the urge for atonement of Third Republican sins may have been strong within Catholic France, and the model of rectitude provided by the Martin family must have been irresistible.

The Carmel at Lisieux retains the notes that Fr. Piat, a Franciscan, amassed in composing this book. He enjoyed a tremendous advantage over all other theresian scholars in being able to draw upon a vast amount of nicely detailed reminiscence set down by Céline. Hers is a document which in itself would deserve publication, but unfortunately the substance of her notes disappeared with Piat. The Archives of Carmel has a typescript of what is left, with painfully large lacunae indicated.

Robo, Etienne. *Two Portraits of Saint Teresa* [sic] *of Lisieux*. Westminster, Md.: Newman, 1957.

A probing, challenging look, first at Pauline's rosewatery image-making—the indignation on this matter is now quite dated—and then with emphasis on Thérèse's unrelenting struggle with her own willful pursuit of sainthood. Robo exalts her so highly that she becomes someone you can admire but not love. He makes too little of her *petitesse* and *faiblesse*, and he neglects the table of bitterness. However imbalanced, this work remains a thoughtful and imposing interpretation of the high cost of saintliness.

Six, Jean-François. *Vie de Thérèse de Lisieux*. Paris: Seuil, 1975.

Well known in France as a biographer of Charles de Foucauld, Six has authored several studies of Thérèse, this one being his condensation of two other efforts. It abounds in lively, even controversial insights and suggestions. For example, he discusses her love of Jesus as an inverted form of the courtly love ethos. He claims that Thérèse and her sisters intended that her autobiography would serve to overcome the calumnious rumors against her family after the confinement of Louis.

Six also takes a number of excursions into the sociology of the time, spending undue length on the reparationist devotion of the Sacred Heart movement, which was of no interest to Thérèse. He also discusses the status of feminism in France during the last year of her life. And he deserves credit for bringing Isidore's anti-semitism squarely into the light but seeing it within its context as well.

About theresian spirituality he argues persuasively that it confounds the implicit pride of effort—the staircase of aristocratic virtue is replaced by the effortless *confiance* in taking the divine elevator—and that Christian love is not to be found in great works nor in institutions but in one's daily life. Six makes Thérèse a foil to both her prioresses, Gonzague and Pauline, who in his estimate saw suffering as a value in itself. As to the dark night, he is respectful of mystery.

Six has published a three-volume edition which arranges all of Thérèse's writings in Carmel by chronology, rather than by genre, an innovative approach which helps the reader to see her development as Carmelite and writer integrally. The volumes of *Thérèse de Lisieux par elle-même* are I. *Scruples et humiliations* (from April 1888 to Christmas of 1894); II. *La confiance et l'amour* (January 1895 to Easter 1896); and III. *L'épreuve et la grâce* (April 1896 to September 1897) (Paris: Desclee de Brouwer, 1996–1997).

Soeur Marie de la Trinité. *Une novice de Sainte Thérèse*, edited by Pierre Descouvement. Paris: Cerf, 1993.

Sometimes called the *Carnet Rouge*, this episodic testimony from one of the four novices trained by Thérèse as their *compagne* proves an invaluable quasi-biographical document on how she did so: how she disciplined, what readings she urged (San Juan de la Cruz), how she dealt with their emotional vicissitudes, what she shared of herself, how she taught them her little way. Adulatory yet didactic in turn, Marie's account shows that unqualified love for Thérèse was not restricted to her natural family.

Van der Meersch, Maxence. *La Petite Thérèse de Lisieux*. Paris: Albin Michel, 1947.

One of the most widely read and controversial profiles, this book caused a lot of consternation upon its appearance. It draws a very unsympathetic portrait of Marie de Gonzague, as though she had forced mortifications upon Thérèse, and makes some wildly errant suppositions, e.g., that Thérèse never knew a spiritual director because Gonzague did not allow her one (p. 84). Sappy in hagiographic moments and full of exclamatory sighs, novelist van der Meersch sobers up to read the little way in Socratic terms, arguing that Thérèse was in a constant struggle for self-knowledge. His sense of chronology is sloppy and his dependence upon *Histoire d'une âme* severely limits this book, but it has some rousing and thoughtful insights, especially in discussing Thérèse's exposure of *calcul* and egotism in even our "good" acts.

SCHOOL FOR SNEERS

As there has long been an open season on Christianity and its Church, it is natural that one of the most prominent of saints, and probably the most beloved, should be subjected to abuse. In the Gospels, Christ is reviled and scorned by men. In our time, women have caught on to the game and have played it with particular relish against Thérèse. To judge from some of the women who review such efforts, I would guess that plenty of readers savor spiteful, black-washing portraits. In an age when vulgarity and mediocrity are given standing ovations, it is hard to accept that someone can be exemplary of singular goodness. Ironically, Thérèse, convinced of her own littleness, offends the more substantial littleness of others.

How would she have responded to criticism, well meant or, as here, otherwise? The word from Avila was that no matter what criticisms a Carmelite hears about herself, even unmerited and malicious ones, they identify only a fraction of her true faults. Thérèse was wise enough to have kept that safeguard of humility offered by Madre Teresa.

Here are a few of the most egregious examples of contempt to date.

Harrison, Kathryn. *Saint Thérèse of Lisieux*. New York: Viking, 2003.

The mathematics in this breezy account does not add up. Harrison notes that 500,000 people attended Thérèse's canonization in Rome, in 1925. From what she writes, we might presume they were affected by the same infantile, repressed, morbid, egotistic urges of the young woman they had come to celebrate, that they too had closed themselves off from life, experience, the democracy of passions. Here is one witheringly dismissive estimate of what Thérèse achieved: "the (reactionary) comfort of traditional, emblematic femininity. Eternally presexual and childlike, Thérèse had chosen a respectable means of power for women: invalidism. Dying of love, she never saw herself—nor was she perceived—as impotent but divinely set apart" (p. 195). She did not, in sum, contribute anything toward the feminist agenda of power and performance in the male-dominated professions. Thoroughly unmodern, she has somehow managed to get millions of people over a century of generations to share in her untimely delusions.

Harrison's impressionistic reading, though sustained by the close documentary work of Msgr. Gaucher and Fr. Clark, warps the facts with gratuitous cruelty time and again. The "adoption" of Pranzini as Thérèse's first child proved "a triumph of sexual repression" (p. 69). Of her determination to enter Carmel: "Louis, along with Céline, was scripted as a possible adversary, his 'dearness' dependent upon his passivity" (pp. 72–73). Well-educated and affluent, the Martin sisters at Carmel "provided worthy adversaries for the proud Marie de Gonzague; they were more satisfying to order around" (p. 90). Thérèse's attempts to learn acceptance of unpleasant tasks became "a game that was over the heads of her sisters, a strategy she would have occasion to use again and again" (p. 93).

Nowhere does Harrison show any interest in the Carmelite tradition which deeply informed Thérèse's spirituality nor, far worse, does she relate that spirituality to Christ and the Gospels. Severed by an arbitrary convenience from those abiding, definitive contexts, Thérèse can easily be portrayed in the grotesque hues of a Freudian send-up.

Rasy, Elisabetta. *La Prima Estasi*. Milan: Mondadori, 1985.

An essayist and journalist, Rasy made her first venture into fiction with this misnamed *romanzo*. It is not a novel so much as a colorful and at times perverse musing on

Thérèse, an editorializing about her life with special attention to its physicality: sleep, eating, the body. Rasy indulges in some slighting—the Martins' "ceremonious and somnolent religiosity" (p. 67), the Carmel's "obtuse petrification of domestic intimacy" (p. 80)—and she makes no effort to reach the Christian source of her subject's spirituality, so that the fact that "her attraction to pain increased with her suffering" (p. 82) is passed off as mere morbidity. It was Christ's leanness on the cross which struck her, as did the dirty laundry water at Carmel, which Rasy reads as "a sinister parody of evangelical waters" (pp. 96, 101).

The deprecations have a striking penetration that seems justified by the sheer force of rhetoric but they are usually short of genuine insight. For instance, Thérèse wanted to become not saintly but *a saint*, "as if, extenuated from a rigid nomenclature, sainthood were only a calendric question, and the saints' calendar a nearly complete repository" (p. 30). Or this: the disappearance of food into her mouth seemed "a corrupt magic, the first of her opaque martyrdoms" (p. 98).

At times, Rasy's flights into fanciful imagery are engaging. She compares the photography with the elevator, both of them altering human proportion and human effort, disconcerting the senses. Of the camera's eye she says: "As if the eye of God were that dark hole capable of transforming the provisional, corruptible chemistry of her body into a lasting and certain chemistry, an inorganic resurrection" (p. 91). And, toward the close, she likens the miscellany of the *Derniers entretiens* in the summer of 1897 to the *disiecta membra* of Teresa of Avila, exhumed and snipped at time and again (p. 131).

Some passages are brilliantly suggestive. The fact of few voices at Carmel and the infrequency of speaking restored to Thérèse the elasticity and power of speech itself, something she had felt compromised about before entering the order (p. 105). On Thérèse's awareness of how intention could be misconstrued by act both in herself and in others, Rasy says, "as if divine grace had arrested judgment or had unmasked its vacuous high-handedness" (p. 106). And the letters of Thérèse depict both a passion and the conditions making it inaccessible (p. 109).

This provocative little book can be safely read only when the reader is familiar with all of Thérèse's own writings.

Sackville-West, Vida. *The Eagle and the Dove.* London: Michael Joseph, 1943.

The title is derived from Richard Crashaw's magnificent celebration of Teresa of Avila, but she is only the eagle here; Thérèse, the dove. A close and informed complementary study of these two major Carmelite writers is not Sackville-West's intent. Rather, she becomes so taken with the golden age of the august, securely reputable Madre Teresa and the exotica of her mysticism that she cannot quite accommodate her own nearly contemporary (and not clearly mystical) Thérèse. She seems to fall into another trap: Madre Teresa was speaking as a mature, deeply experienced woman; Thérèse was by comparison so young as to be all but dismissed. And Sackville-West plays the class card rather too obviously, thus dogging her own insights with snobbery. Likely the populist promotion of Thérèse was not entirely out of this author's remembrance during this writing, and she was writing from *Histoire d'une âme* only.

THEOLOGICAL STUDIES

Balthasar, Hans Urs von. *Thérèse de Lisieux: Histoire d'une mission*. Paris: Médiaspaul, 1972.

A probing and provocative study by a major Jesuit theologian, this book abounds in insights and is generous with quotations from the theresian texts. It is the sort of book with which you can find yourself arguing and yet remain grateful for the engagement. Everyone interested in the theological Thérèse will find much to chew on here, especially in the concluding discussion of mysticism. Balthasar's confusion of her *neant* with hell is just a beginning, and he vacillates brilliantly on the nature of her "solidarity" with the sinners at the table of bitterness.

One exasperating problem persists: Balthasar's book appeared sixteen years after the publication of the autobiographical manuscripts yet he still quotes from a 1940 edition of the *Histoire*, an inexcusable anachronism. For instance, in Manuscript B (5) when Thérèse likens herself to a little bird enveloped in clouds so it cannot see the "Star of Love," she says only that to believe there is nothing but those clouds becomes "le moment de la *joie parfaite*" but Balthasar quotes instead Pauline's explanatory gloss, changing clouds to the cliché "la nuit de cette vie" with this tag on her sister's *joie parfaite*: "le moment de pousser ma confiance jusqu' aux limites extrêmes." That might be fair as interpretation, but it is distracting to have to read Pauline side by side with Thérèse.

Baudry, Père Joseph. *Thérèse et ses théologiens*. Paris: Carmel, 1998.

A collection of basically historiographic reviews and appreciative estimates by current theresian scholars, mostly religious, of their predecessors. Of particular interest is the first essay, Conrad de Meester's detailed review of the making of Thérèse's manuscripts into *L'Histoire d'une âme*; also, Guy Gaucher's on the initial attempt, as early as 1932, to appoint Thérèse a doctor of the church. Pope Pius XI gave a terse refusal: *Obstat sexus*. Also worthy of note is the essay on Erich Przywara, S.J., who wrote a book of *Geistliche Lieder* (1930), lyrical poems celebrating Carmelite spirituality.

Bro, Bernard. *La Gloire et le Mendiant*. Paris: Cerf, 1974.

Known in translation by the misleading title *The Little Way: The Spirituality of Thérèse of Lisieux* (Westminster, Md.: Christian Classics, 1980), this is a thoughtful and challenging work, departing from the usual unloading and analysis of theresian writing. Instead, Fr. Bro affords many insights which take inspiration from Thérèse. Especially biting is his discussion of the modern and fashionable shunning of death, the most obvious datum in anyone's future, and how Thérèse faced it with equanimity, even in her darkness. And he notes that the no-less-fashionable idea that hell does not exist voids the cross of Christ of all significance.

He gives an inordinate, documentary attention to the Pranzini case, though skirting the essential issue which our otherwise blighted age has sensibly brought to the fore, the possibility that Pranzini, Thérèse's first child, was not the "greatest sinner" as she thought, but an innocent man, as he protested to the last. Bro concentrates on how the case manifested the cruel media-summoned urge to punish, which perverts the notion of justice itself into vengeance.

The drawback to this work is that it is thoroughly in-house. Its hortatory tone will not likely reach people who are not Christians.

Clapier, Jean. *Aimer jusqu'à Mourir d'Amour.* Paris: Cerf, 2003.

A very admirable, dense study, this book is especially valuable for its review of theresian theology relative to the cults of the Infant Jesus, the Sacred Heart, and the Holy Face. Clapier, a Carmelite father, gives particularly close heed to the letters and the poems and shows how distant Thérèse stood from and implicitly overcame the vindictive ethos of divine justice current in her time. I cavil, however, with his claim that Louis's time in Bon Sauveur, "l'épreuve familiale," annihilated her voluntarism and prepared her for her darkness of 1896–1897 and yet that this *kenosis* still left her with a "volonté croyante" ["a believing will"]. One could argue that her voluntarism is alive and well in the extravagant claims of Manuscript B and even into C, where she is telling Gonzague how she discovered the true sense of charity. And what is the "néantisation de l'appui majeur de la foi" ["the annihilation of the major prop of faith"] (p. 294) other than "la perte de la foi" ["the loss of faith"]?

Combes, André. *The Spirituality of St. Thérèse,* translated by Msgr. Philip Hallett. New York: P. J. Kennedy & Sons, 1950.

This book appeared nearly a decade before the publication of the autobiographical manuscripts, so it has chiefly historical value. It abounds with insights and helpful caveats. Abbé Combes urges us not to reduce Thérèse to one-liners and catch phrases. He clarifies such loaded terms as *enfance spirituelle* (*esprit d'enfance* is now preferred) and *la petite voie* (NB: she never quotes from *Matthew* 18:3 about the need to become like little children). He reads her work as a fusion of asceticism (excluding the already unfashionable mortification) and mysticism, the latter coming in 1895 with the *offrande* and then the elevator: inspirations and insights rather than ecstatic visions.

The major problem with this book lies in its primary colors of hagiographical assumptions. Theresian spirituality appears forbiddingly seamless and inaccessible thanks to such exalting nonsense as this: "from this pure sanctity, from this heart given over to the pure love of God, from this pure prayer, arises a pure spiritual life, which grows to ever greater strength" (p. 159)—an amazing feat in someone convinced of her paltriness. She would herself have recoiled from this kind of portraiture, as her late remarks on Mary as Queen of Heaven indicate.

He concludes that she stands as antidote to midcentury evils but arguing that convincingly would require another book. She was an innocent in a comparatively innocent age. When he quotes her remark about feeling the same confidence in God even were she to commit every possible crime, her spiritual consciousness being somehow unalterable, he forgets that genocides and world wars have forever altered our awareness of how deep and how warped criminality could become. Mystery apart, suffering has changed its valence to so high a number that it can barely be charted.

De Meester, Conrad. *Dynamique de la Confiance,* 2d ed. Paris: Cerf, 1995.

Although lengthy at 550 pages, this study of the genesis of the little way remains perhaps the best introduction to the spirituality of Thérèse. De Meester handles the texts with careful attention to nuances. He traces the evolution of *l'enfance spirituelle* and distinguishes *confiance* as the maturation of hope in love, thus getting past the lexical fact that Thérèse short-circuits faith and hope, investing all in love.

De Meester's notes are also instructive, particularly in regard to Hans Urs von Balthasar (esp. pp. 389–392), and in an appendix he takes on the delicate issue of Thérèse's scruples in terms of her adolescent sexuality.

De Meester, Conrad. *With Empty Hands: The Message of St. Thérèse of Lisieux*, translated by Mary Seymour. Washington, D.C.: Institute of Carmelite Studies, 2002.

De Meester, having devoted most of his mature life to the study of Thérèse (and of her spiritual sister at the Dijon Carmel, Elizabeth of the Trinity), stresses "the dynamics of hope" in Thérèse's confident love of God. Although he recognizes that for Thérèse love is finally the only road of Christian life, he claims that hope is the source of dynamic life, encouraging self-forgetting and allowing a broader vision and understanding of the future. One wonders whether his own notion of Carmelite spirituality has overly informed his reading of Thérèse, for whom hope is infrequently in lexical usage.

Descouvemont, Abbé Pierre. *Sainte Thérèse de Lisieux, docteur de l'Église: Guide de Lecture.* Paris: Cerf, 1997.

Thérèse had barely been elevated to the position denominated in this title when this book appeared. It is an exhaustive thematic study, heavily referenced and thus frequently repetitive but well indexed. Clearly, the book is meant to ratify the claim that Thérèse is a doctor bona fide, which is fine, but the discussion is rigorously uncritical.

Ouellette, Fernand. *Je serai l'Amour: Trajets sur Thérèse de Lisieux.* Quebec: Fides, 1996.

This lengthy series of meditations on Thérèse offers some very frank assessments, e.g., that Pauline's institutionalization of Thérèse was a means of protecting Thérèse from herself. Ouellette charges that her ecclesiastical interpreters continue in that effort. As for her devotees, the titanic basilica at Lisieux is at the furthest remove from Thérèse's message of silence and hiddenness. This book draws in a number of helpfully suggestive references, particularly to the mystic Henri Suso. Indeed, Ouellette rather too freely identifies Thérèse herself as a mystic without indicating his grounds for that identification. Still, this book offers much to the patient reader and now has a companion volume (see next entry), smaller but with even more helpful insights.

Ouellette, Fernand. *Autres trajets avec Thérèse de Lisieux.* Quebec: Fides, 2001.

This addendum to the author's *Je serai l'Amour* is composed chiefly of essays on Thérèse's implicit roots in the grand tradition of seventeenth-century spirituality. We can only wish Ouellette had probed further, i.e., beyond his exclusive reliance upon Henri Bremond's multivolume *Histoire littéraire du sentiment religieux en France*, and deeper since the affinities are so pronounced, especially with luminaries such as François de Sales and Alexandre Biny, that the Spanish mystical tradition might be offset by extended research. Although influenced by San Juan de la Cruz and quoting him heavily, Thérèse in her sensibility had a truly Gallic family.

Przywara, Erich, S.J. *Humanitas: Der Mensch zwischen gestern und morgen.* Nurnberg: Glock and Lutz, 1952.

This volume is a collection of very short essays which appeared in Przywara's journal, *Humanitas*, over a generation. The scattered references to Thérèse can be found in the index. They tend to be iterative as Przywara pursues the same theme with variations, the burden of the post-Renaissance, post-Reformation, post-Enlightenment era, the void in which one must decide whether one is a child of God or a child of the world alone. His sources are chiefly nineteenth-century offshoots of idealism and Romanticism: Cardinal Newman, Donoso Cortès, Kierkegaard, and above all Nietzsche, whom he sees as a foil to Thérèse. To Nietzsche's *amor fati* as a Dionysian affirmation of contradictions in the turmoil of being, Przywara poses Thérèse's toy ball of Jesus sent rolling in divine love. He neglects the table of bitterness, the emblem of her mature spiritual perception. Even so, this volume as a whole is a rich anatomy of the central intellectual issues of modern religious life. Seldom has Thérèse been put in such heady company of contemporaries but Przywara, two generations before she became a doctor of the Church, makes clear that she can hold her own.

THE SICKNESS

Bancillon, Brigitte. "Le dossier médical de sainte Thérèse de Lisieux," unpublished doctoral dissertation. Université Pierre-et-Marie-Curie, Paris, 1983.

Dr. Bancillon canvasses all available testimony on Thérèse's last illness, arguing that she might have died not from tuberculosis but from another pulmonary infection. She quotes generously from the letters of Marie Guérin (Sr. Marie de l'Eucharistie) to Isidore on Thérèse in her last months. Most important, Bancillon's documentation includes a scathing evaluation of de Cornière from a doctor whom Msgr. Gaucher had consulted for his book *La Passion de Thérèse de Lisieux* (see below).

THE DARKNESS

Gaucher, Guy. *La passion de Thérèse de Lisieux.* Paris: Cerf, 1993.

This study of Thérèse's final illness by a major theresian scholar strives to overcome dolorist readings of Thérèse. Msgr. Gaucher emphasizes the joyful and loving strengths in her which broke the mold of both stiff sanctity and the perverse cult of suffering for its own sake, the counterfeits which have to a degree threatened a just evaluation of Thérèse and her spirituality. Gaucher does not carry this perception into the abyss where she resided at the last, but he has many helpful, corrective insights.

Moré, Marcel. "La Table des Pécheurs." *Dieu Vivant* 24 (1953).

One of the most engaging and insightful works on Thérèse, this 100-page monograph, although written before the publication of the autobiographical manuscripts (he had a peek at them via Abbé Combes), is still worth a close reading. Moré makes clear how central to her spirituality is the table of sinners. The danger to Carmel lay in seeing humanity in two parts, those holy enough for the Fire of Love and those having to deal with divine justice. He argues that Thérèse saw the pharisaism in this view.

According to Moré, her *offrande* was made so that not only she but those counted as sinners would be consumed by divine love. The real grace given her was to get into the skin of sinners and feel their anguish and desolation. This carrying of others' suffering in herself was something other than the standard mortifications. And as the little bird story in Manuscript B shows, suffering is *not* a chastisement from a vengeful, punitive God but an *épreuve* to prompt a sinful heart's cry of love, i.e., suffering is itself integral to salvation.

Moré was writing when Christianity was still deeply informed by Jansenism—as to a degree it continues to be—and he argues that theresian spirituality confounds it. That perspective is commonplace now but during the decade between the Nazi occupation and France's loss of empire in Indochina, sanctimonious reparation for national transgressions was still fashionable: Hitler was the punishment for Third Republican secularism, etc.

Within that historical frame, Moré does further service by his trenchant criticisms of the editors of *Histoire d'une âme*, meaning the Martin sisters. He even charges that Pauline rigged an ecstasy for Thérèse's final moments to make her end accord with the tradition of saintly deaths. She or "they" distorted the manuscript at crucial points, as when the first-person singular is used where Thérèse meant to generalize by using the third. In sum, the point of Thérèse's writing is not to sanctify her life but to show how each of our own can be sanctified. She is an exemplar, not a mediator, and writes on behalf of the sinful, not the pious.

It may be some irony, but Moré's only problem is that of a pious believer: like Thérèse, he cannot imagine a nonbeliever, even a convinced one, *not* languishing in despondency before a godless universe. Do atheists have to live in anguish? Do they look as though they are eating bitter bread? A Christian *cannot* imagine that it is possible to lead a meaningful life without God.

Renault, Emmanuel. *L'Épreuve de la foi: Le combat de Thérèse de Lisieux.* Paris: Cerf, 1991.

A brief but scrupulous study of Thérèse's *téméraire abandon*, her audacious sacrifice of herself, and the fundament of mystery (so acknowledged by Renault) which remains in this young woman's late life and early death. This book is a model of honesty and probity by a Carmelite and scholar. It includes many helpful caveats, e.g., the degree and manner of suffering are determined by one's education but also by one's capacity for reflection and one's openness to grace (p. 33); anyone's testing in faith remains a mystery even for that person herself (p. 35); to be valid, the little way must satisfy many and varied conditions of ordinary people's lives (p. 80); pious urges to palliate Thérèse's *offrande* cannot reach its mystery—what is the point if rewards for it are finally set out as they were for Job (p. 100)? Very highly recommended.

Vasse, Denis. *La souffrance sans jouissance ou le martyre de l'amour.* Paris: Seuil, 1998.

There are many shrewd *aperçus* here about the nature of suffering via Thérèse's experience of it: her breakout from childhood narcissism; the chastity of her suffering which was a love of others through Christ alone and of him through others; by contrast, the perversity in neurosis, which seeks only self-satisfaction. Vasse argues that, taken together, a psychological and spiritual interpretation of Manuscript A ends in what he calls a theological anthropology of the Incarnation, reading the presence of the Holy Spirit only in the flesh.

He emphasizes that Thérèse was called not to suffering but to love, which can only mean dispossession of oneself. Without love, suffering too readily becomes obsessive disquiet, plunged in anger, bitterness, even hatred. But to resist the suffering of *douleur* and *sécheresse* would be to abandon the little way, to presume one can act on one's own to protect oneself instead of allowing God to act within one.

All that is fine, but Vasse clogs the works with some spurious psychobiographical assumptions: Zélie's naming Thérèse after her deceased sister of the year before shows that Zélie's relation to Thérèse was marked by a desire for death (p. 35). Because of her mother's "pulsion de mort" (p. 47), Thérèse could not nurse. The neurotic affection Thérèse showed for those around her, especially Pauline, stemmed from an unconscious horror which Zélie had instilled in her in the form of guilt and denial (p. 48). Rosalie Taille, the wet nurse, became her unconscious figure of God's compassion (p. 51). Do we need this colorful nonsense?

SPECIAL STUDIES

Ahern, Patrick. *Maurice and Thérèse: The Story of a Love.* Garden City, N.Y.:
    Doubleday, 1998.

This wildly popular book is a translation with linking commentary on the ten letters of each correspondent, the troubled, young, soon-to-be friar of the missionary White Order, Maurice Bellière, and Thérèse, to whom Pauline gave him. Bishop Ahern does not make clear that Thérèse had to be tactfully disingenuous with Bellière's struggles in self-doubt, she herself having entered a far deeper void which she of course could not disclose to him.

Chevalier, Emmanuelle, et al. *Thérèse de Lisieux ou la grande saga d'une petite
    soeur, 1897–1997.* Paris: Fayard, 1997.

For the centenary of her death, this book serves as the first "reception history" of Thérèse over a broad canvas. It surveys rather too briskly the groundswell ("vox populi") which pushed Thérèse toward beatification and canonization; then, the substantial cult of her during the First World War when Catholics of Austria and Germany were fighting Catholics of France and both sides sent to Lisieux many ex votos of gratitude for cures or rescues. Thérèse was still only a sister. There is a particularly engaging account of the Martin sisters during the German invasion and occupation, 1940–1944, at the end of which Lisieux was severely bombed and the community had repaired to the basilica. The authors also survey the nettlesome works of Lucie Delarue-Mardrus and Maxence van der Meersch (see above), the former denouncing as early as 1926 the glittering theatrification of Thérèse.

Far more egregious than that charge is the photographic inlay in this volume, which makes clear how the kitschification of Thérèse has proceeded, even to T-shirts.

Lamentations against this commerce—Bernanos denounced Thérèse's "simoniac sisters"—are useless because the kitsch inevitably attends the democratic process of assimilating any "star" personality.

Guitton, Jean. *Le Génie de Thérèse de Lisieux*. Paris: Emmanuel, 1995.

By "genius," Guitton means her simplicity, including the effortless *abandon*, which, he rightly observes, requires much effort from the rest of us. This Thérèse is wholly orthodox, but Guitton finds her the most accessible of saints for Protestants by her attention to grace, her evangelism (meaning her careful reading of Scripture), her appeal to those beyond cloistered life. He is not the first to compare Edith Stein to her: both geniuses of the new, he says, of the direct, the communicable, the simple.

At the close, however, dismay confounds the reader (me, anyway) as Guitton celebrates the crackpot Arminjon, purveyor of apocalyptic fantasies, such as of Asian hordes overwhelming Europe and Jews taking over in Germany. This peculiar hybrid of Gobineau and Jules Verne inspired the youngest Martin sisters in their adolescence—in adulthood only a tabloid reader would be able to keep up with him—with his vision of a celestial amusement park as payoff for the elect. It remains inexplicable that Thérèse ingested this prophetic foolishness in the same years that she was learning by heart the *Imitatio Christi*.

This collection of essays was first published in 1965.

Hermine, Micheline. *Destins de femmes, désir d'absolu: Essai sur Madame Bovary et Thérèse de Lisieux*. Paris: Beauchesne, 1997.

By any reckoning an exceptional book, this bizarre pairing by an established French novelist makes a strong case for the radical insufficiency of life registered in fiction and fact. One might presume its real parallel is drawn between Flaubert and Thérèse. Hermine wastes a lot of space with idle and minute grounds for comparing Emma and Thérèse, and she necessarily ignores *abandon* in Thérèse, a spiritual dynamic wholly absent in the hypertrophically bitter Flaubert and his famous victim. Still, this is a refreshing departure from the usual.

Langlois, Claude. *Les dernières paroles de Thérèse de Lisieux*. Paris: Salvator, 2000.

This work proves to be an admirable piece of sleuthing as Langlois, an eminent historian of what the French call "sciences religieuses," weighs the evidence of Pauline's various editings of her own efforts to record her sister's "last conversations." It becomes clear how much is left to conjecture: it is not even certain that the questions or prompting remarks to which Thérèse was supposedly responding were the ones Pauline actually put to her. In the end, we are sobered by the refractory force and fragilities of memory: Pauline gathered the "corpus" of Thérèse's words but not the "integrality" of the words themselves.

Langlois, Claude. *Le poème de septembre: Lecture du Manuscrit B de Thérèse de Lisieux*. Paris: Cerf, 2002.

An almost pedantically detailed study of Thérèse's handwriting in this central portion of her "autobiography," this book belongs to a specialists' circle, but it sometimes breaks out of its confines and offers a number of helpful insights, chiefly on Thérèse's supersession of *abandon* by a peremptory claim of reciprocity with Christ. Langlois courageously and unflinchingly looks at attendant implications.

Maître, Jacques. *L'Orpheline de la Bérésina: Thérèse de Lisieux (1873–1897)*. Paris: Cerf, 1996.

If you are engaged by psychoanalytic studies of long-dead and never couched analysands, this book can be enthusiastically recommended. Maître draws extensively on the theresian corpus and even fetches up some arcana (the unmentioned paternal grandmother went to live with the unmentioned wet nurse) while crafting some provocative (insightful, if you will) arguments. He fancies that in a constant quest for love to satisfy her narcissism, Thérèse fashioned two selves out of her psyche: an ever-loving, ever-suffering mother (compensatory modeling on Zélie but also inspiration from the Virgin) to a tyrannical son, the petulant Jesus for whom she was a toy to be abused; and the petulant child herself, with regressive infantilism and manipulation, as witnessed in the mysterious illness when she was ten. Theresian littleness becomes a ploy or pretext for eliciting tender and indulgent responses from a feminized God, a kind of celestial Louis. Christ crucified becomes the suffering mother abused by the ungrateful child, us.

Maître writes from such Freudian holiday spots as the Virgin's smile, the Christmas conversion, the dream of the three Spanish mothers. He cites the usual vatic sources (Klein, Lacan, and Him) but gives special attention to British therapist D. W. Winnicott to contend that theresian spirituality derives from the anxieties suffered in separation from her wet nurse and comes full circle in her final weeks when she reverts to infantile talk before her natural sisters. This study has an internal coherence and should satisfy those eager for the reductivism it vigorously affords.

I find it hard to come away from this book without feeling dispirited, chiefly because it unwittingly degrades its subject. The reason lies in Freudianism itself, that whether considered as ideology or ethos it remains pathetically loveless: everything comes down (down, indeed) to the tawdry constituents of sexuality and gender tensions. It is an ignoble reading of the human and rings particularly false in this instance. Proceeding through *L'Orpheline*, I found myself making a kind of mantra from a turned phrase of Bossuet, that she had only love from her pen, because she had only love in her heart. Of course, the child Thérèse was infantile and selfish at times, as who is not? Yes, she was manipulative with Céline. Yes, it might seem that she protested her littleness too much. Maître ignores altogether her attempts to overcome her selfishness; *abandon*, which gets no discussion here, was her certain antidote to *amour-propre*. And grace, the dynamic mechanism in Thérèse's story, is as transcendent mystery wholly alien to Freudian trench work.

Maître's 400-page presentation has no chronology and in the heinous way of French monographs, there is no index. Neither is there an English translation. Fascinating in its way, but beware.

Renault, Emmanuel. *Ce que Thérèse de Lisieux doit à Jean de la Croix*. Paris: Cerf, 2004.

In this dense study of spiritual indebtedness (there is another on the same pairing by Guy Gaucher), Renault suggests why Thérèse looked to the high-flyer and hence loner of Carmelite spirituality rather than to the maternal founder of the reformed order. San Juan wrote in a tone of cocksureness, free from the it-seems-to-me of Madre Teresa. Thus he gave Thérèse the needed ballast for her little boat at crucial points in her spiritual development, when she was integrating herself to Carmel's life in her adolescence and again, toward the end, when she needed to fortify her *confiance* in order to survive the testing darkness.

It is hard to escape the impression that Thérèse read Juan de la Cruz for nuggets, for insights which, taken in aphoristic brevity, took on a sibylline import for her. She cites the same few repeatedly, so they start to read like mottoes: love is paid only by love; God augments our desires by giving; it is our lot to suffer and be despised (the imprisoned Juan was despised, but did anyone ever despise Thérèse?), etc. That is not to diminish their weightiness for her, quite the reverse: the juanist notion that divine love profits even from the evil in us gave her a treasured peace and confers upon her notion of "audace" an ambiguity worth probing. And it was Juan, argues Renault, who gave her the liberating notion of an efficacious Love, that in its ardent purity is itself apostolic. That is how, from within the confines of Carmel, Thérèse could assume a missionary future for herself.

Renault finds close affinity in life and thought between the two saints, "l'accord profond de pensée et de vie" (p. 203), but he candidly notes their differences: Juan had no missionary eagerness to save souls and hence no solidarity with sinners; and Thérèse claimed no glorious exit crowning her life (though Pauline attempted to portray one), which would have been contrary to the humility she wanted to make exemplary for other little people.

Six, Jean-François. *Lumière de la nuit: Les 18 derniers mois de Thérèse de Lisieux.*
    Paris: Seuil, 1995.

A highly contentious study, polemically charged against Pauline, whose recording of the last conversations with her sister is here needlessly set aside as suspect. (For a corrective, see the Langlois study of the *Derniers entretiens*, cited above.) Six has many insights and the richness of his notes alone would justify attention to this study, but he mars the effect of the whole not only by his hostility to Pauline—as in the case of Etienne Robo, the dismay over Pauline's emendations is anachronistic—but by a peculiar failure to give Manuscript C the in-depth analysis it deserves.

Zambelli, Raymond, and Claude Tricot. *Deux mystiques français: Blaise Pascal et*
    Thérèse de Lisieux. A small book-length study published in *Vie thérésienne*
    over six issues: nos. 145, 146, 147 (1997), nos. 151 and 152 (1998),
    and no. 153 (1999).

The value of this carefully detailed exercise is twofold: first, it puts into question the commonplace that Thérèse killed off the Goliath of Jansenism, but it challenges our modern understanding of Jansenism itself by helpful nuances, which to many people might well seem historical or merely academic. Second, it conjoins two of the foremost spiritualities of French Catholicism. The question remains, how forced is their proximity to one another?

Pascal and Thérèse have more in common than one might initially suppose: two provincials, early bereft of their mothers and raised amid sisters by solicitous widowers, both were wracked by illness and isolation in the face of premature deaths, and both sought intimacy with the hidden God. The authors do not help us much with their titular claim that both writers were mystics; both claimed conversion events but one can have a mystical experience without being a mystic. And does the very word have much valence nowadays?

By drawing on such out-of-the-way sources as the letters to Mlle. de Roannez, the authors substantially modify the loveless hair shirt Pascal who is so easily extracted from the major texts. (Tricot and Père Zambelli use the Brunschvicq edition from Hachette, *Pénsees et opuscules*.) Coming from the other direction, they rightly identify the danger of a superficially alluring misreading of "the little way of trust and love," as though it were a vitamin for complacent mediocrity. Neither Pascal nor Thérèse could evade (nor would they have us do so) the centrality of love's bitter suffering as the lot of every Christian. If Pascal's spirituality gives preponderance to divine justice, the theresian emphasis upon God's compassionate love does not confound but complement it.

Beside the emotive first-person élan of Thérèse, the propositional balance weighing of a fastidious mathematical wizard might seem solemn and dry, but both are at least true to the best of French prose style: they write free of sophistry and humbug. On any reader, both impose themselves as truth seekers. This series of essays deserves broad circulation.

CATHOLICISM IN NINETEENTH-CENTURY FRANCE AND BEYOND

Baker, Catherine. *Les contemplatives*. Paris: Stock, 1979.

This sociological profile of Benedictine, Carmelite, Dominican, Ursuline, and Visitandine sisters in modern France is among the most enthralling books I have read in the research for this study. Baker, a young woman with pronounced secular viewpoints, sent out questionnaires and visited many of the conventual sites from which she gathered her responses. The sisters speak anonymously for themselves in sometimes lengthy but consistently engaging ways. The volume is especially pertinent to Thérèse in such matters as the *épreuve de la foi*. Other topics include the assumptions under which the women entered their orders, the maturation of their spirituality, and their views on community, feminine sexuality, God, the Church post–Vatican II. Alas, *Les contemplatives* has never been translated and has long been out of print.

Cholvy, Gérard. *Christianisme et société en France au XIXe siècle, 1790–1914*. Paris: Seuil, 2001.

An excellent survey, dense with primary references, this book does not quite supersede the older generation of church histories (Daniel-Rops, Dansette; see below) but is highly useful. It includes an extensive glossary and the latest in scholarship on ecclesiastical France. It also marks the trend away from strict ecclesial concerns to the sociology of French Catholicism, which means a convincing abundance of statistical profiles of the departments' parishes, their populations, etc.

Daniel-Rops, Henri Petitot. *Un Combat pour Dieu, 1870–1939*. Paris: Fayard, 1963.

Daniel-Rops was the most prolific mid-twentieth-century historian of ecclesiastical France as well as a writer on the primitive Church and the cults of its early martyrs—and a novelist to boot. His unadorned, encyclopedic style should not deter. Seemingly dated, this exhaustively detailed yet not ponderously scholarly study proves still an excellent introduction to the two generations of the Third Republic during which the Church was at bay. Evenhanded, he could discuss the imposing dangers of modernism which the papacy had continuously to oppose and yet see the failings of the Vatican's *integrisme* as well.

The bonus comes at the end of 900 pages in a judicious celebration of Thérèse, whom he regards as the foil to both Marxist materialism and Nietzschean despair. Well and good, but undeveloped, and he regards as immitigable paradox what he miscalls her love of suffering and the eerie peace she attained in "the abyss of despair." His closing remarks on the three cardinal points of her spirituality I shall leave to the reader to discover independently. The English translation is *A Fight for God, 1870–1939*, translated by John Warrington (Garden City, N.Y.: Image Books, 1967).

Dansette, Adrien. *Histoire religieuse de la France contemporaine*. Paris: Flammarion, 1948.

This history, ranging from the Revolution to the end of the Third Republic, has the substantial fault of lacking a bibliography and critical notes; it has only an index. It remains, however, a still-useful chronicle of the contests between the Church and the emergent republicanism of the state. Dansette has been charged with underestimating the degree to which the French populace was alienated from the Church prior to 1789, and he gives little notice to either the ascendant cultish devotional Catholicism of the mid- to late nineteenth-century populace or the extensive missionary work of the Church during that time. Thérèse is given but one paragraph, a fantastic slight.

Soeur Marie de l'Incarnation. *La relation du martyre des seize Carmélites de Compiègne*, edited by William Bush. Paris: Cerf, 1993.

A thorough documentation of the lives of fourteen sisters of Carmel up to nearly the end of the Terror, when they were guillotined on July 17, 1794. Having been disbanded into public life, they had secretly regrouped before they were arrested. Only one of the sisters escaped (or was cheated of) martyrdom—all fourteen have been canonized—and two generations later, she wrote an account of the community.

This story inspired the German novelist (and convert) Gertrud von le Fort to compose *Die letzte am Schafott* [*Last on the Scaffold*] (1931) from which George Bernanos drew for his last masterwork, *Dialogues des Carmélites* (1948), which in turn prompted Francis Poulenc's opera of the same title (1956) and a film by R. L. Bruckberger and Philippe Agostini (1960), for which the dialogues have been reduced to one.

TRANSLATIONS OF THÉRÈSE'S WRITINGS

Bancroft, Alan. *St. Thérèse of Lisieux: Poems*. London: Fount, 1997.

This proves a charmingly perverse little volume, perverse because Bancroft incorporates so many of Pauline's emendations of her sister's verses (not all of them acknowledged) that she might as well have coauthorship; charming, because he wants to overcome some of the banality which weighs heavily in these poems and so he trusses them up with Emily Dickinson–like audacities, which is a stretch. In her very first poem, for example, the flat "sans égal" ["without equal"] is wrenched into a verb, "to out-tower." Her address to the Trinity in her famous "Vivre d'Amour" is transformed from "vous êtes Prisonnière de mon Amour!" ["you're a prisoner of my love"] to "a Prisoner! as so Love-locked by me!" which marks an incontestable improvement.

On the other hand, he himself sometimes flattens: Thérèse's onset of darkness in "la tristesse et l'ennui" becomes merely "I worry and am sad at trouble on its way," in "Mon Chant d'Aujourd'hui." Or he warps: in Céline's canticle, he imports Bernini's famous arrow sent upon Madre Teresa. Where Thérèse writes of Christ's face, "Ton doux regard qui m'a blessée" ["Your sweet look which has wounded me"]. Bancroft inserts, "The arrow-shaft that wounds me so," which is imagery alien to her spirituality and its diction.

It is fine to read these efforts, provided we heed the usual caveats about translation and remember that Thérèse's French is so accessible that it would not take much effort for even the idlest reader to reach for it.

Beever, John. *Story of a Soul*. Garden City, N.Y.: Doubleday Image, 1950.

The most important fact about Beever's translation is that it continues to be in print fifty years after the definitive publication of Thérèse's original version in 1956. This signifies how vital Pauline's version of her sister proved to be—more than 7,000 emendations (mostly minor) of the autobiographical manuscripts—in building up her sister's saintly profile, leaving us to wonder whether Thérèse in her own words could have accomplished as much. Did Pauline perhaps have her finger closer to the pulse of her age than her sister did? And does Pauline *still* speak to Catholicism as eloquently?

Text apart, Beever furnishes a combative, not to say reactionary, self-portrait in his spirited introduction. While this *parti pris* is not convincingly compatible with Thérèse's missionary urge, it suggests that Beever would have been at home with Isidore and the *La Croix* readership at his pharmacy.

Clarke, John. *Letters of St. Thérèse of Lisieux: General Correspondence*, 2 vols. Washington, D.C.: Institute of Carmelite Studies, 1988.

As the letters of Thérèse are an indispensable ancilla to her "autobiographical" writings, this translation by the late Carmelite friar performs a tremendous service. It is in fact a translation of all extant letters both from and to her as published in the 1974 edition from Cerf, *Correspondance générale*. It includes the helpful introductions and the precise, detailed notes for each letter as they appeared in that edition, and even passages from the letters of correspondents, chiefly family members, concerning Thérèse. Behind all that are a biographical guide to all the correspondents, a chronology of important events in Thérèse's life, a table of biblical references within the letters, and—that miraculous event in a French publication—an index.

These two volumes, reasonably priced and in paperback, cannot be commended too highly to anyone seriously interested in this saint.

Kinney, Donald. *The Poetry of Saint Thérèse of Lisieux*. Washington, D.C.: Institute of Carmelite Studies, 1996.

This welcome alternative to Bancroft has two primary, not to say decisive advantages which merit one's preference: Kinney, a Carmelite friar, translates Thérèse and only Thérèse. He does not import Pauline's nor his own language into his renderings. They are so unadorned as to catch the commonplace, even trite language which pervades much of this work. The other advantage is that Fr. Kinney has translated the lengthy and very helpful detailed introductions to each poem as given in the *Nouvelle édition du centenaire* from Cerf. Whereas Bancroft thoughtfully includes some of the verse from the   ·
récréations, he does not include all of Thérèse's poems. Kinney does, and he includes the fragmentary supplementary poems which bring up the rear of the NEC text.

FILMS

Bresson, Robert. *Procès de Jeanne d'Arc*. Pathé Contemporary Films. 1962.

The best cinematic introduction to Thérèse is not about her but her heroine, and the version which speaks closest to her spirituality is Bresson's. (This film is discussed in chapter 6.) Here, in a rendition relentlessly bare of the slightest hint at melodrama, Jeanne is a portrait of spiritual dignity set against indignity, but Bresson divests her judiciary opponents of bogey badness, which means he learned from the grotesque grimacing of Carl Dreyer's judges. The judges in this round proceed through Bresson's innumerable doors with a bemused, almost resigned air, which weirdly underscores the singular nature of Jeanne's trial and the nobility of her enduring it. The only truly dark presence is the whispering malice of the Englishman prodding the French magistrates for condemnation.

As Bresson is arguably one of the great theologians of the twentieth century, it seems fair to mention a few other of his films which are patently theresian in their attention to the acute suffering which attends simplicity and littleness. In my view, the finest of all his thirteen films, *Au hasard Balthasar* (1966), is a Bressonian version of the table of bitterness, with a donkey passing through various masters misshapen by the cruelty of their foibles. It is possibly the most imposing study of evil portrayed on film: it seeks no rationalization nor resolution of evil as mystery, and it leaves grace, the far deeper mystery, at a cruciform juncture in the immortal closing moments.

Two almost unbearably poignant studies of innocence are based upon novels by the great Georges Bernanos, who deeply loved Thérèse, calling her "notre petit chevalier": *Journal d'un curé de compagne* (1951) and *Mouchette* (1967) are also meditations upon the weakness which is at the center of evil. The titular characters convey the *esprit d'enfance* exposed to a blind, uncomprehending world. What finally brings these films into proximity with Thérèse is that they conform to the Carmelite ethos itself, in which the self is obscure, hidden, close to forgotten. As is Bresson himself.

Cavalier, Alain. *Thérèse*. Centre Nationale de la Cinématographie. 1986.

While Catherine Mouchet, the young woman playing Thérèse, has an agreeable energy and sweetness, she does not quite attain a convincing depth: the film, like Thérèse, goes too fast (ninety minutes). It is one of its merits that we would have liked to see and know more, even though Cavalier plays loose with many facts (e.g., here Gonzague, not Pauline, orders the initial writing). The actress-Thérèse's uniform good cheer might be construed as a bourgeois version of the real Thérèse's *joie*, which remains elusive. The few hints of *l'épreuve* toward the close are swaddled in agreeable tones. Was Cavalier afraid of her darkness?

The dramatic pull comes from Gonzague, portrayed as imperious and moody yet affectionate by turns, and from a fictive character, Sr. Lucie (perhaps a partial caricature of Sr. Marthe de Jesus), who is in worldly revolt from the Carmel's constraints and at possessive odds with the Martin sisters over Thérèse. She seems to be there for us and eventually escapes down a rope. But the real presence in this highly acclaimed impression (it won six Césars, the French version of the Oscar) is the Carmelite community, from old to young, in discipline and in banter, from *récréation* to refectory.

Armed with an excellent script, Cavalier interprets Thérèse's story chiefly from within the limits of a secular view, sometimes skeptical and even confrontational, but not once condescending: an anonymous young doctor has a sharp exchange with Gonzague about the apparent inhumanity of denying morphine to Thérèse in her late suffering. But Carmel is given its say, and the prioress's ripostes to the doctor are worth the whole film. Cavalier shows the Carmel as a place occupied by credibly human beings, women who have human failings and human needs, women held together by fundamental charity and obligation. The most delightful scene depicts a Christmas gift giving—a carpenter has sent a wooden baby Jesus carved life-sized, and the sisters take turns holding it as though it were a real infant—which ends with a spontaneous breakout into the Bacchic *euhoe!* from *La Belle Hélène* and dancing. Did Offenbach ever pass within those walls?

With wit, warmth, and balance, Cavalier gives us a gently intriguing film but one more about Carmel than about Thérèse. There is a dubbed version, widely available.

Lonsdale, Michael. *Vous m'appelerez petite Thérèse*, realization de Anne Fournier. ACPA Production (1998).

This film boasts a brilliant economy: three actors perform scenes from Thérèse's life, all set within the gloomy crypt of St. Sulpice, Paris. One actress (Lila Redouane) plays Thérèse; the other (Françoise Thuriès) plays the parts of all the other women; and Lonsdale himself plays all the men, from Pope Leo XIII to the young suitor dancing with Céline at the disastrous marriage banquet. Where Cavalier departed boldly from biographical facts, Lonsdale hugs them close, so that there is a documentary, textual gravity to the sequences which is relieved only by the spontaneity of the performances. The obvious limit to this approach is its presupposition that the viewer has read the autobiography within retrievable memory of many details. Otherwise, frustration with the ellipses will set in fast, and this film runs to more than two hours. No subtitles.

Vanoni, Benoît. *Aventurer sa vie sur le chemin du Carmel*. Production Chrétiens Medias (n.d.).

This extraordinary unembellished documentary on modern Carmelite life affords many little revelatory moments into the perdurance of a spirituality at which most of us can only guess when visiting the great Norman and Gothic cathedrals. It is drawn from the sisters of six Carmels, four of them in Brittany, one of the most stoutly faithful provinces of France. (The production comes from the provincial capital, Rennes.) The sisters, older and younger, reflect individually to the camera in engagingly dispassionately tones about their devoted lives and their faith, including eclipses. We see them at work. Their candor occasionally surprises: one well on in middle age admits to having passed through a twelve-year spell of indifference. The serenity of the older sisters is matchless. I came away wondering how young women in America would respond to the strange beauty and toughness of such a life. No subtitles.

Index

Printed in the USA/Agawam, MA
December 16, 2013

583163.098